RESEARCH LIBRARY
OF
COLONIAL AMERICANA

THE SECRET DIARY

of

WILLIAM BYRD OF WESTOVER

1709 - 1712

EDITED

BY

LOUIS B. WRIGHT AND MARION TINLING

ARNO PRESS

A New York Times Company

New York – 1972

Reprint Edition 1972 by Arno Press Inc.

Copyright © 1941 by Louis B. Wright and
Marion Tinling
Reprinted by permission of Louis B. Wright and
Marion Tinling

Reprinted from a copy in
The State Historical Society of Wisconsin Library

LC# 72-141097
ISBN 0-405-03304-4

Research Library of Colonial Americana
ISBN for complete set: 0-405-03270-6
See last pages of this volume for titles.

Manufactured in the United States of America

The Secret Diary

of

William Byrd of Westover

1709-1712

PAGE FROM THE SHORTHAND JOURNAL

THE SECRET DIARY

of

WILLIAM BYRD OF WESTOVER

1709-1712

EDITED

BY

LOUIS B. WRIGHT AND MARION TINLING

William Byrd of Westover
in Virginia Esq.

1941

THE DIETZ PRESS · RICHMOND, VIRGINIA

Printed in the United States of America.

ACKNOWLEDGMENTS

The editors are indebted to the Director and the Trustees of the Huntington Library for permission to publish the 1709-12 portion of the diary. The transcription was made possible by a grant of funds from the Huntington Library. Professor J. G. deRoulhac Hamilton, of the University of North Carolina, Miss Maude H. Woodfin, of the University of Richmond, Dr. Earl G. Swem, of the College of William and Mary, Dr. Hunter D. Farish, of Colonial Williamsburg, Inc., Miss Norma Cuthbert, of the Huntington Library, and Professor Samuel M. Byrd, of Corpus Christi, Texas, have offered helpful suggestions and advice, for which the editors wish to express their appreciation.

The transcription of the diary from the original shorthand is the work of Mrs. Marion Tinling, of the staff of the Huntington Library, San Marino, California.

INTRODUCTION

I

THE diary of William Byrd of Westover, Virginia, transcribed from the shorthand and published in this volume, belongs to the category of secret journals. Such diaries, written only for the eyes of their authors, are, of all types of writing, the least self-conscious, the least embellished to make an impression on the reader. Because no effect is intended, we can expect to find greater sincerity and more truthful statements in these journals than in more formal writings, even than in personal letters, which, after all, are composed with an eye to the recipient's interpretation. Though men may deceive themselves in their most intimate thoughts, the written record never intended for the public gaze at least approaches complete sincerity, and the rare diaries kept only as safety valves by men and women who felt an imperative urge for this type of self-expression have a peculiar value, both as historical documents and as records of human traits. No one can read the famous diary of Samuel Pepys without gaining a new comprehension of the world the diarist lived in, as well as a deeper understanding of certain universal qualities of mankind.

So rare are intimate diaries kept by personages of historical importance that the discovery of Byrd's lengthy journal is an event of considerable consequence to students of American history. The document is particularly important because it is the earliest extensive diary in the South that has come to light. For some reason, Southern colonists were less introspective and less inclined to trust their thoughts to paper than were their contemporaries in New England. Until Byrd's diary turned up, we had no personal record from the Southern colonies to compare with those of John Winthrop, Samuel Sewall, or Cotton Mather—to mention only the best-known examples of New England diarists. Now at last there is a detailed narrative of early colonial life in the South, a daily journal kept by the greatest

gentleman of Virginia in his time; if he is less inclined to
dissect his soul than was that other diligent diarist, Cotton
Mather, he provides fully as much intimate minutiæ concerning his manner of life. Byrd's diary is at once a contribution to our knowledge of colonial Virginia and a corrective
of some popular but erroneous beliefs. Though it is often
repetitive and tedious, it provides the material from which
we can draw a clear picture of everyday life in Tidewater
Virginia at the beginning of the eighteenth century. Not
least interesting are the clues that the author unconsciously
provides for the interpretation of his own character and
inner being.

William Byrd apparently kept a detailed journal in shorthand throughout most of his adult life, for three portions,
widely separated in date, have come to light. The part of
the diary printed in this volume, dating from February 6,
1709, to September 29, 1712, comes first chronologically.
It was discovered in the Huntington Library in 1939 and
was the first to be transcribed from the shorthand.[1] A
second part of the diary, dating from December 13, 1717,
to May 19, 1721,[2] is in the Virginia Historical Society in
Richmond, where, since 1876, it had been forgotten until
newspaper accounts of the discovery of the earlier portion
caused it to be unearthed. It deals with Byrd's life in
England until December 13, 1719 (when he took ship for
Virginia), with the sea voyage, and with the subsequent
year in the colony. It is a valuable contribution, not only to
Byrd's biography, but to social history. In the interest of
objective scholarship, it is desirable that this part of the
diary be made available to scholars in an unexpurgated
form. The Virginia Historical Society, however, has as yet
declined to permit quotation from, or publication of, this
document. A third portion of the diary, dating from August
10, 1739, to August 31, 1741,[3] is preserved in the University of North Carolina Library. Included in the notebooks
containing the diary are letters and literary exercises in
longhand. Some of the letters date from 1717 and amplify
comments made in the part of the diary in the Virginia
Historical Society. Plans are being made to publish both

Such ᵗˢ by a feme E shall not bar her for twould
be ᵗᵒ ᵗ prejudice of her husband ... ...
be a bar for noby but he will suffer by it.

Middletons case

an ᵗ before Probate may ᵗˢ but not bring ᵗ for
ᵧ ᵗ ~ ᵗ is in him. So if one be obligd to pay a
sum of mony at a day to come ᵧ obligee may ᵗˢ
before ᵧ day but cant bring an action. but if
~ ᵗˢ ~ after E ᵐ this shall be nobar ᵧ ᵗ ~ ᵗ —?

Harrisons case

Debt one upon ᵗ ᵗ be paid before ᵗ for . ~ ᵧ E which
as yet is not broken because such E ~ — never be
broken v than twould be ᵗ ᵧ a z ᵗ ~ have his
just debt ᵧ ~ ᵗ ᵗˢ till such E are broken. ᵗ v
Debts one ᵗ w. ~ ᵗ ᵗ shall be paid for all them.
So ᵗ — . 6 ᵧ to ᵗ . V shall be satisfyd before bonds
in ᵧ n of ᵗ whether they be before or after, because
ᵗˢ ᵗ being matters of higher nature ought to be
satisfyd before ᵗˢ ᵗ ~ ᵗ but private records. v
ᵗ are ᵗ ~ ᵗ ᵗˢ unwilling ᵗ ᵗ ᵗ ᵗ. willingly.

Piggots case

If administration be granted durante minore etate of A
it shall determine when A comes to be 17 years old for
at ᵧ age he is capable to officiate as executour himself.
v n if ᵐ be committed to one durante minore etate
of A v A be then 17 years old it is void.

Princes case

A. seisd of a h for years has J B v C a Dingler he devizes
his h to B v dys leaving C of ᵧ age of 12 years his execu-
trix now ᵐ durante minore etate is committed to ᵧ ᵗ ᵗ
E ᵗ then B dys v ᵧ ᵗˢ of ᵧ ᵗ ᵧ ᵗ ᵧ ᵐ of his ᵗ v sells ᵧ
terme this selling was not lawfull. v such ᵐ dur. min. et.
cant sell any goods unless it be of necessity to pay debts
or unless such goods be perishable for he has ᵧ ᵐ for
the ᵗ v advantage of ᵧ infant v not for his P or loss.
if C had taken ᵗ ᵗ was of full age then such ᵐ would
cease v he should administer for his wife withinage.

PAGE SHOWING SHORTHAND NOTATIONS IN EXCERPTS FROM COKE'S *Reports*

the North Carolina diary and the letter books uniformly
with the present volume. Still other portions of the diary
may come to light, for Byrd seems to have been an inveter-
ate diarist. It should be remembered that Byrd's previously
known writings, including the famous *History of the Dividing Line,* first published in 1841, were based on journals,
and it is probable that he always kept a notebook by him.

The Huntington portion of the diary was found among
the Virginia manuscripts collected by the late R. A. Brock
and purchased from his estate in 1922 by Henry E. Huntington. The document consists of a small octavo volume
containing one hundred and fifty leaves of shorthand entries
and ten leaves of notes in Byrd's handwriting. On one leaf
was written out a religious creed, and on other leaves Byrd
had abridged abstracts from *The Fifth Part of the Reports
of Sir Edward Coke,* in a mixture of long- and shorthand.

The transcription of the diary was undertaken by Mrs.
Marion Tinling, a member of the Huntington Library staff,
who had made a special study of archaic shorthand. By
using as a key the shorthand in the notes from Coke's
Reports, it was possible to decipher enough of the diary to
show its character and prove its authorship. It was then
discovered that Byrd had adapted to his own uses a shorthand developed in the late years of the seventeenth century
by William Mason, the most famous stenographer of his
day, who taught the art in London. In 1672 Mason published a shorthand textbook, entitled *A Pen pluck't from an
Eagle's Wing,* which was reprinted several times and still
further revised to appear as *La Plume Volante* in 1707.
Byrd appears to have used the system set forth in this
revision.

Byrd's shorthand is frequently difficult to read because
he often omitted vowels. Unlike Pepys and other shorthand
diarists, Byrd wrote everything—even proper names—in
shorthand. Although the context helps with ordinary words,
some proper names have defied transliteration. "Mr. G—"
or "Mr. J—n" could stand for any number of contemporary
Virginians. Sometimes internal evidence in the diary and
a knowledge of Byrd's associates help to identify trouble-

some names, but often we have been obliged to leave the skeletons of names as they were indicated in the shorthand, for we have shunned the temptation to guess. Even so, some of the interpretations of the shorthand will inevitably prove to be incorrect.[4]

That Byrd's habit was to write in his diary each day instead of waiting several days for an accumulation of events—as is the practice of some diarists—is implied by the author's own comments. When he has been ill for a few days, he notes, as out of the ordinary, the necessity of catching up with the daily entries.

That he intended these entries for no eyes except his own is made clear by the intimate nature of the revelations. Certainly no man would have recorded some things Byrd mentioned had he believed anyone else would read the document. We may ask why he kept this journal if he expected it to remain a secret. The answer to that question is known only to the seer who can divine the inner workings of the human mind. By some quirk of character a few individuals feel impelled to write down even their meannesses; perhaps it is an instinct for purgation through the confessional. At any rate, Byrd freely admitted his shortcomings. His zeal for confession is more noticeable in the Virginia Historical Society portion of the diary than in the others, perhaps because he had more to confess. After the death of his first wife in London in 1716, he tasted the pleasures of the town with greater zest than discrimination, and methodically listed his amours; the record provides such details as the price of a mistress (two guineas a visit to one Mrs. A-l-c, in 1717, until he dismissed her for infidelity!). Although the periods covered by the Huntington and the North Carolina journals were less strenuous in Byrd's emotional history, these journals also contain many intimate revelations that Byrd could not have intended for the public. But the diaries are by no means a mere *chronique scandaleuse,* and if they enumerate Byrd's passions and meannesses, they also portray qualities that indicate dignity and charm.

II

WILLIAM BYRD, the diarist, who was born in 1674 and died in 1744, belonged to the second generation of his name in Virginia.[5] The elder William Byrd had already established his family as one of the most prominent in the colony when he died in 1704, and young William inherited a fortune and a position as one of the ruling class. Long years in England, first as a pupil at Felsted Grammar School, and later as a member of the Middle Temple, had given Byrd a taste for classical literature, a legal training, a knowledge of the world of fashion, membership in the Royal Society, and a group of distinguished friends among the English gentry and nobility. When he returned to Virginia in 1705 to settle on his estate at Westover, he was already Virginia's most polished and ornamental gentleman.

A political career and public service were the natural inheritance of a young man of Byrd's position. While still a mere youth, in 1692, he was first elected to the House of Burgesses. Subsequently, in 1708, he received an appointment to the all-powerful Council of State, and for the rest of his life, he was an influential member of that body. The post of receiver-general of the royal revenues, which he held from 1706 to 1716, gave him further power and augmented his income. In the latter year, when he was in England and unable to administer this office, he sold it to James Roscow for £500. Three times, for long periods, he represented the colony of Virginia as official agent in London and proved the most urbane of colonial American diplomats. During his second term as agent, from 1718 to 1720, he was engaged in a bitter struggle with Lieutenant-Governor Spotswood, who had proposed changes in the method of collecting the quitrents and had tried to establish courts of oyer and terminer that would have curtailed the judicial power of the Council. Byrd, representing the ruling oligarchy, fought Spotswood's efforts to increase the royal prerogative in Virginia. Neither side won a clear-cut victory, and Byrd and Spotswood were later reconciled. Although Byrd aspired to the governorship of both Virginia and Maryland,

and on one occasion offered £1,000 for the appointment as
lieutenant-governor of Virginia under the titular governor,
the Earl of Orkney, he failed of this culminating honor.
He also sought unsuccessfully for lesser offices that promised
financial rewards, and we find him in 1736 and 1737 begging
Sir Charles Wager, First Lord of the Admiralty, to persuade
Sir Robert Walpole to grant him the post of surveyor of
customs for the Southern District, an office worth £500 a
year. If Byrd failed to gain all the offices he sought, never-
theless few Virginians in his generation exceeded him in
political dignity. In the last year of his life, he was president of the Council, a post of honor if not of profit, which
he might have held earlier had not tough old Commissary
James Blair held on until his eighty-seventh year. To Byrd's
civil honors was added military prestige by reason of his
command of the militia of Charles City and Henrico Counties. Because of his recognized capacity for leadership he
was entrusted with the task of directing the party that, in
1728, surveyed the Virginia-North Carolina boundary, an
adventure that produced his charming *History of the Dividing Line* and gave him a permanent place in American
literature. Again, in 1736, he directed an important survey,
that of the Northern Neck. Throughout his long career,
Byrd was a useful servant of the State, and from all the
evidence available, he was diligent, intelligent, and honest,
even if at times he did seem excessively vigilant for the
financial rewards of office. The diary is filled with allusions
to the performance of his public duties, and we find in it
illuminating sidelights on the administration of public affairs
in the colony.

Byrd's private life was as eventful as his public career.
He was twice married. His first wife, Lucy Parke, whom
he wedded in 1706, was the daughter of the dashing but
rakish Daniel Parke, then governor of the Leeward Islands.
After a tempestuous but not altogether unhappy married
life, Lucy died in London in 1716. She had given Byrd
four children, of whom only two survived infancy. One of
these was his eldest daughter, Evelyn, about whom there has
grown up a romantic legend that her father thwarted her

marriage to the old Earl of Peterborough. The University of North Carolina letter books prove that Evelyn's suitor was a young fortune-hunting baronet, but not the Earl. Byrd mourned his first wife for only a few months and then set out to find another mate—one with a comfortable dowry. London offered many possibilities, and in 1717, Byrd began a violent courtship of one Mary Smith, daughter of John Smith, Esq., a wealthy gentleman of London who was influential enough to get himself buried in Westminster Abbey. Although Byrd was personable and ardent, Miss Smith was under the thumb of her father, who demanded a statement of Byrd's financial position. The suitor submitted an analysis of his property and income with a statement of his honorable descent from the Byrds of Cheshire, but Mr. Smith replied coldly that property on the moon was as acceptable as an estate in Virginia; and presently his daughter accepted the hand of a more eligible Englishman, Sir Edward Des-Bouverie, Bart.[6] After this rebuff, Byrd pursued various women, of high and low degree, and in 1724 married Maria Taylor, daughter of Thomas Taylor, a moderately well-to-do gentleman of Kensington, England. A letter to the bride's mother, preserved in the North Carolina letter book, suggests that the marriage was an elopement. Maria was more placid than Byrd's first wife, but the new mother-in-law was contentious and made trouble over Maria's inheritance. Notwithstanding, Byrd's second marriage was less stormy than his first. Four children were born to Maria Byrd, three daughters and a son, all of whom survived and had families. Maria outlived her husband.

A grave error of business judgment in 1711 cost Byrd many restless nights and thereafter kept him hard up for ready cash. In the preceding year Daniel Parke died, bequeathing his property in Virginia and England to his daughter Frances, married to John Custis, and leaving Lucy Byrd £1,000 in cash. Parke's debts were chargeable against the Virginia property, which had to be sold to satisfy the creditors. Rather than see these lands pass out of the family, Byrd agreed to take them over and assume the debts. This bargain proved a disaster, for the debts turned out to be much larger than he expected. At times he was very hard-pressed for ready money; in 1736 and 1737, he had to sell Negroes and land to fund his debt, and he even sought a buyer for Westover, fortunately in vain. His need for recouping his fortune accounts for a scheme to settle German and Swiss immigrants on his frontier lands.

Despite his financial troubles, Byrd was accounted one of the wealthiest men in the colony. His residence at Westover, which he rebuilt in brick about 1735, was notable among plantation houses for its furnishings and its surroundings. In addition to this estate, he had several other prosperous plantations, notably in the region now occupied by the city of Richmond and on Falling Creek, where he built a dam and operated a mill. On lands in his possession, on September 19, 1733, Byrd "laid the foundation of two large cities," Richmond and Petersburg, at the falls of the James and Appomattox Rivers, places "naturally intended for marts." "Thus," he said, "we did not build castles only, but also cities in the air."[7] Byrd continued the Indian trade his father developed, bought up and shipped tobacco to English markets, and sold imported supplies to his neighbors. Although he deplored the multiplication of Negroes in Virginia, he was at one time interested in the slave trade. A slave ship, the *William and Jane,* of which Byrd was part owner, was captured by a vessel of the French Senegal Company on March 1, 1699, off the coast of Africa. Byrd's petitions to the King in this affair, soliciting the intervention of the British ambassador to France, are preserved in the Huntington Library.[8] At various times he attempted to exploit coal and iron deposits on his lands, and he had hopes of the development of gold mines, but his dream of mineral wealth never materialized. At his death he held title to over 179,000 acres of land. More than one hundred thousand acres of this vast estate lay in the valley of the Dan River, extending to the North Carolina line, and was of great potential value as new ground for sale and settlement. His last years were spent in dreams of peopling this barony with immigrants from Europe. A real estate promotion tract, composed in German by Samuel Jenner and published

in 1737 by the Helvetian Society, described this region as
veritably the earthly paradise. The pamphlet, entitled,
"Newly-Found Eden," was put together from information
supplied by Byrd, whose name Jenner translated for the
benefit of his readers as "Wilhelm Vogel."[9]

III

SUCH, in brief, are the bare outlines of the diarist's career.
His journal supplies innumerable details that throw light
on his manner of life, and, incidentally, on the background
and qualities of the Virginia ruling class. Although we may
wish that he had taken the trouble to write down more
extensive descriptions of many events, the journal provides
much valuable information about manners and customs,
about economic and political conditions, and about the
author's own physical, mental, and spiritual qualities.

The most significant revelations are those that enable us
to recreate the daily life on a great plantation. Once and
for all this journal ought to destroy the romantic illusion
that Cavalier planters lived in silken ease and spent their
days and nights in gaiety and dalliance, a notion that un-
happily persists despite cold facts to the contrary set forth
by sober historians. Byrd's record of his activities shows
that he was an extremely busy man, personally supervising
the management of his properties. That he had overseers,
and servants in abundance, goes without saying, but the
quality of his supervisors was sometimes poor, and his servants, both white and black, were often incompetent, ill-
trained, and slovenly. Byrd's wife Lucy was a bad manager,
and many household duties devolved on her husband, who
grumbled and quarreled about them, but somehow managed
to keep the establishment running with a fair degree of
efficiency. Constantly busy superintending the planting of
crops, orchards, and gardens, the owner of Westover was
not above taking a hand himself in setting out fruit trees
and in other work that excited his particular interest. When
his servants were ill, he visited them and dosed them with
remedies, frequently of his own preparation. Day in and

day out, Byrd labored to improve his sprawling farms and to make them turn a profit. Anyone who has ever tried to maintain a Southern plantation will understand the necessity for the owner's constant supervision. Byrd's activities were typical. Other planters of the same social station exerted a similar personal supervision over their estates, and many must have had to work even harder.

The tribulations incidental to plantation life were numerous, as is obvious from Byrd's comments. Storms destroy the crops; Negroes get sick and die; livestock escape and ruin neighboring fields; the mill dam at Falling Creek breaks during a freshet; an overseer is dishonest and incompetent, has to be discharged, and a new one hired; servants are constantly in some sort of devilment and must be punished. Luxurious ease for the owner was the rarest commodity at Westover.

Servants were a particular trial, and the treatment they received was not altogether gentle, though sentimentalists may generalize too glibly about cruelty from incidents cited in the diary. Byrd clearly disliked punishing his slaves and often tried to get results by making threats. But occasionally he lost his temper—as well as the dignity one conventionally attributes to gentlemen—and in a fit of rage beat a servant. Once he whipped the cook for serving bacon half-raw, and he kicked Prue, the maid, for lighting a candle in the daytime. He sometimes forgot himself so far as to quarrel undignifiedly with the servants. Mrs. Byrd, who had a violent and uncontrollable temper, shocked her husband by the severity of her punishments, as when she beat Jenny with the tongs and branded her with a hot iron. Byrd himself in a few instances meted out what seems to have been cruel punishment: he ordered a slave who pretended sickness to be fastened with a bit in his mouth, and later to be tied up by the leg; he sometimes had slaves whipped for laziness. Although the picture of the punishment of servants is not one that appeals to twentieth century humanitarians, Byrd's slaves received far gentler treatment than that accorded sailors in the royal navy. By eighteenth century standards, the slaves at Westover were little less than spoiled. Certainly Byrd felt that he was a kindly master and inveighed in some of his letters against brutes who mistreat their slaves.

Busy as he was about his private business, Byrd never neglected his public duties. However badly he was needed at Westover, or at some of his other plantations, he dropped everything to attend the meetings of the Council at Williamsburg or to muster the militia which he commanded. In the performance of these public services Byrd derived a great deal of satisfaction. It was part of the obligation of a great gentleman, and Byrd was pleased to be one of this ruling class.

At the game of politics, he was an adept, though an indiscreet utterance occasionally got him into hot water. For example, someone carried to the governor's ears a bit of Byrd's conversation to the effect that no chief magistrate ought to be trusted with as much as £20,000. Governor Spotswood for some time after this affront to his dignity was visibly cool to all of Byrd's overtures. Although Byrd had sought the appointment that Spotswood received, he assiduously cultivated the new governor and sought to retain his friendship in the face of early disagreements, which subsequently ended in a definite break. Though he wished to please the governor, he observes that he would not oblige him in any matter discreditable.

The meetings of the Council, which Byrd was careful not to miss, were something more than a serious duty, as the diary makes abundantly clear. Indeed, descriptions of the drinking, gaming, and horse-play indulged in by the members of the highest civil body in the colony sound scandalous to modern ears. On the occasion of Byrd's induction into the Council, he himself drank too much French wine, played cards, lost twenty shillings, and forgot to say his prayers. Other sessions—in fact many sessions—were more boisterous, with gambling (both cards and dice), drinking, and practical jokes. The diarist records on March 12, 1712, for instance, that members of the Council were merry and almost drunk. Sometimes individuals were entirely drunk, and Byrd himself was now and then half-seas over. If the

meetings of the Council were not altogether edifying, they
at least were seasons of emotional release and conviviality.
It should be noted that these gaieties took place for the
most part in the evening after a day of judicial labor.

Byrd took seriously his duties as militia commander, and
was greatly pleased over honors shown him. Even though
it rained mercilessly when the governor mustered the troops
of Charles City and Henrico Counties on September 21,
1710, Byrd was delighted to be presented officially to the
assembled crowd as "their colonel and commander-in-chief."
A year later, on September 23, 1711, he made note twice in
the same paragraph of the honor accorded him at the
muster, and observed complacently that "everybody treated
me like a king." At this his happiness was complete. But
he was not merely a dress-parade soldier. In August, 1711,
Byrd was exceedingly busy drilling his troops in preparation
for a rumored invasion of the French. In October of the
same year he marched his troops against the Tuscarora
Indians, who had gone on the warpath in North Carolina
and threatened the peace of the Virginia frontier. The
show of strength was sufficient to frighten the Indians into a
treaty, and Byrd and his men went home after they had
"played the wag" with the Indian girls in Nottoway Town.
For these military affairs, the diarist did not conceal his zest.

But Byrd found time for the contemplative as well as the
active life, and one of the most interesting revelations of the
journal is the evidence of the persistence with which he
pursued learning and maintained an interest in literature.
His biographers have all called attention to the magnificent
library accumulated at Westover—the best in America at
that time, with the possible exception of Cotton Mather's.
The diary proves the owner's tremendous interest in his
library and his zeal for scholarship. Throughout the years
covered by the known portions of the journal, 1709 to 1741,
he methodically read Hebrew, Greek, and Latin, and at
intervals read French, Italian, and Dutch. Although he
frequently mentions the names of the authors he is reading
—Homer, Lucian, Herodian, Petronius, Sallust, or some
other classical favorite—he often contents himself with not-

ing the completion of his daily stint in one of the ancient or modern tongues, without naming the work. Byrd never forgot that he had been the familiar friend of members of the Augustan literary set of London, that he had shone in the reflected brilliance of Congreve, Swift, and Pope, and he was determined not to become merely a provincial tobacco grower on a James River plantation. Contemporary writing as well as ancient literature excited his interest, and he kept up with the most recent publications of London. The latest news pamphlets were to be found at Westover, for Byrd's agents and ship-captains had instructions to procure such publications at once. As quickly as ships could bring the *Tatler*, or the pamphlets concerning the Sacheverell trial, Byrd was reading them in his Westover library. But beyond setting down the fact of his reading, unfortunately the diarist rarely comments, and we are left wondering what his reactions were to these years of study and contemplation of letters. That he felt no necessity of stating his views may be a further proof that he was not writing his journal for anyone else to read: he was not trying to impress posterity with his literary appreciation.

Students of American literature have often remarked on the poverty of colonial literature in the South and have wondered why men like Byrd wrote so little. The diary indicates that Byrd wrote more than has hitherto been known. Like the gentlemen of the Renaissance, Virginia aristocrats were not eager to print their thoughts for the multitude, and Byrd never in his lifetime published any literary pieces. Not until the middle of the nineteenth century was the famous *History of the Dividing Line* printed, though it had circulated in manuscript among the author's friends in Virginia and England.

Other works in manuscript were known to Byrd's contemporaries, for he notes in the diary on March 26, 1709, that he entertained the ladies by reading some of his own work. On May 14, 1711, he observes that "we were merry with reading my verse, the 3 W[omen?]." A satirical poem on the House of Burgesses has not survived, but it created a stir in November, 1710. That Byrd was pleased at the production but embarrassed when George Mason got drunk and revealed its author is evident from his comments. Stimulated by the reading of the classics, Byrd undertook several translations. On June 2, 1709, he observes that he had translated some Greek into both Latin and English; on August 23, 1710, he was translating Lucian into English; on May 22, 1711, he was trying his hand at translating Homer; in March, 1712, he was reading Petronius Arbiter almost daily, and, although he does not mention translation at this time, there survives in his notebooks at the University of North Carolina a free translation of the famous story of the Matron of Ephesus from the *Satyricon*. Byrd also mentions on August 27 and 29, 1712, translating the Song of Solomon—whether into prose or verse he does not say.

In the North Carolina notebooks there are a few light verses of Byrd's composition, and a few prose "characters." Some of the letters may also have been literary exercises. A slightly ribald and somewhat amateurish satire on women, entitled "The Female Creed," is preserved in the Huntington Library in a nineteenth century copy. These surviving literary efforts, in addition to the narratives that have now been printed—*The History of the Dividing Line, A Journey to the Land of Eden in the Year 1733,* and *A Progress to the Mines in the Year 1732*—show that Byrd had literary ambitions, even though he made no effort in his lifetime to rush into print. There are indications that he was haunted all his life with the wistful desire to be a man of letters. Why a man of his talents and genius did not produce more is not hard to understand when one has read through the journal: the infinite distractions of his life left little time for creation; only by rigidly adhering to a schedule of daily reading in the morning before breakfast was he able to keep up with his favorite Hebrew and Greek. A settled determination to maintain this schedule is evident from Byrd's expressions of irritation when even these hours were invaded by early rising guests.

His studies were not confined to literature, however. An interest in mathematics led him to spend many days studying geometry. As a student of the law, he continued an interest

in legal learning. The abstracts from Coke's *Reports* in the
preliminary leaves of the Huntington Library portion of the
diary suggest that Byrd was concerned with case law and
precedents. On August 1, 1712, he was busy making a law
abridgment and on another occasion he made a digest of
laws concerned with the militia. His scientific interests,
manifested by his membership in the Royal Society and in
his letters to English scientists, are well known and are
confirmed by evidence in the diary. He makes a trip into
the swamp to look at a humming bird's nest; he collects
seeds for the Bishop of London; he gathers herbs for remedies and makes up doses which he is ready to administer to
anyone with the temerity to experiment on himself. Byrd
seems to have had something of a reputation as an amateur
in medicine, for neighbors sent to him for advice and drugs.
On one occasion he offers to cure a girl of the vapors if she
is placed under his care at Westover. When he himself has
a long spell of malarial fever, he keeps a clinical record of
his symptoms and treatment that would be a credit to a
trained observer.

Although Byrd was in most respects a typical eighteenth
century rationalist, he had a vein of superstition that comes
out in his attitude toward dreams. What the Freudian
psychologist would make of his dreams we do not know, but
no modern specialist in this field could uncover more disturbing theories than Byrd himself imagined. One dream
seems to him a premonition of his wife's death; another
foretells the death of Benjamin Harrison (then ill and
certain to die, as happened a few days later). More than
once he sees in his sleep blazing stars, or flaming swords in
the sky, all foretelling disaster. One night he dreams that
lightning puts out his eyes, but the curse is somewhat alle-
viated because an English lord, not identified in the dream,
shows him favor. The diarist is frank to admit that his
dreams are a source of worry.

Byrd shows little reticence about revealing his domestic
life and personal habits. Every quarrel with his wife Lucy
is mentioned, but the writer is careful to explain that she
was at fault, and that he made the first move toward recon-

ciliation. If he is telling the truth about her shortcomings, she would have been a trial to any man, for she was a petulant, undisciplined, and spoiled girl who knew little or nothing about household management. Furthermore, her health was frail, and her disposition was not improved by the miseries of frequent pregnancies. So angry was Mrs. Byrd on January 31, 1711, that she threatened to kill herself; but her husband calmly reports that she "had more discretion." On February 5, 1711, when she wanted to pluck her eyebrows in preparation for the Governor's ball, a terrific quarrel ensued because her husband objected; he carried his point, as he complacently records, and the next day she was reconciled to going with her brows unplucked. Violent as were the quarrels, they were soon over, and no permanent estrangement occurred, as was the case with Lucy's elder sister Frances, wife of John Custis, who had his marital troubles immortalized on his tombstone.[10] When Lucy died, Byrd wrote a touching letter to Custis telling how proud he had been of her whom his fashionable friends in London had pronounced "an honor to Virginia."[11]

Despite Byrd's self-justification, the evidence he gives against himself is enough to warrant almost any retaliation by his wife. His manner toward Lucy was one of conscious superiority, like that of Adam in *Paradise Lost*. To demonstrate his greater skill at cards on one occasion, Byrd admits that he cheated to win over his wife. Sometimes he annoyed her with petty restrictions. When she wanted a book from the library, he refused to let her have it. Worse still, he did not always disguise his interest in other women. For instance, on November 2, 1709, at Williamsburg, he provoked his wife to tears by kissing Mrs. Chiswell before her—a circumstance that caused him to neglect to say his prayers, "which I should not have done, because I ought to beg pardon for the lust I had for another man's wife." Although he might show remorse over succumbing to temptation, the next pair of eyes made him forget his good resolutions. Nor was he particularly discriminating in his tastes, for on April 21, 1710, he records an effort to lure to his room the maid at the Williamsburg inn—an unsuccessful effort, incidentally—and on October 21, 1711, he asked a Negro girl to kiss him. If, during the period covered by the Huntington Library, he did not abandon himself to the excesses that he confesses in 1717-19, his conduct was far from exemplary.

Although his frailties might make him a sinner, Byrd was sincerely religious throughout his life. Even during the bad years of 1717-19, when he was picking up a woman on the streets of London every few days, he was periodically remorseful and begged God in his prayers to forgive him for his iniquities. In August, 1718, he went to church nearly every day for a week, and prayed regularly. A considerable part of the diary—so much that the document becomes tedious with the repetition—is concerned with the record of Byrd's devotions or with notations of the times when he forgot or neglected his prayers. Obviously these prayers were not merely perfunctory. Although the religious creed that Byrd wrote for himself on the first leaf of the Huntington diary shows a tinge of deistic rationalism,[12] the author had not abandoned supernaturalism. When his slaves suffered an epidemic in the winter of 1710-11, he was convinced that this affliction had been sent as a judgment of God for his own sins. In his later years, the period covered by the North Carolina diary, he made it a custom to talk almost daily with his servants and to pray for them, though even then he occasionally had to confess the strength of his ancient sin, as when, on June 15, 1741, he writes, "In the evening played the fool with Marjorie, God forgive me." Although God did not vouchsafe him the strength to resist passion, Byrd never lost faith in the Almighty's willingness to forgive. A strong religious interest is also evident in his literary taste. Many an evening he spent reading sermons, particularly the works of Archbishop John Tillotson, and he assures us that on May 7, 1710, Dr. Tillotson's sermons moved him to "shed some tears of repentance." Byrd, of course, was a communicant of the Church of England; he attended church regularly; and he carefully recorded his opinion of the sermon, which usually pleased him. Although a staunch Anglican, he showed no taint of bigotry and was tolerant of other religions. Even when, on October 4, 1711, he was forced to fine Quakers because they did not turn out for military service, he made them a kindly speech. In brief, religion to William Byrd was a necessary concomitant of life, and whatever his personal shortcomings may have been, he subscribed to an ideal of piety.

Numerous indications of other traits of the writer's character appear in the diary. He displays a pride in his own social position and demands respect from others. He is pleased when the vestry awards him the best pew in the church; he is angry because Billy Brayne, his nephew, is permitted to run around with a hole in his stocking; when one Tom L-d uses bad language in the presence of Mrs. Byrd, Byrd chases him with his cane; when Colonel Hill and Will Randolph are rude to Mrs. Benjamin Harrison, he tells them that they ought to be put in the stocks for their bad manners. Of himself, Byrd declares complacently on one occasion that he was kind and courteous to everyone. In his own generosity he showed considerable satisfaction and wrote down instances of liberality toward poor people, and of his sizable tips to servants.

His hospitality was generous and free. So numerous were the neighbors, friends, and chance visitors entertained at Westover that one wonders how their host found time for the courtesies he showed them. Food was abundant; wine was liberally served; and visitors enjoyed considerable gaiety and conviviality. It would be a mistake to think, however, that the Byrds entertained with much story-book style. The carelessness of Mrs. Byrd and the poorly trained servants tended to make Westover hospitality more informal than stylish. As a matter of fact, the emphasis on formality in this period of Virginia history has been greatly exaggerated by writers of a later day, and, although Byrd and his contemporaries had a sense of decorum, their code of manners was not that of the next century. That Byrd sometimes found visitors a burden is evident from complaints about their encroachment on his schedule for reading and work. On July 9, 1710, he observes that he has invited nobody home from church because he designed to break up the custom, so that his servants might have leisure on Sunday, but there is no evidence that he succeeded. Whether the master willed it or not, Westover remained a haven for visitors, both on Sundays and weekdays.

Byrd himself was gay and fun-loving, even though he did have a driving conscience that constantly reminded him of his serious responsibilities. For sports and pastimes he somehow found a place in his busy life. He liked to play games, indoors and outdoors: billiards, piquet, whist, and cricket were favorites. He walked a great deal, and during a freeze he and his neighbors slid and skated on the ice. For a time in 1710-11 he enjoyed hunting with bow and arrows. But there is no evidence that hunting claimed much of his attention or that of his neighbors. Hunting as a fashionable event had not yet become important to country gentlemen of Virginia. Dancing was one of Byrd's particular pleasures. During a meeting of the Council in Williamsburg, on November 2, 1711, he suggested a dance, rounded up two fiddlers, and arranged an impromptu ball in the capitol. There is less evidence of music at Westover than one would imagine. Curiously, during the winter of 1710-11, a burst of interest in psalm-singing swept the community; Byrd quarreled with his wife about the new method of singing psalms, but gave in a week later and conceded that the innovation was satisfactory. His love of gaming, one of the notable vices of the day, cost him more than he liked, and on November 24, 1711, he took a solemn vow to quit playing each time his losses reached fifty shillings. Sometimes in convivial company Byrd drank too much, but in general his drinking habits were temperate.

Though feasting was a part of traditional Virginia hospitality, Byrd had dietary and health peculiarities that made him unusually abstemious in that age. At one time he made a rule to confine himself to a single main dish at each meal. Uncharacteristically of the eighteenth century, he drank an incredible quantity of milk, often "warm from the cow," and he recommended a milk diet to ailing neighbors. If his zeal for milk excites the admiration of modern dietitians, the quantities of meat consumed will win no commendation.

Throughout his life, Byrd was greatly preoccupied with his health, and was constantly taking up fads and dosing himself. Methodically he took regular exercise, evidently some sort of calisthenics, as he regularly notes that he has "danced his dance."[13]

Genealogists and Virginia biographers will find much useful information in the allusions and minute detail provided by the diary, for Byrd came in contact with many people; and, even if he is often so vague and laconic in his references that exact identification is sometimes difficult, at least the clues are there to stimulate further investigation. The diary confirms one or two traditions about his own family. That the first William Byrd had a brother who came to Virginia has long been believed, but little has been known about him. The diary refers to an "Uncle Byrd," evidently Thomas Byrd, who died on March 12, 1710; William Byrd had promised his uncle in the preceding February that he could come and live at Westover, but there is no indication in the diary that the nephew felt much grief over his death a month afterward. Byrd's expressions of kinship for some others are more puzzling. He apparently "called cousin" with very remote relations, most of them being related to Lucy Byrd, whose grandmother, Lucy Higginson, married successively Lewis Burwell, William Bernard, and Philip Ludwell, by all of whom she had children. One of them, Jane Ludwell, married Daniel Parke. Byrd calls Philip Ludwell and his wife "uncle" and "aunt"; Elizabeth Harrison and Lucy Berkeley, daughters of Lewis Burwell, "cousin"; Elizabeth Todd, daughter of William Bernard, "cousin." Probably "brother" James Duke was related in this way.

The social historian will find Byrd a useful, if not always a very descriptive, reporter. Contained in the diary is a vast quantity of incidental reference, sometimes more illuminating than their writer would have dreamed. For example, a whole chapter in social relationships is implied in a brief comment on the white boatwright who left Westover in a huff because he was fed cornpone (the diet of slaves) instead of wheat bread. And a great deal of romantic moon-

shine about Cavalier splendor is dispelled by the bald statement that the beds at Colonel Dudley Digges' house stank.
Nor do the virtues of our ancestors seem quite so notable
when we learn that they were often drunk, that even Mrs.
James Blair, wife of the highest official of the Church of
England in the colony, was habitually tipsy. When we are
given an account of Governor Spotswood's ball on the
Queen's birthday and are told that he had to bribe his
servants to stay sober by promising that they could be
drunk the next day by permission, we have new light on the
servant problem in Williamsburg in 1711. When we sit
with Byrd at a meeting of the governors of the College of
William and Mary and listen to discussions of rebuilding
the college or when we hear of Spotswood's displeasure over
the way his palace was built, the history of Williamsburg
takes on a new definiteness. We take pleasure in attending
the launching of Colonel Edward Hill's ship and are pleased
to learn that shortly thereafter he has another keel on the
stocks; we sympathize with Byrd and his fellow planters
over the high cost of freight, the low price of tobacco, and
the loss from storms and pirates. Wistfully, we inquire
with Byrd of each new ship to arrive if there is yet any
hope of peace in Europe. In the pages of this diary, the
whole panorama of early eighteenth century Virginia is
revealed. Even though the entries are often dull, tedious,
and repetitive, they have the authentic ring of truth; they
are not the imaginings of some latter day historian, hope-
fully trying to describe things he has seen only in his mind's
eye. This document, the daily record of a versatile and in-
genious man, once again brings to life an age that is buried in
the graveyard of Westover Parish and Bruton Churchyard.

L. B. W.

The Huntington Library, San Marino, California,
March 16, 1940.

FOOTNOTES

[1]For an announcement of the discovery and a description of the document, catalogued as Brock 61, see "A Shorthand Diary of William Byrd of West-over," *The Huntington Library Quarterly,* II (1939), 489-96. Miss Norma Cuthbert, Chief Cataloguer of Manuscripts in the Huntington Library, first identified the notebook containing the diary as Byrd's from handwriting on the preliminary leaves.

[2]Entries from January 6 to February 13, 1721, are missing. The present editors are under great obligation to Dr. John Stewart Bryan for persuading the Virginia Historical Society to permit them to have a photostatic copy of that portion of the diary for purposes of study, even though direct quotation was forbidden.

[3]Missing from this portion of the diary are entries for September 8 to December 5, 1739, and September 21 to October 21, 1740. Professor Maude H. Woodfin is making a study of these notebooks and expects to edit them for publication as soon as the transcription of the diary from the shorthand is completed by Mrs. Marion Tinling.

[4]All words or phrases which have defied translation, either because the shorthand was baffling or because the manuscript was not clear (the edges of some pages have been rubbed, and there are some blots), have been supplied in brackets, or given in skeleton form. Marks of punctuation have been supplied. Spelling of words, including those that have undergone slight changes in phonography (like "sparrowgrass"), is modern.

[5]The essential facts concerning the life of William Byrd may be found in the *Dictionary of American Biography* in the sketch by Professor Thomas J. Wertenbaker and in the excellent introduction to John Spencer Bassett, *The Writings of Colonel William Byrd* (New York, 1901). More personal details are given in Richmond Croom Beatty's *William Byrd of Westover* (Boston and New York, 1932). For further bibliographical suggestions and interpretations of Byrd, see Louis B. Wright, *The First Gentlemen of Virginia* (San Marino, California, 1940), pp. 312-47.

[6]See Wright, *The First Gentlemen of Virginia,* p. 338, for a note on this episode. The North Carolina letter book contains the documents in the case and confirmation is to be found in the portion of the diary in the Virginia Historical Society. For information about Mr. Smith, see *The Marriage, Baptismal, and Burial Registers of the Collegiate Church or Abbey of St. Peter, Westminster,* ed. and annotated by Joseph Lemuel Chester (London, 1876), pp. 292-93.

[7]*A Journey to the Land of Eden,* in Bassett, *op. cit.,* p. 292.

[8]Huntington Library Manuscripts, Brock 744.

[9]Professor W. J. Mulloy, of the University of California at Los Angeles, has kindly let me see a photostat of this tract, which he has translated. He and Professor R. C. Beatty of Vanderbilt University plan to publish it.

[10]*Memoirs of Washington by his Adopted Son, George Washington Parke Custis, with a Memoir of the Author by His Daughter,* ed. Benson J. Lossing (New York, 1859), p. 17.

[11]*Ibid.,* p. 33.

[12]The creed, as written by Byrd, follows. The manuscript is damaged and some words are illegible. Some words have been supplied in brackets, and the words Byrd crossed out are given in parentheses.

I believe in one eternall and . . . the Worlds by his power and governs . . . who form'd the several orders of creatures . . . be witnesses of his glory and partakers of his . . .

I believe that God made man of the . . . of the . . . insp[ire]d him with a reasonable soul to distinguish betwe[en] Good and Evil. That the Law of nature taught him to . . . the Good and avoid the Evil because the good tends manifestly to his happiness and preservation: but the Evil to his [misery] and destruction.

I believe that by the disobed[ience] of the first Man both he and his posterity became Subject to Sickness . . . while he livd; and afterward to dye and return to the [dust] from which he was taken.

I believe that man must have continu'd under this curse to all eternity had not Jesus Christ the first born of the creation; by whose ministry God made the World, been pleas'd to offer himself to be a propitiatory Sacrifice for . . . mankind.

I believe that for that gracious purpose Jesus Christ . . . down from Heaven, where he had the glory to preside . . . all the orders of angells, Principalitys, and powers, that he condescended to animate a humane Body, to be born of . . . pure Virgin, to lead a life of poverty, contempt & persecut[ion], and, at last to dye a painfull and infamous Death upon [the] Cross to redeem Mankind from the punishment of their sins.

I believe that Jesus Christ while he livd in the World was [the] most perfect Teacher and most perfect Pattern of virtue and holiness, that he evidenc't his divine mission by divers . . . that he recommended Righteousness by the certain . . . of Eternal life, and confirmd his doctrine of mans . . . in another World by his own [resu]rrection.

I believe that by the [Exposition] of Jesus Christ God is . . . to accept of . . . to obey his Laws, . . . allowance for our frailtys, and . . . upon our unfeigned Repentance and . . . [grant] (of our lives). That upon his Intercession he . . . comfort and assist us by his blessed Spirit to overcome the depravity of our nature and to improve our selves in the ways of Vertue and holiness.

I believe that in Gods appointed time we shall be rais'd from the Dead with bodys purgd from the Dreggs and corruptions of mortality. That God by Jesus Christ will judge all Nations & Generations of men with perfect Righteousness, according the Lights & advantages they had received in this World. That those who have led good and holy lives here will be rewarded with unspeakable happiness hereafter. But those who have obstinately & impenitently Rebelld against God and their own consciences shall go into a State of Sorrow & misery.

[13]The occurrence of this phrase as a part of the daily routine suggests that it might be a euphemism for a natural function, but it clearly means just what it says, a dancing exercise that he regularly took, for it occurs in contexts that make its meaning unmistakable.

ABBREVIATIONS

For works frequently cited in the footnotes, we have adopted the following abbreviations:

Bassett: *The Writings of Colonel William Byrd of Westover,*
            ed. J. S. Bassett (N. Y., 1901).

Cal. S. P.: Calendar of Virginia State Papers and Other Manu-
            scripts, 1652-1781, Vol. I, ed. William P. Palmer
            (Richmond, 1875).

Ex. Jour.: Executive Journals of the Council of Colonial Vir-
            ginia, ed. H. R. McIlwaine (Richmond, 1925-30).

Goodwin: Edward L. Goodwin, *The Colonial Church in Vir-
            ginia* (Milwaukee, 1927).

JHB: Journals of the House of Burgesses of Virginia, ed.
            H. R. McIlwaine (Richmond, 1908-15).

LJC: Legislative Journals of the Council of Colonial Vir-
            ginia, ed. H. R. McIlwaine (Richmond, 1918-19).

Va. Biog.: Encyclopedia of Virginia Biography, ed. L. G. Tyler
            (N. Y., 1915).

Va. Mag.: The Virginia Magazine of History and Biography.

Wm. Q. (1): The William and Mary College Quarterly, 1st series.

Wm. Q. (2): The William and Mary College Quarterly, 2nd series.

Note: The spelling in quotations has been modernized except in a
few instances of longhand passages in Byrd's writing.

The Secret Diary of William Byrd of Westover

February, 1709

6. Rose at 7 o'clock and read neither Hebrew nor Greek. I said my prayers not till I came to church. I ate chocolate for breakfast. We went to church, from whence Mr. Anderson,[1] Captain Stith[2] and his wife, Captain F-c and Mistress Anne B-k-r[3] came [with] us to dinner, who all went home in the evening. Daniel[4] came from Falling Creek[5] where all things were well and the sloop almost loaded. I said my prayers. I had good health, good thoughts, and good humor all day, thanks be [to God] Almighty. This day I learned that my sister Duke[6] had miscarried.

7. I rose at 7 o'clock and read a chapter in Hebrew and 200 verses in Homer's *Odyssey*. I said my prayers and ate milk for breakfast. I sent a boat and two hands to Appomattox[7] for the pork. Daniel returned again to Falling Creek this morning. I ate nothing but beef for dinner. I read French. I walked about the plantation in the evening. I said my prayers. I had good thoughts, good health, and good humor, thanks be to God Almighty.

8. I rose at 5 o'clock this morning and read a chapter in

---

[1]The Reverend Charles Anderson, minister of Westover Parish. (*Wm. Q.* (1), IV, 143.)

[2]Both John and Drury Stith, brothers, were captains in the militia of Charles City County. (*Ibid.,* XXI, 181-84.)

[3]Mrs. [or Mistress] Anne B-k-r or B-r-k later married Peter Poythress. (See entry for Mar. 4, 1712.)

[4]Daniel Wilkinson, an employee of Byrd's, later storekeeper for Dr. Blair, and still later employed by Mann Page. (*Va. Mag.,* XXXII, 43.)

[5]Falling Creek, Byrd's plantation on the creek of that name, a few miles below the site of Richmond.

[6]Wife of James Duke, to whom Byrd refers as "my brother." (See Introduction, p. xxiv.)

[7]Appomattox refers to a plantation on that river, not, of course, to the present courthouse site.

Hebrew and 200 verses in Homer's *Odyssey*. I ate milk for breakfast. I said my prayers. Jenny and Eugene[1] were whipped. I danced my dance. I read law in the morning and Italian in the afternoon. I ate tough chicken for dinner. The boat came with the pork from Appomattox and was cut. In the evening I walked about the plantation. I said my prayers. I had good thoughts, good health, and good humor this day, thanks be to God Almighty.

9. I rose at 5 o'clock and read a chapter in Hebrew and 350 verses in Homer's *Odyssey*. I said my [prayers]. I ate milk for breakfast. The people made an end of tarring the house. I ate nothing but pork for dinner. In the evening Mr. H-m brought me a letter from the President[2] about the clerk of Prince George, and signifying that my Lord Lovelace, governor of New York, arrived the ninth of December at his government.[3] I said my prayers. I had good thoughts, good humor, and good health this day, thanks be to God Almighty.

10. I rose at 7 o'clock and read neither Hebrew nor Greek. The river sloop arrived in the night with planks, &c. I ate [not?] much breakfast, being to go abroad. I said my prayers shortly. About 12 o'clock we went to the christening of Mr. Anderson's son, where we met abundance of company. There was a plentiful dinner but I ate nothing but bacon and fowl. Nothing happened particularly but there was dancing and [evident] mirth. Mr. Anderson was beyond measure pleased with the blessing God had sent him. In the evening we returned home. I said my prayers. I had good thoughts, good health, and good humor, thanks be to God Almighty. I [desired Captain] Llewellyn[4] to send his godson to the College.

11. I rose at 4 o'clock this morning and read a chapter

---

[1]House servants, probably negro slaves. It is usually impossible to tell whether the servants mentioned in the diary are negro slaves or white servants.

[2]President of the Council, Colonel Edmund Jenings.

[3]John, Baron Lovelace of Hurley, governor of New York from December 18, 1708, until his death from apoplexy on May 6, 1709.

[4]Probably Daniel Llewellyn.

in Hebrew and 400 verses in Homer's *Odyssey*. I said my prayers. I ate milk for breakfast. I dispatched the river sloop this morning early towards Falling Creek. I danced my dance. I was griped a little this morning and had a loose stool. About 11 o'clock Mr. Harrison,[1] his wife, his brother Henry and his wife [came] to see us. They stayed to dinner, when I transgressed the rule.[2] They told me no news. They went away in the evening. I said my prayers. Just at night Mr. Bland[3] came on his way to Williamsburg, who told me that Prince George court had the third time refused the President's recommendation of Mr. Robin Bolling[4] to be their clerk, without any reason, notwithstanding he had made all the submission that was fit for a gentleman to make. There came a messenger from Dick Cocke[5] signifying that he was extremely ill of the gripes. I had good health, good ·thoughts, and good humor, thanks to God Almighty.

12. I rose at 6 o'clock and read a chapter in Hebrew and 200 verses in Homer's *Odyssey*. I said my prayers and ate chocolate with Mr. Bland for breakfast. He went away this morning. I read law. Tony came to tell me all was well at Appomattox, and also that the hogs were ready. I ate nothing but hashed beef for dinner. In the evening I walked round the plantation. I said my prayers. I had good health, good thoughts, and good humor, and good understanding this day, thanks be to God Almighty. Daniel came to let me know the sloop was almost loaded.

13. I rose at 6 o'clock and read a chapter in Hebrew and 300 verses in Homer. I said my prayers devoutly. I ate milk for breakfast. Daniel let me know Tom Turpin[6] had been sick four days of a fever. I ate pork for dinner, and before afternoon Daniel went away to Colonel Randolph's,[7]

---

[1]Byrd's neighbor, Benjamin Harrison of Berkeley.
[2]Byrd had made a rule to eat of only one dish at a meal.
[3]Richard Bland, living at this time at Jordan's Point, Prince George County, directly across the river from Westover.
[4]Robert Bolling, son of Colonel Robert Bolling.
[5]Richard Cocke, a neighbor.
[6]An overseer; probably the Thomas Turpin who owned 491 acres in Henrico County in 1704. (*Va. Mag.*, XXVIII, 214.)
[7]Colonel William Randolph of Turkey Island, who died in 1711.

where he expected to meet the sloop. In the evening I took a walk and met Dick Cocke's servant who in the absence of the Doctor[1] sent to me for two or three purgatives. I sent him some blackroot sufficient for three doses but refused to send him any laudanum because I think it is bad for the gripes. I said my prayers devoutly, having read a sermon in Dr. Tillotson.[2] I had good health, good thoughts, and good humor, thanks to God Almighty.

14. I rose at 6 o'clock and read a chapter in Hebrew and 300 verses in Homer's *Odyssey*. I said my prayers. I took some epsom salts this morning by way of prevention, which worked very moderately. Colonel Randolph dined with me and I ate chicken for dinner, and our chief business was concerning a ship for his son Isham. After dinner he went away and Captain S-t-k came from below and let me know he had got me three men for my sloop. Daniel came from above and told me the sloop would be down tomorrow. I said my prayers shortly. I had good health, indifferent good humor, and good thoughts, thanks be to God Almighty.

15. I rose at 5 o'clock and read a chapter in Hebrew and 400 verses in Homer's *Odyssey*. I said my prayers, and took epsom salts again, which worked moderately. We made an end of [. . .] winter wheat. Mr. Robin Bolling came to see me and stayed to dinner. I ate nothing but chicken for dinner. In the afternoon Mr. Isham Randolph came to see us, as did also Mr. Parker,[3] but he went away in the evening. The other stayed all night and he, Captain S-t-k and myself played at cards till 10 o'clock. I said my prayers, and had good thoughts, good health, and good humor, thanks be to God Almighty.

16. I rose at 6 o'clock this morning and read a chapter in Hebrew and 200 verses in Homer's *Odyssey*. I said my [prayers] and ate chocolate for breakfast with Mr. Isham

---

[1]Dr. William Oastler, who lived in Westover Parish until his death on December 14, 1709. Byrd mentions him by name only once, on December 17, 1709. (See *Va. Mag.*, XXXV, 376 and W. B. Blanton, *Medicine in Virginia in the Seventeenth Century* [Richmond, 1930], p. 280.)

[2]Archbishop John Tillotson, one of Byrd's favorite authors.

[3]Thomas Parker, a neighbor. (See Aug. 15, 1710 entry and note.)

Randolph, who went away immediately after. I promised him to be engaged of a quarter of a ship for him not exceeding a price of £1000. I wrote my letter to Mr. M-l of Madeira. I prepared a representation concerning the Indian trade to be presented to the Council, to meet on the eighteenth of this month. I ate nothing but beef hash for dinner, and [vented] my passion against Moll for doing everything wrong. In the afternoon Mr. Anderson came to see us and promised to make me some [pulleys] for my windows. When he was gone I walked out in the evening. I said my prayers. I had good thoughts, good health, and indifferent good humor, thanks be to God Almighty. Colonel Miles Cary died this day and was taken sick but yesterday.

17. I rose at 7 o'clock and read neither Hebrew nor Greek because I wrote several letters to send to Williamsburg by Tom, about which I was so busy that I forgot to say my prayers in the morning. I ate milk for breakfast. Mr. Haynes[1] came to give me the account of the tobacco he had received for me. Mr. John Eppes[2] came to make up his sheriff's account with me. He stayed to dinner and I ate nothing but roast pork. Mr. Eppes and I walked to see the sluice which I had drained, which he liked very well. In the evening he went away. I said my prayers. I had good health, good thoughts, and indifferent good humor, thanks be to God Almighty.

18. I rose at 6 o'clock and read a chapter in Hebrew and 400 verses in Homer's *Odyssey*. I said my prayers, and ate milk and hominy for breakfast. I settled accounts with the seamen of the sloop to satisfaction. I finished my dispatch to the Madeiras. Mr. Tom Cocke and his brother came to dine with me today, as did Captain S-t-k and Daniel. I ate fricassee for my dinner. I [read] nothing because of the sloop. In the evening I danced my dance. Captain S-t-k, Mr. M-s-t, and Daniel took part of a bottle and we drank to the prosperity of the voyage. I said my prayers.

---

[1]Perhaps Nicholas Haynes who owned land in Charles City County in 1704. (*Va. Mag.*, XXXI, 315.)
[2]Appointed sheriff of Charles City County April 25, 1707.

I had good health, good thoughts, and good humor, thanks be to God Almighty.

19. I rose at 6 o'clock and read a chapter in Hebrew and 200 verses in Homer's *Odyssey*. I said my prayers, and ate milk for breakfast. I gave Captain S-t-k two shoats and a barrel of corn and I gave Daniel two shoats, a barrel of corn, [. . .] hens and four turkeys toward his voyage. Captain M-s-t received his orders and everything was got ready for sailing. I transgressed my rule at dinner by eating a second dish. Presently after dinner I took leave of Captain S-t-k, Daniel, and Mr. M-s-t and they went aboard and hoisted their sails. I wished them a good voyage and prayed to God for their preservation. In the evening I danced my dance. I said my prayers. I had good thoughts, good health, and good humor, thanks be to God Almighty.

20. I rose at 6 o'clock and read a chapter in Hebrew and 160 verses in Homer's *Odyssey*. I said my prayers and ate hominy for breakfast. I sent away Frank who yesterday brought down an ox from the Falls.[1] He told me of the faults of his overseer and I advised him to tell me any faults of him for which I gave him two blankets. I went to church, where there was a very great congregation. After church Mr. Drury Stith and his wife and Captain Llewellyn came and dined with us. I did not observe my rule at dinner, for which God forgive me. In the evening the company went away. I read a sermon in Dr. Tillotson about [s-n-s-r]. I said my prayers and had good health, good thoughts, and good humor this day, thanks be to God Almighty.

21. I rose at 6 o'clock and read a chapter in Hebrew and 400 verses in Homer's *Odyssey*. I said my prayers with devotion. I ate milk for breakfast. The wind blew hard and it rained all the morning. I read law. I ate nothing for dinner but boiled pork and pie. In the afternoon the Doctor came from Williamsburg and brought me a letter

---

[1]Byrd's plantation at the falls of the James River, the approximate site of the city of Richmond.

from the President, who informed me that Mr. Burwell[1] was by the Council made naval officer of York River in the place of Colonel Cary deceased. In the evening I had a letter from Mr. Parker who sent me a fat steer for a present. I gave the man a crown that brought it. I said my prayers. I had good thoughts, good health, and good humor, thanks be to God Almighty.

22. I rose at 7 o'clock and read a chapter in Hebrew and 200 verses in Homer's *Odyssey*. I said my prayers, and ate milk for breakfast. I threatened Anaka with a whipping if she did not confess the intrigue between Daniel and Nurse, but she prevented by a confession. I chided Nurse severely about it, but she denied, with an impudent face, protesting that Daniel only lay on the bed for the sake of the child. I ate nothing but beef for dinner. The Doctor went to Mr. Dick Cocke who was very dangerously sick. I said my prayers. I had good health, good thoughts, and good humor, thanks be to God Almighty.

23. I rose at 6 o'clock and read a chapter in Hebrew and 100 verses in Homer's *Odyssey*. I said my prayers and ate milk for breakfast. Captain Worsham[2] was here and Mr. Ligon[3] about business. I ate battered eggs and then went to Will Randolph's,[4] who was not at home. From thence I went to Colonel Randolph's, where I met Mr. C-s,[5] a sensible man, who had fled from G-l-s W-l. The Colonel told me that two Nansemond Indians and two Meherrins were sent by the Tuscaroras to see if the English were alive. If they were, the Tuscaroras would send in the offenders. I went to visit Dick Cocke who was a little recovered of his gripes. I returned to Colonel Randolph's again where I ate milk. I said my prayers shortly. I had good thoughts,

---

[1]Nathaniel Burwell.

[2]Member of a large Henrico County family, many representatives of which held local office. (*Va. Mag.*, XXXIII, 184-86.)

[3]Probably Richard Ligon, a surveyor, against whom Byrd brought charges on April 24, 1707, of "evil practices in his office." (*Ex. Jour.*, III, 145.)

[4]Son of Colonel William Randolph of Turkey Island.

[5]Mr. C-s has not been identified. He seems to have been a young lawyer who lived with the Harrisons at Berkeley until he left for Barbados.

good health, and good humor, thanks be to God Almighty.

24. I rose at 6 o'clock. I ate milk for breakfast. I said my prayers. Then I went away and on the way called on Dick Cocke and found him better. From thence I went to Falling Creek, where I found all things well except the dam which had lost several of the stones but without any damage to the dam. In the afternoon I went to the Falls where I did not find things in so good order as I expected. Two of my negroes were sick. In the evening I returned to Falling Creek where I ate milk. I forgot to say my prayers. I had good health and good thoughts, but was out of humor with my affairs.

25. I rose at 6 o'clock. I said my prayers shortly. I ate milk for breakfast. I accounted with several of the work-men. I gave the necessary orders, and after dinner went in the rain to Appomattox, where I found all things well. I ate milk for supper. Here I was told that several persons were sick with the gripes who had drunk of the rum brought over by L-n-n. Those that burned it found a substance at the bottom like lime. I said my prayers shortly. I had good health, good thoughts and good humor, thanks be to God Almighty.

26. I rose at 6 in the morning. I said my prayers shortly. I ate milk for breakfast. It had rained so violently that P-t-r-s-n's mill dam went away. In the afternoon it held up and I went to Colonel Bolling's[1] whom I found very ill of the dropsy. However he was cheerful and though he talked of dying it seemed to be in jest. The Colonel told me a man from North Carolina came to him to buy Indian goods but because he had no pay with him he let him have none. I ate milk for supper. I had good health, good thoughts, and good humor, thanks be to God Almighty.

27. I rose at 6 o'clock and said my prayers and ate milk for breakfast. Robin Bolling came over to see me to consult what was most proper to be done about the clerk's place. He wrote a letter to the President to desire him to appoint

---

[1] Colonel Robert Bolling, whose death Byrd mentions on July 17, 1709.

Mr. Mumford[1] clerk since the justices would not admit him. I recommended the Colonel to God Almighty and returned home. When I [came] to the ferry I saw Mistress Mary Eppes,[2] a pretty girl and capable of impression. When I came home I found all things well.   I ate roast beef for dinner. It rained again in the afternoon. I received a letter from my brother Duke to desire me to lend him £50. I said my prayers. I had good health, good thoughts, and good humor, thanks be to God Almighty.

28. I rose at 6 o'clock and read a chapter in Hebrew and 200 verses in Homer's *Odyssey*. I said my prayers. I ate milk for breakfast. I recommended my family to God Almighty and went the new way to Williamsburg, which seemed very tedious. I got to Mr. Bland's[3] a little after sunset. I ate some rice milk and then went to visit the President where I found Colonel [Rhett][4] and Mr. Robinson.[5] We played at cards till 10 o'clock. Then I went to lie at Mr. Bland's. I said my prayers shortly. I had good thoughts, good health, good humor, thanks be to God Almighty. My sister Custis[6] and Mrs. J-f-r-y[7] came about a week ago over the Bay and say the distemper continues still but not with the same violence it did, but that about [30-] people had died of it this winter in the two counties. It was infectious and killed chiefly poor people. The best remedy for it is sweating and the best way to prevent it is to vomit and purge. This distemper never comes but in winter and as the cold weather abates that abates also.

---

[1]Robert Mumford, justice of the peace in Prince George County.

[2]Probably the daughter of William Eppes, sheriff of Prince George County in 1705. (*Va. Mag.*, III, 394.)

[3]Probably Theodorick Bland, surveyor of Williamsburg.

[4]At a meeting of the Council, on March 1, 1708, when there was a flurry over the danger of French privateers, it was agreed to treat with Colonel William Rhett for the rent of his armed brigantine. This was doubtless Colonel Rhett, the vice-admiral, of South Carolina.

[5]Several Virginians of considerable prominence at this time were named Robinson. There is no indication of which one Byrd means here. He generally confused "Robinson" and "Robertson" in the shorthand.

[6]Byrd's wife's sister, Frances Parke, married John Custis.

[7]Mrs. J-f-r-y later married Parson Dunn. (See Sept. 13, 1709.) There is an unpublished letter to "Dunella" among the Byrd MSS in the University of North Carolina, evidently discussing this lady and her malign influence on Byrd's household.

Abundance of people in Appomattox and upper James River fell sick of the gripes occasioned by rum brought among them by the New England vessels. This is probably because most people that drink a little or much have the gripes unless they can bring it up again. So many people were never known in Virginia to have the gripes at one time. Several have died of it, several lost their limbs. I informed the President and Council of it but they took no notice of it.

March, 1709

1. I rose at 6 o'clock and said my prayers shortly. I ate rice milk for breakfast. Then I went to pay my court to the President. I could not persuade Mr. President to admit Mr. Mumford to be clerk of Prince George. While I stayed there Colonel Carter, Colonel Duke, Mr. Commissary, Colonel Digges, Mr. Lewis, Colonel Bassett, and Colonel Ludwell[1] came over. They all went to Council and I presented a memorial to them, without effect. Mr. Burwell was sworn naval officer of York River and ordered a vessel to be fitted out with 10 guns and 80 men to guard the coast. We all went to dinner at 7 o'clock at night where I ate nothing but beef. Major Burwell[2] dined with us and looked very well by the help of temperance. I said my prayers shortly. I had good health, good thoughts and was out of humor at what Mr. Bland told me about the disorder of Falling Creek. My sea sloop was this day at the mouth of [. . .][3] Hope Creek.

2. I rose at 6 o'clock and went to take my leave of the President. I ate custard for breakfast and then took leave of Mr. Bland and went to the Commissary's where I met my sister Custis and Mrs. J-f-r-y. I was very much surprised to find Mrs. Blair[4] drunk, which is growing pretty common with her, and her relations disguise it under the name of consolation. I ate nothing here but about 12 o'clock waited on the ladies to Green Springs[5] where we found all in good health. I ate nothing but fowl for supper. Then we played

---

[1]Robert Carter, Henry Duke, Commissary James Blair, Dudley Digges, John Lewis, William Bassett, and Philip Ludwell, all members of the Council.
[2]Major Lewis Burwell.
[3]Blotted; possibly Archer's Hope Creek, which is near Williamsburg. The sloop, however, had sailed on February 19.
[4]Wife of Commissary James Blair; she was Sarah, daughter of Colonel Benjamin Harrison. In 1687 she made a solemn promise to marry no man but William Roscow; two months later she married the Commissary. Roscow married Mary Wilson, and died in 1700. (*Va. Mag.*, VII, 278, 286; *Wm. Q. (1)*, 133.)
[5]Green Springs, on the James, at this time the home of Philip Ludwell, whose father had obtained the place on his second marriage, to the widow of Governor Berkeley.

cards till 11 o'clock. I said my prayers shortly. I had good health, good thoughts, and good humor, thanks be to God Almighty.

3. I rose at 6 o'clock and said my prayers and as soon as we had breakfasted we took our leave and went to West-over. By the way we called at the house of one W-l-x [Wilkes?] where we ate bacon and eggs which the people gave us very heartily. I would not give the woman money because it would have been spent in rum but I promised her six pounds of wool. From hence we got home a little after sunset where I found all in good health, thanks be to God. The ladies were not so weary but they ate their supper. I said my prayers. I had good health, good thoughts, and good humor this day, thanks be to God, the giver of all good things.

4. I rose at 6 o'clock and read a chapter in Hebrew and 50 verses in Homer's *Odyssey*. I said my prayers and ate milk for breakfast. I sent Tom to Falling Creek to desire G-r-l[1] to lessen the number of the workmen and to forbid building the house at Westover. Mr. Mumford came to hear the success I had in the business of his being made clerk but he was disappointed. I ate pork for dinner. In the afternoon Mr. Bland came on his way to Williamsburg and was persuaded to stay all night. The Doctor came drunk to dinner. He, Mr. Bland, and I played a pool at piquet[2] and I lost all. I said my prayers. I had good health, good thoughts and good humor this day, thanks be to God Almighty.

5. I rose at 6 o'clock and read a chapter in Hebrew and 100 verses in Homer's *Odyssey*. I said my prayers and ate chocolate for breakfast. Then Mr. Bland went away. Tom brought word that the dam at Falling Creek was much damaged by the fresh and that Abraham had a bloody flux.

---

[1]Overseer at Falling Creek, possibly Richard Grills who in May 1708 brought before the court in behalf of Byrd a young servant of Byrd's "for inspection of age." (Henrico Order Book, 1707-09, p. 49.) In June 1710 Richard Grills deeded land on "Prockter's main branch," Henrico County, to Byrd. (Henrico County Court Records, 1710-14, pp. 6-11.)

[2]A card game popular in the seventeenth and eighteenth centuries.

This morning [Wilkes] came for the six pounds of wool and had it. I ate . . .

[Two pages of MS missing]

. . . and good humor, thanks be to God Almighty.

25. I rose at 6 o'clock and read two chapters in Hebrew and 200 verses in Homer's *Odyssey*. I said my prayers and ate milk for breakfast. I danced my dance. The Doctor went to Williamsburg. I wrote a letter to England. Parson Ware[1] sent to me for a pint of canary, he being sick of the gripes with the New England rum, which I sent him, notwithstanding I have but a little, because I should be glad if I were in his condition to receive such a kindness from another. Mrs. J-f-r-y was sick again today. I ate nothing but hash of beef. In the afternoon I took a nap, contrary to custom. I settled my accounts. In the evening we walked about the plantation. I said my prayers. I had good thoughts, good health, and good humor all day, thanks to God Almighty.

26. I rose at 6 o'clock and read three chapters in Hebrew and 200 verses in Homer's *Odyssey*. I said my prayers, and ate milk for breakfast. I danced my dance. I wrote a letter to England. My river sloop came about noon from Appomattox, with 25 hogsheads of tobacco. I ate tripe for dinner. Before we had dined Mr. Hardiman[2] came to see me but would not eat. In the afternoon Peter Hamlin came also. We played at billiards. In the evening we took a walk about the plantation. I read Italian and some of my own work[3] to the ladies. I had good health, good thoughts, and good humor all day, thanks be to God Almighty. The sloop brought two barrels of tar and 10 hides.

---

[1] Jacob Ware, minister of Henrico Parish, who died before August 1709, when Byrd sued his widow and administratrix, Susanna Ware, for a debt due William Byrd I. (Henrico Order Book, 1707-09, p. 167.) The Mrs. Ware and her daughter "Suky" mentioned later in the diary are evidently the widow and child of Jacob Ware.

[2] Probably John Hardiman, burgess for Prince George County in 1710.

[3] That Byrd was engaged in literary composition at this time is worthy of note. In the University of North Carolina notebook are interspersed "characters" and bits of verse that may be of early composition.

27. I rose at 6 o'clock and read a chapter in Hebrew and two chapters in the Greek 'Testament. I said my prayers and ate fritters for breakfast. I sent away the sloop again to Appomattox for more tobacco. I danced my dance. I had a small looseness this morning. I ate boiled pork for dinner moderately. In the afternoon I walked about the plantation with the ladies. I read nothing in the evening. I said my prayers. I had good health, good thoughts, and good humor this day, thanks be to God Almighty.

28. I rose at 6 o'clock and read a chapter in Hebrew and 250 verses in Homer's *Odyssey*. I neglected to say my prayers this morning, notwithstanding it was my birthday, for which God forgive me. I ate milk for breakfast. About 10 o'clock I got on horseback and rode to Mr. Anderson's on my way to Falling Creek. I called at Colonel Eppes,[1] but he was not at home. I went over the river and called at Dr. Bowman's[2] where was a man sick of the gripes which he got by drinking New England rum. Then I proceeded to Falling Creek where I found Mr. G-r-l drunk and John [full] and the business not in so good order as I expected. I scolded at Mr. G-r-l till he cried and then was peevish. I ate nothing but milk. I said my prayers in bed. I had good health, good thoughts, but was out of humor in the evening.

29. I said my prayers in bed and then rose about 6 o'clock and ate milk for breakfast, and after I had been at the mill I rode with Mr. G-r-l to the Falls, where I found things not extraordinary. Here I went over the river with Mr. G-r-l and Tom Turpin to Shockoe[3] and from thence to the other plantation on that side where matters were not very forward. We took John Blackman with us and went

---

[1]Both Francis and Littlebury Eppes were colonels of the militia at this time.

[2]Dr. John Bowman, a physician practicing in Henrico County at this period. (See Blanton, *Medicine in Virginia in the Seventeenth Century*, p. 263.)

[3]Shockoe plantation, on the site of Richmond. (See Bishop William Meade, *Old Churches, Ministers and Families of Virginia* [Philadelphia, 1857], I, 444.)

to try whether Captain Webb[1] had not encroached on me
and found that he had built his house on my land. We
returned to John Blackman's and ate bacon and eggs and
then went back to Falling Creek, very much tired. I ate a
little [fowl] and went to bed where I said a short prayer.
I had good health, good thoughts, and indifferent good
humor, thanks be to God.

30. It rained very much this morning. I rose about 7
o'clock and said my prayers shortly. I ate milk for breakfast and about 10 I returned from Falling Creek to Mr.
Anderson's, where I ate some fish for dinner, and about
4 o'clock came home in the rain where I found all things in
good order but only Jenny had run into the river last night
but came out again of herself and was severely whipped for
it. In the evening I ate some milk. I neglected to say my
prayers, for which God forgive me. I had good health,
good thoughts, and good humor, thanks be to God Almighty.

31. I rose at 6 o'clock and read a chapter in Hebrew and
200 verses in Homer's *Odyssey*. I said my prayers and ate
milk for breakfast. I danced my dance. Mr. Haynes came
to see me and I appointed him to receive the President's
tobacco. We made an end of sowing the oats. I ate nothing but boiled beef for dinner. My wife was out of humor
for nothing. However I endeavored to please her again,
having consideration for a woman's weakness. I played at
billiards with the ladies. I read Italian. In the evening
we walked about the plantation. My wife was out of order
so we went to bed soon. I had good health, good thoughts,
and good humor, thanks be to God Almighty. I said my
prayers. This month was remarkable for abundance of
rain and wind without frost.

---

[1] Giles Webb of Henrico County.

April, 1709

1. I rose before 6 o'clock and read a chapter in Hebrew and 250 verses in Homer's *Odyssey*. I said my prayers and ate [. . .] for breakfast. John [West] made an end of the two little houses and I settled the account with him. I ate some cold beef and then I waited on the ladies to Mr. Anderson's, where we got about 12 o'clock. About 3 o'clock we ate, and I ate nothing but dry beef, notwithstanding there were several other dishes. We returned home about sunset, and found the Doctor just come from Williamsburg. He brought a good deal of news from Europe and particularly that our last fleet was arrived in England. He told me likewise there was a report that my father Parke[1] was killed by the [l-v-n-t] of a man-of-war in the West Indies, which God grant may not be true. I said my prayers and had a small headache but good thoughts and good humor this day, thanks be to God Almighty.

2. I rose at 6 o'clock and read a chapter in Hebrew and 250 verses in Homer's *Odyssey*. I said my prayers devoutly, and ate milk for breakfast. I danced my dance. I settled my accounts and read Italian. It rained all day. I ate nothing but roast beef for dinner. In the afternoon we played at billiards. In the evening we took a walk. I said my prayers. I had good thoughts, good health, and good humor, thanks be to God Almighty.

3. I rose at 6 o'clock and read a chapter in Hebrew and four chapters in the Greek Testament. I said my prayers devoutly and ate hominy for breakfast. I danced my dance. We prepared to go to church, but the parson did not come, notwithstanding good weather, so I read a sermon in Dr. Tillotson at home. I ate nothing but boiled beef for dinner but a great deal of that. In the evening we took a walk about the plantation. I read again in Dr. Tillotson. I had

---

[1]Daniel Parke, governor of the Leeward Islands, Byrd's father-in-law. This report of his death was not true, but he was killed in an uprising at Antigua on December 7, 1710.

good health, good thoughts, and good humor all day, thanks be to God Almighty. The river sloop arrived before dinner with 24 hogsheads of tobacco.

4. I rose before 6 o'clock and read a chapter in Hebrew and 230 verses in Homer's *Odyssey*. I said my prayers devoutly and ate milk for breakfast. I danced my dance. The sloop was unloaded this morning. Captain Thomson[1] and Captain Littlepage[2] of New Kent came to buy quitrents and dined with me. So did Mr. Parker. While we were at dinner Mr. Bland came and told us abundance of news and particularly that our fleet was arrived safe home. Mr. Harrison, Captain Stith, and Will Randolph came likewise to see me. After dinner we played at billiards. My people set Mr. Bland home and all the company went away. We put everything on board the sloop in order to go to Williamsburg. In the evening we took a walk and I wrote a letter to Mr. Bland about the sloop. I neglected to say my prayers, for which God forgive me. I had good health, good thoughts, and good humor all day, thanks be to God Almighty.

5. I rose at 6 o'clock this morning and read a chapter in Hebrew and 250 verses in Homer's *Odyssey*. I said my prayers and ate milk for breakfast. The sloop sailed away this morning. I danced my dance. I was griped this morning a little and had a loose stool. I settled my accounts and read Italian. I ate hashed beef for dinner only. The Doctor had a fever and ague. We played at billiards. I read more Italian. In the evening we took a walk about the plantation. The brickmaker came this evening. I scolded with John about [managing] the tobacco. I read to the ladies Dr. Lister's *Journey to Paris*.[3] I was ill treated by my wife, at whom I was out of humor. I said my prayers and had good health, good thoughts, and good humor, thanks be to God Almighty.

6. I rose before 6 o'clock and read two chapters in

---

[1] Roger Thomson, appointed sheriff of New Kent County in 1706.
[2] Richard Littlepage. (See Sept. 23, 1712 entry and note.)
[3] Martin Lister, M. D., *A Journey to Paris in the Year 1698* (London, 1699).

Hebrew and 200 verses in Homer's *Odyssey*. I said my prayers devoutly. My wife and I disagreed about employing a gardener. I ate milk for breakfast. John made an end of [trimming] the boat, which he performed very well. I settled my accounts and read Italian. I ate nothing but fish for dinner and a little asparagus. We played at billiards. I read more Italian. In the evening we walked about the plantation after I read in Dr. Lister's book to the ladies. My wife and I continued very cool. I said my prayers, and had good health, good thoughts and good humor, thanks be to God Almighty.

7. I rose before 6 o'clock and read two chapters in Hebrew and 250 verses in Homer's *Odyssey* and made an end of it. I said my prayers devoutly. I ate milk for breakfast. I danced my dance. The men began to work this day to dig for brick. I settled my accounts and read Italian. I reproached my wife with ordering the old beef to be kept and the fresh beef used first, contrary to good management, on which she was pleased to be very angry and this put me out of humor. I ate nothing but boiled beef for dinner. I went away presently after dinner to look after my people. When I returned I read more Italian and then my wife came and begged my pardon and we were friends again. I read in Dr. Lister again very late. I said my prayers. I had good health, good thoughts, and bad humor, unlike a philosopher.

8. I rose after 6 o'clock this morning and read a chapter in Hebrew and 150 verses in Homer's last work. I said my prayers and ate milk for breakfast. I danced my dance. My wife and I had another foolish quarrel about my saying she listened on the top of the stairs, which I suspected, in jest. However, I bore it with patience and she came soon after and begged my pardon. I settled my accounts and read some Dutch. Just before dinner Mr. Custis[1] came and dined with us. He told us that my father Parke instead of being killed was married to his housekeeper which is more improbable. He told us that the distemper continued to

---

[1] John Custis III, Byrd's brother-in-law.

rage extremely on the other side the Bay and had destroyed abundance of people. I did not keep to my rule of eating but the one dish. We played at billiards and walked about the plantation. I said my prayers and had good humor, good health, and good thoughts, thanks be to God Almighty. The Indian woman died this evening, according to a dream I had last night about her.

9. I rose at 5 o'clock and read a chapter in Hebrew and 150 verses in Homer. I said my prayers devoutly and ate milk for breakfast. My wife and I had another scold about mending my shoes but it was soon over by her submission. I settled my accounts and read Dutch. I ate nothing but cold roast beef and asparagus for dinner. In the afternoon Mr. Custis complained of a pain in his side for which he took a sweat of snakeroot. I read more Dutch and took a little nap. In the evening we took a walk about the plantation. My people made an end of planting the corn field. I had an account from Rappahannock that the same distemper began to rage there that had been so fatal on the Eastern Shore. I had good health, good thoughts and good humor, thanks be to God Almighty. I said my prayers.

10. I rose at 6 o'clock and read two chapters in Hebrew and four chapters in the Greek Testament. I said my prayers with great devoutness and ate milk for breakfast. Our maid Jane began to cry out. I danced my dance. Jane was brought to bed of a boy. About 12 o'clock we went to my Cousin Harrison's,[1] where we dined. I ate fowl and bacon for dinner only. Here I heard that Colonel Harrison[2] had been very sick but was now something better and that Colonel Bassett[3] had likewise been sick and Mr. Burwell, but that they were all very well again. Here we stayed till almost sunset when we walked home where we found all things well, thanks be to God. I ate some milk for supper.

---

[1] Byrd referred to Benjamin Harrison of Berkeley as "cousin" and "neighbor." (See Introduction, p. xxiv.)

[2] Colonel Benjamin Harrison of Wakefield, father of the Benjamin Harrison mentioned in the preceding note.

[3] Councillor William Bassett of Eltham, New Kent County.

I said my prayers and had good thoughts, good health, and good humor all day, thanks be to God Almighty.

11. I rose at 5 o'clock and read a chapter in Hebrew and 300 verses in Homer. I said my prayers and ate milk for breakfast. I danced my dance. My brother Custis took a vomit this morning which worked very well. I settled my accounts and read Dutch. I ate nothing but hashed beef for dinner. In the afternoon Ned Randolph[1] came over in order to go to school at Mr. Harrison's. I proffered Colonel Randolph that he might be here for that purpose. This day my neighbor Harrison was taken with the gout in his leg. I packed up my things to send to Williamsburg by Mr. Harrison's boat. In the evening we took a walk about the plantation. I ate some milk. It rained a little this evening. I had good health, good thoughts, and good humor, thanks be to God Almighty.

12. I rose at 5 o'clock and read a chapter in Hebrew and 200 verses in Homer. I said my prayers and ate milk for breakfast. Mr. Harrison's boat called here for my things which I sent to Williamsburg. I danced my dance. I settled my accounts. Before noon Mr. Anderson and his wife and Mistress B-k-r came and dined with us. I ate fish for dinner only. In the afternoon we played at billiards. In the evening they went away and Mr. Bland came on his way to Williamsburg and told us that Colonel Bassett was very ill again. Mr. Bland and I played at piquet. I said my prayers shortly. We went to bed about 10 o'clock. I had good health, good thoughts, and indifferent humor, thanks be to God Almighty.

13. I rose at 5 o'clock this morning and read a chapter in Hebrew and no Greek. I said my prayers and ate milk for breakfast. Mr. M-r-s-l[2] came from Williamsburg, where he had been purchasing the leather. We walked out and saw Mr. Will Randolph calling the ferry. Mr. Bland and I played at piquet before dinner. I ate nothing but boiled beef. After dinner Mr. Tom Randolph[3] came to see me, to

---

[1] Edward, son of Colonel William Randolph of Turkey Island.
[2] An overseer for Byrd, probably Mr. Marshall.
[3] Son of Colonel William Randolph of Turkey Island.

inquire into what land I [or they] had. We played at billiards. In the evening Mr. Mumford came and told me the President had written to the court of Prince George not to sit until they would accept of Mr. Robin Bolling. We walked and I showed Mr. Mumford three hogsheads of bad tobacco of his receiving. I had a great hoarseness. I ate milk. I neglected to say my prayers. I had good health, good thoughts and good humor, thanks be to God Almighty.

14. I rose at 6 o'clock and read a chapter in Hebrew and 100 verses in Homer. I neglected to say my prayers. I ate milk for breakfast. About 10 o'clock my brother and sister Custis went away, and presently after Mr. Mumford like-wise. Captain Llewellyn came to see me and stayed about an hour. The Doctor came home. I paid the old wire man for what work he had done at Falling Creek. I ate only honey and bread for dinner and drank milk and water. Last night three moons were seen about 10 o'clock. We played at billiards. I read some Dutch. In the evening it rained very much. I ate milk for supper but in the night it made me a little feverish and my spirits were strangely disturbed. Our daughter[1] was taken ill at night of a fever. I neglected to say my prayers. I had good thoughts, in-different health, and good thoughts [sic], thanks be to God Almighty.

15. I rose about 6 o'clock and read a chapter in Hebrew and 150 verses in Homer. I said my prayers and ate milk for breakfast. I had a little looseness. I gave some men leave to fish at the bay. I prepared my accounts against the General Court. I read some Dutch. My hoarseness was something better. The child continued to have her fever till about noon and then she fell into a sweat which drove out red spots. At noon I ate nothing but squirrel and asparagus for dinner. We played at billiards in the after-noon. Then I mended the locks of my closet and secretary. In the evening we took a walk to the bay to see the men fishing. We had a letter from my sister Custis by which we

---

[1]Evelyn, born June 16, 1707.

learned that Crapeau[1] is come into our cape and taken a vessel. I neglected to say my prayers. I had good health, good thoughts, and good humor, thanks be to God Almighty.

16. I rose before 6 o'clock and read a chapter in Hebrew and 150 verses in Homer. I said my prayers and ate milk for breakfast. The child was a great deal better and had no fever this day. I prepared my accounts for Williamsburg and read some Dutch. Mr. Harrison's boat brought my [chains] from Williamsburg. I ate nothing at dinner but pork and peas which were salty and made me dry all the afternoon. We played at billiards, and I won a bit of the Doctor. I read more Dutch. In the evening I walked about the plantation and showed John what work I would have done when I was gone to Williamsburg. At night I wrote a letter to Falling Creek to send by Henry, who is to go tomorrow morning. I said my prayers. I had good health, good thoughts, and good humor, thanks be to God Almighty.

17. I rose at 5 o'clock and read a chapter in Hebrew and 150 verses in Homer. I said my prayers, and ate milk for breakfast. I danced my dance. The child had her fever again last night for which I gave her a vomit this morning, which worked very well. Anaka was whipped yesterday for stealing the rum and filling the bottle up with water. I went to church, where were abundance of people, among whom was Mrs. H-m-l-n, a very handsome woman. Colonel Eppes and his wife, with Captain Worsham came to dine with me, who told me that Tom Haynes[2] was gone out of his wits. I sent Tom and Eugene to Mr. Harvey's[3] to meet me tomorrow morning. I took a walk about the plantation. I said my prayers. I had good health, good thoughts, and good humor, thanks be to God Almighty.

18. I rose at 3 o'clock and after committing my family

---

[1]Captain Crapeau, a French privateer. (See *Ex. Jour.*, III, 205.)

[2]On December 24, 1714, the Council received a petition of guardianship from George Hunt for "Thomas Haynes of Charles City County a lunatic." (*Ex. Jour.*, III, 394.)

[3]Probably William Harvey of Surry County. (*Wm. Q. (1)*, XI, 83, and *Cal. S. P.*, 141.)

to the divine protection, I went in the boat to Mr. Harvey's, where I got by break of day. Mr. Harvey's mother met me on the shore and desired me to persuade her son to be more kind to her, which I promised I would. From thence I proceeded to Williamsburg, where I got about 10 o'clock. I waited on the President, where I saw Mr. Blair and Colonel Duke. Then I went to Mr. Bland's where I ate some custard. Then I went to court where I presented a petition to the General Court for Captain Webb's land as lapsed.[1] When the court rose I went to dinner to C-t Y-n with the Council, where I ate nothing but boiled beef. Then we went to the President's where we played at cards till 10 o'clock. I won 25 shillings. I went and lay at my new lodgings. I had good health, good thoughts, and good humor, thanks be to God Almighty.

19. I rose at 5 o'clock and read in Homer and a chapter in Hebrew. I said my prayers and ate rice milk for breakfast. About 10 o'clock I went to court where I paid Mr. Conner[2] 40 shillings instead of the note for £7 drawn by Daniel Wilkinson. He told me his sloop came the last of March from Barbados, and brings word that the King of France was dead and that my father Parke was well and not married. I read in Justin. In the afternoon I played at piquet with Mr. W-l-s. We dined very late and I ate nothing but fowl and bacon. When that was over we went to Mr. David Bray's[3] where we danced till midnight. I had Mrs. Mary Thomson[4] for my partner. I recommended myself to the divine protection. I had good thoughts, good health, and good humor, thanks to God

---

[1] For the transactions involving Captain Giles Webb's land, see letters of William Byrd I in *Va. Mag.*, XXV, 262, 352, 355; XXVI, 21, 27; also *Edward Pleasants Valentine Papers*, ed. Clayton Torrence (Richmond, 1927), p. 1,409.

[2] Lewis Conner of Norfolk County owned a vessel trading to Curaçao and St. Thomas's. He is referred to in connection with illegal trading with these islands in a letter of Spotswood. (*Va. Mag.*, XXX, 22; *Official Letters of Alexander Spotswood*, ed. R. A. Brock [Richmond, 1882], I, 87.)

[3] Colonel David Bray, resident of Bruton Parish, was appointed sheriff of James City County May 11, 1706.

[4] Probably the daughter of Stevens Thomson, attorney general. (*Wm. Q.* (*1*), X, 141.)

Almighty. This day I learned that one of my new negroes died of a fever. God's will be done.

20. I rose at 7 o'clock and read a chapter in Hebrew and looked over two books of Homer. I said my prayers and ate rice milk for breakfast. Mr. [Claiborne][1] came to my chambers and we had some words about a protested bill of exchange of his. I went to court and did a great deal of business all day. The news was confirmed of the King of France's death. We did not dine till 6 o'clock [when] I ate nothing but boiled beef. I was at a meeting of the College where we chose Colonel Randolph [rector]. We had Mr. Luke[2] before us about his accounts, who could not justify them, nor say anything in his excuse. Afterwards we played at whist with the President and I lost £ . . . I said my prayers shortly, had good health, and good thoughts, and good humor, thanks be to God Almighty.

21. Rose at 6 o'clock and read three books of Homer. I said my prayers and ate milk for breakfast. I did a great deal of business this day. We dined about 3 o'clock and I ate fowl and bacon for dinner. Afterwards we went to whist £5.10 [sic] and then I played at dice and lost 50 shillings and John Bolling won £10. I wrote a letter to my wife to let her know my health. We sat up till 12 o'clock. I had good health, good thoughts, and good humor all day, thanks be to God Almighty.

22. I rose at 6 o'clock and read two books in Homer and said my prayers. I ate rice milk for breakfast and did some business. Then I went to church, it being Good Friday, where the Commissary preached. After church I went with abundance of company to dine at the Commissary's, where I ate with moderation. In the evening I returned into the town and played at whist and won 8:10 of Colonel Smith.[3] We sat up till 12 o'clock and then separated. I had good health, good thoughts, and good humor,

---

[1]Possibly Thomas Claiborne, of Sweet Hall, King William County.
[2]George Luke, collector of customs, Lower District of the James River. (*Ex. Jour.*, III, 200.)
[3]John Smith, of Gloucester County, appointed to the Council in 1704.

thanks be to God Almighty. Here we saw Mistress H-l-y who is a great instance of human decay.

23. I rose at 6 o'clock and read two books in Homer. I said my prayers, and ate milk for breakfast. I went to the President's, where I learned that the Tuscarora Indians would not deliver up the men we demanded and Colonel Harrison now wrote that now it was his opinion the trade should be open, contrary to what he thought before. I did a great deal of business and dined with the President because it was St. George his day. Then I went with Colonel Ludwell to Green Springs with Colonel Carter, where we danced and were very merry. I neglected to say my prayers. I had good thoughts, good humor, and good health, thanks be to God Almighty.

24. I rose at 6 o'clock and said my prayers very shortly. We breakfasted about 10 o'clock and I ate nothing but bread and butter and sack. We rode to Jamestown Church, where Mr. Commissary preached. When church was done I gave 10 shillings to the poor. Nothing could hinder me from sleeping at church, though I took a great deal of pains against it. We rode home to Colonel Ludwell's again where we dined and I ate fish and asparagus. In the afternoon we took a walk and saw the carcasses of 50 cows which had been burnt in a house belonging to Colonel Ludwell. Mr. W-l-s ran two races and beat John Custis and Mr. [Hawkins][1]. He likewise jumped over the fence which was a very great jump. Colonel Carter returned to town with Mr. Harrison and we stayed and ate syllabub for supper. I neglected to say my prayers. I had good thoughts, good humor, and good health, thanks be to God Almighty.

25. I rose at 6 o'clock and said my prayers shortly. Mr. W-l-s and I fenced and I beat him. Then we played at cricket. Mr. W-l-s and John Custis against me and Mr. [Hawkins], but we were beaten. I ate nothing but milk for breakfast and then we returned to Williamsburg, where

---

[1]Possibly John Hawkins, a burgess from Essex County in 1710 and later.

we received the news that the Governor[1] was returned to France, not being able to get his exchange, and that he could not be here before the fall, and that tobacco was very low and that the Lord Somers[2] was president of the Council. I did a great deal of business. About 5 o'clock we went to dinner and I ate nothing but boiled beef. In the evening I took a walk and then went to Mr. Bland's, where I examined my godson[3] and Johnny Randolph[4] and found the last well improved. I said my prayers shortly and went to bed in good time to recover my lost sleep. I had good health, good thoughts, and good humor all day, thanks to God Almighty.

26. I rose at 6 o'clock and read two books in Homer and two chapters in Hebrew. I said my prayers, and ate milk for breakfast. We went to the Council where it was agreed to open the Indian trade. I did a great deal of business. The sheriffs were appointed this day. They passed several accounts. About 4 o'clock we went to dinner and I ate nothing but beef. Then I took a walk and came to Mr. Bland's, from whence Mr. Will Randolph and I went to Colonel Bray's, where we found abundance of ladies and gentlemen dancing. We did not dance but got some kisses among them. About 11 o'clock we returned home. I recommended myself to the divine protection. I had good health, good thoughts, and good humor, thanks be to God Almighty.

27. I rose at 6 o'clock and read two books in Homer and a chapter in Hebrew. I said my prayers and ate milk for breakfast. I wrote a letter to my wife by Will Randolph. I did abundance of business. My sister Custis came to town on her way to Major Burwell's. I went to wait on her at

---

[1]Robert Hunter, commissioned lieutenant governor of Virginia on August 14, 1707, was captured by French privateers and never arrived in Virginia. He was taken to France, but later returned to England in an exchange of prisoners. He was appointed governor of New York and arrived there on June 14, 1710, where he remained as governor until 1719. (See later entries in the diary, especially June 20, 1709, and January 2, 1710.)
[2]John, Lord Somers, sworn president of the Privy Council November 25, 1708.
[3]Perhaps Drury Stith's son John, whom Byrd mentions later as a godson.
[4]Son of William Randolph of Turkey Island; later Sir John Randolph.

Mr. Bland's, where came abundance of other ladies. I stayed with them two hours. My brother and sister Custis went away. I paid several of the Council their money. I agreed with Captain C-l to give him bills for money at five guineas per cent. I went to dinner where I ate nothing but mutton hash. After dinner we played at cricket and then went to whist and I lost 30 shillings. I went home about 11 o'clock. I had good health, good thoughts, and good humor all day, thanks be to God Almighty.

28. I rose at 6 o'clock and read two books in Homer and a chapter in Hebrew. I said my prayers and ate milk for breakfast. Mr. President and Colonel Duke came to see me at my chambers where we talked about the accounts. I did abundance of business and got all the warrants ready. It was 5 o'clock before we went to dinner and I ate mutton and asparagus. After dinner I went to the President's, and then took a walk. Then I went to Mr. Bland's, where I found Mr. Harrison and Mr. Robinson. I went to bed early and committed myself to God's protection. I had good health, good thoughts, and good humor, thanks be to God Almighty. It rained much this night.

29. I rose at 6 o'clock and read a chapter in Hebrew and a book in Homer. I had not time to say my prayers in form, and ate milk for breakfast. I received £600 of Captain C-l for bills at five guineas per cent. About noon my spouse arrived and left all things well at home this morning, thanks be to God. We dined at Mr. Bland's and then rode to Mr. Commissary Blair's and were overtaken with a gust of thunder and rain. Mrs. Blair was sick and talked very [simply]. We were kindly entertained. About 10 o'clock we went to bed, where I lay in my wife's arms. I had good health, good thoughts, and good humor, thanks be to God Almighty.

30. I rose at 6 o'clock and read nothing, nor did I say my prayers, for which God forgive me. I drank two dishes of chocolate and after it some broth. About 8 o'clock we walked to the capitol, where my warrants were signed. I ate about 12 o'clock some hashed mutton with the President,

and then took my leave of the Council. When the ladies had put their things in order we went into the vault and drank a glass of Rhenish wine and sugar. Then we rode to Kings Creek to Major Burwell's. We found him at dinner with my brother and sister Custis and Mistress Betty Todd[1]. We ate with them. I ate nothing but boiled beef. The Major had the gout in one foot, very moderately because of his temperance. We took a walk to the marsh lately drained by a dam and sluice. We went to bed about 9 o'clock. I had good health, good thoughts, and good humor, thanks be to God Almighty. I prayed shortly.

---

[1] Probably Elizabeth Todd, sometimes called "cousin Todd," a descendant of Lucy Higginson and William Bernard, whose daughter Elizabeth Bernard married Thomas Todd. (See Introduction, p. xxiv.)

May, 1709

1.[1] I rose about 6 o'clock and read in Lucian. I recommended myself to God in a short prayer. My wife was a little indisposed and out of humor. I ate bread and butter for breakfast. We went to church over the creek and Mr. Taylor[2] preached a good sermon. As soon as we came into church it began to rain and continued to rain all day very much. However I was not wet. When we returned my wife was something better. I ate roast beef for dinner. After dinner we were forced to keep house because of the rain. I endeavored to learn all I could from Major Burwell who is a sensible man skilled in matters relating to tobacco. In the evening we talked about religion and my wife and her sister had a fierce dispute about the infallibility of the Bible. I neglected to say my prayers. However, I had good health, good thoughts, and good humor, thanks be to God Almighty.

2. I rose at 6 o'clock and read in Lucian. I recommended myself to God in a short prayer, and ate meat for breakfast. The women went to romping and I and my brother romped with them. About 12 o'clock my brother and sister Custis went on board their frigate in order to sail to Accomac. Then we went over the river to Carter's Creek and found Mr. Burwell[3] indisposed with a cold and his lady ready to lie in. We ate boiled beef for supper. After supper I found myself very sleepy. About 10 o'clock we went to bed. I had good health, good humor, and good thoughts, thanks be to God Almighty.

3. I rose about 6 o'clock and read in Lucian. I recommended myself to heaven in a short prayer and ate milk

---

[1]The figure "31" under April is changed to "1" and at the bottom of the page is a note in longhand: "Note ye 31. of April is a mistake & shoud be ye 1st of May."
[2]Reverend Daniel Taylor, minister of Blissland Parish, New Kent County, 1700-1724. (*Va. Mag.,* VIII, 62.)
[3]Nathaniel Burwell, of Carter's Creek, Gloucester County, whose wife was Elizabeth, daughter of Robert Carter.

for breakfast. I went to see Mr. Burwell's tobacco, which seemed to be very heavy. I ate fish for dinner, which they called trout. In the afternoon we went to see my cousin Berkeley.[1] We found her big with child. Their house was very neat. We stayed about two hours and then returned to Mr. Burwell's, where we found Mr. Evans.[2] Mrs. Burwell is a very pretty, good-humored woman but seemed to be a little melancholy, as he did likewise, I know not for what reason. I went to bed about 10 o'clock, notwithstanding my cousin sat in the room. I had good health, good thoughts, and good humor, thanks be to God.

4. I rose at 6 o'clock and read in Lucian, ate milk for breakfast, and walked out and said my prayers in the open. A ship arrived in York River about 9 o'clock. Captain Berkeley came to see us, who is a very good-humored man. We walked in the garden about an hour; then we went to dinner and I ate boiled beef. In the afternoon we danced a minuet and then took our leave and returned over the river again to Major Burwell's[3] where we found Colonel Bassett and his lady who are very good people. In the evening we saw a great ship sail up the river. The Major sent on board for his letters which brought no news. We sat up talking till 10 o'clock. I had good health, good thoughts, and good humor, thanks be to God Almighty.

5. I rose at 6 o'clock and ate milk for breakfast, and neglected to say my prayers, for which God forgive me. I read in Lucian. About 11 o'clock I ate some bread and butter and sack, and then took leave of Major Burwell and rode to Williamsburg with Colonel Bassett. On the way we met Mr. Ingles[4] with his wife and daughter who were going to see us. When we came to Williamsburg, I de-

---

[1]Lucy, daughter of Major Lewis Burwell (and sister of Nathaniel), married Edmund Berkeley of Petsworth Parish, Gloucester County, later of Barn Elms, Middlesex County. Their daughter Lucy was born in May 1709. (*Va. Mag.,* XXXV, 34-38; see Introduction, p. xxiv.)

[2]Perhaps John Evans, an Indian trader. (*Ex. Jour.,* III, 198.)

[3]Major Lewis Burwell, of King's Creek.

[4]Mungo Ingles, grammar master of William and Mary College, 1693-1705, and 1716-19. His wife was Anne, daughter of James Bray. (*Va. Biog.,* I, 263.)

livered to Mr. Bland £600 in money to pay for the use of
the vessel to guard the country. I gave Colonel Bassett a
bottle of wine and then took our leave of him and Mr.
Bland and proceeded to Green Springs where we found Nat
Harrison[1] and his wife and Mr. Edwards.[2] I ate mutton
and sallet for supper. About 11 o'clock we went to bed.
I had good health, good thoughts, and good humor, thanks
be to God Almighty.

6. I rose about 6 o'clock and Colonel Ludwell, Nat
Harrison, Mr. Edwards and myself played at cricket, and
I won a bit.[3] Then we played at whist and I won. About
10 o'clock we went to breakfast and I ate some boiled rice.
Then Colonel Ludwell went to Jamestown court and then
we played at [l-n-s-n-t][4] and I lost £4, most of which Nat
Harrison won. In the afternoon Colonel Ludwell returned
and brought us the bad news that Captain Morgan[5] had
lost his ship in Margate Roads by a storm as likewise had
several others. My loss was very great in this ship where I
had seven hogsheads of skins and 60 hogsheads of heavy
tobacco. The Lord gives and the Lord has taken away—
blessed be the name of the Lord. In the evening Mr.
Clayton[6] and Mr. Robinson came and confirmed the same
bad news. However I ate a good supper of mutton and
asparagus. Then we went to dance away sorrow. I had
good health, good thoughts, and good humor, notwithstanding my misfortune, thanks be to God Almighty.

7. We rose at break of day and were on horseback before
sunrise to return home, after taking leave of our friends.
We had nothing extraordinary happen in our journey but
only that my wife had a pain in her belly which made me
afraid she would miscarry. However we made shift to get
her home and after some rest she recovered. We found all

---

[1]Son of Colonel Benjamin Harrison of Wakefield.
[2]Probably William Edwards, burgess for Surry in 1706, who married
Colonel Harrison's daughter Elizabeth. (*Wm. Q. (1)*, XV, 80.)
[3]A bit—one-eighth of a Spanish dollar.
[4]Perhaps lansquenet, a card game of German origin.
[5]James Morgan, captain of a merchant ship in 1706, is mentioned in
Ex. Jour., III, 95.
[6]John Clayton, later attorney general for Virginia.

things well, thanks be to God, and the servants in good order. Mr. Salle[1] had been here four days to speak with me about the disorder of Manakin Town occasioned by the parson. I ate bacon and pigeon for dinner. In the afternoon Mr. Salle returned toward home and I took a walk to [M-n-s] and ate some cherries, which began to be ripe. In the evening I ate some strawberries and milk. I neglected to give thanks to God for the health of my family and myself returned home, for which God forgive me. I had good thoughts, good health, and good humor, thanks be to God.

8. I rose at 5 o'clock and read a chapter in Hebrew and four chapters in the Greek Testament. I ate strawberries and milk for breakfast and neglected to say my prayers, for which God forgive me. Mr. Mumford came about 10 o'clock and let me know all was well at Appomattox. He told me Mr. Bolling had agreed with Mr. Goodrich[2] that he be clerk on the consideration he should have half the profit for three years. I ate bacon and chicken for dinner. In the afternoon I wrote a letter to the President to recommend Mr. Mumford to be clerk of Prince George. Caleb [Ware] came from Falling Creek and let me know Mr. G-r-l was very sick of the gripes ever since Tuesday last. I sent him the best directions I could and ordered Caleb to call at Colonel Randolph's for the Doctor. In the evening I took a walk. I had good health, good thoughts, and good humor, thanks be to God Almighty, but neglected to say my prayers.

9. I rose at 5 o'clock and read two chapters in Hebrew and two leaves in Plutarch's *Morals*. I said my prayers and ate milk for breakfast. I danced my dance. About 10 o'clock Dick Cocke came to see me and I paid him for 70 bushels of wheat that Daniel had of him. He dined

[1] Abraham Salle, leader of a faction opposed to the French minister, Claude Phillipe de Richborough, at Manakin Town. The latter was a Huguenot settlement some twenty miles above the site of Richmond, on the south side of the James River. (See *Documents Relating to the Huguenot Emigration,* ed. R. A. Brock [Richmond, 1886], *passim,* and *Ex. Jour.,* III, 222, 225.)

[2] Edward Goodrich, burgess from Prince George County in 1711 and later.

with me and I ate roast mutton for dinner. Just after dinner Mr. Bland's man brought me a letter from Daniel written the 5 of April about 360 leagues from the Cape. He said he had a terrible voyage so far but that all was well. Captain C-l came in his boat from Williamsburg to see me. He is a sensible man and knows the world. In the evening we took a walk about the plantation. I had an express from Falling Creek to tell me my uncle Byrd[1] was dangerously sick and that Mr. G-r-l continued bad. I had good health, good thoughts, and good humor, thanks be to God Almighty.

10. I rose at 5 o'clock and read a chapter in Hebrew and some Greek in Josephus. I said my prayers and ate milk for breakfast. About 9 o'clock Captain C-l returned to Williamsburg in his boat. I ate bacon for dinner. In the afternoon I wrote a petition for Mr. Salle that the clerk of the vestry might return the books. In the evening I walked about the plantation. I ate abundance of cherries. Mrs. J-f-r-y took a vomit, which worked very well. I neglected to say my prayers. I had good health, good thoughts, and good humor, thanks be to God Almighty. Mr. Mumford returned here about 10 o'clock at night.

11. I rose at 5 o'clock and read a chapter in Hebrew and some Greek in Josephus. I said my prayers and ate milk for breakfast. Mr. Mumford brought me a letter from the President in which he was pleased to compliment me with the name of the clerk of Prince George. Mr. Cary came to see me. About 11 o'clock I went to Falling Creek, and called at Mr. Anderson's by the way but he was not at home, but his lady was, with whom I stayed about an hour; then I went over the river and at the Hundred[2] met Will Randolph who gave me an account of the court business. About 4 o'clock I got to Falling Creek and the Doctor was got there before me and had given Mr. G-r-l some physic that passed through him and gave him some ease. His

---

[1] Thomas, brother of William Byrd I. (See references to his death and estate, March 13, 1710, ff., and note on Mrs. Byrd, March 16, 1710.) The inventory of Thomas Byrd's estate was filed in Henrico County June 1, 1710. (Henrico County Court Records, 1710-14, pp. 12-14.)

[2] Bermuda Hundred, on the south side of the James.

brother was come to supply his place while he continued sick. I found things in good order, only two of the negroes were sick. The Doctor refused to go to my uncle Byrd on pretence of much business. I ate roast pig for supper. The Doctor and I lay together. I had good health, good thoughts, and good humor, thanks be to God Almighty.

12. I rose about 6 o'clock and read some Greek. I said my prayers and ate milk for breakfast. Mr. G-r-l was something better. I went to see the tannery which was in a good forwardness. I viewed everything and went to see the sick negroes, who were both a little better. Then I proceeded to the Falls and went to see my uncle who was much better than he had been. I gave him the best advice I could and then went to view my plantation. The people were all planting because it was a rainy day. Everything was in good order but because I would not hinder the people's planting I returned to Falling Creek, and by the way called on my uncle and there ate bacon and eggs. I likewise called on the Dutchman who I understood was sick, but I found him not at home. But I saw his wife, who was mad again. When I came to Falling Creek I had some complaints against Robin Easely[1] which seemed to be the effect of quarrelling. However I desired Mr. G-r-l to keep a watch on him. About 4 o'clock I returned home but did not find Mr. Anderson, who was gone to Tom the tailor's wedding. I found all well at home, thank God. I had good health, good thoughts, but was out of humor. When I came home I ate some strawberries and wine.

13. I rose at 6 o'clock and read a chapter in Hebrew and some Greek in Josephus. I said my prayers and ate milk for breakfast. I danced my dance and settled my accounts. I ate red herring and sallet for dinner. In the afternoon I settled my accounts again. Nurse came home from the wedding where she had stayed all night, contrary to her mistress' orders, for which I was in too great a passion with

---

[1]In 1706 Robert Easely petitioned for the return of his land rights, having patented land in Henrico County which proved to be included in Colonel Byrd's property. (*Ex. Jour.*, III, 92.)

her, but she gave me as good as I brought and she was so impudent to her mistress that she could not forbear beating her. In the evening I took a walk about the plantation and in the garden where I ate abundance of cherries. My horse Star got a thorn in his foot and was lame. I had good health and good thoughts but was out of humor with Nurse.

14. I rose at 5 o'clock and read a chapter in Hebrew and some Greek in Josephus. I said my prayers and ate milk and strawberries for breakfast. I danced my dance. Settled my accounts. I ate roast mutton and sallet for dinner. In the afternoon I read more in Josephus. In the evening I took a walk about the plantation. I said my prayers. Jacky came from Falling Creek and brought me news that all was well and that Mr. G-r-l was much better than he had been. I had good thoughts, good health, and good humor, thanks be to God Almighty.

15. I rose at 5 o'clock and read two chapters in Hebrew and some Greek in Josephus. I said my prayers and ate strawberries and milk for breakfast. We went to church, where the congregation was very small because it was like to rain. Mr. Anderson came from church to dine with us and complained he was out of order but by the symptoms he found the disorder to be nothing but hunger. I ate gammon and chicken for dinner. My river sloop came from Appomattox with 26 hogsheads of tobacco. Mr. Anderson went away in the evening and we took a walk about the plantation. Captain Stith was not at the church because he had the whooping cough. I had good health, good thoughts, and good humor, thanks be to God. I said my prayers.

16. I rose at 5 o'clock and read a chapter in Hebrew and some Greek in Josephus. I said my prayers and ate milk for breakfast. I danced my dance. The tobacco was taken out of the sloop in good order and several things were put on board to be sent up to Falling Creek. My man Jack was taken lame in his foot for which I gave him a purge which worked very well. I ate boiled beef and asparagus for dinner. The sloop sailed up with a good wind about 3 o'clock. We played at billiards. At 5 o'clock

Will [Bridger]¹ came to see me to buy the quitrents of his county. He ate but would not stay all night and therefore my people set him over the river just as it was dark. I said my prayers. I had good health, good thoughts, and was out of humor about Ned Randolph's complaining that he had not victuals enough.

17. I rose at 5 o'clock and read a chapter in Hebrew and some Greek in Josephus. I said my prayers and ate milk for breakfast. I danced my dance. I put my man Jack into a tub to sweat him but he found no service by it. I ate nothing but bacon for dinner. In the afternoon Mr. Mumford came to tell me that the justices of Prince George had resolved to accept of Mr. Bolling for their clerk on condition he would allow Mr. Goodrich half the profit and that Mr. Harrison had advised them to this because the President would not grant a commission to Mr. Goodrich according to Mr. Bolling's recommendation. Upon this I gave Mr. Mumford the commission which the President had sent me and he went away with it immediately. I played at billiards with the Doctor and won 15 pence. In the evening there was a storm so that I could not walk. I said my prayers and had good thoughts, good health, and good humor, thanks be to God Almighty.

18. I rose at 5 o'clock and read two chapters in Hebrew and some Greek in Josephus. I said my prayers and ate milk for breakfast. I danced my dance. This was fast day to pray to God to remove the fatal sickness with which this country has been of late afflicted. There was the most people at church I ever saw there. Mr. Harrison was in deep consultation with Colonel Hardiman and Mr. Anderson, I suppose about the clerk's place of Prince George. Isham Eppes and his wife and Robin Bolling's wife came home and dined with us. I ate nothing but bacon for dinner. In the evening they went away and I walked about the plantation. I said my prayers and had good health, good thoughts, and good humor all day, thanks be to God Almighty.

---

¹Perhaps William Bridger, burgess for Isle of Wight in 1712.

19. I rose at 5 o'clock and read a chapter in Hebrew and some Greek in Josephus. I said my prayers and ate milk for breakfast. I danced my dance. The nurse was in great haste to go and complain to Mr. Harrison that [I should call her whore] but was commanded not to go. I wrote to Mr. Mumford not to come to any terms with Mr. Goodrich about the clerk's place of Prince George. I ate nothing for dinner but fish. In the afternoon we played at billiards. I took a nap. In the evening I walked about the plantation. My man Jack's knee began to swell which makes it look like the gout. I gave him some oil. I sent John to foment it, which gave him some ease. I said my prayers. I had good health, good thoughts, and good humor this day, thanks be to God Almighty.

20. I rose at 5 o'clock and read a chapter in Hebrew and some Greek in Josephus. I said my prayers and ate milk for breakfast. This morning about 2 o'clock there happened a violent storm of thunder, wind and hail. The nurse went to Mr. Harrison to complain but met with no comfort there. John Pleasants and Isham Randolph came to see me and dined with us. I ate no meat for dinner. In the afternoon we played at billiards and I won half a crown of Isham Randolph. Then we walked in the garden and ate some cherries. In the evening Mr. Randolph went home. My man Jack continued lame and seemed to have the gout. My horse Star was taken very ill. I said my prayers. I had good health, good thoughts, and good humor, thanks be to God.

21. I rose at 5 o'clock and read a chapter in Hebrew and some Greek in Josephus. I said my prayers and ate milk for breakfast. I danced my dance. About 12 o'clock Mr. Bland came from Williamsburg and brought me some letters from England and an account from Mr. Perry[1] of £7 a hogshead. He gave me the comfort that the skins and 350 hogsheads of tobacco were saved out of the *Perry and Lane* and some tobacco out of the other ships that were lost in

---

[1] Micajah Perry, a great merchant of London, who was agent for many Virginia planters.

the storm that happened in January last in England. The [hatter] brought some [hats] from Appomattox. They both dined with us. I ate mutton and sallet for dinner. In the afternoon we played at billiards. In the evening they went away and I took a walk about the plantation. I was out of humor at my wife's climbing over the pales of the garden, now she is with child. I recommended my all to God. I had good health, good thoughts, and good humor, thanks be to God Almighty.

22. I rose at 5 o'clock and read two chapters in Hebrew and some Greek in Josephus. I said my prayers and ate milk for breakfast. Mr. Harrison sent for us to dine there but the rain hindered us from going. I sent for Mr. G-n [Jones?] to take care of my horse and gave him several medicines with little or no effect. I ate bacon for dinner. In the afternoon I wrote a letter to the President. In the evening I walked in the garden. I read some news. I said my prayers. I had good health, good thoughts, and good humor, thanks be to God Almighty.

23. I rose at 5 o'clock and read a chapter in Hebrew and some Greek in Josephus. I said my prayers and ate milk for breakfast. My horse died this morning. John Woodson[1] came in the rain about paying me some money and left his papers at home; so he returned as wise as he came. My man Jack continued lame in his foot. I ate nothing for dinner but mutton boiled with turnips. In the afternoon we played at billiards. I read news till the evening and then I took a walk about the plantation. Moll was whipped for a hundred faults. I said my prayers and had good health, good thoughts, and good humor, thanks be to God Almighty. I danced my dance.

24. I rose at 5 o'clock and read a chapter in Hebrew and some Greek in Josephus. I said my prayers and ate milk for breakfast. I danced my dance. Mr. Mumford came and let me know the justices of Prince George had resolved to admit nobody except he would give Mr. Goodrich half

---

[1] See Aug. 18, 1709 note.

the profit which showed almost unreasonable partiality and
not according to the oath a justice takes to distribute equal
justice to all men. Mr. Bland called here on his way to
Williamsburg. He told me that Mr. Bolling had had the
humility to agree to give half the profit to Goodrich as long
as this [secretary] continues in place and then to surrender
on condition the justices would admit him in opposition to
Mr. Mumford. I ate mutton and green peas for dinner.
In the afternoon we played at billiards and in the evening I
walked about the plantation. Mr. Harrison and his lady
were at our house while I walked out but I came back before
they went away, which was at 9· o'clock. I recommended
myself to God. I had good health, good thoughts, and
good humor, thanks be to God.

25. I rose at 5 o'clock and read a chapter in Hebrew and
some Greek in Josephus. I said my prayers and I ate milk
for breakfast. I discovered that Jack had a rheumatism
which made me resolve not to have him salivated according
to Mr. Harrison's advice, but had him let blood and put
[c-ler leaves] to his joint, by which means he grew much
better. I gave him nothing to eat but very thin [diet] to
cool the heat of his blood and parsley boiled in it. I ate
hashed mutton for dinner. In the afternoon we played at
billiards. In the evening we took a walk about the plantation. I neglected to say my prayers, for which God forgive
me. I had good thoughts and good health and good humor
this day, thanks to God Almighty.

26. I rose at 5 o'clock and read a chapter in Hebrew and
some Greek in Josephus. I said my prayers and ate milk
for breakfast. I danced my dance, and then went to see
Jack and found that he had slept very well without pain, for
which reason I caused him to be let blood again and continued the same medicine. About 12 o'clock Mr. Parker
came to see me and dined with us. I ate nothing but beans
and bacon for dinner. Mr. Parker told me he lost a negro
by salivating him for the rheumatism and Mr. Harrison lost
another by applying a hot dressing and stupe to the part
affected. In the afternoon we played at billiards and I won

a bit. He went away in the evening and I walked about the plantation. I said my prayers and had good health, good thoughts, but was out of humor with Tom for the disorder of the garden.

27. I rose at 5 o'clock and read a chapter in Hebrew and some Greek in Josephus. I said my prayers and ate milk for breakfast. I danced my dance. Jack was much better this morning and I gave him a gentle purge of syrup of roses, which did not work at all but made him hot all day. I read some Latin. When we were at dinner Mr. Will Randolph came from Williamsburg and brought me two letters from England, one of which told me a sad story of the misfortune of our last fleet by the storm but there are some hopes that the *Perry and Lane* is not lost as we had been informed, though she was in great danger. In the afternoon we played at billiards. He stayed till the evening and then went home and I took a walk about the plantation. I said my prayers and had good thoughts, good humor, and good health, thanks be to God Almighty.

28. I rose at 5 o'clock and read a chapter in Hebrew and some Greek in Josephus. I said my prayers and ate milk for breakfast. I danced my dance. My man Jack was better and began to walk. I read some Latin. The Doctor returned from over the river, where he had been to see Frank Mallory[1] who has the gripes. This distemper has been more common this spring than ever was known in this country. I ate bacon fraise for dinner. In the evening I took a walk about the plantation. I said my prayers and had good health, good thoughts, and good humor, thanks be to God Almighty.

29. I rose at 5 o'clock and read a chapter in Hebrew and some Greek in Josephus. I said my prayers and ate milk for breakfast. Mr. G-r-l came late last night and told me all was well at Falling Creek. He desired more help to finish the dam while the season permits. I was out of humor with the proposal but agreed at last to send him some help.

---

[1]Francis Mallory was sheriff of Prince George County in 1707.

He returned home and I went to church and heard Mr.
Anderson preach. After church I invited Mr. Drury Stith,
Mr. C-s, and Mrs. L—[1] home to dine with us. I ate green
goose for dinner. In the evening they went away and I
walked about the plantation. My man Jack ventured to
come down today and made his foot swell, for which I chid
him. I said my prayers and had good health, good thoughts,
and good humor, thanks be to God Almighty.

30. I rose at 5 o'clock and read a chapter in Hebrew and
some Greek in Josephus. I said my prayers and ate milk
for breakfast. I danced my dance. I gave Jack some
epsom salts and Tom a vomit, both which worked very well.
I made my creed.[2] I ate beans and bacon for dinner.
While we were at dinner Colonel Harrison came to see me
and told me there was a privateer at the Cape of 16 guns.
He would not eat with us but stayed till about 4 o'clock and
then went over the river again because his son was not at
home. We played at billiards. In the evening I read in
Homer and went to walk about the plantation. My wife
was out of order all day with a headache. I recommended
myself to heaven. I had good health, good thoughts, and
good humor, thanks be God Almighty.

31. I rose at 5 o'clock and read a chapter in Hebrew and
some Greek in Josephus. I said my prayers and ate milk
for breakfast. I danced my dance. This day we sheared
the sheep. My man Jack was better and the swelling of his
foot abated. We began to shear the sheep but the rain
interrupted us. I read some Latin. I ate roast chicken for
dinner and green peas. In the afternoon we played at
billiards and I read more Latin and Greek and wrote on
articles of faith. In the evening I walked about the plantation and went to see them hang the tobacco. I said my
prayers and had good health, good thoughts, and good
humor, thanks be to God Almighty.

---

[1] A Mrs. Low owned land in Prince George County in 1704. (*Va. Mag.*,
XXVIII, 333.)
[2] The first page of the manuscript volume of this diary consists of a creed in
Byrd's handwriting, perhaps written at this time. (See Introduction, p. xviii.)

June, 1709

1. I rose at 5 o'clock and read two chapters in Hebrew and some Greek in Josephus. I said my prayers and ate milk for breakfast. I danced my dance. I agreed with B-r-k to fetch me a load of shingles. He brought me a letter from the President by which he discovered his mean satisfaction in yielding to his enemies rather than his friends in the business of Prince George. My man Jack was better today. Our people made an end of shearing the sheep. I read some Latin and Greek in Homer. I ate boiled beef for dinner. I was out of humor about Mrs. J-f-r-y so that I would not let my wife go abroad. In the evening I took a walk about the plantation and went to the brick house where the people hung tobacco and some of it was extremely bad. I said my prayers and had good health, good thoughts, and good humor, thanks be to God Almighty.

2. I rose at 6 o'clock and read two chapters in Hebrew and some Greek in Josephus. I said my prayers and ate milk for breakfast. I danced my dance. I was out of humor with my wife for trusting Anaka with rum to steal when she was so given to drinking, but it was soon over. My man Jack grew better and better, thanks be to God Almighty. He took a purge today that worked very well. I read some Latin. I ate nothing but beans and bacon for dinner. In the afternoon we played at billiards, and I translated some Greek into Latin and into English. In the evening we rode out to take the air. When we returned I took a walk in the garden till it was dark. I said my prayers and had good health, good thoughts, and good humor, thanks be to God Almighty.

3. I rose at 5 o'clock and read two chapters in Hebrew and some Greek in Josephus. I said my prayers and ate milk for breakfast. I danced my dance. My man Jack was still better, having lost all the symptoms of his dis-

temper. About 11 o'clock Mr. Harrison, Mr. Parker, and Mr. Harwood[1] came to see me, as did Captain Llewellyn and Colonel Eppes and stayed about half an hour. Mr. Parker came to tell me there was a petition against me for stopping the way against the people on the other side the creek. Only Mr. Parker dined with me today. I ate a fricassee of chicken for dinner. In the afternoon Mr. Parker and I played at billiards and I won 15 pence. About 4 o'clock Mr. Randolph came and told me the jury above had given me a shilling damages against Phil Pursell.[2] In the evening they went away and I walked about the plantation. I said my prayers and had good thoughts, good humor, and good health, thanks be to God Almighty.

4. I rose at 5 o'clock and read a chapter in Hebrew and some Greek in Josephus. I said my prayers and ate milk for breakfast. I danced my dance. My man Jack was pretty well. We made some wine of the common cherry for an experiment. It was extremely hot this day. I was out of humor with my wife for not minding her business. I ate roast shoat and sallet for dinner. In the afternoon I read some Latin and some Greek in Homer. In the evening Mr. C-s came to see me, who is a man of good understanding, and Ned Randolph brought me a letter from Mr. Bland in which he told me that the Lord Lovelace was dead at New York. We took a walk. I said my prayers and had good health, good thoughts, and good humor, thanks be to God Almighty.

5. I rose at 6 o'clock and read two chapters in Hebrew and some Greek in Josephus. I said my prayers and ate milk for breakfast. I gave my man Jack a purge which worked very well. He began to come down stairs. About

---

[1]Samuel Harwood was burgess for Charles City County in 1710 and later; his brother Joseph was a burgess in 1715. Evidently Byrd is referring to one of this family.

[2]Byrd had sued Philip Pursell for £10 damages for having dug up and carried away 60 young apple trees of the value of £3 sterling. William Randolph, Jr., served as Byrd's attorney in this and other cases. (Henrico County Court Records, 1707-09, pp. 145-50.)

12 o'clock Mr. C-s and Mr. Doyley[1] came to dine with us.
I ate pork and turnips for dinner. They stayed here till
5 o'clock. I read some Greek in Homer. About 6 o'clock
there began a terrible gust with thunder and rain which
lasted about an hour with great violence, but no harm was
done here, thanks be to God. I said my prayers and had
good thoughts, good humor, and good health, thanks be to
God Almighty.

6. I rose at 5 o'clock and read two chapters in Hebrew
and some Greek in Josephus. I said my prayers and ate
milk for breakfast, and raspberries. I danced my dance.
It thundered and rained this morning violently till 8 o'clock.
I read some Latin and Greek in Homer and wrote a prayer.
I ate pork and turnips for dinner. Just after dinner Mr.
Mumford came with the Doctor and he told me that five
justices of Prince George had written to the President in
behalf of Mr. Bolling, contrary to their former resolution
and the President upon that wrote a letter in favor of Mr.
Bolling, notwithstanding the commission he had granted to
Mumford by which Mr. Bolling's commission was made
void. He likewise told me that Mr. Bolling did not stick
to speak things very much to my disadvantage, against
all truth and reason. I wrote to Mr. Bolling to let him
know I did resent it. Mumford went away about 5 o'clock
and I walked in the garden. I said my prayers and had
good health, good thoughts and good humor, thanks be to
God Almighty.

7. I rose at 5 o'clock and read two chapters in Hebrew
and some Greek in Josephus. I said not my prayers this
morning because Colonel Randolph came and prevented me.
I ate milk for breakfast. I had a quarrel with Ned Ran-

---

[1]Son of Reverend Cope Doyley (or D'Oyley), minister of Bruton Parish,
1697-1704. At his death in 1704 his two minor sons, Charles and Cope, were
apparently bound by the York County Court to Benjamin Harrison. In July
1709 their uncle, Robert D'Oyley, petitioned the Queen to have them sent to
him in England, claiming that their land and personal property had been
seized by Harrison, and that they were kept among slaves. However, they
seem to have remained in Virginia. (*Va. Mag.*, XII, 300-301.) In 1705
Charles was a student at William and Mary College. (*Wm. Q. (1)*, XVI,
193.)

dolph about his complaining that he was starved and because he ran about without my knowing anything of it and would not come to me when I sent to him, of all which I told his father who [threatened] him if he should dare to do so again. The Colonel and I made up accounts. Mr. Blacka-more[1] came to meet the Colonel here because he did not dare to come by himself, for I had reprimanded him for his being drunk. They both dined with me. I ate beans and bacon for dinner. In the afternoon we played at billiards and I lost two bits. About 5 o'clock they went away and I walked about the plantation. I said my prayers and had good health, good thoughts, and good humor, thanks be to God Almighty.

8. I rose at 5 o'clock and read two chapters in Hebrew and some Greek in Josephus. I said my prayers and ate milk for breakfast. About 10 o'clock we rode to see Colonel Eppes and Mrs. Anderson met us there. We were enter-tained very courteously. I ate bacon and fowl for dinner. The Colonel and I balanced accounts. In the evening as we returned home we met Mr. Anderson, who came that morn-ing from Williamsburg. He brought news that there were 13 men of war arrived at New England with design to attempt the taking of Canada. We likewise met Mr. Ran-dolph who came from Prince George Court and said the court had sworn Mr. Bolling, contrary to their first and repeated resolves, notwithstanding Mr. Mumford had a commission and Bolling only a letter. We found all things well at home, thank God. I recommended myself and family to heaven, and had good health, good thoughts, and good humor, thanks be to God Almighty.

9. I rose at 5 o'clock and read two chapters in Hebrew and some Greek in Josephus. I neglected to say my prayers, for which God forgive me. I ate milk for breakfast. I received a very foolish letter from Robin Bolling which contained many ridiculous arguments to justify his late

---

[1]Reverend Arthur Blackamore, headmaster of the grammar school of William and Mary College, 1706-1716. (See Byrd's remarks on October 28, 29, 1709; and references in *Wm. Q. (2)*, XIX.)

foolish proceedings, to which I sent him a full answer. I ate mutton and sallet for dinner. My Eugene ran away this morning for no reason but because he had not done anything yesterday. I sent my people after him but in vain. The sloop came from Falling Creek with copper, timber, and planks. In the evening Captain Keeling[1] came to see us to account with me for the quitrents of New Kent. I ate some supper with him, contrary to custom. I neglected to say my prayers, for which God forgive me. I had good health, good thoughts, and good humor, thanks be to God Almighty. I danced my dance.

10. I rose at 5 o'clock this morning but could not read anything because of Captain Keeling, but I played at billiards with him and won half a crown of him and the Doctor. George B-th brought home my boy Eugene. I ate milk for breakfast, but neglected to say my prayers, for which God forgive me. The Captain and I had some discourse about the philosopher's stone which he [is following with great diligence]. He stayed to dinner. I ate mutton for dinner. In the afternoon he went away. I read some Greek in Homer. In the evening I took a walk about the plantation. Eugene was whipped for running away and had the [bit][2] put on him. I said my prayers and had good health, good thoughts, and good humor, thanks be to God Almighty.

11. I rose at 5 o'clock this morning and read a chapter in Hebrew and some Greek in Josephus. I said my prayers and ate milk for breakfast. I danced my dance. My wife was [g-r-n-t] with the headache all day. I read some Latin. I ate hashed mutton for dinner. In the afternoon I read some Greek in Homer. In the evening I took a walk about the plantation. I settled accounts with Mr. Randolph. When I came home I found Dick Hamlin[3] and [Mistress] who had been taken by [a slow poison] about five years ago. I neglected to say my prayers, for which God forgive me.

---

[1]George Keeling, sheriff of New Kent County. (*Ex. Jour.*, III, 215.)

[2]This shorthand symbol may stand for *bit* or *boot*. This is one indication of occasional harsh punishment meted out to servants.

[3]Richard Hamlin of Prince George County married Anne, daughter of Thomas Harrison. (*Wm. Q. (1)*, XI, 60.)

I had good health, good thoughts, and good humor, thanks be to God Almighty.

12. I rose at 5 o'clock and read two chapters in Hebrew and some Greek in Josephus. I said my prayers and ate milk for breakfast. I received a letter from my dear friend Admiral Wager[1] from Jamaica which signified his health and the continuance of his friendship. We went to church and heard a sermon. Nobody came home with us but Mr. Gee.[2] I ate mutton pie for dinner. Mr. Gee stayed here till the evening and according to his custom spoke against several people like any woman. I walked about the plantation. The weather was grown much cooler. I said my prayers and had good health, good thoughts, and good humor, thanks be to God Almighty.

13. I rose at 5 o'clock and read two chapters in Hebrew but no Greek by reason that Captain Collins[3] came to see me, who came out of England about seven weeks ago and says the fleet came out 13 days before him and may be every day expected because they had been above nine weeks out of England. He brought me some letters from England. I had a great deal of discourse with him and drank chocolate for breakfast. I said my prayers. About 11 o'clock we rode to Drury Stith's where we met Mr. Anderson and his wife and Mr. Eppes. I ate pork and turnips for dinner. Then we played at nine-pins. In the evening Mr. Harrison and Colonel Eppes came to us, having been around the neighborhood of Chickahominy. We returned home and found all well, thanks be to God. I neglected to say my prayers. I had good health, good thoughts, and good humor, thanks be to God Almighty.

14. I rose at 5 o'clock and read a chapter in Hebrew and some Greek in Josephus. I said my prayers and ate chocolate for breakfast. We heard guns this morning, by which

---

[1]Rear-Admiral Sir Charles Wager, who accumulated a vast fortune by the capture of Spanish prizes in the West Indies. Byrd had known him in England.
[2]Probably Henry Gee, who owned lands in Henrico County.
[3]Captain Edward Collins, master of a merchant ship plying between England and Virginia. (*Va. Mag.*, IX, 255-56.)

we understood that the fleet was come in and I learned the same from Mr. Anderson. I ate bacon and chicken for dinner. I began to have the piles. I read some Greek in Homer. I heard guns from Swinyard's and sent my boat for my letters. In the meanwhile I walked about the plantation. In the evening the boat returned and brought some letters for me from England, with an invoice of things sent [for?] by my wife which are enough to make a man mad. It put me out of humor very much. I neglected to say my prayers, for which God forgive me. I had good thoughts, good health, and good humor, thanks be to God Almighty.

15. I rose at 5 o'clock and read two chapters in Hebrew and some Greek in Josephus. I said my prayers and ate milk for breakfast. Captain C-l-t[1] brought me some letters from England and offered me freight in his ship. He brought a parson with him, Mr. Goodwin.[2] He ate his breakfast here and went away about 9 o'clock. I ate dry beef for dinner, and chicken. While we were at dinner Captain M-r-n[3] came with some more letters. He brought me a coaler[4] recommended by Colonel Blakiston.[5] He brought me also some goods for my wife, to an extravagant value. My letters gave me a sad prospect of the tobacco trade in England. My wife continued very ill. I sent Tommy to Williamsburg to inquire for my letters. I took a walk about the plantation. I said my prayers and had good thoughts, good humor and good health, thanks be to God Almighty, only I feared I was going to have the piles.

16. I rose at 5 o'clock and read a chapter in Hebrew and a little Greek. I neglected to say my prayers and ate milk

---

[1]This may stand for Captain Richard Cutlet, master of the *Corbin* out of London. (*Va. Mag.,* IX, 257.)

[2]Reverend Benjamin Goodwin, licensed by the Bishop of London to preach in Virginia, March 5, 1709. (*Va. Mag.,* VII, 312.) He became minister of St. Peter's Parish, New Kent County, then of Yorkhampton Parish, York County, and was chaplain of the House of Burgesses in 1714. (Goodwin; *Va. Mag.,* II, 2, 15.)

[3]Possibly Captain Thomas Markin, master of the *Providence* out of London. (*Va. Mag.,* IX, 259.)

[4]From later diary entries the coaler's name appears to be George Smith.

[5]Nathaniel Blakiston, appointed by the Council on August 16, 1705, as agent for the colony in England. (*Ex. Jour.,* III, 27 and *passim.*)

for breakfast. Mr. Bland's boy brought me abundance of letters from Williamsburg, out of the men-of-war. I spent all the morning in reading them. My orders for being of the Council arrived among the rest.[1] By these letters I learned that tobacco was good for nothing, that protested bills would ruin the country, that our trade with the Carolina Indians was adjusted in England, that my sister Braynes[2] was in [prison by the cruelty of C-r-l-y], that my salary was in a fair way of being increased, that the College was like to be rebuilt by the Queen's bounty, that there was a probability of a peace next winter. I ate mutton for dinner. While we were at dinner, Colonel Harrison, Mr. Commissary, and Mr. Wormeley[3] came to see us, but would not eat with us. They likewise brought me some letters. Captain Wilcox[4] dined with us. His people brought me a box of [. . .] from P-r-c-r. I walked about the plantation. Mr. Wormeley and I played at billiards and I won half a crown. I said my prayers. All the company went away. I had good health, good thoughts, and good humor, thank God Almighty.

17. I rose at 5 o'clock and read some Greek in Josephus and perused some of my new books. I said my prayers, and ate milk for breakfast. I settled my accounts. We expected some company but they disappointed us. I ate roast mutton for dinner. In the afternoon we rode to my neighbor Harrison's where we stayed till the evening with Mr. [Gee]. Here I ate some apple pie. Mr. Harrison had the same bad account of tobacco in England and advised me to ship none by this ship. I promised to give no more than £12 per ton. He told me that several gentlemen were extremely in debt with Mr. Perry. In the evening we returned home, where we found all very well, thanks be to God Almighty. I said my prayers and had good health, good thoughts, and good humor, thanks be to God Almighty.

---

[1]Byrd was nominated to the Council on August 15, 1705, but was not sworn in until September 12, 1709.
[2]Byrd's sister Susan married John Brayne and lived in England.
[3]Probably Ralph Wormeley III, of Rosegill, sheriff of Middlesex in 1704.
[4]Captain John Wilcox, a sea-captain of Rotherhill, England, who settled in Charles City County. (*Wm. Q. (1)*, XI, 59.)

18. I rose at 5 o'clock and read two chapters in Hebrew and some Greek in Josephus. I said my prayers and ate milk for breakfast. I gave my man George a purge. I prepared my accounts for Williamsburg. I ate hashed mutton for dinner. In the afternoon I was busy about my accounts and then read some Greek in Homer. Mr. Dick Randolph[1] and Mr. Jackson[2] came to see me on their way to Williamsburg. I took a walk about the plantation and discoursed my man George. I said my prayers and had good health, good thoughts, and good humor, thanks be to God Almighty.

19. I rose at 6 o'clock and read two chapters in Hebrew and some Greek in Josephus. I said my prayers and ate milk for breakfast. I danced my dance. Mr. Mumford came to see me and let me know that Jack Bolling did all he could to persuade people not to pay their debts and several low contrivances against me and my wife which were false. I ate boiled mutton and turnips for dinner. Soon after dinner Captain S-t-k came from below to let me understand he intended to sail in three days and gave me to understand that he wanted more money, but I was deaf. Mr. C-s came likewise to see me and they all stayed till the evening and then went away, and I prepared my things for my journey and sent away my man and horse to Weyanoke. I said my prayers and had good health, good thoughts, and good humor, thanks be to God Almighty.

20. I rose at 3 o'clock and went in my boat to Weyanoke where I arrived at 5 o'clock and got on my horse and rode to Williamsburg, where I got by 9 o'clock. I went to Mr. Bland's where I found Dick Cocke and Isham Randolph. Here I ate some milk and then went to my chambers, where I slept sweetly for two hours. I dined at Mr. Bland's and ate beans and bacon for dinner. In the evening I sent for Mr. Clayton from the coffeehouse, to whom I gave a bottle of white wine. I did not go to see the President but sent

---

[1] One of the numerous sons of Colonel William Randolph of Turkey Island.
[2] Possibly Christopher Jackson, who was made surveyor of James City County in 1717.

for some letters he had of mine by Johnny Blair.[1] By my letters I learned that the Governor[2] was released and that the Queen had granted £500 to the College. I had a letter from Mr. Southwell[3] that told me Lady Betty was like to die of a consumption. I neglected to say my prayers. I had good health, good thoughts, and good humor, thanks be to God Almighty.

21. I rose at 5 o'clock and while I was dressing of me, the President had the humility to come and visit me. I thanked him for the exact performance of his promise about the clerk's place. He had very little to say for himself, but told me Robin Bolling had written him word that he never employed me to get the commission for Mr. Mumford, which is a cursed lie. The President [courted] me to pass it by, but I continued out of humor. I neglected to say my prayers and ate milk for breakfast. Then I went to the capitol about my business. Then I went to the President's where I met several of the Council. They met about 12 o'clock, and I was before them concerning my accounts. They expected I would produce the Queen's letter for my being of the Council but I was not in haste. I went and dined with Mr. Bland and then returned to the Council at the President's, where I met the captains of the men-of-war, who were pretty gentlemen. We played at piquet till midnight and I went to my lodgings. I neglected to say my prayers. I had good health, good thoughts, and good humor, thanks be to God Almighty.

22. I rose at 4 o'clock and got on horseback and rode to Mr. Harvey's and was courteously entertained by Mrs. Harvey till my boat came and then I came home, where I found all well, thanks be to God. I ate dry beef for dinner, though with the heat I ate but little. I slept in the afternoon. I wrote several letters to England. Captain Wilcox

---

[1]Son of Dr. Archibald Blair, and nephew of the Commissary.
[2]Governor Hunter, who had been held by French privateers.
[3]Edward Southwell, son of Byrd's patron, Sir Robert Southwell. In 1703 he married Lady Elizabeth Cromwell, apparently the "Lady Betty" of this reference; the *Dictionary of National Biography* states that she died in childbirth on March 31, 1709.

came to see me and told me he was going to Williamsburg. In the evening I took a walk about the plantation and found all things in good order. I neglected to say my prayers, for which God forgive me. When I was at town I ended my disagreement with Mr. Robinson. I had good health, good thoughts, and good humor, thanks be to God Almighty.

23. I rose at 5 o'clock and read nothing but wrote several letters to England. I neglected to say my prayers and ate [. . .] for breakfast. I ate bacon for dinner and continued to write more letters to England. In the evening Captain [. . .] came with several flats to fetch 36 hogsheads of tobacco, which he was content to take at £12 per ton. The seamen told John they did not come to roll tobacco, which made me give them a good scolding and I would not let them have the tobacco that night. The Captain returned to Mr. Harrison's, to whom I told the rudeness of his men. He promised to make them roll it tomorrow and went away. I neglected to say my prayers. I had good health, good thoughts, and good humor, thanks be to God Almighty.

24. I rose at 5 o'clock and read two chapters in Hebrew and some Greek in Josephus. I neglected to say my prayers, for which God forgive me. I ate milk for breakfast. I read some news. I ate dry beef and [pig] for dinner. In the afternoon I read more news and some Greek in Homer. Mr. Blackamore came to see me with Johnny Randolph. He told me that Mr. Will Randolph[1] was to bring up his wife to Captain Stith's this night. He was married on Tuesday last. They went away about 6 o'clock. I took a walk about the plantation. I said my prayers and had good health, good thoughts, and good humor, thanks be to God Almighty. Captain Collins was here this morning and stayed till 11 o'clock till I was weary of him.

25. I rose at 6 o'clock this morning and read two chapters in Hebrew and some Greek in Josephus. I said my prayers and ate milk for breakfast. I danced my dance. Tom S-d-s-n came from Falling Creek and told me the stone

---

[1]Will Randolph married Elizabeth, second daughter of Peter Beverley, of Gloucester County. (*Va. Mag.*, III, 263.)

cutter was dead [w-l m-l-r].[1] I read some Latin and some news. I ate some bacon fraise for dinner. In the afternoon Mr. Bland's sloop brought my things from aboard Captain M-r-n's ship, which had received no damage. My man John got drunk, for which I reprimanded him severely. I walked about the plantation in the evening. I said my prayers and had good thoughts, good health, and good humor, thanks be to God Almighty.

26. I rose at 5 o'clock and read two chapters in Hebrew and some Greek in Josephus. I said my prayers and ate milk for breakfast. We went to church and heard a sermon. After church Colonel Eppes and his wife and Captain Wilcox came home and dined with us. I ate bacon and roast shoat for dinner. In the afternoon we drank some tea. About 6 o'clock the company went away. I took a walk about the plantation. I recommended myself to God in a short prayer. I had good health, good thoughts, and good humor, thanks be to God Almighty.

27. I rose at 5 o'clock and read two chapters in Hebrew and some Greek in Josephus. I said my prayers and ate milk for breakfast. I danced my dance. I made an invoice of the things that my wife could spare to be sold. I settled the accounts of protested bills. I ate mutton for dinner. My wife was in tears about her [cargo] but I gave her some comfort after dinner. Mr. Bland came with Henry Randolph[2] to see me and soon after Mr. Harrison and his wife and daughter. They stayed till 7 o'clock and then went away. In the evening we took a walk [about] the plantation. I recommended myself to God in a short prayer. I had good health, good thoughts, and good humor, thanks be to God Almighty. Tom was whipped for not telling me that he was sick.

28. I rose at 5 o'clock and read two chapters in Hebrew and some Greek in Josephus. I said my prayers and ate milk for breakfast. The sloop came up with my things from Cap-

---

[1] This may stand for a name—Will Miller?
[2] Another son of Colonel William Randolph of Turkey Island.

tain Browne[1] with my goods which were not so much damaged as I expected. I was angry with the people for staying
so long. They sailed away this morning with George the coaler to Falling Creek. I ate cold mutton and sallet for dinner.
In the afternoon I read some news and some Latin and also
some Greek in Homer. In the evening I took a walk about
the plantation. I said my prayers. I had good health, good
thoughts, and good humor, thanks be to God Almighty.

29. I rose at 5 o'clock and read only some Greek in
Josephus, because I was hindered by Daniel who came last
night from Williamsburg where the sea sloop is safe arrived,
thanks be to God Almighty. Two of her men were pressed
by the men-of-war, notwithstanding the proclamation.
Wheat sold for about six shillings a bushel in Madeira and
wine for £8 a pipe with the exchange. Captain Browne and
Captain Collins came to see me. I said my prayers and ate
milk for breakfast. I began to reap my wheat. I ate bacon
and pork for dinner. In the afternoon Mr. Bland came to
counsel the proper measures to be taken with the sloop and
it was agreed he should go down to take care of the cargo
and he went accordingly and was caught in a great shower
of rain. Daniel behaved himself very foolishly. In the
evening the rain hindered my walking and lasted above an
hour. I said my prayers. I had good health, good thoughts,
and good humor, thanks be to God Almighty.

30. I rose at 5 o'clock and read two chapters in Hebrew
and some Greek in Josephus. I said my prayers and ate milk
for breakfast. Daniel went this morning early down to the
sloop. I wrote a letter to England. Mr. Salle came from
Manakin Town to see me. I gave him two bottles of wine to
make an [n-t-r-m-n] for his son. He dined with us and I ate
hushed pork for dinner. In the afternoon we played at billiards. I read some Greek in Homer. I made an end of
reaping my wheat this day.. I walked about the plantation in
the evening. I said my prayers and had good health, good
thoughts, but indifferent humor, thanks be to God Almighty.

---

[1]Probably Captain Henry Browne, master of the *Loyalty* out of Liverpool.
(*Va. Mag.*, IX, 256.)

July, 1709

1. I rose at 5 o'clock and read two chapters in Hebrew and some Greek in Josephus. I said my prayers and ate milk for breakfast. I danced my dance. I wrote a letter to England. George began to plaster the house. I read some Latin. I ate broiled pork for dinner. In the afternoon I wrote more letters to England and read more Latin and some Greek in Homer. Then I took a walk about the plantation. I said my prayers and had good health, good thoughts, and good humor, thanks be to God Almighty.

2. I rose at 5 o'clock and read a chapter in Hebrew and some Greek in Josephus. I said my prayers and ate milk for breakfast. I danced my dance. I wrote a letter to England. I read some Latin. The cooper and I parted because I would not let him have three holidays as he desired. John G-r-l[1] took a vomit which worked very well. Just before dinner Mr. Anderson called here but would not stay. Captain John Eppes dined with us. I ate nothing but eggs for dinner. In the afternoon we played at billiards. In the evening Mrs. L— came to see us but went away presently. I took a walk about the plantation. I neglected to say my prayers. I had good health, good thoughts, and good humor, thanks be to God Almighty.

3. I rose at 5 o'clock and read two chapters in Hebrew and some Greek in Josephus. I said my prayers and ate milk for breakfast. I wrote a letter to England, notwithstanding it was Sunday. About 12 o'clock we went in the coach to Mr. Harrison's where we dined and Mrs. L— was there. I ate boiled shoat for dinner. We were very friendly together. Mr. Anderson and Captain Hamlin called there on their way. In the evening we returned home where we found all things well, thank God. I recommended myself to God in a short prayer. I had good health, good thoughts, and good humor, thanks be to God Almighty.

---

[1]Employed at Westover, probably as an apprentice or secretary. No relationship is mentioned between this boy and the G-r-l who was overseer at Falling Creek.

4. I rose at 5 o'clock and read two chapters in Hebrew and some Greek in Josephus. I said my prayers and ate milk for breakfast. I wrote a letter to England. Captain C-l-t came to see me, as did Will Randolph and John Bolling and Captain Wilcox. I went to court to answer the petition against me about the landing of the people on the other side the creek and prevailed with the court to order their landing at Major Marshall's[1]. The two captains and Frank Eppes dined with me and several others came after dinner. I ate fricassee of chicken for dinner. In the afternoon we played at billiards. Robin Bolling was at court but had not the confidence to look toward me. In the evening the company went away and I took a walk about the plantation. I neglected to say my prayers. I had good health, good thoughts, and good humor, thanks be to God Almighty.

5. I rose at 5 o'clock and read a chapter in Hebrew and some Greek in Josephus. I said my prayers and ate milk for breakfast. I danced my dance. Captain Wilcox came and brought me some oatmeal. I wrote a letter to England and read a little Latin. I ate nothing but eggs for dinner. In the afternoon Indian Peter brought me a letter from the President in which he desired me to send him his account and my bill for the balance, which I did accordingly and also sent several letters which I desired him to convey by the men-of-war. In the afternoon I wrote more letters to England and read a little Greek in Homer. I reproved George for being drunk yesterday. We took a walk about the plantation and I threatened L-s-n for galling the harrow horse. I recommended myself to God. I had good health, good thoughts, and good humor, thanks be to God Almighty.

6. I rose at 5 o'clock and read two chapters in Hebrew and some Greek in Josephus. I said my prayers and ate milk for breakfast. Peter went this morning to Williamsburg with my letters. I wrote more letters to England. I read some Latin and ate bacon for dinner that did not agree

---

[1] Perhaps Alexander Marshall who married Mrs. Elizabeth Ligon. She owned land in Henrico County in 1704 and he later acquired much land in the county. (*Wm. Q. (1)*, XXV, 94.)

with me. In the afternoon I wrote more letters to England, read more Latin and some Greek in Homer. Then I took a walk about the plantation. I said my prayers. Mrs. J-f-r-y went away by moonshine to Williamsburg and my wife was very much concerned at her going. I had good health, good thoughts, and good humor, thanks be to God Almighty. It was extremely hot.

7. I rose at 5 o'clock and read a chapter in Hebrew and some Greek in Josephus. I said my prayers and ate milk for breakfast. I danced my dance, and settled my accounts. I read some Latin. It was extremely hot. I ate stewed mutton for dinner. In the afternoon it began to rain and blow very violently so that it blew down my fence. It likewise thundered. In all the time I have been in Virginia I never heard it blow harder. I read Latin again and Greek in Homer. In the evening we took a walk in the garden. I said my prayers and had good health, good humor and good thoughts, thanks be to God Almighty.

8. I rose at 5 o'clock and read a chapter in Hebrew and some Greek in Josephus. I said my prayers and ate milk for breakfast. I danced my dance. I read some Latin. Tom returned from Williamsburg and brought me a letter from Mr. Bland which told me the wine came out very well. I ate nothing but pudding for dinner. In the afternoon I read some more Latin and Greek in Homer. Then I took a walk about the plantation. I said my prayers and had good health, good thoughts, and good humor, thanks be to God Almighty.

9. I rose at 5 o'clock and read two chapters in Hebrew and some Greek in Josephus. I said my prayers and ate milk and apples for breakfast with Captain Wilcox who called here this morning. I danced my dance. I wrote a letter to England and read some Latin. I ate roast chicken for dinner. In the afternoon I saluted my wife and took a nap. I read more Latin and Greek in Homer. Then I took a walk about the plantation. I neglected to say my prayers. I had good health, good thoughts, and good humor, thanks be to God Almighty.

10. I rose at 5 o'clock and read two chapters in Hebrew and some Greek in Josephus. I neglected to say my prayers and ate milk for breakfast. I received a letter from poor Captain C-l-v who gave me to understand that he had been run down by another ship and that all the tobacco was lost. My part of this misfortune was 36 hogsheads. God gives and God takes away—blessed be the name of the Lord. Mr. Bland and Daniel came and told me they had lost a whole pipe of wine in getting it into the vat. We went to church, from whence only Captain Wilcox and Mr. Bland came home with me. Daniel and Mr. M-s-t came to dine with me also. Captain Wilcox was so kind as to offer his pinnace to go down to see if anything was saved of the Captain C-l-v lading. He likewise offered me to set a new mast in the "Evelyn." I ate chicken pie for dinner. The sloop came up about noon. It rained a good shower, thank God. Mr. Bland lay here this night. I neglected to say my prayers. I had good health, good thoughts, and indifferent good humor, thanks be to God Almighty.

11. I rose at 5 o'clock and read nothing because Mr. Bland and I settled the sloop accounts. Mr. Mumford came this morning and brought his fine horse for me to try. I neglected to say my prayers, for which God forgive me. I ate milk for breakfast. I had my wine unloaded out of the sloop in good order. About 12 o'clock [came] Mr. Harrison and lady and Mr. James Burwell[1] who all dined with us. I ate goose for dinner. In the afternoon they played at billiards. I was very angry with Bannister[2] for letting Daniel have the key of the store, because he went away with it so that George could not get paint that he wanted. In the evening all the company went away except Mr. Mumford. I was extremely out of humor and scolded with Bannister before the company, and my wife thought me angry with her, which made her very melancholy. I had good health and indifferent thoughts and very bad humor.

---

[1] Of Kings Creek, York County. He was a son of Major Lewis Burwell, and was Mrs. Harrison's brother.
[2] John Bannister, an apprentice or secretary at Westover.

12. I rose at 5 o'clock and rode out with Mr. Mumford to try his horse and liked him very well. I settled the sloop accounts with Daniel whom I asked to go again in the sloop but he denied me, so I took him at his word. I read a chapter in Hebrew and some Greek in Josephus. I neglected to say my prayers and ate milk for breakfast. I ate pig for dinner and ate too much. I took a nap and was out of order over it. My wife was very melancholy, but I comforted her as well as I could and was troubled to see her so. I played at billiards with the Doctor and lost. In the evening I took a walk about the plantation. I recommended myself to God Almighty. I was a little out of order but had much better humor than yesterday, thank God for it.

13. I rose at 6 o'clock and read two chapters in Hebrew and some Greek in Josephus. I said my prayers and ate milk for breakfast. Will Randolph called here and I gave him some sweetmeats for his lady. Captain Wilcox likewise called here and proffered more assistance to my sloop. He confessed it lay in my power to set the freight and desired me to do it, but I excused it by good reason. Mrs. Harrison came here just before dinner and dined with us. I ate pigeon for dinner. In the evening Captain Wilcox and Mr. Bland came and had some victuals. The captain went away and Mr. Bland stayed all night. My sloop sailed to Swinyards to have her new mast put in. I said my prayers. I had good health, good thoughts, and good humor, thanks be to God Almighty.

14. I rose at 5 o'clock but could read nothing because Mr. Bland was here. I ate chocolate with him for breakfast. I played at billiards with the Doctor and won three bits. I wrote an account of things I sent to town for Mr. Bland to sell. I ate pork for dinner. In the afternoon I read some Latin and Greek in Homer. In the evening I rode out with my new horse and he had like to have broken my neck by running away and [raising up an end], but I did not fall, thank God. When I came home I said my prayers, and had good health and good humor and good thoughts, thanks be to God Almighty.

15. I rose at 5 o'clock and read a chapter in Hebrew and some Greek in Josephus. I said my prayers and ate milk for breakfast. I danced my dance. I was very sore with my ride last night which hindered my activity. I had a bad dream this morning which seemed to foretell the death of some of my family. I thought I saw my yard full of people and when I came into the house I could not find my wife. God avert her death. I read some Latin. I gave Ben O-d-s-n a vomit which worked very well. I ate boiled pork and rice for dinner. In the afternoon I wrote some letters for the Doctor to carry to the north. I read news and some Greek in Homer. In the evening I took a walk about the plantation. I said my prayers and had good health, good thoughts, and good humor, thanks be to God Almighty.

16. I rose at 5 o'clock and read two chapters in Hebrew and some Greek in Josephus. I said my prayers and ate milk for breakfast. This day my daughter Evelyn is two years old. Pray God send his blessing on her. Old Ben was extremely sick. I gave him a sweat that worked abundantly, which made him something better. I read some Latin. I ate some pork for dinner. In the afternoon I sent Mr. Harvey a bottle of wine and some [s-p-s] for his wife who was ready to lie in. I read more Latin and some Greek in Homer. In the evening I took a walk about the plantation. I neglected to say my prayers. I had good health, good thoughts, and good humor, thanks be to God Almighty.

17. I rose at 6 o'clock and read two chapters in Hebrew and some Greek in Josephus. I said my prayers and ate milk for breakfast. I sent back Mr. Mumford's fine horse because it is dangerous to ride him. Colonel Bolling[1] died this morning after a long sickness. I read a sermon of Dr. Tillotson's. I ate roast pigeon for dinner. In the afternoon Mr. C-s and Mr. Doyley came to see me and stayed till the evening. I walked a little way with them. Old Ben had his fever again this afternoon and it remitted in the evening. I

---

[1]Colonel Robert Bolling of Kippax, Charles City County, father of the "Robin" Bolling with whom Byrd at this time had a feud.

said my prayers and had good health, good thoughts, and good humor, thanks be to God Almighty.

18. I rose at 5 o'clock and read two chapters in Hebrew and some Greek in Josephus. I said my prayers and ate milk for breakfast. I sent the boatmaker to Falling Creek to build me a little boat for my sea sloop. I read some Latin. Tom returned from Falling Creek and brought me word all was well there and that the coaler found the coal mine very good and sufficient to furnish several generations.[1] I ate cold chicken for dinner. In the afternoon Captain Wilcox came from Williamsburg and brought news several ships were come in and one was coming up this river. He was out of humor about the freight. In the evening it rained a little that I could not walk about the plantation. I said my prayers and had good health, good thoughts, and good humor, thanks be to God Almighty.

19. I rose at 6 o'clock and read two chapters in Hebrew and some Greek in Josephus. Robin Hix[2] came over this morning, with whom I had some discourse about the Indian trade. I said my prayers and ate milk for breakfast. I read some geometry. I ate roast mutton for dinner. In the afternoon I read more geometry and some Greek in Homer. It rained a little in the evening, with thunder and lightning. Peter Hamlin came to see me. I could not now walk because of the rain. Captain Wilcox was not kind to my people when I sent them to desire some things of him. I said my prayers and had good health, good thoughts, and good humor, thanks be to God Almighty.

20. I rose at 5 o'clock and read two chapters in Hebrew and some Greek in Josephus. I said my prayers and ate milk for breakfast. I sent Tom to Williamsburg for John B-r-d to work on my sloop. Old Ben was very ill and I gave him a vomit which worked very well and he was something better after it. I read some geometry. I ate nothing but

---

[1] Byrd was interested throughout his life in the possibility of developing mines of various sorts on his property. (See his *A Progress to the Mines in the Year 1732*.)

[2] Robert Hix (or Hicks) was an Indian trader.

hashed mutton for dinner. It was exceedingly hot and I was very dry. In the afternoon I took a nap and read more geometry. In the evening Captain Wilcox came and brought me a letter from Colonel Harrison, who is resolved not to give above £12 a ton. I read it to Captain Wilcox, on which he determined to go round to York River. We drank some syllabub. I said my prayers, and had good health, good thoughts, and good humor, thanks be to God Almighty. I danced my dance.

21. I rose at 5 o'clock and read two chapters in Hebrew and some Greek in Josephus. I said my prayers and ate milk for breakfast. I danced my dance. Old Ben was better this morning. Tom returned from Williamsburg with a letter from Mr. Bland. I read some geometry. I ate roast mutton for dinner. Soon after dinner Captain Wilcox came to take his leave of us. I gave him a letter of recommendation to Colonel Bassett which he desired. I offered to give his carpenters ten shillings each, but he would not let me but promised me he would give them a gallon of rum and some sugar on my account. I read more geometry and some Greek in Homer. In the evening I walked about the plantation. I said my prayers and had good health, good thoughts, and good humor, thanks be to God Almighty.

22. I rose at 5 o'clock and read two chapters in Hebrew and some Greek in Josephus. I said my prayers and ate milk for breakfast. John B-r-d came in the night from Williamsburg in order to work on my sloop. Old Ben was bad this morning. I read some geometry. Frank Eppes came and dined with us. I ate nothing but pudding and stewed apples for dinner. It was exceedingly hot. Mr. Eppes came from Will Randolph's, where he left abundance of company. Here we had a little rain. God send more for everything needs it much. He went away in the evening, and I took a walk about the plantation. I said my prayers and had good health, good thoughts, and good humor, thanks be to God Almighty.

23. I rose at 5 o'clock and read two chapters in Hebrew and some Greek in Josephus. I neglected to say my prayers,

for which God forgive me. I ate milk and apples for breakfast. Captain C-l-t came and lamented that we would not come up to his freight. Captain Wilcox went down with his ship and was so gallant as to give us five guns at parting. I ate dry beef for dinner. Robin Jones came from above and told me all was spoiled at my plantation for want of rain. I read some Greek in Homer and walked about the plantation. It was exceedingly hot. I neglected to say my prayers again. I had good health, good thoughts, but indifferent bad humor. Old Ben was very ill.

24. I rose at 5 o'clock and read two chapters in Hebrew and some Greek in Josephus. Mr. G-r-l came last night and told me all his business was well but that the plantations were brown for want of rain. I said my prayers and ate milk for breakfast. Old Ben was better this morning. It was so very hot that I omitted going to church. Dick Cocke called here before church to drink. Mr. G-r-l told me of all my affairs and went away before dinner. I ate ham and [chicken] for dinner. In the afternoon I was in great hopes of rain but it went away, but it grew cool and I walked about the plantation. I said my prayers and had good health, good thoughts, and good humor, thanks be to God Almighty. Abundance of the N-t-s Indians came here this evening.

25. I rose at 5 o'clock and read two chapters in Hebrew and some Greek in Josephus. I said my prayers and ate milk for breakfast. I danced my dance. The Indians went away this morning and I set them over the river in my boat. I was invited to Colonel Bolling's funeral who is to be buried tomorrow. I read some geometry. Old Ben was very ill but would not take a vomit. I ate broiled chicken for dinner. In the afternoon it began to rain and rained four hours together, thank God. I read more geometry and some Greek in Homer. In the evening it left off raining and I walked in the garden. I said my prayers shortly. I had good health, good thoughts, and good humor, thanks be to God Almighty.

26. I rose at 5 o'clock and read two chapters in Hebrew and some Greek in Josephus. I said my prayers and ate milk for breakfast. Old Ben had a great looseness and was very ill. I read and wrote some geometry. Mr. Harrison came home and sent me two letters from England which informed of the likelihood of peace. I ate roast mutton for dinner. In the afternoon it rained violently and continued till the evening, thanks be to God, so that I could not walk. I recommended my affairs to God, and had good health, good thoughts, and good humor, thanks be to God Almighty.

27. I rose at 5 o'clock and read a chapter in Hebrew and some Greek in Josephus. I said my prayers and ate milk for breakfast. I danced my dance. My wife was not well all day which made me send for Mrs. B-t-s [or P-t-s]. I read and wrote some geometry. It was fair weather today and tolerably cool. Old Ben was something better, grew sensible again. I ate roast mutton for my dinner. In the afternoon I played at piquet with my wife. I read more geometry. In the evening I took a walk about the plantation. I recommended myself to God and had good health, good thoughts, and good humor, thanks be to God Almighty.

28. I rose at 5 o'clock and read two chapters in Hebrew and some Greek in Josephus. I said my prayers and ate milk for breakfast. Old Ben was better and began to be sensible and to eat. Daniel came this morning and brought me a letter from Mr. Bland who told me the news that poor Captain Harrison[1] was dead. I wrote a letter to England. About 12 o'clock Mrs. B-t-s came over. I ate no good dinner because our mutton was spoiled; however I ate some of it. In the afternoon we played at piquet. I read some geometry and a little Greek in Homer. In the evening I walked about the plantation. I neglected to say my prayers, but I had good health, good thoughts, but indifferent good humor, thanks be to God Almighty.

29. I rose at 5 o'clock and read two chapters in Hebrew

---

[1]Perhaps John Harrison, master of a merchant ship. (*Ex. Jour.*, III, 95.)

and some Greek in Josephus. I said my prayers and ate milk for breakfast. Old Ben was something better and seemed to have lost his fever, thank God. I read some geometry. It was very hot again. Anaka lost her fits today; however I continued to give her the bark. I ate tongue and chicken for dinner. In the afternoon my wife and I played at piquet. I wrote to Major Allen[1] for a permit to load my sloop and sent Daniel with the letter. I read some Greek in Homer. I walked about the plantation. I neglected to say my prayers, for which God forgive me. I had good health, good thoughts, and good humor, thanks be to God Almighty.

30. I rose at 5 o'clock and read a chapter in Hebrew and some Greek in Josephus. I said my prayers and ate milk for breakfast. Old Ben was better and without any fever. I read some geometry. It was exceedingly hot. My wife continued well. We loaded the sloop. I ate fish for dinner. In the afternoon my wife and I played at piquet. I read and wrote more geometry. I took a walk about the plantation. I had old Ben taken up and cleaned and he sat up an hour. Daniel brought my permit from Major Allen. I said my prayers and had good health, good thoughts, and good humor, thanks be to God Almighty.

31. I rose at 5 o'clock and read a chapter in Hebrew and some Greek in Josephus. I said my prayers and ate milk for breakfast. I threatened Moll with a good whipping again tomorrow for her many faults. Old Ben grew better and better. I read a sermon in Dr. Tillotson. I took a little nap before dinner. I ate roast pork for dinner. In the afternoon I read some geometry. In the evening Mr. C-s came to see me and we drank a syllabub. We walked in the garden till late. I said my prayers and had good health, good thoughts, and good humor, thanks be to God Almighty.

---

[1]Arthur Allen, of Bacon's Castle, naval officer of the Upper District of the James River.

August, 1709

1. I rose at break of day and drank some warm milk and rode to Mr. Harrison's, where I got a permit to load tobacco on board my sloop. There I found Mr. Anderson. I ate some watermelon and stayed till about 9 o'clock, when I returned and read a chapter in Hebrew and some Greek in Josephus. I said my prayers and went to see old Ben and found him much better. I read some geometry. I ate fish for dinner. In the afternoon the Doctor and my wife played at piquet. Joe Wilkinson[1] came and gave me an account of the tobacco that he raised this year and I agreed with him to be my overseer at Burkland[2] the next year. I read some Greek in Homer and took a walk about the plantation. I neglected to say my prayers. I had good health, good thoughts, and good humor, thanks be to God Almighty.

2. I rose at 5 o'clock and read two chapters in Hebrew and some Greek in Josephus. I said my prayers and drank whey for breakfast. It was terribly hot. I wrote a letter to the Governor of Barbados,[3] to whom I intend to consign my sloop and cargo. The old Ben was still better and began to complain he was hungry. I ate chicken for my dinner. In the afternoon my wife and the Doctor played at piquet and the Doctor was beat. My neighbor Harrison had the ague but was something better this day. I wrote more letters to Barbados. I walked about the plantation. Mrs. Hamlin was to see us. I said a short prayer. It rained a little. I had good health, good thoughts, and good humor, thanks be to God Almighty.

3. I rose at 5 o'clock and read a chapter in Hebrew and some Greek in Josephus. I said my prayers and ate milk

---

[1]Joseph Wilkinson owned land in Henrico County. (*Va. Mag.*, XXVIII, 217.)

[2]A plat from the Byrd Title Book (reproduced in *Va. Mag.*, XXVI, 36) shows "Burkland"; in later maps and in the will of William Byrd III (*Va. Mag.*, XXXVIII, 60), there is a "Buckland" plantation. These may not be the same. The shorthand symbol includes the letter *r*.

[3]Mitford Crow was governor of Barbados from 1707 to 1710.

for breakfast. The old man was better. Colonel Randolph came to see me, as did Mr. Anderson and several others. It rained a little; however we resolved to go to town tomorrow to the meeting of the College. Mr. Harrison continued sick. Colonel Randolph, Mr. Anderson and Will Randolph and Tom dined with me. I ate hung beef for dinner. Will Randolph said his wife had a fever. In the evening Colonel Randolph went to Captain Stith's and the rest of the company went away except Mr. Anderson. I neglected to say my prayers. I had good health, good thoughts, and good humor, thanks be to God Almighty.

4. We rose at 2 o'clock this morning and went in the sloop's boat to Mr. Harvey's, where we arrived by break of day and our horses were ready for us. We rode to town and got there before 10 o'clock, notwithstanding we called at Green Springs, but Colonel Ludwell was not at home. At Mr. Bland's I ate some milk and then went to see the President, who persuaded me to be sworn in Council but I refused. From hence we went to the school house where we at last determined to build the college on the old walls and appointed workmen to view them and [compute] the charge. From hence we went to the Commissary's to dinner where we found Mrs. Ludwell. In the evening we rode to Green Springs and lay there all night. But this hurry made me neglect to say my prayers, for which God forgive me. However, I had good health, good thoughts, and good humor, thanks be to God Almighty.

5. We rose at break of day and without ceremony rode away and got to the ferry before sunrise, and to Mr. Harvey's before 8 o'clock where we found the boat and got home before 10 o'clock, where we found Dr. Blair.[1] He had been [sent] for to set a negro boy's leg which was broken this morning by the fall of the door in the brick house. He and Mr. Anderson dined with us and went away in the afternoon to see Mr. Harrison and his wife, that were both sick. I wrote letters to Barbados. In the evening I

---

[1]Dr. Archibald Blair, brother of Commissary James Blair. He practiced medicine at Jamestown and Williamsburg for many years and died in 1736.

walked about the plantation. I said a short prayer and had good health, good thoughts, and good humor, thanks be to God Almighty.

6. I rose at 5 o'clock and read a chapter in Hebrew but no Greek. I read nothing more all day but wrote the rest of my letters to Barbados. Old Ben began to come down stairs, and the boy that broke his leg was easy. Mr. Harrison missed his fits this day. I ate hashed mutton for dinner. In the afternoon I wrote more letters to Barbados. In the evening I walked about the plantation. I neglected to say my prayers, for which God forgive me. I had good health, good thoughts, and good humor, thanks be to God Almighty.

7. I rose at 5 o'clock and read a chapter in Hebrew and some Greek in Josephus. I said my prayers and ate milk for breakfast. It was so hot I could not go to church, but ordered G-r-l to desire Mr. Anderson and his wife and Mr. C-s to come and dine with me, which they did accordingly. I ate fish for dinner. Mr. Parker also dined with us. One of my fawns died of poison. In the evening all the company went away and I took a walk about the plantation. It grew much cooler with a northwest wind. I neglected to say my prayers, but had good thoughts, good humor, and good health, thanks be to God Almighty.

8. I rose at 5 o'clock and read a chapter in Hebrew and some Greek in Josephus. My sloop sailed this morning for Barbados, God send her a good and expeditious voyage. I was angry with B-l-n-m and he ran away. I likewise chastised Tom. I said my prayers and ate milk for breakfast. I walked out to see my people at work at the ditch. I read a little geometry. I ate mutton for dinner. In the evening I took a little nap, and I read Mr. Woodson's[1] pretense against me. I walked to the ditch again. In the evening I said my prayers. My man Jack was lame again. I had

---

[1]John Woodson, of Henrico County. On April 26, 1707, Byrd, as receiver general of Her Majesty's revenue, had incurred the enmity of Woodson by charging him with occupying more land near Manakin Town than his patent authorized. (*Ex. Jour.*, III, 147.)

good health, good thoughts, and good humor, thanks be to God Almighty.

9. I rose at 5 o'clock and read two chapters in Hebrew and some Greek in Josephus. I said my prayers and ate milk for breakfast. Colonel Harrison, Nat Harrison, Hal Harrison[1] and Mr. Cargill[2] came to see me. We played a little at billiar   but Colonel Harrison as so much in haste to go that we had no time for dive.ion. They all went away about 10 o'clock. Old Ben's leg began to swell and made him very lame. I ate some shoat for dinner. In the afternoon Hal Randolph came and told me G-l-s W-l was recovered. I read some Greek in Homer and then took a walk about the plantation. Colonel Ludwell and his lady came over from Mr. Harrison's and told us Mr. Harrison and his wife were better. I neglected to say my prayers. I had good health, good thoughts, and good humor, thanks be to God Almighty.

10. I rose at 5 o'clock and read two chapters in Hebrew and some Greek in Homer. I said my prayers and ate milk for breakfast. I could not persuade Old Ben to take a purge but Jack took a purge to carry away his lameness. Colonel Ludwell, the Doctor, and I played at billiards. Mr. Mumford came and played likewise at billiards. We drank some Rhenish wine and sugar. Captain Collins came just before dinner but would not stay and dine with us. I ate some roast goose for dinner, and we were served very well, but Colonel Ludwell's boy broke a glass. In the afternoon we played again at billiards. It rained a little towards the evening but not enough to hinder the company from going away. I neglected to say my prayers but only in short. I had good health, good humor, and good thoughts, thanks be to God Almighty.

11. I rose at 5 o'clock and read two chapters in Hebrew and some Greek in Josephus. I said my prayers and ate milk for breakfast. I read some geometry and removed

---

[1] Captain Henry Harrison.
[2] Reverend John Cargill, minister of Southwark Parish, Surry, 1708-23 *et seq.* (Goodwin, pp. 258-59.)

some of my books into the library. I gave Bannister leave
to go see his mother. I ate goose giblets for dinner. In
the afternoon I read some Greek in Homer. I gave old
Ben a purge which worked very well. It looked as if it
would rain but it did not. I said a short prayer and had
good health, good thoughts, and good humor, thanks be to
God Almighty.

12. I rose at 5 o'clock and read two chapters in Hebrew
and some Greek in Josephus. I said my prayers and ate
milk for breakfast. I removed more of my books into the
library. I read some geometry. I danced my dance. It
was a very cold day but did not rain. Old Ben had his leg
bathed in milk and mullein and found ease. I ate boiled
shoat for dinner. In the afternoon I put up my books and
then read some Greek in Homer and some Italian. In the
evening I took a walk about the plantation. I neglected to
say my prayers but had good health, good thoughts, and
good humor, thanks be to God Almighty.

13. I rose at 5 o'clock and read a chapter in Hebrew and
some Greek in Josephus. I said my prayers and ate bread
and butter for breakfast. Twelve Pamunkey Indians came
over. We gave them some victuals and some rum and put
them over the river. I danced my dance. I removed more
books into the library. I read some geometry and walked
to see the people at work. I ate fish for dinner. I was
almost the whole afternoon in putting up my books. In the
evening John Blackman came from the Falls and brought
me word some of my people were sick and that my coaler
was sick at the coal mine. I scolded with him about the little
work he had done this summer. I took a walk about the
plantation. I had a little scold with the Doctor about his
boy. I said my prayers and had good health, good thoughts,
and good humor, thanks be to God Almighty.

14. I rose at 5 o'clock and read a chapter in Hebrew and
some Greek in Josephus. I said my prayers and ate milk
for breakfast. I sent away my sloop which came yesterday
to Falling Creek. John Blackman returned to the Falls.

The old man grew better in his lameness and the boy who broke his leg was much better, thanks be to God. I ate boiled mutton for dinner. In the afternoon I took a nap. My cousin Betty Harrison[1] came over and stayed till the evening. I took a walk about the plantation with my wife who has not quarrelled with me a great while. I said my prayers shortly and had good health, good thoughts, and good humor, thanks be to God Almighty.

15. I rose at 5 o'clock and read two chapters in Hebrew and some Greek in Josephus. I said my prayers and ate milk for breakfast. I removed two cases of books into the library. I read some geometry. Old Ben walked a little today which made his leg swell again. Jack was better of his lameness. Mr. Isham Randolph came and dined with us. I ate fish for dinner. In the afternoon I put my books into the cases in the library, notwithstanding Mr. Randolph was here. He said Captain Webb was very bad. In the evening I took a walk about the plantation. I said my prayers and had good health, good thoughts, and good humor, thanks be to God Almighty.

16. I rose at 5 o'clock and read a chapter in Hebrew and some Greek in Josephus. I said no prayers this morning because my cousin Harrison came and hindered me. I ate milk for breakfast. I removed the rest of my books into the library. My cousin Harrison dined with us, and I ate mutton for dinner. In the afternoon I set up all my books and then came in to the rest of the company. In the evening my cousin Harrison went home and I took a walk about the plantation. I said my prayers shortly and had good health, good thoughts, and good humor, thanks be to God Almighty. One of Mrs. Taylor's daughters was married to Mr. John Hardiman.[2]

17. I rose at 5 o'clock and read a chapter in Hebrew and some Greek in Josephus. I said my prayers and ate milk for

---

[1]Wife (or possibly daughter) of Benjamin Harrison of Berkeley.
[2]Henrietta Maria, daughter of John Taylor of Charles City County (who died in 1707), married John Hardiman. Her sister Sarah, mentioned later in the diary, married John Hardiman's brother Francis. (*Va. Mag.*, VII, 354.)

breakfast. Mr. C-k of Plymouth was here and so was Mr. N-r-t-n from below, who told me my sloop was sailed out of the Cape. God send her a good voyage. I ate hashed mutton for dinner. In the afternoon I settled some accounts and read some Greek in Homer. In the evening I took a walk about the plantation and found that some of my good neighbors had dug down the bank of my ditch to let their hogs into my pasture, for which I was out of humor. However I said my prayers shortly and had good health and good thoughts, thanks be to God Almighty.

18. I rose at 5 o'clock and read nothing because I prepared to go to Falling Creek. I said my prayers and ate milk for breakfast. About 8 o'clock got on my horse and rode to Will Randolph's where I saw his wife and gave her joy. She seems to be a good-humored woman and is handsome. Here I dined and ate boiled beef for dinner. In the afternoon I took my leave and walked to Colonel Randolph's where I only saw Mrs. Randolph because the Colonel was gone to see Captain Webb who was recovered. Mrs. Randolph and I talked of the debt which the Colonel owes to Mr. Perry. From hence Isham Randolph and I proceeded to Falling Creek, where I found all well and had the pleasure to hear that my coaler was recovered. I ate milk for supper and had good health, good thoughts, and good humor, thanks be to God Almighty.

19. I rose at 6 o'clock and Mr. Randolph and I walked to the tannery, with which we were both pleased. Then we went and viewed all the work at the dam. Then we ate milk for breakfast and rode to the Falls where we found a good crop considering the great drought. From hence we rode to Kensington[1] where there is a very poor crop. Here we waded over the river, stepping from one rock to the other and so got to Burkland where John Blackman had little to show for his year's work. Here we ate bacon and eggs. From hence we proceeded to walk to [Byrd Park] where was the worst crop of all. Then we walked on to Shockoe

---

[1]The plantations mentioned here are all in the vicinity of what is now Richmond.

where the crop was something better. Here we crossed the river in a canoe and rode to Falling Creek where we ate chicken pie for supper. I recommended myself to heaven in a short prayer and had good health, good thoughts, but indifferent humor.

20. I rose at 6 o'clock and said a short prayer and then we ate milk for breakfast and I gave audience to some of the workmen and then rode towards the Hundred. We called on board Captain Collins but we could not meet with the Captain. Then we crossed the river to Colonel Hill's[1] where we found nobody at home. Then we rode to Colonel Eppes but we found only his wife. After staying a little there we rode to each of our homes. I found all well, thanks be to God Almighty. I ate fish for dinner. In the afternoon I enjoyed my wife. I read some Greek in Homer and took a walk about the plantation. I neglected to say my prayers. I had good health, good thoughts, and good humor, thanks be to God Almighty.

21. I rose at 5 o'clock and read two chapters in Hebrew and some Greek in Josephus. I said my prayers and ate milk for breakfast. I went to church where Mr. Anderson preached, from whence I invited Mr. Bland, Mr. Isham Randolph, and Mr. Gee to dinner. I ate boiled pork and rice for dinner. Mr. Randolph sent us a sturgeon and Mr. Mumford sent us some peaches. In the evening all the company went away and were caught in a rain, there being a good shower, thank God, which hindered my walk. My man John sprained his ankle in running after the hogs. I said my prayers and had good health, good thoughts, and good humor, thanks be to God Almighty.

22. I rose at 5 o'clock and read two chapters in Hebrew and some Greek in Josephus. I said my prayers and ate milk for breakfast. Mr. Mumford sent to the Doctor to carry him something for a fever and ague, of which he had had two fits. Daniel went away this morning to Williams-

---

[1]Colonel Edward Hill, of Shirley, was at this time in England. His return to Virginia is mentioned in January, 1710.

burg to keep Dr. Blair's store and I gave him a letter of recommendation. I walked to see my people. I read some geometry. I ate boiled pork and rice for dinner. In the afternoon I played at cards with my own wife. I read more geometry and some Greek in Homer. I took a walk about the plantation. I said my prayers and had good health, good thoughts, and good humor, thanks be to God Almighty.

23. I rose at 5 o'clock and read two chapters in Hebrew and some Greek in Josephus. I said my prayers and ate milk for breakfast. I danced my dance. My wife was indisposed all day. I began to read geometry but was interrupted by the coming of Mr. Will Randolph and his wife and Mrs. Cocke. I was as courteous as possible to them to give Mrs. Randolph a good impression of this part of the country. They dined with us and I ate blue wing for dinner. In the afternoon we played at billiards. In the evening the company went away and I took a walk about the plantation. I said my prayers and had good health, good thoughts, and good humor, thanks be to God Almighty.

24. I rose at 5 o'clock and read a chapter in Hebrew and some Greek in Josephus. I said my prayers and ate milk for breakfast. I danced my dance. I settled some accounts. I read some geometry. I was a little angry with Bannister for hiding a glass in the cellar. I ate roast mutton for dinner. In the afternoon I read more geometry and in the evening walked about the plantation. My wife complained all day very much of her belly, but to no purpose. I said my prayers in bed and had good health, good thoughts, and good humor, thanks be to God Almighty.

25. I rose at 5 o'clock and read two chapters in Hebrew and some Greek in Josephus. I said my prayers and ate milk for breakfast. I danced my dance and settled some accounts. I read some geometry. My wife was something better. I ate mutton for dinner. In the afternoon I played at cards with my own wife. I read more geometry and a little Greek in Homer. Then I took a walk about the plantation. I said my prayers and had good health, good thoughts, and good humor, thanks be to God Almighty.

26. I rose at 5 o'clock and read a chapter in Hebrew and some Greek in Josephus. I said my prayers and ate milk for breakfast. I danced my dance. Mr. Frank Eppes and the [hatter] came over. The first brought a mare that he had bought for me. We played at billiards and I won. They stayed and dined with us. I ate roast mutton for dinner. In the afternoon the company went away and I read some Greek in Homer. I took a walk about the plantation. I said my prayers and had good health, good thoughts, and good humor, thanks be to God Almighty.

27. I rose at 5 o'clock and read two chapters in Hebrew and some Greek in Josephus. I said my prayers and ate milk for breakfast. I danced my dance. I had like to have whipped my maid Anaka for her laziness but I forgave her. I read a little geometry. I denied my man G-r-l to go to a horse race because there was nothing but swearing and drinking there. I ate roast mutton for dinner. In the afternoon I played at piquet with my own wife and made her out of humor by cheating her. I read some Greek in Homer. Then I walked about the plantation. I lent John H-ch £7 in his distress. I said my prayers and had good health, good thoughts, and good humor, thanks be to God Almighty.

28. I rose at 5 o'clock and read two chapters in Hebrew and some Greek in Josephus. I said my prayers and ate milk for breakfast. I danced my dance. Mr. Bland's shallop brought me some things and some letters of an old date from England. I ate chicken for dinner. In the afternoon Mr. Harrison and his wife and daughter and two of Colonel Bassett's daughters came to see us and stayed till the evening and then I walked with them to their boat. I said my prayers and had good health, good thoughts, and good humor, thanks be to God Almighty.

29. I rose at 5 o'clock and read two chapters in Hebrew and some Greek in Josephus. I said my prayers devoutly and ate milk for breakfast. I danced my dance. I read some geometry. I ate dry beef for dinner. Mr. Dennis[1]

---

[1] Probably Richard Dennis, who was appointed sheriff of Charles City County on April 28, 1714.

came just before dinner but would not eat with us. He came with a letter of recommendation from Colonel Randolph to be the receiver of my tobacco above. I put him off as courteously as I could. He told me a sad story of the badness of his crop because of the great drouth. God send rain. I read a little in Homer. I took a walk about my plantation in the evening. I said my prayers. My wife was out of order. I had good health, good thoughts, and good humor, thanks be to God Almighty.

30. I rose at 5 o'clock and read two chapters in Hebrew and some Greek in Josephus. I said my prayers and ate milk for breakfast. I danced my dance. I was angry with G-r-l for letting some of the bacon spoil for want of making a fire. My brother Duke's[1] boy came and brought me several letters, some of which were from England. My sloop came from Falling Creek with the closets and other things. The Dutchman also came from thence and told me all was well above. I ate pork for dinner. In the afternoon I played at piquet with my own wife. I read a little Greek in Homer. It began to rain, thanks be to God, which hindered me from walking. I said my prayers and had good health, good thoughts, and good humor, thanks be to God Almighty.

31. I rose at 5 o'clock and read two chapters in Hebrew and some Greek in Josephus. I said my prayers and ate milk for breakfast. I wrote several letters to go by the sloop which sailed away to Appomattox. It rained very much and blew hard. I read some geometry. I ate roast pork for dinner. In the afternoon I read some news that came to hand, by which I found there is a great likelihood of peace. I read some Greek in Homer and in the evening took a walk about the plantation. I said my prayers shortly. I had good health, good thoughts, and good humor, thanks be to God Almighty. My letters from England tell me tobacco is sold for nothing there and skins for very little,

---

[1]James Duke. The tie between the two families has not been found.

that hardly any bills are paid, and very little goods will come by the next fleet. It is time there should be peace to remedy these misfortunes. Mrs. B-t-s taught me to reckon 20 weeks from the time a woman is quick when she will seldom fail to be brought to bed. In this reckoning there are seven days in a week.

September, 1709

1. I rose at 5 o'clock and read two chapters in Hebrew and some Greek in Josephus. I said my prayers and ate milk for breakfast. I danced my dance. I read some geometry and some news. The Dutchman returned to Falling Creek again. I ate peas and bacon for dinner. In the afternoon I played at cards with my own wife. I read more news and some Greek in Homer, and a little geometry. In the evening I took a walk about the plantation. I neglected to say my prayers, for which God forgive me. I had good health, good thoughts, and good humor, thanks be to God Almighty.

2. I rose at 5 o'clock and read a chapter in Hebrew and some Greek in Josephus. I said my prayers and ate milk for breakfast. I danced my dance. It rained again this day, thanks be to God for his great goodness, who sent us rain almost all day and all the night following. I read some geometry. Notwithstanding the rain Mrs. Ware[1] came to desire me to take tobacco for her debt to me but I refused because tobacco was good for nothing. I ate hashed pork for dinner. In the afternoon Mr. Taylor[2] came from Surry about his bill of exchange. He told me there was news by way of Barbados that the peace was expected there to be already concluded. The rain kept him here all night but Mrs. Ware went away. I neglected to say my prayers but I had good health, good thoughts, and good humor, thanks be to God Almighty.

3. I rose at 5 o'clock and was hindered from reading Hebrew by the company; however, I read some Greek in Josephus. I said my prayers and ate chocolate with Mr. Taylor for breakfast. Then he went away. I read some geometry. We had no court this day. My wife was indisposed again but not to much purpose. I ate roast chicken

---

[1]Susanna, widow of Rev. Jacob Ware. (See note, March 25, 1709.)
[2]Probably Ethelred Taylor, appointed sheriff of Surry County April 27, 1710.

for dinner. In the afternoon I beat Jenny for throwing water on the couch. I took a walk to Mr. Harrison's who told me he heard the peace was concluded in the last month. After I had been courteously entertained with wine and cake I returned home, where I found all well, thank God. I neglected to say my prayers but had good health, good thoughts, and good humor, thanks be to God Almighty.

4. I rose at 5 o'clock and read a chapter in Hebrew and some Greek in Josephus. I said my prayers and ate milk for breakfast. It rained abundantly in the night. I went to church and was devout and heard a good sermon of Mr. Anderson. Colonel Eppes and his wife came home and dined with us. I ate fish for dinner, which Mr. Parker was so kind to send us. They stayed here till the evening, when my wife and I took a walk about the plantation. I gave Mr. Parker's boy two bits that brought the fish. I neglected to say my prayers but I had good health, good thoughts, and good humor, thanks be to God Almighty. Two [travellers] were entertained here this night.

5. I rose at 5 o'clock and read some Greek in Josephus and a chapter in Hebrew. I said my prayers and ate milk for breakfast. I danced my dance. My wife was much out of order and had frequent returns of her pains. I read some geometry. I ate roast mutton for dinner. In the afternoon I wrote a letter to England and I read some Greek in Homer. Then in the evening I took a walk about the plantation and when I returned I found my wife very bad. I sent for Mrs. Hamlin and my cousin Harrison about 9 o'clock and I said my prayers heartily for my wife's happy delivery, and had good health, good thoughts, and good humor, thanks be to God Almighty. I went to bed about 10 o'clock and left the women full of expectation with my wife.

6. About one o'clock this morning my wife was happily delivered of a son,[1] thanks be to God Almighty. I was awake in a blink and rose and my cousin Harrison met me

---

[1]The child, named Parke, after his maternal grandfather, died on July 3, 1710. (See entry in the diary.)

on the stairs and told me it was a boy. We drank some French wine and went to bed again and rose at 7 o'clock. I read a chapter in Hebrew and then drank chocolate with the women for breakfast. I returned God humble thanks for so great a blessing and recommended my young son to His divine protection. My cousin Harrison and Mrs. Hamlin went away about 9 o'clock and I made my [satisfaction] to them for that kindness. I sent Peter away who brought me a summons to the Council. I read some geometry. The Doctor brought me two letters from England from Captain Stith. I ate roast mutton for dinner. In the afternoon I wrote a letter to England and took a walk about the plantation. I said my prayers and had good health and good thoughts, thanks be to God Almighty.

7. I rose at 5 o'clock and read a chapter in Hebrew and some Greek in Josephus. I said my prayers and ate milk for breakfast. My wife grew much better. I danced my dance. It rained in the night and likewise this day. I broached another pipe of wine, the other having lasted about half a year. I wrote a letter to England and read a little geometry. I ate roast pigeon for dinner. Just as we had dined Joe Wilkinson[1] came to justify himself against some accusation he thought had been brought against him. Captain Collins came over for his protested bills of my endorsement and I renewed them. In the evening Mr. Clayton came and brought me a letter from my father Parke in which he signified he received all my letters and expressed himself well satisfied with us. We drank a bottle of wine. I neglected to say my prayers, but had good health, good thoughts, and good humor, thanks be to God Almighty.

8.[2] I rose at 5 o'clock and read a chapter in Hebrew and some Greek in Josephus. I neglected to say my prayers, and ate chocolate for breakfast. Mr. Clayton and the Doctor and myself went to Mr. Anderson's where we stayed till the evening. I ate bacon and chicken for dinner. We

---

[1] The overseer of Burkland later proved unsatisfactory and had to be discharged. (See later entries in the diary.)
[2] The entries for the 8th and the 9th are reversed in the manuscript.

talked politics abundantly and returned in the evening. Then we played at cards till 12 o'clock at night. My wife was very well, thank God. I said my prayers shortly and had good health, good thoughts, and good humor, thanks be to God Almighty.

9. I rose at 5 o'clock and read a chapter in Hebrew and some Greek in Josephus. I said my prayers and ate chocolate for breakfast. Mr. Clayton told me the Governor of Maryland died about a month ago very suddenly.[1] Mr. Dennis also came, as likewise did Mr. Anderson and they all dined with us. I ate fricassee for dinner. In the afternoon we talked politics till the evening, when all the company but Mr. Clayton went away. Then we went again to cards and I had bad luck. I neglected to say my prayers but had good health, good thoughts, and good humor, thanks be to God Almighty. Mrs. B-t-s went away this day.

10. I rose at 5 o'clock and read a chapter in Hebrew and some Greek Greek [sic] in Josephus. Mr. Clayton went away this morning without his breakfast because he was to call at Mr. Harrison's. Old Ben grew much swelled in his leg and had a great cough. I wrote a letter to England. I ate bacon for dinner. In the afternoon I wrote more letters to England and read some Greek in Homer. Captain Collins came over this evening, to whom I delivered a letter to my uncle Rand.[2] I gave him some physic for some of his men that were sick. He went away. I said my prayers and had good health, good thoughts, and good humor, thanks be to God Almighty.

11. I rose at 5 o'clock and read a chapter in Hebrew and some Greek in Josephus. I said my prayers and ate milk for breakfast. My wife and child were extremely well, thanks to God Almighty, who I hope will please to keep them so. I recommended my family to the divine protection

---

[1]Governor John Seymour died on July 30, 1709.

[2]Byrd's aunt, Ursula Horsemanden, married a Mr. Rand, who lived near Deal, England. In December, 1719, just before sailing for Virginia, Byrd visited the Rands. (He mentions the visit in the part of the diary in the Virginia Historical Society.)

and passed over the creek and then rode to my brother
Duke's whom I found just recovered of the ague by means
of my physic. Here I ate some roast beef for dinner, and
then proceeded to Colonel Duke's, whom I found indisposed. He entertained me very courteously and I said my
prayers and had good health, good thoughts, and good
humor, thanks be to God Almighty.

12. I rose at 5 o'clock and said my prayers and then the
Colonel and I discoursed about his debt to Mr. Perry in
which I promised to be the mediator. I ate milk for dinner
[*sic*] and then I met Colonel Bassett and with him rode to
Williamsburg. We called at Mr. Blair's but nobody was at
home. Then went to Mr. Bland's where I found all well.
Then I went to Mr. President's, where I found several of
the Council. The President persuaded me to be sworn,
which I agreed to, and accordingly went to Council where I
was sworn a member of the Council. God grant I may
distinguish myself with honor and good conscience. We
dined together and I ate beef for dinner. In the evening we
went to the President's where I drank too much French wine
and played at cards and I lost 20 shillings. I went home
about 12 o'clock at night. I neglected to say my prayers
and had good health, good thoughts, and good humor,
thanks be to God Almighty.

13. I rose at 5 o'clock and read some Greek in Lucian
and a little Latin in Terence. I neglected to say my prayers
and ate rice milk for breakfast. Several people came to see
me and Mr. Commissary desired me to frame a letter to the
Lord Treasurer which I did and then went to the meeting
of the College where after some debate the majority were
for building on the old wall; I was against this and was for
a new one for several reasons. We heard that my sister
Custis was brought to bed of a daughter[1] and that Mrs.
J-f-r-y was married to Parson Dunn.[2] I ate bacon and

---

[1] Frances Custis.
[2] Minister of Hungar's Parish, Northampton County (Goodwin, p. 266).
Little is known of him. In 1706 the Bishop of London licensed a William
Dunn to preach in Carolina, but whether he came to Virginia is uncertain
(*Va. Mag.*, VII, 311). Dunn seems to have removed to Henrico County in

chicken for dinner. I received some protested bills and then we went to the President's and played at cards and I lost £4 about 10 o'clock and went home. I neglected to say my prayers and had good health, good thoughts, and good humor, thanks be [to] God Almighty.

14. I rose at 5 o'clock and Colonel Randolph came to see me to discourse about his debt to Mr. Perry. Then I went to take leave of the President and Mr. Bland and rode to Colonel Ludwell's, whom I overtook on the road. I ate rice milk for breakfast. I presented Mrs. Bland with a keg of sweetmeats. Colonel Ludwell and I discoursed about my father Parke's business. I ate bacon and chicken for dinner. About 3 o'clock I rode towards home, where I got about 8 o'clock and found all well, thanks be to God Almighty. By the way every time my horse went through the water he was lame for a little time. I said my prayers shortly, and had good health, good thoughts, and good humor, thanks be to God Almighty.

15. I rose at 6 o'clock and read a chapter in Hebrew and some Greek in Josephus. I neglected to say my prayers because Mr. John Bolling came to see me. I ate milk for breakfast. I received him very coldly because he [is a sharper]. However, we played at billiards. I ate blue wing for dinner. In the afternoon Will Randolph brought me Mrs. Ware's debt and Mr. Salle came likewise to see me and we all played at billiards. In the evening all except Mr. Salle went away. Mr. Salle came about the contest with the parson, who is a pestilent fellow. I took a walk about the plantation. I read some Greek in Homer. I said my prayers shortly, and had good health, good thoughts, and good humor, thanks be to God Almighty.

1710, and from a letter in the Byrd letter book at the University of North Carolina, it appears that he abandoned his wife, who lived thereafter in the Byrd household. There is a jocular letter from Byrd to John Custis, dated October, 1709, saying "How is Madam Dunn? For there goes a prophecy about, that in the eastern parts of Virginia a parson's wife will, in the year of our Lord 1710, have four children at a birth, one of which will be an admiral, and another Archbishop of Canterbury . . ." (*Va. Mag.*, XX, 379-80.)

16. I rose at 3 o'clock and read two chapters in Hebrew and some Greek in Josephus. I said my prayers and ate milk for breakfast. I wrote a letter to England to make interest for the government of Maryland; God send good success. Jenny was whipped for abundance of faults. I ate fresh beef for dinner. In the afternoon I played at cards with my wife who was something indisposed. Then I wrote other letters to England. In the evening I took a walk about the plantation and met Mr. Mumford who came to see me and told me all was well at Appomattox. I neglected to say my prayers, but had good health, good thoughts, and good humor, thanks be to God Almighty.

17. I rose at 2 o'clock and read two chapters in Hebrew and some Greek in Josephus. I said my prayers and ate milk for breakfast. I read some geometry. Mr. Mumford and I played at billiards almost all the morning and I lost half a crown. I ate roast beef for dinner. In the afternoon Mr. Mumford and I played at billiards again. In the evening he went away. Mr. Anderson just called here. Robin [Craddock] came and made his peace with me, and I forgave him and promised if he behaved himself well he should not be turned off his plantation. I neglected to say my prayers and had good health, good thoughts, and good humor, thanks be to God Almighty.

18. I rose at 3 o'clock and read a chapter in Hebrew and some Greek in Josephus. I said my prayers and ate milk for breakfast. I danced my dance. I went to church and heard Mr. Anderson preach a sermon, from whence Mr. Drury Stith and his wife and Mrs. Harrison and his [sic] daughter came to dine with us. I ate blue wing for dinner. In the evening the company went away and I took a walk. I read a little Greek in Homer. I said my prayers and had good health, good thoughts, and good humor, thanks be to God Almighty.

19. I rose at 4 o'clock and read a chapter in Hebrew and some Greek in Josephus. I said my prayers and ate milk for breakfast. I danced my dance. I beat Anaka for letting the child piss in bed. I wrote a letter to England

for the government of Maryland. I read some law. I ate blue wing for dinner. In the afternoon I wrote another letter to England and then took a walk about the plantation. My wife was something better, thank God. I said my prayers and had good health, good thoughts, and good humor, thanks be to God Almighty. I read some Greek in Homer.

20. I rose at 4 o'clock and read two chapters in Hebrew and some Greek in Josephus. I said my prayers and ate milk for breakfast. Captain Wilcox came to see me but would not stay. I wrote two letters to England and read some law. I ate roast pigeon for dinner. In the afternoon I played at cards with my own wife and then wrote another letter to England. I agreed with John L— to let him shoot in the marsh provided he brings me the meat and keeps the feathers for himself. In the evening I took a walk about the plantation. I neglected to say my prayers but had good health, good thoughts, and good humor, thanks be to God Almighty. I read some Greek in Homer.

21. I rose at 4 o'clock and read two chapters in Hebrew and some Greek in Josephus. I said my prayers and ate broth for breakfast. I danced my dance. My boat went down to Green Springs for Colonel Ludwell and his lady and Major Burwell and I went in it as far as Mr. Parker's, who was very sick. I stayed with him most all day and ate fish for dinner. He lent me a horse back again and in the evening I got home where I found all well, thanks be to God Almighty. I ate some roast beef for supper, and then read some Greek in Homer. I said my prayers and had good health, good thoughts, and indifferent good humor.

22. I rose at 5 o'clock and read two chapters in Hebrew and some Greek in Josephus. I said my prayers and ate milk for breakfast. I danced my dance. Phil Pursell came to speak with me and I treated him as he deserved. It rained very hard all day. I had another quarrel with my maid Anaka. Mr. Will Eppes came to see me and stayed to dinner. I ate roast mutton for dinner. In the afternoon Mr. Eppes went away in the rain though I persuaded him

to stay. In the evening the rain hindered me from walking. I said my prayers and had good health, good humor, and good thoughts, thanks be to God Almighty. I was angry with Bannister for writing a foolish letter to Charles Doyley.

23. I rose at 6 o'clock and read a chapter in Hebrew and some Greek in Josephus. I said my prayers and ate boiled milk for breakfast. Last night my boat returned without the company I expected because both my Aunt Ludwell[1] and Major Burwell were indisposed. I danced my dance. I wrote a letter to England. I read some law. I ate blue wing for dinner. In the afternoon I was angry with G-r-l for being sick and not telling me of it and with Tom for not doing well in the garden. I wrote another letter to England and read some Greek in Homer. It rained pretty much this day. I said my prayers and had good health, good thoughts, and good humor, thanks be to God Almighty.

24. I rose at 3 o'clock and read three chapters in Hebrew and some Greek in Homer. I said my prayers and ate milk for breakfast. I danced my dance. I wrote a letter to England. About 11 o'clock Colonel Randolph came and brought me an answer to Mr. Perry's claim against him, by which it appeared that the interest was twice as much as the principal. The Colonel dined with me and I ate mutton for dinner. In the afternoon Mr. Harrison and his wife came to see us and the company all went away in the evening and I walked part of the way with my cousin Harrison. I said my prayers and had good thoughts, good health, and good humor, thanks be to God Almighty.

25. I rose at 4 o'clock and read two chapters in Hebrew and three chapters in the Greek Testament. I said my prayers devoutly and ate boiled milk for breakfast. I danced my dance. I wrote a letter to England. I ate fish for dinner. In the afternoon I wrote another letter to England. In the evening I rode out to try my new horse which I bought of Mr. Parker. When I returned I walked about the plantation. I said my prayers and had good

---

[1] Mrs. Philip Ludwell. (See Introduction, p. xxiv.)

health, good thoughts, and good humor, thanks be to God
Almighty.

26. I rose at 4 o'clock and read two chapters in Hebrew
and some Greek in Homer. I said my prayers and ate
boiled milk for breakfast. I danced my dance. I wrote a
long letter to England. About 10 o'clock Mrs. Cocke came
and about 12 Mr. Anderson, his wife, and Colonel Eppes
and his wife came to see us and dined with us. I ate boiled
beef for dinner. In the afternoon we played at billiards.
About 5 o'clock they all went away. I took a walk about
the plantation and when I returned Captain R-b-n,[1] Captain
Cook[2] and Mr. Robinson arrived from Williamsburg. I
gave them some blue wing and partridge for supper. I
neglected to say my prayers, but had good health, good
thoughts, and good humor, thanks be to God Almighty.

27. I rose at 6 o'clock but could read nothing because of
my company. I said my prayers shortly and ate milk for
breakfast. The company drank chocolate. Then we played
at billiards and I showed them a rattlesnake. After this we
played at cards. I played at piquet till dinner. We had a
very handsome dinner, and particularly a fine dessert which
the company admired. After dinner we played at piquet
again till 12 o'clock at night. I had a cold which troubled
me. Mr. Isham Randolph came over. I asked the captains
to be godfathers, which they kindly accepted. I neglected
to say my prayers but had good health, good thoughts, and
good humor, thanks be to God Almighty.

28. I rose at 6 o'clock and read nothing because of the
company. I said my prayers shortly and ate milk for breakfast. It rained much in the night and also this morning, for
which reason my company went to cards again. About 11
o'clock Mr. Anderson came and soon after Mr. Harrison,
his wife, and daughter. About 12 o'clock our son was
christened and his name was Parke. God grant him grace
to be a good man. The two captains of the men-of-war

---

[1]Byrd probably referred to Captain John Roberts, commander of the
warship *Southsea Castle* which arrived in June, 1709, to serve as a convoy.
[2]Captain Cook, commander of the warship *Garland.*

were godfathers. When this was over we played at cards again till dinner. I ate blue wing for dinner. In the afternoon we went to cards again and played till 10 o'clock. In the meanwhile Mr. Harrison and his wife and Mr. Anderson went away. My cold continued .with some violence. I had good health, good thoughts, and good humor, thanks be to God Almighty. Mrs. Betty Harrison was godmother.

29. I rose at 6 o'clock this morning and the two Captains and Mr. Robinson went away early. I read two chapters in Hebrew and some Greek in Josephus. I danced my dance, and ate milk for breakfast. My cold continued with violence so that I could not write. I ate blue wing for dinner. In the afternoon Mr. Dennis came over. I read nothing but in the evening I rode out and met the [d-r]. Mr. Peter Hamlin came after it was dark. I neglected to say my prayers but I had good health, good thoughts, and good humor, thanks be to God Almighty.

30. I rose at 8 o'clock because my cold was bad. I read nothing. I said my prayers shortly and ate milk for breakfast. I resolved to go to Falling Creek. I gave my wife a flourish this morning. About 12 o'clock I rode to Mr. Anderson's where I ate some roast beef. Then I went over the river and proceeded to Falling Creek where I arrived about 5 o'clock and found things in good order. I ate some chicken pie for supper. After supper I discoursed G-r-l about my affairs. I recommended myself to heaven in a short prayer. I had good health, good thoughts, and good humor, thanks be to God Almighty.

October, 1709

1. I rose at 6 o'clock and read nothing because I got ready to go see the quarters. I ate milk for breakfast and said my prayers shortly. I went to see Westminster who had a pain in his back, to which I ordered to apply some cold water. About 9 o'clock I rode to [Warwick] where I found Tom Turpin and Joe Wilkinson. I took the last with me to the Falls where things were in good order. We went over the river and found that Blackman left everything in a sad condition for which reason I refused to pay him. I stayed on this side till 5 o'clock and returned by the Falls to Falling Creek. Frank Eppes came to us but too late to survey the land in dispute between Captain Webb and me. We ate beef for supper. Frank Eppes lay with me. I neglected to say my prayers, but had good health, good thoughts, and good humor, thanks be to God Almighty.

2. I rose at 6 o'clock and prepared to return home. I ate milk for breakfast and about 8 o'clock I rode towards the Hundred. By the way I met Will Bass who gave me a sad account of Robin Easely, who is a lazy fellow. I said my prayers on my horse. I called at Doctor Bowman's who gave me some apples. I got home about noon, where I found all well, thanks be to God Almighty. I ate beef for dinner. In the afternoon I took a nap and then went to see the Doctor, who had an ague. In the evening I took a walk about the plantation. I neglected to say my prayers but had good health, good thoughts, and good humor, thanks be to God Almighty.

3. I rose at 7 o'clock and read a chapter in Hebrew and some Greek in Josephus. I said my prayers and ate chicken broth for breakfast. I danced my dance. The Frenchman came to demand some tools which I detained for a debt he owes me and so I refused to deliver it to him. I went to see the Doctor, who was something better. Mr. Salle and his wife came over, as did John Woodson, while we were at

dinner. I ate blue wing for dinner. In the afternoon Mr. Salle and I played at billiards. In the evening we got some supper for our company and I ate some myself. I neglected to say my prayers, but had good health, good thoughts, and good humor, thanks be to God Almighty.

4. I rose at 6 o'clock and read a chapter in Hebrew and some Greek in Josephus. I said my prayers and ate [chocolate] for breakfast. Mr. Salle and I played at billiards again and he beat me. The Doctor had his fever violently again. Dick Randolph came from Williamsburg with some letters for me but would not stay to dinner. I ate some blue wing for dinner. In the afternoon our company went away. I wrote some business. I walked about the plantation. In the evening Mr. Evans came for the Doctor to his father, who is very sick. I could not persuade him to eat anything. I neglected to say my prayers but had good health, good thoughts and good humor, thanks be to God Almighty.

5. I rose at 6 o'clock and prepared to go to Williamsburg. I said my prayers and ate milk and potatoes for breakfast. The Doctor was something better this morning. I was set over the creek and from thence rode to Green Springs where I found Mr. Ludwell sick and Mrs. Wormeley not well recovered. The Colonel had been at general muster and brought home two of his captains with him. I ate boiled beef for dinner. Then we played at whist till bed time. I said my prayers and had good health, good thoughts, and good humor, thanks be to God Almighty.

6. I rose at 6 o'clock and said my prayers and ate milk for breakfast. Then I proceeded to Williamsburg, where I found all well. I went to the capitol where I sent for the wench to clean my room and when I came I kissed her and felt her, for which God forgive me. Then I went to see the President, whom I found indisposed in his ears. I dined with him on beef on beef [sic]. Then we went to his house and played at piquet where Mr. Clayton came to us. We had much to do to get a bottle of French wine. About

10 o'clock I went to my lodgings. I had good health but wicked thoughts, God forgive me.

7. I rose at 6 o'clock and ate milk for breakfast. The President and Mr. Clayton came to see me. When they were gone I wrote several letters to England. I could get nobody to go with me to Kiquotan and therefore I forbore the journey. I went to the President's and dined with him again. Then took my leave and rode to Green Springs where I found Mr. Ludwell worse. I wrote a letter to England and received one from Mrs. Dunn directed to my wife by which I found out some handy dealings which put me out of humor. About 10 o'clock I went to bed and said my prayers shortly. I had good health, good thoughts, and good humor, thank God.

8. I rose at 6 o'clock and said my prayers and ate milk for breakfast. I took my leave and rode towards home where I got about noon and found all things well but I heard bad news from Falling Creek for S-t-n had been almost killed by having a tree fall on him. God's will be done. I ate fish for dinner. The Doctor had been very sick and continued so. In the afternoon Daniel came to see the Doctor who had taken a great quantity of laudanum. I thanked God for my safe return home. I had good health, good thoughts, and good humor, thanks be to God Almighty. The President told me Mr. P-r-r was turned parson and had a good holding.

9. I rose at 3 o'clock and read a chapter in Hebrew and some Greek in Josephus. I said my prayers and ate milk for breakfast. I danced my dance. The Doctor was very ill so that I thought he would die. Captain Stith came to see the Doctor and [f-r f-r-m s-k] came to see me. He stayed and dined with us, and Mr. Dennis likewise. In the afternoon I sent for the parson and Mr. Harrison to see the Doctor and they were both of opinion he would die. Mr. Anderson stayed all night and about 7 o'clock his fever began to go off. We prayed by him. We gave him Dr.

Goddard's Drops,[1] which seemed to do him great service. We had sent for Dr. Blair but he could not come because of Mrs. Ludwell who was very ill. The Doctor [extremely] much better and took the bark.[2] I had good thoughts, good health, and good humor, thanks be to God Almighty.

10. I rose at 6 o'clock and read a chapter in Hebrew and some Greek in Josephus. I neglected to say my prayers but not to eat milk for breakfast. I danced my dance. The Doctor was much better and continued to take the bark with great profit. Captain Stith came again and found the Doctor well enough to make a codicil to give B-l-n-m to his son, which he persuaded him with great importunity to do. I heard from Falling Creek that S-t-n was something better but a cripple and that the plantation began to want corn. I wrote very sharp letters about it. I neglected to say my prayers but had good health, good thoughts, and indifferent good humor, thanks be to God Almighty.

11. Rose at 3 o'clock and read a chapter in Hebrew and some Greek [in] Cassius.[3] I said my prayers and ate milk for breakfast. I danced my dance. The Doctor was much better. Daniel went back to Williamsburg much out of humor with the Doctor because he would not lend him a book notwithstanding the care he had taken with him. About noon Colonel Randolph came to visit the Doctor, and dined with me. I ate roast beef for dinner. He went away in the afternoon and I played at piquet with my own wife. It rained a little this day so that I could not walk. I said my prayers and had good health, good thoughts, and good humor, thanks be to God Almighty.

12. I rose at 4 o'clock and read two chapters in Hebrew and some Greek in Cassius. I said my prayers and ate milk for breakfast. Mr. G-r-l came over to talk about some

---

[1] A popular proprietary medicine. (See W. B. Blanton, *Medicine in Virginia in the Seventeenth Century*, p. 115.)

[2] Cinchona bark, the source of quinine.

[3] Dion Cassius, a Greek, born in 155 A. D., who wrote a celebrated history of Rome. Byrd's library contained the work in two volumes, as well as Xiphilin's epitome of it.

things at Falling Creek. Mr. Holloway[1] sent me two negroes of Colonel W-l-k-s [Walker's[2]] estate for part of my debt. Captain Llewellyn, Mr. Randolph, Mr. Anderson and his wife, Mr. Harrison, Captain Stith, and Captain [Brown] came to see us, of which Captain Llewellyn only dined with us. The Doctor was much better but honed after strong drink very much. All the company went away in the evening. I said my prayers and read some Greek in Homer. I had good health, good thoughts, and good humor, thanks be to God.

13. I rose at 4 o'clock and read a chapter in Hebrew and some Greek in Cassius. I ate chocolate with Mr. Frank Eppes for breakfast, who came to give me a plat of the land of mine which he surveyed. My sloop came from Falling Creek with the partitions for my closet. Mr. Eppes went away. I wrote letters to Falling Creek. I ate pork for dinner. In the afternoon I played at cards with my own wife. The Doctor was much better this day. I said my prayers. I read some Greek in Homer. I had good thoughts, good health, good humor, thanks be to God Almighty.

14. I rose at 5 o'clock and read a chapter in Hebrew and some Greek in Cassius. I said my prayers and ate milk for breakfast. It rained hard so that I could not go to Williamsburg as I intended. The sloop returned to Falling Creek this morning. I ate fresh pork and sallet for dinner. In the afternoon I played at piquet with my wife. The Doctor was abundantly better. Mr. Anderson called here principally to see the Doctor. In the evening I took a walk in the garden. I put up my things with design to go very early to Williamsburg. I said my prayers and had good thoughts, good humor, and good health, thanks be to God Almighty.

15. I rose at 3 o'clock and recommended my family to the divine protection. Then I was set over the creek and

---

[1]John Holloway of York County, a lawyer of some note and first mayor of Williamsburg.
[2]Possibly Colonel John Walker, mentioned in April 17, 1713, as "late of King and Queen [County] deceased." (*Ex. Jour.*, III, 334.)

proceeded towards Williamsburg by moonshine. I got as far as C-ler before the rising of the sun and to Williamsburg by 10 o'clock. I waited on the President and found five of the Council there. A letter came from Colonel Parke that informed us that he had like to have been assassinated by a negro hired for that purpose who shot at him and broke his arm.[1] I was sworn a judge of the General Court and took my place on the bench. I dined at Mr. Bland's with Mrs. Stith and Captain Llewellyn and ate beef for dinner. In the evening the President, Mr. Bland and I played a pool at piquet. I said my prayers and had good health, good thoughts, and good humor, thanks be to God Almighty.

16. I rose at 6 o'clock and read some Greek in Lucian and said my prayers and ate milk for breakfast. Then I went to the President's and waited on him to church where we heard Mr. Gray[2] preach, who did not attack his sermon well. It rained much in the night and good part of the day. I dined with the President and ate roast chicken for dinner and then ran through the rain home. In the evening I read some Latin in Terence. I said my prayers and had good health, good thoughts, and good humor, thanks be to God Almighty.

17. I rose at 6 o'clock and read some Greek in Lucian. I said my prayers and ate milk for breakfast. Mr. Bland came to see me. I went to court and discoursed Mr. Hollo-way about my law affairs. About 10 o'clock the court sat. There was little business for want of a jury because it rained almost all day and blew very hard. About noon I returned to my chambers and ate some biscuits and butter. Then I returned again to the court and we rose about 3 o'clock and went to dinner. I ate boiled beef for dinner. Then we went to whisk[3] and I won 4 pounds 10 shillings. Then I went home and read some Latin in Terence. I said

---

[1] Colonel Daniel Parke. The attempted assassination took place on September 5. (*Calendar of State Papers, America and West Indies, 1708-1709*, pp. 469-71.)

[2] The Reverend Samuel Gray, minister of St. Peters Parish, New Kent. He died in 1709 or 1710. (*Ex. Jour.*, III, 245.)

[3] *I. e.*, whist.

my prayers and had good health, good thoughts, and good humor, thanks be to God Almighty.

18. I rose at 6 o'clock and read some Greek in Lucian. Mr. Bland came and hindered me from saying my prayers. I ate milk for breakfast. About 10 o'clock the court sat. About noon I returned to my chambers and ate biscuits and butter; then I returned to court again. About 4 o'clock the court rose and we went to dinner. I ate mutton and turnips for dinner. Colonel Bassett, Colonel Duke, and Colonel Lewis came to dinner with us. In the evening I went to my chambers and read some Latin in Terence. I said my prayers and had good health, good thoughts, and good humor, thanks be to God Almighty.

19. I rose at 6 o'clock and could not say my prayers because Colonel Bassett and Colonel Duke came to see me. For the same reason I could read nothing. I ate milk for breakfast. About ten o'clock we went to court where a man was tried for ravishing a very homely woman. There were abundance of women in the gallery. I recommended myself to God before I went into court. About one o'clock I went to my chambers for a little refreshment. The court rose about 4 o'clock and I dined with the Council. I ate boiled beef for dinner. I gave myself the liberty to talk very lewdly, for which God forgive me. I said my prayers and had good health, good thoughts, and good humor, thanks be to God Almighty.

20. I rose at 6 o'clock and read two chapters in Hebrew and some Greek in Lucian. I said my prayers and ate milk for breakfast. I went to court, where I sat almost all day without anything remarkable. About 4 o'clock the court rose and we went to dinner. I ate boiled beef for dinner. In the evening we played at cards at Mr. President's, and I won 35 shillings. About 8 o'clock I returned home where I read a little in Terence. I said my prayers and had good health, good thoughts, and good humor, thanks be to God Almighty.

21. I rose at 6 o'clock and read two chapters in Hebrew and some Greek in Lucian. I said my prayers and ate milk for breakfast. About 10 o'clock I went to court and sat till noon when I went up to my office and did some business. About 3 o'clock we went to Council about the Indians. About 4 I went home with Mr. Blair where I found abundance of ladies. I ate boiled pork for dinner. We stayed here till 7 o'clock when I returned to Mr. Bland's. Here I sat about an hour and went home to my lodgings. I said my prayers and had good health, good thoughts, and good humor, thanks be to God Almighty.

22. I rose at 6 o'clock and read two chapters in Hebrew and some Greek in Lucian. I said my prayers and ate milk for breakfast. Colonel Bassett came to see me and we went to visit R-b-r-s-n [Robertson?] where we found Colonel Duke. About 10 o'clock we went to Council and heard the dispute between Parson Slater and his parish and between the parson and vestry of Manakin Town,[1] but nothing was decided. Several of the Council went home. We just went to adjourn the court and then went to dinner. I ate beef for dinner. In the evening I went to Mr. Bland's where the President came likewise and we played at cards. About 10 o'clock I went home. I said my prayers and had good health, good thoughts, and good humor, thanks be to God Almighty.

23. I rose at 6 o'clock and read two chapters in Hebrew and some Greek in Lucian. I said my prayers devoutly and ate milk for breakfast. Daniel came and shaved my head. About 11 o'clock I waited on the President and Colonel Harrison to church, where Mr. Cargill preached a good sermon. After church Colonel Harrison asked me to go to Mr. Blair's to dinner. I ate fish and goose for dinner. I went in the evening to Colonel Bray's where we found abundance of company and agreed to meet there the next

---

[1]The Reverend James Slater of Charles Parish, York County, was so disliked by his parishioners that they barred the door of the church against him. The dispute between Parson Phillipe and the vestry of Manakin Town was over the election of vestrymen. (See *Ex. Jour.,* III, 143, 225.)

day and have a dance. About 10 o'clock I came home and neglected to say my prayers and for that reason was guilty of uncleanness. I had bad thoughts, good health and good humor, thanks be to God Almighty.

24. I rose at 6 o'clock and read nothing because Mr. Bland came and gave in his accounts. I said my prayers and ate milk for breakfast. I had a letter from Colonel Lee[1] with his accounts. I went to court where I sat till noon and then returned to my chambers and ate some biscuits and neat's tongue. I did some business and about 4 o'clock went to Mr. Bland's and from thence to Colonel Bray's where we found abundance of company. We danced till 2 o'clock in the morning. We then played at [l-t-l p-l-y] and then returned home. I said my prayers very shortly and had good health, and good thoughts, thanks be to God Almighty.

25. I rose at 6 o'clock and read a chapter in Hebrew and then was disturbed with company. However I said my prayers and ate milk for breakfast. I went to the capitol about 10 o'clock where I found Colonel Carter. I sat about three hours and then went again to my chambers and ate a bite and did more business and came to court again. About 4 we went to dinner and I ate beef for dinner. Then we played at cards and I won £3 of Colonel Smith. I said my prayers and had good health, good thoughts, and good humor, thanks be to God Almighty.

26. I rose at 6 o'clock and read a chapter in Hebrew and some Greek in Lucian. I said my prayers and ate milk for breakfast. I went to Council, when my warrants were signed. Then we went to court about 12 o'clock and sat till 4. Then we went to dinner and I ate goose for dinner. In the evening we played at cards and I lost 40 shillings. I went home about 10 o'clock and said my prayers. I had good health, good thoughts, and indifferent good humor, thanks be to God Almighty.

---

[1]Possibly Colonel Richard Lee II of Westmoreland County.

27. I rose at 6 o'clock and read a chapter in Hebrew and some Greek in Lucian. I said my prayers and ate milk for breakfast. The President was so kind to offer to put off passing the accounts till my order came for increasing my salary. We went to court and sat till 4 o'clock. Then we went to dinner and I ate boiled beef for my dinner. In the evening we played at cards and I won £5. We drank some of Will Robinson's[1] cider till we were very merry and then went to the coffeehouse and pulled poor Colonel Churchill[2] out of bed. I went home about one o'clock in the morning. I neglected to say my prayers but had good health, good thoughts, and good humor, thanks be to God Almighty.

28. I rose at 6 o'clock but read nothing because Colonel Randolph came to see me in the morning. I neglected to say my prayers but I ate milk for breakfast. Colonel Harrison's vessel came in from Madeira and brought abundance of letters and among the rest I had ten from Mr. Perry with a sad account of tobacco. We went to court but much time was taken up in reading our letters and not much business was done. About 3 we rose and had a meeting of the College in which it was agreed to turn Mr. Blackamore out from being master of the school for being so great a sot. I ate boiled beef for dinner and in the evening went home after walking with Colonel Bassett. I said my prayers and had good health, good thoughts, and good humor, thanks be to God Almighty.

29. I rose at 6 o'clock and read nothing because the governors of the College were to meet again. However I said my prayers and ate milk for breakfast. When we met Mr. Blackamore presented a petition in which he set forth that if the governors of the College would forgive him what was past, he would for the time to come mend his conduct. On which the governors at last agreed to keep him on, on trial, some time longer. Then we went to court where we sat till about 3 o'clock and then I learned that my

[1]This may be William Robinson, sheriff of Richmond County, or William Robertson, clerk of the Assembly. Byrd wrote both names alike.
[2]Colonel William Churchill of Middlesex County, a member of the Council.

sister Custis was at Mr. Bland's. I went to her and there was also Mrs. Chiswell.[1] I went with them to Doctor B-r-t [Barret?][2] and ate beef for dinner. Here I stayed till 8 o'clock and then walked home. I said my prayers and had good health, good thoughts, and good humor, thanks be to God Almighty.

30. I rose at 6 o'clock but read nothing because by the time I was dressed Mr. Holloway, Mrs. Chiswell, and Mrs. Custis came to see me. However I said my prayers and ate milk for breakfast. I gave them a bottle of sack and as soon as they went away I waited on the President to church where Mr. Goodwin preached a good sermon. After church I went to Mr. Blair's to dinner with all the Council in attendance. I ate boiled beef for dinner. About 5 o'clock we returned home and then went to the coffeehouse where we sat an hour and then went home. I neglected to say my prayers, for which God forgive me. I had good health, good thoughts, and good humor, thanks be to God Almighty.

31. I rose at 6 o'clock and read two chapters in Hebrew and some Greek in Lucian. I said my prayers and ate milk for breakfast. About 10 o'clock we went to court. The committee met to receive proposals for the building the College and Mr. Tullitt[3] undertook it for £2,000 provided he might wood off the College land and all assistants from England to come at the College's risk. We sat in court till about 4 o'clock and then I rode to Green Springs to meet my wife. I found her there and had the pleasure to learn that all was well at home, thanks be to God. There was likewise Mrs. Chiswell. I ate boiled beef for supper. Then

---

[1]Probably the wife of Charles Chiswell, appointed clerk of the General Court in 1706. On his "progress to the mines" in 1732 Byrd visited the Chiswells at Fredericksburg, when he remarked, "I had not seen Mrs. Chiswell in twenty-four years, which, alas! had made great havoc with her pretty face, and plowed very deep furrows in her fair skin." (Bassett, p. 343.)

[2]Possibly Charles Barret, who married Mary Chiswell. In 1716 a Mr. Chiswell petitioned on behalf of Mrs. Mary [Chiswell?] Barrett offering to undertake the keeping of the table at William and Mary College. (Wm. Q. (1), IX, 242.)

[3]John Tullitt in 1700 was authorized to supply brick for the new capitol. (Wm. Q. (1), X, 80, 81.) He bought 17,650 acres of William Byrd's land in Henrico County in 1705. (Ex. Jour., III, 49.)

we danced and were merry till about 10 o'clock. I neglected
to say my prayers but had good health, good thoughts, and
good humor, thanks be to God Almighty. This month I
took above 400 of Colonel Quarry[1] [*or* Cary] in money
for bills at an allowance of 10 per cent.

---

[1]Probably Robert Quarry, surveyor general of customs.

November, 1709

1. I rose at 8 o'clock because I could not leave my wife sooner. Then I ate milk for breakfast. I neglected to say my [prayers] nor could I read anything. About 11 o'clock I went to Williamsburg and about 12 took my place in court. I sat there till about 4 and could not go out of town because I had accounts to settle with several people. About 5 o'clock we went to dinner and I ate boiled beef. Then the President took us home to his house, where I played at cards and won 35 shillings. We were very merry and in that condition went to the coffeehouse and again disturbed Colonel Churchill. About 11 o'clock I went home and said a short prayer. I had good health, good thoughts, and good humor, thanks be to God Almighty.

2. I rose at 6 o'clock and read a chapter in Hebrew and some Greek in Lucian. I said my prayers and ate milk for breakfast, and settled some accounts, and then went to court where we made an end of the business. We went to dinner about 4 o'clock and I ate boiled beef again. In the evening I went to Dr. [Barret's] where my wife came this afternoon. Here I found Mrs. Chiswell, my sister Custis, and other ladies. We sat and talked till about 11 o'clock and then retired to our chambers. I played at [r-m] with Mrs. Chiswell and kissed her on the bed till she was angry and my wife also was uneasy about it, and cried as soon as the company was gone. I neglected to say my prayers, which I should not have done, because I ought to beg pardon for the lust I had for another man's wife. However I had good health, good thoughts, and good humor, thanks be to God Almighty.

3. I rose at 6 o'clock and without ceremony went away to court to hear the orders read. However I ate my breakfast in milk first. We had likewise a short Council. I settled accounts with Colonel Digges and Mr. President. Then I took leave of the Council and returned to Dr. [Barret's],

from whence I waited on the ladies to Queen's Creek[1] where my mother Parke's things were divided between my wife and her sister. My uncle Ludwell was there with us. Then we went to Mr. Blair's where we found Mr. Holloway and Mr. Robinson. I ate boiled pork for supper. Then we played at cards and about 10 o'clock went to bed. I neglected to say my prayers but had good health, good thoughts, and good humor, thanks be to God Almighty.

4. I rose at 6 o'clock but neglected to say my prayers because Mr. Commissary kept me to hear a verse he had made for the College. I ate chocolate for breakfast. Mr. Holloway and Mr. Clayton came over this morning. We went to dinner about 12 o'clock and I ate some hash. Then we went to Mr. Bland's where we found letters from England but no news. Then we rode to Major Burwell's where we found turkey for supper. We sat and talked till 10 o'clock and then went to bed. I neglected to say my prayers but had good health, good thoughts, and good humor, thanks be to God Almighty.

5. I rose at 7 o'clock and read a little in my commonplace,[2] but I neglected to say my prayers. I drank posset for breakfast. Then I took a walk about the plantation. About one o'clock we went to dinner. I ate boiled beef and pudding. About 3 o'clock we went over the river to Mr. Burwell's where we arrived about 5. In the evening we drank two bottles of French claret. I was so sleepy I could not keep my eyes open. However we did not go to bed before 10 o'clock. I neglected to say my prayers but had good health, good thoughts, and good humor, thanks be to God Almighty.

6. I rose at 7 o'clock and read a little in my commonplace. I neglected to say my prayers. However I ate milk for breakfast. About 11 o'clock we rode to the church of Abingdon Parish which is the best church I have seen in the

---

[1]York County. John and Frances (Parke) Custis were living there at this time.

[2]Byrd apparently kept notebooks in addition to his diary. The University of North Carolina notebooks probably represent only a fragment of an extensive series.

country.[1] We heard a sermon of Parson Smith.[2] After church we returned to Mr. Burwell's and Mr. Berkeley and his wife with us. We dined late and I ate boiled beef and pudding. In the evening we sat and talked till 10 o'clock and I told abundance of lies by way of diversion. Then we went to bed. I said my prayers and had good health, good thoughts, and good humor, thanks be to God Almighty.

7. I rose at 7 o'clock and said my prayers. I ate chocolate for breakfast. We walked about till dinner and then I ate roast beef. We had intended to go over the river again but my sister Custis asked me to [move] her over the Bay[3] and I said I would if Mr. Burwell would. He said he would if his wife would, and she agreed to go and drew us all into the frolic. In the afternoon we rode to my Cousin Berkeley's with design to take him and his wife with us but he escaped by being from home. His wife was at home and gave us a good supper. I ate boiled beef. Then we had some cherries which had been scalded in hot water which did not boil and then [put] in bottles without water in them. They were exceedingly good. I neglected to say my prayers but had good health, good humor, good thoughts, and good humor [sic], thanks be to God Almighty.

8. I rose at 7 o'clock and said a short prayer. I ate chocolate for breakfast. Then we took our leave of Mrs. Berkeley and went in a [boat] to York where there is a stone church. Then we went over the river to Gloucester Town[4] and about noon went aboard the shallop and sailed down the river with a fair wind. When we came to the mouth of the river it grew calm so that we came to anchor

---

[1]Abingdon Church in Gloucester County. The present building, built some time in the middle of the eighteenth century, replaced the one admired by Byrd. (See Henry Irving Brock, *Colonial Churches in Virginia* [Richmond, 1930], p. 72.)
[2]The Reverend Guy Smith, minister of Abingdon Parish, 1702-1719. (Goodwin, p. 308.)
[3]The old Custis home was at Arlington, Northampton County, across Chesapeake Bay.
[4]Byrd and his party crossed the James River to Yorktown, visited the stone church (see Brock, *Colonial Churches*, p. 32), and crossed back again to Gloucester Point. (*Wm. Q. (1)*, XV, 222). Early maps show York and Gloucester as towns almost opposite each other.

but soon after the wind began to blow again. We saw a [c-l-n] sloop in the bay which soon put aboard us and the men were so rude we kept them off because we took them for privateers. I ate roast beef for dinner, but the women were frightened with the boat that they could not eat. We lay in the shallop all night but about 5 o'clock in the morning we dropped anchor in [Pigot's] Hole.[1] I recommended myself and all the company to God Almighty and had good health, good thoughts, and good humor, thanks be to God Almighty.

9. I turned out about 7 o'clock and Mr. Burwell and I rowed ourselves ashore because the men were all gone for horses. We went to Mr. Littleton's[2] where I ate milk for breakfast. About 10 o'clock the horses came from my brother Custis and we rode to Arlington which is a great house within sight of the Bay and really a pleasant plantation but not kept very nicely. We walked all over the plantation in which the hogs had done great damage. My brother Custis received us kindly. I ate goose for dinner. In the afternoon we walked again and in the evening Mr. Dunn and his wife came to see us. We ate oysters and were merry together till about 11 o'clock. I neglected to say my prayers but had good health, good thoughts, and good humor, thanks be to God Almighty.

10. I rose about 7 o'clock and read some Greek in Anacreon. I said my prayers shortly and ate roasted potatoes for breakfast. About 10 o'clock we rode to the Cape with design to go to Smith Island but it blew too hard. Among the [. . .] here and everywhere on this shore is a tree called [p-l] tree, a suffusion of whose bark will cause a salivation. The leaves and berries smell of spice. We were

---

[1] The Pigot or Pickett family were residents and landowners on the Eastern Shore. "Pigot's Hole" has not been located on any available map.
[2] The Littleton family were descendants of the famous judge, Sir Thomas Littleton, whose son Nathaniel emigrated to Virginia and settled at Nadua [or Nandua] Creek, now in Accomac County, which was the family seat for several generations. The Littleton and Custis families were related by marriage. (Va. Mag., XVIII, 20-23.)

kindly treated at George Freshwater's[1] where I ate beef
and potatoes for dinner. Parson Dunn was sick here, who
is a man of no polite conversation, notwithstanding he be a
good Latin scholar. From hence we rode to Mr. [Harris]
who gave us a bottle of good wine, of which he was very
generous. Then we went home, where we were merry till
11 o'clock. I neglected to say my prayers but had good
health, good thoughts, and good humor, thanks be to God
Almighty.

11. I rose at 7 o'clock and read some Greek in Anacreon.
I said a short prayer and about 11 o'clock we went to
breakfast and I ate goose. In the afternoon we went to
visit Colonel Waters,[2] a very honest man, who lives about
six miles off. He gave us some good wine called [Saint
George's] wine. We took a walk by the side of the Bay
and then went to supper and I ate some roast beef. Then
we returned in the dark to Arlington where we found some
of the women sick and some out of humor and particularly
my wife quarreled with Mr. Dunn and me for talking Latin
and called it bad manners. This put me out of humor with
her which set her to crying. I wholly made the reconciliation. The parson was more affronted than I, and went to
bed. I neglected to say my prayers but had good health,
good thoughts, and indifferent good humor, thanks be to
God Almighty.

12. I rose about 7 o'clock and read some Greek in Anacreon. I said a short prayer and about 11 o'clock ate some
goose for breakfast again. Then we rode on bad horses to
Hungars to visit Colonel Custis[3] who is 20 miles off Arlington. It began to rain before we got there. We were very
kindly received by all the family. The Colonel is an honest
well-meaning man. About 3 o'clock we went to dinner and
I ate boiled beef. Then we took a walk about the plan-

---

[1]George Freshwater owned 200 acres in Northampton County in 1704.
(*Va. Mag.*, XXXIV, 315.)
[2]William Waters, a justice of the peace of Northampton County, later
naval officer of the Eastern Shore.
[3]John Custis II, father of Byrd's brother-in-law. (*Wm. Q. (1)*, III,
258-61.)

tation. Colonel Waters met us here. In the evening we danced and were very merry till about 10 o'clock. I neglected to say my prayers but had good health, good thoughts, and good humor, thanks be to God Almighty.

13. I rose about 7 o'clock but could read nothing because we were in haste to go to church. I ate milk for breakfast notwithstanding it was here not very good. About 10 o'clock we rode to church which is six miles off. There was the biggest congregation I ever saw in the country. The people look half dead since the sickness which they had last year. Mr. Dunn preached a good sermon. After church we returned to Colonel Custis' again. About 3 o'clock we dined and I ate boiled beef. In the evening we drank a bottle of wine pretty freely and were full of mirth and good humor and particularly Colonel Waters. However we were merry and wise and went to bed in good time by my means. I neglected to say my prayers but had good health, good thoughts, and good humor, thanks be to God Almighty.

14. Before I rose this morning I made a [Quaker] song on John Pleasants and rose about 7 o'clock. I said a short prayer and drank chocolate for breakfast. Then I read a little in Anacreon. About 12 o'clock we went to dinner and I ate goose, which are very good and in great plenty here. In the afternoon we paid a visit to Mr. Hamilton[1] who lives across the creek. He is a man of a bad character and he got the estate nobody knows how. We walked about his plantation and saw a pretty shallop he was building. He was very courteous to us and provided a supper but we could not stay to eat it because it grew dark and it was dangerous to stay late for fear of the dogs which are fierce at Colonel Custis'. In the evening we all designed to be merry but were all out of humor by consent and would neither dance nor drink. About 8 o'clock we went to supper and I ate some mince pie. I neglected to say my prayers

---

[1] Andrew Hamilton. A deed dated March 13, 1713, conveys from Hamilton to Colonel Waters 500 acres on the north side of Hungars Creek. Hamilton is said to have gone thence to Philadelphia, where he became a noted lawyer. (*Va. Mag.*, XX, 118-19.)

but had good health, good thoughts, and good humor, thanks be to God Almighty.

15. I rose about 7 o'clock with design to return to Arlington but the rain prevented. I said my prayers and read a great deal in Anacreon. About 10 o'clock we went to breakfast and I ate some goose, of which they have great plenty here. The rain did not hold up till towards evening when I took a walk in the garden. Then we went to a play called [burning coals] at which we ran much and were very merry. However some of the women were out of humor, as was natural among so many. About 7 o'clock we went to supper and I ate mutton. Colonel Waters stayed with us to the last. I neglected to say my prayers but had good health, good thoughts, and good humor, thanks be to God Almighty.

16. I rose about 7 o'clock and said my prayers. I read a little in Anacreon. About 9 o'clock we went to breakfast and I ate goose again. It rained a little but that did not discourage us from going; but we took leave of the good company. Then we rode very hard because it rained. Colonel Custis lent me the only good horse I met with on this shore. About 2 o'clock we came to Arlington. I got a pain in my loins I suppose by cold and my brother Custis had a [remembrance] of the gripes. In the evening we were all very dull and therefore we went to bed early. I neglected to say my prayers but had good health, good thoughts, and good humor, thanks be to God Almighty. It blew extremely hard this night.

17. I rose about 8 o'clock and read in Anacreon. The wind was directly contrary so that we could not think of embarking to return over the Bay. I neglected to say my prayers. I ate milk for breakfast, which is hard to be got here. We took a walk about the plantation. About 3 o'clock we went to dinner and I ate goose again. In the afternoon we took a walk of about three miles. In the evening I read some Latin in Horace. We were very merry till about 10 o'clock, notwithstanding my wife was much incommoded with her term which came away in great abun-

dance. I neglected to say my prayers but had good health, good thoughts, and good humor,.thanks be to God Almighty.

18. I rose about 8 o'clock and said a short prayer. I read some Greek in Anacreon and some Latin in Horace. I ate milk for breakfast. The contrary wind continued, at which my sister Custis was very uneasy and quarrelled with Mrs. Dunn for persuading my wife to stay so long at Hungars. Here are the worst servants that ever I saw in my life. My wife continued indisposed with a great flux of blood. I took a walk about the plantation. About 3 o'clock we went to dinner. Wine was very scarce here so that we were very moderate. I ate boiled beef. In the afternoon we walked very fast to the church and almost killed Parson Dunn, who was forced to run all the way to keep up with us. In the evening we were as merry as we could till about 9 o'clock. I neglected to say my prayers but had good health, good thoughts, and good humor, thanks be to God Almighty.

19. I rose at [. . .] o'clock on the news the wind was fair, but it soon came contrary again. I said my prayers and ate milk for breakfast. I read some Greek in Anacreon and some Latin in Horace. My sister continued out of humor with us and especially with Mrs. Dunn. About 11 o'clock I took a walk about the plantation, notwithstanding it was very cold. About 2 o'clock we went to dinner and I ate roast beef. The wind blew very cold at northwest. In the afternoon I took a walk again with my friend Horace. In the evening we were as merry as we could. I neglected to say my prayers but had good health, good thoughts, and good humor, thanks be to God Almighty.

20. I rose at 8 o'clock and I read nothing because we dressed to go to church, notwithstanding it was extremely cold, but the women did not go but only Mrs. Dunn. I deferred saying my prayers till I came to church. I ate milk for breakfast. About 11 I walked to church where Mr. Dunn gave us a good sermon. I accosted a man by mistake and put him out of countenance. Colonel Waters' daughter went home with us. About 2 o'clock we went to dinner and I ate goose. In the afternoon we took a walk

to see my sister Custis' child who had a great cold. In the evening Mistress Waters went home. We were very merry till about 9 o'clock. Then I neglected to say my prayers but had good health, good thoughts, and good humor, thanks be to God Almighty.

21. I rose about 8 o'clock and said my prayers. Then I read some Greek in Anacreon and some Latin in Horace. I ate milk for breakfast. The wind continued contrary to us. About 12 o'clock I took a walk about the plantation with my wife. I received a letter from Colonel Custis with a present of [wax] and a kind invitation to make him another visit. I returned my satisfaction by a letter. About 3 o'clock we went to dinner and I ate hashed goose. In the afternoon I took another walk with my wife. In the evening I read some Greek in Homer. About 9 o'clock we returned to our chamber where I read some more Latin in Horace. I neglected to say my prayers and had good health, good thoughts, and good humor, thanks be to God Almighty.

22. I rose about 9 o'clock because the wind continued contrary. I said my prayers and ate milk for breakfast. I read some Greek in Homer and Latin in Horace. Then I took a walk about the plantation. Mr. Dunn and his wife went away out of humor with my sister for her unkind usage. About 3 o'clock we went to dinner and I ate wild duck, which are not so good here as on our shore. In the afternoon we walked again. In the evening [I] read some English verse aloud to the ladies. I went to visit a negro of Mr. Custis' who was very sick. I said my prayers and had good health, good thoughts, and good humor, thanks be to God Almighty.

23. I rose about 8 o'clock and said my prayers. Then I ate milk for breakfast and read some Greek in Homer. The wind continued contrary to us. About 11 o'clock I took a walk with my wife and read in Collier against the stage.[1] About 2 o'clock we went to dinner. The negro that was sick

---

[1]Jeremy Collier, *Short View of the Immorality and Profaneness of the English Stage* (1698).

called Ch-n-s died this morning. He was one of the best my brother had. I ate goose for dinner. About 4 o'clock we took another walk about the plantation. In the evening I read again in Collier. Every day at dinner we had a bottle of good wine first and then a bottle of bad. I said a short prayer and had good health, good thoughts, and good humor, thanks be to God Almighty.

24. I rose at 7 o'clock because they told us the wind was fair. I said my prayers and ate milk for breakfast. Then I read some Greek in Homer. The women scolded at my brother Custis so much that he resolved to get the sloop out of the creek, which he did and carried her into [Pigot's] Hole, 3 miles off. We all rode there to try whether we could go, but the wind turned directly contrary. Then we rode back again and about 3 o'clock we went to dinner and I ate boiled beef. In the afternoon I took a walk and read in Homer. In the evening I read aloud to the ladies in Collier. I said my prayers and had good health, good thoughts, and good humor, thanks be to God Almighty.

25. I rose about 6 o'clock because the wind was come fair again. I said a short prayer, gave the servants money, and we all rode away to the Hole with expedition. About 8 we took leave of Mr. Custis and went on board the shallop, notwithstanding the wind was very scanty and blew hard. This made us all very sick and particularly the women. In about five hours we made a shift to reach Back River,[1] for the wind would not permit us to reach York. We went ashore at Mr. Wallace's[2] who was not at home himself, but his wife was very kind to us and gave us a good supper. I ate roast beef. In the evening Mr. Wallace came home and gave us some excellent cider. I said a short prayer and had good health, good thoughts, and good humor, thank God Almighty.

26. I rose about 7 o'clock and because we were in haste to go I neglected to say my prayers. I [ate] toast and cider

---

[1]The section of the James between Jamestown Island and the mainland.
[2]Reverend James Wallace, minister of Elizabeth City Parish; he owned a place on Back River, where he is buried. (*Wm. Q. (1)*, V, 266; Goodwin, p. 314.)

for breakfast. The parson was so kind as to provide us with six horses and would hardly part with us so that it was noon before we could get away. He lives very neatly and is very kind to all that come to his house. At 12 we mounted and it was my fortune to have a horse that would not run away with me. We all got safe in the evening to Major Burwell's, where we found abundance of company. I was grieved to hear my daughter had received a fall and hurt her forehead but I was comforted again with a letter from Bannister that told me she and all the family was well. I ate exceedingly much boiled beef for supper. I neglected to say my prayers but had good health, good thoughts, and good humor, thanks be to God Almighty.

27. I rose about 7 o'clock but neglected to say my prayers. I could read nothing but wrote some notes for Major Burwell. So soon as Mr. Burwell sent my [papers] over the river I thought to go away, but I ate milk for breakfast and likewise stayed to dinner and I ate mutton. About 4 o'clock we took leave of Major Burwell and Mrs. Burwell, who is a well-humored woman that I had not seen once out of humor since our voyage. We rode to Williamsburg and had a little rain by the way. Mr. [?] nor his wife were at home so that we were forced to tarry till it was dark, when they came. Here I saw honest Mr. Clayton, Mr. Jones, and Mr. Robinson. Mr. Clayton was so kind as to lend me his horse to Green Springs, because mine was lame. We got there about 7 o'clock. Here I was a little out of humor without any reason. I neglected to say my prayers but had good health and good thoughts, thanks be to God Almighty.

28. I rose about 7 o'clock and said a short prayer. About 8 o'clock we played at cricket and lost five shillings. At 10 o'clock we went to breakfast and I ate goose. We stayed till noon and then took our leave of all the company. My wife was uneasy and much out of humor by the way. We got home by 5 o'clock where we found all well, thanks be to God. Poor old Ben died ten days ago and I learned that Mr. Isham Eppes died likewise about the same time. I examined into all my business and was well satisfied with

it. I ate some milk for supper. I neglected to say my prayers in form, but had good health, good thoughts, and good humor, thanks be to God Almighty.

29. I rose about 7 o'clock and settled some accounts and put all my matters in order. I neglected to say my prayers but did not neglect to eat milk for breakfast. I thought to go to Falling Creek but I learned that G-r-l had laid a wager that he would saw 1,000 feet of planks in ten hours with two saws and by way of [. . .] afterwards performed it in six hours, to the confusion of Webb and Woodson, that had laid with him. I ate fish for dinner. In the afternoon I walked about the plantation to see what my negroes had done and was not displeased. In the evening I read some Greek in Homer and a chapter in Hebrew. I said my prayers and had good health, good thoughts, and good humor, thanks be to God Almighty.

30. I rose at 3 o'clock and read two chapters in Hebrew and some Greek in Cassius. I went to bed again and lay till 7. I said my prayers, danced my dance, and ate milk for breakfast. Eugene was whipped for pissing in bed and Jenny for concealing it. I settled several accounts. I ate boiled beef for dinner. In the afternoon I played at billiards with my wife and then took a walk about the plantation to look over my affairs. I said my prayers. In the evening I read some Italian. About 8 o'clock we went to bed and I had good health, good thoughts, and good humor, thanks be to God Almighty.

December, 1709

1. I rose at 4 o'clock and read two chapters in Hebrew and some Greek in Cassius. I said my prayers and ate milk for breakfast. I danced my dance. Eugene was whipped again for pissing in bed and Jenny for concealing it. About 11 o'clock came Captain Stith and his wife, not on a visit but Mrs. Stith came to desire me justify her to Mrs. Harrison that she had not told me that Mrs. Harrison was delivered of two children before her time. I wrote to Mrs. Harrison to assure her that Mrs. Stith had never told me any such thing. But my wife could not deny but she had told that Mrs. Stith told her so. Thus women will be [p-r-t]. I denied her and so did Mrs. Mallory and Bannister's sister. In the afternoon the company went away. I took a walk [about] the plantation. In the evening I read Italian. I said my prayers and had good health, good thoughts, and good humor, thanks be to God Almighty.

2. I rose at 5 o'clock and read a chapter in Hebrew and some Greek in Cassius. I said my prayers and ate milk for breakfast. I danced my dance. I settled some accounts and read news. My wife was very much vexed with the conversation she had yesterday with Mrs. Stith. I ate fish for dinner which we catch in great quantity. It rained a little in the afternoon. I settled more accounts and played at billiards with my wife. In the evening I read more Italian and washed my feet. I said my prayers and had good health, good thoughts, and good humor, thanks be to God Almighty.

3. I rose at 5 o'clock and read two chapters in Hebrew and some Greek in Cassius. I said my prayers and ate milk for breakfast. I danced my dance. Eugene pissed abed again for which I made him drink a pint of piss. I settled some accounts and read some news. About 12 o'clock I went to court where I found little good company. However I persuaded Mr. Anderson and Colonel Eppes to come and

dine with me. I ate a venison pasty for dinner. In the evening Mr. Anderson and I walked to Mr. Harrison's where we found Frank W-l-s and James Burwell and Isham Randolph. Here I ate custard and was merry. I stayed till 9 o'clock and when I came home my wife was in bed. I neglected to say my prayers and had good health, good thoughts, and good humor, thanks be to God Almighty.

4. I rose at 5 o'clock and read a chapter in Hebrew and some Greek in Cassius. I said my prayers and ate milk for breakfast. I danced my dance, and then took a walk in the garden because the weather was very tempting for so late in the year. God continue it for the service of those that have but little corn. I ate boiled beef for dinner. In the afternoon I ate an apple and then took a long walk about the great pasture with my wife and I found [they finished stacking]. In the evening I read some Italian and said my prayers shortly and had good health, good thoughts, and good humor, thanks be to God Almighty.

5. I rose at 3 o'clock and read a chapter in Hebrew and some Greek in Cassius. I said my prayers shortly and ate milk for breakfast. About 10 o'clock Mrs. Harrison and her daughter came and soon after Mr. Harrison, Frank W-l-s and James Burwell and Isham Randolph. I gave them some strong water. Then we went and played at billiards and I won half a crown. About one we went to dinner and I ate fish. Mrs. [Ware] managed with great [order]. In the afternoon we shot in a bow but none of us could hit the mark. My wife was guilty in reproaching Frank W-l-s for swearing and he was out of humor for it. They went away just as it was dark. In the evening I read some Italian, said my prayers, and had good health, good thoughts, and good humor, thanks be to God Almighty.

6. I rose at 4 o'clock and read two chapters in Hebrew and some Greek in Cassius. I said my prayers and ate milk for breakfast. I danced my dance. Then I took a walk about the plantation. About 10 o'clock Mr. Isham Randolph came in order to go with me to Falling Creek. But

Mr. Mumford came and told me that Mr. G-r-l was to come down over this day and accordingly he came about 12 o'clock and told me all was well above, as Mr. Mumford did that all was well at Appomattox. We played at billiards and I won half a crown. I ate boiled beef for dinner. In the afternoon Mr. Mumford went away in the rain but the other two stayed here all night. In the evening we drank a bottle of wine and were merry. I neglected to say my prayers and had good health, good thoughts, and good humor, thanks be to God Almighty.

7. I rose at 5 o'clock and read two chapters in Hebrew and some Greek in Cassius. I said my prayers and drank some chocolate with Isham Randolph. About 8 o'clock he went away. I danced my dance. Mr. G-r-l went away in the night. About 10 o'clock I rode to Captain Stith's to see the Doctor who lay there very ill. Here I met Colonel Randolph who was going to Williamsburg. I ate some roast beef here and then proceeded with Colonel Randolph over S-n-s Bridge[1] to Colonel Duke's. It was exceedingly cold. We did not get over till after sunset. We found the Colonel under great fear of the distemper, which he said was very violent in the neighborhood. Here I ate some milk for supper by my own choice. I said my prayers shortly and had good health, good thoughts, and good humor, thanks be to God Almighty.

8. I rose about 7 o'clock and neglected not to say my prayers. I ate milk for breakfast. About 9 o'clock we proceeded to Williamsburg and by the way called at Mr. Blair's, who was already gone. Then we went to Mr. Bland's, who was sick. From hence I went to the Presi-dent's where a council was held concerning the loss of the man-of-war which ran ashore near Coratuck Inlet on the 29th of the last month about one o'clock in the morning.[2] All the men were saved except 12 who had been overset in

---

[1]Perhaps at Soane's Warehouse.
[2]The ship "Garland", Captain Cook, which foundered in Coratuck (or Currituck) Inlet, off the North Carolina coast. Some months later the ship's bell was brought, by Spotswood's orders, to Bruton Church, where it thereafter served to call the people to church. (See *The Official Letters of Alexander Spotswood,* ed. R. A. Brock [Richmond, 1882], I, 67.)

a yawl. Orders had been sent to Colonel Wilson[1] to press a sloop to go to the assistance of the men to save the stores and rigging. The Council also considered about taking off the protection of corn but agreed not to do it. They also agreed to give directions to the Attorney General to prosecute the vestry of Charles Parish for disturbing divine services, and then a general fast was appointed on account of the sickness. Then we went to dinner and I ate boiled beef. In the afternoon we had a meeting of the College to confirm the agreement with John Tullitt to build the College. The President received a letter from Colonel Wilson which said that several of the men belonging to the unfortunate man-of-war had left the captain and were come to Kiquotan and were [distressed] for victuals. The Council sat till 8 o'clock when I went to Queen's Creek, notwithstanding the great cold, where I found my sister in the middle of her [m-d]. About 10 o'clock we went to bed. I said my prayers shortly and had good health, good thoughts, and good humor, thanks be to God Almighty.

9. I rose at 7 o'clock and said a short prayer. It had frozen very hard. I discoursed with my brother about plantation matters and then ate milk for breakfast. About 10 o'clock I rode to Colonel Duke's but it was so cold I was forced to walk twice to give myself a heat. About one I got there, but Colonel Randolph did not meet me according to his promise because Mr. Bland was very sick. About 3 o'clock we dined and I ate boiled beef for dinner. Then we rode to my brother Duke's and took some of Mr. B-s' [Boush's?] cider by the way. I ate milk for supper but too great a quantity which therefore did not agree with me. I said my prayers and had good health, good thoughts, and good humor, thanks be to God Almighty.

10. I rose at 7 o'clock and said a short prayer. Then I walked with my brother to see the dam he was making for a mill. I ate milk for breakfast. About 10 o'clock I took my leave and Colonel Duke was so complaisant that he came

---

[1]Colonel William Wilson, naval officer of the Lower District of the James River.

about three miles with me. About 1 o'clock I got home,
where I found all well, thanks be to God. Eugene had
pissed in bed for which I gave him a pint of piss to drink.
I ate fish for dinner. In the afternoon Mr. C-s came to
visit me. We played at billiards and then took a walk.
In the afternoon I read a little Italian and said a short
prayer. I had good health, good thoughts, and good humor,
thanks be to God Almighty.

11. I rose at 5 o'clock and read a chapter in Hebrew and
another in the Greek testament. I ate milk for breakfast
and said a short prayer. I had a little quarrel with my wife
but it soon went over. About 11 o'clock we went to church,
where Mr. Anderson gave us a sermon. Captain Stith told
me the Doctor was very sick and in great danger. Colonel
Eppes, Captain Llewellyn, Mr. Dick Cocke, Mr. Hamlin
and Mrs. L— came and dined with us. I ate fish for dinner.
About 4 o'clock the company went away and I took a walk.
In the evening I read a sermon of Mr. Norris.[1] I neglected
to say my prayers but had good health, good thoughts, and
good humor, thanks be to God Almighty.

12. I rose at 2 o'clock in the morning and read two
chapters in Hebrew and some Greek in Cassius, and then
went to bed again and rose at 7 o'clock. I said my prayers
and ate milk for breakfast. I danced my dance. I read
some Latin and settled some accounts. About 12 o'clock
Mrs. Hamlin and Mrs. B-r-d-r came over and stayed to
dinner. I ate some boiled beef for dinner. The company
went away about 3 o'clock and I took a walk about the
plantation. Then I read more Latin and then walked again.
In the evening Tom returned from Captain Stith's and
brought me word the Doctor grew worse and likewise a
letter from Mr. Bland by which I learned that he was almost
recovered, and that little of the rigging and stores of the
man-of-war was saved because of the unruliness of the sea-

---

[1]The Reverend John Norris, rector of Bemerton, near Salisbury, the author
of several popular volumes of meditations and reflections. Byrd had in his
library Norris' *Collection of Miscellanies* (1687), containing poems, essays,
and sermons.

men. In the evening I also said my prayers and had good health, good thoughts, and good humor, thanks be to God Almighty.

13. I rose at 5 o'clock and read a chapter in Hebrew and some Greek in Cassius. I said my prayers and ate milk for breakfast. I danced my dance. Last night I gave my wife a flourish and this morning I quarreled with her about her neglect of the family. I settled some accounts. About 12 o'clock Mr. J—[Gee ?] came and dined with me. He told me the Doctor was extremely ill, which made me resolve to go there in the afternoon. I ate fish for dinner and as soon as I had dined I rode with Mr. J— to Captain Stith's where I found the Doctor in a very weak condition. We prayed by him and I took my leave, committing him to God, before whom he was likely to appear very soon. Then I returned home with Mr. Harrison, and Mr. Anderson, and Mr. Cocke who had all been to take leave of the poor Doctor. In the evening I read some Latin. I neglected to say my prayers, but had good health, good thoughts, and good humor, thanks be to God Almighty.

14. I rose at 5 o'clock and read two chapters in Hebrew and some Greek in Cassius. I said my prayers and ate milk for breakfast. I danced my dance. I sent Tom to know how the Doctor did and he brought word he died about 5 o'clock last night. His distemper was first a fever, of which he recovered but went too soon to Major Allen's and was sick again there but made a shift to get back again and recovered again, and then he went to Captain Stith's where he got what strong drink he pleased and lay in the house [n-l-y p-l-s-t-r][1] and got cold and that brought intermittent fever and short breath which killed him. He was a good natured man but too much addicted to drink. I settled some accounts. I ate hashed mutton for dinner. In the [afternoon] I played at piquet with my own wife and in the evening walked about the plantation. I read some Latin verse, then I said my prayers and had good health, good thoughts, and good humor, thanks be to God Almighty.

---

[1]This may be read "newly plastered."

15. I rose at 6 o'clock and read a chapter in Hebrew and some Greek in Cassius. I neglected to say my prayers because company came in. I ate milk for breakfast. About 10 o'clock Mr. Harrison, Dr. Blair, and Jimmy Burwell came over to see some of the Doctor's things and took some account of them, but they went away about 12 and I and my wife went to Mr. Harrison's, where we dined. I ate boiled mutton for dinner. We were very merry and stayed till about 4 o'clock and then returned home where we found all well, thanks be to God. In the evening I read nothing but only wrote two letters to Williamsburg. I neglected to say my prayers and had good health, good thoughts, good humor, thanks be to God Almighty.

16. I rose at 5 o'clock and read a chapter in Hebrew and some Greek in Cassius. I said my prayers and ate [milk for] breakfast. My wife had a great pain in her belly and so took a purge which worked very well. Eugene was whipped for doing nothing yesterday. I danced my dance. I settled several accounts. I ate roast mutton for dinner. My [wife] was better after her physic, which worked 12 times. In the afternoon I played at piquet with my wife to divert her. Peter Hamlin came over. In the evening I took a walk about the plantation and found things in good order. I read some Latin. I said my prayers and had good thoughts, good humor, and good health, thanks be to God Almighty.

17. I rose at 5 o'clock and read a chapter in Hebrew and some Greek in Cassius. I said my prayers and ate milk for breakfast. I danced my dance. About 10 o'clock I ate some hashed mutton in order to go to Dr. Oastler's funeral. Accordingly about 11 o'clock we went to Captain Stith's and there heard a sermon on the occasion preached by Mr. Anderson and then followed him to his grave. About 3 o'clock we returned and found that one of my negro women had broken her leg and another had sprained herself. But thank God Daniel came home with us and did great service in setting the broken leg and dressing the other. In the

evening my cousin P—,[1] lieutenant of the lost man-of-man, came over. I made him very welcome. I neglected to say my prayers but had good health, good thoughts, and good humor, thanks be to God Almighty.

18. I rose at 5 o'clock and read two chapters in Hebrew and some Greek in Cassius. I neglected to say my prayers and ate chocolate for breakfast. My cousin and I played at billiards because there seemed to be no more harm in it than in talk. Then we took a walk about the plantation. I ate roast goose for dinner. In the afternoon we walked again about the plantation. My cousin P— is a good humored man and has seen abundance of the world. In the evening we sat and talked till 9 o'clock and then went to bed. I said a short prayer and had good health, good thoughts, and good humor, thanks be to God Almighty.

19. I rose at 4 o'clock and read two chapters in Hebrew and some Greek in Cassius. I said my prayers shortly and ate chocolate for breakfast. My river sloop came from Falling Creek with planks. Mr. P— and I played at billiards and then took a walk about the plantation, notwithstanding it rained a little. I ate beef for dinner. In the afternoon we played again at billiards and it rained still. Joe Wilkinson returned home this morning. He told me several faults of my negroes under his care, of which one died this day called S-r-y. In the evening we drank a bottle of wine but Mr. P— was very moderate. I neglected to say my prayers but had good thoughts, good humor, and good health, thanks be to God Almighty.

20. I rose at 5 o'clock and read a chapter in Hebrew and some Greek in Cassius. I said my prayers and ate toast and cider for breakfast with Mr. P—. About 12 o'clock we mounted in order to ride to Falling Creek and about two got to Will Randolph's. Here we stayed about an hour and

---

[1] "Mr. Pye" was in command of the sloop of war "Diamond" in March, 1709. On March 21, the Council issued a proclamation for all seamen of the lost ship "Garland" to go on board the "Diamond." Whether this is the cousin P— of the entry is not certain. (*Ex. Jour.*, III, 235.) Cousin John P—, evidently a connection of the Horsemanden family in England, is mentioned by Byrd in the diary for December, 1719. (Va. Hist. Soc.)

then went to visit Colonel Randolph who had the gout in his hand. In about an hour we returned again to Will Randolph's to supper. I ate boiled pork. In the evening we played at cards and I was very sleepy so that I lost half a crown. I neglected to say my prayers but had good health, good thoughts, and good humor, thanks be to God Almighty.

21. I rose about 8 o'clock but neglected to say my prayers because Mr. P— lay with me. He is a merry good humored man as can be. About 10 o'clock we went to breakfast and I ate sausage and chocolate. Then we took our leave and went to Colonel Randolph's but there it began to rain so that we went to cards again. About one we went to dinner and I ate roast beef. In the afternoon we played at cards again because the rain prevented our departure. We continued to play till 11 o'clock and then went to bed. I neglected to say my prayers but recommended myself to God. I had good health, good thoughts, and good humor, thanks be to God Almighty.

22. I rose about 8 o'clock but continued to neglect my prayers because Mr. P— lay with me. About 10 o'clock we went to breakfast. I ate pickled oysters and chocolate. Then we thought to take our leave, but the rain prevented us again. However we sent for John Pleasants with whom Mr. P— had some business. We played at cards again and about 3 o'clock went to dinner. I ate broiled pork. In the afternoon because the rain continued we played at cards again. In the evening Mrs. Randolph gave us some apples. We played at cards till 10 o'clock and then went to bed. I neglected to say my prayers but had good health, good thoughts, and good humor, thanks be to God Almighty.

23. I rose at 7 o'clock and said my prayers shortly. I ate milk for breakfast. About 8 o'clock we took leave and proceeded with Mr. P— and Isham Randolph to Falling Creek. Here I found matters in good order. Mr. P— was well pleased with the sawmill and other matters at Falling Creek. We stayed here about two hours and ate some milk and then rode away to the Hundred where we were forced

to wait above an hour because the boat was not at home, for which Captain Worsham came and made an excuse. However, we got over the river in Isham Eppes' boat and about 5 o'clock were at Colonel Hill's, where we found Mr. Anderson and all the family. In less than an hour we went to supper over a turkey pie. We sat and were merry till 9 o'clock. I neglected to say my prayers but had good health, good thoughts, and good humor, thanks be to God Almighty.

24. I rose about 8 o'clock and read in my commonplace and said my prayers. I cast water over a negro maid that was passing under the window. I ate custard for breakfast. Then we took a walk about the pasture and about 11 o'clock went to dinner. I ate [sh-ler]. Then we took our leave and got home about 2 o'clock where I found all well, thanks be to God. About 3 o'clock came Dick Randolph and Mr. Jackson from Williamsburg and brought me a letter from Mr. Bland who was much better. About 6 o'clock we went to supper and I ate turkey. We sat up till about 9 o'clock. I neglected to say my prayers but had good health, good thoughts, and good humor, thanks be to God Almighty.

25. I rose at 7 o'clock and ate milk for breakfast. I neglected to say my prayers because of my company. I ate milk for breakfast. About 11 o'clock the rest of the company ate some broiled turkey for their breakfast. Then we went to church, notwithstanding it rained a little, where Mr. Anderson preached a good sermon for the occasion. I received the Sacrament with great devoutness. After church the same company went to dine with me and I ate roast beef for dinner. In the afternoon Dick Randolph and Mr. Jackson went away and Mr. Jackson rode sidelong like a woman. Then we took a walk about the plantation, but a great fog soon drove us into the house again. In the evening we were merry with nonsense and so were my servants. I said my prayers shortly and had good health, good thoughts, and good humor, thanks be to God Almighty.

26. I rose about 4 o'clock and read two chapters in Hebrew and some Greek in Cassius. I said my prayers and

ate milk for breakfast. I wrote several letters to Falling Creek which I sent by Dick. It rained very hard all night. We played at billiards till about 12 o'clock when Mr. Harrison and his wife came to dine with us. I ate boiled beef for dinner. We were not very merry because the weather had some effect over us. They went away in the evening and Mr. P——, Mr. Isham Randolph, and I took a walk about the plantation, and then played at cards till 10 o'clock. I neglected to say my prayers but had good health, good thoughts, and good humor, thanks be to God Almighty.

27. I rose at 5 o'clock and read a chapter in Hebrew and some Greek in Cassius. I said my prayers and ate milk for breakfast. I danced my dance. When the company came down I ate chocolate likewise with them. Then we played at billiards and tried some of our [tokay]. About 12 o'clock we went to Mr. Harrison's, notwithstanding it was extremely cold and the wind blew very hard. About 2 o'clock we went to dinner and I ate some goose. In the afternoon we were very merry by a good fire till 5 o'clock. Then we returned home, where I found all well, thank God. In the evening we played at cards till about 10 o'clock and I lost a crown. I neglected to say my prayers and had good health, good thoughts, and good humor, thanks be to God Almighty.

28. I rose at 6 o'clock and read two chapters in Hebrew and some Greek in Cassius. I said my prayers and ate milk for breakfast. I danced my dance. It continued very cold with a strong wind. About 10 o'clock I ate some chocolate with the rest of the company. Then we played at billiards and I lost. When I was beat out I read something in Dr. Day.[1] About one we went to dinner and I ate boiled pork. In the afternoon we played again at billiards till we lost one of the balls. Then we walked about the plantation and took a slide on the ice. In the evening we played at cards till

---

[1] Perhaps Henry Day, *A Thanksgiving Sermon* (1696) or Martin Day, *Sermons* (1640).

about 10 o'clock. I said my prayers and had good health, good thoughts, and good humor, thanks be to God Almighty.

29. I rose at 5 o'clock and read two chapters in Hebrew and some Greek in Cassius. I said my prayers and ate milk for breakfast. I danced my dance. About 9 o'clock I ate again some chocolate with the company. Then we took a walk and I slid on skates, notwithstanding there was a thaw. Then we returned and played at billiards till dinner. I ate boiled beef for dinner. In the afternoon we played at billiards again and in the evening took another walk and gave Mr. Isham Randolph two bits to venture on the ice. He ventured and the ice broke with him and took him up to the mid-leg. Then we came home and played a little at whisk but I was so sleepy we soon left off. I said my prayers and I had good health, good thoughts, and good humor, thanks be to God Almighty.

[There are no entries for December 30 and 31.]

January, 1710

1. I rose at 6 o'clock and read a chapter in Hebrew and two chapters in the Greek Testament. I neglected to say my prayers because Mr. G-r-l kept me in discourse till the company came down. Mr. Isham Randolph went away this morning. I ate milk for breakfast. Mr. G-r-l went away likewise. Mr. C-s and Mr. Mumford came over, the first before and the last after dinner. I ate boiled pork. In the afternoon we took a walk about the plantation. The weather was very warm. In the evening we drank a bottle of wine and were merry. I said my prayers and had good health, good thoughts, and good humor, thanks be to God Almighty. I gave my wife a flourish this morning.

2. I rose at 6 o'clock and wrote several letters to recommend my Cousin P— to a ship. I said my prayers and ate milk for breakfast. News was brought that Colonel Hill was come from England and came to his house last night. He came in a ship by way of Bristol. Mr. P— and Mr. Mumford played at billiards. I ate boiled beef for dinner. In the afternoon I sent Mr. Mumford to compliment Colonel Hill on his return from England and by him I learned that our Governor Colonel Hunter has quit this government for that of New York, and that there is no likelihood of a peace or of the fleet's coming over. In the evening Mr. C-s came to visit us and we drank a bottle of wine. I said my prayers and had good thoughts, good health, and good humor, thanks be to God Almighty.

3. I gave my wife a flourish and then rose at 7 o'clock. I read nothing because my Cousin P— went away and I sent my man Tom to Williamsburg. News was brought that the distemper was at Captain Stith's where he had ten negroes sick of it. God of his excessive goodness deliver from it! Mr. Mumford and I played at billiards till dinner after we had settled our accounts. My wife was very sick. I ate hashed turkey. My son began to breed teeth which

disordered him.   In the afternoon Mr. Mumford went away
and I took a walk about the plantation and when I came
home I gave a vomit to six of my people by way of prevention. God send it may succeed. Their vomits worked
very well. I said my prayers and had good health, good
thoughts, and good humor, thanks be to God Almighty.

4. I rose at 4 o'clock and read much in Hebrew and some
Greek in Cassius. I said a short prayer and ate milk for
breakfast. About 10 o'clock I went to bid Colonel Hill
welcome to Virginia. There was abundance of company, on
the same account, and among the rest Parson Robinson
[*i. e.* Robertson].[1] The Colonel was very courteous and
complaisant. About 3 o'clock we went to dinner and I ate
boiled beef. I could stay but a little while after dinner and
then took leave and returned home and found all well,
thanks be to God. One from the Falls brought me some
venison and told me all was well and Tom returned from
Williamsburg and brought me a letter from Mr. Bland by
which I learned that he was recovered. Mrs. Ware sent her
daughter over to live with my wife. In the evening I read
some French. I neglected to say my prayers in form, but
had good hope, good thoughts, and good humor, thanks be
to God Almighty.

5. About 4 o'clock this morning I dreamed that my sloop
was arrived from Barbados. God send it may prove true as
sometimes dreams have been true. I rose about 6 o'clock
and read a chapter in Hebrew and some Greek in Cassius. I
said my prayers and ate milk for breakfast. I danced my
dance. My wife was very much indisposed in her head. I
ate boiled beef for dinner. In the afternoon read some
news and settled some accounts. In the evening I took a
walk about the plantation and gave several of my people
vomits to prevent the distemper. Jimmy came from Falling
Creek and told me all were well above, thanks be to God
Almighty. I read some Italian. Then I said my prayers

[1]The Reverend George Robertson, minister of Bristol Parish, 1693-1739.
(Goodwin, p. 302.)

and had good health, good thoughts, and good humor, thanks be to God Almighty.

6. I rose at 6 o'clock and read a chapter in Hebrew and some Greek in Cassius. I said my prayers and ate milk for breakfast. I beat Jenny severely. I danced my dance, and wrote a long letter to England. I sent Jimmy away to Falling Creek. My wife was very much out of order. I ate some boiled pork for dinner. In the afternoon I played at piquet with my wife to divert her. Then I went and took a long walk about the plantation and looked over my people. In the evening I wrote a letter to my sister Custis about Mr. Dunn. Then I gave a vomit to several more of my people to prevent the distemper. I said my prayers and had good health, good thoughts, and good humor, thanks be to God Almighty.

7. I rose at 7 o'clock and read a chapter in Hebrew and some Greek in Cassius. I said my prayers and ate milk for breakfast. I danced my dance. I gave a vomit to my negro children to prevent the distemper. I settled some accounts and prepared some accounts to send to England. I ate roast pork for dinner. In the afternoon I played at cards with my wife. Then I took a walk about the plantation to see what the people were doing. In the evening I gave the rest of the servants a vomit to prevent the distemper which is come as far as G-l-s Ordinary. I read some Latin in Terence with which I was very much pleased. I said my prayers and had good health, good thoughts, and good humor, thanks be to God Almighty.

8. I rose at 5 o'clock and read a chapter in Hebrew and some Greek in Cassius. I said my prayers and ate milk for breakfast. I danced my dance. About 11 o'clock I went to church where I met Colonel Hill who told me he had six people that had the distemper and he had such a pain in the head that he was forced to return home before church. Mr. Drury Stith and Mr. C-s came home and dined with me. I ate boiled beef for dinner. They stayed till about 4 o'clock; then Mr. Stith returned home and Mr. C-s went to walk with me and my wife. In the evening I caused several

of my people to be let blood for prevention. I read some Latin in Terence. I said my prayers and had good health, good thoughts, and good humor, thanks be to God Almighty.

9. I rose at 6 o'clock and read two chapters in Hebrew and some Greek in Cassius. I said my prayers and ate milk for breakfast. I danced my dance. About 10 o'clock Mr. Harrison came over as I thought to surrender the Doctor's things to me for 30 pounds but we could not agree. Afterwards Colonel Hill and Mr. Anderson came. We played at billiards till dinner. I ate boiled pork. Mr. Jackson and Dick Randolph called here on their way to Williamsburg. The company stayed here till about sunset and then returned home. Colonel Hill told me the distemper was at his house and that five people had it. I took a walk about the plantation. In the evening I read in Terence and gave Nurse a vomit, and likewise to Suky Ware. I said my prayers and had good health, good thoughts, and good humor, thanks be to God Almighty.

10. I rose at 4 o'clock and read two chapters in Hebrew and some Greek in Cassius. I said my prayers and ate milk for breakfast. I danced my dance. My sloop returned from Chickahominy with shingles which I caused to be unloaded. My wife continued indisposed in her head. I wrote a letter to England and read some Latin in Terence. I ate chicken and hashed mutton for dinner. In the afternoon I played at piquet with my wife and she fell down which increased the pain in her head. I took a walk and endeavored to kill a partridge for my wife but could not. In the evening Mr. Salle came down and told me all was well at Falling Creek and put me out of humor by putting stories into my head of several people, I cannot tell with what design. However I discouraged him as much as I could. I said my prayers shortly and had good health, good thoughts, but ill humor, for which God forgive me.

11. I rose at 6 o'clock and read a chapter in Hebrew and some Greek in Cassius. I said my prayers and ate milk for breakfast. This day was appointed for a fast and notwithstanding it rained, abundance of people came to church and

when I came there I was surprised to find Mr. Clayton and
Mr. Robinson there, who had laid at Mr. Harrison's that
night. Mr. Anderson gave us a good sermon on the occasion. These two gentlemen went home with me. They
knew no news at all. I ate roast beef for dinner. In the
afternoon we took a walk about the plantation. The weather was very warm. Joe W-l-s-n [Wilkinson ?] sent me a
swine from the Falls. In the evening we drank a bottle of
wine and were merry. I said a short prayer and had good
health, good thoughts, and good humor, thanks be to God
Almighty.

12. I rose at 7 o'clock and read a chapter in Hebrew and
some Greek in Cassius. I neglected to say my prayers and
ate chocolate for breakfast with my company. Then we took
a walk and after that played at billiards. I sent my sloop
away to Falling Creek. I ate roast swine for dinner. In
the afternoon we took another walk about the plantation.
Mr. Salle went away. In the evening we played at cards
and drank a bottle of wine till 12 o'clock at night. My
daughter Evelyn was indisposed and took a purge which did
not work very well. My wife was better, thank God, but
did not come out to the company. I neglected to say my
prayers in form, but said them shortly. I had good health,
good thoughts, and good humor, thanks be to God Almighty.

13. I rose at 7 o'clock and read a chapter in Hebrew and
some Greek in Cassius. I said my prayers and ate chocolate
with the company for breakfast. About 9 o'clock they went
away to Williamsburg and I sent some letters by them. My
wife was better today. I danced my dance. I took a walk
about the plantation. I ate hashed mutton for dinner. My
daughter was not well and took a purge which did not work
much. My wife was severe to her because she was fretful.
In the afternoon I danced more dances, and then took a
walk again about the plantation with my bow and arrow.
In the evening I [reproached] Bannister for his pride. I
read some Latin in Terence. I said my prayers and had
good health, good thoughts, and good humor, thanks be to
God Almighty.

14. I rose at 4 o'clock and read two chapters in Hebrew and some Greek in Cassius. I said my prayers and ate milk for breakfast. I danced my dance. I read some Latin in Terence. Then I took a walk about the plantation to overlook my people. I ate roast pork for dinner. In the afternoon I danced more dances and then took another walk about the plantation. Jack returned with the boat from Appomattox with the rest of the hogs [or hogsheads] and told me all was well there. In the evening I read some Latin in Terence. I said my prayers and had good health, good thoughts, and good humor, thanks be to God Almighty.

15. I rose at 7 o'clock and read two chapters in Hebrew and four chapters in the Greek Testament. Mrs. Ware's daughter got up in the night and went away without any cause in the world. I danced my dance and said my prayers. I ate milk for breakfast. About 12 o'clock Mr. G-r-l came from Falling Creek and said two of my negroes were sick of the distemper. God send them well. I ate boiled beef for dinner. In the afternoon Mr. G-r-l went away. I sent my English letters over the river to Peter Hamlin who will go on Tuesday next to England. In the evening I took a walk about the plantation. I read some French about the [experience] of some people in the [savannahs]. I said my prayers and had good health, good thoughts, and good humor, thanks be to God Almighty.

16. I rose at 4 o'clock and read two chapters in Hebrew and some Greek in Cassius. I said my prayers and ate milk for breakfast. My wife was much better, thanks be to God. I read some Latin in Terence and wrote a letter to England. I danced my dance and then took a walk to overlook my people. I ate hashed beef for dinner. In the afternoon I read some news and then took another walk about the plantation. It grew a little cold this day, the wind at northwest. In the evening I read some Latin in Terence. I said my prayers and had good health, good thoughts, and good humor, thanks be to God Almighty.

17. I rose at 5 o'clock and read two chapters in Hebrew and some Greek in Cassius. I said my prayers and ate milk

for breakfast. I danced my dance. Two of my negro children were sick and took a vomit which worked very well. I wrote a letter to the President and read some Latin in Terence. It began to rain a little with an east wind. I ate roast pork for dinner. In the afternoon I played at piquet with my wife and then read some news. It continued to rain so that I could not walk about the plantation. In the evening I read some Latin in Terence. I neglected to say my prayers but had good health, good thoughts, and good humor, thanks be to God Almighty.

18. I rose at 3 o'clock and read two chapters in Hebrew and some Greek in Cassius. I said my prayers and ate milk for breakfast. I danced my dance. It rained much this night and continued almost all day. I settled some accounts and then read some Latin. I ate boiled pork for dinner. In the afternoon I played at cards with my wife. Then I settled more accounts and read more Latin. Then I danced my dance again because it rained that I could not walk out. In the evening I read Latin in Terence. I said my prayers devoutly and had good health, good thoughts, and good humor, thanks be to God's will.

19. I rose at 5 o'clock and read two chapters in Hebrew and some Greek in Cassius. I said my prayers and ate milk for breakfast. I danced my dance. Colonel Kemp [?][1] came to see me from Mr. Harrison to desire me to have patience about the protested bill of exchange which I agreed to. He went away presently and I walked to my people to overlook them. When I returned I read some Latin in Terence. I ate roast mutton for dinner. In the afternoon I played at cards with my wife. Dick Randolph came and brought me a letter from England by which I learned the Queen's letter was sent to Carolina to forbid them from meddling with our traders. I ordered my people to set him up to Mr. Bland's. I took a walk with my wife about the plantation. In the evening I read some Latin in Terence, and said my prayers and had good health, good thoughts, and good humor, thanks be to God Almighty.

---

[1] Possibly Richard Kemp, appointed sheriff of Middlesex County in 1710.

20. I rose at 5 o'clock and read two chapters in Hebrew and some Greek in Cassius. I said my prayers and ate milk for breakfast. I danced my dance. I wrote a letter to the President and to Mr. Bland to send by Dick Randolph. About 9 o'clock John Anderson came over with a note on me of Mr. G-r-l's for £20. About 11 he went away. I gave G-r-l leave to go see his mother. I ate boiled pork for dinner. In the afternoon I played at cards with my wife. Dick Randolph came from the other side the river about 3 o'clock and went away presently to Williamsburg. I took a walk about the plantation. An express came from my brother Custis with the news that they had lost four negroes of the distemper and desired me to send more ipecac. In the evening I wrote a letter to my brother Custis. I said my prayers and had good health, good thoughts, and good humor, thanks be to God Almighty.

21. I rose at 5 o'clock and read two chapters in Hebrew and some Greek in Cassius. I said my prayers and ate milk for breakfast. I danced my dance and then sent away my brother Custis' boy with the things he came for. I settled some accounts and then took a walk. I ate pork and peas for dinner. In the afternoon I read some Latin. About 3 o'clock my cousin Betty Harrison came to see us and told us they had lost a negro man. Then Mr. C-s came over. We drank a bottle of French wine and after that took a walk about the plantation. In the evening I read some Latin in Terence and said my prayers. I had good health, good thoughts, and good humor, thanks be to God Almighty.

22. I rose at 6 o'clock and read a chapter in Hebrew and a chapter in the Greek Testament. I said my prayers and ate milk for breakfast. I danced my dance. About 11 o'clock we went to church and before we went in Mr. Harrison's horse ran away with his coach and broke down my mother's tombstone.[1] Mr. Anderson gave us a good sermon and after church he and Colonel Hill and Mrs. Anderson and Mrs. B-k-r came and dined with us and so

---

[1] William Byrd I and his wife Mary were buried in the churchyard of Westover Parish. (*Wm. Q. (1)*, IV, 144, 150.)

did Mr. C-s. I ate beef for dinner but ate too much. They went away about 4 o'clock and then Mr. C-s and I took a walk about the plantation. My daughter was indisposed and had a fever, for which I gave her a vomit of the tincture of ipecac. One of my negroes came from the Falls where all was well, thank God. I scolded at G-r-l for staying so long with his mother. I said my prayers and had good health, good thoughts, and good humor, thanks be to God Almighty.

23. I rose at 5 o'clock and read a chapter in Hebrew and some Greek in Cassius. I wrote two letters to send to the Falls. I said my prayers and ate milk for breakfast. My daughter slept very well this night and was well this morning, thank God. I danced my dance. Mr. M-r-s-l [Marshall ?] came to bring his accounts of Shockoe and I found fault with his management. About 12 o'clock Mrs. Hamlin came and went away presently. Then came Mr. Mumford and Mr. G-r-l who dined with me. In the afternoon Mr. G-r-l put on the locks in the library. In the evening we took a walk and then came back and settled some long accounts which kept us till 10 o'clock at night. I neglected to say my prayers, but had good health, good thoughts, and good humor, thanks be to God Almighty.

24. I could not sleep all night for the disturbance my daughter gave me. I rose at 6 o'clock but could read nothing because I settled accounts with Mr. M-r-s-l. I fell out with him very much about his accounts and other management. I neglected to say my prayers but ate milk for breakfast. Mr. G-r-l and I quarrelled about Mr. M-r-s-l because I had told him that Mr. G-r-l said he was lazy. I had my father's grave opened to see him but he was so wasted there was not anything to be distinguished. I ate fish for dinner. In the afternoon the company went away and I took a walk about the plantation. I said my prayers. In the evening I read nothing by my wife's desire. I had good health, good thoughts, and good humor, thanks be to God Almighty.

25. I rose at 6 o'clock and read two chapters in Hebrew and some Greek in Cassius. I said my prayers and ate milk

for breakfast. I danced my dance. The weather continued very warm and the sickness abated, thanks be to God. I walked about the plantation and overlooked the people. Then I read a little Latin in Terence but was interrupted by Mother S-m-s-n about her debt which I forgave her because she complained she was poor. I ate hashed turkey for dinner. In the afternoon I played at cards with my wife. Then I gave some physic to a woman that was here. Then I read some Latin and took another walk about the plantation. In the evening I read more Latin and said my prayers and had good health, good thoughts, and good humor, thanks be to God Almighty.

26. I rose at 4 o'clock and read a chapter in Hebrew and some Greek in Cassius. I said my prayers and ate milk for breakfast. I danced my dance. The weather changed and it snowed all morning. I settled some accounts of my workmen at Falling Creek. I read a little Latin in Terence. I ate some hashed mutton. In the afternoon we played at piquet and then I settled more accounts and read more Latin in Terence. Then I took a walk about the plantation. In the evening I said my prayers, ate some milk, and read more Latin in Terence. I had good health, good thoughts, and good humor, thanks be to God Almighty.

27. I rose at 6 o'clock and read a chapter in Hebrew and some Greek in Cassius. I said my prayers and ate milk for breakfast. I danced my dance. Then I took a walk about the plantation. I wrote a letter to Colonel Hill in answer to his about ready money. I ate roast mutton for dinner. In the afternoon I played at cards with my wife, then I settled some Falling Creek accounts and afterwards went to walk about the plantation. In the evening I read some Latin in Terence and likewise in the C-r-t-c. Then I said my prayers and had good health, good thoughts, and good humor, thanks be to God Almighty. The weather was warm again.

28. I rose at 4 o'clock and read a chapter in Hebrew and some Greek in Cassius. I said my prayers and ate milk for breakfast. I danced my dance. My wife was out of order

today. I settled some accounts. I received some letters from England with a sad account of tobacco. I took a walk about the plantation. I ate partridge for dinner. In the afternoon I played at cards with my wife but we quarrelled and she cried. About 3 o'clock Mrs. Harrison and Mr. Gee came to see us and stayed about two hours. George made an end of setting up my father's tomb. In the evening my river sloop came from Falling Creek, loaded with pales. I read some Latin in C-l-r-c. I said my prayers and had good health, good thoughts, and good humor, thanks be to God Almighty.

29. I rose at 6 o'clock and read two chapters in Hebrew and some Greek in the Greek Testament. I said my prayers and danced my dance. Mr. Anderson came to be set over the river, which my people did for him. I ate milk for breakfast. About 12 o'clock we went in the coach to my cousin Harrison's and dined there. I ate boiled beef for dinner. Mr. Harrison was not at home. In the afternoon we sat and talked till 4 o'clock. Then my wife rode home and I walked round the plantation. When I came home I found Joe Wilkinson who told me all was well above, thanks be to God. He came to tell me that he was to bring a steer down for me but he got away again. I neglected to say my prayers but had good thoughts, good humor, and good health, thank God Almighty. I had a cold in my head.

30. I rose at 5 o'clock and read 8 Psalms in Hebrew and some Greek in Cassius. My cold continued. I said my prayers and ate milk for breakfast. I danced my dance. I caused the river sloop to be unloaded. Then I took a walk to see all my matters. I wrote a letter to England. I ate boiled pork for dinner. In the afternoon I played at piquet with my wife. My cold continued very violently. I walked about the plantation with my wife who was very much out of order all day. I said my prayers. In the evening I read some in the R-t C-r-t-c. I had good health, good thoughts, and good humor, thanks be to God Almighty.

31. I rose at 7 o'clock by reason of my cold. I said my prayers and ate milk for breakfast. I read nothing because

I rode to Colonel Randolph's, where I arrived about 12 o'clock. The Colonel had the gout severely but the rest of the family were well. Here I stayed till the evening and then I went to Will Randolph's and Isham Randolph with us. There I ate some beef for supper. We sat and talked about my case in Henrico court and of other things till about 9 o'clock and then retired to bed. I proffered Isham Randolph to teach him French if he would come to our house, which he promised he would very thankfully. I said my prayers shortly. My cold continued bad. I had in other respects good health, good thoughts, and good humor, thanks be to God Almighty. Generally this month the wind was from the south and the weather extraordinarily warm for the time of year, which was very happy considering the distemper is worse in cold weather and considering the great want of corn in the country.

February, 1710

1. I rose about [. . .] o'clock and read a little in my commonplace. I said my prayers shortly and found my cold bad, which made me resolve not to go to court but I recommended my business to Will Randolph and wrote to Mr. G-r-l. Then we went to breakfast with Colonel Randolph and stayed till 11 o'clock, and then Isham Randolph and I rode to Colonel Hill's. The Colonel and Mr. Harrison were just going to court but I stayed with Mr. Anderson and he and Colonel Eppes played with Isham Randolph and me at cricket but we beat them. About 4 o'clock I returned home, where I found all well, thanks be to God. In the evening Mr. C-s came to visit me. I ate some roast duck for supper. He went away about 9 o'clock. I said my prayers and had good health, good thoughts, and good humor, thanks be to God Almighty.

2. I rose at 7 o'clock and read some Hebrew and some Greek in Cassius. I said my prayers and ate milk for breakfast. I gave Bannister leave to visit his father-in-law who was sick and sent him some physic. It was very warm weather. I took a walk about the plantation. I ate boiled beef for dinner, and was out of humor with my wife about stewed cherries. In the afternoon I read some Latin in C-r-t-c. Then I walked again about the plantation to overlook my people. In the evening I ate some milk and read more Latin. I said my prayers and had good health, good thoughts, and good humor, thanks be to God Almighty.

3. I rose at 5 o'clock and read some Greek in Cassius and some Hebrew. I said my prayers and ate milk for breakfast. I danced my dance. About 10 o'clock Mr. Parker came to see me and told me that George Carter had left some shoes and nails at his quarters which he thought might have been stolen from me. Soon after Colonel Hill and Mr. Anderson and Captain Llewelyn came. When we had drunk a glass of wine we went to court, where we stayed

about an hour and then came home to dinner and Isham Randolph with us. Here I found Captain Keeling to buy quitrents. I ate roast beef for dinner. Then we went to the vestry where we ordered the church yard to be paled in for 8,000 pounds of tobacco by Mr. Parker. Then my boat set Colonel Hill and Mr. Anderson to Mrs. Taylor's.[1] I took a walk about the plantation. My man Tony brought me an Indian boy called Harry. In the evening I read some Latin. Then I said my prayers and had good health, good thoughts, and good humor, thanks be to God Almighty.

4. I rose at 4 o'clock and read four Psalms in Hebrew and some Greek in Cassius. I said my prayers and ate milk for breakfast. I danced my dance. The sheriff of Isle of Wight[2] was here about the quitrents which I ordered him to sell by inch of candle.[3] I took a walk about the plantation, and then read some Latin in Terence. I ate some ox feet for dinner. In the afternoon I played at piquet with my wife. I read more Latin in Terence and then took a walk about the plantation again and in returning met Colonel Hill and Mr. Anderson riding home. In the evening Bannister returned home and told me his father-in-law was very ill. I read some Latin and said my prayers and had good health, good thoughts, and good humor, thanks be to God Almighty.

5. I rose at 7 o'clock and read the Psalms in Hebrew and two chapters in the Greek Testament. I neglected to say my prayers. I ate milk for breakfast. About 11 o'clock I went to church and heard a good sermon from Mr. Anderson. After church Mr. Bland and Captain Llewellyn went home with me to dinner. I ate boiled beef. In the afternoon the company went away and I took a walk about the plantation.

---

[1] Probably the widow of Captain John Taylor, of Charles City County, who died in 1707.

[2] Henry Applewhite was appointed sheriff for the ensuing year on April 18, 1709.

[3] The instructions to the governors of Virginia specified that the quitrents should be sold "by inch of candle"—i. e., at public auction, bidding to stop at the burning out of an inch-long candle (*Va. Mag.*, IV, 53; XXI, 356), but this method was now being given up, and the quitrents sold by the auditor and the receiver general themselves. (*Ex. Jour.*, III, 248.)

Mr. Bland told me the sickness continued about Williamsburg very violently. In the evening I read some French [miracles]. I said my prayers and had good health, good thoughts and good humor, thanks be to God Almighty.

6. I rose at 4 o'clock and read the Psalms in Hebrew and some Greek in Cassius. I said my prayers and ate milk for breakfast. I danced my dance. The weather continued very moderate, thank God. I settled some accounts and then took a walk about the plantation. About 11 o'clock Mrs. Harrison, Mrs. L— and other gentlewomen came over and so did Mr. Bland. They all dined here, notwithstanding we had but an indifferent dinner. I ate boiled pork for dinner. In the afternoon the women played at billiards and Mr. Bland went away. My wife and I walked with my cousin Harrison home and stayed there about an hour. Mr. C-s returned home with me and stayed till 9 o'clock. I neglected to say my prayers, but had good thoughts, good health, and good humor, thanks be to God Almighty.

7. I rose at 6 o'clock and read the Psalms and some Greek in Cassius. I said my prayers and ate milk for breakfast. I danced my dance. The wind was easterly and it rained a little. My wife was very much out of order. I settled some accounts and took a walk to overlook my people. I ate boiled beef for dinner. In the afternoon I played at cards with my wife and then took a walk about the plantation. When I returned I found Major Merriweather come from over the river to get some rights.[1] I had wine brought but he drank no strong drink. In the evening I read some Latin. I said my prayers and had good health, good thoughts, and good humor, thanks be to God Almighty.

8. I rose at 6 o'clock and read the Psalms and some Greek in Cassius; I said my prayers and ate milk for breakfast. I danced my dance. I settled some accounts and then Mr. Harrison and Dr. Blair came, the first to sell me the Doctor's things and the last to buy some of the medicine.

---

[1] Nicholas Merriweather, of New Kent County. The "rights" he sought were certificates of treasury rights, sold by the receiver general, permitting the holder to take up certain Crown lands. (*Ex. Jour.*, III, 434-35.)

About 11 o'clock they went away again. Then I surveyed the Doctor's things and found them not so many as I expected. I ate boiled beef for dinner. In the afternoon I played at billiards with my wife and then removed some of the Doctor's books. Then I took a walk about the plantation to overlook my people. In the evening I ate some milk and read some Latin. Then I said my prayers and had good health, good thoughts, and good humor, thanks be to God Almighty.

9. I rose at 6 o'clock and read the Psalms and some Latin [sic] in Cassius. I said my prayers and ate milk for breakfast. I danced my dance. My wife was indisposed. The wind at northwest. I settled some accounts and removed the Doctor's books. Then Captain Eppes came to make up his accounts. He stayed at dinner. I ate some roast pig. In the afternoon my uncle Byrd came to speculate about [seizing] his things to secure himself in case the hour should come. Mr. Eppes went away and I took a walk about the plantation to overlook my people. When I returned I found Mr. C-s here. I ate roast beef for supper with my uncle. Then I said my prayers and had good health, good thoughts, and good humor, thanks be to God Almighty. My wife found herself very much out of order because I forgot to give her a glass of physic when she desired it.

10. I rose at 5 o'clock and read the Psalms and some Greek in Cassius. I said my prayers and ate milk for breakfast. I danced my dance. I settled some accounts. I desired my uncle to stay this day, which he agreed to. I gave a poor man some physic for his sick child. I ate boiled beef for dinner. In the afternoon Mr. [Henry] Goodrich and Bannister came over and Mr. Isham Randolph came over to [. . .] with me to learn French. He and I took a walk about the plantation. In the·evening we sat and talked. I said my prayers and had good health, good thoughts, and good humor, thanks be to God Almighty. My wife continued indisposed.

11. I rose at 7 o'clock and read nothing because I had company. I neglected to say my prayers for the same reason. I ate milk for breakfast. I settled some accounts and Mr. Randolph began his French. My uncle went away pretty well satisfied because I told him he might come and live with me. I ate hashed beef for dinner. Mr. Bland called here on his way to Williamsburg with his shallop. In the afternoon I settled some of the Doctor's affairs and then Mr. Randolph and I took a long walk about the plantation. In the evening I read some Latin and taught Mr. Randolph his lesson. I said my prayers and had good health, good thoughts, and good humor, thanks be to God Almighty.

12. I rose at 6 o'clock and read the Psalms and two chapters in the Greek Testament. I said my prayers and ate milk for breakfast. I danced my dance. My wife was much better, thank God. I took a walk with my wife and daughter and Mr. Randolph. I ate boiled beef for dinner. In the afternoon I read about an hour, then Mr. C-s came to see us and we drank a bottle of white wine. He stayed till 9 o'clock, then I said my prayers and had good thoughts, good humor, and good health, thanks be to God Almighty.

13. I rose at 6 o'clock and read the Psalms and some Greek in Cassius. I said my prayers and ate milk for breakfast. I danced my dance. I settled some of the Doctor's affairs and amended my [creed]. I wrote a letter to Colonel Duke and another to my brother Duke in answer to a letter I received from them. I ate roast beef for dinner. In the afternoon I played at billiards with Mr. Randolph and then removed several of the Doctor's things into my closet. Then we went to take a walk and were taken in the rain but were not very wet. In the evening I instructed Mr. Randolph in his French. I said my prayers and had good health, good thoughts, and good humor, thanks be to God Almighty. As soon as we were in bed my wife complained of great pains in her belly. I persuaded her to be bled and I rose to call G-r-l to let her blood. She refused a long time; at last she agreed, but there was no one appeared.

However, she was more at ease and we went to bed again and she was easy all night, thank God.

14. I rose at 7 o'clock and read the Psalms and some Greek in Cassius. My wife miscarried this morning. I said my prayers and ate milk for breakfast. I danced my dance. My cousin Harrison and Mrs. Anderson came to see my wife to comfort her in her affliction. They stayed and dined with me. I ate roast shoat. In the afternoon they went away and Mr. Randolph and I walked to Mr. Harrison's where we found Colonel Hill extremely troubled with a headache. We stayed about two hours and then Colonel Hill and Mrs. Anderson went over the river and Mr. Randolph and I took a walk. In the evening my spouse was better. I read some Latin and said my prayers, and had good health, good thoughts, and good humor, thanks be to God Almighty. My wife slept very well tonight.

15. I rose at 6 o'clock and read the Psalms and some Greek in Cassius. I said my prayers and ate milk for breakfast. My wife was indisposed again today so that I sent for Mrs. Hamlin. I danced my dance. About 10 o'clock Mrs. Hamlin came and soon after her Mrs. Bolling, the widow. She came for some physic which the Doctor had prepared for her and would have paid me for it but I would not take it. They both stayed and dined with me. I ate boiled beef for dinner. In the afternoon I read some Latin and put the Doctor's medicines in order. About 3 o'clock the gentlewomen went away and I and Mr. Randolph took a walk about the plantation. In the evening I instructed him in his French and I read some Latin. I said my prayers and had good health, good thoughts, and good humor, thanks be to God Almighty.

16. I rose at 7 o'clock and read the Psalms and some Greek in Cassius. I said my prayers and ate milk for breakfast. Then I danced my dance. My wife was better, thank God. I removed several things out of the Doctor's closet. I taught Mr. Randolph French in which he made good improvement. I ate roast beef for dinner. In the

afternoon Mr. Randolph and I played at billiards and then Captain Cook came from Williamsburg to see me, where there was no news. He ate some roast beef and then we took a walk about the plantation. He is a very good-humored man and has been very unfortunate. In the evening we played at piquet till 9 o'clock. I said my prayers and had good health, good thoughts, and good humor, thanks be to God Almighty.

17. I rose at 6 o'clock and read the Psalms and some Greek in Cassius. I said my prayers and ate milk for breakfast. I danced my dance. One of my negroes was taken sick at the quarters, to whom I gave a vomit which worked very well. I settled some of the Doctor's things. About 11 o'clock came Mr. Parker with a [cooper] but I could not agree with him. We played at billiards. I ate fish for dinner which Captain Mallory sent us. My wife was a little better, thank God. We played at billiards again and then took a walk about the plantation. In the evening we played at piquet till 10 o'clock. I said my prayers and had good health, good thoughts, and good humor, thanks be to God Almighty. About 8 o'clock there blew a gust and the wind came about to northwest with hail and rain.

18. I rose at 6 o'clock and read the Psalms and some Greek in Cassius. I said my prayers and ate milk for breakfast. Mr. Parker went away before breakfast and only drank a dram. The wind blew hard at northwest. I drank besides my milk some chocolate. Then we played at billiards by turns and I put the Doctor's things in order. I had a letter from John Bolling by which he desired my leave to kill his hogs on my land but I denied him. I ate boiled pork for dinner. In the afternoon we played at billiards again and then took a walk about the plantation. In the evening we played at piquet till 10 o'clock and drank a bottle of wine. I said my prayers and had good health, good thoughts, and good humor, thanks be to God Almighty.

19. I rose at 6 o'clock and read the Psalms and some Greek in Cassius. I neglected to say my prayers and ate

milk for breakfast. I danced my dance. I drank chocolate with the company. About 11 o'clock we went to church and heard a good sermon from Mr. Anderson. After church Colonel Hill, Mr. Anderson and his wife came home with us to dinner. I ate boiled beef for my dinner. The company stayed with us till after 5 o'clock and then we took a long walk about the plantation. In the evening we drank a bottle of wine and were merry till 10 o'clock. I said my prayers and had good health, good thoughts, and good humor, thanks be to God Almighty.

20. I rose at 6 o'clock and read the Psalms and some Greek in Cassius. I said my prayers and ate milk for breakfast. My maid Anaka was taken sick yesterday but I gave her a vomit that worked very much and she was better this day. Then I had her sweated and bled which gave her some ease. However her fever continued violently. We rode to Colonel Hill's where we were kindly received. We played at cricket and I sprained my backside. I ate bacon and fowl for dinner. In the afternoon we played at the same sport again but I could not run. When we came away I was forced to get on my horse by a chair. We found my wife not very well. In the evening we played at piquet. I said my prayers and had good health, good thoughts, and good humor, thanks be to God Almighty.

21. I rose at 6 o'clock and read the Psalms and some Greek in Cassius. I neglected to say my prayers and ate milk for breakfast. We played at billiards all the morning. The Captain received letters from a gentleman of North Carolina about the man-of-war that was lost. I ate pork and rice for dinner. In the afternoon we shot with bow and arrow and I hit the mark. Mr. C-s came to see us. We took a walk in the evening. When we returned we drank two bottles of wine and I was very merry. I said my prayers and had good health, good thoughts, and good humor, thanks be to God Almighty. My maid Anaka was better, thank God.

22. I rose at 6 o'clock and read the Psalms and some Greek in Cassius. I neglected to say my prayers and ate

milk for breakfast. We played at billiards. About 11
o'clock Colonel Hill and Mr. Anderson came over and I
invited Mr. Harrison and his wife but they could not come.
We sweated my maid Anaka which did her much good. We
played at billiards. By Mr. Anderson's advice I put a
plaster [or blister] to Moll's side, which did her good.
I ate dry beef for dinner. In the afternoon Colonel Randolph came. We played at cricket and then Colonel
Randolph and Mr. Anderson went away. In the evening
Colonel Hill, the Captain, my wife, and I played a pool at
piquet and the Captain won it. I said my prayers and had
good health, good thoughts, and good humor, thanks be to
God Almighty.

23. I rose at 6 o'clock and read the Psalms and some
Greek in Cassius. I said my prayers and ate milk for breakfast. My maid Anaka was better, thank God. The Captain's bitch killed a lamb yesterday, for which we put her
into a house with a ram that beat her violently to break her
of that bad custom. We played at billiards. It rained with
a northeast wind. I ate roast beef for dinner. In the afternoon we played at cards and were very merry. The pool
lasted so long that we played till 11 o'clock at night. I
neglected to say my prayers, but had good health, good
thoughts, and good humor, thanks be to God Almighty.

24. I rose at 6 o'clock and read the Psalms and some
Greek in Cassius. I neglected to say my prayers but ate
milk for breakfast. Mr. Harrison invited us to dinner and
we went, notwithstanding it was bad weather and snowed a
little. Colonel Hill had been sick very much. We found
Mrs. John Stith at Mr. Harrison's, who dined with us. I
ate fowl and bacon for dinner. In the afternoon the Colonel
returned home but we stayed till it was evening. Then we
returned home where I found all well, thank God, and
Anaka had been sweated again with success. In the evening
we played at piquet till 10 o'clock and ate some roast beef
for supper. I neglected to say my prayers but had good
health, good thoughts, and good humor, thanks be to God

Almighty. Mr. G-r-l, Tom Turpin, and George Smith came from above, where all were well.

25. I rose at 6 o'clock and read the Psalms and some Greek in Cassius. I neglected to say my prayers but ate milk for breakfast. Mr. G-r-l put up the pales round my father's and mother's tombs and the others. Tom went away after breakfast. We played at billiards till 12 o'clock; then Mr. Harrison, his wife, and Mrs. Stith came and soon after them Robin Mumford and Captain Hamlin who all dined with us. I ate boiled beef for dinner. In the afternoon they played at cricket, at which the Captain sprained his thigh. About 5 o'clock the company went away and Mr. Harrison seemed to be very gallant to Mrs. Stith. In ·the evening we played at piquet till 10 o'clock. I neglected to say my prayers but had good health, good thoughts, and good humor, thanks be to God Almighty.

26. I rose at 8 o'clock and read nothing because of my company. I neglected to say my prayers, for which God forgive me. I ate milk for breakfast. Then we took a walk about the plantation till it was time to go to dinner. I ate fish for dinner. In the afternoon we saw a good battle between a stallion and Robin about the mare, but at last the stallion had the advantage and covered the mare three times. The Captain's bitch killed another lamb for which she was beat very much. We took another walk about the plantation. My maid Anaka was very well again, thank God, and so was Moll at the quarters. My wife was out of humor with us for going to see so filthy a sight as the horse to cover the mare. In the evening we drank a bottle of wine and were very merry till 9 o'clock. I neglected to say my prayers but had good health, good thoughts, and good humor, thanks be to God Almighty.

27. I rose at 7 o'clock and read nothing because Colonel Hill came early to see us to take us over the river. I neglected to say my prayers but ate milk for breakfast. It was no good weather to go abroad; however, for fear of disappointing the Colonel we agreed to go with him to his ship.

Accordingly about 10 o'clock we went, notwithstanding it snowed. Just before we went into the boat Captain John Bolling and Tom Randolph came but did not stop us. When we got over the river we walked to Mrs. Taylor's to see Colonel Hill's ship and then dined with Mrs. Taylor. In the afternoon we stayed till 4 o'clock and then returned the same way we came and got home before dark, where I found all well, thank God. We had roast pigeon for supper and then were merry till about 10 o'clock. I neglected to say my prayers but had good health, good thoughts, and good humor, thanks be to God Almighty.

28. I rose at 7 o'clock and read the Psalms and some Greek in Cassius. I said my prayers and ate milk for breakfast. Captain Cook went away this morning about 8 o'clock. I danced my dance. I took a walk about the plantation. The weather was very cold. My horse Robin was melancholy because the mare was shut up with the stone horse and would not eat but stood at the fence all day to look at her. I ate duck for dinner and in the afternoon in pure pity let the mare come out to Robin who was glad to have her again though he could do nothing to her but keep her company as a Platonic lover. I set some of the Doctor's things in order in my closet and then took a walk with Mr. Randolph, but it was very cold. In the evening I read some Latin and ate some milk with my wife. I said my prayers and had good health, good thoughts, and good humor, thanks be to God Almighty. The weather has been warm the greatest part of this month and the sickness is favorable in this neighborhood, thank God. Mr. Drury Stith lost a very good slave and some others have died for want of using remedies in time. I received a summons to Council the 8th of next month.

March, 1710

1. I rose at 8 o'clock and read the Psalms and some Greek in Cassius. I said my prayers and ate milk for breakfast. Then I danced my dance. I wrote a letter to my father Parke to be sent by way of Barbados. Then I took a little walk before dinner. I ate hashed mutton for dinner. In the afternoon set some things in order in the Doctor's closet. About 4 o'clock Tom H-n-s came for some physic for his father who has a cancer in his lip, which I gave him. Then Mr. Randolph and I took a walk about the plantation. In the evening I read some Latin. I said my prayers and had good health, good thoughts, and good humor, thank God Almighty.

2. I rose at 6 o'clock and read the Psalms and some Greek in Cassius. I said my prayers and ate milk for breakfast. I danced my dance. About 12 o'clock we rode to Colonel Hill's where we dined. Then we went over the river in the ferry boat though the Colonel proffered to set us over in his boat. In the afternoon we rode up to Falling Creek where we found all things well, thank God. In the evening we ate some milk for supper. I was better satisfied than I used to be with the affairs of this place. I neglected to say my prayers but had good health, good thoughts, and good humor, thanks be to God Almighty.

3. I rose at 7 o'clock and read a little in my commonplace. I said a short prayer and ate milk for breakfast. We took a walk to the mill and then proceeded to the Falls where we ate some milk and pone. From hence we rode to Kensington where I reprimanded Robin for not looking after the cattle better. Here we went over the river to Burkland where things were in good order. Then we walked to [Byrd Park] where I had several of the negroes whipped for stealing the hogs [or hogsheads]. From hence we walked to Shockoe where things were in good condition. Then we went over the river again to the Falls and from thence to Falling Creek, where we ate venison for supper.

I neglected to say my prayers but had good health, good thoughts, and good humor, thank God Almighty.

4. I rose at 7 o'clock and said a short prayer. Then I discoursed Mr. G-r-l about several things and likewise Tom Turpin. Then we walked to the mill where we looked over everything. Then we ate milk for breakfast. Then we rode to Dr. Bowman's who showed me some of his physic. From thence we rode to the Hundred and went over the river to Colonel Hill's where we dined. I ate boiled bacon for dinner. In the afternoon we played at cricket and then rode home where I found all well, thank God, and my sister Custis come from Queen's Creek. In the evening we talked till 10 o'clock. I neglected to say my prayers but had good thoughts, good humor, and good health, thanks be to God Almighty.

5. I rose about 7 o'clock and I read nothing because of the company. I ate some milk for breakfast. My man C-n-g-y was taken very sick of the distemper with a great pain in his breast. I put Dr. Bowman's plaster to his breast and some of his powder. About 11 o'clock we went to church, where there was but a small congregation. Mr. Anderson gave us a good sermon. After church nobody came home with us but Mr. C-s. I ate boiled pork for dinner. In the afternoon we talked a little while and then took a walk about the plantation. We met Mr. James Burwell and Mr. Doyley, who came home with us. We drank a bottle of wine and were merry for about an hour in the evening. I said my prayers and had good health, good thoughts, and good humor, thanks be to God Almighty.

6. I rose at 7 o'clock and read the Psalms and some Greek in Cassius. I neglected to say my prayers. About 10 o'clock John Pleasants, Mr. Will Randolph, and Mr. Dick Cocke came to see me and stayed about an hour and then returned. C-n-g-y continued very bad and Mary was also taken sick. They were both put into a tub and sweated. About 12 o'clock Mr. Doyley came to tell us my cousin Harrison was very sick. I ate boiled beef for dinner. In the afternoon we went to see Mrs. Harrison where we

stayed till the evening and then returned home. I said my prayers and had good health, good thoughts, and good humor, thanks be to God Almighty.

7. I rose at 7 o'clock and read the Psalms and some Greek in Cassius. I said my prayers and had John Bannister take physic. C-n-g-y continued very sick but Mary was better. I ate milk for breakfast. It rained all the morning which, together with my sick family, made me resolve not to go to Williamsburg to Council. I danced my dance. I ate hashed beef for dinner. In the afternoon my sister Custis went away and I put my closet in order. I danced my dance again. It rained in the evening that I could not walk about the plantation, but I read some Latin and ate some roast beef. I said my prayers devoutly and had good health, good thoughts, and good humor, thanks be to God Almighty. Mr. Isham Randolph went away this afternoon.

8. I rose at 6 o'clock and read the Psalms and some Greek in Cassius. I said my prayers and ate milk for breakfast. I danced my dance. It rained this morning again. My man C-n-g-y continued very sick, but Bannister was better, thank God, and so was Moll. I settled some accounts and then set my closet in order. I ate boiled beef for dinner. In the afternoon I played at piquet with my wife. My man C-n-g-y grew worse. In the evening we took a walk about the plantation. Then I said my prayers and read some English. I had good thoughts, good humor, and good health, thanks be to God Almighty.

9. I rose at 7 o'clock and read the Psalms and some Greek in Cassius. Poor C-n-g-y died this morning before day. I said my prayers and ate milk for breakfast. I danced my dance, and settled some accounts. I set the Doctor's closet in order. It rained a little in the morning. Mrs. Taylor was married to Mr. Platt[1] on Tuesday last, notwithstanding her exceedingly grave fear of the death of her last husband. I ate some cold roast beef for dinner.

---

[1]Randle (or Randolph) Platt, appointed sheriff of Prince George County on August 22, 1712. (*Ex. Jour.*, III, 305.) Mrs. Taylor probably was the widow of John Taylor, who died in 1707.

In the afternoon put the Doctor's closet in order again and then with my wife took a walk about the plantation. In the evening I read some Latin. I said my prayers and had good health, good thoughts, and good humor, thanks be to God Almighty.

10. I rose at 6 o'clock and read the Psalms and some Greek in Cassius. I said my prayers and ate milk for breakfast. I set the Doctor's closet in order. About 11 Colonel Hill, Mr. Anderson, and his wife came to see us but Mr. Harrison could not come because his wife was sick and he himself had the gout. About 12 Mr. Isham Randolph came. They walked in the garden till dinner. I ate boiled beef. In the afternoon we played at cricket a little while but Mr. Anderson was sent for to Mrs. Harrison who was worse. In the evening we took a walk about the plantation and then Mr. Anderson came back to us, and Mr. C-s came soon after. We drank two bottles of wine and were merry till 10 o'clock. I said my prayers and had good health, good thoughts, and good humor, thanks be to God Almighty.

11. I rose at 6 o'clock and read the Psalms and some Greek in Cassius. I said my prayers shortly because of my company. Isham Randolph went away very early. I ate milk for breakfast. Mr. Anderson and I were busy mending one of my [globes]. Colonel Hill had the headache severely. About 12 o'clock we walked to Mr. Harrison's where we found my cousin better. I ate fowl and bacon for dinner. In the afternoon Mr. Gee came over from our house, where he found nobody at home, and so did Dick Cocke. We were merry till almost 6 o'clock; then we walked home. In the evening I read some Latin. I said my prayers and had good health, good thoughts, and good humor, thanks be to God Almighty.

12. I rose at 8 o'clock and read the Psalms and some Greek in Cassius. I said my prayers shortly and ate milk for breakfast. I took a little walk before dinner, when I ate fish. We had no company with us. In the afternoon we walked again about the pasture and then Mr. C-s and Mrs. Hamlin came to see us. While they were here we heard

guns as if a ship was come to Swinyards. Mrs. Hamlin went away soon but Mr. C-s stayed till 8 o'clock. We drank a bottle of wine and were merry. I said my prayers and read some English. I had good health, good thoughts, and good humor, thanks be to God Almighty.

13. I rose at 6 o'clock and read the Psalms and some Greek in Cassius. I said my prayers and ate milk for breakfast. I danced my dance. I read some Latin. I received news about my uncle Byrd's death; he [died] yesterday morning a little before day. All my people were well, thank God, at Falling Creek. I ate boiled beef for dinner. In the afternoon I played at piquet with my wife. Then I read some Dutch. Then I took a walk about the plantation. My wife was melancholy; therefore I made her walk with me. In the evening I read some English. I said my prayers and had good health, good thoughts, and good humor, thanks be to God Almighty.

14. I rose at 6 o'clock and read the Psalms and some Greek in Anacreon. I said my prayers and ate milk for breakfast. I received a letter by Captain Posford[1] from Mr. Bland by which I learned that my sloop was taken into Martinique. Captain Ned Bolling died of the smallpox at sea and so did Ch-s-t-r, both pretty young men. The death of this last makes way for Isham Randolph to command Colonel Hill's ship, for which he shall have my recommendation. My wife was melancholy, which made me weep. I danced my dance. I ate roast mutton for dinner. In the afternoon we played at piquet, then I read more Dutch. Then I took a walk about the plantation. In the evening I read some English. I said my prayers and had good health, good thoughts, and good humor, thanks be to God Almighty.

15. I rose at 6 o'clock and read the Psalms and some Greek in Anacreon. I said my prayers and ate milk for breakfast. I danced my dance. George made an end of

---

[1] In 1737 Mr. Posford was mentioned in a letter of Byrd's as "commander of the ship 'Harrison'." (*Wm. Q. (2)*, I, 194.) A letter to him [printed "Porford"] from Byrd is to be found in the *Va. Mag.*, IX, 128.

painting the library and gave in his account, which was a very reasonable one. The boatwright was here to mend the boat. Mr. Harrison invited us to dinner but my wife had a cold and could not go. But I went about 12 o'clock with Colonel Eppes who came over for some physic which I gave him. I found Colonel Hill, Mr. Anderson, his wife, and Mr. Gee. Mrs. Harrison was better but he was not very well. I ate fish for dinner. In the afternoon we played at cricket but Mr. Harrison was soon tired. Then we drank a bottle of wine and about 5 o'clock the company parted and I walked home with Mr. C-s who stayed with me till 8 o'clock. I said my prayers and had good health, good thoughts, and good humor, thanks be to God Almighty.

16. I rose at 6 o'clock and read the Psalms and some Greek in Anacreon. I said my prayers and ate chocolate with Colonel Hill who came this morning to see me. I put him in mind of his promise to Isham Randolph concerning his ship, for which he promised to use his interest but he thought Mr. Platt would be against it. I danced my dance. Colonel Hill went away over the river about 9 o'clock. My wife was out of order and melancholy. I ate hashed mutton for dinner. In the afternoon I wrote a letter to Barbados and then took a walk about the plantation. In the evening I had an express from Falling Creek to let me know Mrs. Byrd[1] was dead. I said my prayers and had good health, good thoughts, and good humor, thank God Almighty.

17. I rose at 6 o'clock and read the Psalms and some Greek in Anacreon. I said my prayers and ate milk for breakfast. I danced my dance. I took a walk this fine morning, then I wrote a letter to Barbados, and after that set the Doctor's closet in order. About 12 o'clock Mr. Isham Randolph came. I ate boiled beef for dinner. In the afternoon Mr. Will Randolph and Robin Mumford came. We played at cricket. I committed my business con-

---

[1]Mrs. Mary Byrd's will was admitted to probate, June 1, 1710, on petition of her son by an earlier marriage, Thomas Howlett (Stanard, Henrico Records, p. 211). Mary Howlett is mentioned in 1685 as administratrix of Thomas Howlett (Henrico County Records, 1677-92, pp. 356-7). Perhaps Mary Byrd was the wife of Thomas Byrd, who predeceased her by three days.

cerning my uncle Byrd to Will Randolph. In the evening they went away and Colonel Hill came. I applied to him again in behalf of Isham Randolph and he expressed himself very kindly. We walked with him some part of his way. We ate some mutton. I neglected to say my prayers but had good thoughts, good humor, and good health, thanks be to God Almighty.

18. I rose at 6 o'clock and read the Psalms and some Greek in Anacreon. I said my prayers and ate milk for breakfast. I wrote a letter to Barbados, while Mr. Randolph and Mr. Mumford played at billiards. About 11 o'clock we ate some duck and then went over the river in my boat to visit Mr. Platt and his wife to give them joy, and to recommend Mr. Randolph. Mr. Platt was not at home but his wife was. We stayed about two hours and then returned home, where I found Mr. C-s who stayed here till 8 o'clock. We ate some fish. My wife was very much disordered with her cold. I said my prayers and had good health, good thoughts, and good humor, thanks be to God Almighty.

19. I rose at 6 o'clock and read the Psalms and four chapters in the Greek Testament. I said my prayers and ate milk for breakfast. My wife continued disordered with her cold. About 11 o'clock I went to church, where I heard that Captain B-r-k was dead suddenly. It rained a little before church. After sermon I invited Colonel Eppes and his wife and the sheriff and Mr. C-s to dinner. I ate fish. In the afternoon the company went away and soon after there came a great gust of wind and rain to punish them for not staying. It likewise thundered a little. In the evening I neglected to say my prayers but had good health, good thoughts, and good humor, thanks be to God Almighty. Nurse was taken sick at church.

20. I rose at 6 o'clock and read the Psalms and some Greek in Anacreon. I said my prayers and ate milk for breakfast. The sloop came over and S-k-f-r was sick. It brought a boy sick from the Falls. It rained much in the night and often in the day. My wife was indisposed and

took a sweat and so did Nurse and it did them both service. I ate fish for dinner. In the afternoon Mr. Randolph and I played at billiards. I was amicable with my wife in her sickness. In the evening I took a short walk and when it was dark Mr. Randolph and my wife played at piquet. I neglected to say my prayers, had good health, good thoughts, and indifferent good humor, thank God Almighty.

21. I rose at 6 o'clock and read the Psalms and some Greek in Anacreon. I said my prayers and ate milk for breakfast. I danced my dance. My wife was better and so were Nurse and S-k-f-r, thank God. It rained a little today. I wrote a letter to England. I ate fish for dinner. In the afternoon Captain Posford came and presented us with 12 bottles of wine. He bespoke some planks of me and I agreed to give him £12 a ton. I set the Doctor's closet to rights. In the evening we took a walk about the plantation. Then I had a messenger from above with news that the gust on Sunday last blew down three houses, which I bore with a submission to God Almighty who knows best what to do for us. I neglected to say my prayers but had good health, good thoughts, and good humor, thanks be to God Almighty.

22. I rose at 6 o'clock and read the Psalms and some Greek in Anacreon. I said my prayers and ate milk for breakfast. I wrote several letters to send to the quarters. I ordered Bannister to dispatch the sloop because S-k-f-r was well and then we rode to Colonel Hill's where we found abundance of company, more than we expected and among the rest Mr. Harrison who was not well. About 2 o'clock we went to dinner and I ate bacon and fowl. In the afternoon played at cricket, four of a side, and Mr. Harrison among us, who looked exceedingly red a great while after it. In the evening most of the company went away and we recommended Mr. Randolph to Mr. Platt who was very equable and suave. He made, however, some difficulty of the matter but with the air of consent. About 10 o'clock we went to bed. I neglected to say my prayers but had good health, good thoughts, and good humor, thank God Almighty.

23. I rose at 7 o'clock and read a little in Homer and said a short prayer. Then we drank chocolate for breakfast. Then we drank a dram of cherry brandy. Then we played several games of cricket and after a little rest played several more games till it began to rain. About 2 o'clock we went to dinner and I ate boiled beef for dinner. In the afternoon we danced and were merry till the evening. Then we sat and talked till about 10 o'clock but in the evening my wife began to have a pain in her breast. I neglected to say my prayers but had good health, good thoughts, and good humor, thanks be to God Almighty. Mr. Harrison was taken sick this morning before day.

24. I rose at 7 o'clock and read nothing. I said my prayers shortly and ate milk for breakfast. There came an express for Mr. Anderson to Mr. Harrison who was very sick and he went to him. We took a walk in the morning, then we had some sack and toast, after which we took leave and returned home where we found all well, thank God. I ate pigeon and asparagus for dinner. In the afternoon I took a little nap. Then Mr. Randolph and I took a walk to Mr. Harrison's who had been very sick but was something better, and young Drury Stith was sick there likewise. We stayed there about an hour and then walked home and walked with my wife in the garden. I said my prayers and had good health, good thoughts, and good humor, thank God Almighty.

25. I rose at 6 o'clock and read the Psalms and some Greek in Anacreon. I said my prayers and ate milk for breakfast. I danced my dance. My wife was out of order a little. I sent to know how Mr. Harrison did and received word that he was worse, but it rained so all day that I could not go to see him. I settled some accounts and then put the Doctor's closet in order. I ate fish for dinner. In the afternoon I played at piquet and retired to my library. It continued to rain all day. In the evening I sent again to know how Mr. Harrison did and received word that he was better and that Doctor Blair was come up to him, who brought me a letter from England that told me the "An-

gelica" foundered at sea.[1] I said my prayers and read some Dutch. I had good health, good thoughts, and good humor, thanks be to God Almighty.

26. I rose at 7 o'clock and read the Psalms and three chapters in the Greek Testament. I said my prayers and ate milk for breakfast. I danced my dance. I received an express from Mr. Harrison that he was better and I sent him some red lead plasters.[2] It rained again almost all day, the wind at northeast. I read two sermons in Dr. Tillotson. My wife was better. I ate boiled beef for dinner. In the afternoon Mr. Randolph and I walked to see Mr. Harrison and found him better. Here we found his two brothers,[3] Colonel Hill, and Mr. Anderson with Dr. Blair. We stayed till the evening and then took our leave and returned home where we found all well, thank God. We sat and talked. I said my prayers and had good health, good thoughts, and good humor, thanks be to God Almighty.

27. I rose at 6 o'clock and read a chapter in Hebrew and some Greek in Anacreon. I ate milk for breakfast which gave me a looseness. I began to say my prayers but was interrupted. About 10 o'clock Dr. Blair, Mr. James Burwell and Major and Captain Harrison came to see us. After I had given them a glass of sack we played at cricket and after that at billiards till dinner. I ate boiled beef for my dinner. In the afternoon we played at billiards. John Bolling and young Woodson came. Then we played at shooting with arrows till about 4 o'clock when we went all to Mr. Harrison's, whom we found better. Here we went to cricket again till dark; then we returned home where I [found] Jenny sick. I said my prayers and had good health, good thoughts, and good humor, thank God Almighty.

---

[1]James Bray, owner of a ship "Angelica", petitioned the Council for leave to clear for England on February 4, 1708. Presumably this is the ship that foundered. (*Ex. Jour.*, III, 166.)

[2]E. Smith, *The Compleat Housewife* (1742), pp. 175 and 203, recommends "plaster of red lead."

[3]Nathaniel and Henry Harrison.

28. I rose at 6 o'clock and read a chapter in Hebrew and some Greek in Anacreon. I ate milk for breakfast and said my prayers. I danced my dance. About 10 o'clock Major Harrison, Hal Harrison, James Burwell and Mr. Doyley came to play at cricket. Isham Randolph, Mr. Doyley, and I played with them three for a crown. We won one game, they won two. Then we played at billiards till dinner, before which Colonel Ludwell came on his way to Mr. Harrison's. They all dined with us and I ate boiled pork. Soon after dinner the company went away and I took a nap. Then we walked to Mr. Harrison's, whom we found better. We played a game at cricket again. I took leave about 8 and returned home where I found Jenny better. I caused her to be cupped and then gave her [m-t-y] pills. This was my birthday, on which I am 36 years old, and I bless God for granting me so many years. I wish I had spent them better. I neglected to say my prayers but had good health, good thoughts, and good humor, thank God Almighty.

29. I rose at 7 o'clock and read a chapter in Hebrew and some Greek in Anacreon. I said my prayers and ate milk for breakfast. I danced my dance. I settled my matters to go to Falling Creek, but first we ate our dinner and then after recommending my family to the protection of the Almighty, we rode to Colonel Hill's. With him and Mr. Anderson we talked and were merry all the afternoon and all the evening, but on our way over I met one of Mr. Harrison's people that told me his master was much better. We went to bed soon because I rose early the next morning. I said my prayers and had good health, good thoughts, and good humor, thanks be to God Almighty.

30. I rose at 3 o'clock and ate milk about 4 and then we went over the river and were a-horseback by 5 and so rode to Falling Creek, where we got about 7, and we found Mr. G-r-l getting ready the mill for a wager and a little after 8 o'clock the mill began to saw and sawed 2,000 feet in five hours and finished the rest in four hours more by which we won a wager of £40 of John Woodson, who laid that the mill could not saw 3,000 feet of planks in ten hours. There

was abundance of company there, the best of which I treated with wine. About 5 o'clock we returned to Colonel Hill's where we were told that Mr. Harrison was relapsed again and in great danger. I ate some milk and said my prayers both morning and evening, and had good thoughts, good humor, and good health, thanks be to God Almighty.

31. I rose at 7 o'clock and read some Greek in bed. I said my prayers and ate milk for breakfast. Then about 8 o'clock we got a-horseback and rode to Mr. Harrison's and found him very ill but sensible. Here I met Mr. Bland, who brought me several letters from England and among the rest two from Colonel Blakiston who had endeavored to procure the government of Virginia for me at the price of £1,000 of my Lady Orkney[1] and that my Lord [agreed] but the Duke of Marlborough declared that no one but soldiers should have the government of a plantation, so I was disappointed. God's will be done. From hence I came home where I found all well, thank God. I ate fish for dinner. In the afternoon I went again with my wife to Mr. Harrison's who continued very bad so that I resolved to stay with him all night, which I did with Mr. Anderson and Nat Burwell. He was in the same bad condition till he vomited and then he was more easy. In the morning early I returned home and went to bed. It is remarkable that Mrs. Burwell dreamed this night that she saw a person that with money scales weighed time and declared that there was no more than 18 pennies worth of time to come, which seems to be a dream with some significance either concerning the world or a sick person. In my letters from England I learned that the Bishop of Worcester was of opinion that in the year 1715 the city of Rome would be burnt to the ground, that before the year 1745 the popish religion would be routed out of the world, that before the year 1790 the Jews and Gentiles would be converted to the Christianity and then would begin the millenium.

---

[1] Lord George Hamilton, Earl of Orkney, was appointed in 1704 governor of Virginia for life, but never came to the colony. He died in 1737. During that period various lieutenant governors ruled. On July 23, 1710, Alexander Spotswood received the appointment sought by Byrd.

April, 1710

1. Before sunrise I returned home and after recommending myself and the sick man to the divine protection, I went to bed and lay till 12 o'clock at noon. Then I rose and read a chapter in Hebrew and some Greek. I ate milk for breakfast. About 2 o'clock we went to dinner and I ate a little fish. In the afternoon I went to visit Mr. Harrison and found him a little better. I stayed about an hour and then returned home. A man coming from Kiquotan brought me more letters from England. I neglected to say my prayers but had good health, good thoughts, and good humor, thank God Almighty.

2. I rose about 7 o'clock and read two chapters in Hebrew and four chapters in the Greek Testament. I said my prayers and ate milk for breakfast. I sent to know how Mr. Harrison did and received word that he was a little better. About 11 o'clock I went to church and heard a sermon of Mr. Anderson. After church I invited Nat Burwell and his wife and several others to dinner and treated them very well. I ate boiled beef for dinner. They stayed till the evening and then I went to see Mr. Harrison, who seemed to be better but his fever still on him. I stayed about an hour and then returned home. We sat up with my Cousin Burwell till about 11 o'clock. I said my prayers and had good health, good thoughts, and good humor, thanks be to God Almighty. Abraham Bayley[1] came over this night from above.

3. I rose about 7 o'clock and read a chapter in Hebrew and some Greek. I said my prayers and ate milk for breakfast. I danced my dance; then I sent to know how Mr. Harrison did and received word that he had slept badly this night, though he drank a great deal of the tea which I sent him. Colonel Eppes came about 11 o'clock and said

---

[1]Abraham Bayley is listed as owning 542 acres in Henrico County in 1704. (*Va. Mag.*, XXVIII, 209.)

Mr. Harrison was very bad. Mr. Parker came likewise; then came Mr. Burwell, Colonel Hill, and Nat Harrison and they all gave a bad account of Mr. Harrison. We played at billiards till dinner. I ate roast beef for dinner. In the afternoon we shot with a bow and then played at cricket. In the evening we walked to Mr. Harrison's, with whom I had intended to watch but there were several that came for that purpose. He was very ill. Then I returned home. I neglected to say my prayers but had good health, good thoughts, and good humor, thanks be to God Almighty.

4. I rose at 6 o'clock and read a chapter in Hebrew and some Greek in Anacreon. I said my prayers and ate milk for breakfast. I danced my dance. I sent to inquire how Mr. Harrison did and received word that he was no better notwithstanding he had slept much in the night by the help of laudanum. My wife was indisposed this morning and I took a walk with her. I ate fish for dinner. In the afternoon I settled the Doctor's closet and then read some news. Mr. C-s came and told me Mr. Harrison continued extremely bad. About 5 I walked there with him and found him in a bad condition, sometimes dozing then waking with groaning and frenzy. I found Mrs. Hamlin and Mrs. Stith there and likewise Colonel Hill. I ate milk about 8 o'clock and then went into the chamber and sat up with him all night. His fever was very high and he began to break out in pimples but was very restless all night. We gave him tea with ten drops of spirits of saffron. I stayed till 5 o'clock in the morning and then returned home and went to bed. I said a short prayer and had good health, good thoughts, and good humor, thanks be to God Almighty.

5. I rose about 10 o'clock and read only a chapter in Hebrew, being interrupted by Mr. Bland who brought word my cousin Harrison continued bad and that Dr. Blair was with him and despaired of his life. I settled accounts with Mr. Bland. My wife took a vomit which worked very well but did not remove the pain in her side. I ate milk for breakfast. I had abundance of discourse with Mr. Bland concerning our store at Williamsburg. I ate hashed mutton

for dinner. In the afternoon Mr. Bland and I read some news till Mrs. Hamlin came and told us Mr. Harrison was still very bad. Mr. Bland went away and I walked to Mr. Harrison's where I found him better and broken out extremely but his fever still very high. Mr. Blair and his wife, with Colonel Harrison, was there. I stayed till 8 o'clock and then returned home where I found my wife complaining of the pain in her breast. I said my prayers and had good health, good thoughts, and good humor, thank God Almighty.

6. I rose at 7 o'clock and read a chapter in Hebrew and some Greek. I ate milk for breakfast and neglected to say my prayers. I sent to know how Mr. Harrison did and received word that he seemed to be a little better, which was confirmed by Mr. Anderson whom I sent for to let me blood because of a little pain I found in my side. He sucked about a pint of blood from me which gave me ease, but my wife would not be let blood notwithstanding the pain in her breast. I ate boiled beef for dinner but very moderately. In the afternoon I read some news and played at piquet with my wife to divert her. In the evening I took a walk about the plantation but was not very well. I read more news and then sent to know how Mr. Harrison did and received word that he was worse. I said my prayers and had indifferent good health, good thoughts, and good humor, thank God Almighty.

7. I rose at 5 o'clock and read a chapter in Hebrew and some Greek. I said my prayers and then took a purge of laxative salts, as did also my wife who was much indisposed with her breast. I sent to inquire how Mr. Harrison did and received word that he was still worse. I sent him some spirits of saffron. My purge did not work much but made me hot and out of order. I set my closet in order. My godson John Stith came to see me and I examined him and found he had made a good progress. I ate chicken for dinner. In the afternoon I played at cards with my wife and then ordered the coach to go visit Mr. Harrison. I found him better in appearance and everybody full of hope.

In the evening I returned home. I neglected to say my prayers but had good health, good thoughts, and good humor, thank God Almighty.

8. I rose at 6 o'clock and read nothing because I took physic, and Mr. Anderson came from Mr. Harrison's and told me that he was much better and that he had good hopes of him. I neglected to say my prayers and ate broth for breakfast. About 8 o'clock Mr. Anderson went away and I put my closet in order. I took Epsom salts which worked little but very easy. I ate boiled chicken again for dinner. In the afternoon I sent Nurse to Mr. Harrison's and he [*sic*] brought word Mr. Harrison was growing worse again, on which I ordered her to go watch with him all night. I played at cards with Mrs. Byrd and then set my closet in order again. Then I took a walk about the plantation. In the evening I received a letter from my plantation above and learned that all was well there, thank God. I neglected to say my prayers but had good health, good thoughts, and good humor, thank God Almighty.

9. I rose at 6 o'clock and read a chapter in Hebrew and a chapter in the Greek Testament. I said my prayers and ate caudle for breakfast. I received an account that Mr. Harrison was very ill and was confirmed in the same account. Went to church. We heard a good sermon from Mr. Anderson and after received the Sacrament with great devoutness. Mr. Harrison had a mind to partridge, which I sent him, and he ate one of them. We had nobody but our own family at dinner. I ate roast beef. As soon as we had dined we went to Mr. Harrison's, who we found past all hopes, and a very melancholy family. We stayed till the evening and then returned home. Mr. G-r-l came this afternoon and let me understand all was well at Falling Creek. I said my prayers and had good health, good thoughts, and good humor, thank God Almighty.

10. I rose at 6 o'clock and wrote several letters to my overseers. I sent early to inquire after Mr. Harrison and received word that he died about 4 o'clock this morning, which completed the 18th day of his sickness, according to

Mrs. Burwell's dream exactly. Just before his death he was sensible and desired Mrs. L— with importunity to open the door because he wanted to go out and could not go till the door was open and as soon as the door was opened he died. The country has lost a very useful man and [one] who was both an advantage and an ornament to it, and I have lost a good neighbor, but God's will be done. I said my prayers and ate caudle for breakfast. I danced my dance. My wife rode to Mrs. Harrison's to comfort her and to assure her that I should be always ready to do her all manner of service. My wife returned before dinner. I ate tripe for dinner. In the afternoon we played at piquet. Then I prepared my matters for the General Court. It rained, with the wind at northeast, and it was very cold, and in the night it snowed. I read news. I said my prayers and had good health, good thoughts, and good humor, thank God Almighty.

11. I rose at 6 o'clock and found snow on the ground. I read a chapter in Hebrew and some Greek in Anacreon. I neglected to say my prayers and ate milk for breakfast. The wind changed and it grew good weather about 10 o'clock. I prepared my accounts against the General Court. I took a walk before dinner. Then I ate hashed beef. In the afternoon my wife went to visit the widow to comfort her and stayed with her all the afternoon. In the meantime I wrote out more accounts against the General Court. In the evening I took a walk about the plantation. My wife came home in the evening and I wrote a letter to England. I said a short prayer and had good health, good thoughts, and good humor, thanks be to God Almighty.

12. I rose at 6 o'clock and read a chapter in Hebrew and some Greek in Anacreon. I said my prayers and ate milk for breakfast. My sloop arrived last night from Falling Creek with boat timber and was unloaded this day. I danced my dance. My boat set Mr. Randolph and Mr. Rogers[1] over the river because they could not get the ferry-

[1] Mr. Robert Rogers is mentioned in the Henrico County court records as an attorney.

boat. Mr. C-s came over to invite to Mr. Harrison's funeral. I invited him in case he left Mrs. Harrison to come and live with me. I settled my accounts against I go to Williamsburg. I ate hashed beef for dinner. In the afternoon I played at piquet with my wife and then wrote more accounts. In the evening I took a walk about the plantation. Mr. Mumford came and I ate some supper with him. I said a short prayer and had good health, good thoughts, and good humor, thanks be to God Almighty.

13. I rose at 5 o'clock and read a chapter in Hebrew and some Greek in Anacreon. I said my prayers and ate milk for breakfast. I danced my dance. I wrote my accounts and Mr. Mumford helped me. Then we took a walk to see the mare in the great pasture. Then we played at billiards. I ate hashed beef for dinner. In the afternoon Mr. Mumford went away. Captain Posford came to see me and offered me his boat to carry my things to Williamsburg. Mr. Doyley came over to borrow some black wax but I had none. I was much troubled with wind since I took physic. In the evening we took a walk and in the meantime Mr. Clayton and Mr. Robinson came in order to go the next day to the funeral. I ate some fish with them for supper. I said a short prayer and had good health, good thoughts, and good humor, thanks be to God Almighty.

14. I rose at 6 o'clock and read some Hebrew and no Greek. I neglected to say my prayers but ate milk for breakfast, but the rest of the company ate meat. About 10 o'clock we walked to Mrs. Harrison's to the funeral, where we found abundance of company of all sorts. Wine and cake were served very plentifully. At one o'clock the corpse began to move and the ship "Harrison" fired a gun every half minute. When we came to church the prayers were first read; then we had a sermon which was an extravagant panegyric or [eulogy]. At every turn he called him "this great man," and not only covered his faults but gave him virtues which he never possessed as well as magnified those which he had. When [the] sermon was done the funeral service was read and the poor widow trembled extremely.

When all was over I put the widow, her daughter, and two sisters[1] into my coach and Colonel Randolph, his wife, Colonel Hill, Mrs. Anderson, and the two B-r-k-s[2] went home with us and I invited several others who would not come. I ate roast beef for dinner. It rained most of the afternoon; however Colonel Hill and Mrs. Anderson went away. I neglected to say my prayers but had good health, good thoughts, and good humor, thanks be to God Almighty.

15. I rose at 6 o'clock but it rained and so I would not go to Williamsburg. I neglected to say my prayers but drank chocolate for breakfast with the company. It rained a little in the morning; however I sent some tobacco on board the "Harrison" in my sloop. Colonel Randolph and I took a little walk. I ate boiled beef for dinner. In the afternoon the company went away and Mr. C-s who dined with us likewise stayed till the evening. We took a walk about the plantation with my wife. Mr. C-s sat and talked with us till 8 o'clock. I neglected to say my prayers but had good health, good thoughts, and good humor, thanks be to God Almighty.

16. I rose at 7 o'clock and read a chapter in Hebrew and some Greek in the Testament. I said my prayers and ate milk for breakfast. I danced my dance. My wife was indisposed in her breast which made her melancholy. We took a walk by the [hedge] where I found that John had cut down two trees for which I was angry. I ate boiled beef for dinner. In the afternoon we went in the coach to Mrs. Harrison's. We found her melancholy. Her two brothers were with her and so was Mrs. Berkeley. We stayed there till the evening when we returned home. I prepared to go to Williamsburg. I said a short prayer and had good health, good thoughts, and good humor, thanks be to God Almighty.

---

[1]Mrs. James Blair and Mrs. Philip Ludwell were sisters of Mr. Harrison. Mrs. Harrison's sisters were Mrs. Henry Armistead, Mrs. William Bassett, and Mrs. Edmund Berkeley.
[2]Probably Edmund Berkeley and his wife (Lucy Burwell) Berkeley.

17. I rose at 4 o'clock and sent my horses over the creek and followed them about 5 o'clock, after committing my wife and family to the protection of the Almighty. I likewise, left orders with my family what to do. Nothing happened by the way extraordinary, so that I got to Williamsburg about 10 o'clock, where I found several letters from England, and among the rest one from Mr. Perry who told me that my father's accounts were passed and that my salary was increased to 5 per cent with one year's retrospect.[1] I had also a letter from Lady G-s by which I learned how much I am obliged to her for endeavoring to get for me the governorship of Maryland. About 12 o'clock we went to court and finished the business of the day by 4 o'clock. I went to dinner soon after. I ate boiled beef for dinner. Then we went to the President's where we drank some of his French wine. In the evening Captain Cook came and I ate some broiled beef with them. Then I went home. I said a short prayer and had good health, good thoughts, and good humor, thanks be to God Almighty.

18. I rose at 5 o'clock and read two chapters in Hebrew and some Greek in Homer. I said my prayers and ate rice milk for breakfast. Then I went to the capitol about 8 o'clock and settled my accounts till 9. Then I went to the President's where I found several of the Council and about 10 we went to Council where among other things we directed the negroes to be arraigned for high treason.[2] We continued in Council till 4 o'clock and then went to court where we sat till 5. Then I went with my brother Custis to Dr. [Barret's] where my sister was, Mr. Dunn and his wife and Mrs. Chiswell. About 7 o'clock we went to supper and I ate roast mutton. About 9 o'clock I returned home and read a little Latin. I neglected to say my prayers but had good health, good thoughts, and good humor, thank God Almighty.

---

[1]Byrd's salary as receiver general had hitherto been three per cent.

[2]Some excitement had been caused in the colony by a rumored plot of certain slaves to rise against their masters. The negroes on trial were accused of this conspiracy. (*Ex. Jour.*, III, 235-36.)

19. I rose at 5 o'clock and read two chapters in Hebrew and some Greek in Homer. I said my prayers and ate some rice milk for breakfast. I had abundance of company before I could get out of my chamber. I settled my accounts till about 11 o'clock and then went to court, where the negroes were arraigned for treason. About 3 o'clock we had news that the captain[1] of the man-of-war called the "Enterprise" was come to town and soon after he came to the capitol and the Council was called about him where it was concluded that he should have orders to stay and cruise at the Cape to protect the country but he seemed resolved to sail to New York. About 5 o'clock we went to dinner and I ate boiled beef. In the evening I took a walk and then returned home. I read some Latin; then I said my prayers and had good health, good thoughts, and good humor, thanks be to God Almighty.

20. I rose at 5 o'clock and read two chapters in Hebrew and some Greek in Homer. I said my prayers and ate custard for breakfast. I had several gentlemen come to see me. Then I went to the capitol where I wrote a letter to England and settled some accounts. Then I went to court where three persons were tried for felony and acquitted. I returned again to my chambers and settled more business. About 6 o'clock the court rose and went to dinner. Then Colonel Basset and I took a walk and then went and drank cider at Will Robinson's chambers. Then I returned home and read a little Greek in Homer. I said my prayers and had good health, good thoughts, and good humor, thanks be to God Almighty.

21. I rose at 5 o'clock and read two chapters in Hebrew and some Greek in Homer. I said my prayers and ate milk for breakfast. I had abundance of people come to see me. About 8 o'clock I went to see the President and then went to court. I settled some accounts first. Two of the negroes were tried and convicted for treason. I wrote a letter to England and then went to court again. About 3 o'clock I

---

[1]Captain Nicholas Smith. (*Ex. Jour.*, III, 237-38.)

returned to my chambers again and found above a girl who I persuaded to go with me into my chambers but she would not. I ate some cake and cheese and then went to Mr. Bland's where I ate some boiled beef. Then I went to the President's where we were merry till 11 o'clock. Then I stole away. I said a short prayer but notwithstanding committed uncleanness in bed. I had good health, bad thoughts, and good humor, thanks be to God Almighty.

22. I rose at 5 o'clock and read a chapter in Hebrew and some Greek in Homer. I said my prayers and ate milk for breakfast. I went to the capitol where I settled some business. Then I went to court where I stayed a little and then returned again to my chambers where I wrote two letters to England. About 12 o'clock I ate some cake and cheese and about 5 o'clock I went to Mr. Bland's where I ate some fish. In the evening we went to the President's where we played at piquet till about 10 o'clock. Then I went to my chambers and read some news. I recommended myself to Heaven and had good thoughts, good health, and good humor, thanks be to God Almighty.

23. I rose at 5 o'clock and read a chapter in Hebrew and some Greek in Homer. I said my prayers and ate milk for breakfast. About 11 o'clock my sister Custis called on me to desire me to go to Green Springs with her, but I excused myself. Then I went to the President's where I found some of the Council; then we went to the church, where Mr. Anderson told me all was well at my house, thanks be to God Almighty. He gave us a good sermon. After church we went and dined with the President. In the afternoon we took a walk and then I went home with Colonel Duke where I sat till 9 o'clock. Then I went home and recommended myself to heaven in a short prayer. I had good health, good thoughts, and good humor, thanks be to God Almighty.

24. I rose at 5 o'clock and read two chapters in Hebrew and some Greek in Homer. I said my prayers and ate milk for breakfast. I had much company at my chambers. About 10 o'clock I went to the President's and about 12 there was

a Council where they passed my accounts and Mr. Commissary and I had a dispute about paying money to the College and the Council were of my opinion except Colonel Ludwell. Then I went and read my letters. About 4 o'clock we went to dinner. I ate mutton pie for dinner. In the afternoon it rained and we went to the President's where my sister Custis sent to me to Mr. Bland's. I went and stayed with her till 10 o'clock and Colonel Randolph was there. Then I went home, where I recommended myself to heaven and had good health, good thoughts, and good humor, thanks be to God Almighty.

25. I rose at 5 o'clock and read a chapter and no Greek because my head was full of business. I said my prayers and ate milk for breakfast. Several people were at my chambers. About 9 o'clock went to Mr. Bland's to my sister Custis and from thence to the President's. Then I went to court where I settled several accounts. About 12 o'clock I ate some cake and then went to court again. About 5 o'clock we had a meeting of the College where they made it appear that they ought to pay the Queen's bounty in money and not in bills. We chose Mr. Clayton and Mr. Bland two new members. About 7 o'clock we went to dinner and I ate fowl and bacon. Then I went to the President's where I found Captain Cook just come from Kiquotan. I said my prayers and had good health, good thoughts, and good humor, thanks be to God Almighty.

26. I rose at 5 o'clock and read a chapter in Hebrew and some Greek in Homer. I neglected to say my prayers and ate milk for breakfast. I had company with me this morning. About 8 o'clock I went to court where I settled much business. I wrote to my wife by Mr. Anderson. Then I went into court. About 2 o'clock I went to my chambers where I did more business and then ate some cake. About 6 o'clock I went to Mr. Bland's where I ate some bacon. Then I went to C-t where I drank my bottle of wine with the Council. About 9 o'clock I returned home and read a new play. I said my prayers and had good health, good thoughts, and good humor, thanks be to God Almighty.

27. I rose at 5 o'clock and read a chapter in Hebrew and some Greek in Homer. Then I went to Council where my warrants passed and several other matters of consequence were done. About 12 o'clock I ate some tongue and then we tried an unfortunate man who had against his will killed his nephew and he was found guilty of manslaughter. I was appointed commander in chief of two counties. I received a letter from my father Parke of an old date. About 5 o'clock we dined. I ate roast beef for dinner. Then we sat in Council again till 9 o'clock. I had good health, good thoughts, and good humor, thank God Almighty, and said my prayers.

28. I rose at 5 o'clock and read a chapter in Hebrew and no Greek because I had company. I said a short prayer and ate milk for breakfast. Then I went to the capitol and settled some accounts. Then I went to court where I sat till 12 o'clock. Then I went to my office and did more business and settled Captain Cook's account which was in very great confusion. Then we went to dinner and I ate boiled mutton. Several of the Council went out of town. In the evening I agreed with Mr. Ingles to lend him £200 on good security, for which he was very thankful. Then I went to the President's and stayed there till about 10 o'clock. I said my prayers and had good health, good thoughts, and good humor, thanks be to God Almighty.

29. I rose at 5 o'clock and read a chapter in Hebrew and some Greek in Homer. I said my prayers and ate rice milk for breakfast. Then I went to court to hear the orders read, after which we went to Council and settled some affairs. Then I gave Captain Cook a certificate of the truth of his account and took leave of him and of the gentlemen of the Council. I settled some accounts with the President and Mr. Robinson. About 12 o'clock I ate some cake and cheese. About 3 o'clock my man brought my horse and a letter from home that told me all was well, thank God. Then Mr. Custis and I rode to Mr. Blair's where I ate some roast mutton for dinner. Then we went to Queen's Creek where I was received very kindly. I was much tired.

I neglected to say my prayers but had good health, good thoughts, and good humor, thanks be to God Almighty.

30. I rose at 7 o'clock and said my prayers. Then I ate rice milk for breakfast. I read nothing because I had no books with me. I wrote a letter of excuse to Major Burwell for not going to see him as I ought to do. I also excused myself to my uncle Ludwell for the same purpose. About 11 o'clock I took my leave and rode to Colonel Duke's where I came about 2 o'clock. There I found my brother Duke, who told me all was well at his house. I ate some cold beef and salad. In the afternoon it rained exceedingly and thundered terribly for about an hour. However it did not prevent me from proceeding to my brother Duke's, where we came before sunset. My sister and her child were very well. I ate milk for supper. I said a short prayer and had good health, good thoughts, and good humor, thanks be to God Almighty. Colonel Duke told me that Ben Goodrich[1] died at night and was well that morning two days since. The distemper continues violent in some parts. This was a very backward spring, notwithstanding we had a favorable winter.

---

[1] In 1704 Benjamin Goodrich owned 1,650 acres in James City County. (*Va. Mag.*, XXXI, 156.) He left two daughters, Anne and Elizabeth. (*Wm. Q. (1)*, XXVII, 210.)

May, 1710

1. I rose at 7 o'clock and read in a book about breeding of horses. I neglected to say my prayers and ate milk for breakfast. We took a walk to see my brother's mill dam. About 11 o'clock I took my leave and rode to Mr. Gee's, who was not at home. From thence I proceeded home, where I came about 2 o'clock and found all well, thanks be to God Almighty. I ate some hashed beef for dinner. In the afternoon I gave my wife a flourish. I sent to Captain Posford to send his boat to Williamsburg to fetch my trunk which he very readily performed this night. In the evening I walked about the plantation and found everything in pretty good order. I said my prayers and had good health, good thoughts, and good humor, thanks be to God Almighty.

2. I rose at 7 o'clock and read a chapter in Hebrew and some Greek in Anacreon. I said my prayers and ate milk for breakfast. I danced my dance. I settled some accounts and put things in order. About 11 o'clock Captain Posford came to see me and made me a present of some raisins. He stayed and dined with us. I ate roast mutton and sallet. He went away soon after dinner. Then we went in the coach to see my disconsolate cousin Harrison, where we found Colonel Bassett and his wife. I proffered my service to my cousin Harrison in everything she should please to command me. We stayed here till evening, when we walked home, where we found all well, thank God. I said my prayers and had good health, good thoughts, and good humor, thanks be to God Almighty.

3. I rose at 6 o'clock and read a chapter in Hebrew and some Greek in Anacreon. I said my prayers and ate milk for breakfast. I danced my dance. It rained a little all the morning [near] afternoon. However some people came to court and got drunk in defiance of the sickness and the bad weather, among whom was Joe Harwood and Mr. Dennis, two great examples of virtue. Robin B-r-k came to account

with me but put me out of humor with his roguery. I ate
roast beef for dinner, which I ate little of because it was not
enough done. In the afternoon Will Eppes and Colonel
Eppes came to see me through the rain. In the evening I
took a walk and saw several drunk people in the churchyard.
Mr. C-s came in the evening and stayed till 9 o'clock. I said
a short prayer and had good health, good thoughts, and
good humor, thank God Almighty.

4. I rose at 6 o'clock and read a chapter in Hebrew and
some Greek in Anacreon. I said my prayers and ate milk
for breakfast. Eugene and another boy were sick and my
wife was not well. I danced my dance. My sloop came
from Falling Creek, where she left all well, thank God. I
settled some accounts and then took a walk before dinner.
I ate hashed mutton. In the afternoon my wife and I
played at billiards and then took a nap. I settled more
accounts and then took another walk about the plantation.
The two boys grew better. In the evening I read some
French. I said my prayers and had good health, good
thoughts, and good humor, thank God Almighty. My sloop
went this night to Appomattox for tobacco.

5. I rose at 7 o'clock and read a chapter in Hebrew and
some Greek in Anacreon. I said my prayers and ate milk
for breakfast. I danced my dance. My sick boys were a
little better. The wind blew cold at northwest. I settled
several accounts. About 11 o'clock there came abundance
of people to visit us and among them Mr. Goodwin and his
wife. We played at billiards till dinner. I ate boiled beef
for dinner. In the afternoon we played again at billiards.
The company stayed till about 6 o'clock and then took leave
and went away. Then my wife and I took a walk to Mrs.
Harrison's, who was indisposed with a cold. We stayed
there about half an hour and then walked back again. I
read some French. I said my prayers and had good health,
good thoughts, and good humor, thank God Almighty.

6. I rose at 6 o'clock and read a chapter in Hebrew and
some Greek in Anacreon. I said my prayers and ate milk

for breakfast. I danced my dance. About 10 o'clock I got ready to ride to Colonel Hill's. I found the Colonel indisposed of the headache, but Mr. Anderson was better but not altogether well. There was the master of the New England vessel [to enter]. About 2 o'clock we went to dinner and I ate heartily of a chicken pie. We had no diversion but talk, which we did till about 5 o'clock, and then I rode to my cousin Harrison's with design to meet my wife there but she failed. My cousin was pretty well but still very disconsolate. Here I ate some strawberries and wine. Then I walked home where I found Mr. C-s. We stayed till 9 o'clock. I neglected to say my prayers but had good health, good thoughts, and good·humor, thanks be to God Almighty. My wife began to have her term.

7. I rose at 6 o'clock and read two chapters in Hebrew and two chapters in the Greek Testament. I said my prayers and ate milk for breakfast. I danced my dance. Then I read a sermon of Dr. Tillotson's which affected me very much and made me shed some tears of repentance. The weather grew very hot. The sick boys were a little better. I ate [moderately] of roast beef for dinner. In the afternoon my wife and I took a long sleep which discomposed me. Then I read another sermon in Dr. Tillotson, after which we took a walk and met Mr. C-s who walked with us and told us several strangers were come to my cousin Harrison's. He stayed here till 9 o'clock. I neglected to say my prayers but had good health, good thoughts, and good humor, thanks be to God Almighty.

8. I rose at 7 o'clock, having slept ill in the night. I read a chapter in Hebrew and some Greek in Anacreon. I said my prayers and ate milk and strawberries for breakfast. I danced my dance. I accounted with old [Higbee] and promised him my good word to be sexton. I settled some accounts. About 11 or 12 o'clock our cousins R-d, Betty Bassett,[1] and Betty Harrison came to see us and were forced to be content with our own dinner. I ate bacon and pigeon

---

[1] Daughter of Councillor William Bassett. The Bassetts were "cousins" through Mrs. Bassett, who had been Joanna Burwell.

for dinner. In the afternoon we played at billiards and diverted the company as well as we could. In the evening they went away and we walked with them some part of the way. I was out of humor, I knew not why. I neglected to say my prayers and had indifferent health, humor, and thoughts, for which God Almighty forgive me and for the future enable [me] to have better. I had a colt dead soon after he was gelt.

9. I rose at 6 o'clock and read two chapters in Hebrew and some Greek in Anacreon. I said my prayers and ate milk for breakfast. I danced my dance. I settled some accounts. The wind was at northeast and rained a little, but it soon cleared up again. About 1 o'clock Colonel Ludwell, Mrs. Hal Harrison, [Mrs.] Armistead,[1] and Mrs. Hamlin came over to dinner. I ate boiled beef for dinner. In the afternoon we played at billiards and ate cherries, and were as merry as we could. In the evening they returned to Mrs. Harrison's and I and my wife walked with them, where we found Nat Harrison and Nat Burwell and Mr. Armistead and Mr. Blair. We stayed about half an hour and then walked home. I said my prayers and had good health, good thoughts, and good humor, thank God Almighty.

10. I rose at 7 o'clock and read a chapter in Hebrew and some Greek in Anacreon. I said my prayers and ate milk for breakfast. I danced my dance. Mr. Randolph came to see me on his way to Prince George Court. Sam M-r-k-m likewise was here, who was taken in my sloop. I wrote two letters to Williamsburg. About 12 o'clock Mr. Blair and Nat Burwell came to dine with us. I ate boiled beef for dinner. In the afternoon we played at billiards and were very merry till the evening. Then I walked with them to Mrs. Harrison's, where I stayed till night, when I returned home, where I found Will Randolph and Robin Mumford. I ate a little supper with them and then talked till 9 o'clock. I said my prayers and had good health, good thoughts, and

---

[1]Probably Martha, wife of Henry Armistead of Hesse in Gloucester County. She, too, was a daughter of Lewis Burwell.

good humor, thanks be to God Almighty. The sloop came with tobacco from Appomattox.

11. I rose at 6 o'clock and read two chapters in Hebrew and some Greek in Anacreon. I said my prayers and ate milk for breakfast. I danced my dance, and then played at billiards in my turn with Mr. Randolph and Robin Mumford and when I was out I read in my commonplace. I ate roast mutton and sallet for dinner. In the afternoon we played at billiards again till about 5 o'clock when the company went away. Then we took a walk about the plantation and overlooked the quarters. In the evening I read in Dr. Tillotson. Then I said my prayers and had good thoughts, good humor, and good health, thanks be to God Almighty.

12. I rose at 5 o'clock and read three chapters in Hebrew and some Greek in Anacreon. I said my prayers and ate milk for breakfast. I danced my dance. I settled some accounts. Then I settled my closet. It was very hot this day, and the first day of summer. I read some news. I ate boiled beef for dinner. In the afternoon I cut some [sage][1] and then read a sermon in Tillotson. I also read some news. Then my wife and I took a walk about the plantation; when we returned we found our son[2] very sick of a fever and he began to break out terribly. We gave him some treacle water. I said my prayers and had good health, good thoughts, and indifferent good humor, thanks be to God Almighty.

13. I rose at 7 o'clock because I did not sleep well in the night. However, I read a chapter in Hebrew and some Greek in Anacreon. I said my prayers and ate milk and strawberries for breakfast. I wrote two letters. Then I danced my dance. I settled some accounts and read some Italian. About 12 o'clock Mr. Parker came and told me his parish had agreed with Mr. Dunn and would give him [?]. I ate sallet and shad for dinner. Soon after dinner Mr.

---

[1] This symbol, s-c or s-k, closely resembles the symbol translated "physic." Apparently Byrd was preparing a supply of sage (or some other herb) for medicinal use.
[2] Parke.

Parker went away and then my wife and I cut [sage]. Our child was a little better, thank God. I read more Italian. In the evening we took a walk about the plantation. I said my prayers and had good health, good thoughts, and good humor, thanks be to God Almighty.

14. I rose at 7 o'clock and read two chapters in Hebrew and some Greek in the Testament. I said my prayers and ate milk and strawberries for breakfast. My wife had the headache very much this morning and our child continued bad. About 11 o'clock I went to church without my wife and heard a sermon from Mr. Anderson. After church I invited Mr. Drury Stith and his wife, Colonel Eppes and his. wife, and John Eppes to dinner. I ate roast mutton for dinner. In the afternoon I persuaded Drury Stith to be a justice of peace. About 5 o'clock the company went away and my wife and I walked about the plantation. I neglected to say my prayers, and had good health, good thoughts, and good humor, thanks be to God Almighty.

15. I rose at 5 o'clock and prepared to ride to Falling Creek, notwithstanding it rained a little. I said my prayers and ate milk and strawberries for breakfast. The child continued sick. I pray God restore him to his health again. About 7 o'clock I got on my horse but before I got four miles it rained very hard and I was wet to the skin, but when I came to Colonel Randolph's they gave me clothes. Here I had an opportunity to converse with Mr. Finney[1] the minister, who is a sober, ingenuous man. About 12 o'clock we went to dinner and I ate some chicken fricassee. In the afternoon I proceeded with Will Randolph and Isham Randolph to Falling Creek. Mr. G-r-l was not returned from Carolina, nor was his brother there as he promised. It rained violently in the evening and all night. We went and looked about and all things were in order except the dam, in which there was a leak. We ate some milk. I neglected to say my prayers and had good thoughts, good health, and good humor, thanks be to God Almighty.

---

[1]Probably the Reverend William Finney, minister of Henrico Parish, 1714, or before, to 1727. (Goodwin, p. 269.)

16. We lay in bed till 9 o'clock because it rained and we knew not what to do up. We ate milk for breakfast. I said a short prayer; then we walked to the mill and about 12 o'clock departed. Will Randolph went home and Isham and I rode to Colonel Hill's where I ate some broiled chicken. After dinner we ate cherries and talked till about 6 o'clock and then I took leave and rode home, where I found all my family well except my son, who had still a fever. It had rained very much till about 2 o'clock. I took a walk about the garden. I said my prayers and had good health, good thoughts, and good humor, thanks be to God Almighty.

17. I rose at 5 o'clock and read two chapters in Hebrew and some Greek in Anacreon. I ate milk and strawberries for breakfast. My son was a little worse, which made me send for Mr. Anderson. My express met him on the road and he came about 10 o'clock. He advised some oil of juniper which did him good. I ate some sack and toast with him. About 12 o'clock he went away. I danced my dance. I ate fish for dinner. In the afternoon my wife and I cut some [sage]. In the evening took a walk to Mrs. Harrison's to inquire if they had any service for me. I stayed about an hour and Mr. C-s came home with me and stayed till about 9 o'clock. I said my prayers and had good health, good thoughts, and good humor, thanks be to God Almighty. My sloop came this evening from Appomattox.

18. I rose at 5 o'clock and read two chapters in Hebrew and some Greek in Anacreon. I said my prayers and ate milk and strawberries for breakfast. I danced my dance. About 9 o'clock Colonel Hill called on his way over the river. I gave him some strong water. When he went away Mrs. Hamlin came to see the child, whose fever continued. I sent my sloop to Falling Creek. I read some Italian. A little before dinner Mr. Randolph came and dined with us. I ate hashed mutton for dinner. The company stayed almost all the afternoon. I read more Italian and then with my wife took a walk about the plantation. My little boy was a little better, thank God. I gave a poor woman some physic

for her daughter. I said my prayers and had good health, good thoughts, and good humor, thanks be to God Almighty.

19. I rose at 5 o'clock and wrote a letter to Mr. Bland by his sloop. I read two chapters in Hebrew and some Greek in Anacreon. I said my prayers and ate milk for breakfast. I danced my dance. My little boy was better, thank God Almighty. I read some Italian and ate abundance of cherries. I ate fish for dinner. In the afternoon my wife and I cut a little [sage] but were interrupted by a visit we had from Colonel Hill, Mr. Anderson, and his wife, who stayed with us all the afternoon. The Colonel was out of order and I gave him some physic. I read more Italian and in the evening took a walk about the plantation and met Major C-s who came home with us and stayed till 9 o'clock. The child was a little better, thank God. I said a short prayer and had good health, good [thoughts], and good humor, thanks be to God Almighty.

20. I rose at 5 o'clock and read two chapters in Hebrew and some Greek in Anacreon. I said my prayers and ate milk and strawberries for breakfast. I danced my dance. I settled the Doctor's closet. Then I read some Italian and ate some cherries. The child continued indisposed. I ate roast shoat for dinner. In the afternoon my wife and I cut some [sage]. Then I settled my closet again. In the evening I took a walk about the plantation. I received letters from above that gave an account of the appraisal of my uncle's estate and that Mr. G-r-l was not returned from Carolina and that the dam was out of order. I said my prayers and had good health, good thoughts, and indifferent good humor, thank God Almighty.

21. I rose at 5 o'clock and read a chapter in Hebrew and some Greek in the Testament. I said my prayers and ate milk and strawberries for breakfast. I danced my dance. I wrote two letters to the Falls. The child continued indisposed. I read two sermons in Tillotson, which edified me very much. I ate roast shoat for dinner, and Miss Sarah Taylor[1] dined with us. I was out of humor with my wife

---

[1] Daughter of John Taylor, who died in 1707.

for forcing Evie to eat against her will. In the afternoon
we went in the coach to Mrs. Harrison's and found her very
disconsolate. Mr. Anderson came there likewise. We ate
some cherries. I comforted my cousin as well as I could.
In the evening we walked home and found Evie in a great
fever and to increase [it] they had given her milk. I
remembered both my children in my prayers and had good
health, good thoughts, and good humor, thanks be to God
Almighty.

22. I rose by 5 o'clock and sent our excuses to Colonel
Hill for not going with him to Colonel Harrison's because
our children were both sick. However, they came to see us
in our affliction. I read two chapters in Hebrew but no
Greek because the company hindered me. We ate milk and
strawberries for breakfast. Then we played at billiards till
about 11 o'clock when Mr. Woodson came to see me. We
ate cherries and talked of many things. I ate beef for
dinner but ate too much. In the afternoon we drank some
tea and ate more cherries. Tom Randolph came and brought
me word that Colonel Randolph had the gout in his stomach,
for which I sent him some [b-v-r mineral].[1] In the evening
the children were a little better, and the company went away.
I took a little walk with my wife. I was out of order with
eating too much. I said my prayers and had good health,
good thoughts, and good humor, thanks be to God Almighty.

23. I rose at 5 o'clock and read two chapters in Hebrew
and some Greek in Anacreon. The children were a little
better, thank God. I said my prayers and ate milk and
strawberries for breakfast. I danced my dance. My daughter was very ill, but the boy had lost his fever, thank God.
I settled some accounts and wrote some commonplace. I
ate hashed shoat for dinner. In the afternoon Evie had a
sweat that worked pretty well but not long enough, for
which I was out of humor with my wife. I read some
Italian and some news and then took a walk about the
plantation. When I returned I had a great quarrel with my

---

[1]Possibly "beaver mineral," *i. e.*, *castoreum.*

wife, in which she was to blame altogether; however I made the first step to a reconciliation, to [which] she with much difficulty consented. I said a short prayer and had good health, good thoughts, and good humor, thank God Almighty.

24. I rose at 5 o'clock and read a chapter in Hebrew and some Greek in Anacreon. I said my prayers and ate milk and strawberries for breakfast. I sent for my cousin Harrison to let Evie blood who was ill. When she came she took away about four ounces. We put on blisters and gave her a glyster which worked very well. Her blood was extremely thick, which is common in distemper of this constitution. About 12 o'clock she began to sweat of herself, which we prompted by tincture of saffron and sage and snakeroot. This made her sweat extremely, in which she continued little or more all night. I ate some fish for dinner. In the afternoon Mr. Anderson whom I had sent for came and approved of what I had done. I persuaded him to stay all night which he agreed to. It rained in the evening. We stayed up till 12 o'clock and Bannister sat up with the child till 12 o'clock and G-r-l till break of day. I said my prayers and had good health, good thoughts, and good humor, thanks be to God Almighty.

25. I rose at 5 o'clock and read a chapter in Hebrew and some Greek in Anacreon. I said my prayers and ate milk and strawberries with Mr. Anderson for breakfast. Evie was much better, thank God Almighty, and had lost her fever. The boy was better likewise but was restless. It was very hot today. I read some Italian. I ate green peas for dinner. In the afternoon my wife and I cut some [sage] and then I read more Italian. In the evening Mr. C-s came over and we took a walk about the plantation. When we came home Mr. C-s had some milk. He stayed here till 9 o'clock and I was pleased with his conversation. I never was more incommoded with heat in my whole life. I neglected to say my prayers and had good health, good thoughts, and good humor, thanks be to God Almighty.

26. I rose at 5 o'clock and read two chapters in Hebrew and some Greek in Anacreon. I said my prayers and ate milk and strawberries with Captain Posford for breakfast. He told me that a ship was arrived with negroes and offered his service to fetch my wine from Williamsburg. Evie was better but the boy was worse, with a cold and fever for which we gave him a sweat which worked very well and continued all day. About 9 o'clock Mr. J— came to buy some glass and stayed here about an hour. The wind was northeast and was cold again. I wrote a letter to England. I ate beef and sallet for dinner. In the afternoon we cut some [sage]. Then I read some [Italian] and in the evening took a walk about the plantation. I scolded at G-r-l for telling a lie. I said my prayers and had good health, good thoughts, and good humor, thanks be to God Almighty.

27. I rose at 5 o'clock and read two chapters in Hebrew and some Greek in Anacreon. I said my prayers and ate milk for breakfast. I danced my dance. Evie took a purge which worked but a little and my son had a little fever. Mr. [i. e. Mrs.?] Hamlin came to see them. I went about 11 o'clock to Colonel Randolph's to visit him because he was sick, and I found him better than he had been. We had bacon and green peas for dinner. I let the Colonel know anything I had was at his service and took my leave about 5 o'clock and got home about 7 where I found the boy in his fever but Evie was better, thank God Almighty. Mr. C-s was at our house to borrow a horse to go to Major Burwell's. He stayed till 9 o'clock. I neglected to say my prayers but had good health, good thoughts, and good humor, thanks be to God Almighty.

28. I rose at 6 o'clock and read two chapters in Hebrew and some Greek in the Christian part of Anacreon.[1] I said my prayers and ate bread and butter for breakfast. The boy was still ill of his fever. Joe Wilkinson came from above where all was well, thank God. We went to church

---

[1]St. Gregory of Nanzianus and other church fathers wrote so-called "pious anacreontics." Byrd may refer to some of these imitations of Anacreon, whose own verses are the very antithesis of Christian.

and heard a sermon and received the Sacrament.   I heard at
church that Colonel Ludwell had lost 3 or 4 negroes more.
I invited nobody home this day.   I ate beans and bacon for
dinner.   In the afternoon I discoursed with Joe Wilkinson
about my affairs and learned that all went well.   In the
evening Mr. G-r-l came with a heavy heart and cried on my
reproaching him for staying so long in Carolina and not leaving his brother in his stead as he promised me, and offered to
make me any reparation.   He told me of the breaking of
the dam, which was like my fortune.   It put me very much
out of humor.   In the evening I took a walk.   I said my
prayers and had good health, indifferent humor, and good
thoughts, thanks be to God Almighty.

29. I rose at 5 o'clock and read a chapter in Hebrew and
some Greek in Anacreon.   I said my prayers and ate milk
and strawberries for breakfast.   I danced my dance.   I
agreed with Joe Wilkinson to be my overseer four years.   I
ordered Mr. G-r-l to repair the break in the dam as soon as
possible.   Then they both went away.   The boy continued
very ill of the fever.   I read some Italian.   I ate roast
mutton for dinner.   In the afternoon we cut [sage].   My
belly ached exceedingly and continued so till the evening and
gave me many stools.   I took a long walk about the plantation.   I neglected to say my prayers but had good health,
good thoughts, and good humor, thanks be to God Almighty.
My boy appeared to be a little better this evening, blessed
be God for it.

30. I rose at 6 o'clock and read two chapters in Hebrew
and some Greek in Anacreon.   I said my prayers and ate
bread and butter for breakfast.   I danced my dance.   The
boy was better, thank God, and I began to give him the
bark.   About 10 o'clock Captain Browne[1] came to pay for
the quitrents of Surry, which he had bought.   Captain
Posford's boat brought three pipes of wine from Williamsburg which came in good order.   I ate some chicken for

---

[1] Probably Captain William Browne of Surry County, who speculated in
land. (*Ex. Jour.*, III, 79 and *passim*.)

dinner. In the afternoon Tom Howlett[1] came. I sent Captain Posford some green peas. In the evening we thought the child better. I took a walk about the plantation. Mr. C-s returned from Major Burwell's with the horse which I lent him. I said my prayers and had good health, good thoughts, and good humor, thank God Almighty.

31. I rose at 5 o'clock and read a chapter in Hebrew and some Greek in Anacreon. I said my prayers and ate milk for breakfast. The child had a fever still. I danced my dance. I read some Italian and wrote a letter. I ate hashed mutton for dinner. In the afternoon I played at billiards with my wife and was exceedingly griped in my belly. I ate as many cherries as I could get for it, but they did no good. I read more Italian, and in the evening took a walk to my cousin Harrison's, whom I found very melancholy. She told me she was much alone and little company came near her. When I returned I found the child a little better. I said my prayers and had good health, good thoughts, and good humor, thanks be to God Almighty. The weather of this month was generally cold, notwithstanding for about a week of it, it was very hot. The wind was often east and northeast and northwest, which did much injury to the fruit trees and made the weather unseasonable and the people sickly.

---

[1]Son of Mrs. Mary Byrd. (See note for March 16, 1710.)

June, 1710

1. I rose at 6 o'clock and because I was not easy in my belly I took some [purge l-p of scurvy grass]. They worked but little. I read a chapter in Hebrew and some Greek in Anacreon. I said my prayers and drank some broth for breakfast. The child was a little better. Colonel Hill and Mr. Anderson called to see us on their way over the river. I wrote a letter to England. My purge worked but a little. I ate some boiled chicken for dinner. In the afternoon we played at billiards and then cut some [sage]. Then I set my closet in order. In the evening I took a walk and met the new negroes which Mr. Bland had bought for me to the number of 26 for £23 apiece. This evening the sloop likewise came from above where all was well. I said my prayers and had good health, good thoughts, and good humor, thanks be to God Almighty.

2. I rose at 6 o'clock and read a chapter in Hebrew and some Greek in Pindar. I said my prayers and ate bread and butter for breakfast. I sent away the sloop to Appomattox. The child was worse and his nurse was very ill. I gave her a vomit which worked very well. Colonel Eppes called here. I ate cold mutton for dinner. In the afternoon I read some English. About 5 o'clock Robin Hix and Robin Mumford came to discourse about the skin trade. We gave them some mutton and sallet for supper. In the evening I did not walk because of my company. Robin Hix asked me to pay £70 for two negroes which he intended to buy of John [Evans] which I agreed to in hope of gaining the trade. I neglected to say my prayers but was griped in my belly and had indifferent bad humor.

3. I rose at 6 o'clock and as soon as I came out news was brought that the child[1] was very ill. We went out and found him just ready to die and he died about 8 o'clock in the morning. God gives and God takes away; blessed be the

---

[1] His infant son Parke.

name of God. Mrs. Harrison and Mr. Anderson and his wife and some other company came to see us in our affliction. My wife was much afflicted but I submitted to His judgment better, notwithstanding I was very sensible of my loss, but God's will be done. Mr. Anderson and his wife with Mrs. B-k-r dined here. I ate roast mutton. In the afternoon I was griped in my belly very much but it grew better towards the night. In the afternoon it rained and was fair again in the evening. My poor wife and I walked in the garden. In the evening I neglected to say my prayers, had indifferent health, good thoughts, and good humor, thanks be to God Almighty.

4. I rose at 6 o'clock and read nothing because I took physic which did not work. I said my prayers and ate water gruel. I had no more than two stools but was a little griped. I was so indisposed that I could not settle to anything. My wife had several fits of tears for our dear son but kept within the bounds of submission. I ate hashed mutton for dinner. In the afternoon we walked a little abroad but it was so hot we soon returned. My dinner griped me again but not so much as it did. My man Tom returned from Williamsburg and brought me letters from Green Springs and Queen's Creek. Jimmy brought a coffin from Falling Creek made of walnut tree. In the evening we took a walk. I said my prayers and had good thoughts, good humor, and indifferent good health, thank God Almighty.

5. I rose at 6 o'clock and read a chapter in Hebrew and some Greek in Pindar. I said my prayers and ate water gruel for breakfast. Mrs. Ann B-k-r came to assist my wife. I gave John W-l-r-c a note to Colonel Digges for a negro. My gripes continued still, and made me uneasy. About 12 o'clock my brother Custis came without my sister who could not come because she was big with child. He could tell no news. I ate roast veal for breakfast [sic]. In the afternoon I was worse of my gripes. My wife continued very melancholy, notwithstanding I comforted her as well as I could. I took a glyster in the evening which worked a little. Then we walked in the garden. I said my prayers

and had good thoughts, good humor, but indifferent health, thank God Almighty.

6. I rose at 6 o'clock and read two chapters in Hebrew and no Greek because we prepared to receive company for the funeral. I said my prayers and ate cake and water gruel for breakfast. About 10 o'clock Colonel Hill, Mr. Anderson and his wife came. Half an hour after my sister Duke came without my brother who could not leave his business, and about 11 came my cousin Harrison with her son and daughter, Mr. C-s and Mr. Doyley. We gave them burnt claret and cake. About 2 o'clock we went with the corpse to the churchyard and as soon as the service was begun it rained very hard so that we were forced to leave the parson and go into the church porch but Mr. Anderson stayed till the service was finished. About 3 o'clock we went to dinner and I ate boiled beef for dinner. The company stayed till the evening and then went away. Mr. Custis and I took a walk about the plantation. Two of the new negroes were taken sick and I gave each of them a vomit which worked well. I said my prayers and had good health, good thoughts, and better health [*sic*], thank God Almighty.

7. I rose at 6 o'clock and read a chapter in Hebrew and some Greek in Pindar. My brother Custis went away before I was up. I said my prayers and ate cake for breakfast. I danced my dance. My gripes were better, thank God. I wrote a letter to England. My wife continued to be exceedingly afflicted for the loss of her child, notwithstanding I comforted her as well as I could. I ate calf's head for dinner. In the afternoon my gripes returned again and made me uneasy. I drank several strong things for them but they did no good. Robin Jones came from above where all was well, thank God. I took a walk in the evening and met Colonel Harrison and Nat Harrison going to my neighbor's. They told me that about eight weeks since our fleet was ready to sail with a Governor and that there was no sign of a peace. I took some [Lady Kent's] powders, which did me good. I said my prayers and had good

thoughts, good humor, but indifferent health, thank God Almighty.

8. I rose at 7 o'clock and read a chapter in Hebrew and some Greek in Pindar. It rained much in the night. I said my prayers and ate water gruel for breakfast. I wrote some letters to my quarters. Then I wrote a letter to England. I was a little better of the gripes, thank God. My wife continued disconsolate. The two new negroes that had been sick were well again. I ate roast veal for dinner. It rained all day. In the afternoon I wrote more letters to England. My gripes returned again in the afternoon but not so violently. In the evening the rain would not let me walk abroad and therefore I walked in the library. I said my prayers and had good thoughts, good humor, and indifferent good health, thank God Almighty.

9. I rose at 7 o'clock and read some Hebrew and some Greek in Pindar. Colonel Harrison and his son Nat came before I was up. I drank some canary and toast with them and settled accounts with the Colonel. They stayed about an hour and then went over the river. I said my prayers and danced my dance. I wrote a letter to England. My wife continued melancholy. I ate some beans and bacon for dinner. I was better of the gripes in my belly, thank God, though not free from it. I wrote more letters to England. In the afternoon my sister went to see Mrs. Harrison and my wife and I rode out about the pasture and when we returned I ate some cold veal with my wife. I said my prayers and had good health, good thoughts, and good humor, thank God Almighty.

10. I rose at 6 o'clock and read a chapter in Hebrew and some Greek in Pindar. I said my prayers and ate bread and butter for breakfast. Captain Posford called to tell me he should sail on Monday. My sloop came from Appomattox with tobacco. It rained much this day, and was very cold. I was better of the gripes, thank God. I wrote many letters for England. Just before dinner Mr. Bland came from Williamsburg and told us that Colonel Parke was

recalled from his Governorship. I ate minced veal for dinner. In afternoon I wrote more letters to England. In the evening Mr. C-s came and stayed till 9 o'clock and told me all was well at the next house. My belly was not quite well. I neglected to say my prayers but had good thoughts, good humor, and indifferent good health, thank God.

11. I rose at 7 o'clock and read two chapters in Hebrew and three chapters in the Greek Testament. I said my prayers and ate water gruel for breakfast. It continued to rain so that we could not go to church. My wife was still disconsolate. I was better, thank God. It rained almost all day. Colonel Hill sent his man to know if I had any service at Williamsburg. I ate roast veal for dinner. In the afternoon we took a little walk but the rain soon sent us home. I read a sermon of Tillotson's. In the evening we took a walk in the garden because the grass was wet. I wrote two letters for England. I said my prayers, had good health, good thoughts, and good humor, thank God Almighty.

12. I rose at 6 o'clock and Captain Posford called to take leave. I settled my business with him and the ship sailed away about 8 o'clock. I read a chapter in Hebrew and some Greek in Pindar. The sloop was unloaded. Several of the new [negroes] were sick and I ordered them a vomit, which worked very well. I said my prayers and ate water gruel for breakfast. I danced my dance. Captain John Eppes came over and dined with us. I ate roast shoat for dinner. John Eppes went away soon after dinner. In the afternoon I read some Italian. My wife was out of humor with me for [n-r-s m-n]. In the evening we took a walk about the plantation. I said my prayers and had good health, good thoughts, and good humor, thanks be to God Almighty.

13. I rose at 6 o'clock and read a chapter in Hebrew and some Greek in Pindar. I said my prayers and ate milk for breakfast. I read nothing because I was hindered by Frank Eppes who came to see me. I drew off some brandy that came from Madeira that was very good. Mr. Eppes came from Captain Stith's and therefore would not eat with us.

I ate boiled chicken for dinner. In the afternoon Frank discovered the reason of his visit, which was to borrow money to pay a protested bill of his for £20. Because I had a kindness for him I lent him £41 and in the evening he went away and I took a walk about the plantation. I neglected to say my prayers and had, good health, good thoughts, and good humor, thanks be to God Almighty.

14. I rose at 5 o'clock and read a chapter in Hebrew and some Greek in Thucydides. I said my prayers and ate milk for breakfast. I danced my dance. I read some Italian. My wife began to be comforted, thank God, and I lost my gripes. A poor woman brought her daughter over that was troubled with the vapors extremely. I let her know if her daughter would come and stay here for two months I would endeavor to cure her. I ate cold chicken for dinner. In the afternoon I read some physics. About 4 o'clock Dick Cocke came from Prince George court where he saw Captain [Goodwin] just come from Barbados loaded at £9 per ton. The weather grew very hot again. In the evening I took a walk about the plantation and when I returned I found Mr. C-s here. I encouraged him to pursue the law without being discouraged and he resolved he would. I said my prayers and had good health, good thoughts, and good humor, thanks be to God Almighty.

15. I rose at 5 o'clock and read a chapter in Hebrew and some Greek in Thucydides. I said my prayers and ate milk for breakfast. The weather was very hot. I wrote a letter to England. I ate some broiled pork for dinner. In the afternoon my gripes returned on me and continued till the evening with some violence. Hot things did it no good but in the evening I drank some warm milk from the cow which eased me immediately. It rained this afternoon very hard with a little wind and thunder. This hindered my walking anywhere but in the garden. I foretold by my cellar stinking that it would rain. I impute my gripes to cherry wine, or else pulling my coat off about noon. I said my prayers and had good thoughts, good humor, but indifferent good health, thank God Almighty.

16. I rose at 5 o'clock and drank some milk warm from the cow. I read a chapter in Hebrew and some Greek in Thucydides. I said my prayers and danced my dance. About 10 o'clock Captain Drury Stith and his wife came to make us a visit, notwithstanding it was very hot. I was glad to see them because I think them excellent people. We played at billiards till dinner. I ate boiled pork. In the afternoon we passed away the time pleasantly till about 6 o'clock and then they went home. In the evening I took a walk with my wife. We made a little cider of the G-n-t-n apples, which yielded but little juice. I was better of my gripes, thank God. I neglected to say my prayers but had good health, good thoughts, and good humor, thank God Almighty.

17. I rose at 5 o'clock and drank some milk hot from the cow. I read a chapter in Hebrew and some Greek in Thucydides. I said my prayers and danced my dance. About 8 o'clock Mr. Anderson came on his way over the river. He told me the quarrel was made up between Parson Slater and his vestry without coming to trial. He stayed about half an hour. Colonel Hill sent his man with a basket of apricots, of which my wife ate twelve immediately and I ate eight which however did not make my gripes return. I set my closet right. I ate tongue, and chicken for dinner. In the afternoon I caused L-s-n to be whipped for beating his wife and Jenny was whipped for being his whore. In the evening the sloop came from Appomattox with tobacco. I took a walk about the plantation. I said my prayers and drank some new milk from the cow. I had good health, good thoughts, and good humor, thanks be to God Almighty.

18. I rose at 5 o'clock and drank some new milk from the cow. I read a chapter in Hebrew and some Greek in Thucydides. I said my prayers. It was extremely hot. I read a sermon in Dr. Tillotson about angels. I wrote a letter to Williamsburg to send by my sloop which I sent for rum, wine, and sugar from thence and that this might come safely I resolved to send Bannister with the sloop. I ate chicken for dinner but very little because I had no appetite.

In the afternoon my wife told me a dream she had two nights. She thought she saw a scroll in the sky in form of a light cloud with writing on it. It ran extremely fast from west to east with great swiftness. The writing she could not read but there was a woman before her that told her there would be a great dearth because of want of rain and after that a pestilence for that the seasons were changed and time inverted. Mr. James Burwell and Charles Doyley came and in the evening I took a walk with them. Our nurse went away in the sloop. I said my prayers and had good health, good thoughts, and good humor, thanks be to God Almighty.

19. I rose at 5 o'clock and read a chapter in Hebrew and some Greek in Thucydides. I drank some warm milk from the cow. I said my prayers and danced my dance. About 10 o'clock came Isham Randolph and Mr. Finney to see us. They told me Colonel Randolph was very ill and very melancholy. We played at billiards till dinner. I ate fish for dinner. In the afternoon Mr. Stith came over with my cousin Berkeley, who all stayed here till the evening and then they all went away but Mr. Finney. In the evening we took a walk. Mr. Finney is a sensible man and good natured. He told me that Major Allen died on Thursday last. In our walk we met Mr. C-s who came home with us. I neglected to say my prayers but had good health, good thoughts, and good humor, thank God Almighty.

20. I rose at 5 o'clock and drank milk from the cow. I read a chapter in Hebrew and some Greek in Thucydides. I said my prayers and danced my dance. Mr. Finney returned home without any breakfast but I gave him some strong water. Colonel Hill sent us another present of apricots. I wrote a letter to England. I ate five apricots which put my belly out of order. I ate roast mutton for dinner. In the afternoon my belly was griped. I played with my wife at piquet and then I ordered the boat to carry us to my cousin Harrison's where we found my cousin Berkeley and Jimmy Burwell. I was out of order in my belly. About 8 o'clock we returned home where we found all well, thank

God. I said my prayers and had good health, good thoughts, and good humor, thanks be to God Almighty.

21. I rose at 5 o'clock and drank milk from the cow. I read a chapter in Hebrew and some Greek in Thucydides. I said my prayers and danced my dance. My wife was indisposed. I sent Tom to Appomattox to desire Mr. Mumford to go to the outcry of my uncle's estate. About five nights since I dreamed I saw a flaming star in the air at which I was much frightened and called some others to see it but when they came it disappeared. I fear this portends some judgment to this country or at least to myself. I ate roast mutton for dinner. In the afternoon I settled the closet. About 5 o'clock I received an express from Mr. Clayton that the Governor, Colonel Spotswood, with two men-of-war arrived last night at Kiquotan with several other ships. I sent word of this to Mrs. Harrison and then prepared to go to Williamsburg tomorrow. In the evening I took a walk about the plantation. I said my prayers and had good thoughts, good humor, and good health, thank God Almighty.

22. I rose at 6 o'clock because it rained in the morning which I thought would hinder my voyage. But when I was up I resolved to go. I ate milk for breakfast and about 8 o'clock got on my horse on the other side the creek. I neglected to say my prayers before I came out but afterwards I committed my family to God Almighty. About 12 o'clock I got to the ferry, where I heard the Governor was at Green Springs. Just before I came there I changed my clothes and about one o'clock arrived at Green Springs where I found abundance of company. I complimented the Governor who seemed to be a very good man and was very courteous to me and told me I had been recommended to him by several of my friends in England. I met likewise with Dr. Cocke,[1] my old school-fellow. The Governor brought with him a niece, a pretty woman. I ate boiled [. . .] for dinner. In the evening I danced a minuet. The

---

[1] Dr. William Cocke, frequently mentioned hereafter. On June 12, 1712, he was sworn in as Secretary of State for the colony of Virginia.

mosquitoes bit me extremely. I neglected to say my prayers but had good health, good thoughts, and good humor, thanks be to God Almighty.

23. I rose at 7 o'clock and got the Governor's man to shave me. I neglected to say my prayers because I was never alone. I read some of my letters, by which I found a sad account of tobacco and abundance of protested bills. I ate nothing but bread and butter and drank tea and milk for breakfast. About 10 o'clock we waited on the Governor to Williamsburg and he was met out of town by the President and abundance of people. From thence we went to town and then to Council where I found I was left out of the instructions; however after a dispute I was allowed to be sworn among the rest till further news from England, which nobody seemed to oppose but the President.[1] The Governor was [r-n-s-t] for my [seat]. The Governor made a courteous speech and told the Council that he was come with a full disposition to do the Queen and country service and hoped we should all concur with him in that good design. Then we went to dinner at C-t where the President treated us. I ate calf's head for dinner. In the afternoon we retired to the President's to drink the Queen's health, where I drank some French wine that did not agree with me but gave me the gripes. In the evening we returned to Green Springs with the Governor but I could not enjoy him because of my indisposition. However he always distinguished me with his courtesy. I took leave of the Governor this night, because I resolved to go early in the morning. I neglected to say my prayers but had good health, good thoughts, and good humor, thank God Almighty.

24. I rose at 3 o'clock and Major Harrison with me and away we went and got to the ferry at four o'clock and the Major and I parted a little after we got over. I proceeded, however, and got home about 8 o'clock in the morning, where I found all well except that a negro woman and seven cattle were gone away. I ate some milk and [m-l-y]

---

[1]See *Ex. Jour.*, III, 247-8. The omission was an error, which was later rectified.

for breakfast. Then I read my letters and was much concerned to find no sign of any goods from Williamsburg. I ate hashed mutton for dinner. In the afternoon Mr. Mumford came and gave me an account of the outcry. My sloop came from Williamsburg with the wine and rum and she was unloaded in the evening, when Mr. C-s came over and gave me an account of the rencounter with Charles Doyley. We took a walk and drank some new milk. I neglected to say my prayers and was out of humor extremely and had indifferent health and thoughts, but God send me better if it please his good will.

25. I rose at 6 o'clock and found myself a little hot and therefore I took a vomit of infused ipecac, which worked but moderately. I neglected to say my prayers. I ate some toast and canary for breakfast. I could not go to church nor would my wife leave me but I sent several letters to people there. After church Will Randolph came over and told me his father was better. I ate poached eggs for dinner. In the afternoon I found myself a little better and then Will Randolph went away and my wife and I took a walk and met Mr. C-s who came home with us and told us of the unkindness of Mrs. Harrison. I was so tired with walking that I could not hold open my eyes. My people could not find the negro woman but found her hoe by the church land. I neglected to say my prayers but had indifferent health, humor, and thoughts; God send me better. This morning the hogshead of molasses looked above half out.

26. I rose about 6 o'clock and took a purge of [p-l c-ch] which worked very extremely. I neglected to say my prayers, for which God forgive me. I had eight stools and my fundament was swelled with a sharp humor and very sore. I drank some water gruel. They began to reap this day. I read a chapter in Hebrew. I ate some boiled chicken for dinner. In the afternoon I took a nap which refreshed me a little. The violence of the purge gave me the piles extremely which they say is the property of [a-l-s] which is the chief ingredient of [p-l c-ch]. Mr. Gee came to see me and

in the evening Mr. Bland came up in his shallop from Williamsburg and expected to find his cargo but I told him it was not come. I said a short prayer and had bad health, good thoughts, and indifferent good humor, thank God Almighty.

27. I lay in bed till 9 o'clock because of the piles, and read a chapter in Hebrew and some Greek in the Testament. I said my prayers and ate milk and [m-l-y] for breakfast. My wife anointed my fundament with tobacco oil and balsam of saltpeter mixed together. It was very much swelled and very painful so that I could not sit nor stand. I settled my closet. I ate hashed pork for dinner. In the afternoon I read some news. About 4 o'clock Mrs. Anderson, Colonel Hill, and Mr. Anderson came to see me and condoled my sore backside and advised me to use linseed oil made hot. As soon as they were gone I tried their medicine and soon after went to bed, but was in exceeding pain so that I was forced to take an opiate and could hardly sleep with that. I said a short prayer. Mr. Mumford came this evening. I had good thoughts, good humor, but indifferent health, thank God Almighty.

28. I lay abed till 10 o'clock and read some letters which Mr. Mumford brought me. Then I read some news. I said a short prayer and ate boiled milk and [m-l-y] for breakfast. My wife anointed my bum with hot linseed oil which had done it some good. However it was not easy yet. Captain Broadwater brought over my sister Brayne's two children[1] who were much below my expectation, being very ordinary. I thanked him for his kindness to the children. About 12 o'clock came Captain Burbydge[2] and Mr. J—, who both dined here. I ate fish for dinner. In the afternoon the company went away. I went to bed early and had my breech anointed. The negro woman was found again that they thought had drowned herself. I said a short

---

[1]William and Susan Brayne, the children of Byrd's sister Susan. William was sent to the College of William and Mary in 1712.

[2]Captain William Broadwater and Captain Richard Burbydge were both on a committee to inspect a damaged ship in the James River on August 14, 1710. (*Cal. S. P.,* p. 141.)

prayer and had good health, good thoughts, and good humor, thank God Almighty.

29. I did not rise till 10 o'clock because my bum was still sore. I read a chapter in Hebrew and some Greek in Thucydides. I said a short prayer and ate milk and [m-l-y] for breakfast. About 11 o'clock Captain Broadwater came over and offered to send and rescue my sloop in York River. Colonel Hill came about 12 o'clock and told me Mr. Anderson was sick. I ate boiled shoat for dinner. I offered to bring the Colonel's tobacco from York River. They stayed here till the evening when Mr. Bland and Mr. Mumford came over and we consulted about dividing the goods between them. I ate some broiled pork with them and sat up late. Mr. Bland told me Mrs. G-r-t had had a child at Williamsburg. I neglected to say my prayers and had indifferent good health, good thoughts, and good humor, thanks be to God Almighty.

30. I rose at 7 o'clock and read a chapter in Hebrew and some Greek in Thucydides. I neglected to say my prayers and ate milk for breakfast. Mr. Bland and Mr. Mumford settled their matters. I wrote a letter to Mr. Perry to desire him to send Mr. Bland's goods by the fall fleet. My bum was better, thank God, and I was well again. I ate roast mutton for dinner. In the afternoon the sloop came from Appomattox with tobacco and the other sloop from the ship with my goods and Mr. Bland and Mr. Mumford went aboard to part them between them and in the evening they made an end. I ate some bread and butter for supper. In the evening I said a short prayer and had good health, good thoughts, and good humor, thank God. I gave my wife a flourish. My cousin Betty Harrison was here this evening and told us Colonel Harrison was very ill of a fever.

July, 1710

1. I rose at 6 o'clock and read a chapter in Hebrew and some Greek in Thucydides. I said my prayers and ate milk for breakfast with Mr. Mumford. Soon after he went aboard my sloop with design to go up with the goods that were put into her. I read news. Mr. C-s came a little before dinner. I ate boiled mutton for dinner. In the afternoon Colonel Eppes came over from the courthouse. About 4 o'clock they both went away. I ate so many pears that I was a little griped in the evening. I read some news and then took a walk with my wife. It was exceedingly hot. The negro woman ran away again with the [bit] on her mouth. I said my prayers and had indifferent health, good thoughts, and good humor, thank God Almighty.

2. I rose at 6 o'clock and read two chapters in Hebrew and some Greek in Thucydides. I said my prayers and ate milk and [m-l-y] for breakfast. It was very hot. I read a sermon in Dr. Tillotson which affected me very much. I ate boiled mutton for dinner. In the afternoon Mr. Doyley and Ben Harrison came over and stayed almost all the afternoon. They told me that Colonel Harrison was better. In the evening I took a walk about the plantation. My bum was well recovered but I had a little gripes in my belly. The negro woman ran away again with the [bit] in her mouth and my people could not find her. I said my prayers and had good health, good thoughts, and good humor, thanks be to God Almighty. Captain Harvey[1] and Captain Burbydge came over in their boat this night.

3. I rose at 6 o'clock and read a chapter in Hebrew but had no time to read any Greek. I ate milk and apples for breakfast. About nine Captain Burbydge came with another master and after that Colonel Hill and Mr. Anderson with many others because it was court day. Some of us played at

---

[1] A Captain Harvey was commander of a merchant ship from Virginia, captured late in 1709 by French privateers and carried into France. (*Cal. S. P.*, p. 138.)

billiards. We had abundance of people dine with me and I ate some mutton hash as good as ever I ate in my life. We did not settle the freight. The company all went away in the evening, when my cousin Harrison came over to inquire if I would buy any goods, for which I thanked her and walked home with her, as did also my wife. We stayed there till 10 o'clock and then walked home where I said a short prayer and had good health, good thoughts, and good humor, thanks be to God Almighty.

4. I rose at 4 o'clock, and dressed me because I expected Colonel Hill and Captain Burbydge in his boat to carry us to Colonel Ludwell's bay, where I said a short prayer and then we went about 6 o'clock. We called aboard his ship and took some bread and cheese and wine in the boat and then went to breakfast. About 11 o'clock we called at Major Tooker's[1] where we stayed about half an hour and then proceeded to Major Harrison's, but neither he nor his lady were at home. However, we went in and had some victuals. About 5 o'clock Mrs. Harrison came home and we had just [time] to take leave of her and proceed to Green Springs, where we arrived as soon as it was dark. The Colonel was melancholy because his daughter was sick. I ate cold veal for supper. I recommended myself to heaven and had good health, good thoughts, and good humor, thank God Almighty.

5. I rose about 6 o'clock and read nothing but said a short prayer and got ready to go to Williamsburg, but it was necessary to eat milk for breakfast. About 9 o'clock we took leave of the Colonel and rode to town and when we came to Mr. Bland's he told us my chest of linen sent to his store had been plundered before it came to him. This was according to my whole fortune, which I must try to bear with patience till God shall please to better it. Then we waited on the Governor and drank coffee with him. Then the rest of the Council came and we went to Council, where the Governor's instructions were read, one of which was to suffer the people have the settlement of the habeas corpus

---

[1] Probably Major Henry Tooker, of Surry County.

act. Many things were debated and Major Harrison was appointed naval officer[1] and I and Colonel Hill were his securities. About 3 o'clock we dined with the Governor where everything was very polite and well served. I ate boiled beef for dinner. In the evening we took leave and returned to my lodgings. I said my prayers and had good health, good thoughts, and good humor, thank God Almighty.

6. I rose at 4 o'clock and settled some bills of exchange. Mr. Randolph came to introduce him to the Governor and recommend him to be clerk of the House of Burgesses, which I did in the best manner and the Governor promised him. Mr. Bland and Mr. Clayton also came to my chambers. When I went to wait on the Governor I found most of the Council there. Then I drank some coffee and ate bread and butter. Then we went to Council where we stayed till about 2 o'clock in the afternoon. Then we went to dine with the Governor where everything was extremely polite and I ate fish and then we took leave of the Governor and rode to Green Springs where we found Hannah Ludwell very ill and the family melancholy. We stayed about half an hour and then went in the boat to Major Harrison's where we arrived about 8 o'clock and the Major soon after. I ate some apple pie for supper and then said my prayers and had good health, good thoughts, and good humor, thanks be to God Almighty.

7. I rose about 6 o'clock and read some of the *Tatler*. I said my prayers and drank chocolate for breakfast. We had a long debate with the captains about freight and at last I generously offered them £10 per ton, which they received with negation but I believe must submit to it. We dined about 11 o'clock and I ate boiled mutton for dinner. About 2 o'clock the Major and I rode to Colonel Harrison's to make him a visit in his sickness and found him abroad in his store but very weak. I stayed there about two hours therefore and then rode home, where I found all well, thank God.

---

[1]Nathaniel Harrison, appointed naval officer of the Upper District of the James River in place of Major Arthur Allen, deceased. (*Ex. Jour.*, III, 249.)

My sloop was just come with tobacco. I drank some hot milk from the cow. I neglected to say my prayers but had good thoughts, good humor, and good health, thank God Almighty.

8. I rose at 6 o'clock and read a chapter in Hebrew and some Greek in Thucydides. I said my prayers and ate milk for breakfast. I settled several accounts. It rained gently all day. I sent away the sloop to Falling Creek. I was out of humor with Bannister and G-r-l for spoiling the curtains of the bed. I ate roast pork for dinner. Messrs. C-s and Chamberlayne dined with us. In the afternoon I unpacked several things in the afternoon [*sic*] and then gave my wife a flourish and then read in the *Tatler*. Two negroes of mine brought five of the cows that strayed away from hence and told me all was well above, but that Joe Wilkinson was very often absent from his business. It rained all the afternoon, that I could not walk. The negro woman was found and tied but ran away again in the night. I said my prayers but had good health, good thoughts, and indifferent good humor, thank God Almighty.

9. I rose at 5 o'clock and read two chapters in Hebrew and some Greek in Thucydides. I [said] my prayers and ate bread and butter for breakfast. I wrote three letters to the plantations. Captain Burbydge came over before church. About 11 o'clock we went to church and had a good sermon. After church I invited nobody home because I design to break that custom that my people may go to church. I ate boiled pork for dinner. In the afternoon my wife and I had a terrible quarrel about the things she had come in[1] but at length she submitted because she was in the wrong. For my part I kept my temper very well. In the evening Mr. C-s and I took a walk about the plantation and on our return Mr. M-r-s-l overtook us and told me all was well at Falling Creek. He told me that my two overseers above fought and that Joe Wilkinson was to blame for desiring Mr. G-r-l to bid for some things at the outcry and before anybody could bid above him Joe gave him the goods. Tom

---

[1] "Come in" was a common phrase referring to goods imported.

Turpin told him this was not fair, which made the quarrel between them. I said my prayers and had good health, good thoughts, and indifferent good humor, thank God Almighty.

10. I rose at 5 o'clock and read a chapter in Hebrew and a little Greek in Thucydides. I ate boiled milk for breakfast, but neglected to say my prayers. More goods came up from the ship. About 10 o'clock, Mr. Anderson and his wife came to help me and my wife work. About 12 o'clock Mrs. Betty Todd and Betty Harrison came and so did Colonel Eppes and the captain of the Plymouth ship. They all dined with us, and I ate pigeon for dinner. In the afternoon we went to work again and finished about 4. Then we talked till 6 when the company went away and we walked in the garden. I said my prayers and had good health, good thoughts, and good humor, thanks be to God Almighty.

11. I rose at 6 o'clock and read two chapters in Hebrew and a little Greek in Thucydides. I said my prayers and ate boiled milk for breakfast. Mr. C-s and I worked on the [b-t-r-k] almost all day. There came a workman with an account from Falling Creek of work, which I sent away with some passion because I had ordered G-r-l to employ no workmen. I ate roast pig for dinner. In the afternoon we went to work again till the evening, when Mr. Clayton, Dr. Cocke, and Mr. Bland came over. We took a walk together about the plantation and the Doctor seemed to be well pleased with the place. We gave them some supper but it was [late first] and I ate some roast veal with him. I neglected to say my prayers but had good health, good thoughts, and good humor, thanks be to God Almighty.

12. I rose at 5 o'clock and read a chapter in Hebrew and some Greek in Thucydides. I said a short prayer and had milk tea and bread and butter for breakfast. The Doctor, who is a man of learning, was pleased with the library. Mr. Clayton and Mr. Bland went to Prince George court, but the Doctor stayed here. About 10 o'clock Captain Broadwater came over about his freight but I could resolve noth-

ing but advised him to take the common freight. He went
likewise to court. I ate boiled beef for dinner. In the
afternoon Mr. Allen and Justice [Pigeon ?][1] came about a
protested bill of exchange but without success. Dr. Cocke
and I played at piquet and I won. In the evening Major
Harrison, John Bolling, and Captain Burbydge came over
and went away again in half an hour. We had a hash of
lamb for supper and drank a bottle of claret. I said my
prayers and had good health, good thoughts, and good
humor, thanks be to God Almighty.

13. I rose at 5 o'clock and read a chapter in Hebrew and
a little Greek in Thucydides. I said my prayers and ate
milk tea and bread and butter for breakfast. I danced my
dance. It rained almost the whole day; however it did not
hinder Mr. Clayton from going to Mrs. Harrison's and the
Doctor and me from going to Colonel Hill's. When we
came there nobody was at home but the ladies but about
2 o'clock the Colonel came home and we went to dinner and
I ate sheep's head and bacon for dinner. In the afternoon
we talked till about 6 o'clock and then we returned home,
where we found Mr. Blair and Mr. Bland. We drank a
bottle of wine and then retired to bed. I neglected to say
my prayers but had good health, good thoughts, and good
humor, thanks be to God Almighty.

14. I rose at 5 o'clock and read a chapter in Hebrew and
some Greek in Thucydides. I neglected to say my prayers
but ate bread and butter and milk tea for breakfast. Then
the gentlemen took their leave and I went with them to
Mrs. Harrison's where we ate again. Then they all went
away and I looked into the library and bought as many
books as cost £10. About 2 o'clock I returned home and
found Mr. Parker there. He came to pay me interest for
the money he owes me. About 4 o'clock he went away.
Billy Brayne and I had a quarrel because he would not learn
his books and I whipped him extremely. In the evening we
took a walk and I drank some milk warm from the cow. I

[1] Perhaps Richard Pigeon, who owned land in Prince George County in
1704. (*Va. Mag.*, XXVIII, 335.)

neglected to say my prayers but had good health, good thoughts, and indifferent good humor, thank God Almighty.

15. I rose at 5 o'clock and read two chapters in Hebrew and some Greek in Thucydides. I said my prayers and ate milk and pears for breakfast. About 7 o'clock the negro boy [or Betty] that ran away was brought home. My wife against my will caused little Jenny to be burned with a hot iron, for which I quarreled with her. It was so hot today that I did not intend to go to the launching of Colonel Hill's ship but about 9 o'clock the Colonel was so kind as to come and call us. My wife would not go at first but with much entreaty she at last consented. About 12 o'clock we went and found abundance of company at the ship and about one she was launched and went off very well, notwithstanding several had believed the contrary. When this was over we went to Mr. Platt's to dinner and I ate boiled beef. We stayed till about 5 o'clock and then returned home, where all was well. I found an express from above with a letter from Joe Wilkinson desiring to be discharged from my service when his year was out. I neglected to say my prayers and had good health, good thoughts, and good humor, thank God Almighty.

16. I rose at 5 o'clock and read a chapter in Hebrew and some Greek in Thucydides. I said my prayers and ate milk and pears for breakfast. Mr. G-r-l came last night after we went to bed. He told me all was well above. We did not quarrel this time. I sent my sloop to Appomattox for tobacco. I ate chicken for dinner. In the afternoon I took a nap for half an hour. I read some divinity. In the evening we took a walk about the plantation. It was exceedingly hot. I said my prayers and had good health, good thoughts, and good humor, thanks be to God Almighty.

17. I rose at 5 o'clock and read a chapter in Hebrew and some Greek in Thucydides. I said my prayers and ate milk and pears for breakfast. I settled my library till 11 o'clock and then Captain Burbydge came to see me but we could not settle the freight. He stayed to dinner. I ate neat's tongue

for dinner. My wife went this morning to Mrs. Harrison's and stayed all day because my cousin Todd was there. About 3 o'clock the Captain went to Mrs. Harrison's and I unpacked some goods till the evening and then we took a walk about the plantation and I went to Mrs. Harrison's to fetch my wife. There I drank some syllabub and stayed till about 10 o'clock. I neglected to say my prayers but had good health, good thoughts, and good humor, thanks be to God Almighty.

18. I rose at 5 o'clock and wrote a letter to the Governor to beg him to intercede with the men-of-war to let Colonel Hill's ship have men. I read a chapter in Hebrew and some Greek in Thucydides. I said my prayers and ate milk and pears for breakfast. I settled my cases in the library till about 11 o'clock when Major Chamberlayne came to see me, who is one of the biggest men in Virginia. I ate dry beef for dinner. In the afternoon I caused some of the goods to be unpacked. About 4 o'clock Isham Randolph came to see me. I gave him a letter to the Governor in his favor and sent a squirrel to Mrs. Russell.[1] In the evening Mr. C-s and I went into the river. Then I drank some warm milk. Several of my negroes were taken sick. I neglected to say my prayers and had good health, good thoughts, and good humor, thanks be to God Almighty.

19. I rose at 5 o'clock and read two chapters in Hebrew and some Greek in Thucydides. I said my prayers and ate milk and pears for breakfast. I danced my dance. Three of my people were sick of fever. I settled my library. My negro boy [or Betty] ran away again but was soon caught. I was angry with John G-r-l for losing the screw of the [bit]. I ate roast pork for dinner. In the afternoon I settled my library again. Then I wrote a letter to England. Then in the evening we took a walk about the plantation. Then Mr. C-s and I went into the river and afterwards

---

[1]Mrs. Katharine Russell, described as the niece of Governor Spotswood, presided over his household. That there was some gossip about her and Spotswood is evident from later entries, and from an allusion in one of Spotswood's letters. (Official Letters of Alexander Spotswood, II, 243.)

drank some syllabub. I neglected to say my prayers but had good health, good thoughts, and good humor, thanks be to God Almighty.

20. I rose at 5 o'clock and read two chapters in Hebrew and some Greek in Thucydides. I said my prayers and ate milk and pears for breakfast. I danced my dance. I spent almost all the morning in settling my books. About 12 o'clock John Blackman [came] for his money which I paid him to his content. I ate hashed 'pork for dinner. In the afternoon I settled my books again. Several of my negroes were sick. We [b-t] some cider. In the evening we took a walk about the plantation. I neglected to say my prayers but had good health, good thoughts, and good humor, thanks be to God Almighty.

21. I rose at 5 o'clock and read two chapters in Hebrew and some Greek in Thucydides. I said my prayers and ate milk and apples for breakfast. I danced my dance. I settled my books again till almost 12 o'clock. Then I wrote a letter to England. About eight nights ago I dreamed that several of my negroes lay sick on the floor and one Indian among the rest and now it came exactly to pass. I ate roast chicken for dinner. In the afternoon I settled my books again till the evening and then took a walk with Mr. C-s about the plantation. I drank some milk and water after I came out of the river where I had been to swim. I said my prayers and had good health, good thoughts, and good humor, thanks be to God Almighty.

22. I rose at 5 o'clock and read two chapters in Hebrew and some Greek in Thucydides. I said my prayers and ate milk and pears for breakfast. I danced my dance. The Indian continued very ill. I settled my books till about 12 o'clock, when Captain Burbydge came to see us. I gave him a bottle of cider. I ate lamb for dinner. In the afternoon while the Captain smoked his pipe I settled my books again and then came in again. About 6 o'clock he went away and I walked along with him to the Point. He and the rest of the masters agreed at last to go at £10 per ton. A negro

came from Falling Creek to tell me all was well. I said my prayers and had good health, good thoughts, and good humor, thank God Almighty.

23. I rose at 5 o'clock and read two chapters in Hebrew and some Greek in Thucydides. I said my prayers and ate milk and pears for breakfast. I wrote two letters to Falling Creek. About 11 o'clock we went to church and heard Mr. Anderson preach. We invited nobody home because we would not make our people work too much of a Sunday. I ate hashed lamb for dinner but my wife was indisposed and ate but little. In the afternoon I took a little nap and then read some Latin. In the evening I took a walk. The Indian was a little better. I neglected to say my prayers but had good health, good thoughts, and good humor, thanks be to God Almighty.

24. I rose at 5 o'clock and read two chapters in Hebrew and some Greek in Thucydides. I said my prayers and ate milk and pears for breakfast. I danced my dance. The sloop came with tobacco from Appomattox. The Indian was a little better, thank God. My wife was also better, notwithstanding the impression she had that she should die. I sent this morning 15 hogsheads of tobacco on board Captain Burbydge. I settled my books. I wrote a letter to England. I ate roast shoat for dinner. In the afternoon I settled my books again. In the evening I quarrelled with my wife for not taking care of the sick woman, which she took very ill of me and was out of humor over it. I scolded at S-k-f-r for losing his tide. Mr. C-s and I took a walk and could hardly persuade my wife to walk with us. I neglected to say my prayers and had good health, good thoughts, but indifferent good humor, thank God Almighty.

25. I rose at 5 o'clock and read a chapter in Hebrew and a little Greek in Thucydides. I wrote letters to my overseers above. I said no prayers this morning but ate milk and apples for breakfast. Then I went to the store and opened some things there. I sent 15 hogsheads more of tobacco on board Captain Burbydge. I ate dry beef for

dinner. In the afternoon my sloop returned and was loaded again with 15 hogsheads to send to Captain Bradby.[1] There happened a gust very violent but it did no damage. I settled my books again. In the evening Mr. C-s took a walk about the plantation. My wife was out of humor this evening for nothing, which I bore very well and was willing to be reconciled. I neglected to say my prayers but had good thoughts, good humor, and good health, thank God Almighty.

26. I rose at 7 o'clock and read two chapters in Hebrew and some Greek in Thucydides. It rained very much. I said my prayers and ate bread and butter for breakfast, which made me very [dull]. I settled my books in the library. The Indian was better, thank God, and so were all that were sick. I ate hashed pork for dinner. In the afternoon I settled my library again and read some Latin. In the evening my wife and I took a walk about the plantation and were good friends. Mr. C-s went to Mrs. Harrison's. I said my prayers and had good health, good thoughts, and good humor, thanks be to God Almighty. I gave my wife a flourish.

27. I rose at 5 o'clock and read a chapter in Hebrew and some Greek in Thucydides. I said my prayers and ate milk for breakfast. I danced my dance. Colonel Hill came this morning and stayed about an hour. Then came Colonel Randolph who was just recovered of a dangerous sickness. My sloop came from Sandy Point and I sent more tobacco on board Captain Bradby. I ate boiled pork for dinner. In the afternoon I received letters from Falling Creek, where all was well, thank God. Our maid Moll was taken sick and so was Tom, to both whom I gave vomits which worked very well. About 5 o'clock Colonel Randolph went away. Then I wrote several letters to my overseer above. In the evening Mr. C-s and I took a walk about the plantation. I neglected to say my prayers but had good health, good thoughts, and indifferent good humor, thank God Almighty.

---

[1]Captain Joseph Bradby was one of the shipmasters captured by the French in 1709. (*Cal. S. P.,* p. 138.)

28. I rose at 5 o'clock and read two chapters in Hebrew and some Greek in Thucydides. I said my prayers and ate milk for breakfast. I danced my dance. Moll continued sick but Tom was better. I wrote several letters to Barbados and sent Mr. C-s a present of bacon, cherries, and apples. Mr. Will Eppes came to see me but went away before dinner. I ate boiled mutton for dinner. In the afternoon my wife and I had a little quarrel because she moved my letters. Captain Burbydge came to see us and told me my great sloop was come round. I sent ten hogsheads more on board him. I walked with him some part of the way towards Mrs. Harrison's. When we came home my wife was pleased to be out of humor. I neglected to say my prayers but had good health, good thoughts, and good humor, thanks be to God Almighty. Ned Chamberlayne came over this evening.

29. I rose at 5 o'clock and read a chapter in Hebrew and a little Greek in Thucydides. I said my prayers and ate milk for breakfast. It rained this morning till 10 o'clock. I went to the store to put up some things to send to Williamsburg and gave John some rope for the press. About 1 o'clock Captain Broadwater came over in my sloop and dined with us. I ate some stewed pigeon. In the afternoon the Captain agreed to depart from his charter and take £10 per ton. I persuaded him to take my sloop with him and do some necessary things to her. I loaded my small sloop with 15 hogsheads for Captain Harvey. In the evening we took a walk about the plantation. I neglected to say my prayers but had good health, good thoughts, and good humor, thank God Almighty.

30. I rose at 5 o'clock and wrote a letter to Major Burwell about his boat which Captain Broadwater's people had brought round and sent Tom with it. I read two chapters in Hebrew and some Greek in Thucydides. I said my prayers and ate boiled milk for breakfast. I danced my dance. I read a sermon in Dr. Tillotson and then took a little [nap]. I ate fish for dinner. In the afternoon my wife and I had a little quarrel which I reconciled with a

flourish. Then she read a sermon in Dr. Tillotson to me. It is to be observed that the flourish was performed on the billiard table. I read a little Latin. In the evening we took a walk about the plantation. I neglected to say my prayers but had good health, good thoughts, and good humor, thanks be to God. This month there were many people sick of fever and pain in their heads; perhaps this might be caused by the cold weather which we had this month, which was indeed the coldest that ever was known in July in this country. Several of my people have been sick, but none died, thank God.

31. I rose at 5 o'clock and read two chapters in Hebrew and some Greek in Thucydides. I said my prayers and ate boiled milk for breakfast. I danced my dance. My daughter was taken sick of a fever this morning and I gave her a vomit which worked very well and brought away great curds out of her stomach and made her well again. My people were all well again, thank God. I went to the store and unpacked some things. About 12 o'clock Captain Burbydge and Captain Broadwater came over. The first went away to Colonel Randolph's; the other stayed to dine with us. I ate hashed mutton for dinner. In the afternoon Dick Randolph came from Williamsburg and brought me the bad news that much of my wine was run out. God's will be done. In the evening Mrs. Harrison and her daughter came over. However I took a little walk. I said a short prayer and had good health, good thoughts, and good humor, thanks be to God Almighty.

1. I rose at 5 o'clock and read two chapters in Hebrew and some Greek in Thucydides. I said my prayers and ate boiled milk for breakfast. I danced my dance. About 9 o'clock Colonel Hill called here but would not stay. The child was better, thank God. It grew very hot again. I wrote several letters to Williamsburg and then read some Italian. I ate some boiled mutton for dinner. In the afternoon I settled the library and then wrote more letters to the Eastern Shore. My daughter was taken sick again. About 5 o'clock there happened a gust [with] much rain and thunder. When that was over I took a walk to see the boatwright at work. I said a short prayer and had good health, good thoughts, and indifferent good humor, thank God Almighty.

2. I rose at 5 o'clock and read two chapters in Hebrew and some Greek in Thucydides. I said my prayers and ate boiled milk for breakfast. My daughter was worse this morning and my wife gave her another vomit of tartar emetic which worked much both up and down. She continued very ill all day and was not sensible. I wrote a letter and read some French. About 1 o'clock Ned Randolph came and Hal Randolph. The last stayed and dined with us, but the first went away immediately. I ate hashed mutton for dinner. In the afternoon Mr. C-s came home with his face swelled with a toothache. Colonel Eppes came and stayed about an hour. I read more French. In the evening three captains of the ships came and Mrs. Harrison to see the child, who had blisters put on. I ate some mutton with the captains. I said a short prayer and had good health, good thoughts, and good humor, thank God Almighty. My wife had a headache almost all day.

3. I rose at 5 o'clock and read a chapter in Hebrew and a little Greek in Thucydides. I said my prayers and ate milk and apples for breakfast. The child was better, thank

God Almighty, whose name be praised for ever. Two of the captains went to Mrs. Harrison's. I had much company come over. About 12 o'clock I went to court and after staying there about an hour I returned and brought several gentlemen with me to dinner. The child was very sick again. I ate calf's head for dinner. In the afternoon I sent for Mr. Stith to bleed my daughter. He came from court very readily and bled her. She continued very ill. In the evening I took a little walk. The boatwright was taken sick. I said a short prayer and had good health, good thoughts, and good humor, thanks be to God Almighty.

4. I rose at 5 o'clock and found my daughter very ill, so that I sent for Dr. Cocke. I read a chapter in Hebrew and a little Greek in Thucydides. I said my prayers but ate no breakfast, I was so concerned for my daughter. I read French but could not keep my mind steady. Mr. Anderson came to the next house and would not be so kind as to call to see the child. I ate some minced veal for dinner. In the afternoon I took a little [nap] and then read more French. I sent for Dr. Cocke, but a gust hindered him from coming and me from taking a walk. In the evening my daughter began to be better and had a sort of a looseness which abated her distemper. Mr C-s was better of his toothache. I said my prayers and had good health, good thoughts, and good humor, thanks be to God Almighty.

5. I rose at 5 o'clock and read two chapters in Hebrew and some Greek in Thucydides. I said my prayers and ate milk boiled for my breakfast. My child was better, thank God Almighty. About 10 o'clock the Doctor came but found the child in no danger. Dr. Bowman came to tell me that my negro boy which he had was too big for him to manage, and therefore desired me to send for him, which I did. The Doctor ordered the child oil of bitters drunk three times a day. About 10 o'clock Mr. Anderson and his wife and Mrs. Harrison came to see us. I scolded at Mr. Anderson for not coming to see the child, but I was satisfied with his excuse. All but my cousin Harrison stayed to dinner with us. I ate some roast veal. In the afternoon the

child continued without fever, thank God. Mr. Anderson and the Doctor were pleased with each other. In the evening the company went away and the Doctor and I took a walk. I neglected to say my prayers but had good health, good thoughts, and good humor, thank God Almighty.

6. I rose at 5 o'clock and read two chapters in Hebrew and some Greek in Thucydides. I said my prayers and ate boiled milk for breakfast. Mrs. John Stith sent my wife some grapes. The Doctor took part of them. The child was much better and [I] gave the Doctor four pieces of gold and desired him to accept of them. He went away about 9 o'clock. About 11 o'clock I went to church and heard a sermon from Mr. Anderson. After church Mr. Bland came home with me and so did Drury Stith to draw Mr. C-s' tooth. I ate roast veal for dinner. In the afternoon we ate some fruit and about 5 o'clock the company went away and Mr. C-s and I took a walk about the plantation. I said my prayers and had good health, good thoughts, and good humor, thanks be to God Almighty. I gave my wife a flourish on the couch in the library.

7. I rose at 5 o'clock and read three chapters in Hebrew and some Greek in Thucydides. I said my prayers and ate boiled milk for breakfast. I danced my dance. My sloop came from Williamsburg and without staying proceeded to Appomattox. The child slept but indifferently last night. However, she was something better. I wrote a letter to England and then read some French. I ate broiled pork for dinner. In the afternoon I settled my library and then read more French. About 6 o'clock there was very loud thunder but no rain here. However it hindered us from taking our evening walk. We drank some syllabub. I said a short prayer and had good health, good thoughts, and good humor, thank God Almighty.

8. I rose at 5 o'clock and read two chapters in Hebrew and some Greek in Thucydides. I said my prayers and ate boiled milk for breakfast. The child had rested very ill tonight and drank abundance of water. However she had

little fever and was hungry. Colonel Hill and Mr. Anderson called here on their way over the river. About 10 o'clock Captain Burbydge came with his boat and I went with him over the river to choose burgesses for Prince George. When we came there we found abundance of people met together and about 2 o'clock they chose Colonel Hardiman[1] and Robin Bolling. I stayed there till 5 o'clock and then went to Mrs. Harrison's where we found Major Burwell. We supped here and I ate fowl and bacon for supper. I stayed here till 9 o'clock and then went home where I found all well, thank God. I neglected to say my prayers but had good health, good thoughts, and good humor, thank God Almighty.

9. I rose at 5 o'clock and read two chapters in Hebrew and some Greek in Thucydides. I said my prayers and ate boiled milk for breakfast. I paid the builder of my sloop £60 which was £10 more than I agreed for. I settled my public accounts. My daughter was better, thank God, but was a little bloated. I was very much out of humor for nothing by reason of the weather or my constitution. I ate boiled lamb for dinner. In the afternoon I read some French. Mr. Salle came and told me that my coaler had the ague and that my shoemaker was sick at his own house. I drank some syllabub and after that ate some beef with him for supper. I said a short prayer and had good health, good thoughts, but indifferent humor, thank God Almighty.

10. I rose at 5 o'clock and read two chapters in Hebrew and some Greek in Thucydides. I said my prayers and ate boiled milk for breakfast. I danced my dance. About 10 o'clock my cousin Harrison, Major Burwell, and Captain Burbydge came over and soon after them Mr. [Gee] with a present of grapes. They came in the rain and were a little wet. My cousin's John brought home my negro G-l

---

[1]John Hardiman died before the opening of the second session and was succeeded in the House of Burgesses by Edward Goodrich. (*JHB*, 1702-1712, p. viii.)

[girl?]¹ that ran away three weeks ago. Mr. [Massot]² came and settled his accounts with me. I ate boiled beef for dinner. In the afternoon we walked about the garden and Major Burwell was very well pleased with everything. He and the rest of the company stayed till the evening when we walked in the garden. I said a short prayer and had good health, good thoughts, and good humor, thank God Almighty.

11. I rose at 5 o'clock and read two chapters in Hebrew and some Greek in Lucian. I said my prayers and ate boiled milk for breakfast. I danced my dance. I settled my accounts and then read some French. Then I settled my library till dinner. I ate fowl and bacon for dinner. In the afternoon I received a letter from Williamsburg which told me the Governor's family began to be sick, and Mrs. Russell was the first of them and was sick of a fever. I wrote an answer and sent it by Indian Peter and sent it immediately. Then I settled my library. It rained very hard for an hour, so that I was forced to walk in the library. I said my prayers and had good health, good thoughts, and good humor, thanks be to God Almighty.

12. I rose at 5 o'clock and read a chapter in Hebrew and some. Greek in Lucian. I said my prayers and ate boiled milk for breakfast. I danced my dance. I had a quarrel with my wife about her servants who did little work. I wrote a long and smart letter to Mr. Perry, wherein I found several faults with his management of the tobacco I sent him and with mistakes he had committed in my affairs. My sloop brought some tobacco from Appomattox. Mr. Bland came over and dined with us on his way to Williamsburg. I ate roast shoat for dinner. In the afternoon Mr. Bland went away and I wrote more letters. I put some tobacco into the sloop for Captain Harvey. It rained and hindered our walk; however we walked a little in the garden. I neg-

---

¹See entries for July 15 and 19, 1710.
²Later (Oct. 2, 1711) identified as "one of the French"—probably Massot, vestryman of Manakin Town.

lected to say my prayers but had good health, good thoughts, and good humor, thank God Almighty.

13. I felt a pain in my fundament which lasted half an hour in the night. I rose at 5 o'clock and read two chapters in Hebrew and six chapters in the Greek Testament. My sloop sailed away this morning. I ate abundance of peaches and figs before dinner. I read in a good book. I ate boiled beef for dinner. In the afternoon I took a nap, which disordered me. Then I read more in my good book. I ate abundance more fruit but drank some canary after it. About 6 o'clock we took a walk about the plantation. Henry brought me a letter from Falling Creek by which I learned that many of my folks were sick above, though without danger. I neglected to say my prayers but had good health, good thoughts, and good humor, thank God Almighty.

14. I rose at 5 o'clock and read a chapter in Hebrew and some Greek in Lucian. I said my prayers and ate boiled milk for breakfast. I danced my dance. I wrote a letter to England. Walter Scott[1] came to offer himself to be my overseer at Burkland but I could not give him any answer till I see Joe Wilkinson. The weather was hotter this day than it had been a good while. I ate some muskmelon before dinner and then I ate some hashed mutton. In the afternoon I settled my library. Then I read some Latin and afterwards wrote another letter to England. In the evening Mr. C-s and I took a walk about the plantation and ate a good many peaches. I said my prayers and had good health, good thoughts, good humor, thanks be to God Almighty. My sloop came from putting tobacco on board Captain Harvey.

15. I rose at 5 o'clock and read two chapters in Hebrew and some Greek in Lucian. I said my prayers and ate boiled milk for breakfast. I sent my flat with several goods to Appomattox. About 11 o'clock Mr. Drury Stith and his wife came to our house and not long after came Colonel Hill and Mr. Anderson with Mrs. Anderson, &c. About 12

---

[1] A landowner in Henrico County. (*Va. Mag.*, XXVIII, 215.)

o'clock we went to the courthouse where the freeholders were met to choose burgesses. After a great deal of persuading the choice fell on Colonel Eppes and Sam Harwood, notwithstanding Mr. Parker thought he should have carried it.[1] But Colonel Hill used his endeavors to make the people vote for Colonel Eppes and he had it by one vote. Nothing remarkable happened but that the disappointment gave Mr. Parker a fever. We did not dine till 4 o'clock and then had so much company that there was no pleasure. I ate stewed eggs. In the evening the company went away. I walked to the courthouse, where the people were most of them drunk and Mr. Doyley gave me some letters which he brought from Williamsburg, among which was one from Colonel Parke which told us he was going to England but was not put out of his government and though he was dismissed he should not be put out if he could justify himself from the accusation against him. I neglected to say my prayers but had good thoughts, good health, and good humor, thanks be to God Almighty.

16. I rose at 5 o'clock and read a chapter in Hebrew and some Greek in Lucian. I said my prayers and ate boiled milk for breakfast. I danced my dance. I wrote a letter to England and then sent Tom to Williamsburg with my letters about 12 o'clock. I ate bacon for dinner. In the afternoon Mr. Bland's boy brought me a letter from Barbados by which I learned that I had some goods from thence. I wrote him an answer immediately. I sent my people to fetch up the great sloop from Swinyards. In the evening Mistress Betty Harrison came over and I took a walk about the plantation and met Mr. C-s who had [been] at Mrs. Harrison's to settle accounts. I drank some syllabub. I neglected to say my prayers but had good health, good thoughts, and good humor, thanks be to God Almighty.

17. I rose at 5 o'clock and read two chapters in Hebrew and some Greek in Lucian. I said my prayers and ate

---

[1]On contest, Thomas Parker was declared elected in place of Littlebury Eppes. Parker died in November, however, and was succeeded in the House by Eppes. (*JHB*, 1702-1712, p. viii.)

boiled milk for breakfast. I danced my dance. I read some Latin and settled my closet. It was very hot. My great sloop came up about noon. I ate some lamb for dinner. In the afternoon I went on board my sloop and liked her very well. Then I caused my people to unrig the old sloop with design to burn her. Then I caused several things to be put on board the new sloop to send to Falling Creek. In the evening I took a walk about the plantation. Several people came from Falling Creek that told me Mr. G-r-l had the ague, and that Mr. M-r-s-l was likewise sick. I said my prayers and had good health, good thoughts, and good humor, thank God Almighty.

18. I rose at 5 o'clock and settled accounts with several people from Falling Creek. As soon as I had done with one, another came, so that I could read nothing this morning. About 9 o'clock Mr. Tom D-k came to renew some bills of exchange. Captain Randolph came over to get some iron and some rope. I said my prayers and ate boiled milk for breakfast. About 11 o'clock Colonel Hill came in order to go on board Captain Burbydge who sent his boat for us about 12 o'clock. My wife and child went with us, and Mr. C-s. When we came there we were equably treated and had a good dinner and I ate abundance of pease porridge. Mr. Platt and his wife and Mr. Cargill came to us; we stayed till 6 o'clock and then went away in the Captain's boat. He gave us nine guns at parting. We went to Mr. Cargill's, where we had some syllabub. It was terribly hot. I neglected to say my prayers but I had good thoughts, good health, and good humor, thank God Almighty.

19. I rose at 6 o'clock and read nothing. I ate some milk for breakfast. I neglected to say my prayers. We took a walk about the plantation. I ate two apples and some watermelon. We diverted ourselves till about 11 o'clock and then went to dinner. I ate fowl and bacon. In the afternoon Mr. Anderson came on his way to preach at [Weyanoke]. Colonel Hill came to us in the morning. About 1 o'clock we rode to Mr. Platt's, in whose field there was a race. There was Captain Burbydge and some other

company. Here was another dinner provided but I could eat nothing but a little lamb. About 5 o'clock we went home in our boat, which came for us about 4 o'clock and Colonel took a passage with us. We found all well but old Jane who had a fever. We went into the river. I neglected to say my prayers but had good health, good thoughts, and good humor, thank God Almighty.

20. I rose at 5 o'clock and read a chapter in Hebrew and some Greek in the Greek Testament. It was exceedingly hot. I said my prayers and ate boiled milk for breakfast. About 11 o'clock we went to church and had a good sermon from Mr. Anderson. Cope Doyley died yesterday morning at Mrs. Harrison's of an imposthume in his head. We had some watermelon in the churchyard and some cider to refresh the people. We asked nobody to go home with us, that our servants might have some leisure. I ate roast veal for dinner. In the afternoon I read in Grotius' *Truth of the Christian Religion*.[1] About 4 o'clock there happened a small gust with little rain. I heard Mr. Drury Stith was sick and I gave a man some Jesuit's bark. In the evening we took a walk but only in the garden for fear of the rain. I neglected to say my prayers but had good health, good thoughts, and good humor, thanks be to God Almighty.

21. I rose at 5 o'clock and rode to see Drury Stith who I found with a small fever and his wife and child with great colds. I ate some milk there and stayed about an hour and then returned home. Then I read a chapter in Hebrew and some Greek in Lucian. About 12 o'clock Harry Cary[2] came and Mrs. Sarah Taylor. They stayed to dinner and I ate some hashed veal. In the afternoon the company went away John Bannister fell down stairs and hurt himself this morning. The Indian Harry had a fever. About 4 o'clock there came a gust with much thunder and rain which hindered our walk this evening. I read in Grotius. In the evening I

---

[1] There were many editions in both Latin and English of Hugo Grotius' popular work.

[2] Henry Cary was overseer of the construction of several public buildings including the capitol and the Governor's house in Williamsburg. (See note under Dec. 7, 1711.)

neglected to say my prayers but had good thoughts, good humor, and good health, thank God Almighty.

22. I rose at 5 o'clock and read two chapters in Hebrew and some Greek in Lucian. I said my prayers and ate boiled milk for breakfast. John G-r-l was taken sick of a fever. About 9 o'clock Mrs. Harrison came to ask my advice concerning her overseer and those people who sold them drink. I offered my service to wait on her to her quarters which she accepted of. When we came there we saw the overseer and I threatened him severely so that he promised never to neglect his business more. Then we went to C-t Ch-r-n[1] and I threatened him likewise if he ever entertained any of Mrs. Harrison's people any more. He promised, very frightened, too, and then we returned home. I ate whole hominy for dinner. In the afternoon I settled some accounts and then read a little in Grotius. In the evening I had a severe quarrel with little Jenny and beat her too much for which I was sorry. I went into the river. I said a short prayer and had good health, good thoughts, and good humor, thanks be to God Almighty.

23. I rose at 5 o'clock and read two chapters in Hebrew and some Greek in Lucian. I said my prayers and ate boiled milk for breakfast. This morning I gave Harry another vomit and likewise G-r-l another which worked very well. About 9 o'clock Nurse came over from [below] and told us Colonel Hill's lady was dead. She plead innocence as to her having a child as was reported.[2] I translated some of Lucian. I ate boiled shoat for dinner. In the afternoon I translated more of Lucian and then read in Grotius. Nurse was for going away but I bade her stay. In the evening I took a walk about the plantation. I ate some cake and drank some milk and water. I neglected to say my prayers but had good health, good thoughts, and good humor, thank God Almighty.

---

[1]Possibly one of the Christian family of Charles City County.
[2]See entry for June 29. These references seem to indicate that "Nurse" was "Mrs. G-r-t," possibly the Mrs. Joanna Jarrett, at this time a widow, who had been housekeeper for Byrd's father and a witness of his will in 1704.

24. I rose at 5 o'clock and read two chapters in Hebrew and some Greek in Lucian. I said my prayers and ate boiled milk for breakfast. I danced my dance. I gave Suky Braynes a vomit which worked very well. The Indian boy Harry continued very ill of a fever. I settled some accounts and then translated some in Lucian. Then I read in Grotius. It was exceedingly hot. I ate some apple pudding for dinner. In the afternoon I put up some other pictures and went and translated more of Lucian. Then I read in Grotius again and some Latin. In the evening we took a walk about the plantation and called to Captain Burbydge as he went by in his boat, who stayed with us till 8 o'clock. I neglected to say my prayers but had good thoughts, good health, and good humor, thank God Almighty.

25. I rose at 5 o'clock and read two chapters in Hebrew and some Greek in Lucian. I said my prayers and ate boiled milk for breakfast. I gave Suky Brayne a purge. Indian Harry continued ill and so did John G-r-l. I went to the store about 10 o'clock with Bannister and was angry with him for letting the tar run out. We unpacked several things. I read some Latin. Captain Llewellyn came over but would not dine with us. I ate some dried beef. In the afternoon the Captain went away and I received a letter from Colonel Hunter. Mrs. Harrison sent to desire me to go see her in the evening, which I did and found her indisposed in her side. Her business was to speak with me concerning some iron which she had come in. I wrote a letter for her to George Walker about it. I drank some syllabub and about 9 o'clock returned home. I neglected to say my prayers and had good health, good thoughts, and good humor, thank God Almighty.

26. I rose at 5 o'clock and read two chapters in Hebrew and some Greek in Lucian. I said my prayers and ate boiled milk for breakfast. The sick people continued so and the Indian was very ill. It was exceedingly hot again. I settled some accounts. About 11 o'clock Captain Burbydge came and stayed here to dinner. I ate some hashed pork. In the afternoon he stayed here so that I could do nothing. In the

evening I took a walk about the plantation. My people made an end of shelling the corn. G-s-p-r came from Falling Creek and told me all was well, thank God. I said my prayers and then we walked by moonlight for almost an hour. I had good health, good thoughts, and good humor, thank God Almighty.

27. I rose at 5 o'clock and wrote letters to Falling Creek. Then I read two chapters in Hebrew and two chapters in the Greek Testament. I said my prayers and ate boiled milk for breakfast. The people continued sick and L-s-n was also sick, and took a purge. I danced my dance. I translated Solomon's Song. It was very hot again. I ate fish for dinner. In the afternoon Captain Burbydge came again and about 4 o'clock we went in his boat to see my cousin Harrison. On the way we took up Mr. Anderson, who [told] us Colonel Hill was very disconsolate for the loss of his wife. I drank some syllabub and returned in the boat about 9 o'clock. I said my prayers and had good health, good thoughts, and good humor, thank God Almighty.

28. I rose at 5 o'clock and read two chapters in Hebrew and some Greek in Lucian. I said my prayers and ate boiled milk for breakfast. I intended to go to Drury Stith's but the rain prevented me. I danced my dance. About 10 o'clock the rain left off and Mr. C-s and I rode to see Mr. Drury Stith. We found him much better than when I saw him last and all the family were well likewise. After we had been there about an hour Mr. Stith and I went to look for some flowers in the wood and found several, which I brought home. About 3 o'clock we went to dinner and I ate some chicken. We stayed till about 6 o'clock and then returned home where all was well, thank God, except the sick people, and they were better. I said my prayers and had good health, good thoughts, and good humor, thank God Almighty.

29. I rose at 5 o'clock and read two chapters in Hebrew and some Greek in Lucian. I said my prayers and ate milk for breakfast. The sick people were better, thank God. I danced my dance. I dreamed last night that the lightning

almost put out one of my eyes, that I won a tun full of money and might win more if I had ventured, that I was great with my Lord Marlborough. I settled my accounts and then translated out of Hebrew. I ate roast mutton for dinner. While we were at dinner Mr. Bland came and brought me some English letters, but without news of a peace. He stayed here till 5 o'clock and then went over the river. I read some news. In the evening I and my wife took a walk about the plantation. She hurt her hand [with a-c-f-r-t-s]. I said my prayers and had good health, good thoughts, and good humor, thank God Almighty.

30. I rose at 5 o'clock and read a chapter in Hebrew and some Greek in Lucian. I said my prayers and ate boiled milk for breakfast. The sick people were better, thank God, but not well. I settled my accounts till dinner and wrote a letter in answer to one from Mr. Anderson. I ate [b-l] for dinner. In the afternoon I settled my accounts again. Billy Brayne's face was much swelled but Mr. C-s beat him, for which I reproved Mr. C-s. About 5 o'clock I rode to Mrs. Harrison's to tell her what news I had. I ate some peaches and drank some wine there and about 7 o'clock returned home where all was well, thank God Almighty. In the evening I read some news. I said a short prayer and had good health, good thoughts, and good humor, thank God Almighty.

31. I rose at 5 o'clock and read two chapters in Hebrew, some Greek in Lucian. I said my prayers and ate milk for breakfast. I danced my dance. The sick people were better, thank God. Eugene was whipped for cheating in his work and so was little Jenny. About 11 o'clock I went to see Colonel Hill to condole him over the death of his wife, who died in England. I found him in great concern; however he came out to me and talked a little. Mr. Drury Stith came [there] likewise on the same errand. About 3 o'clock we went to dinner and.I ate boiled pork for dinner. I stayed there till about 6 o'clock and then rode home, where I found all well and the sick people better. In the evening I said my prayers and read some news. I had good health, good thoughts, and good humor, thanks be to God Almighty.

September, 1710

1. I rose at 5 o'clock and read a chapter in Hebrew and some Greek in Lucian. I said my prayers and ate boiled milk for breakfast. I danced my dance. My wife and I had a quarrel because she neglected to give the child the bitter drink. I settled some accounts. About 11 o'clock Captain Burbydge came and he and I played at billiards. I had a letter from Joe Wilkinson which told me he was sick. I ate roast pigeon for dinner. In the afternoon Captain Burbydge went away to my cousin Harrison's. Colonel Randolph and Captain Bolling were chosen burgesses for the upper county.[1] My wife and I took a long walk about the plantation. In the evening I read a sermon of Dr. Sacheverell,[2] and had good health, good thoughts, and good humor, thank God Almighty.

2. I rose at 5 o'clock and found it extremely cold. I read a chapter in Hebrew and some Greek in Lucian. I said my prayers and ate boiled milk for breakfast. I danced my dance. I settled some accounts and read some Latin. Several of my people were sick and Indian Ned among the rest. It was exceedingly cold. I ate fish for dinner. In the afternoon Mr. C-s came from above and brought me an English letter, and Colonel Eppes came and gave me two other English letters, but no news. I sent Captain Llewellyn a dose of physic. Colonel Eppes stayed about [an hour]. In the evening we took a walk and Jimmy from Falling Creek brought me word that Mr. G-r-l was very ill of the gripes. All the people were well. In the evening I read some English and had good health, good thoughts, and good humor, thank God Almighty.

---

[1] John Bolling and Colonel William Randolph, burgesses for Henrico County. Colonel Randolph died before the opening of the second session and was succeeded in the House by Francis Eppes. (*JHB*, 1702-1712, p. viii.)

[2] Dr. Henry Sacheverell, impeached in the House of Lords on March 20, 1710, for violent sermons attacking the religious tendencies of the Whigs. The sermons were printed, and in 1710 there appeared *The Answer of Henry Sacheverell, D. D. to the Articles of Impeachment.*

3. I rose at 5 o'clock and found the sloop here. It stayed so long because the master was arrested by Captain [W—]. I read a chapter in Hebrew and a chapter in the Greek Testament. About 11 o'clock Jimmy Burwell came over with my cousin Betty Harrison. A little after we went to church and heard Mr. Anderson preach a good sermon. When we came home we found the child sick, and our maid Anaka. I ate some roast veal for dinner. In the afternoon I read some divinity, and about 6 o'clock took a walk about the plantation. In the evening [I read] the speech of the Bishop of Sarum against Dr. Sacheverell.[1] I neglected to say my prayers but had good health, good thoughts, and good humor, thank God Almighty.

4. I rose at 5 o'clock and read a chapter in Hebrew and some Greek in Lucian. I said my prayers and ate boiled milk for breakfast. My daughter was a little better. About 10 o'clock Mr. Bland came and Captain Drury Stith and several other gentlemen, among the rest Parson Robinson who was charmed with my library. About one o'clock my cousin Harrison came and desired me to go with her to court, which I did and she there took letters of administration and was bound in £12,000 security. About 3 o'clock we came home and went to dinner and I ate calf's head. In the afternoon the company went away and my wife was taken with a violent colic which lasted till the evening. Mr. C-s and I took a little walk. My man Tom was taken with an ague. I neglected to say my prayers but had good health, good thoughts, and good humor, thank God Almighty.

5. I rose at 6 o'clock and read two chapters in Hebrew and some Greek in Lucian. I said my prayers and ate milk for breakfast. I danced my dance. My wife was still indisposed but not so much as to keep me from going to Falling Creek, because Mr. G-r-l was sick of the gripes and it was necessary to get my sloop dispatched. So about 11 o'clock I recommended my family to God Almighty and went to Falling Creek, where I arrived about 3 o'clock and found

_____

[1] Gilbert Burnet, *The Bishop of Salisbury His Speech in the House of Lords on the First Article of the Impeachment of Dr. Sacheverell* (1710).

Mr. G-r-l very bad of the gripes. I found things in an in-different condition. I went to the tannery, which is a very good one. I ate nothing but milk for supper, and soon after went to my chamber where I said my prayers and had good health, good thoughts, and good humor, thank God Al-mighty.

6. I rose at 6 o'clock and said a short prayer and ate boiled milk for breakfast. Mr. G-r-l continued ill. About 8 o'clock I rode to the Falls where things were in good order and there seemed to be abundance of tobacco and corn but the tobacco is injured by too much rain. About 10 o'clock I rode from hence to Kensington where things were well. From thence we went over the river to Burkland where I found Joe Wilkinson sick. However I scolded at him for neglecting his business. He excused all with the good crop which indeed he showed me everywhere. There I ate some potatoes and milk and then proceeded to [Byrd Park] where there was a very good crop. Then I went to Shockoe where there was a good crop likewise. I made [. . .] stay his year out and two months besides. From hence we went over the river to the Falls where I understood that my man Tom had an ague. I went by myself to Falling Creek where Mr. G-r-l continued bad. I ate some shoat and then recom-mended Mr. G-r-l to God Almighty and then went to bed. I neglected to say my prayers and had good health, good thoughts, and good humor, thank God.

7. I rose at 6 o'clock and settled accounts with several men. I ate milk for breakfast but neglected to say my prayers. Captain Webb came to see me. I had some words with him but at last by his fair speaking we parted friends. Mr. Laforce[1] came likewise but could not pay me the money he owes. Mr. G-r-l was still bad. I returned home about 9 o'clock and got to Colonel Hill's about 12, where I dined and ate boiled shoat for dinner. It rained all the afternoon. However I went home about 5 o'clock and found several of my family sick but without danger. I scolded at John for

---

[1] In 1711 Byrd sued René Laforce for £12 sterling due him on a bond. (Henrico Order Book, 1710-14, pp. 90, 98; see later entries in the diary.)

letting five of the cattle stray away. I prepared some physic for Mr. G-r-l. I neglected to say my prayers but had good health, good thoughts, and good humor, thank God Almighty.

8. I rose at 6 o'clock and dispatched the express to Falling Creek with physic. Mr. [Bridger] came to settle an account with me and went away about 8 o'clock. I read a chapter in Hebrew and some Greek in Lucian. I neglected to say my prayers and ate milk for breakfast. I danced my dance, and sent John to look for the cattle that had strayed away but he could not find them, nor could he find Indian Ned that was run away. I settled some accounts. My wife and I had a small quarrel. I ate hashed veal for dinner. In the afternoon I settled accounts with Hal Gee who came from above for that purpose. In the evening I took a walk about the plantation. Then I read some Latin. I said my prayers and had good health, good thoughts, but indifferent good humor, thank God Almighty.

9. I rose at 6 o'clock and read two chapters in Hebrew and some Greek in Lucian. I said my prayers and ate boiled milk for breakfast. I danced my dance. No news yet of Indian Ned. Several of my family were sick. I translated some of Lucian and settled some accounts. I ate veal for dinner. In the afternoon I translated more of Lucian. My daughter had her fever again. In the evening I took a walk about the plantation. I received a letter from above where all was well, thank God. I read some news. I neglected to say my prayers but had good health, good thoughts, and good humor, thank God Almighty.

10. I rose at 6 o'clock and wrote a letter to my overseers above. I read two chapters in Hebrew and five chapters in the Greek Testament. I said my prayers and ate boiled milk for breakfast. I gave physic to several of my people, which [worked] very well. I danced my dance. Then I read a sermon [in] Dr. Tillotson. I ate chicken pie for dinner. In the afternoon I took a flourish with my wife and then read a sermon in Tillotson. In the evening we took a

walk. Mr. C-s had the headache very badly but towards the evening was better. It was very hot again this day. I said a short prayer and had good health, good thoughts, and good humor, thank God Almighty.

11. I rose at 6 o'clock and read a chapter in Hebrew and some Greek in Lucian. Tom the tailor came to alter the sleeves of my coat. I said my prayers and ate boiled milk for breakfast. I danced my dance. Dick C-k came to see if my wire wanted mending. It rained a little before dinner. I settled some accounts. The sick people were better, thank God. I ate boiled mutton for dinner and Captain Broadwater dined with us but went away presently. After dinner I settled my accounts again. My wife and I played at billiards. In the evening I took a walk and met T-r-y who brought home Indian Ned. My wife and I walked in the garden. In the evening I read some news. I neglected to say my prayers but had good health, good thoughts, and good humor, thank God Almighty.

12. I rose at 6 o'clock and read two chapters in Hebrew but no Greek. I said my prayers and ate boiled milk for breakfast. The weather threatened rain. However, it did not discourage me from going to Williamsburg. After I had settled my business I went over the creek and about 1 o'clock got to my brother Duke's where I found my sister but he was not at home. Here I met with Dr. Burbage.[1] We ate some bread and butter and about 3 o'clock went over the river. I just called at Colonel Duke's but did not light off my horse and got to Queen's Creek about 7 o'clock where I found my sister Custis but my brother was gone to the upper plantation. I ate some broiled shoat. My sister told me four of their negroes were run away. About 9 o'clock I went to bed, said a short prayer, and had good thoughts, good health, and good humor, thank God Almighty.

13. I rose at 6 o'clock and read in my commonplace book. I said my prayers and ate boiled milk for breakfast. I slept

---

[1] Dr. Robert Burbage, a physician of New Kent County.

very ill last night which was occasioned by eating so late.
About 9 o'clock I rode to town and after I had talked with
Mr. Bland and adjusted myself I went about 11 to wait on
the Governor. He received me very courteously. The Doctor was sick of an ague. Mr. Hyde, the governor of North
Carolina,[1] came likewise there and dined with us. He seems
to be a jolly, good-natured man but no valiant politician. I
ate several things for dinner. In the afternoon came Mr.
Blair and his wife and Mrs. Hyde,[2] who is a woman of
abundance of life. They all went away about 7 o'clock but
I stayed till 9 and played at piquet with the Governor.
Several of his family were sick. I neglected to say my
prayers but had good health, good thoughts, and good
humor, thank God Almighty.

14. I rose at 6 o'clock and read a chapter in Hebrew and
some Greek in Homer. I said my prayers and ate milk for
breakfast. Mr. Clayton came to see me and told me the
difficulty of getting bills renewed. Mr. Bland came likewise
to see me and we settled some accounts together. I sent to
know how the Doctor did and they sent me word that he
was very ill. About 12 o'clock I went to the Governor's.
We had much conversation till dinner. I ate roast mutton.
In the afternoon we drank two bottles of the best claret I
ever drank in the country. The Governor entertained with
the history of the war. I stayed till 6 o'clock and then
returned to my lodgings, where Mr. Bland came to see me
and stayed about an hour. Then I read in *Hudibras,* which
the Governor presented me with, about half an hour. Then
I said a short prayer and had good health, good thoughts,
and good humor, thank God Almighty.

15. I rose at 6 o'clock and read two chapters in Hebrew
and some Greek in Homer. I said my prayers and ate
boiled milk for breakfast. My brother Custis came to see
me and gave me a bill of exchange. About 10 o'clock I went
to wait on the Governor and found Mr. S-c-r-y there. Soon

---

[1]Edward Hyde, appointed deputy governor in 1709; governor in 1710.
For his career, see the *Dictionary of American Biography.*
[2]The Governor's wife. (See entry and note for July 27, 1711.)

after came several gentlemen of the Council. We drank chocolate and then went to the capitol to Council where among other things it was agreed that the ships should stay till the 15th of October. About 4 o'clock we went to dine with the Governor and I ate boiled beef for dinner. About 7 o'clock I took leave of the Governor and went to Mr. Bland's where I stayed about an hour, and then went home, where I said a short prayer and had good health, good thoughts, and good humor, thank God Almighty.

16. I rose at 6 o'clock and read a little Greek in Homer. Then I prepared to go out of town. I said my prayers and ate boiled milk for breakfast. I left some directions concerning my house with Mr. Bland and then took my leave of him and his wife and about 8 o'clock rode to Colonel Ludwell's where I ate some fricassee of chicken. About 11 o'clock I went towards home and by the way called on Mr. Gee where I stayed about an hour and then proceeded home where I arrived about 6 o'clock and found several of my family sick, and my daughter among them. I ate some milk and quince. Since I went Captain Lee,[1] one of the captains of the men-of-war, was here and brought me a letter from my cousin H-s. I said my prayers and had good health, good thoughts, and good humor, thank God Almighty.

17. I rose at 7 o'clock and read two chapters in Hebrew and some Greek in the Greek Testament. I ate boiled milk for breakfast, and said my prayers. It rained hard all the morning that nobody came to church. I read a sermon in Dr. Tillotson. About 11 o'clock came Captain Burbydge to inquire what news. I desired him to let his boat be ready to receive the Governor on Wednesday next. He stayed. At dinner I ate roast beef. In the afternoon my sloop came over. We walked and talked till the evening when we drank a syllabub and then he went away. In the evening I wrote letters to the officers of the militia to be ready against the

---

[1] Probably Captain Lee of the galley *Bedford*, who escorted Colonel Spotswood from Kiquotan to Jamestown on June 21. (See *Official Letters of Alexander Spotswood*, I, 1.)

Governor's coming. I neglected to say my prayers but had good health, good thoughts, and good humor, thank God Almighty.

18. I rose at 6 o'clock and read a chapter in Hebrew and some Greek in Lucian. I said my prayers and ate milk for breakfast. I danced my dance. I [took] some of the tobacco out of the sloop and put in other instead of it and then the sloop [. . .] on board Captain Randolph. About 11 o'clock Mrs. Hamlin came over. I sent John G-r-l with orders to Colonel Randolph and Colonel Eppes to summon the militia of the two counties for the Governor to review. I ate boiled beef for dinner. In the afternoon Mrs. Hamlin went away. We fired several pistols to teach my horse to stand fire. Captain Randolph came over to give notes for more tobacco for my sloop to fetch and went away in the evening again. I read some news. I neglected to say my prayers and had good health, good thoughts, and good humor, thank God Almighty.

19. I rose at 6 o'clock and read a chapter in Hebrew and some Greek in Lucian. I said my prayers and ate boiled milk for breakfast. I danced my dance. The house and ground was made clean to receive the Governor. We gave the child the bark which put away her fit. Several of the negroes were sick. I ate roast beef for dinner. In the afternoon I caused all the rut to be cut away that lay at the woodpile and the pasture to be made clean. I caused a hogshead of punch to be made for the people when they should come to muster. Joe Wilkinson sent us some strawberries and peaches by little Peter who told me all the people were well and that Joe Wilkinson carried all the cider away. In the evening I took a walk. I neglected to say my prayers but had good health, good thoughts, and good humor, thank God Almighty.

20. I rose at 6 o'clock and read nothing because I prepared for the Governor's coming in the evening. I neglected to say my prayers but ate milk for breakfast. I settled several things in my library. All the wood was removed

from the place where it used to lay to a better place. I sent John to kill some blue wing and he had good luck. I ate some boiled beef for dinner. In the afternoon all things were put into the best order because Captain Burbydge sent word that the Governor would be here at 4 o'clock but he did not come till 5. Captain Burbydge sent his boat for him and fired as he came up the river. I received at the landing with Mr. C-s and gave him three guns. Mr. Clayton and Mr. Robinson came with him. After he had drunk some wine he walked in the garden and into the library till it was dark. Then we went to supper and ate some blue wing. After supper we sat and talked till 9 o'clock. I neglected to say my prayers but had good health, good thoughts, and good humor, thank God Almighty.

21. I rose at 6 o'clock and read nothing but got ready to receive the company. About 8 o'clock the Governor came down. I offered him some of my [fine water]. Then we had milk tea and bread and butter for breakfast. The Governor was pleased with everything and very complaisant. About 10 o'clock Captain Stith came and soon after him Colonel Hill, Mr. Anderson, and several others of the militia officers. The Governor was extremely courteous to them. About 12 o'clock Mr. Clayton went to Mrs. Harrison's and then orders were given to bring all the men into the pasture to muster. Just as we got on our horses it began to rain hard; however, this did not discourage the Governor but away we rode to the men. It rained half an hour and the Governor mustered them all the while and he presented me to the people to be their colonel and commander-in-chief. About 3 o'clock we returned to the house and as many of the officers as could sit at the table stayed to dine with the Governor, and the rest went to take part of the hogshead in the churchyard. We had a good dinner, well served, with which the Governor seemed to be well pleased. I ate venison for dinner. In the evening all the company went away and we took a walk and found a comic freak of a man that was drunk that hung on the pales. Then we went home and played at piquet and I won the pool. About 9 the Governor

went to bed. I had good health, good thoughts, and good humor, thank God, but neglected to say my prayers.

22. I rose at 6 o'clock but read nothing. About 8 the Governor appeared and we had nothing but milk tea for breakfast, and bread and butter. I neglected to say my prayers. About 10 o'clock we got on our horses and rode towards Henrico to see the militia. Colonel Randolph with a troop met us at Pleasant's mill and conducted us to his plantation, where all the men were drawn up in good order. The Governor was pleased with them and exercised them for two or three hours together. He presented me likewise to them to be their commander-in-chief [who] received me with an huzzah. About 3 o'clock we went to Colonel Randolph's house and had a dinner and several of the officers dined with us and my hogshead of punch entertained all the people and made them drunk and fighting all the evening, but without much mischief. Some of the French came to wait on the Governor and Mr. Salle made him a speech. We sat up till 10 o'clock. I neglected to say my prayers but had good health, good thoughts, and good humor, thank God Almighty.

23. I rose about 7 o'clock but read nothing. About 8 the Governor appeared and several of the French came to wait on the Governor. He recommended to them, and particularly to Mr. Salle and to the parson, to live in peace and to be reconciled to one another. The parson [seemed] more difficult to be reconciled than anybody, which the Governor resented and told them if they put him to the trouble of hearing their disagreement he would never forgive them that were in fault. This frightened them into an agreement and they promised that they would forgive what was past and for the future live with kindness to one another. Mr. Anderson made them a speech to that purpose. We had breakfast about 10 o'clock and I ate blue wing. Then the French company was exercised and performed very well and the Governor made out of them a troop of dragoons with orders that Mr. Salle should command them as well as the foot. About 3 o'clock we went

from hence to Colonel Hill's where we supped and I ate roast beef. We sat up till 9 o'clock but I was sleepy before that. I neglected to say my prayers but had good health, good thoughts, and good humor, thank God Almighty.

24. I rose at 6 o'clock and shaved myself and said a short prayer. The Governor's horses got away but Colonel Hill sent men after them and got them again. We had chocolate for breakfast and about 10 o'clock rode home to my house, where we refreshed ourselves and then the Governor and I went to church in the coach and my wife was terribly out of humor because she could not go likewise. Mr. Anderson preached very well and pleased the Governor. After church I invited abundance of gentlemen home where we had a good dinner. My wife after much persuasion came to dinner with us. The company went away in the evening and the Governor and I took a walk on the river side. The Governor was very willing to favor the iron works. We sat up till 9 o'clock. I neglected to say my prayers but had good health, good thoughts, and good humor, thank God Almighty.

25. I rose at 6 o'clock but read nothing. The Governor appeared about 8 o'clock and we had milk tea and bread and butter for breakfast. About 10 the Governor went away and I waited on him to Captain Stith's where several gentlemen came. About 12 o'clock we dined and I ate nothing but beef. About 2 o'clock we went from hence and I conducted the Governor as far as [Bridgewater's] mill, and so did Colonel Hill. On our return we called at Mr. Gee's but he was not at home. From thence I returned home where I found Jenny very sick but bleeding and [m-th-y] pills made her better. In the evening I took a walk about the plantation. I read some news. About 8 o'clock we went to bed, where I gave my wife a flourish. I neglected to say my prayers but had good health, good thoughts, and good humor, thank God Almighty.

26. I rose about 6 o'clock and read a chapter in Hebrew and some Greek in Lucian. I said my prayers and ate boiled

milk for breakfast. I danced my dance, and then wrote a letter to New England to Colonel Dudley.[1] I settled some accounts. About 12 o'clock a man came to get some physic which I gave him. Then came the doctor of Captain Broadwater's ship, who is a sensible man. I asked him to stay to dinner. I ate some boiled beef. In the afternoon came Captain Burbydge to take his leave and I gave him a sheep and some corn. Mrs. Harrison came to settle accounts and Jimmy Burwell came with her. They stayed here about an hour. Then they went away and I took a walk about the plantation. In the evening I read a little English. I neglected to say my prayers but had good health, good thoughts, and good humor, thank God Almighty.

27. I rose about 6 o'clock and read three chapters in Hebrew and some Greek in Lucian. I said my prayers and ate boiled milk for breakfast. I danced my dance. About 9 o'clock Peter Hamlin came over who came lately from England in the ship "Betty." I lent him a horse to Colonel Hill's. About 11 o'clock came a man from above who told me all was well at Falling Creek. There came likewise the shipwright that came from England in the "Betty." I ate some boiled beef for dinner. In the afternoon I sent six hogsheads tobacco on board Captain Randolph. Mr. Mumford came over and told me all was well at Appomattox. We took a walk in the evening. I ate some boiled beef with him for supper. I neglected to say my prayers, but had good health, good thoughts, and good humor, thank God Almighty.

28. I rose at 6 o'clock and read a chapter in Hebrew and some Greek in Lucian. I said my prayers shortly and ate milk for breakfast. I settled some matters for Mr. Mumford. About 10 o'clock Mrs. Harrison came to go with us to Colonel Harrison's but I ate some fish first. About 12 o'clock we got over the river and then proceeded to Colonel Harrison's where we got about 3 o'clock and found the Colonel pretty well. About 4 we went to dinner and I ate

---

[1]Probably Joseph Dudley, Governor of Massachusetts, 1702-15.

some boiled beef. Then we sat and talked about several matters till 8 o'clock and then we went to bed. I neglected to say my prayers but had good health, good thoughts, and good humor, thank God Almighty.

29. I rose at 6 o'clock and read some Greek but nothing else. I shaved myself and about 8 o'clock I drank some chocolate. Then I went to the Colonel and he talked abundantly about the old affairs of Governor Nicholson, with whose successor he is already well pleased. Captain Harrison was gone to Gloucester but his lady was here. I presented my wife with some Indian goods to the value of 4 pounds 10 shillings. I ate some fricassee of chicken for dinner. In the afternoon we took our leave and returned home where we came about 6 o'clock and found all well, thank God. Then we had some blue wing for supper and Mrs. Harrison supped with us and then returned home. I neglected to say my prayers but had good health, good thoughts, and good humor, thank God Almighty.

30. I rose at 6 o'clock and read two chapters in Hebrew and some Greek in Lucian. I said my prayers and ate milk for breakfast. I danced my dance. I settled some accounts and then wrote a letter to England. I sent to Appomattox for some powder and shot by my boat. I ate fish for dinner. In the afternoon I wrote more letters to England till Mr. G-r-l came from Falling Creek and told me all was well there and that Jimmy was better and out of danger. I scolded at him for wasting the provisions but he justified himself pretty well. I discoursed with him about several matters there. In the evening we took a walk about the plantation. Billy Brayne was taken sick again this afternoon. I said a short prayer and had good thoughts, good health, and good humor, thank God Almighty.

October, 1710

1. I rose at 12 o'clock and read two chapters in Hebrew and five leaves in Lucian (Greek and French). About 3 I went to bed again and lay till 6. I said my prayers and ate potatoes for breakfast. I danced my dance, and wrote several letters to my overseers above. Then my wife and I fell out. Mr. G-r-l went away about 10 o'clock. About 11 we went to church where we found Nat Burwell and Mr. Cole.[1] I took the Sacrament and then invited Nat Burwell, Mr. Cole and several others home to dinner. I ate pigeon for dinner. In the afternoon the company went away and my wife and Mr. C-s and I took a walk about the plantation. I said a short prayer and had good health, good thoughts, and good humor, thank God Almighty.

2. I rose at 12 o'clock and read two chapters in Hebrew and five leaves in Lucian (Greek and French). About 3 I went to bed again and rose at 7. I said my prayers and ate milk for breakfast. I danced my dance. It rained almost the whole night and this whole morning till noon. I wrote several long letters to England. I ate hashed pork for dinner. In the afternoon I wrote more letters to England. It grew very cold. In the evening I took a walk about the plantation and then read some of the trial of Dr. Sacheverell. I said my prayers and had good health, good thoughts, and good humor, thank God Almighty.

3. I rose at 4 o'clock and read two chapters in Hebrew and some Greek in Lucian and also some French. Then I went to bed again and lay till 7 o'clock. I said my prayers and ate boiled milk for breakfast. I danced my dance. It was cold this morning. I wrote a letter for England. About 9 o'clock came Mr. Bland in his shallop to know [if] I had any business at Williamsburg. Then came Captain Bolling

---

[1]William Cole, son of William Cole, the Secretary of State of Virginia, and Martha (Lear) Cole, who married, secondly, Lewis Burwell. (*Wm. Q. (1)*, V, 178.)

with whom I accounted, and then Colonel Randolph and many more and I went to court with them. About 2 o'clock several gentlemen came home with me to dinner. I ate pork and peas. In the afternoon came Captain Broadwater with whom we all accounted and the poor Captain was arrested. About [. . .] o'clock they all went away. I neglected to say my prayers but had good health, good thoughts, and good humor, thank God Almighty.

4. I rose at 4 o'clock and read two chapters in Hebrew and some Greek in Lucian. Then I went to bed again and lay till 7 o'clock. I said my prayers and ate boiled milk for breakfast. I danced my dance. Mr. C-s came to me to complain of his bad fortune in getting any business and talked of going to England. My wife told me that she conceived this morning by the token that she voided some blood. I wrote several letters to England. About 10 o'clock Mrs. Harrison came and we settled the disagreement between her and Mr. C-s and she went away soon after. I ate hash of pork for dinner. In the afternoon I wrote more letters to England and in the evening took a walk about the plantation. Then I read a little and [n-t]. I neglected to say my prayers but had good health, good thoughts, and good humor, thank God Almighty.

5. I rose at 2 o'clock and read a chapter in Hebrew and six leaves in Lucian (Greek and French). I said my prayers and ate boiled milk for breakfast. I danced my dance. I wrote several letters to England. About 10 o'clock Drury Stith came over from the court martial, but I was so busy I could not go there. However I invited the commanders of the militia to dinner and they came accordingly. I ate boiled pork for dinner. Soon after dinner they went away and I went to write more letters to England. Then I went and took a walk about the plantation. I read a little in Dr. Sacheverell's trial. I said a short prayer and had good health, good thoughts, and good humor, thank God Almighty.

6. I rose at 12 o'clock and read two chapters in Hebrew, and Greek in Lucian, and also the French. I went to bed again about 2 and lay till almost [. . .]. I said my prayers and ate boiled milk for breakfast. I danced my dance. I wrote more letters to England till we went to dinner. I ate boiled beef for dinner. In the afternoon my wife and I played at billiards. Then came Frank Eppes to give me a bill of exchange and he told me that Joe Wilkinson was willing to stay with me. I wrote more letters to England and Frank went away. In the evening I took a walk about the plantation. I sent Drury Stith some Madeira brandy and he sent me some peach brandy. I sealed up my letters. I said my prayers and had good health, good thoughts, and good humor, thank God Almighty.

7. I rose at 3 o'clock and read two chapters in Hebrew and some of Lucian in Greek and French. About 5 I went to bed again and rose before 7. I said my prayers and ate boiled milk for breakfast. I danced my dance. Then I wrote letters to England and wrote my general accounts. I danced a second time with my wife. About 12 o'clock my sloop went down to the shipyards. I ate roast beef for dinner. In the afternoon came Joe Wilkinson who told me all things were well above. Then came Frank Eppes and stayed here about two hours. In the evening I took a walk about the plantation. Then I wrote more letters to England. I read a little in *Hudibras*. I neglected to say my prayers but had good health, good thoughts, and good humor, thank God Almighty.

8. I rose at 3 o'clock and read two chapters in Hebrew and five leaves in Lucian (Greek and French). About 5 I went to bed again and lay till 7. I said my prayers and ate boiled milk for breakfast. I whipped Sue Braynes for [sh-t] herself and Anaka for lying, and Prue for losing the [scroll]. I danced my dance. Then I wrote a letter to England till dinner. In the afternoon I wrote more letters to England and in the evening prepared all my things for my journey to Williamsburg. Then I took a walk about the plantation with my wife. At night I settled accounts

with Mr. C-s who [talks] of going to England with Captain Randolph. I neglected to say my prayers but had good health, good thoughts, and good humor, thank God Almighty.

9. I rose about 5 o'clock and got myself ready for my journey, and about 6 o'clock [I] recommended my wife and my family to God's protection, and after my people had set me over the creek, I got on horseback about 7 and proceeded to Williamsburg where I arrived about 12. About one I went to wait on the Governor, where I found Colonel Digges and several other gentlemen. My wife sent a present of blue wing which were kindly accepted. I ate some roast beef for dinner. In the afternoon we drank a bottle of claret and then we took leave of the Governor and went to the coffeehouse where after we had settled some accounts of the naval officers we played at cards till 11 o'clock. Then I went to my lodgings but my man was gone to bed and I was shut out. However I called him and beat him for it. I neglected to say my prayers but had good thoughts, good health, and good humor, thank God Almighty.

10. I rose about 6 o'clock and read nothing because I prepared my matters against the Council. I neglected to say my prayers but ate boiled milk for breakfast. I settled accounts with several people and then went to the Governor's where several of the Council were. Here I drank chocolate and then we all went to Council, where several matters were debated, and particularly we had the journal of the commissioners for settling the bounds between this colony and Carolina,[1] which made the business much in our favor. About 4 o'clock we went to dine with the Governor and I ate boiled beef and several other things. After dinner we went to cards and I won half a crown. About 9 o'clock we went home. I neglected to say my prayers but had good thoughts, good health, and good humor, thank God Almighty.

[1] See *Ex. Jour.*, III, 256-58. Seventeen years later Byrd commanded the party of Virginians on the joint commission to survey the boundary between Virginia and North Carolina.

11. I rose about 6 o'clock and read nothing because Colonel Digges came to settle accounts with me. I neglected to say my prayers but ate boiled milk for breakfast about 9 o'clock, and went to the Governor's where I drank tea with him and then settled accounts with him and gave him bills. About 11 I took my leave and Dr. Cocke and I rode to visit my sister Custis, whom we found very well but Mr. Custis was not at home. Here we stayed about two hours and then proceeded to Green Springs. Mrs. Ludwell was gone to Surry but the Colonel was there. In the evening I ate some boiled beef for supper and then the Doctor and I played at cards and I lost half a crown. About 10 o'clock we went to bed. I neglected to say my prayers but had good health, good thoughts, and good humor, thank God Almighty.

12. I rose at 7 o'clock but read nothing. I neglected to say my prayers but ate milk for breakfast. The Doctor and I played at piquet and I lost half a crown. About 10 o'clock we parted and I proceeded to Mr. J-k who entertained me very courteously. I dined here and ate fried chicken. Then went home but was taken in the rain before I got there. I found all well, thank God, and Mr. Dunn was there. My sloop was not discharged from Colonel Hill's sloop till this day, when she was loaded with shingles and sent to Williamsburg and Nurse went in her. Mr. Dunn and I had a great deal of talk till 9 o'clock and then we went to bed. I neglected to say my prayers but had good health, good thoughts, and good humor, thank God Almighty. After we were in bed my wife and I had a terrible quarrel about nothing, so that we both got out of bed and were above an hour before we could persuade one another to go to bed again.

13. I rose about 6 o'clock and read a chapter in Hebrew and a little Greek in Lucian. I said my prayers and ate boiled milk for breakfast. I danced my dance. Then I wrote a letter to England. About 10 o'clock Mr. Dunn went away and I advised him to reconcile the differences of his parish as much as possible. About 12 o'clock John

Woodson came to see me and complained he was not well. He stayed but would not dine with us. I ate roast pork. In the afternoon John Woodson went away and I wrote another letter to England. In the evening I took a walk about the plantation. At night I wrote another letter to England. I neglected to say my prayers but had good health, good thoughts, and good humor, thank God Almighty. Billy came from the Falls, where all was well, thank God.

14. I rose at 2 o'clock and read two chapters in Hebrew and four leaves in Greek and French Lucian. I went to bed again and lay till 7. I said my prayers and ate boiled milk for breakfast. I danced my dance. Then I wrote a letter to England and put up some seeds for the Bishop of London. About 11 o'clock my cousin Harrison came to see me and desired me to carry some letters for her to Williamsburg. I ate boiled pork for dinner. In the afternoon my cousin Harrison went away and I wrote more letters to England. In the evening I took a walk about the plantation and then wrote some warrants against the general court. I said my prayers and had good thoughts, good health, and good humor, thank God Almighty.

15. I rose at 3 o'clock and read two chapters in Hebrew and five leaves in Lucian (Greek and French). I went to bed again and rose about 7 o'clock. I said my prayers and ate [b-l] for breakfast. I danced my dance. I received a letter from Joe Wilkinson who told me all was well above. To this I wrote an answer. About 11 o'clock I went to church and heard a sermon of Mr. Anderson. Captain Isham Randolph and Colonel Eppes came to dinner with us. I ate boiled beef. About 3 o'clock they went away and in the evening Captain Randolph's boat came to fetch Mr. C-s and his things. I gave Mr. C-s a letter to the Bishop of London and took my leave of him. Then my wife and I took a walk about the plantation. About 8 o'clock Frank Eppes and

Billy Kennon[1] came. I said my prayers and had good health, good thoughts, and good humor, thank God Almighty.

16. I rose about 5 o'clock and ate milk for breakfast. I neglected to say my prayers. About 6 o'clock we were set over the creek and proceeded to Williamsburg, after I had recommended my wife and family to God's protection. About 12 we got to Williamsburg. There I ate some cakes and butter and then went to court where we were sworn again. Here we sat till 4 o'clock and then the Governor asked most of the Council to go to dinner and me among the rest. I ate blue wing for dinner. Then we drank a bottle of wine and about 8 o'clock we returned to our lodgings where I read a little in Greek. I said my prayers and had good health, good thoughts, and good humor, thank God Almighty. I sent away my horse by Tom to Colonel Ludwell's in order to return home in the morning.

17. I rose at 5 o'clock and read two chapters in Hebrew and some Greek in Lucian. I said my prayers and ate boiled milk for breakfast. About 8 o'clock Frank Eppes came to my lodgings and I went with him to the Governor to get him a commission to go to the mountains, which he readily gave him. Here I drank some milk tea. About 9 o'clock we went to court where we sat till 12 and then adjourned to see the horse race and I lost 35 shillings. About 4 o'clock we went to dinner at C-t, where I ate boiled beef for dinner. Then we took a little walk and after that had a meeting of the College and then Colonel Digges and I went to the Governor's, where we drank a bottle of claret and were merry till 10 o'clock. Then I returned to my lodgings where I said my prayers and had good health, good thoughts, and good humor, thank God Almighty.

18. I rose at 6 o'clock and read a chapter in Hebrew and some Greek in Lucian. I neglected to say my prayers but ate milk for breakfast. About 7 o'clock Robin Beverley

---

[1]Son of Richard Kennon (d. 1696), of Conjurer's Neck on the Appomattox. Justice of the peace in 1710. (*Wm. Q. (1)*, XIV, 132-33.)

came to my lodgings and stayed till 8. Then I went with the governors of the College to wait on the Governor to desire him to accept of our choosing him one of the governors, which he did with an assurance that he would do us all the service he could. Here we drank chocolate. Then I went home and settled some business till 11 o'clock and then went to court, where we stayed till 5 before we went to dinner. I ate boiled chicken and bacon. Then I returned to my lodgings, where I did a great deal of business. I said my prayers and had good health, good thoughts, and good humor, thank God Almighty.

19. I rose at 6 o'clock and read a chapter in Hebrew and some Greek in Homer. I said my prayers and ate boiled milk for breakfast. I settled accounts with several people. About 11 o'clock I went to court, it being the day appointed for trying the criminals. After we had stayed there about two hours we went into Council and then came down to court again, where we stayed till 4 o'clock and then adjourned. Then I went to dine at the Governor's, where I ate boiled beef for dinner. In the evening we played at cards and I lost 25 shillings. We played at basset.[1] About 11 o'clock I returned to my lodgings. I recommended to the Governor to get some men from the men-of-war for Colonel Hill's ship. I said my prayers and had good health, good thoughts, and good humor, thank God Almighty.

20. I rose at 6 o'clock and read a chapter in Hebrew and 100 verses in Homer. I said my prayers and ate boiled milk for breakfast. I wrote a letter to England. I settled accounts with several. About 10 o'clock I took leave of Captain Isham Randolph, who came to see me. Then I went to court and gave my judgment in several cases. About one o'clock I took some sage and snake-root. Then I returned into court again and there we sat till 3. Then I wrote a letter to my wife and after that went to dinner and ate roast beef for dinner. Then I went to the coffeehouse,

---

[1]"An obsolete game at cards, resembling faro, first played at Venice."
—*New English Dictionary.*

where I played at hazard[1] and lost £7 and returned home very peaceful. I said my prayers and had good health, good thoughts, and good humor, thank God Almighty.

21. I rose at 6 o'clock and read a chapter in Hebrew and 200 verses in Homer. I settled some accounts. Then I said my prayers and ate boiled milk for breakfast. About 10 I was sent for to Council and went accordingly. Here we were about an hour and then went to court, where we sat till 3. Then I went with the Governor to dinner and ate roast beef for dinner which had been basted with vinegar to make it tender and good. After dinner I went to make a visit to Mrs. Russell in her chamber and drank some tea with her. Then we went down and played at piquet and I lost 10 shillings. The Governor had a letter that the Commodore[2] was come from New York. About 9 o'clock I went home where I said my prayers and had good health, good thoughts, and good humor, thank God Almighty.

22. I rose at 5 o'clock and read a chapter in Hebrew and 200 verses in Homer. I wrote a letter to England. I neglected to say my prayers but ate milk for breakfast. Mr. Bland made me a visit. About 11 o'clock I went to church and heard Mr. Whately[3] preach a sermon. It was very cold this morning and rained much last night. I went with Colonel Harrison and Colonel Duke to Mr. Blair's to dinner. I ate boiled beef for dinner. Here I stayed till about 5 o'clock and then I walked from thence to Mr. Bland's where I stayed about an hour and then returned to my chambers where I wrote a letter to England. I said my prayers and had good health, good thoughts, and good humor, thank God Almighty.

23. I rose at 6 o'clock and read a chapter in Hebrew and 50 verses in Homer. I settled accounts with several. I said my prayers and ate boiled milk for breakfast. Mr. Bland

---

[1] A game at dice.
[2] Captain John Roberts, commodore of the Virginia fleet. (*Ex. Jour.*, III, 570; *Cal. S. P.*, p. 132.)
[3] The Reverend Solomon Whately, minister of Bruton Parish, 1702-10; Byrd refers to his funeral on November 19, 1710.

brought me some bills of exchange. About 9 o'clock I went
to wait on the Governor, where I found Colonel Custis. I
read my proposal about naval stores to the Governor and
he approved of it. Then we went to court. I sat a little
while and then returned to my lodgings and prepared my
public accounts and continued at them till 3 o'clock. Then
I went to C-t to dinner and ate boiled mutton for dinner.
Then Colonel Duke and I took a walk and then went to the
coffeehouse. There I stayed till 7 o'clock and went home
and wrote a letter to England. I said my prayers but I committed uncleanness, for which God forgive me. However I
had good health and good humor, thank God Almighty.

24. I rose at 5 o'clock and read a chapter in Hebrew and
250 verses in Homer. I neglected to say my prayers but
ate boiled milk for breakfast. I settled accounts with Mr.
Clayton and with some others. The Commodore came to
town last night. About 9 o'clock I went to Council where
the Governor read his speech to us and about 11 we went to
court and [sat] till one. Then I went home to write and
settle accounts with Colonel Digges. About 3 o'clock we
went to dinner and I ate boiled beef. Then I went to the
coffeehouse where I saw Captain Robinson[1] and a [lieuten-
ant] of the [marines]. I went with them to the Governor's
where we supped and played at cards till 10 o'clock. Then
I returned to my lodgings, where I said my prayers and had
good health, good thoughts, and good humor, thank God
Almighty.

25. I rose at 6 o'clock and read nothing because I wished
to finish my public accounts. I said my prayers and ate
boiled milk for breakfast. About 9 o'clock we went to
Council to consult about the writ of alias capias[2], and at
last we carried 7 to 5. Then we went to court where we sat
till 3. Then I went to dine at the Governor's where was

---

[1]Captain Tancred Robinson commanded the man-of-war *Deptford*, in
which Spotswood came to Virginia. (*Official Letters of Alexander Spotswood*,
I, 1.)
[2]There is no mention in Hening's *Statutes* or in any of the Assembly
records of this date concerning writs of *alias capias*. Possibly it was an error
on Byrd's part for *habeas corpus*, the benefits of which had just been extended
to the colonists by the Queen. (*JHB*, 1702-1712, p. 240.)

the Commodore and Mr. Hamilton[1] the postmaster general, and Captain Garlington.[2] I ate wild duck for dinner. Soon after dinner I waited on the Governor to the capitol where the House of Burgesses were met and chose Major Beverley for speaker, 21 against 16 who were for Mr. Holloway.[3] Then we went to the coffeehouse and about 8 o'clock I went to my lodgings to write. I neglected to say my prayers but had good health, good thoughts, and good humor, thank God Almighty.

26. I rose at 6 o'clock and read nothing because I wrote. I neglected to say my prayers but ate boiled milk for breakfast. About 8 o'clock I went to the Governor's where I found the Commodore ready to depart to Kiquotan. I let the Doctor have a bill of exchange for £10 for money. About 9 o'clock we went to court and from thence to Council where the Governor approved of the choice the House of Burgesses made of their speaker. Then he made a speech and delivered it with the best grace I ever saw anybody speak in my life.[4] They passed my accounts of 2 shillings a hogshead. Then we went to court, where we sat till 4 and then went to dinner. I ate boiled beef. Then I went to the coffeehouse and from thence home. I received a letter from the Falls where all was well, thank God, but Joe Wilkinson was gone off. I settled some accounts and said my prayers and had good health, good thoughts, and good humor, thank God Almighty.

27. I rose at 6 o'clock and read a chapter in Hebrew and 200 verses in Homer. I neglected to say my prayers and ate boiled milk for breakfast. I wrote letters to England and settled all my business. Mr. Bland came over this morning. About 10 o'clock I went to court, where we sat

---

[1] John Hamilton, agent for the posts on the continent of America. (*Journal of the Commissioners for Trade and Plantations*, 1708-1715, p. 439.)

[2] "Captain Garlington" is mentioned twice in the *Official Letters of Alexander Spotswood*, according to the Index, but the references were not found, nor has any other work consulted yielded any information as to this ship captain. A Garlington family lived in Northumberland County.

[3] Peter Beverley of Gloucester County; John Holloway of King and Queen County.

[4] For the Governor's speech, see *JHB*, 1702-1712, pp. 240-41.

till 4 o'clock; then we went to Council for half an hour. I
went to dine at the Governor's where I ate roast mutton for
dinner. After dinner we drank a bottle of wine and then
took our leave. I went to the coffeehouse where I found
several of the Council playing at dice and I played with
them and won 40 shillings. Then I went home, where I
wrote 2 letters to my overseers. I said my prayers and had
good health, good thoughts, and good humor, thank God
Almighty.

28. I rose at 6 o'clock and read two chapters in Hebrew
and some Greek in Homer. I neglected to say my prayers
but ate milk for breakfast. Several people came to my lodgings. About 10 o'clock I went to court, where we sat about
an hour and then adjourned because several of us were to
go to the christening of my sister Custis' child.[1] The Governor and I were godfathers, and Mrs. Ludwell was godmother. I went there in the President's coach and the Governor soon after. About 2 o'clock the ceremony was performed and about 3 we went to dinner and I ate roast beef.
I gave the midwife 10 shillings. About 6 o'clock I returned
on my brother Custis' horse and when I came home I found
Tom who told me all was well at home, thank God, and
brought me a letter from my wife and some fish for Mrs.
Russell. I wrote a letter to my wife. I said my prayers and
had good health, good thoughts, and good humor, thank
God Almighty.

29. I rose at 6 o'clock and sent away my man Tom home
with a letter to my wife. I read two chapters in Hebrew
and some Greek in Homer. I said my prayers and ate
boiled milk for breakfast. I went to church about 11 o'clock
and heard a sermon of Mr. Taylor. Then Colonel Duke
and I went to Mr. Commissary's to dinner and Mr. Hamilton the general postmaster with us. I ate roast mutton. I
had a great deal of wit this day, more than ordinary. My
cousin Harrison and her daughter were here. About 5
o'clock we took our leave and walked to the coffeehouse

[1]Daniel Parke, only son of John Custis, born October 15. His widow,
Martha Dandridge, married George Washington.

where I drank two dishes of tea. Here I sat till 8 o'clock and then returned to my chambers where I read some verses of the Commissary's making. I said my prayers and had good health, good thoughts, and good humor, thank God Almighty. I committed uncleanness this night, for which God forgive me.

30. I rose at 5 o'clock and read two chapters in Hebrew and 200 verses in Homer. I said my prayers and ate boiled milk for breakfast. I read some French. About 10 o'clock Mr. Bland came to see me. Soon after I went to court but when I found nobody there I went to my chamber in the capitol where I read some Latin. About 12 o'clock we went to court and determined two cases and then went to Council, where several petitions were read and some discourse had about the post. About 4 o'clock we went to dinner and I ate roast goose. I returned to my chambers and drew up a bill against the masters that abuse hogsheads of tobacco.[1] I read some French. Then I said my prayers and had good health, good thoughts, and good humor, thank God Almighty. The fleet was not sailed this morning. The weather grew very cold this evening.

31. I rose at 5 o'clock and read a chapter in Hebrew and 200 verses in Hebrew [sic]. I said my prayers and ate boiled milk for breakfast. I read French. I drew an attack against the masters that abuse tobacco hogsheads. About 9 o'clock Mr. Bland came to see me. Then we went to court, where we sat about two hours and then went to Council and then back again to the court, where we sat till 4 o'clock. Then we went to dinner and I ate turkey. Then Colonel Lewis and I walked to see the Governor's house[2] and then went to the President's where we played at cards and I lost 35 shillings. I wrote a letter to Colonel Hunter[3] which Mr. Hamilton undertook to carry to him. Then

---

[1] See *JHB* and *LJC* for November 9, 1710, ff.

[2] The finishing of a house for the governor was one of the projects in which Spotswood was especially interested.

[3] Governor of New York.

several of us went to the coffeehouse where we played at
hazard and I won 23 shillings.   I wrote a letter to my wife.
I did not come home till 11 o'clock; however, I said my
prayers and had good health, good thoughts, and good
humor, thank God Almighty.   The fleet is not yet sailed.

November, 1710

1. I rose at 7 o'clock and read a chapter in Hebrew and 100 verses in Homer. I said my prayers and ate boiled milk for breakfast. About 8 o'clock I went to see Mr. Hamilton at Marot's[1] and went with him to the Governor's where we ate bread and butter and drank tea. About 9 o'clock I came to court where we sat till 4 and Mr. W-r-t-n was reproved for speaking disrespectfully to Mr. Commissary and telling him that he expressed himself as well as another did in the pulpit. We went to Council for half an hour and then Colonel Carter and I dined at the Governor's. I ate mutton for dinner. Then we drank three bottles of French wine. It rained very hard so that we went home about 8 o'clock in the Governor's coach and Colonel Carter set Colonel Corbin[2] and me down at the coffeehouse where we made Colonel Digges treat us. I said my prayers and had good health, good thoughts, and good humor, thank God Almighty.

2. I rose at 6 o'clock and read a chapter in Hebrew and 300 verses in Homer. I said my prayers and ate boiled milk for breakfast. Will Randolph and Mr. Bland came to see me and the first told me of several proceedings of the House of Burgesses. About 10 o'clock I went to court where we sat till about 12 o'clock and then adjourned because Mr. Holloway's trial came on before the committee, who were of opinion that it was a void election.[3] About 4 o'clock we went to dinner, and I ate roast beef. Then I took a little walk with Colonel Duke and then came to the coffeehouse, where I sat till 8 o'clock and then returned to my lodgings. Soon after I went from the coffeehouse there happened a

---

[1]Jean Marot came to Virginia in 1700 and in 1704 was secretary to Byrd's father at Westover. In 1705 he opened an ordinary in Williamsburg.

[2]Gawin Corbin, naval officer of the Rappahannock River district.

[3]The election of William Bird (not the diarist) and John Holloway as burgesses from King and Queen County was contested and declared void. However, they continued to serve, and were later declared duly elected. (*JHB,* 1702-1712, pp. 256, 332. See *Va. Mag.,* V, 356.)

quarrel between Colonel Smith and Mr. Holloway, but Mr. Holloway seemed to be in the wrong. I wrote my judgment concerning the minister and parishioners of Charles Parish which had been referred to me. Colonel Hill came from Kiquotan and told us the fleet sailed this day and his ship among the rest. I neglected to say my prayers and had good health, good thoughts, and good humor, thank God Almighty.

3. I rose at 6 o'clock and read a chapter in Hebrew and then company came to me. Indian Peter brought me a letter from home [which] told me that my wife was not like to come down because my daughter was sick. About 9 o'clock I went to court and we sat till one o'clock and then adjourned because Mr. Holloway was called away to the House of Burgesses for his trial and the House judged it a void election. I dined with the Governor and ate fish for dinner. The Governor learned that I intended home to-morrow and so sent a fine [case] to my daughter which I was unwilling to accept but he would have me take it. About [. . .] o'clock we went to the coffeehouse where I stayed about an hour and then went home. I said my prayers and had good thoughts, good humor, and good health, thank God Almighty.

4. I rose at 7 o'clock but read nothing because I prepared to go home this day. I said my prayers and ate boiled milk for breakfast. About 8 o'clock I went to court where I sat till 11 o'clock and took horses, which I borrowed of Mr. Clayton and Mr. Jackson, and rode home, where I came about 5 o'clock. I found all my family well except my daughter, who had a little fever but was much better than she had been. I found Mrs. Hamlin there to see the child. I ate some wild duck for supper and then examined how everything stood. I was very weary and so went to bed about 8 o'clock. I neglected to say my prayers in form but had good health, good thoughts, and good humor, thank God Almighty. I gave my wife a flourish in which she had a great deal of pleasure.

5. I rose at 8 o'clock and read nothing because I walked about. I said a short prayer and had ate [sic] boiled milk for breakfast. My daughter did not sleep well last night but was, however, better than she was, thank God. I wrote two letters to my overseers. I settled some things with Mr. G-r-l, who told me all was well at Falling Creek. About 11 o'clock he and I took a walk to see a fine enclosure which Mrs. Harrison put about her husband's grave which cost abundance of money but will not last. Mrs. Hamlin stayed and dined with us and I ate boiled pork. In the afternoon Mrs. Hamlin went away and I took a long walk about the plantation and found all things in good order. In the evening my daughter was better, thank God. I said my prayers and had good thoughts, good humor, and good health, thank God Almighty.

6. I rose at 8 o'clock after I had given my wife a flourish. I read two chapters in Hebrew and some Greek in Lucian. I said my prayers and ate boiled milk for breakfast. I danced my dance. I cleaned my head and was shaved. I ate cold roast beef for dinner. In the afternoon the wind was northeast and in the evening it began to rain. I danced my dance again and said my prayers. I sent for the tailor to cut my coat shorter. At night my wife and I played at piquet and had a small quarrel about [our count]. We ate some pears and milk for supper. I wrote a letter to Mr. Will Eppes and sent him some [sage] to cure his looseness. I prepared for my journey to Williamsburg. I had good health, good thoughts, and good humor, thank God Almighty. The negro woman ran away again.

7. I rose at 7 o'clock and read two chapters in Hebrew and some Greek in Lucian. I said my prayers and ate boiled milk for breakfast. I danced my dance. I settled several accounts. It rained exceedingly all night and likewise all this morning. The wind was northwest. My daughter was much better, thank God Almighty. I ate some sheldrake for dinner. In the afternoon I walked to Mrs. Harrison's to see how her family did in her absence and found two of her women sick. Then I went to see my people work where

they were clearing a new corn field. In the evening I ate some milk for supper. The wind was northwest and cleared away all the rain. I said my prayers, and had good health, good thoughts, and good humor, thank God Almighty.

8. I rose at 6 o'clock and prepared for my journey to Williamsburg. About 7 o'clock I recommended my family to the divine protection and took leave of my wife and took horse about half an hour after. I ate some boiled milk. I met with nothing remarkable on the way but got to Williamsburg about 12. I sent some fish to the Governor and Mrs. Russell invited me to dinner. About 3 o'clock I went to the Governor's where I dined and ate fish. Here I stayed till about 8 and then went to the coffeehouse where I played at cards till about 9, when the Doctor and the President came. We drank out Colonel Digges' brandy and were merry till 12 o'clock. Then I went home to bed. I neglected to say my prayers but had good health, good thoughts, and good humor, thank God Almighty.

9. I rose at 7 o'clock and read a chapter in Hebrew and some Greek in Homer. I said my prayers and ate boiled milk for breakfast. Several gentlemen came to visit me and I settled some accounts with some of them. About 11 o'clock I went to the coffeehouse and from thence to the capitol. Then we went into Council. We continued there till 4 o'clock and then went to dinner. I ate chicken and bacon for dinner. After that Colonel Smith and I walked to see the Governor's house and visited Mr. Cary. In an hour we returned to the coffeehouse where we played at cards and I won [18] shillings. I ate some bread and butter for supper. The bill for settling the money passed the House of Burgesses this day.[1] I said my prayers and had good health, good thoughts, and good humor, thank God Almighty.

10. I rose at 7 o'clock and read two chapters in Hebrew and 250 verses in Homer. I neglected to say my prayers

---

[1] "The bill for settling and ascertaining the current rates of foreign coins in this dominion." (*JHB*, 1702-1712, p. 262.)

and ate boiled milk for breakfast. Major Harrison and Will Randolph came to see me. About 10 o'clock I went to see the Governor and drank tea with him and discoursed with him concerning several matters. About 12 o'clock we came to the capitol and went into the Council, where two bills were read of no consequence. Colonel Lewis was very drunk with drinking canary. About 4 o'clock we went to dinner and I ate boiled beef. Then we went to the coffeehouse where I lost 40 shillings at cards and dice. Mrs. Russell was indisposed again. I said my prayers and had good health, good thoughts, and good humor, thank God Almighty.

11. I rose at 6 o'clock and read two chapters in Hebrew and some Greek in Homer. I said my prayers and ate boiled milk for breakfast. Several people came over to see me. I settled some accounts which kept me so late that I could not go to the capitol. About 12 o'clock I went to the coffeehouse and found several gentlemen there that got me to cards till about 2 o'clock and then I went with Colonel Digges in his chaise with the Doctor and several others to Colonel Digges his house where we went to supper about 6 o'clock. I ate boiled beef. Then we played at cards and dice till 10 o'clock, and then drank a merry bottle of wine till about 11. When we went to bed it smelled so bad I could hardly endure it. I neglected to say my prayers but had good thoughts, good health, and good humor, thank God Almighty.

12. I rose at 8 o'clock and read nothing nor [did] I say my prayers but very shortly. I ate oysters for breakfast. About 10 o'clock we went in the chariot to church, but the Doctor was sent for to Captain Berkeley.[1] It rained a little till the evening. Mr. Taylor preached a short sermon but it was very good. We returned to Colonel Digges' to dinner. I ate boiled mutton for dinner. In the evening the Doctor came to us and told us Mr. Berkeley was better and that Mrs. Burwell was likewise very bad and also Colonel

---

[1] On November 4, 1710, Edmund Berkeley drew up his will, "being sick and weak of body," but he lived until 1718. (*Wm. Q. (1)*, VII, 84.)

Churchill. At night we played at cards in the belief that there was no hurt in it. We drank very little and about 10 o'clock went to bed. I neglected to say my prayers but had good thoughts, good humor, and good health, thank God Almighty.

13. I rose at 7 o'clock and said a short prayer. Then I took a little walk about the plantation. I ate toast and cider for breakfast. Colonel Digges sent for a white negro for us to see who except the color was featured like other negroes. She told us that in her country, which is called Aboh near Calabar,[1] there were many whites as well as blacks. We played at dice till about 12 o'clock and then we [went] to Williamsburg, but I was so dusted with dirt that I was forced to change my clothes. Yesterday Mr. Ingles had a child burnt to death by fire taking hold of its clothes.[2] We went to the capitol and stayed there about two hours and then I went and dined with the Governor where I ate roast mutton. I had a letter from home which told me all was well except a negro woman who ran away and was found dead. I said my prayers and had good thoughts, good health, and good humor, thank God Almighty.

14. I rose at 7 o'clock and read two chapters in Hebrew and a little Greek in Homer. I said my prayers and ate boiled milk for breakfast. Mr. Salle and several others were to see me this morning. We had news that Mr. Parker was dead and that Colonel Churchill was speechless. About 11 o'clock I went to the capitol and Mr. Jacquelin[3] sent me 24 oranges. We had several disputes in Council concerning the coin. The Governor on several occasions discovered a great inclination to hold the royal P[reroga-tive?]. About 4 o'clock we went to dinner and I ate boiled pork for dinner. In the evening I took a walk about the

---

[1]Aboh is a town about 80 miles from the sea on the Niger River. Calabar is the old name for the region now known as Nigeria. This interest in the white negro calls to mind Byrd's first contribution to the Royal Society, an article on an albino negro.
[2]Anne, daughter of Mungo Ingles, died November 12, 1710. (*Wm. Q. (1)*, XIII, 268.)
[3]Edward Jacquelin, sheriff of James City County.

town and then went to the coffeehouse and played at cards
and lost 30 shillings. About 11 o'clock I returned to my
lodgings where I said my prayers and had good health, good
thoughts, and good humor, thank God Almighty. I wrote
two letters to my wife.

15. I rose at 7 o'clock and read two chapters in Hebrew
and 200 verses in Homer. I said my prayers and ate boiled
milk for breakfast. Several people came to visit me, among
[them] the President. I went to court about 11 o'clock
where we had several bills read to us and particularly the
bill for settling the rate of money and we were all of
opinion to settle at 16 pennyweights to the crown. About 4
o'clock we went to dinner and I ate salt fish for dinner.
Then we went to the coffeehouse where I wrote a sham
letter to Dr. Cocke under the name of Mary F-x. Soon
after he came and the letter was delivered to him. Then
we played at cards and I lost 10 shillings. About 9 o'clock
I came home, where I said my prayers and had good health,
good thoughts, and good humor, thank God Almighty.

16. I rose at 7 o'clock and read a chapter in Hebrew
and 100 verses in Homer. I neglected to say my prayers
and ate boiled milk for breakfast. Several people came to
see me and Mr. Salle among the rest, who desired me to
look over the petition of the French to have their 5000
acres of land laid out, in which I assisted them.[1] Major
Harrison came to town and told us that Mr. Parker died
on Tuesday morning. About 9 o'clock I went to prepare
the bill about the money according to the amendment of the
Council. About 12 o'clock we went to Council. Colonel
Carter came to us and told us that Colonel Churchill was a
little better. About 4 o'clock we went to dinner, and I ate
boiled beef. Then I took a long walk without the town and
returned to the coffeehouse where I played at cards and lost
£3 to Colonel Smith. About 9 o'clock I went home where
I said my prayers and had good thoughts, good humor, and
good health, thank God Almighty.

---

[1] *Ex. Jour.*, III, 261-63.

17. I rose at 7 o'clock and read a chapter in Hebrew and 100 verses in Homer. I said a short prayer and ate rice milk for breakfast. About 10 o'clock I went to wait on the Governor and found several of the House of Burgesses there with a message to know what he would have done to the house for the Governor. I went with them to the Governor's house where he showed them all the conveniences he proposed. It rained this morning as it had done also in the night. About 1 o'clock I went to the capitol where we amended the bill concerning the tobacco hogsheads. We sat till about 4 and then I waited on the Governor to dinner. I ate fish for dinner. About 8 o'clock we went to the coffee-house where I played at cards and lost 40 shillings. Captain Smith and Captain Garlington came this night from Kiquotan. About 11 o'clock I returned to my lodgings where I said my prayers and had good health, good thoughts, and good humor, thank God Almighty.

18. I rose at 7 o'clock and read a chapter in Hebrew and 160 verses of Homer. I neglected to say my prayers and ate boiled milk for breakfast. Several people came to visit me this morning and Colonel Bassett among the rest. About 10 o'clock I went with him to the Governor's and on the way met the two captains of the men-of-war, Captain Smith and Captain Garlington. They told us there was a change in the ministry in England, that a fleet of three men-of-war and 50 merchant ships were expected about Christmas. [W—] we went to the Governor's, where we drank chocolate. About 12 o'clock we came to the capitol and sent the money bill and the hogshead bill to the House of Burgesses with amendments. About 4 o'clock we went to dinner and I ate goose. In the evening I went to see Colonel Duke, who was sick of a fever. Then we went to the coffeehouse where we stayed about two hours and then went home. I said my prayers and had good health, good thoughts, and good humor, thank God Almighty.

19. I rose at 7 o'clock and read two chapters in Hebrew and 100 verses in Homer. I neglected to say my prayers but ate rice milk for breakfast. Daniel came to shave me.

About 11 o'clock I walked to church but came there too soon. Colonel Carter and I went to see Colonel Duke and found him still with a fever with the addition of a looseness. Mr. Wallace preached this day but flattered the Governor and recommended the College which did not please at all. After church Colonel Harrison took Colonel Carter and me to dine at Mr. Blair's where I ate boiled beef for dinner. In the afternoon we walked to church again to hear Mr. Blair preach Mr. Whately's funeral sermon, which he performed very well. After this ceremony was over we walked to the coffeehouse, where we stayed the rest of the evening. About 11 o'clock I went home where I said my prayers and had good health, good thoughts, and good humor, thank God Almighty.

20. I rose at 7 o'clock and read a chapter in Hebrew and 150 verses in Homer. I said my prayers and ate boiled milk for breakfast. Mr. Mumford sent to me for the sheriff's place of Prince George for Peter Jones in the room of Will Eppes who died on the 16 of this month, but it was disposed of. About 11 o'clock I went to the Governor's but found nobody. I wrote a letter to Barbados which I gave to Captain Smith when he gets leave of the Governor to go there. I ate some toast and cider with Colonel Carter at Marot's. About 1 o'clock we went to the capitol where we did very little. About 4 o'clock we went to dinner and I ate boiled beef for dinner. In the evening I went to see Colonel Duke who was much better and there I found my brother Duke. Then I went to the coffeehouse and played at cards till 12 o'clock. I said my prayers and had good health, good thoughts, and good humor, thank God Almighty.

21. I rose at 7 o'clock and read a chapter in Hebrew and 100 verses in Homer. I said a short prayer and ate boiled milk for breakfast. About 8 o'clock I had some visitors and Mr. Blair brought his accounts for me to examine. About 10 o'clock I went to court where most of our time was taken up in these accounts so that we did little business in the upper house. In the House of Burgesses they threw out our

hogshead bill and also the bill for dividing our county.[1] Colonel Duke was better and rode out of town. About 4 o'clock we went to dinner and I ate roast goose. In the evening I took a walk and returned in an hour to the coffee-house where I played at cards and lost my money and went home about 9 o'clock and wrote some verses on the House of Burgesses. I neglected to say my prayers but had good thoughts, good humor, and good health, thank God Almighty.

22. I rose at 7 o'clock and read nothing because I wrote some verses and then was interrupted by Mr. Blair who plagued me again with his accounts. I neglected to say my prayers and ate boiled milk for breakfast. I went to court about 10 when we had more dispute about Mr. Harrison's accounts and Mr. Blair was in the right. We did very little business and about 4 went to dinner and ate roast beef. In the evening I walked for half an hour and then came to the coffeehouse and lost 40 shillings. About 9 I went home where I found my man from Westover with letters which told me my daughter and all the family was well, thank God, but only Harry the Indian boy died four days ago. I said my prayers and had good health, good thoughts, and good humor, thank God Almighty.

23. I rose at 7 o'clock and read nothing but wrote two letters home to send by my man Tom. I neglected to say my prayers because company came in on me but ate boiled milk for breakfast. Several gentlemen came to see me and about 10 I went to the coffeehouse and from thence to the capitol. When we had our instructions from the Council we went on the conference with the Burgesses concerning the money bill and used abundance of arguments with them but to no purpose, so that at last we parted and reported what we had done to the Council. About 4 o'clock Colonel Carter and I went to dine with the Governor and I ate wild fowl. One of the burgesses told us that the House had agreed to our amendment of the money bill. We drank two

---

[1] This was a plan for adding part of James City County to Charles City County. (*JHB*, 1702-1712, p. 273.)

bottles of claret and then went to the coffeehouse where I stayed about an hour and then went home where I said my prayers and had good health, good thoughts, and good humor, thank God Almighty.

24. I rose at 7 o'clock and read two chapters in Hebrew and 100 verses in Homer. I said my prayers and ate rice milk for breakfast. Several persons came to see me, among whom was Mr. Cary to satisfy me about his accounts. Then I went to court where we did some business. I directed a letter to Nat Burwell with a lampoon in it and threw it into the capitol and Mr. Simons[1] found it and gave it him, which put the House of Burgesses into a ferment,[2] but I discovered to nobody that I had a hand in it. I went to my chamber in the capitol and danced my dance. About 4 o'clock we went to dinner and I ate boiled pork. Then we went to the coffee-house where I played at cards and I lost my money but was diverted to see some of the burgesses so concerned at the lampoon. About 10 o'clock I went home where I said my prayers and had good thoughts, good health, and good humor, thank God Almighty. It rained this evening moderately.

25. I rose at 7 o'clock but read nothing because I wrote a poem. I said my prayers shortly and ate [b-l] for breakfast. It rained all night and almost all the morning. Colonel Lewis and Mr. Bland came to see me. About 11 o'clock I went to the capitol where we met and read a bill for the impositions[3] which the Governor thought fit to find fault with. It rained still and hindered us from going on our frolic. About 3 o'clock we went and dined with the Governor where I ate some beefsteak. In the evening we went to cards and were merry but I lost about a crown. About 10 o'clock I got home, where I said my prayers and had good thoughts, good health, and good humor, thank God Almighty.

---

[1]John Simons, burgess for Surry.
[2]The "ferment" in the House took the form of an order "that a scandalous paper lately found be privately kept by the clerk and that the author thereof, if discovered, be liable to the censure of this House." (*JHB*, 1702-1712, p. 280.)
[3]"Act for raising a duty on liquors and slaves." (*LJC*, I, 502.)

26. I rose at 7 o'clock and read two chapters in Hebrew and 140 verses in Hebrew [*sic*]. I said my prayers and ate rice milk for breakfast. It rained all night and this morning so as to hinder my going to church. I wrote several things till about two o'clock and then went to Marot's to dinner with the burgesses. I ate roast goose for dinner. In the afternoon we sat and drank a bottle of cider till about 5 o'clock and then adjourned to the coffeehouse. Before we had been there long, in came George Mason[1] very drunk and told me before all the company that it was I that wrote the lampoon and that Will Robinson dropped it. I put it off as well as I could but it was all in vain for he swore it. About 9 o'clock I went home and said my prayers and had good thoughts, good health, and good humor, thank God Almighty.

27. I rose at 7 o'clock and read two chapters in Hebrew and 100 verses in Homer. I neglected to say my prayers but ate boiled milk for breakfast. I wrote more verses against the burgesses. About 9 o'clock Colonel Randolph and Mr. Bland came to see me. About 10 o'clock I went to the coffeehouse where I found several of the Council and from thence went to the capitol where we read several taxes and the Governor sent them several messages which they did not like.[2] It rained again all day. Colonel Carter received the news of his family's sickness which obliged him to ask leave of the Governor to go home. About 4 o'clock five of the Council went to dine at the Governor's where I ate boiled beef. In the evening we went to cards and I won 10 shillings. We stayed till 10 o'clock and then the President's coach carried us to the coffeehouse where I stayed

---

[1]Burgess for Stafford County, grandfather of George Mason of Revolutionary War fame.

[2]A message from Spotswood likely to arouse the ire of Virginians was one urging the repeal of a high duty on negro slaves, a trade that Her Majesty was "graciously pleased to countenance." Spotswood pointed out that the Virginia law also made a distinction between Virginian and British owners, a thing reprehensible to Her Majesty. (*JHB* 1702-1712, p. 281.)

He rebuked them also for usurping Her Majesty's royal prerogative in dividing counties and parishes. (*Ibid.*)

about half an hour and then returned home, where I said my prayers and had good health, good thoughts, and good humor, thank God Almighty.

28. I rose at 7 o'clock and read nothing but some English because the head speaker and Colonel Randolph came to see me to discourse about the Governor's message. I said my prayers and ate boiled milk for breakfast. About 11 o'clock I went to the capitol where we dispatched some business. About 2 o'clock the Governor came to us and I endeavored to soften him concerning the passing of the land bill,[1] but in vain, for notwithstanding he be a gentleman that means well, yet he is too obstinate and [w-l f-t] his own sentiments. About 3 o'clock Colonel Digges and I dined with the Governor again and I ate fish for dinner. In the evening we drank a bottle of wine till 9 o'clock and then I went to the coffee-house where I stayed half an hour and then returned home, where I said my prayers and had good health, good thoughts, and good humor, thank God Almighty. The weather was good again this day. Colonel Churchill died this morning.

29. I rose at 7 o'clock and read a chapter in Hebrew and some Greek in Homer. I said my prayers and ate boiled milk for breakfast. About 9 o'clock John G-r-l came over and told me my wife was at Queen's Creek where she came last night. He told me all was well at home. I sent to borrow the Governor's coach to fetch her to Williamsburg and went in it myself about 1 o'clock. When I came there I had a sham reprimand for not meeting my wife last night. I caused her to make haste to the Governor's to dinner. We took our leave in half an hour and carried Mrs. Dunn with us to the Governor's who entertained us very handsomely. I ate roast venison for dinner. In the evening we played at cards and the Governor would lend us his coach next day to go to Major Burwell's. About 10 o'clock we took leave and I carried my wife to my lodgings and Mr.

---

[1] "An act for settling titles and bounds of lands and for preventing unlawful shooting and ranging thereupon"—legislation which Spotswood believed was the prerogative not of the Assembly but of the Queen. (*LJC*, I, 506.)

Dunn and his wife to Mr. Bland's. I neglected to say my prayers but had good health, good humor, and good thoughts, thank God Almighty. I gave my wife a flourish.

30. We rose at 7 o'clock and I read nothing and neglected to say my prayers. About 8 o'clock Mrs. Dunn came to us. I drank some mulled wine for breakfast. About 9 o'clock the Governor's coach and six horses came to my lodgings to carry us to Major Burwell's and we went soon after and got there about 11. We found the Major very sick and despaired of by Dr. Cocke. I ate some oysters there. There was a consultation between Dr. Blair and Dr. Cocke about him and they agreed on the method to treat him. We stayed here till 2 o'clock and before we came away Nat Burwell told us his wife was sick of the gripes. About 4 o'clock we got to the Governor's where we dined and I ate boiled goose and onions. In the evening we played at cards and my wife received very great charity from the Governor and Mrs. Russell. We stayed till 10 o'clock and were set home in the coach to our lodgings. I neglected to say my prayers and had good thoughts, good humor, and good health, thank God Almighty. Almost all this [month] was very fine weather and not cold considering the time of year.

December, 1710

1. I rose at 7 o'clock but read nothing because my wife hindered me. However I said my prayers and ate boiled milk for breakfast. Then I dressed me and went to the capitol where I danced my dance. My wife went with Mrs. Russell in the coach and four horses to Queen's Creek to visit my sister. I went into Council where we did a great deal of business till 4 o'clock and then I went home with the Governor to dinner. Mrs. Russell and my wife on their way to Queen's Creek called on Mrs. Blair who talked very strangely. They returned to the Governor's about 5 o'clock. I ate fish for dinner. Then we played at cards and were merry till 10 o'clock. The Governor was so courteous as to send us home in the coach and I gave the coachman 5 shillings. I neglected to say my prayers but had good health, good thoughts, and good humor, thank God Almighty.

2. Before I rose this morning I gave my wife a flourish and rose about 8 o'clock. I read nothing and neglected to say my prayers. My wife intended to proceed to Green Springs but the rain prevented her. We ate milk for breakfast. About 11 o'clock I went to the capitol where we dispatched several bills and the land bill among the rest. We [sat] till about 3 o'clock and then the Governor did me the honor to go to our lodgings to see my wife and I went with him in his coach. He stayed a little while there and invited the women to dinner. Mrs. Russell and Mrs. Dunn were with my wife. We dined at the Governor's and I ate boiled beef for dinner. We diverted ourselves with nothing but conversation till about 10 o'clock and the coach set my wife and Mrs. Dunn home and I walked home. I neglected to say my prayers and had good health, good thoughts, and good humor, thank God Almighty. It thundered in the evening.

3. We rose about 7 o'clock but I read nothing because the women hindered me. I neglected to say my prayers and

drank mulled wine for breakfast. About 11 o'clock Mrs. Russell came with the coach to visit my wife and to go with her to Green Springs, and with Mrs. Dunn. In half an hour I took my leave of my wife and I went to church where Mr. Blair preached on the subject of the world spirit. After church I went with my brother Custis home to dine with my sister and found her indisposed. I ate boiled pork for dinner. I stayed there till almost 5 o'clock and then rode to town and went to my lodgings, where I read a chapter in Hebrew and some Greek in Homer. The weather was very warm after the rain, and clear. I said my prayers and had good health, good thoughts, and good humor, thank God Almighty.

4. I rose at 7 o'clock and read two chapters in Hebrew and 150 verses in Homer. I neglected to say my prayers and ate boiled milk for breakfast. Several gentlemen came to see me at my lodgings. I desired Mr. Bland to give his vote for the Commissary to be minister of Bruton Parish and he promised he would and accordingly his vote carried it at night against the inclination of Mr. President. About 11 o'clock I went to the capitol and I learned by Colonel Ludwell that my wife stayed at Green Springs this day but I could not go there to her because I was ordered to draw an address to the Governor. About 4 o'clock we all went to dine at the Governor's, where Mrs. Russell was indisposed. I ate giblet pie. We stayed till about 8 o'clock and went to the coffeehouse where we played at cards and I won about £4. It was one o'clock before I got to bed. I neglected to say my prayers but had good health, good thoughts, and good humor, thank God Almighty.

5. I rose about 7 o'clock and read nothing because I was busy in drawing the address to the Governor. I said my prayers and ate boiled milk for breakfast. Several were to see me this morning and particularly Mr. Commissary to thank me for my good offices in procuring him this parish. Mr. Eppes came to see me and told me he had been at the mountains and found them easy to be passed in several places. About 11 o'clock I went to the capitol where we

stayed till 4 o'clock and my address was read and approved by the Council. We read the Book of Claims and then went to dinner at C-t where I ate boiled mutton. Then we went to the coffeehouse where we played at cards and I won 20 shillings. About 10 o'clock I returned home. I had good health, good thoughts, and good humor, thank God Almighty. It rained hard for about two hours in the middle of the day.

6. I rose about 7 o'clock and read a chapter in Hebrew but no Greek because I was hindered by Mr. Eppes who came to give me an account of his journey to the mountains. I ate boiled milk for breakfast but neglected to say my prayers. About 9 o'clock I went with Mr. Eppes to the Governor's and drank chocolate. We stayed there till 10 and then I went to the capitol, where we did a great deal of business till about 4 o'clock, and then I and the Commissary went and dined with the Governor where I ate fish for dinner. We drank a bottle after dinner till about 8 o'clock and then went to the coffeehouse where I stayed talking till about 10 with several gentlemen and Mr. Burwell among the rest, who told me that his wife and father were better. I said my prayers and had good thoughts, good humor, and good health, thank God Almighty.

7. I rose about 7 o'clock and read a chapter in Hebrew but no Greek because Mr. Eppes came and hindered me. I neglected to say my prayers but ate boiled milk for breakfast. About 10 o'clock I went to see Mr. Holloway and to settle accounts with him but was much disturbed to find how much he had charged me for fees. From thence I went to the capitol where I danced my dance and read some Latin. We settled the commissions of the peace and finished about 4 o'clock. Then we went to dinner at C-t where I ate roast beef for dinner. Then we took a walk about the town till it was dark, and then I went to my lodgings, where I read some Greek in Homèr and some English till 9 o'clock. I said my prayers and had good health, good thoughts, and good humor, thank God Almighty.

8. I rose at 7 o'clock and read two chapters in Hebrew and 50 verses in Homer. I said my prayers and ate boiled milk for breakfast. Mr. Eppes was with me again. About 10 o'clock I went to the capitol where I wrote a letter to my wife. Then I went up stairs and danced my dance. I caused a lampoon to be directed to Colonel Smith. About 3 o'clock we went home with the Governor but the servants were out of the way, but when they came the Governor chastised them. I ate boiled pork for dinner. In the evening we drank a bottle till about 9 o'clock and the Governor gave us some oranges which he had sent him from Barbados. From thence we went to the coffeehouse where I lost 40 shillings at cards. About 12 o'clock I went home where I said my prayers and had good health, good thoughts, and good humor, thank God Almighty.

9. I rose about 7 o'clock and read a chapter in Hebrew but no Greek because I had company come in to visit me. I said my prayers and ate boiled milk for breakfast. About 9 o'clock Mrs. Russell sent lemons and citrons to my wife. About 10 o'clock I went to the capitol where I met Mr. Holloway and reasoned with him about his accounts but he was on the high rope and gave me back my papers and would have nothing to do with my business which he had but half done. I took him at his word and sent my papers to Robin Beverley. The Governor prorogued the Assembly till April. Then a particular company of us went to dine at the French ordinary where I ate some fish for dinner. We were exceedingly merry and stayed there till about 7 o'clock and then rode to Williamsburg. We stayed at the coffeehouse till 10 o'clock and then I went home. I said my prayers and had good thoughts, good health, and good humor, thank God Almighty.

10. I rose about 7 o'clock and read two chapters in Hebrew and 200 verses in Homer. I said my prayers and ate boiled milk for breakfast. I read some French. About 11 o'clock I went to visit the President at his lodgings and went with him and Mr. Clayton to church where parson Taylor preached a short sermon. From church I went with

the Governor and Mrs. Russell in the coach to dinner. I ate chine and turkey for dinner. In the afternoon we drank a bottle of wine till about 4 o'clock and then I took my leave. The Doctor returned from Major Burwell's who was very sick again and Frederick Jones was also sick of a palsy. I took a walk about the town. The weather was exceedingly warm for the time of year. About 5 o'clock I returned to my chambers and Mr. Bland [came] and sat with me two hours. Then I read some English. I said my prayers and had good health, good thoughts, and good humor, thank God Almighty.

11. I rose at 7 o'clock and read two chapters in Hebrew and 180 verses in Homer. I said my prayers and ate boiled milk for breakfast. It rained much last night. There was a great noise of people drunk in the street good part of the night. About 10 o'clock I borrowed Mr. Clayton's horse to ride to Major Burwell's and got there before 12. I found him with a fever on him but not violent, but he was apprehensive of dying and desired extremely to live a little longer. He begged of me to pray for him and if after his death there should happen a disagreement among his children he conjured me [to] make it up, which I promised him I would. I found there several of his daughters. About 3 o'clock it began to rain and a little after we went to dinner and I ate some roast pig. Then about 4 o'clock I recommended Major Burwell to the protection of the Almighty and took my leave. It rained again before I got to the end of my journey. When I returned I found several letters from England by which I learned that my sister Brayne was dead. I said my prayers, in which I prayed for Major Burwell, and had good health, good thoughts, and good humor, thank God Almighty.

12. I rose at 7 o'clock and read two chapters in Hebrew and 120 verses in Homer. I said my prayers and ate boiled milk for breakfast. It rained again very hard all night, and about 3 o'clock the wind came to northwest which turned the rain into snow about break of day. Several gentlemen came to see me at my lodgings. About 11 o'clock

I went to the coffeehouse where I found several gentlemen of the Council.   From thence we went to the Court of Oyer and Terminer and adjourned as soon as we had sworn the jury and went to dine at the Governor's, where I ate some boiled goose and onion sauce.   About 4 o'clock we returned to court and one criminal was arraigned for killing a woman after a new fashion.   Then we went to the Governor's again, it being the Governor's birth night, and stayed till 10 o'clock and drank a bowl of punch.   I desired the Doctor to give six of the Governor's servants £3 and returned to my lodgings and said my prayers and had good health, good thoughts, and good humor, thank God Almighty.

13. I rose at 7 o'clock and read 50 verses in Homer but no Hebrew because some company came in on me.   I said my prayers and ate boiled milk for breakfast.   [It] froze hard last night.   I settled some accounts with Mr. Bland.   About 10 o'clock I went to the capitol to the Court of Oyer and Terminer where we proceeded to try the person accused of killing the woman and the jury found him guilty of manslaughter.   Then we went to Council where some little matters were dispatched.   Then I went to dine with the Governor where I ate boiled beef.   After dinner about 4 o'clock my man came from home with the horses and told me my wife was indisposed with a cold and fever.   Several of the Council went home and some of us stayed with the Governor till about 9 o'clock.   Then I took my leave of the Governor and Mrs. Russell and returned to my lodgings, where I said my prayers and had good thoughts, good humor, and good health, thank God Almighty.

14. I rose at 7 o'clock and read nothing because I was preparing to return home to Westover.   I said my prayers and ate boiled milk for breakfast.   It was very cold weather.   However I was resolved to go home because my wife was indisposed.   Accordingly I went and took leave of Mrs. Bland and thanked her for all her kindness to me and my servants.   About 10 o'clock I took horse and rode away, without calling anywhere till I got home, where I arrived about 4 o'clock and found my wife better and the rest of

the family pretty well only two people were sick without danger. I came just as my wife was at dinner with Mr. Dunn and his wife and ate some wild duck. In the evening I looked about me a little and found things in pretty good order. In the rest of the evening I read nothing because of the company that was here. I neglected to say my prayers but had good health, good thoughts, and good humor, thank God Almighty. I gave my wife a flourish, notwithstanding she was indisposed.

15. I rose at 8 o'clock and read nothing because of the company that was here. I neglected to say my prayers but had boiled milk for breakfast. My wife was better, thank God, but the child was out of order with a cold. I put the pictures in the library and walked about till dinner. Colonel Hill and Colonel Eppes came just time enough to dine with us. I ate roast beef for dinner. In the afternoon I went with the two colonels to the church to hear the people sing Psalms and there the singing master gave me two books, one for me and one for my wife. Mr. Dunn went away and left his wife at our house. In the evening I walked about the plantation to see what work the people had done and found things pretty well. Then I returned home and wrote some verses in the rest of the evening till 9 o'clock. The child was very dull all day and her eyes ran. I neglected to say my prayers but had good health, good thoughts, and good humor, thank God Almighty.

16. I rose at 8 o'clock, having first rogered my wife. I read a chapter in Hebrew and some Greek in Lucian. I said my prayers and ate boiled milk for breakfast. I danced my dance and I set things in order in my library. Mrs. Dunn took physic and so did several of my people. The child continued out of order and Nurse was troubled with sore eyes. I ate boiled beef for dinner. In the afternoon my wife and I had a quarrel about learning to sing Psalms, in which she was wholly in the wrong, even in the opinion of Mrs. Dunn who was witness of it. Dick C-k the wiremaker came to settle his accounts with me. In the evening I took a walk about the plantation. When I came home I ate some

milk and potatoes and wrote some verses. I neglected to say my prayers but had good health, good thoughts, and good humor, thank God Almighty. The weather grew more moderate and the wind turned southwest.

17. I rose about 8 o'clock and read two chapters in Hebrew and two chapters in the Greek Testament. I said my prayers and ate boiled milk for breakfast. The weather continued warm and my child was better, thank God. My other sick people were better likewise. I danced my dance. I took a walk in the garden. I ate boiled [pork] for dinner. In the afternoon we walked to visit Mrs. Harrison but she was gone to see Major Burwell so that we returned home without rest. In the evening it threatened rain. Mrs. Dunn read a sermon in Bishop Latimer which was written in a very comic style. Then we sat and talked till 8 o'clock when we went to bed because I intended to rise in the morning before day. My daughter lay with me. I said my prayers and had good health, good thoughts, and good humor, thank God Almighty.

18. I rose about 3 o'clock and read a chapter in Hebrew and six pages in Lucian. About 6 I went to bed again and lay till 8. I said my prayers and ate boiled milk for breakfast. I danced my dance. The weather was warm again. About 10 o'clock Mr. Bland came from Williamsburg and brought me two letters from England which came from New York but no news. About 12 o'clock came Dick Ward from above to settle accounts with me. He did not tell me that some part of the dam was gone, but Ralph G-p-l-n did tell me there was three feet of it gone. About 1 o'clock I went to the vestry, who gave me the best pew in the church. About 3 o'clock I returned home to dinner and ate roast duck. In the evening I sent my boat with Mr. Bland home to his house. In the evening I wrote some verses and was very much out of humor. I neglected to say my prayers but had good health, good thoughts, but indifferent humor, without much provocation.

19. I rose about 7 o'clock and read nothing because I prepared to go to Falling Creek. I continued exceedingly out of humor, which was increased by the news of my dam being broken. About 10 o'clock I had a quarrel with my wife about lending my gun to John and about telling me I lied. However I was reconciled before I went away. About 11 o'clock I got on horseback and rode to Colonel Hill's where I only found Mr. Anderson at home with Mr. Finney the minister. About 1 o'clock we went to dinner and I ate some salt beef. About 2 o'clock I went over the river and rode in two hours and a half to Falling Creek where I found a break in the dam but everything else was well besides. Mr. G-r-l was in much concern about the dam. I ate boiled milk for supper and then talked with Mr. G-r-l till 9 o'clock. I said a short prayer and notwithstanding I had but indifferent humor yet I had good health and good thoughts, thank God Almighty.

20. I rose at 7 o'clock and neglected to say my prayers but remembered to eat boiled milk for breakfast. Then I walked about and looked over everything. About 8 o'clock I rode to the Falls where I found things in good order. About 11 o'clock we went over the river and learned that Joe Wilkinson was not on the plantation but was gone with Mr. Laforce to look after his hogs. He had spoiled all the tobacco by house burn and carried several things that belong to me home to his house, for all which reasons I wrote to him to forbear coming any more to my service and appointed Tom Turpin to take care of everything till I sent an overseer. I walked to all the plantation on that side the river and the tobacco was most of it spoiled. In the evening I returned to Falling Creek and left orders with Mr. G-r-l to discharge S-c-f-r and put Jimmy into the sloop. I ate boiled milk again for supper. I neglected to say my prayers but had good health, good thoughts, and good humor, thank God Almighty.

21. I rose about 7 o'clock and neglected to say my prayers but remembered to eat milk for breakfast. About

8 o'clock Tom Osborne[1] came and I agreed to let him be
overseer in the room of Joe Wilkinson for £25 a year.
Then I took my leave and rode away to Appomattox where
I got about 11 o'clock but did not find Mr. Mumford at
home. I [found r-s] about the house and so ate cold beef
for dinner. Soon after dinner I went away towards home,
where I arrived about 4 o'clock but made some verses on
the road. I found several of my family sick and little
M-n-g-y dead. I ate milk for supper and wrote verses in
the evening. I neglected to say my prayers and had good
health, good thoughts, but indifferent humor. However I
rogered my wife when we got to bed.

22. I rose about 8 o'clock but·read nothing because the
sloop came and I was busy in loading her and in punishing
Johnny and scolding at S-k-f-r for bringing goods for Mr.
Tullitt contrary to my orders. About 10 o'clock I sent her
away. It rained this morning. I ate boiled milk for breakfast. I neglected to say my prayers. I settled several things
which took up all the morning. Some of the sick people
grew better and some others fell sick. I ate raspberries for
dinner. In the afternoon my wife and I played at billiards
and I laid her down and rogered her on the [trestle]. About
4 o'clock Mr. Bland came on his way to Williamsburg but
I persuaded him to stay all night. We sat and talked all the
evening. I neglected to say my prayers but had good
thoughts, good health, and good humor, thank God Almighty.

23. I rose about 5 o'clock and read a chapter in Hebrew
and some Greek in Lucian. I said my prayers and ate boiled
milk for breakfast. About 8 o'clock Mr. Bland went away.
Our maid Jenny was taken this night with a pleurisy. Our
daughter began to take drops of ginseng.[2] It was still fair
warm weather. We were invited this day to the funeral of
Major Burwell, but could not go. I wrote some verses

---

[1]The Osborne family settled in Henrico County in the seventeenth century.
In 1704 a Thomas Osbourn paid quitrents on 288 acres. (*Va. Mag.*, IV,
247-48; XXVIII, 214.)
[2]This is the first reference in the diary to the use of ginseng as a drug.
Byrd's letters are filled with comments on the efficacy of this herb.

before dinner. I ate some fish for dinner. In the afternoon my wife and I played at billiards and then I went and took a walk about the plantation to see how everything stood. In the evening a negro came from above with venison and wild turkey and told me all was well there. At night I wrote a letter to the Governor to send with a present of venison and turkey. George the coaler came likewise from the coal-pit and told me all was well there. My wife and I had a little quarrel about nothing. I said my prayers and had good health, good thoughts, and good humor, thank God Almighty.

24. I rose at 5 o'clock and read two chapters in Hebrew and some Greek in Lucian. I said my prayers and ate boiled milk for breakfast. Billy Brayne was taken sick in the night and another negro boy. The woman that was sick was mad this morning. I danced my dance. About 11 o'clock we went to church and took possession of the pew which the vestry gave us. We began to give in to the new way of singing Psalms. I had nobody home with me to dinner. I ate venison. The weather continued warm. In the afternoon my wife and I took a walk about the plantation. In the evening I read a sermon and wrote a letter to Williamsburg. My daughter was a little better, thank God. She drank cider in which rhubarb was infused. I said my prayers and had good health, good thoughts, and good humor, thank God Almighty.

25. I rose at 5 o'clock and read a chapter in Hebrew and some Greek in Lucian. About 7 o'clock the negro woman died that was mad yesterday. I said my prayers and ate boiled milk for breakfast. The wind blew very strong and it rained exceedingly. I danced my dance. About 11 o'clock we went to church where we had prayers and the Holy Sacrament which I took devoutly. We brought nobody home to dinner. I ate boiled venison. The child was a little better. In the afternoon I took a long walk and I saw several parts of the fence blown down with the wind, which blew very hard last night. In the evening I read a sermon in Mr. Norris but a quarrel which I had with my wife hin-

dered my taking much notice of it. However we were reconciled before we went to bed, but I made the first advance. I neglected to say my prayers but not to eat some milk. I had good health, good thoughts, and indifferent good humor, thank God Almighty.

26. I rose about 5 o'clock and read two chapters in Hebrew and ten pages in Lucian. I neglected to say my prayers but ate boiled milk for breakfast. I danced my dance. My sick continued so and another sick girl came down. It was very cold this day. I was busy all the morning and read nothing before dinner. I ate roast pork. In the afternoon I read more in Lucian. Then took a walk about the plantation to see how things were and did not find Jack who had not been at home since the morning. However he came home about 7 o'clock and said he had been to meet Nurse. I wrote a key of the *Atlantis*.[1] I said my prayers and had good health, good thoughts, and good humor, thank God Almighty.

27. I rose about 5 o'clock and read two chapters in Hebrew and 12 pages in Lucian. I said my prayers and ate boiled milk for breakfast. The weather was a little warmer. I had two sick people come down. I danced my dance. One of the negro girls that was taken sick yesterday morning died this morning very suddenly. I settled some accounts. I had more sick people come down. I read some French till dinner. I ate some roast venison. The weather was warmer. In the afternoon I read more French and in the evening took a walk about the plantation to look over everything. More of my people were taken sick. At night I

---

[1] The *New Atlantis*, by Mrs. Mary de la Riviere Manley (the first volume, called *Secret Memoirs and Manners of Several Persons of Quality*, published 1709), is described by G. M. Trevelyan (*England under Queen Anne*, III [London, 1934], 38) as "the publication that did most harm to the Ministry that year . . . brutal stories, for the most part entirely false, about public men and their wives, especially Whigs." Mrs. Manley was arrested but she was bailed out and the prosecution was dropped. Byrd, with his numerous connections in England, would have been especially interested in identifying his friends and enemies in this gossipy work.

wrote the key of the *Atlantis* and then read some of it. I
said my prayers and had good health, good thoughts, and
good humor, thank God Almighty.

28. I rose at 4 o'clock and read two chapters in Hebrew
and eight pages in Lucian. I went to bed again and lay till
7 and rogered my wife. I said my prayers and ate boiled
milk for breakfast. I danced my dance. Then I read some
French and settled some accounts till about 12 o'clock when
Mr. Mumford came and let me know all was well at
Appomattox. There were more sick people come down.
I ate roast venison for dinner. In the afternoon Mr. Mumford and I took a walk about the plantation and looked over
the flocks. My daughter had a fever again and could not
eat. At night I gave the best orders I could concerning the
sick people and then we ate some oysters and drank some
cider. Then we sat and talked till 9 o'clock. I said my
prayers and had good health, good thoughts, and good
humor, thank God Almighty.

29. I rose at 5 o'clock and read two chapters in Hebrew
and four pages in Lucian. I said my prayers and ate boiled
milk for breakfast. Then I danced my dance. Mr. Mumford ate some fried oysters for breakfast and then we went
to play at billiards for the rest of the morning. I had two
more sick people come down. These poor people suffer for
my sins; God forgive me all my offenses and restore them to
their health if it be consistent with His holy will. I ate wild
turkey for dinner. In the afternoon Mr. Mumford went
away. My poor child continued to have a fever, from which
God of his excessive goodness deliver her. In the evening
I took a walk about the plantation and was very melancholy
on account of the unkindness of my wife. I read several
leaves in the *Atlantis* and was much affected with it. I said
my prayers and had good health, good thoughts, and good
humor, thank God Almighty.

30. I rose about 4 o'clock and read two chapters in
Hebrew and 12 pages in Lucian. I said my prayers and ate
boiled milk for breakfast. I danced my dance. The weather

continued warm and fair. I had more sick people come down from the quarters. I caused them all to be let blood by which they grew better, thank God. Dick came from Falling Creek and told me an old negro of mine was dead and the boy that goes in the sloop very sick. I sent him back with orders to let all my people blood by way of prevention. I read some French till dinner. In the afternoon I read some English and then my wife and I made some punch of [lemons], white sack, and Madeira brandy, and I put it into bottles. In the evening I took a walk with my wife about the plantation. The weather was exceedingly warm. My people seemed to be all better, thank God. At night I read some English in the *Atlantis* till 8 o'clock. I said my prayers and had good health, good thoughts, and good humor, thank God Almighty.

31. I rose at 5 o'clock and read a chapter in Hebrew and four leaves in Lucian. I said my prayers and ate boiled milk for breakfast. My daughter was very sick all night and vomited a great deal but was a little better this morning. All my sick people were better, thank God, and I had another girl come down sick from the quarters. I danced my dance. Then I read a sermon in Dr. Tillotson and after that walked in the garden till dinner. I ate roast venison. In the afternoon I looked over my sick people and then took a walk about the plantation. The weather was very warm still. My wife walked with me and when she came back she was very much indisposed and went to bed. In the evening I read another sermon in Dr. Tillotson. About 8 o'clock the wind came to northwest and it began to be cold. I said my prayers and had good health, good thoughts, and good humor, thank God Almighty.

Some night this month I dreamed that I saw a flaming sword in the sky and called some company to see it but before they could come it was disappeared, and about a week after my wife and I were walking and we discovered in the clouds a shining cloud exactly in the shape of a dart and seemed to be over my plantation but it soon disappeared likewise. Both these appearances seemed to foretell some misfortune to me which afterwards came to pass in the death of several of my negroes after a very unusual manner. My wife about two months since dreamed she saw an angel in the shape of a big woman who told her the time was altered and the seasons were changed and that several calamities would follow that confusion. God avert his judgment from this poor country.

January, 1711

1. I rose about 4 o'clock and read two chapters in Hebrew and 12 pages in Lucian. I said my prayers and ate boiled milk for breakfast. I danced my dance. My wife was something better and so was my child, but the negro man C-l-y was very ill; God Almighty cure him if it be his holy will. My wife took a purge which worked much with her. I read some English till dinner. In the afternoon I took what care I could of my sick people and then took a walk about the plantation. Frank came from above with a steer, where he says all were well, thank God. My wife had a [flux] in her eye. In the evening came old Harry Cary[1] and Mr. Jackson from Williamsburg and brought me a letter from the Governor, very complaisant. I sat and talked with them till 9 o'clock and then went to bed without saying my prayers. However, I had good thoughts, good health, and good humor, thank God Almighty for it.

2. I rose at 5 o'clock and read a chapter in Hebrew and nothing in Greek because of the company that was here. I said my prayers and ate boiled milk for breakfast. I had six sick negroes come down from the quarters. About 9 o'clock my company went away. My wife was a little better and so was my child, thank God, but C-l-y was extremely ill and so was A-g-y. I tended them as much as I could but God is pleased to afflict me with his judgment for my sins. His holy will be done. I ate some wild turkey. The wind was northeast and it was cold. In the afternoon I read a little English but could not be easy because poor C-l-y was so very ill. I took a melancholy walk. In the evening about 6 o'clock C-l-y died and all the people was [sic] grieved at it. I read a little English and gave the necessary orders about the sick people who were 12 in number. I said my prayers and had good health, good thoughts, and good humor, thank God Almighty.

---

[1]Probably the father of Henry Cary the overseer of the building of the governor's house.

3. I rose at 4 o'clock and read two chapters in Hebrew and 14 pages in Lucian. I said my prayers and ate boiled milk for breakfast. I danced my dance. I looked over my sick people and one boy was near his death. About 10 o'clock Mr. Clayton came from Mrs. Harrison's where he lay last night. Soon after him came Captain Drury Stith and then Mr. Cary and Colonel Hill and Mr. John Pleasants. Mrs. Harrison came, likewise Mrs. Taylor and Mrs. Anderson, but the latter [or ladies] and Colonel Hill went away before dinner. The rest except Drury Stith and John Pleasants dined here. The negro boy died while we were at dinner. God's will be done. I ate roast beef for dinner. In the afternoon Mr. Cary went away but Mr. Clayton and Tom Jones stayed. We played at billiards and then took a walk till night and then we drank a bottle of wine till about 10 o'clock. My wife was indisposed in her eyes, that she could not see the company. I said a short prayer and had good health, good thoughts, and good humor, thank God Almighty.

4. I rose about 7 o'clock and read nothing because I had company here. I said my prayers and ate boiled milk for breakfast. I danced my dance. The company went away about 9 o'clock. Several of the sick people complained of pain in the side and breast and poor A-g-y was very ill. About 11 o'clock Mr. Dunn and his wife came. I spent most of my time in looking after the sick; God grant them a recovery. About 12 o'clock I received a letter from my brother Duke that told me they were all well. I ate roast beef for dinner. In the afternoon Mr. Dunn and I played at billiards a little and then I returned to look after the sick again. Then I took a walk about the plantation. In the evening we sat and talked and drank some cider. I said a short prayer and had good health, good thoughts, and good humor, thank God Almighty. George Smith returned from Williamsburg.

5. I rose about 3 o'clock and read two chapters in Hebrew and some Greek in Lucian. I said my prayers and ate boiled milk for breakfast. I danced my dance. My sick

people seemed to be all mending except Jenny and A-g-y, God grant them their recovery, if it be his holy will. The child seemed a little [. . .] and so was my wife, who would not dine with us. I ate fish for dinner. I played at billiards in the afternoon with my cousin [Guy][1] who belongs to the man-of-war and came to see me this morning by the leave of his captain. Then I returned to look after my people. Then my cousin and I took a walk about the plantation but it rained before we came back. The wind was at northeast and threatened bad weather. A-g-y voided three worms, which gave her some ease but did not remove the pain in her side. Upon this, I gave to all the sick people the wormseed because I believed their sickness proceeded from worms in some measure. I said my prayers and had good health, good thoughts, and good humor, thank God Almighty.

6. I rose at 5 o'clock and read two chapters in Hebrew and six leaves in Lucian. I said my prayers and ate boiled milk for breakfast. Poor old S-r-y died this night to make up the number of the dead. God save the rest. A-g-y seemed to be a little better and so did the rest of the sick, God be praised, except Jenny and she seemed to be worse. The weather threatened rain all day. I removed several things out of the Doctor's closet into mine and was very little with my cousin. I was out of humor with my wife. I ate boiled pork for dinner. In the afternoon Mrs. Dunn went away in the rain. I spent most of my time in looking after my sick. In the evening it rained extremely, and all night. My cousin and I took a walk about the plantation. I said my prayers and had good health, good thoughts, and good humor, thank God Almighty.

7. I rose at 5 o'clock and read two chapters in Hebrew and some Greek in Lucian. I said my prayers and ate boiled milk for breakfast. My sick people were some worse and some well enough to go home to the quarters. Jenny and A-g-y were much as they were. The weather held up so

---

[1] Mary Byrd, sister of William Byrd I, married a Mr. Guy in England. This may have been one of the family. (*Va. Mag.*, XXVI, 127.)

that I and my cousin [Guy] went to church, but my wife was afflicted with the headache and stayed at home. People condoled the sickness of my family. Mr. Anderson gave us a sermon. After church I carried him home with me to dinner and to see my sick people. I ate fish for dinner. Mr. Anderson advised me to give my people cordials since other physic failed, which I did. In the afternoon I did nothing but mind them. In the evening my cousin and we talked till 8 o'clock. I said a short prayer and had good health, good thoughts, and good humor, thank God Almighty.

8. I rose about 5 o'clock and read two chapters in Hebrew and some Greek in Lucian. I said my prayers and ate boiled milk for breakfast. My people continued sick and particularly A-g-y was very ill and so were some of the others. My wife was indisposed, rather out of humor with me and everybody else. Dick Randolph called here on his way to Williamsburg to know if I had any service and several other people came about business. I set my closet in order. I ate boiled pork for dinner. A-g-y was a little better, thank God Almighty. In the afternoon I settled accounts with John [Faile][1] and Will Bass who came from above and left all my people well. In the evening my cousin [Guy] and I walked about the plantation. At night I looked over all my people and found one woman very well. I said my prayers and had good health, good thoughts, and good humor, thank God.

9. I rose about 5 and read a chapter in Hebrew and eight leaves in Lucian. I said my prayers and ate boiled milk for breakfast. My people continued sick and one woman very sick, but A-g-y was better, thank God. I tended them diligently and went to the quarters to see the negroes there and gave the necessary orders about them. The child was very sick again. I set my closet in order till dinner. I ate roast beef. In the afternoon Mr. [Guy] and I played at billiards. I visited my people again and had one woman

---

[1]John Faile owned 240 acres in Henrico County in 1704. (*Va. Mag.,* XXVIII, 212.)

extremely sick. In the evening Joe Wilkinson's [wife] came to beg for her husband but I would not speak to her for fear of being persuaded by her tears which women have always ready at command. At night I read some news and drank a bottle of cider. I said my prayers and had good health, good thoughts, and good humor, thank God Almighty.

10. I rose at 4 o'clock and read a chapter in Hebrew and 14 pages in Lucian. I said my prayers and ate boiled milk for breakfast. I danced my dance. My people were all better except one woman that was extremely sick of the headache. About 11 o'clock Colonel Eppes came and he and I played at billiards till dinner. I ate fish. In the afternoon I returned to looking after my people and one woman was extremely sick. Colonel Eppes went away soon after dinner and I was going to Mrs. Harrison's but on the walk met Nat Harrison and Hal Harrison who were coming to visit me. I brought them home with me and entertained them as courteously as I could. They stayed about two hours and then went away. In the evening came Colonel Ludwell and Mr. Clayton but had supped. I said my prayers and had good health, good thoughts, and good humor, thank God Almighty.

11. I rose about 6 o'clock but read nothing because of my company, who went away about 8 o'clock. I said my prayers and ate chocolate for breakfast. Two of my people were very ill. I quarreled with my wife for being cruel to Suky Brayne, though she deserved it. I wrote several letters to Williamsburg to go by Mr. Clayton. The weather was very warm and I had another boy taken sick. I ate roast mutton for dinner. In the afternoon after giving the necessary orders about my people [I] walked to Mrs. Harrison's where was a great deal of company. They were going to dinner but I could eat nothing with them but a little pudding. I stayed till it was almost dark and then returned home where I found my family in the same condition. In the evening I read some news and said my prayers and had good health, good thoughts, and good humor, thank God Almighty.

12. I rose about 3 o'clock and read two chapters in Hebrew and 14 pages in Lucian. I said my prayers and ate boiled milk for breakfast. My family continued in a bad condition and Mary and another woman came down sick. I gave the necessary orders about them and then walked to Mrs. Harrison's to see Mr. Perry's papers delivered to Mr. Clayton. I stayed there till about 11 o'clock and then returned home, where I found Tom L-d who gave my wife bad language and I gave him chase with my cane but could not overtake him. It rained a little this day. I ate boiled squirrel and onions for dinner. In the afternoon I looked after my people and one woman died of the [m-d t-c-d-c]. In the evening Mary was a little better, thank God. At night my wife and I ate some roast beef. I neglected to say my prayers but had good health, good thoughts, and good humor, thank God Almighty.

13. I rose at 5 o'clock and read a chapter in Hebrew and some Greek in Lucian. I said my prayers and ate boiled milk for breakfast. Mr. Tullitt came here about some business and went away again. None of our negroes seemed to be in danger except one girl, thank God. The rest were better. I went with my people to replant trees. Then I wrote articles between Tom Turpin and me and after read some news till dinner. I ate roast beef for dinner. In the afternoon we planted more trees till the evening and then Dick came from the Falls and told me all the people were well there, thank God Almighty. At night I wrote a letter to Tom Turpin to tell him the terms that I would give him. My cousin [Guy] and I drank some cider. I said my prayers and had good thoughts, good health, and good humor, thank God Almighty.

14. I rose about 5 o'clock and read two chapters in Hebrew and three chapters in the Greek Testament. Then I wrote a letter to Mr. G-r-l to send by Dick to whose care I committed 18 new negroes to be carried up to the Falls. They went away about 8 o'clock. I said my prayers and ate boiled milk for breakfast. All my sick people grew better, thank God, only one girl was extremely ill. About 10

o'clock Tom Osborne came down to settle our bargain. He stayed till about 12 o'clock and then returned home but had something to eat first. I danced my dance and took a walk before dinner. I ate boiled beef. In the afternoon we took a walk with the child who was a little better but very fretful. I read a sermon of Dr. Tillotson, and in the evening took a walk. At night we had another negro girl dead; God's will be done. We drank a bottle of punch. I said my prayers and had good health, good thoughts, and good humor, thank God Almighty.

15. I rose about 6 o'clock and read a chapter in Hebrew and some Greek in Lucian. I said my prayers and ate boiled milk for breakfast. I danced my dance. My sick people were much as they were yesterday, only N-n-y was worse at the quarters. I wrote articles between Tom Turpin and me and settled several accounts. The wind was northeast and threatened snow but towards noon got about to the south. I read some news till dinner. I ate hashed mutton for dinner. In the afternoon I went into the field to see my people at work and when I returned I learned one of the negroes was grown worse. I danced with my wife, who was very merry today and in the evening took a walk with her. Then I took care of all the sick. At night I read some English. About 7 o'clock Tom returned from carrying the new negroes to the Falls and told me they were all well, thank God. I neglected to say my prayers in form but had good thoughts, good health, and good humor, thank God Almighty.

16. I rose at 5 o'clock and read two chapters in Hebrew and ten pages in Lucian. I said my prayers and ate boiled milk for breakfast. I danced my dance. My sick people were better this morning, thank God. I settled some accounts. It rained a little in the morning but soon held up. About 10 o'clock I went with the people to plant trees and then read some English. I wrote several letters till dinner time. I ate roast beef for dinner. In the afternoon Mrs. Hamlin came to see us and to have some salt. We planted trees again till just night. Then I went and took a walk

about the plantation. At night I read some English. The wind came to northwest and it grew very cold. My people were better, thank God. I said my prayers and had good health, good thoughts, and good humor, thank God Almighty.

17. I rose at 6 o'clock and read two chapters in Hebrew and some Greek in Lucian. I said my prayers and ate boiled milk for breakfast. My people all grew better, thank God. I danced my dance. It was cold today. My cousin [Guy] went away this morning and seemed to be much concerned for parting with Nurse. I wrote several letters and read some French and settled some accounts. I ate mutton pie for dinner. In the afternoon I took a walk to visit Mrs. Harrison but she was gone to the Colonel's in Surry. I found Mistress Betty at home but did not stay long with her but returned home and by the way looked for some cedar trees to plant in my pasture. My sick people grew still better. At night I read some English. I said my prayers but had good health, good thoughts, and good humor, thank God Almighty.

18. I rose at 4 o'clock and read two chapters in Hebrew and some Greek in Lucian. I said my prayers and ate boiled milk for breakfast. I danced my dance. Negro Peter came from above and told me all was well except one new negro that was sick. I wrote a letter to Tom Turpin and to Tom Osborne. About 10 o'clock I went out to get some cedar trees to plant in my pasture and while I was about it came Colonel Hill and Mr. Anderson, who made me leave the work and go to them. My sick people were much as they were. I ate fish for dinner. In the afternoon I gave them some of my punch which they liked very well. In the evening they went away and I and my wife took a walk about the plantation. At night I read some English. I said my prayers and had good health, good thoughts, and good humor, thank God Almighty.

19. I rose about 5 o'clock and read two chapters in Hebrew and some Greek in Lucian. I said my prayers and ate boiled milk for breakfast. I danced my dance. My

sick people continued as they were. It rained all night and
a little this morning. Mr. Bland's shallop came last night
and brought me 42 hides and 50 pounds of [tallow]. I
settled some accounts and wrote a letter to Madeira. Then
I went to plant trees in the garden, and in the pasture. I
ate boiled beef for dinner. I wrote several orders on the
sheriff for Colonel Hill who sent to me for them. Then
I went and planted more trees and afterwards took a walk
about the plantation. Nick Haynes[1] died last night. At
night I read some English. My sick negroes all mended
except S-n-y who seemed worse. I said my prayers and had
good health, good thoughts, and good humor, thank God
Almighty.

20. I rose at 5 o'clock and read two chapters in Hebrew
and some Greek in Lucian. I said my prayers and ate
boiled milk for breakfast. I danced my dance. My sick
people continued to mend except S-n-y. The weather was
very warm and cloudy. I settled many of my accounts, then
I read some French. About 12 o'clock Robin Burton[2] came
to speak with me. I ate roast mutton for dinner. In the
afternoon I went with my people to plant some cedar trees.
About 3 o'clock Dick Randolph came with a letter from
Mr. Bland to tell me that my friend Colonel Digges was
dead yesterday of the fever; upon this I wrote to the Governor to engage him to assist me in getting the two places
joined again,[3] and sent Tom with the letter because the
express was not to return till tomorrow. In the evening I
took a walk about the plantation and at night read some
English. I neglected to say my prayers but had good health,
good thoughts, and good humor, thank God Almighty.

---

[1]A Nicholas Haynes owned land in Charles City County in 1704. (*Va.
Mag.*, XXXI, 315.)

[2]Robert Burton owned 1,350 acres in Henrico County in 1704. (*Va. Mag.*,
XXVIII, 209.)

[3]William Byrd I had held both offices of auditor and receiver, and on
Sept. 4, 1705, the diarist was sworn auditor and receiver; a few months later
the two places were separated and Dudley Digges was sworn deputy for
William Blathwayt, auditor and surveyor general for Her Majesty's revenues.
(*Ex. Jour.*, III, 29, 70.)

21. I rose at 5 o'clock and read two chapters in Hebrew and some Greek in Lucian. I said my prayers and ate boiled milk for breakfast. I danced my dance. In the night S-n-y died, which made 12 slaves that I have lost this winter. The rest of my sick people were better, thank God. It rained all day so that we did not go to church because nobody came. I read one of Dr. Tillotson's sermons at home. I ate boiled beef for dinner. In the afternoon the boatwright came from Falling Creek and told me that Westminster's wife was sick and that Mr. G-r-l would be here tomorrow. In the evening the sloop came over with planks, &c. At night I read some English about the soul being a spirit. I said my prayers and had good health, good thoughts, but indifferent good humor, thank God Almighty.

22. I rose at 3 o'clock and read a chapter in Hebrew and some Greek in Lucian. I said my prayers and ate boiled milk for breakfast. I danced my dance. I ordered the sloop to be unloaded. Redskin Peter pretended to be sick and I put a [branding-iron] on the place he complained of and put the [bit] upon him. The boy called the Doc was sent from Falling Creek with a swollen thigh. My sick people were better, thank God Almighty. I received a courteous letter from the Governor by Tom, who brought no news. I ate boiled pork for dinner. Mr. Mumford came down after dinner and told me all was well at Appomattox. When he had got some victuals we took a walk to see the people load the sloop and afterwards about the plantation. In the evening G-r-l came and let me know things were well at Falling Creek. He brought me a letter from Tom Turpin in which he agreed to stay with me for £25 a year. I ate some roast beef for supper. I neglected to say my prayers, but had good health, good thoughts, and good humor, thank God.

23. I rose at 5 o'clock and read a chapter in Hebrew and some Greek in Lucian. I said my prayers and ate boiled milk for breakfast. I danced my dance. My sick people were better, thank God, and Redskin Peter was particularly

well and worked as well as anybody. We dispatched the sloop away to Williamsburg. Then I reckoned with Mr. G-r-l and surprised him when he found himself so much in debt. I settled accounts with S-k-f-r and discharged him. Captain Llewellyn came to see my wife and I settled accounts with him. I ate fat goose for dinner. In the afternoon Mr. G-r-l and Mr. Mumford went away and in the evening Will Bass came again to amend his accounts. In the evening I took a walk about the plantation. My wife was extremely out of humor, for I know not what. At night I read some English. I said my prayers and had good health, good thoughts, and good humor, thank God Almighty.

24. I rose at 6 o'clock and only read two chapters in Hebrew and no Greek. I said my prayers and ate boiled milk for breakfast. I danced my dance. Then I settled accounts with Will Bass. My wife came into good humor again of herself. The wind was northeast and was very cold. I settled several other accounts and did several little things about the house till dinner. My sick people were all mending, thank God. I ate roast [. . .] and mutton for dinner. In the afternoon I went about the planting of trees and in the evening took a walk about the plantation. It was very cold. At night I ate some oysters and then played at piquet with my wife to oblige her, notwithstanding it was against my inclination. I said my prayers and had good health, good thoughts, and good humor, thank God Almighty.

25. I rose at 5 o'clock and read two chapters in Hebrew and some Greek in Lucian. I said my prayers and ate boiled milk for breakfast. I danced my dance. I settled several accounts till about 10 o'clock and then I read some English. About 11 o'clock Colonel Hill came and told me the rest of his family were singing at church. He told me the ship that is arrived in York River brings an account that our fleet was in the Downs ready to sail in October last. Colonel Hill since the news of his wife's death, which was in July last, has eaten no flesh, which agrees well with him. I ate hog's

haslet for dinner. In the afternoon the Colonel went away and I went to plant trees. My two boys, Bannister and G-r-l, began to learn to sing Psalms. In the evening I took a walk. At night it rained and the wind continued at northeast. I read some English. I said my prayers and had good health, good thoughts, and good humor, thank God Almighty.

26. I rose at 6 o'clock and read a chapter in Hebrew and some Greek in Lucian. I said my prayers and ate boiled milk for breakfast. I danced my dance. It rained almost all night and the wind continued at northeast. I settled several accounts and read some English. The rain confined me in the house all day. I ate roast shoat for dinner. In the afternoon I looked over my letters from England in order to answer them. My wife and I danced together. It rained all day without holding up one minute. My people kept holiday because of the weather, having nothing within doors to do. At night I read some English and read my old letters. I said my prayers and had good health, good thoughts, and good humor, thank God Almighty.

27. I rose at 5 o'clock and read two chapters in Hebrew and some Greek in Lucian. I said my prayers and ate boiled milk for breakfast. I danced my dance. It rained all night but held up about 8 o'clock this morning. My sick people were all better, thank God Almighty. I settled several accounts; then I read some English which gave me great light into the nature of spirit. I ordered Tom to plant some [l-c-s] seed. I ate goose giblets for dinner. In the afternoon my wife and I took a little walk and then danced together. Then I read some more English. At night I read some Italian and then played at piquet with my wife. Peter came from the Falls and brought me some venison. My overseer wrote me word one of my new negroes was in danger. I said my prayers and had good health, good thoughts, and good humor, thank God Almighty.

28. I rose at 5 o'clock and read two chapters in Hebrew and some Greek in Lucian. I said my prayers and ate

boiled milk for breakfast. I danced my dance. I wrote
two letters to the Falls. I read some English about the
nature of spirit. It rained small rain almost all day. My
sick people were better, thank God. I exercised my memory
with getting things by heart. I thought a great deal about
religion. I ate nothing but sallet for dinner. In the afternoon I rogered my wife on the couch. Then I took a little
nap. After that I read some more English about the soul
and then took a walk, but the rain made me return soon. At
night I read more English. Jenny's child was taken sick of
a looseness and vomiting. I said my prayers devoutly and
had good thoughts, good humor, and good health, thank
God Almighty.

29. I rose at 5 o'clock and read a chapter in Hebrew and
some Greek in Lucian. I said my prayers and ate boiled
milk for breakfast. I danced my dance. Our cook Moll
was taken sick. I caused her to be bled and vomited. Then
I went to plant trees and worked very hard about it, notwithstanding the rain, but I had the precaution to change my
stockings. Then I read some English till dinner. I ate cold
roast beef. In the afternoon I went to plant more trees.
We heard several guns fired at a great distance. In the
evening the boatwright and I came to a bargain by which he
was to teach John to build a flat for £10. The wind continued northeast still, notwithstanding it began to clear up
and be fine weather. My wife was taken sick this afternoon
of a kind of ague and our cook Moll continued very sick.
At night I read some English. I said my prayers and had
good health, good thoughts, and good humor, thank God
Almighty.

30. I rose at 5 o'clock and read a chapter in Hebrew and
some Greek in Lucian. I wrote several letters to my people
above but neglected to say my prayers but did not neglect
to eat boiled milk for breakfast. My wife was a little better
and so was my cook-maid. It rained again this morning.
My sloop returned from Williamsburg and was dispatched
away presently because the wind was northeast. This was

appointed to be kept as a fast[1] and so my people did not go to work. About 11 o'clock we went to church and heard a sermon. After church it rained but I could not persuade anybody to go home with me and it was well I did not, for I found no fire, everything else out of order. My wife was out of order and so could justify her want of good humor. I ate nothing but milk for dinner but was likewise much out of humor. In the afternoon I read some English and in the evening danced my dance. At night I read more English and ate some toast and mead. My wife and I were good friends again. I said my prayers and had good health, good thoughts, and good humor, thank God Almighty.

31. I rose at 5 o'clock and read two chapters in Hebrew and some Greek in Lucian. I said my prayers and ate boiled milk for breakfast. My wife quarreled with me about not sending for Mrs. Dunn when it rained to [lend her John]. She threatened to kill herself but had more discretion. I danced my dance and then read some English about [love]. It rained again all the morning. I ate some roast shoat for dinner. In the afternoon Nurse was taken sick of a [purging]. I took a walk to see the boatwright at work. My wife came into good humor again and we resolved to live for the future in love and peace. At night I ate some battered eggs with her and drank some cider. I said my prayers and had good health, good thoughts, and good humor, thank God Almighty. The wind was still northeast as it was when the moon was at full and since that a good deal of rain has fallen. The boy whose thigh was swollen grew worse.

---

[1]According to the Governor's proclamation, the day was "set apart by public authority for commemorating the martyrdom of King Charles I" and also for imploring God's mercy for "our own sins and the grievous sickness which now rages amongst us." (*Cal. State Papers, Colonial, America and the West Indies*, 1710-1711, p. 411.)

February, 1711

1. I rose at 5 o'clock and read two chapters in Hebrew and some Greek in Lucian. I said my prayers and ate boiled milk for breakfast. I danced my dance. I beat my cousin Susan for not learning to read. The weather began to clear up, thank God, and was very warm weather and very pleasant. I settled several accounts. About 11 o'clock Mr. Dunn and his wife came. They met G-r-l whom I sent for Mrs. Dunn to help her prepare to go to Williamsburg. We had pork for dinner. In the afternoon Mr. Dunn and I walked about the plantation and saw the people at work, and in the evening my wife and Mrs. Dunn walked likewise. I read a little English. At night we drank some cider. I neglected to say my prayers but had good health, good thoughts, and good humor, thank God Almighty.

2. I rose at 5 o'clock and read a chapter in Hebrew and some Greek in Lucian. I said my prayers and ate boiled milk for breakfast. I danced my dance. I chastised Moll and Eugene for not doing their business on pretence of sickness. It was very fine weather and warm, thank God. I settled some accounts and then wrote a letter to Falling Creek. Then I read a little English. Then Mr. Dunn and I played at billiards and I gave him three and a go and beat him. I ate some boiled beef for dinner. In the afternoon Mr. Dunn and I went to Mrs. Harrison's where we found Colonel Hill and Mr. Gee and Mrs. Anderson. I bought two negroes of Mrs. Harrison for the Governor for £63. She was out of humor about her accounts. In the evening we returned home where we found all well. We drank some cider. I said my prayers and had good health, good thoughts, and good humor, thank God Almighty.

3. I rose at 5 o'clock and read a chapter in Hebrew and some Greek in Lucian. I said my prayers and ate boiled milk for breakfast. I danced my dance. It continued fine weather and the wind at northwest. I settled several ac-

counts and wrote a letter to the Governor to send with the negroes which I bought for him. Then I took a walk about the plantation. I played at billiards with Mr. Dunn till dinner. I ate roast beef for dinner. In the afternoon Mrs. Harrison came about business, and I wrote a letter to one of the sheriffs on her complaint that she could not get the quitrents. In the evening Tom Turpin came from the Falls and told me that two of my negroes were dead. God's will be done. At night we drank some mead and ate toast. I said my prayers and had good health, good thoughts, and good humor, thank God Almighty.

4. I rose at 5 o'clock and read a chapter in Hebrew and some Greek in Lucian. I said my prayers and ate boiled milk for breakfast. I gave my necessary orders to Tom Turpin and he went away about 10 o'clock. About 11 we walked to church and heard a good sermon of Mr. Anderson. After church we ate some toast and drank some mead and went over the creek with our horses where the water was very high and I was very wet and got a violent cold. Mrs. Dunn returned home and we rode to my brother Duke's where we found all well. My sister did not ask us to eat till my brother came home and then I got some milk and potatoes. My cold grew worse. About 9 o'clock we went to bed. I said a short prayer and had good thoughts, good humor, and indifferent good health, thank God Almighty.

5. I rose about 8 o'clock and found my cold still worse. I said my prayers and ate milk and potatoes for breakfast. My wife and I quarreled about her pulling her brows. She threatened she would not go to Williamsburg if she might not pull them; I refused, however, and got the better of her, and maintained my authority. About 10 o'clock we went over the river and got to Colonel Duke's about 11. There I ate some toast and canary. Then we proceeded to Queen's Creek, where we found all well, thank God. We ate roast goose for supper. The women prepared to go to the Governor's the next day and my brother and I talked of old stories. My cold grew exceedingly bad so that I thought

I should be sick. My sister gave me some sage tea and leaves of [s-m-n-k] which made me mad all night so that I could not sleep but was much disordered by it. I neglected to say my prayers in form but had good thoughts, good humor, and indifferent health, thank God Almighty.

6. I rose about 9 o'clock but was so bad I thought I should not have been in condition to go to Williamsburg, and my wife was so kind to [say] she would stay with me, but rather than keep her from going I resolved to go if possible. I was shaved with a very dull razor, and ate some boiled milk for breakfast but neglected to say my prayers. About 10 o'clock I went to Williamsburg without the ladies. As soon as I got there it began to rain, which hindered about [sic] the company from coming. I went to the President's where I drank tea and went with him to the Governor's and found him at home. Several gentlemen were there and about 12 o'clock several ladies came. My wife and her sister came about 2. We had a short Council but more for form than for business. There was no other appointed in the room of Colonel Digges. My cold was a little better so that I ventured among the ladies, and Colonel Carter's wife and daughter were among them. It was night before we went to supper, which was very fine and in good order. It rained so that several did not come that were expected. About 7 o'clock the company went in coaches from the Governor's house to the capitol where the Governor opened the ball with a French dance with my wife. Then I danced with Mrs. Russell and then several others and among the rest Colonel Smith's son, who made a sad freak. Then we danced country dances for an hour and the company was carried into another room where was a very fine collation of sweetmeats. The Governor was very gallant to the ladies and very courteous to the gentlemen. About 2 o'clock the company returned in the coaches and because the drive was dirty the Governor carried the ladies into their coaches. My wife and I lay at my lodgings. Colonel Carter's family and Mr. Blair were stopped by the unruliness of the horses and Daniel Wilkinson was so gallant as to lead the horses

himself through all the dirt and rain to Mr. Blair's house. My cold continued bad. I neglected to say my prayers and had good thoughts, good humor, but indifferent health, thank God Almighty. It rained all day and all night. The President had the worst clothes of anybody there.

7. I rose at 8 o'clock and found my cold continued. I said my prayers and ate boiled milk for breakfast. I went to see Mr. Clayton who lay sick of the gout. About 11 o'clock my wife and I went to wait on the Governor in the President's coach. We went there to take our leave but were forced to stay all day. The Governor had made a bargain with his servants that if they would forbear to drink upon the Queen's birthday, they might be drunk this day. They observed their contract and did their business very well and got very drunk today, in such a manner that Mrs. Russell's maid was forced to lay the cloth, but the cook in that condition made a shift to send in a pretty little dinner. I ate some mutton cutlets. In the afternoon I persuaded my wife to stay all night in town and so it was resolved to spend the evening in cards. My cold was very bad and I lost my money. About 10 o'clock the Governor's coach carried us home to our lodgings where my wife was out of humor and I out of order. I said a short prayer and had good thoughts and good humor, thank God Almighty.

8. I rose at 7 o'clock and we both got ready to go. I said my prayers and ate boiled milk for breakfast. We expected the Governor at my lodgings and he came about 9 o'clock. We stayed there a little while and then I walked with him to the house that is building for the Governor where he showed me abundance of faults and found great exception to the proceedings of the workmen. The Governor was pleased to tell me his thoughts about the auditor's place and told me several had made application for it and that one gentleman (that I took to be Holloway) had offered £500 for it. The Governor assisted my wife to get on her horse and then we took leave and rode to Mr. Blair's where we had some milk tea. Then we proceeded to Colonel Duke's where I got 50 black cherry trees for the

Governor. We ate some boiled beef for dinner and then sat and talked all the evening. I neglected to say my prayers but had good thoughts, good humor, and indifferent good health, thank God Almighty.

9. I rose at 9 o'clock because it rained and ate boiled milk for breakfast. I wrote a letter to the Governor and to my brother Custis about the auditor's place, and then another to Mr. Bland. Then I ate some roast turkey for dinner. My cold was better, thank God. About one o'clock we rode to my brother Duke's and just called to know how they did and then because it was late proceeded on our journey home. The roads were exceedingly bad because of the abundance of rain that had fallen. At Mr. B-s we saw a pretty girl called Mistress King[1] who had £400 to her fortune. About 6 o'clock we got home, where we found all well, thank God Almighty, and my little girl was much recovered in her color. I ate some boiled milk when I came home and was pretty well of my cold but my wife had got a cold in her turn. I said my prayers and had good health, good thoughts, and good humor, thank God Almighty.

10. I rose about 7 o'clock and ate boiled milk for breakfast. I said my prayers and ate boiled milk for breakfast [sic]. My cold was much better, thank God. I danced my dance. I gave rights to several people but read nothing. About 10 o'clock Mr. G-r-t-l came to see me and I sent my boat to Mrs. Hamlin's for his wife. Soon after came Colonel Hill and Mr. Anderson. The Colonel came to purchase some iron but I had none to spare. They all stayed to dinner and I ate pork. In the afternoon it rained but that did not hinder the company from going away, all except Colonel Hill who was so kind as to stay with us. We drank some mead which was very good and talked of several things and among others I encouraged him to endeavor for the auditor's place. The Colonel is a man of no great ambition but a man of honor and good nature. He complained that his head began to ache. Mr. M-r-s-l came from

---

[1]Mary King, who married Dr. Robert Burbage on August 12, 1711.

Falling Creek and told me all was well there. I neglected to say my prayers but had good health, good thoughts, and good humor, thank God Almighty. Tom Turpin sent a deer and two turkeys. It snowed a little this evening.

11. I rose about 7 o'clock and read nothing because of the company that was here. However I wrote several letters to my overseers above. I neglected to say my prayers but ate boiled milk for breakfast. Poor Colonel Hill had a headache exceedingly. However he went home about 9 o'clock without it. Mr. M-r-s-l and I settled accounts and I bought a horse of him for £10. He went away about 11 o'clock, notwithstanding the rain. I danced my dance, and read a little English. I ate some roast pig for dinner. In the afternoon my wife and I took a little walk but the rain soon drove us in again. I read more English till the evening; then I read a sermon in Mr. Norris and ate some milk with my wife. The weather continued very wet. I said my prayers and had good health, good thoughts, and good humor, thank God Almighty.

12. I rose about 3 o'clock and read two chapters in Hebrew and six leaves in Lucian. I said my prayers and ate boiled milk for breakfast. I danced my dance. It rained very hard all night and all this morning likewise. I settled several accounts. A man came from New Kent for rights in the rain but had not money enough. However I trusted him and ordered him some victuals. I read some English before dinner. I ate roast mutton. In the afternoon I took a walk to see my people and met two men who wanted rights. I returned home and gave them what they wanted and gave them a bottle of cider. In the evening I took a walk about the plantation because the weather grew fair. At night I wrote a letter to Mr. C-s in Barbados and ate some milk for supper. I said my prayers and had good health, good thoughts, and good humor, thank God Almighty.

13. I rose about 5 o'clock and read two chapters in Hebrew and some Greek in Lucian. I said my prayers and ate boiled milk for breakfast. The weather was fair. I

danced my dance. Then I wrote two letters to England to go by way of Barbados. Then I ate some battered eggs and prepared to go to Prince George court. About 12 o'clock I got there and met several people there to do business with and gave my letters to Peter Hamlin. I sold above 100 rights there and saved the people the trouble of coming over the river. Here I saw Mr. Randolph and told him the Governor was displeased with him for not making more haste with the laws.[1] There was also Mr. Bland, who brought no news from Williamsburg. Mr. Mumford and Mr. Kennon helped me write the certificates of rights. About 3 o'clock I returned home and carried over Colonel Hill, Colonel Eppes, and Mrs. Harrison in my boat to Mrs. Harrison's house where we supped and I ate roast turkey. I stayed there till about 7 o'clock and then walked home, where I found all well, thank God Almighty. I neglected to say my prayers and had good health, good thoughts, and good humor, thank God Almighty.

14. I rose about 5 o'clock and read a chapter in Hebrew and some Greek in Lucian. I said my prayers and ate boiled milk for breakfast. I danced my dance, and then settled some accounts. The weather was fair and cold all day. I wrote a letter to Commissary Blair and sent him the balance of his account in bills of exchange. Two men came to me for rights. I ate roast venison for dinner. In the afternoon I took a walk about the plantation. Dick Cocke sent to me for linseed oil but I could not spare any. In the evening a woman came from the Falls to settle accounts and told me all was well there, but that Tom Turpin has lost his [negro] and his wife was very sick. At night I ate some milk for supper and read a little English. I said my prayers and had good health, good thoughts, and good humor, thank God Almighty.

---

[1]William Randolph apparently was employed to make fair copies of the laws passed at the previous Assembly, for on November 14, 1711, he presented a petition to the House of Burgesses, "praying an allowance for four copies of the laws and journal of the last Assembly delivered unto the Honorable the Lieut. Governor, as also for a copy of the laws sent to the Secretary's office." (*JHB*, 1702-1712, p. 307.)

15. I rose at 4 o'clock and read two chapters in Hebrew and six leaves in Lucian. I said my prayers and ate boiled milk for breakfast. I danced my dance. The weather was fair and warm. I wrote to the Falls to order a steer down. I heard news of another negro dead at the Falls. God's will be done. I granted rights to several people. I was out of humor and denied some men to catch their hogs on my land because they had bred them there. I read some English and took a walk in the garden. I ate roast mutton for dinner. In the afternoon I walked about the plantation till the evening and then my cousin Harrison came and when she had stayed here about an hour my wife and I walked home with her and did not return home till 8 o'clock. Then I ate some milk and wrote some rights that a man came for this evening. I neglected to say my prayers and had good thoughts, good humor, and good health, thank God Almighty. Colonel Eppes was taken very sick last night.

16. I rose at 5 o'clock and read a chapter in Hebrew and some Greek in Lucian. I said my prayers and ate boiled milk for breakfast. I danced my dance, then granted 44 rights of land. The weather was warm. I settled some accounts. About 11 o'clock I had a messenger from the Falls to tell me that several of my negroes were sick and that the steer I sent for died on the road and Tom Turpin told me he could not stay except I [sell a negro] and I wrote him word that he might go away. I ate fish for dinner. In the afternoon I took a walk with my wife who was melancholy for her misfortunes and wished herself a freak for which I rebuked her. I read some English. In the evening there came a man for rights. I granted him eight. He told me Hal Harrison was extremely sick. I desired him to stay all night but he excused himself. I read more English at night. I neglected to say my prayers but had good health, good thoughts, and good humor, thank God Almighty.

17. I rose about 5 o'clock and read a chapter in Hebrew and some Greek in Lucian. I said my prayers and ate boiled milk for breakfast. I danced my dance. The weather was warm, the wind southeast. I settled several accounts and

granted several rights of land. I took a walk about the plantation. I read some English. The carter brought a steer from above and told me that another negro was dead at the Falls. God's will be done. I ate steak for dinner. In the afternoon I rode my new horse to see Colonel Eppes and found him extremely bad. From thence I went to see Colonel Hill's ship which he is building and then called at his house to see him and stayed about half an hour. Then I returned home and found all well, thank God. I wrote two [memoranda] for Will Wilkins. I said my prayers and had good thoughts, good humor, and good health, thank God Almighty.

18. I rose about 6 o'clock and read a chapter in Hebrew and no Greek. I said my prayers and ate boiled milk for breakfast. I danced my dance. The weather was warm and fair. I wrote a letter to Falling Creek. About 11 o'clock I went to church and heard a sermon of Mr. Anderson. Mr. Bland was at church and I brought him home to dinner. I ate some wild turkey for dinner. In the afternoon I walked with Mr. Bland almost to Mrs. Harrison's. Mrs. Eppes sent to me for some things for her husband, which I sent. Mistress Sarah Taylor came also with us from church. In the evening we took a walk. Mistress Sarah stayed with us all night. At night we talked of several things and drank a bottle of cider. I said my prayers and had good health, good thoughts, and good humor, thank God Almighty.

19. I rose about 6 o'clock and read a chapter in Hebrew and some Greek in Lucian. I said my prayers and ate boiled milk for breakfast. I danced my dance. I had abundance of people with me for rights and I granted more than a hundred and among others Mr. John Simons came for some. I spent all the morning in this business, only I read a little English. I heard that Mr. Hal Harrison was better by a man that came from Surry. I ate roast beef for dinner. In the afternoon I granted more rights. I was very courteous to everybody that came and trusted one poor man because he came a great way. John G-r-l came from Appomattox and told me Mr. Mumford and all beside were well

there. In the evening I took a walk about the plantation and at night John Bannister and I fell out and I gave him a severe reprimand for speaking surlily to me. I found Mr. B-n taking too much care of his horse. I said my prayers and had good health, good thoughts, and good humor, thank God Almighty.

20. I rose about 4 o'clock and read a chapter in Hebrew and some Greek in Lucian. I said my prayers and ate boiled milk for breakfast. I danced my dance. John Bannister and I were good friends again this morning. [Si] the negro boy was sick this morning and I gave him a vomit which worked well and recovered him a little. I sold 23 rights this morning. Then I wrote a letter to England. Then I read a little English likewise. My daughter was indisposed of a terrible cold. I ate roast mutton for dinner. In the afternoon we took a walk to see the boats that are building. Then I read some more English and afterwards took a walk about the plantation to see my people at work. At night I read a little French and had some milk for supper. I said my prayers and had good health, good thoughts, and good humor, thank God Almighty.

21. I rose about 5 o'clock and read two chapters in Hebrew and some Greek in Lucian. I said my prayers and ate boiled milk for breakfast. I danced my dance. My daughter was taken with a pain in her side and a violent fever. I sent for Drury Stith to let her blood and he was so kind as to do it though he tried twice first. When he had done he went away and would not stay to dinner. Mr. Dunn and his wife came about 12 o'clock. I ate some wild turkey for dinner, but ate too much. In the afternoon Mr. Dunn and I played at billiards. He told me that he heard Hal Harrison was dead. My poor daughter continued sick. I caused her to be put into a sweat which gave her some ease. In the evening I took a walk about the plantation and at night drank some cider with my friend. Mr. Dunn received a letter that made him resolve to go home that night. I said my prayers and had health, good thoughts, and good humor, thank God Almighty.

22. I rose about 5 o'clock and read a chapter in Hebrew and some Greek in Lucian. I said my prayers and ate boiled milk for breakfast. I danced my dance. My daughter continued very sick and complained of her side for which Mrs. Dunn let her blood but she bled but a little, but about 10 o'clock she grew better, thank God Almighty; and I sold 13 rights this morning. Then I read some English. Mr. Doyley came a little before dinner and dined with us. I ate roast beef. In the afternoon Mr. Doyley went away and I read more English and then wrote a letter to England. It rained almost all day so that I could not walk about. At night we ate some bread and cheese and drank some punch and were merry. I said my prayers and had good health, good thoughts, and good humor, thank God Almighty.

23. I rose about 5 o'clock and read a chapter in Hebrew and some Greek in Lucian. I said my prayers and ate boiled milk for breakfast. I danced my dance, and then went to see my child and found her much better, thank God Almighty. The lame boy was also better. There came a man for six rights who told me Hal Harrison was better. It snowed in the night but the snow melted in the morning and the weather cleared up. I read some English and then wrote a letter to England. I ate some boiled beef for dinner. In the afternoon I took a walk and trimmed some trees in the pasture. Then I read some more English till the evening and took another walk and met a man that wanted more rights. I granted him six. At night I read more English. My girl was better. I said my prayers and had good health, good thoughts, and good humor, thank God Almighty.

24. I rose about 5 o'clock and read a chapter in Hebrew and some Greek in Lucian. I said my prayers and ate boiled milk for breakfast. I danced my dance. My girl was better, thank God. The weather threatened rain or snow, the wind being northeast, but it did neither. Mr. Drury Stith called on his way over the river where he was going to see his sister Bolling[1] who was sick. Mr. Wilkins came to bind

---

[1] Anne (Stith), widow of Colonel Robert Bolling.

his son and several men came for rights and I sold about 20.
Mr. Will Randolph sent me a copy of the laws for which I
sent him my thanks. Mrs. Dunn went away this morning.
I ate broiled beef for dinner. In the afternoon Mr. G-r-l
came from Falling Creek and told me all was well there,
thank God. He put up some brass locks for me. In the
evening I took a walk about the plantation. At night I ate
some milk with my wife. We sat up till 10 o'clock. I said
my prayers and had good health, good thoughts, and good
humor, thank God Almighty.

25. I rose at 8 o'clock and read nothing because I discoursed Mr. G-r-l. I neglected to say my prayers but not
to eat my boiled milk for breakfast. I sent my lame boy
with Mr. G-r-l to Mrs. [Hancock] to be cured. We took a
walk to see the place I propose to keep my boats in, and the
place where I intend to set the gates. About 11 o'clock my
sloop came with planks and soon after Mr. G-r-l went away
in my boat. The sloop brought me a letter from Appomattox where all things were well, and a load of tobacco
ready. I ate roast beef for dinner. In the afternoon I took
a walk about the plantation and met negro P-t-s-n who had
been off the plantation and brought some bacon with him,
for which I threatened to whip him. Then I found also that
John was riding out with the stallion without leave, for
which I threatened him likewise. Then I returned home and
read some English and then walked out with my wife. At
night I read some English. I said my prayers and had good
health, good thoughts, and good humor, thank God Almighty.

26. I rose about 5 o'clock and read two chapters in
Hebrew and some Greek in Lucian. I said my prayers and
ate boiled milk for breakfast. Then I danced my dance.
My people unloaded the sloop of the planks with which she
was loaded. I wrote a letter to England. The weather was
fair and warm. About 12 o'clock Mr. Bland came on his
way to Williamsburg. I troubled him with several letters.
He stayed to dinner. I ate roast pork. In the afternoon
Mr. Bland went away and I went to give orders to my
people to pile the planks in the brick house where I spent

all the afternoon. In the evening I had not time to walk. At night I read some English and ate some milk. I said my prayers and had good health, good thoughts, and good humor, thank God Almighty.

27. I rose at 6 o'clock and read two chapters in Hebrew and some Greek in Lucian. I said my prayers and ate boiled milk for breakfast. I danced my dance and then went to the brick house to see my people pile the planks and found them all idle for which I threatened them soundly but did not whip them. The weather was cold and the wind at northeast. I wrote a letter to England. Then I read some English till 12 o'clock when Mr. Dunn and his wife came. I ate boiled beef for dinner. In the afternoon Mr. Dunn and I played at billiards. Then we took a long walk about the plantation and looked over all my business. In the evening my wife and little Jenny had a great quarrel in which my wife got the worst but at last by the help of the family Jenny was overcome and soundly whipped. At night I ate some bread and cheese. I said my prayers and had good health, good thoughts, and good humor, thank God Almighty.

28. I rose at 5 o'clock and read two chapters in Hebrew and some Greek in Lucian. I said my prayers and ate boiled milk for breakfast. I danced my dance. The weather was clear and warm till about 10 o'clock and then grew cold and cloudy. I wrote a letter to England and about 11 o'clock rode with Mr. Dunn to visit Colonel Eppes. We found him well recovered. A certain woman that was there had a child that could just go alone who had been with some of the children in the morning but could not be found. All the people on the plantation were looking for it and I went likewise to look [for] it and at last found it, for which the woman gave me abundance of blessings. Then we went to Colonel Hill's where we dined. I ate some fowl and bacon. Several of the Colonel's family were sick and he had lost a young fellow worth £100. We stayed here till 5 o'clock and then rode home where we found all well. I said my prayers and had good health, good thoughts, and good humor, thank God Almighty.

March, 1711

1. I rose at 5 o'clock and read a chapter in Hebrew and some Greek in Lucian. I said my prayers and ate boiled milk for breakfast. I danced my dance. The weather was cold and the wind northeast. I wrote a letter to England. The weather would not permit us to go to Mr. Platt's according to invitation. I took a walk about the plantation. Then I wrote another letter to England and after read some English. I ate boiled pork for dinner. In the afternoon I played at billiards with Mr. Dunn and then I wrote another letter to England. Then we took a walk about the plantation. I gave my wife a flourish this afternoon. At night I ate some [broiled] pudding, and had good health, good thoughts, and good humor, thank God Almighty. I sold four rights.

2. I rose at 4 o'clock and read two chapters in Hebrew and some Greek in Lucian. I said my prayers and ate boiled milk for breakfast. I danced my dance. I wrote a letter to England. A boy from Frank Eppes brought me some venison. The boatwright was affronted that I gave him pone instead of English bread for breakfast and took his horse and rode away without saying anything a word [sic]. Mr. Hal Randolph came to see me with a letter from Captain Webb. I ate roast beef for dinner. In the afternoon I received two letters from Williamsburg by which I learned that Colonel Jenings intends to go to England in the "Lion." I read some English and then took a walk about the plantation. I gave a vomit to John, L-s-n, and Tom by way of prevention. I said my prayers and had good health, good thoughts, and good humor, thank God Almighty.

3. I rose at 5 o'clock and read a chapter in Hebrew and some Greek in Lucian. I said my prayers and ate boiled milk for breakfast. It rained all the morning. I danced my dance. The boatwright returned last night again. Mr. Dunn and Mr. Randolph played 30 games at billiards. I

wrote a letter to England and settled some accounts between Captain Webb and me. I read a little English. I ate boiled pork for dinner. My wife endeavored to cut a bone of pork but Mr. Dunn took the dish and cut it for himself, which put my wife into great disorder and made her void blood so that [she] seemed to be going to miscarry and Mr. Dunn had not the manners to ask pardon. He went away in the rain this afternoon and so did Mr. Randolph. In the evening it snowed very much. At night we ate some bread and butter. I said my prayers and had good health, good thoughts, and good humor, thank God. I gave John, Tom, and L-s-n a vomit for their colds.

4. I rose at 8 o'clock and read two chapters in Hebrew and some Greek in Lucian. I said my prayers and ate boiled milk for breakfast. I danced my dance. My [wife] continued still disordered in her back and belly. However she went to church with Mrs. Dunn in the coach and I walked there. Mr. Anderson gave us a good sermon. After church nobody came home with us. Little Peter came from above and brought news another negro died, which makes 17 this winter; God's will be done. Several others are sick. The Lord have mercy on them, and spare them if it be His will. I ate boiled beef for dinner. In the afternoon Mrs. Dunn went away and I was at the trouble to send John home with her, who did not come back till 8 o'clock. He had a great cold still. In the evening I took a walk about the plantation. In the evening I read a little English. I said my prayers and had good health, good thoughts, and indifferent humor, thank God Almighty.

5. I rose at 4 o'clock and read two chapters in Hebrew and some Greek in Lucian. I said my prayers and ate boiled milk for breakfast. I danced my dance. I wrote several letters to the quarters and sent Suky to Manakin Town to Mr. Salle. The weather was warm. I wrote a letter to England. I sold eight rights. I ate some broiled beef for dinner. In the afternoon I removed several of the pictures. I received a letter from Mr. Bland that gave me an account of ill success of our forces in Spain and that some ships

were cleared and gone out without the Governor's knowledge and against the orders of the Council, and it is believed it was contrived by Colonel Corbin to be beforehand in his petition for the auditor's place. I was [not c-r-n-t] all day. In the evening my wife and I took a walk to see the boat, where John complained of a pain at the root of his tongue, for which I caused him to be let blood, which gave him ease. At night I ate some milk. I said my prayers and had good health, good thoughts, and good humor, thank God Almighty.

6. I rose at 7 o'clock and before I got up gave my wife a flourish. I read a chapter in Hebrew and some Greek in Lucian. I said my prayers and ate boiled milk for breakfast. It rained much in the night and a little this morning. John was better, thank God. I wrote the public accounts for the Governor. I resolved to eat no meat today and so I dined on potatoes and butter. In the afternoon I settled some accounts and then went and took a walk about the plantation. My wife was a little indisposed in her belly and in her teeth. At night I sealed up my letters and prepared everything for my journey tomorrow. I said my prayers and had good health, good thoughts, and good humor, thank God Almighty.

7. I rose at 6 o'clock but read nothing because of my journey to Williamsburg. I said my prayers and ate boiled milk for breakfast. I danced my dance, and gave the necessary orders to Bannister. The weather was clear and not very cold. About 9 o'clock I got on horseback and rode to Mr. Gee's where I had appointed to meet Colonel Hill, who came according to his time. We ate bacon and eggs and then proceeded to my brother Duke's. He was not at home but my sister was and gave us a cast over the river and from thence we rode to Colonel Duke's where we came about 5 o'clock. He could tell us no news. He received us, according to custom, very courteously. We had milk for supper and sat talking till about 9 o'clock before we went to bed. I said my prayers and had good health, good thoughts, and good humor, thank God Almighty.

8. I rose about 8 o'clock but read nothing because Colonel Hill lay with me. However, I said my prayers and ate milk and potatoes for breakfast. The moon changed this morning with a south wind. About 10 o'clock we took leave and rode to Williamsburg and by the way met Mr. Clayton who told us the fleet was come in but knew no particulars. Then we proceeded to Williamsburg, first to Mr. Bland's, who could tell us no more than Mr. Clayton. After I had set myself in order, and Colonel Hill had likewise, we went to wait on the Governor, who received us very courteously and with a particular distinction. He told us two ships of the fleet were come in and the rest, with the two men-of-war, were at hand. We dined there and I ate some roast beef for dinner. In the afternoon I walked with the Governor to the new house, where he showed the improvements he had made. Then I went home with the Governor and stayed with him till 9 o'clock tête-à-tête. Then I went to my lodgings where I said my prayers and had good health, good thoughts, and good humor, thank God Almighty. The Doctor was gone to the north.

9. I rose about 7 o'clock and read a chapter in Hebrew and some Greek in Homer. I ate some boiled milk for breakfast. Mr. Bland came to me about 9 o'clock. I went to the Governor's about 10 and drank some tea with him and Mrs. Russell. About 11 o'clock I walked with him to the new house where Captain [Berkeley] came to wait on the Governor, just come from England, who told him the fleet he left about 500 leagues off. The whole fleet consisted 20 sails besides the men-of-war. He said that Mr. Page[1] was come with him, that Mr. Lane, partner to Mr. Perry, was dead, that Colonel Parke was not arrived in England. We went to dine with the Governor, where I ate some salt fish, but Mr. Holloway dined there likewise, which put me out of humor. I sent my letters by Peter to Kiquotan to overtake the ships that were going out. About 5 o'clock I took leave of the Governor and went with Colonel Hill to

---

[1]Probably Mann Page, of Rosewell, Gloucester County, who had been at school in England.

see my sister Custis who was indisposed with a cold. About 9 o'clock we went to bed. I said a short prayer, and had good health, good thoughts, and good humor, thank God Almighty.

10. I rose about 8 o'clock and read nothing but I said my prayers and ate boiled milk for breakfast. My brother and Colonel Hill went to Yorktown this morning. My sister was under great apprehension lest her husband should return again to the Eastern Shore. I promised her in case of Mr. Burwell's death, who was sick, I would use my interest with the Governor to get him the place of naval officer. About 9 o'clock Mr. Clayton came to give me an account of my business in his hands. Among other things we talked of Colonel Digges' family and I desired him to offer Mr. Digges in my name that my wife would take care of his sister[1] because she had nobody to take care of her, which Mr. Clayton thought very kind. About 11 o'clock I took leave of him and my sister Custis and rode to Colonel Duke's, where I got about 2 o'clock and soon after came Colonel Bassett and his wife who dined there with us. I ate boiled beef for my dinner. Colonel Bassett told me the family of Major Burwell was not like to fall out because they had adjusted their differences. About 4 o'clock he and his wife went home and Colonel Duke and I took a walk. We talked till 9 o'clock and then I said my prayers and had good health, good thoughts, and good humor, thank God Almighty.

11. I rose about 7 o'clock and read nothing because I wished to shave myself. I said my prayers and ate milk and potatoes for breakfast. The weather was clear and warm. About 10 o'clock Colonel Hill came but brought me no letters but told us very bad news of the fleet which wanted some vessels, that six of them were taken and two burnt but he could not tell which they were, that Mr. Lane was dead, that tobacco was worth nothing, that the King of France had coined money which thus [necessitated] anew a begin-

---

[1]Probably Elizabeth, only daughter of Colonel Dudley Digges. Her mother died in 1708.

ning of war. Then we went to church and heard Mr.
Goodwin preach a good sermon. After church Mr. Goodwin invited us to dinner and I ate fish. Here we saw a fine
widow Mrs. O-s-b-r-n who had been handsome in her time.
From hence we went to Mr. B-s where we drank cider and
saw Molly King, a pretty black[1] girl. Then we went over
the river to my brother Duke's. I was not very well because
I had eaten too much. I said my prayers and had good
health, good thoughts, and good humor, thank God Almighty. Colonel Duke went over the river with us.

12. I rose about 6 o'clock and read nothing. However
I said my prayers and ate boiled milk for breakfast. About
8 o'clock we took our leave and called upon Mr. Gee and
took him with us to Mr. Drury Stith's. We found his wife
and son indisposed. It was very hot weather. About 12
o'clock we ate some [brains] for dinner and about 2 we took
our leave and I returned home, where I found all well, thank
God, except a negro boy called [Si] who had a fever and
violent cold. There had been no bad news from above since
I went from home. In the evening I took a walk about the
plantation and found everything in order. I had a small
quarrel with the boatwright about his making a [horse],
which he told me was not his business. I said my prayers
and had good health, good thoughts, and good humor, thank
God Almighty.

13. I rose at 8 o'clock and read nothing because Mr.
Peter Hamlin came to see me and told me the "Harrison"
was come in and had abundance of goods for me. I lent
him a horse to go to Colonel Hill's. Then I said my prayers
and ate boiled milk for breakfast. I wrote a letter to Falling Creek. About 10 o'clock came Captain Posford and
Captain Wilcox, the last of which gentlemen had lost his
ship this voyage. They brought me several letters and an
account of a great cargo for Williamsburg. These gentlemen parted with their convoy 500 leagues off which was
wrong in them because they had much goods in their ships.

---

[1]That is, a brunette. Shakespeare could refer to the lady of the sonnets as
being "black as hell," when he merely meant that she was not a blonde.

About 11 o'clock I went to court. I ate fish for dinner. In the afternoon I put up a picture and in the evening took a walk about the plantation. The negro boy was worse. At night I read some English. I said my prayers and had good health, good thoughts, and good humor, thank God Almighty.

14. I rose at 6 o'clock and read a chapter in Hebrew and some Greek in Lucian. I said my prayers and ate boiled milk for breakfast. I settled some accounts and then read some French. I put up a picture. About 12 o'clock came Captain John Eppes and stayed to dinner with us. I ate boiled beef for dinner. In the afternoon I talked with Captain Eppes till 4 o'clock. Then I put up a picture in the bed chamber. The negro boy was worse. In the evening I took a walk about the plantation and we missed a cow, who was mired somewhere. At night I read some English and then wrote some English. I said my prayers and had good health, good thoughts, and good humor, thank God Almighty. I danced my dance.

15. I rose at 6 o'clock and read a chapter in Hebrew and some Greek in Lucian. I said my prayers and ate boiled milk for breakfast. I danced my dance. The negro boy was a little better, thank God Almighty. We found the cow that was mired. The weather was cloudy and rained a little but soon cleared up again. The wind was west and it was a little cooler than yesterday. I looked over some of the new books that came lately from England by the "Harrison." We rummaged the cellar to know our stock of wine. I wrote a letter to England and then read a little English. I ate mutton for dinner. In the afternoon I unpacked some things. About 3 o'clock my cousin Harrison came to see us. The negro boy was something better, thank God. In the evening I took a walk about the plantation. At night I ate some milk and then said my prayers and had good health, good thoughts, and good humor, thank God Almighty.

16. I rose about 6 o'clock and read two chapters in Hebrew and some Greek in Lucian. I said my prayers and ate boiled milk for breakfast. I danced my dance. The

negro boy was better. We unpacked the beer that came from England and a great deal was run out. I wrote a letter to England. Captain Posford sent for some planks of oak of 25 feet long but I had none so long. I ate boiled pork for dinner. Moll spoiled a good plum pudding, for which I chastised her. In the afternoon Mr. Bland came from Williamsburg but brought no news nor letters. He came for the ship's [notice]. I discoursed him about the cargo. He would not stay under pretence of being at Williamsburg early tomorrow. I took a walk about the plantation. At night I read in the *Tatler*. I said my prayers and had good health, good thoughts, and good humor, thank God Almighty.

17. I rose at 6 o'clock and read a chapter in Hebrew and some Greek in Lucian. I said my prayers and ate boiled milk for breakfast. I danced my dance. Mr. Mumford came and told me all was well at Appomattox. I sold him several rights. About 12 o'clock Dick Hamlin came for rights likewise. Just before we went to dinner came Mr. Finney and Tom Randolph, who dined with us. They told me Colonel Randolph had the gout very much. I ate some broiled roast beef [*sic*]. I settled Colonel Randolph's account. One of my folks came from the Falls and told me three more of my people were dead. God's will be done. In the evening I rode a little way with Mr. Finney to see how they had mended the road. In the evening I read in the *Tatler* and then said my prayers, and had good health, good thoughts, and good humor, thank God Almighty.

18. I rose at 6 o'clock and read a chapter in Hebrew but no Greek. I said my prayers and ate boiled milk for breakfast. I danced my dance. My negro boy was much better, thank God. The weather was clear and warm. About 11 o'clock I went to church and heard Mr. Anderson preach a good sermon. After church I asked Captain Posford to come home to dinner. I ate roast beef. In the afternoon the Captain stayed till about 4 o'clock and then he took his leave. Then I took a walk about the plantation and found Mrs. Harrison's horses had broken my fence four times in

two days. My wife took a long walk with me and was much tired. Captain Posford told me Captain Stith was much [troubled] that I should sell him planks. At night I read some English and had good health, good thoughts, and good humor, thank God Almighty.

19. I rose at 6 o'clock and read two chapters in Hebrew and some Greek in Lucian. I said my prayers without much devoutness and ate boiled milk for breakfast. I danced my dance. About 9 o'clock Mr. Rogers came with some bills of exchange which I knew would be protested, and so I would not take them. Then I took a walk to see my people work. Then I wrote a long letter to England. I ate some boiled beef for dinner. In the afternoon I took another walk to see my people. Mr. C-k came to set up the wire. I wrote another letter to England. In the evening I took a walk about the plantation and found my people had done a great deal of work. At night I wrote another letter to England. I said my prayers and had good health, good thoughts, and good humor, thank God Almighty.

20. I rose at 6 o'clock and read two chapters in Hebrew and some Greek in Lucian. I said my prayers and ate boiled milk for breakfast. I danced my dance. Captain Isham Eppes sent for rights but I sent him none because he sent no money. I took a walk to see my people at work. The weather was cold, the wind being northeast. My negro boy was better, thank God. I wrote another long letter to England, about increasing my salary to 400 a year, in which I hope to succeed because I have some friends in the Treasury. I took a walk to see my people at work. Captain Posford sent some of my things up. I made an indifferent dinner this day because Moll had not boiled the bacon half enough, for which I gave her some stripes under which she [b-s-t] herself. I wrote another letter to England in the afternoon. In the evening I took a walk about the plantation with my wife. At night I read in the *Tatler* and ate some bread and new butter. I said my prayers and had good health, good thoughts, and good humor, thank God Almighty.

21. I rose at 7 o'clock and read two chapters in Hebrew and some Greek in Lucian. I said my prayers and ate boiled milk for breakfast. I danced my dance. The weather was very cold with a northeast wind. I wrote a letter to England. Then I took a walk about the plantation. About 12 o'clock Captain Wilcox came and brought me some letters from England and one from the Governor which told me Colonel Hill's ship was arrived in England. I ate fish for dinner. In the afternoon came Captain Posford and hired one of my flats. He stayed with me about an hour and went away. I wrote another letter to England and then took a walk about the plantation. Negro Frank came with a steer from above and told me all the people were well, thank God. At night I wrote two more letters to England. I said my prayers and had good health, good thoughts, and good humor, thank God Almighty.

22. I rose at 6 o'clock and read two chapters in Hebrew and some Greek in Lucian. I said my prayers and ate boiled milk for breakfast. I sent away my letters by Captain Posford's man. I wrote two letters to my overseers. I danced my dance. It continued cold still. About 10 Colonel Hill and Mr. Anderson [came] to see me. I gave them news to read and entertained them with showing them some new books. We rejoiced together at the news of Colonel Hill's ship's safe arrival in England. I ate some beefsteak for dinner. In the afternoon we talked till about 5 o'clock and then they returned home and I took my gun and endeavored to shoot some partridges but could not. At night I read in the *Tatler*. I said my prayers and had good health, good thoughts, and good humor, thank God Almighty.

23. I rose at 6 o'clock and read a chapter in Hebrew and some Greek in Lucian. I said my prayers and ate boiled milk for breakfast. I danced my dance. It continued cold and fair weather. I settled some accounts. I read some English in the *Tatler*. I ate some roast beef for dinner. In the afternoon Johnny Randolph came and brought me a letter from Williamsburg without any news. He said the Governor came out of Williamsburg on Wednesday and

would be here on Saturday. I examined him in Greek and found he had made a great progress. He told me Captain Stith had the dropsy. About 4 o'clock he went away and I took a walk with my gun to kill some partridge, but could not. At night I read some English. I said my prayers and had good health, good thoughts, and good humor, thank God Almighty.

24. I rose at 7 o'clock and read nothing because I was to go meet the Governor. I said my prayers and ate boiled milk for breakfast. The weather was clear and about 9 o'clock I rode in form to Captain Drury Stith's, where I had appointed several gentlemen to go and meet the Governor. Here we ate some bread and butter and about 12 o'clock proceeded to [Chickahominy Bridge] and found him just arrived there, with Colonel Bassett and some few gentlemen. After the Governor and Mrs. Russell had rested a little we returned with the Governor to Captain Stith's where we stopped to drink a peach dram, and then went on to my house at Westover where [. . .] gentlemen went to wait on the Governor. It was evening before we got there and about 7 o'clock before we went to supper. We had eight dishes beside the dessert every day. I ate some beef. I gave them several sorts of wine and made them as welcome as I could. After supper all the gentlemen went home and the Governor and the Doctor and I drank two bottles of French wine and talked of many things. The Governor seemed satisfied with his entertainment. I said a short prayer and had good health, good thoughts, and good humor, thank God Almighty.

25. I rose at 7 o'clock and read nothing because of the company. I said my prayers and ate boiled milk for breakfast. About 8 o'clock the Governor came down stairs and about 9 drank some tea and ate bread and butter. It was 12 o'clock before the Governor and the ladies were dressed and then we went to church and heard Mr. Anderson preach. He and three other gentlemen came and dined with us. I would have no more company for fear of crowding the Governor. I ate some tongue for dinner. The Governor's

cook dressed dinner and so it was in good order. The sloop came last night, loaded with planks. After dinner the company stayed till 5 o'clock and then took leave. The Governor and I took a walk about the plantation. He told me that Colonel Bassett agreed to come into the Council again and that he had written to England about it. At night we drank several things but French wine was the chief. About 9 o'clock we went to bed. I neglected to say my prayers but had good thoughts, good humor, and good health, thank God Almighty.

26. I rose at 6 o'clock and read nothing. I neglected to say my prayers and ate boiled milk for breakfast and at 9 o'clock I took some milk tea with the company. Several Indians came here yesterday to complain that the Nottoway Indians and several northern Indians had conferred together to cut them off. I told the Governor of it and he sent an order to the Nottoways to forbid them and ordered Colonel Harrison to cause some of the northern Indians to come to him to declare their business. About 10 o'clock several gentlemen came to wait on the Governor, who stayed to dinner, and among the rest Captain Wilcox, who told me Captain John Stith was very bad. We had a very handsome dinner; I ate a partridge. About 5 the gentlemen went away and the Governor, the Doctor, and I took a walk. At night the Doctor was sent for to Captain Stith's and went about 8 o'clock at night. We drank several things. My sister and Mrs. Dunn came this afternoon. I neglected to say my prayers but had good health, good thoughts, and good humor, thank God Almighty.

27. I rose at 6 o'clock and prepared for to wait on the Governor some part of his journey. We ate some bread and fresh butter for breakfast and then rode to Colonel Hill's where the Governor saw Colonel Hill's ship and we ate some roast beef. Here the Doctor came to us and about 10 o'clock we went over the river where we found several gentlemen ready to go with the Governor, among whom was Colonel Frank Eppes. We rode away to Falling Creek where we got about 12 o'clock. The Governor observed my

sawmill and dam very nearly and the Doctor was much pleased with it. I brought some wine with me with which I entertained the company. Then we rode to the falls of the river with which the Governor was well pleased. Here all my people and affairs were well. From hence we returned to Captain Webb's who was sick of the gout. However we were very well entertained by his wife who is an excellent woman. I ate some fowl and bacon for supper. We had several gentlemen come over with us and three parsons. The Doctor and I lay together. I neglected to say my prayers but had good health, good thoughts, and good humor, thank God Almighty.

28. I rose about 7 o'clock and was shaved. I neglected to say my prayers but ate some hashed turkey for breakfast. Captain Webb did not sleep because of the pain he was in. The weather was very cold and snowed a little. However the Governor was resolved to go on and about 10 o'clock we took leave and rode by [Pamunkey] where we passed Chickahominy Swamp and so went to Major Merriweather's, which is a journey of about 26 miles.[1] The Major was a little surprised and was not prepared much for such guests; however he did as well as he could and for fear of the worst I had brought two bottles of wine with me. The Major told the Governor he had not made above one visit in 16 years and that was to a man that was sick. I ate some boiled beef for dinner. The Major sat at the upper end of the table and helped himself first. His wife did not appear. The Doctor's horse was foundered so that he could not go; however he would not believe it. After supper I took a little walk about the plantation, which is level. Our diversion was chiefly in laughing at the Doctor about his horse and he was at last a little angry. I neglected to say my prayers but had good health, good thoughts, and good humor, thank God Almighty. The Doctor and I lay together.

29. I rose about 7 o'clock and neglected to say my prayers. The Governor made me a compliment and would

---

[1] They were in the part of New Kent County now Hanover, where Nicholas Merriweather, burgess for the county, owned many acres.

permit me to go with him no farther but the Doctor endeavored to persuade me to it. About 9 o'clock I ate boiled beef for breakfast. About 10 I took leave of the Governor and when I had seen him [to] Pamunkey River, I and the gentlemen with me returned and had one of the Major's sons for our guide as far as Mr. Fleming's[1] where we drank abundance of cider but we could not see his pretty daughters because they were gone to a meeting. Mr. Fleming himself went with us to show us the way to the bridge where I took leave of the gentlemen that had been with me to wait on the Governor and I rode by myself home, where I arrived about 9 o'clock and found all well, thank God Almighty. I gave Mrs. Russell an account of the Governor's health and of his journey and that the Doctor was to ride on her horse because he had foundered his own which she was very sorry for. In the evening we drank a bottle of mead and I ate some toast. My gray horse carried me this journey very well and so did Ch-s-r which Bannister rode for he had taken good care of them. I said my prayers and had good health, good thoughts, and good humor, thank God Almighty. I rogered my wife with vigor.

30. I rose about 6 o'clock and read two chapters in Hebrew and some Greek in Lucian. I said my prayers and ate boiled milk for breakfast. My wife and I paid all possible respect to Mrs. Russell and I entertained her as well as I could and her conversation was very agreeable. The women drank tea but I drank none with them. About 11 o'clock came Captain Posford and we settled the freight at £12 per ton and I engaged for 100 hogsheads. He told me that Captain Stith was better. He stayed with us at dinner and I ate fish which made me very dry. In the afternoon the Captain went away and I wrote my journal. About 4 o'clock I drank some coffee with the women and talked with them till the evening. Then I took a walk about the plantation. At night we drank a bottle of cider and talked

---

[1]Charles Fleming, of St. Peter's Parish, New Kent County, a large land-owner. His pretty daughters were probably Judith, who married (in 1712) Tom Randolph; and Susannah, who married John Bates. (*Va. Mag.*, XXIII, 325.)

till about 9 o'clock and then the ladies went to bed. I said my prayers and had good health, good thoughts, and good humor, thank God Almighty. I rogered my wife again.

31. I rose about 6 o'clock and read two chapters in Hebrew and some Greek in Lucian. I said my prayers and ate boiled milk for breakfast. My wife told me of the misfortunes of Mrs. Dunn—that her husband had beat her, and that she had complained to Mr. Gee of it, who made Mr. Dunn swear that he would never beat her again; that he threatened to kill her and abused her extremely and told her he would go from her. I was sorry to hear it and told my wife if he did go from her she might come here. I read some news till dinner. I ate boiled beef for dinner. In the afternoon we made a cold tincture. In the evening I took a long walk about the plantation. At night we drank a bottle of French wine. I said my prayers and had good health, good thoughts, and good humor, thank God Almighty. Mrs. Russell has good sense and very good breeding but can hardly forbear being hysterical, notwithstanding it is with good manners.

April, 1711

1. I rose at 6 o'clock and said my prayers with devoutness but read nothing because I drank tea and ate bread and butter with the ladies. I danced my dance. The ladies were dressed by 11 o'clock and we went to church with two coaches and heard Mr. Anderson preach a good sermon. We received the Sacrament with devoutness except Mrs. Russell, who I waited upon to her coach as soon as church was done. My cousin Harrison went home with us and gave herself airs of fainting because Mr. Gee came into the room, whom I had invited over to dinner. I ate boiled beef again. In the afternoon Betty Harrison and Betty Bassett came to see us. Poor Mr. Gee was melancholy because Mrs. Harrison appeared uneasy at his company. In the evening he went away by himself except his little ganymede that was with him. In the evening we drank a bottle of cider and the conversation went current on till 9 o'clock. Then I said my prayers shortly and had good health, good thoughts, and good humor, thank God Almighty.

2. I rose at 7 o'clock and read a chapter in Hebrew and some Greek in Lucian. I said my prayers and ate boiled milk for breakfast. I danced my dance. It threatened rain, with the wind at northeast, but without effect till about 3 o'clock in the afternoon. I read some law in Coke on Littleton. Our ladies were not dressed till one o'clock and then they went in the coach to Mrs. Harrison's and I walked. Mistress Betty Harrison was extremely recovered by the cure that Doctor Cocke had put her in. Colonel Bassett's two daughters were there.[1] About 3 o'clock we went to dinner and I ate some partridge. In the afternoon we sat and talked and my sister received an account that my brother was come to our house which made her impatient to go to him. I returned with her in the coach and afterwards sent it again for Mrs. Russell because of the rain. As soon as it

---

[1] Betty and Lucy.

was dark Mr. Dunn and his wife came. I neglected to say my prayers but had good thoughts, good health, and good humor, thank God Almighty.

3. I rose at 6 o'clock and read a chapter in Hebrew and some Greek in Lucian. I said my prayers and ate boiled milk for breakfast. It rained again this morning and prevented me from waiting on Mrs. Russell to Colonel Hill's as was intended. However I sent word we could not come. Mr. Dunn and I played at billiards and then we read some news while the ladies spent three hours in dressing, according to custom. About half an hour after one o'clock we went to dinner and I ate some boiled pork. In the afternoon I carried Mrs. Russell into the billiard table and to the library and showed her some prints. It rained almost all day and prevented our walk. I read in the *Dispensary*[1] to the ladies till night and then we played at piquet and I won all. I neglected to say my prayers but had good health, good thoughts, and good humor, thank God Almighty.

4. I rose at 6 o'clock and read two chapters in Hebrew and some Greek in Lucian. I said my prayers and ate boiled milk for breakfast. I danced my dance. It rained again very hard and the wind was northeast. This was court day but the rain hindered people from coming. We played at billiards and I won half a crown. Captain Posford came and told me at first he could have £14 per ton, but I let him know I would not give it and so at last he agreed to take mine at £12. I ate some mutton-pie for dinner. In the afternoon it began to clear up and my brother Custis and I and Mr. Dunn walked into the churchyard where we saw several people drunk, notwithstanding the late law.[2] In the evening came Mr. Clayton and Tom Jones. I employed him in my action against Joe Wilkinson. He told me Colonel Randolph was very sick. At night we drank two

[1] Sir Samuel Garth's *The Dispensary, A Poem* (1699), a popular mock epic describing a battle between the physicians and the apothecaries.

[2] On December 9, 1710, the Governor signed "An act for the further restraint of tippling houses and other disorderly places." (*JHB*, 1702-1712, p. 298.)

bottles of wine and were very merry. I neglected to say my prayers but had good health, good thoughts, and good humor, thank God Almighty.

5. I rose about 6 o'clock but read nothing because I prepared to go to Colonel Hill's with Mrs. Russell. I said my prayers and ate boiled milk for breakfast. Mr. Clayton and Mr. Jones who went last night to Mrs. Harrison's came again this morning to drink tea. About 10 we put two of our horses to the Governor's [coach] and my wife rode in the coach with Mrs. Russell and the rest went on horseback to Colonel Hill's except Mr. Clayton, Mr. Jones, and my brother Custis, who all went to Williamsburg. We got to Colonel Hill's in about an hour, notwithstanding the roads were dirty. We were very courteously entertained. I ate bacon and fowl for dinner. In the afternoon we walked to the ship and Mrs. Russell had a little of her ague which I was very sorry for. About 5 o'clock we returned home and the coach performed it in an hour. When we came home we drank a bottle of French wine and then went to bed. I said my prayers and had good health, good thoughts, and good humor, thank God Almighty. Nurse had an ague.

6. I rose about 7 o'clock and read a chapter in Hebrew and some Greek in Lucian. I said my prayers and ate boiled milk for breakfast. I danced my dance. Mr. Dunn went away this morning and is to begin to keep school next Monday. The weather was very warm and pleasant. Mrs. Russell was much disordered. About 11 o'clock came Mr. Bland, just from Colonel Randolph's, who he said was very sick. He told me the things got well to Williamsburg for his store. About 12 came Mrs. D-k and Mistress Sarah Taylor but the women were not dressed in a good while so that I was forced to entertain them. Mrs. Russell was so indisposed that she could eat no dinner. I ate roast veal. In the afternoon Mr. Bland went away and soon after him the ladies. About 4 o'clock Mrs. Russell was better and ate some veal broth. In the evening I took a walk about the plantation. At night we drank some Rhenish wine and ate

some bread and butter and were very merry till 10 o'clock. I said my prayers and had good health, good thoughts, and good humor, thank God Almighty.

7. I rose at 6 o'clock and read a chapter in Hebrew and some Greek in Lucian. I said my prayers and ate boiled milk for breakfast. I danced my dance. I ordered my lambs to be cut and Gilbert[1] assisted my people. I read some English. Mrs. Russell had her fever. About 11 o'clock we went to Captain Stith's, some in the coach and some on horseback. We were courteously entertained and found the Captain much better than he had been. The Governor's men came over with the horses to carry Mrs. Russell to Williamsburg and they brought me a letter from Mr. Clayton that told me Captain Smith in the man-of-war was come from the West Indies but no ship with him and that Colonel Harrison's vessel was taken with two others. I ate some cake before dinner and then some fowl and bacon. Mrs. Russell was much out of order and could eat nothing. About 5 o'clock we returned home and Mrs. Russell went immediately to bed. We ate some bread and butter. I said my prayers and had good health, good thoughts, and good humor, thank God Almighty.

8. I rose at 6 o'clock and read two chapters in Hebrew and some Greek in Lucian. I said my prayers and ate boiled milk for breakfast. I danced my dance. The weather was very warm. I sent away little Peter who brought me word all was well above. Mrs. Russell continued much indisposed and began again to take the bark again [sic] which she has taken nine months without losing her ague above 14 days together. I read a sermon in Doctor Tillotson and afterwards some news till dinner. Mrs. Russell could not come to dinner. I ate boiled mutton. In the afternoon I read some English. Mrs. Russell came down about 4 o'clock and ate some broth but soon brought it up again. In the evening I took a walk about the plantation and at night we drank some cider and I ate some apple pie.

[1] The Governor's coachman.

We all endeavored to divert Mrs. Russell. I said a short prayer and had good health, good thoughts, and good humor, thank God Almighty.

9. I rose about 5 o'clock and read the Psalms in Hebrew and some Greek in Lucian. I said my prayers and ate boiled milk for breakfast. I danced my dance. About 7 o'clock Mrs. Russell, after eating bread and butter and drinking some coffee, went away in the Governor's coach and six horses and my sister Custis with her. She was a little better this morning. I excused myself from waiting on her because the General Court was so near. The weather was very hot for them to travel in. I gave the Governor's servants some strong beer before they went and put some meat and wine in the coach for the ladies and their men and some corn also for the horses. John H-s-t came to settle accounts with me and about 12 o'clock Mr. M-r-s-l came and I was very angry with him for losing his time so much as to come in the middle of the week and would not speak with him. I ate roast veal for dinner. In the afternoon I read the news till the evening and then I took a walk about the plantation with my wife and Mrs. Dunn, and the air was very sweet and the birds very merry. I said my prayers and had good health, good thoughts, and good humor, thank God Almighty.

10. I rose at 6 o'clock and read the Psalms in Hebrew and some Greek in Lucian. I said my prayers and ate boiled milk for breakfast. I danced my dance. The weather was not so warm as yesterday, and threatened rain but without effect. Several people came to me this morning and among the rest John Randolph that told me his father was very sick and desired a bottle of sack, which I sent him. I read some news till dinner. I ate roast mutton and sallet. In the afternoon came Colonel Bassett who flattered everything and soon after him Will Randolph and Major Harrison, the last of which gentlemen told me Mrs. Parker had desired him to take up my mortgage on her estate but he would do nothing without acquainting me first with it. I took this charity very kindly and answered him I had no view but to be paid and should be glad to have so good a paymaster as

himself. They went away in the evening and my wife and I took a walk about the plantation. Captain Posford and Captain L-th-n came to see me in the morning. Mrs. Dunn went home likewise. I said my prayers and had good health, good thoughts, and good humor, thank God Almighty.

11. I rose about 6 o'clock and read the Psalms in Hebrew and some Greek in Lucian. I said my prayers and ate boiled milk for breakfast. I danced my dance. It rained a little this morning, the wind northeast, but soon left off. I wrote a memorandum by which Will Eppes was to be bound to me. Then I settled some accounts till dinner. I ate some roast veal for dinner. In the afternoon Colonel Hardiman came with Will Eppes to bind him but that could not be done because his mother was not here. Then I weighed some money. In the evening I took a walk about the plantation. My wife walked with me, notwithstanding she was a little indisposed. At night I read some news till almost 9 o'clock. I said my prayers and had good health, good thoughts, and good humor, thank God Almighty.

12.[1] I rose about 6 o'clock and read the Psalms in Hebrew and some Greek in Lucian. I said my prayers and ate boiled milk for breakfast. I danced my dance. I received a letter this morning from Mr. C-s in Barbados which told me the sad news that my father Parke was shot through the head in the Leeward Islands.[2] He told me no particulars because it was a melancholy subject. I told it my wife as gently as I could and it affected her very much but I comforted her as well as I could by telling her that his enemies killed him because he should not make their villainy appear in England. My wife could eat nothing at dinner, but I ate some boiled veal and bacon. In the afternoon I weighed some money and then came my cousin Betty Harrison and Sarah Taylor and stayed about an hour. In the evening it rained and blew hard, the wind northeast so

---

[1]In the margin opposite this entry there is a sketch of a pointing hand.
[2]The tragedy occurred on December 7, 1710.

that I could not walk. At night I read some news. I said a short prayer and had good health, good thoughts, and good humor, thank God Almighty.

13. I rose about 6 o'clock and read the Psalms in Hebrew and some Greek in Lucian. I said my prayers and ate boiled milk for breakfast. I danced my dance. It rained almost all night. I settled accounts with the boatwright and parted very good friends with him. I let out a nine hogshead flat to Captain L-th-m and his people took her away this morning. I wrote several things and settled some accounts till dinner, only about 11 o'clock Mr. Bland came in his way to Williamsburg but went away again before dinner. About one o'clock Mrs. Bassett, my cousin Harrison, Betty Harrison and Sarah Taylor came to dine with us. My wife could not come out for grief. I ate roast mutton for dinner. In the afternoon came Frank Eppes and Will Kennon to visit me and in the evening Robin Mumford who persuaded the other gentlemen to stay all night. About 5 o'clock the ladies went away and with the men I took a walk about the plantation. At night we went to supper and I ate a little veal. I neglected to say my prayers but had good health, good thoughts, and good humor, thank God Almighty.

14. I rose at 6 o'clock and read nothing because of the company. I neglected to say my prayers and ate boiled milk for breakfast. Then I played at billiards with Mr. Mumford. I settled some accounts. About 11 o'clock Frank Eppes and Mr. Kennon went away but Mr. Mumford stayed. John Randolph called here on his way to Williamsburg. Captain Posford sent his boat to fetch Eugene and my trunk to carry them to Williamsburg. Mr. Mumford and I took a walk about the plantation till dinner. I ate some roast mutton for dinner. In the afternoon Mr. Mumford went away and Mr. Gee came and I gave him some seeds of the [u-n-y] tree. He stayed about an hour and then went away. Then came Captain L-th-m for some planks and drank some strong beer. In the evening it rained and hindered me from walking. Mr. G-r-l came and told me all was well. I ate some supper with him and gave him

some strong beer. I neglected to say my prayers but had good health, good thoughts, and good humor, thank God Almighty.

15. I rose about 7 o'clock and read the Psalms in Hebrew and two chapters in the Greek Testament. I said my prayers and ate boiled milk for breakfast. It rained this morning so that we could not go to church. Mr. G-r-l and I had abundance of discourse about the affairs at Falling Creek and had a little quarrel but it was soon over. I had a letter from the Falls which told me another negro was like to die. God preserve her and all the rest. I ate some bacon and eggs for dinner. Presently after dinner I recommended my wife and family to God Almighty and went over the creek to my brother Duke's where I found all well and from thence to Colonel Duke's where I ate some custard for supper. It rained by the way. I said my prayers and had good health, good thoughts, and good humor, thank God Almighty. My brother Duke came with me to Colonel Duke's.

16. I rose about 6 o'clock and read nothing because I prepared for my journey to Williamsburg. I said my prayers and ate milk and bread for breakfast. We stayed here till about 8 o'clock and then Colonel Duke and I took leave of my brother and then rode to Williamsburg where we arrived about 11 o'clock. I set myself in order and then went to court. I sent my man Tom home with a letter to my wife to comfort her for her father's death. I found the news came not only from Barbados but also from Jamaica and Bermudas by which it appeared that he was murdered after a most barbarous manner. The court rose about 2 o'clock. We stayed at the coffeehouse till 4 o'clock and then went and dined with the Governor. I ate fowl and bacon for dinner. Mrs. Russell was very inquisitive after the health of my family but was not well herself. About 8 o'clock I went home where I said my prayers and had good health, good thoughts, and good humor, thank God Almighty.

17. I rose about 6 o'clock and read a chapter in Hebrew and some Greek in Homer. I neglected to say my prayers because company came in on me. I ate boiled milk for breakfast. I had several gentlemen come to see me and among the rest Mr. Le Fevre[1] a Frenchman of great learning. Colonel Ludwell came also to learn to be auditor.[2] About 10 o'clock I went to court. While I was there I received a letter from my brother Custis which told me he was not well. We rose about one o'clock and then walked to the Governor's house where we stayed till 4 and then I went with Colonel Ludwell and dined with the Commissary where I ate roast beef for dinner. Mrs. Ludwell was there and very courteous to me. I stayed there till 6 o'clock and then took my leave, notwithstanding they asked me to stay there, but I went home where I wrote till about 9 o'clock and settled some accounts. Then I said my prayers and had good health, good thoughts, and good humor, thank God Almighty.

18. I rose at 6 o'clock and read a chapter in Hebrew and some Greek in Homer. I said a short prayer and ate boiled milk for breakfast. Several gentlemen came to see me. About 9 o'clock I went to wait on the Governor and saw Mrs. Russell who had her ague again. About 10 we went to court where we sat till about 3 o'clock and nothing remarkable happened and I went with some of my brothers to dine with the Governor. I ate some fowl and bacon. About 5 o'clock we went away and took a walk to the new house and from thence went to the coffeehouse. There came

---

[1]Byrd's entry of January 28, 1712, gives us the name of this gentleman as Tanaquil Faber (or LeFevre). He was licensed to preach in Virginia June 19, 1709. (*Va. Mag.*, VII, 312.) The delay in his coming to the colony is explained by a letter of Spotswood, written in August 1710, which reports that Mr. Faber had become entangled with an "idle hussy." (*Official Letters of Alexander Spotswood*, I, 4.) When he finally arrived in Virginia, he had the woman with him. Although he was elected (April 25) professor of mathematics and philosophy at the College, he was discharged in the next January for unbecoming conduct. Spotswood deported the woman, and the reformation of the professor is described by the Governor on May 8, 1712. (*Ibid.*, I, 103, 156-8.) In 1724 he was preaching at Jamestown. (*Wm. Q. (1)*, VI, 85.)

[2]Philip Ludwell was sworn deputy auditor on July 21, 1712. (*Ex. Jour.*, III, 318.)

several of the [courteous] young men and we went to gaming and I won five pounds. We played till about 10 o'clock and then I went to my lodgings where I settled some accounts. I said my prayers and had good health, good thoughts, and good humor, thank God Almighty. Mr. Holloway and I had some discourse but could not settle our account.

19. I rose about 7 o'clock and read two chapters in Hebrew and no Greek because there came much company to my lodgings. I said a short prayer and ate rice milk for breakfast. I settled some accounts and about 10 o'clock went to court where nothing remarkable happened but that Mr. S-l-n was prosecuted for beating of George Walker. We had no criminals this court. The court rose about 4 o'clock and some of us went to dinner at Mrs. G-r-t's where we had good victuals and no drink. After dinner Colonel Smith and I took a walk and overtook the Governor and walked with him to the Governor's new house. We walked with him till it was dark and then took our leave and went to the coffeehouse. I stayed here about half an hour and then went home to my lodgings. I wrote a little and then said my prayers and had good health, good thoughts, and good humor, thank God Almighty.

20. I rose about 6 o'clock and read two chapters in Hebrew and some Greek in Lucian. I said my prayers and ate boiled milk for breakfast. I had several gentlemen come to my lodgings. Both my overseers came likewise and told me that all was well above but one woman that was sick. I wrote a letter to my wife in the morning and another in the afternoon. About 9 o'clock I went into court where we sat till past 5 dispensing justice. My case against Joe Wilkinson was called but not tried this day. I went to dine with the Governor and ate roast mutton for dinner. While I was there the Doctor returned from his journey and told me all were well at Westover and that Colonel Randolph was extremely sick and in great danger. At night I walked to the coffeehouse and drank two dishes of tea. Then I returned

to my lodgings where I said my prayers and had good health, good thoughts, and good humor, thank God Almighty. I had several letters from England.

21. I rose at 6 o'clock and read nothing because my head was full of my case. I said my prayers and recommended my case to God to direct it according to equity and justice. I ate boiled milk for breakfast. Several gentlemen came to see me and Colonel Beverley among the rest. I recived an account from England that two ships were lost in which I lost 60 hogsheads of tobacco. God's will be done. About 9 o'clock I went to court and my case against Joe Wilkinson came on and the jury found for me and 3000 pounds of tobacco damages and John Bolling offered to pay it. About 2 o'clock I went out of court and did some business and then returned again and we sat till about 5 o'clock. Then I went to dine at the Governor's and ate tripe for dinner. Colonel Randolph died this evening about 5 o'clock.[1] I went early to my lodgings and did some business with Colonel Robinson. I said a short prayer and had good health, good thoughts, and good humor, thank God Almighty.

22. I rose about 7 o'clock and read a chapter in Hebrew and some Greek in Lucian. I said my prayers and ate boiled milk for breakfast. Robin Beverley came to see me this morning and told me his son Billy was come in and had a quartan ague, that he was pretty well improved in his learning but seemed to have bad health. About 11 o'clock Mr. Clayton and Mr. D-r-k came to see me in order to go with me to church. The first of these gentlemen asked me if it was worth my while to be escheator in the place of Colonel Randolph. I thanked him and considered of it. Then we walked to church and heard Mr. Anderson preach. After church I borrowed a horse of Mr. Clayton and rode to Queen's Creek where I found all pretty well and at dinner. I ate some roast beef for dinner. I stayed there with them till almost sunset and then returned to Williamsburg where

---

[1]Colonel William Randolph of Turkey Island, father of numerous Randolphs mentioned throughout the diary.

I made a visit to Mrs. Bland[1] to console the death of her father. I stayed there all the evening and then went to my lodgings. I said my prayers and had good health, good thoughts, and good humor, thank God Almighty.

23. I rose about 6 o'clock and read a chapter in Hebrew but no Greek because I had company. I said a short prayer and ate boiled milk for breakfast. About 9 o'clock I went to wait on the Governor and asked him for the escheator's place. He would not promise me but gave me great hope by the compliments he was pleased to make me. I also begged leave of him to go to England to manage Colonel Parke's affairs. He was pleased to tell me he would always be ready to grant me that and likewise to make any man my deputy that I pleased. John Bolling desired my interest with the Governor for the escheator's place but I told him honestly that I had asked for it myself. Then we went to court where we sat till 5 o'clock and then all the council went to dine with the Governor because it was Saint George's day. I ate boiled beef. We were very merry in the evening in drinking the healths and in making the Commissary drink them by the help of Colonel Harrison that sat next him. About 9 o'clock we took leave and some of us went to Colonel Bray's where some company was dancing. I stayed there about an hour and then went home. I neglected to say my prayers but had good health, good thoughts, and very good humor, thank God Almighty.

24. I rose about 6 o'clock and read two chapters in Hebrew and some Greek in Homer. I said my prayers and ate boiled milk for breakfast. I had abundance of people come to see me about business. About 9 o'clock I went to Council where I procured a patent for the gold mines[2] for Colonel Hill. Then I went to my office above stairs and settled some accounts. About one o'clock the court sat and a new trial was ordered in Branch[3] his case concerning his

---

[1]Mrs. Richard Bland was Elizabeth, daughter of Colonel Randolph.
[2]The so-called "gold mines" were found to be "no other than a kind of Taulk." They lay in New Kent County. (*Executive Journals*, III, 266-7.)
[3]The Branch family for generations owned Kingsland on the south side of the James River, between Falling Creek and Kingsland Creek.

land near Falling Creek. Mr. Holloway was very sullen
against me. The court rose about 5 o'clock and I went to
dine with the Governor. I ate roast beef for dinner. At
night we diverted ourselves with some Indians. Then I
returned to my lodgings where I settled some accounts. I
said my prayers and had good health, good thoughts, and
good humor, thank God Almighty.

25. I rose about 6 o'clock and read nothing because I had
company come in as soon as I was up. I said a short prayer
and ate boiled milk for breakfast. I settled accounts with
abundance of people. About 9 o'clock I went to Council
where the Governor heard several disputes about entering
for land. About noon we went to court and sat till about
4 o'clock and then the governors of the College met and
chose five new members and the Governor was chosen
Rector but he was displeased that we did not turn Mr.
Blackamore out of the school and Mr. Le Fevre in. He
also showed abundance of disorder because we did not
choose Dr. Cocke one of the College but we excused ourselves because he was not an inhabitant. We chose Mr. Le
Fevre professor of philosophy and mathematics with a
salary of £80 a year. Colonel Smith and I dined at Marot's
and I ate roast beef. I went about 11 o'clock home and
said my prayers and had good health, good thoughts, and
good humor, thank God Almighty.

26. I rose about 6 o'clock and read a chapter in Hebrew
and no Greek. I neglected to say my prayers and ate boiled
milk for breakfast. Abundance of company came to see me
about business so that I could not go to court till 10 o'clock.
I did not stay there long but went off the bench again about
my accounts. The court sat till about 5 o'clock and I went
to Mrs. G-r-t's to dinner and ate boiled beef. I paid for all
the days I had been absent, three bits for every day. Then
Colonel Smith and I took a walk to take the air. In the
evening I went home to my lodgings and did a great deal of
business and settled abundance of accounts but could read

nothing. About 10 o'clock I went to bed and said my prayers and had good health, good thoughts, and good humor, thank God Almighty.

27. I rose about 6 o'clock and read nothing because I had my public accounts to write. I said a short prayer and ate boiled milk for breakfast. Several people came to me; however I used no ceremony but wrote on till I had finished my business and then I went to court where I just saved my day, because the court was just on rising. Then we went to Council and Colonel Ludwell examined my account and found an error in it which cost me some trouble to rectify. About 6 o'clock the Council rose and I went to dinner with the Governor where I ate boiled beef. It rained a little in the evening. At night I went to the coffeehouse where I stayed about an hour and then went to my lodgings where I settled some accounts. I neglected to say my prayers for which reason I was guilty of uncleanness. I had good health, good thoughts, and good humor, thank God Almighty.

28. I rose about 6 and read nothing because we were to go by 7 o'clock to Council. This made me neglect to say my prayers though not to eat boiled milk for breakfast. They passed my quitrent accounts in Council and got the warrants signed. I settled the Governor's account and adjusted several other matters and took leave of several of the members of the council. Mr. Commissary got £5 as ordinary by his [teaching] us.[1] I dined with the Governor and ate salt fish for dinner. In the afternoon my man came with my horse and brought me word all was well at home, thank God. I took leave of the Governor and Mrs. Russell and then took a walk and afterwards went to the coffeehouse where I took leave of more of my friends and then went to my lodgings where I settled some accounts. I said my prayers and had good health, good thoughts, and good humor, thank God Almighty. I gave the Governor's men 5 shillings apiece.

---

[1]Possibly a somewhat sarcastic reference to Blair's salary as president of the College of William and Mary. Some of the colonists complained bitterly against Blair's salary, which began before the College was built and in session.

29. I rose about 6 o'clock and read nothing because I wished to prepare for my going out of town. I said my prayers and ate rice milk for breakfast. I settled all my affairs and then went to Mr. Bland's to take my leave, which I did about 9 o'clock. Then I rode to my sister Custis' and found them pretty well, only my sister was melancholy. I comforted her as well as I could and then took a walk with my sister and brother in the orchard. About one o'clock Dr. Cocke came from Williamsburg and soon after we went to dinner and I ate boiled beef. In the afternoon we sat and talked till 3 o'clock and then I took my leave and went to Green Springs, and the Doctor returned home. I found a great deal of company with Colonel Ludwell who went away in the evening and we took a walk and romped with the girls at night. I ate some partridge and about 10 went to bed. I said a short prayer and had good health, good thoughts, and good humor, thank God Almighty. I had wicked inclinations to Mistress Sarah Taylor.

30. I rose at 5 o'clock and said a short prayer and then drank two dishes of chocolate. Then I took my leave about 6 o'clock and found it very cold. I met with nothing extraordinary in my journey and got home about 11 o'clock and found all well, only my wife was melancholy. We took a walk in the garden and pasture. We discovered that by the contrivance of Nurse and Anaka Prue got in at the cellar window and stole some strong beer and cider and wine. I turned Nurse away upon it and punished Anaka. I ate some fish for dinner. In the afternoon I caused Jack and John to be whipped for drinking at John [Cross][1] all last Sunday. In the evening I took a walk about the plantation and found things in good order. At night I ate some bread and butter. I said my prayers and had good health, good thoughts, and good humor, thank God Almighty. The weather was very cold for the season. I gave my wife a powerful flourish and gave her great ecstasy and refreshment.

---

[1]Possibly the John Cross whose widow, Jane, married Francis Hardiman.

May, 1711

1. I rose about 8 o'clock because the child had disturbed me in the night and read a chapter in Hebrew and some Greek in Lucian. I said my prayers and ate boiled milk for breakfast. I wrote to Mr. Randolph to have some copies of his county records and sent G-r-l with the letter. I caused Bannister to draw off a hogshead of cider which was very good. I danced my dance. I ate fish for dinner. In the afternoon came Colonel Eppes and his wife and brought me two [country letters]. They stayed here about an hour. Then I took a walk about the plantation and went to see John at work about the boat. I forgave Anaka, on my wife's and sister's persuasion, but I caused Prue to be whipped severely and she told many things of John G-r-l for which he was to blame, particularly that he lost the key of the wine cellar and got in at the window and opened the door and then because he had not the key the door was left open and anybody went in and stole the beer and wine &c. In the evening I took a walk with my wife and sister. At night I ate some bread and butter. I said my prayers and had good health, good thoughts, and good humor, thank God Almighty. I received a letter with some records from Will Randolph. I gave my wife a short flourish.

2. I rose about 7 o'clock and read a chapter in Hebrew and some Greek in Lucian. I said my prayers and ate cold milk for breakfast. I danced my dance. Three of my negroes were sick and I took the best care of them I could. About 11 o'clock came Mr. Randolph and told me concerning my affairs above. Soon after came Colonel Hill and Drury Stith and several others and when we went to dinner Captain Posford and Captain L-th-m came. I ate dry beef for dinner. In the afternoon came Frank and Isham Eppes. I settled some accounts and particularly with George Carter whom I scolded at for drinking with my people at John [Cross]. In the evening my sister went to Colonel Eppes' and my wife and I took a walk about the plantation. I said

my prayers at night and had good health, good thoughts, and good humor, thank God Almighty. There was no drinking at [court].

3. I rose about 6 o'clock and I read a chapter in Hebrew and some Greek in Lucian. I said my prayers and ate boiled milk for breakfast. I danced my dance. One of my sick people was better, thank God. It threatened rain this morning and it did rain a little, but soon cleared up again. I settled several accounts and then read some English till dinner. I ate some bacon and pigeon. In the afternoon I took a walk to see my people and then returned and wrote some things. Then I read some law and searched for precedents. In the evening my wife and I took a walk about the plantation and when we returned we found Captain Posford's boat come with my things from Williamsburg. By that came some letters from England which told me the Duke of Argyle was made General in Spain. I neglected to say my prayers but had good health, good thoughts, and good humor, thank God Almighty.

4. I rose about 6 o'clock and read two chapters in Hebrew and some Greek in Lucian. I said my prayers and ate boiled milk for breakfast. I danced my dance. The weather was cold. I sent G-r-l with a letter to Colonel Hill which came from Mr. Perry concerning his ship. Nurse sent for her things which were delivered. I settled some accounts. My sick people were better, thank God Almighty. My sister Duke and Colonel Eppes came and stayed to dinner. I ate pork and peas for dinner. In the afternoon my sister went home and the Colonel went away and then I went and read some law till evening. Then I took a walk about the plantation to see how everything was but my wife stayed at home and was melancholy. At night I read more law. I said my prayers and had good health, good thoughts, and good humor, thank God Almighty. I gave my wife a flourish.

5. I rose about 6 o'clock and read two chapters in Hebrew and some Greek in Lucian. I said my prayers and

ate boiled milk for breakfast. I danced my dance. My people were better, thank God, only my wife was a little indisposed with a cold. The weather was more warm than it had been. I read some law and then some other English till dinner. I ate some pigeon and bacon. In the afternoon I took a walk to see what John was doing and then returned home and read more law till the evening, when my wife was well enough to walk with me about the plantation. Just as it was dark came Mr. Clayton from Williamsburg and brought no news only that Mrs. Russell was going to Pennsylvania for her recovery which some think is to lay a great belly there but this is a malicious idea. At night we ate bread and butter and drank some wine till about 10 o'clock. I neglected to say my prayers because of company but I had good health, good thoughts, and good humor, thank God Almighty for it. Captain Posford was here this afternoon and told me our nurse was drunk aboard his ship and the smith lay with her.

6. I rose about 6 o'clock and read a chapter in Hebrew and some Greek in Lucian. I said my prayers and ate some bread and butter and tea for breakfast. I danced my dance. My sick people were better. It threatened rain this morning and was very warm but it failed. Mr. Clayton and I went into the library to consult some law books concerning my case with John Giles.[1] We stayed there till dinner. I ate tongue for dinner. In the afternoon Mr. Clayton and I walked to Mrs. Harrison's who looked a little grave but afterwards she cleared up and was in good humor. She gave us some strawberries and milk. In the evening we returned home. My sick people were better. At night we drank a bottle of wine and my wife with us. I neglected to say my prayers but had good health, good thoughts, and good humor, thank God Almighty.

7. I rose about 5 o'clock and read a chapter in Hebrew and some Greek in Lucian. I said my prayers and ate boiled

---

[1] In September, 1711, John Giles of Henrico County, carpenter, deeded to Byrd for £20 current money of Virginia two tracts of land on the upper and lower sides of Falling Creek which had been formerly conveyed to Byrd's father by William Giles. (Henrico County Court Records, 1710-14, p. 97.)

milk for breakfast. It rained this morning, which hindered me from going to the court above to hear my case but Mr. Clayton went, however, in the rain. They could not unload the sloop because of the rain. I settled some accounts till dinner. I ate broiled mutton. In the afternoon I settled more accounts and then took a walk to the brick house to see them [manage] tobacco and I found P-t-s-n smoking there for which I drubbed him very much. In the evening it held up a little and we got 40 hogsheads ashore. My wife and I walked in the garden. At night I read some English and then my wife and I ate some roast mutton with great pleasure. I neglected to say my prayers but had good health, good humor, and good thoughts, thank God Almighty.

8. I rose about 6 o'clock and read a chapter in Hebrew and some Greek in Lucian. I said my prayers and ate boiled milk for breakfast. I danced my dance. It rained again; however we made an end to unloading our sloop and sent her away. About 9 o'clock came Captain Posford and Mr. Rogers and the last [offered] his service as a lawyer and I promised to employ him in Henrico. He then desired to know whether I would take Spanish money for Mrs. Parker's debt. I told him I would. They went away soon. About 12 came Mr. Clayton and let me know the court above had done me all the injustice they could in my case. I ate pigeon and bacon for dinner. In the afternoon Mr. Clayton went to Mrs. Harrison's and I took a walk about the plantation. In the evening I could not walk for fear of rain and so I read in the *Tatler*. At night came Mr. Mumford and Mr. Clayton returned from Mrs. Harrison's. We drank a bottle of claret. I neglected to say my prayers but had good health, good thoughts, and good humor, thank God Almighty.

9. I rose about 6 o'clock and read a chapter in Hebrew and some Greek in Lucian. I said my prayers and ate boiled milk for breakfast. I danced my dance. It rained but neither Mr. Mumford nor Mr. Clayton was stopped by it but they went away about 9 o'clock, after I had done my

business with them. I took a walk into the garden and ate some cherries. My wife and daughter were both indisposed, the first with breeding, and the last with a fever. I settled some accounts till dinner. I ate some pork and peas. In the afternoon I took another walk and then returned and settled my accounts. Then I read in the *Tatler* till the evening and then my wife, being better, took a walk with me in the garden. My daughter vomited very much. I said my prayers and had good health, good thoughts, and good humor, thank God Almighty.

10. I rose about 6 o'clock and read two chapters in Hebrew and some Greek in Lucian. I said my prayers and ate boiled milk for breakfast. I danced my dance. It continued to rain till about 8 and then cleared up for a little while. I took a walk to look over my people. Then I returned and settled several of my accounts. My daughter was a little better, thank God, but my wife was indisposed by fits as women are in her condition. I went into the garden and ate some cherries. I ate some boiled mutton for dinner. In the afternoon it rained again and hindered my taking a walk so that I took a nap. I slept. In the next place I read some Greek in the new edition of Homer. In the evening I took a walk and ate some cherries at M-n-s. The season has happened so late this year that cherries are three weeks more backward than they used to be. I neglected to say my prayers but had good health, good thoughts, and good humor, thank God Almighty. I wrote a letter to the Governor to send by Tom with some cherries.

11. I rose about 6 o'clock and read a chapter in Hebrew and some Greek in Homer. I said my prayers and ate boiled milk for breakfast. I danced my dance. I sent Tom with some cherries and green peas to the Governor at Williamsburg. I dreamt last night that I received letters from England with a paper of funeral biscuits, by which I expect letters from thence to tell me of the death of Colonel Parke very soon. I settled several accounts and then went and ate some cherries. Dr. Cocke came just before dinner and so did Colonel Hill and Mr. Anderson. They brought no news

but that Mrs. Russell was gone to Pennsylvania for her health in order to leave her distemper there and put it out to nurse. I ate fish for dinner. In the afternoon we diverted ourselves till about 6 o'clock and then Colonel Hill and Mr. Anderson went home, notwithstanding I invited them to stay. In the evening we took a walk about the plantation and then at night drank a bottle of wine and were very merry till about 10 o'clock. I neglected to say my prayers and had good health, good thoughts, and good humor, thank God Almighty.

12. I rose about 5 o'clock and read a chapter in Hebrew and some Greek in Homer. I said my prayers and ate boiled milk for breakfast. I danced my dance. It was very warm this morning; however we resolved to go to Colonel Hill's and accordingly about 10 o'clock I recommended my family to heaven and then the Doctor and I rode to Colonel Hill's where we ate cherries and were very merry till about 2 o'clock when we went to dinner and I ate bacon and strawberries and milk. In the afternoon we walked to the ship which is much advanced. Then we returned to the house and ate more cherries and Mr. Anderson mended my watch till it would not go at all. About 6 o'clock we returned home and found all well. We took a little walk and at night drank a bottle of wine. I neglected to say my prayers but had good thoughts, good health, and good humor, thank God Almighty.

13. I rose about 6 o'clock and read a chapter in Hebrew but no Greek because the Doctor interrupted me. Neither did I say my prayers but ate boiled milk for breakfast. It rained very much in the night and almost all the morning. However we went to church and heard Mr. Anderson preach. After church it rained extremely and I sent Mrs. Harrison and Mrs. Armistead and Betty Harrison to my house and the [ch—] returned and carried us men. I invited the whole congregation to go to our house but nobody else went but I sent them a bottle of wine. I ate dry beef for dinner. The company stayed till the evening and then because of the rain I sent them home in the coach.

In the evening we walked in the garden and at night we drank a bottle of wine. I neglected to say my prayers but had good health, good thoughts, and good humor, thank God Almighty.

14. I rose about 6 o'clock and read two chapters in Hebrew and some Greek in Homer. I said my prayers and ate boiled milk for breakfast. I danced my dance. The weather was clear and cold. I ate some cherries. We were merry with reading my verse, the 3 W. My wife could not be persuaded to be let blood neither by the Doctor or me to prevent miscarriage. However she promised [she] would forbear eating much to breed blood since she was so unwilling to part with it. About 12 o'clock we got ready and went in the coach to Mrs. Harrison's to dinner. I ate some bacon and chicken. In the afternoon the Doctor and I went into the study and bought some books. In the evening we rode home and found all well. Then we drank a bottle of wine and about 9 o'clock retired. I neglected to say my prayers but had good health, good thoughts, and good humor, thank God Almighty.

15. I rose about 5 o'clock and read a chapter in Hebrew and some Greek in Homer. I said my prayers and ate milk and strawberries for breakfast. I wrote a letter to the Governor concerning the [mare which we have b-g-r] the Doctor, who went away about 9 o'clock. Captain Posford came and complained that the family of the Harrisons used him very ill because he would not take their tobacco at £10 a ton and feared they would complain against him in England. I told him if they would be so unjust I would endeavor to right him there. I ate beans and bacon for dinner. My wife was much indisposed in her breeding. In the afternoon I took a walk about the plantation and threatened those of my negroes that stole some eggs from my wife. I read some English and in the evening took another walk with my wife about the plantation. I said my prayers and had good health, good thoughts, and good humor, thank God Almighty. About 9 o'clock just as I went to bed came Mr. G-r-l but I did not see him so late.

16. I rose about 5 o'clock and read a chapter in Hebrew and some Greek in Homer. I said my prayers and ate boiled milk for breakfast. I danced my dance. Mr. G-r-l told me all was well at Falling Creek but that the sloop did not get up till Saturday, notwithstanding they sailed with a good wind the Tuesday before. Mr. G-r-l went about hanging the gates and I took a walk to him. Then I went into the garden to eat some cherries. My wife was sick still but something better than yesterday. I ate some roast shoat for dinner. In the afternoon came Frank Eppes to bring me his father's bills for the quitrents. He stayed here till about 6 o'clock and then went with me to see the gates and my wife came and walked with me. Just as I was going to bed the Captain of the salt ship came and stayed about half an hour with me and I gave him a bottle of cider. I said my prayers and had good health, good thoughts, and good humor, thank God Almighty. I rogered my wife, in which she took but little pleasure in her condition.

17. I rose about 5 o'clock and read two chapters in Hebrew and some Greek in Homer. I said my prayers and ate boiled milk for breakfast. I danced my dance. I settled accounts with old C-r-n-r who lay here last night. It rained this morning a little. I took a walk to see Mr. G-r-l put up the gates but was driven in again by the rain. About 11 o'clock came Mr. [Gee] to endeavor to get me to be his security for being sheriff but I put him off as courteously as I could. About one o'clock came Mr. Burwell and his wife, Mistress Judy Wormeley,[1] Mrs. Harrison and her daughter to dine. I ate salt fish. In the afternoon it rained very hard so that my people could not proceed to put up the gates. However we were as merry as we could. In the evening Mrs. Harrison and her daughter went away in the coach and the rest of the company stayed. We ate a little supper at night, and were merry till about 10 o'clock. I neglected to say my prayers but had good health, good thoughts, and good humor, thank God Almighty.

---

[1]Judith, daughter of Ralph Wormeley II. She married, in July 1712, young Mann Page.

18. I rose about 6 o'clock and read no Hebrew but 200 verses in Homer. I neglected to say my prayers and ate strawberries and milk for breakfast. We took a walk to see the mare and then returned and ate some cherries. It rained several times this morning; however that could not discourage Mr. Burwell and the rest of the company from going away, notwithstanding all the reasons I could use for their staying. I took a little nap before dinner. I ate some beans and bacon. In the afternoon I took a walk and then returned and read some English in the *Tatler*. About 4 o'clock it rained prodigiously hard and I doubted not but our friends were in it to their great [refreshment]. A man came with a register to be signed from Williamsburg and told me there was no news. I asked him to eat but he would not. In the evening I took a short walk to see what my people had done. I said my prayers and had good health, good thoughts, and good humor, thank God Almighty. It was exceedingly cold.

19. I rose at 5 o'clock and read a chapter in Hebrew and 300 verses in Homer. I said my prayers and ate boiled milk for breakfast. I danced my dance. It continued very cold, sometimes threatened rain and sometimes did rain showers as in April. I settled some accounts. About 11 o'clock came a man with a note of Mr. M-r-s-l which I had paid before. Then I ate some cherries. About 12 o'clock came Tom Butts[1] to purchase the quitrents of New Kent but we could not agree. However I asked him to dine and soon after we sat down came Mr. Chapman and sat down with us also. I ate some bacon and sallet for dinner. In the afternoon I learned that Chapman's wife was in the church-yard and I sent her a bottle of English beer. I sold Chapman some rights and then he went away and so did Tom Butts. In the evening I took a walk and saw my people at work about the gates and then I walked to see the [mare b-t-n]. Chapman told me that our Commodore was arrived

---

[1]Appointed sheriff of New Kent County in 1712. (*Ex. Jour.*, III, 305.)

from Barbados but could tell no particulars.[1] My wife was a little better, thank God. I said my prayers and had good health, good thoughts, and good humor, thank God Almighty.

20. I rose about 6 o'clock and read a chapter in Hebrew and some Greek in Homer. I said my prayers devoutly and danced my dance. I gave all the people a dram. I ate boiled milk for breakfast. I ate some strawberries. We had no sermon here, notwithstanding it was Whitsunday because Mr. Anderson had [f-l] often to preach on the other [side] the river.[2] I ate some green peas for dinner and was out of humor because the butter was melted oil and scolded at Moll for it. After dinner I took a walk about the plantation to see how everything stood. Then I ate some cherries. My wife was much out of order. I read some English in the *Tatler* and then my wife and I took a walk about the plantation. She was much out of humor with her indisposition, as she generally is. I said my prayers and had good health, good thoughts, and good humor, thank God Almighty.

21. I rose about 6 o'clock and read a chapter in Hebrew and some Greek in Lucian. I said my prayers and ate boiled milk for breakfast. I danced my dance. I wrote a letter to the Governor and sent Tom with some cherries and [r-t-r-c]. I wrote also to Mr. Bland. My wife was still indisposed and much out of humor. The weather was very warm again. About 12 o'clock came Mr. Mumford and told me all was well at Appomattox. I ate some beans and bacon for dinner. In the afternoon Mr. Mumford and I played at billiards and I won a bit. Then we went and got some cherries but we found to our great surprise that the wild pigeons had eaten all the black-hearts. Then we took a

---

[1]On March 20, 1711, Spotswood wrote to the Board of Trade and Plantations that several of the fleet had arrived in Virginia but that "the Reserve (which was Commodore) being in want of water, and several men sick, was forced to bear away to Barbadoes." (*Official Letters of Alexander Spotswood*, I, 74.)

[2]Probably Mr. Anderson supplied Martin's Brandon Parish, at this time vacant. (Goodwin, p. 337.)

walk about the plantation and particularly saw the colt. It was very hot this afternoon. At night we sat and talked till 9 o'clock. I said my prayers and had good health, good thoughts, and good humor, thank God Almighty.

22. I rose about 6 o'clock and read a chapter in Hebrew and some Greek in Homer. I said my prayers and had boiled milk for breakfast. I danced my dance. Mr. Mumford cut my young horse and then he and I went and shot wild pigeons with bows and arrows and then wrote some verses to try if I could translate Homer with any success. A little before dinner came Mrs. Dunn and told us her husband wished to go to Stafford to live. I ate green peas for dinner. In the afternoon Tom returned and brought me a kind letter from the Governor but no news. Mr. Mumford and I played at billiards and he won a bit and then went away. I read some English in the *Tatler* and then went with my wife and Mrs. Dunn to walk about the plantation. At night we drank some syllabub. I said my prayers and had good health, good thoughts, and good humor, thank God Almighty.

23. I rose about 5 o'clock and read a chapter in Hebrew and some Greek in Homer. I said my prayers and ate milk and strawberries for breakfast. I danced my dance. The salt came this morning, about 400 barrels which I ordered to be taken ashore. It was very hot. I began this day to make my will, which I never had done before in my life. I ate bacon and pigeon for dinner. We consulted by what means to persuade Mr. Dunn not to go away to Stafford County to live and agreed the best way would be to persuade him to go to England. About 3 o'clock Mrs. Dunn went home. It thundered and threatened rain but it did not rain. In the evening the master of the salt ship came and he agreed next week to send up 100 barrels of salt to my store at Appomattox. I walked with him in the garden and said my prayers. I had good health, good thoughts, and good humor, thank God Almighty.

24. I rose about 5 o'clock and read a chapter in Hebrew and some Greek [in] Homer. I said my prayers and ate

milk for breakfast. I danced my dance. My sheep began this day to be sheared. It threatened rain this morning and about 11 o'clock rained so that we were forced to leave shearing. I wrote more of my will. My sloop came from Falling Creek with planks and other shipping. I ate some beans and bacon for dinner. In the afternoon Captain Posford called here and told me Mr. Blair was at next house. About 3 o'clock there came a terrible gust of wind and rain that blew up several trees by the roots and tore many more and threw down my fence. However it did no mischief to the house nor to my sloop but it was soon over, thank God. In the evening I took a walk about the plantation to see what damage I had sustained. In the evening I read some English in the *Tatler* till it was time to go to bed. I said my prayers and had good health, good thoughts, and good humor, thank God Almighty.

25. I rose about 6 o'clock and read a chapter in Hebrew and some Greek in Homer. I said my prayers and ate boiled milk for breakfast. I danced my dance. About 10 o'clock Mr. Blair, his wife, and Mrs. Harrison called here and at the same time came Mr. Cairon,[1] the minister sent for Manakin Town. He gave me two letters from the Bishop of London and one from the Leeward Islands containing a copy of my father Parke's will, in which, I thank him, he gave me nothing but gave his estate in this country to my sister Custis and his estate in the Island to the daughter of Mrs. Chester.[2] We gave the company some cherries, coffee, and wine, but [they] did not stay above an hour and then went away to Colonel Hill's but the French

---

[1] John Cairon, minister of King William Parish, Manakin Town, 1710-1715. (Goodwin, p. 257.)

[2] Apparently the wife of Edward Chester; he was agent for the Royal African Company and member of the Antigua Assembly, and a mortal enemy of Parke. Parke describes Mrs. Chester as "in a deep consumption," wanting "a nurse more than a gallant, and has the fate to be married to a cruel madman and a fool." She overheard, in her own house, a plot to assassinate Parke, and warned him of it. (Parke to the Board of Trade and Plantations, March 21 and Sept. 9, 1710, *Cal. State Papers, Colonial, America and West Indies*, 1710-11, pp. 61, 206.) Parke's will, drawn in January 1710, left his estate in the islands to "Mrs. Lucy Chester being the daughter of Mrs. Katherine Chester though she is not yet christened." (*Va. Mag.*, XX, 372-73.)

minister, who stayed to dinner. About 12 o'clock came Captain Posford to dine with me. I ate some beans and bacon. In the afternoon the French minister went towards Falling Creek and the Captain went away. About 4 o'clock Mr. Bland came on his way to Jordans but had no news only that a rich ship from Carolina was taken by the Cape. In the evening I caused him to be set over the river and then took a walk about the plantation. At night I read in the *Tatler*. I said my prayers and had good health, good thoughts, and good humor, thank God Almighty.

26. I rose about 6 o'clock and read a chapter in Hebrew and some Greek in Homer. I said my prayers and ate boiled milk for breakfast. I danced my dance. I sent the sloop to Appomattox for tobacco. We made an end of shearing our sheep. I cleaned my razor and [mended] the lock of my closet. I ate some boiled mutton for dinner. In the afternoon I wrote more of my will and then read more Greek in Homer till the evening. Then my wife and I took a walk about the plantation. My wife continues very sick and peevish in her breeding and uses but little exercise. The wind was east and pretty cold. At night I read in the *Tatler*. I said my prayers and had good health, good thoughts, and good humor, thank God Almighty.

27. I rose about 6 o'clock and read a chapter in Hebrew and some Greek in Homer. I said my prayers and ate boiled milk for breakfast. I danced my dance. My wife was pretty well this morning. The weather was cold and the wind northeast. About 11 o'clock we went in the coach to church and heard a good sermon of Mr. Anderson. Then we received the Sacrament and there were more communicants than ever I saw here. We invited nobody to dinner. I ate roast pigeon and asparagus. In the afternoon came my cousin Betty Harrison by whom I sent a letter to Colonel Bassett because she was to go there tomorrow. Then I ate some cherries with her but she would drink nothing. In the evening I took a walk about the plantation. At night I read in the *Tatler*. Then I said my prayers and had good health, good thoughts, and good humor, thank God Almighty.

28. I rose at 5 o'clock and read nothing because I prepared for my journey to Falling Creek, but I said my prayers and ate boiled milk for breakfast. About 7 o'clock I had got everything ready and rode on M-r-s-l to Colonel Randolph's to visit the poor widow who desired my good offices with Mr. Perry in her behalf, which I promised. Here I met Mr. Anderson, Mr. Finney, and Mr. Brodie[1] who were going to the Manakin Town and they persuaded me to go there with them. Here we ate some roast shoat. Then we took leave and rode to Falling Creek, where I found all well, but heard that S-r-y a negro woman was dead at Burkland. God's will be done. On the way I saw Mr. Laforce and demanded the debt of him but he gave me no satisfaction and I threatened to sue him. The three parsons stayed with me at Falling Creek till 6 o'clock and then they went to Mr. Tullitt's and I stayed here and ate for supper some chicken pie. I talked with Mr. G-r-l about my business and then said a short prayer and had good health, good thoughts, and indifferent good humor, thank God Almighty.

29. I rose about 6 o'clock and read a little in Homer. I said my prayers and ate boiled milk for breakfast. Then I walked to the mill where I took horse and rode to Mr. Tullitt's to call for my company. Here I saw abundance of work done and many conveniences made. The company went to breakfast but I could eat nothing with them and therefore walked in the garden. About 10 o'clock we mounted and proceeded to the Manakin Town but they rode very slowly. Mr. Finney and I went to Mr. Salle's and ate some eggs, and then went to Mr. Phillipe's[2] and from thence to the coalpit where we found all well and George told me they had pressed through the rock and found very good coal. We stayed here about half an hour and then returned, the parsons to Mr. Phillipe's and I to Mr. Salle's. But they came to me in about an hour. Mr. Anderson and Mr. Finney stayed to supper with us but Mr. Brodie went over

---

[1]Reverend William Brodie, minister of St. Peter's Parish, New Kent, 1710-1720. (Goodwin, p. 254.)
[2]Reverend Claude Phillipe de Richbourgh, minister of Manakin Town, 1704-1710.

the river with Tom Randolph and fell out of the boat and hurt himself. We had some French cookery for supper. Mr. Finney went over the river but Mr. Anderson stayed and lay with me, no very clean bedfellow. I said a short prayer and had good health, good thoughts, and good humor, thank God Almighty.

30. I rose at 6 o'clock and Mr. Finney came to us and told us of the misfortune of Mr. Brodie. Mr. Anderson went to him to let him blood and returned in an hour and told me he could not ride with us. There was a very good breakfast but I ate nothing but milk. About 8 o'clock we took our leave and rode very slowly to Falling Creek. Mr. Anderson's horse was very poor. While of the expedition among the French, I recommended peace and union to them and conjured them to be courteous to Mr. Phillipe notwithstanding he was removed, which Mr. Salle promised me they would. We got to Falling Creek about 12 o'clock, where I made a bargain for some good land. Captain Webb came there and about one we went to dinner and I ate some chicken pie. About 2 o'clock we rode away and came to the Hundred about 5 o'clock. I stayed at Colonel Hill's and ate some milk and raspberries and then took my leave and got home just as it was dark, and found all well only they told me old P-r-s-n was dead. I was tired exceedingly. I said a short prayer and had good health, good thoughts, and good humor, thank God Almighty.

31. I rose about 7 o'clock and read a chapter in Hebrew and some Greek in Homer. I said my prayers and ate milk and raspberries for breakfast. I danced my dance. My wife was indisposed and had been ever since I went from home. Tom was sick and I gave him a purge which worked very well. I believe his sickness proceeded from my threatening to whip him for not taking care of the horses. It was exceedingly hot today. I ate salt fish for dinner but had no great stomach because I breakfasted too late. In the afternoon I wrote some of my will till the evening. I sent Cap-

tain Posford some cherries and some beans. In the evening I ate some cherries and then took a walk about the plantation, and my wife was with me very sick. At night I read some English in the *Tatler*. I said my prayers and had good health, good thoughts, and good humor, thank God Almighty.

June, 1711

1. I rose about 6 o'clock and read a chapter in Hebrew and some Greek in Homer. I said my prayers and ate boiled milk for breakfast. I danced my dance. My wife was a little better this day. I wrote a letter to the Governor to give him an account of my expedition to Manakin Town. It was very hot again. I settled some accounts. Then I read some French till dinner. I ate some broiled pork and green peas. In the afternoon I took a nap and then read some English till the evening and then with my wife took a walk about the plantation. My wife was a little better, which she thought was because she drank some sage tea. Mrs. Dunn came about 6 o'clock and told us that the Governor would not recommend her husband to the parish in Stafford. We had a syllabub. I said my prayers and had good health, good thoughts, and good humor, thank God Almighty.

2. I rose about 5 o'clock and read a chapter in Hebrew and some Greek in Homer. I said my prayers and ate boiled milk for breakfast. I danced my dance. I read some English and then settled some accounts. My wife was again indisposed and it was very hot and threatened rain. Captain L-th-m sent home the boat which he had hired of me. I searched for the bond of Laforce but could not find it. I ate beans and bacon for dinner. In the afternoon I searched again but in vain. About 4 o'clock it thundered and rained very much. I read some English in the *Tatler*. In the evening we walked in the garden, because it was too wet to walk about the plantation. I ate some hot pone and milk. My wife complained extremely of her head. I said my prayers and had good health, good thoughts, and good humor, thank God Almighty.

3. I rose at 7 o'clock and read two chapters in Hebrew and 300 verses in Homer. I said my prayers and ate milk and raspberries for breakfast. My wife was better today

than she has been this month. It was very hot weather. I received a complaint that one of my steers had broken in again to Mrs. Harrison's cornfield. I had put a yoke on his neck and put him into the great pasture but he jumped out notwithstanding, on which I resolved to kill him rather than keep anything injurious to my neighbor. I ate a broiled pigeon for dinner. In the afternoon I searched for the bond again and found it at last to my great satisfaction. I read some Latin. In the evening Mrs. Dunn went home, and I took a walk about the plantation. I said no prayers and had good health, good thoughts, and good humor, thank God Almighty.

4. I rose at 5 o'clock and read two chapters in Hebrew and 200 verses in Homer. I said my prayers and ate boiled milk for breakfast. I danced my dance. I wrote two letters which I sent by Bannister to [Henrico Court]. I threatened Will Wilkins for stealing the apples and denying it when he had done, but I forgave him. It was extremely hot. I practiced some arithmetic till dinner. I ate some dry beef but had no stomach to eat. In the afternoon I began to write my will fair and about half did it. In the evening I took a walk with my wife who had been pretty well all day. At night I caused the steer to be killed that had broken into my cousin Harrison's cornfield and sent her part of it to make her amends. I said my prayers and had good health, good thoughts, and good humor, thank God Almighty.

5. I rose about 5 o'clock and read about 500 verses in Homer and two chapters in Hebrew. I said my prayers and ate cold milk for breakfast. I danced my dance, notwithstanding it was so hot. My wife was something better. Young Woodson brought me a letter from Charles Fleming concerning the quitrents of New Kent and I wrote an answer. Woodson would not stay to dinner. I ate some roast beef for dinner. In the afternoon I ciphered a little and slept for it was so hot I could do nothing else. In the afternoon I read a little in the *Tatler* and then went and took a walk about the plantation and saw John build the boat. We moved the sheep-pen with the ox down the walk

by the river. At night I said my prayers and had good thoughts, good health, and good thoughts [*sic*], thank God Almighty.

6. I rose about 5 o'clock and read two chapters in Hebrew and 300 verses in Homer. I said my prayers and ate cold milk for breakfast. About 9 o'clock came Mr. Bland on his way to Williamsburg and I sent a letter to the Governor. We gave Mr. Bland some milk and raspberries for breakfast. About 10 o'clock came Colonel Hill and Captain [. . .] who brought his ship from Kiquotan to load her at £10 a ton. About 12 o'clock I went to court and swore to my judgment against Captain B-r-k. I stayed there about an hour and then brought several gentlemen to dinner. We had several things but I only ate boiled pork. Captain S-c-r would have hired my sloop but I would not let him have it under 5 shillings per hogshead. In the evening Will Randolph came and the French parson who told me that Captain Smith on his way from New York had taken a privateer of 90 men. We had a gust in the evening but little rain. Mrs. Harrison and Mrs. Eppes called here. At night the French parson and his three sons went on board their boat to go up the river. I walked in the garden because I could not walk in the pasture. I said my prayers and had good health, good thoughts, and good humor, thank God Almighty.

7. I rose about 6 o'clock and read a chapter in Hebrew and some Greek in Homer. I said my prayers and ate cold milk for breakfast. It was so hot I could not dance. The French parson and his three sons could not go last night and so came and ate some raspberries and milk here and when they went away I gave them some roast beef and bread. About 11 o'clock came Colonel Eppes. I got him to be a witness to my will. There came a man for my advice about a boy that had received a kick from a horse, which I gave him as well as I could. Colonel Eppes stayed to dinner and I ate some steer feet. In the afternoon the Colonel went away and I read some Greek and some English in the library. In the evening I took a walk about the plantation.

Then I drank some syllabub. I said my prayers and had good health, good thoughts, and good humor, thank God Almighty.

8. I rose about 5 o'clock and read a chapter in Hebrew and some Greek in Homer. I said my prayers and ate cold milk for breakfast. I danced my dance. It was very hot again. I received news that one of my mares was killed by a snake or spider for she was swelled much. I had also an account of one of my negro's death above by Will Bass who came over to account with me. I read some English till dinner. I ate some boiled beef. In the afternoon I took a small nap and did some ciphering. Then I read more English till the evening when I took a walk about the plantation and ordered the colt that had lost his mother to be brought home and fed with milk. I drank some syllabub at night and then said my prayers and had good health, good thoughts, and good humor, thank God Almighty. My sloop came this evening from Appomattox with tobacco.

9. I rose about 5 o'clock and read a chapter in Hebrew and 300 verses in Homer. I said my prayers and ate cold milk for breakfast. I danced my dance, and my sloop was unloaded. About 10 o'clock came Captain Jones[1] to visit me and I showed him my library with which he was pleased. About 11 o'clock Mrs. [Hancock] came with a negro boy that she had in care [or cure] and I gave her five pounds for his care. About 12 came Captain Posford and Captain L-th-m to dine with me. I ate boiled beef for dinner. In the afternoon I took a nap and then did some ciphering. Then I read some English till the evening and then with my wife took a walk about the plantation. I said my prayers and had good health, good thoughts, and good humor, thank God Almighty. Peter came from above and informed me that everybody was well.

10. I read a chapter in Hebrew and a chapter in the Greek Testament. Then I wrote letters to my overseers

---

[1]Spotswood mentions the arrival of Captain Jones in January 1711; possibly Francis Jones, master of a merchant ship in 1706. (*Official Letters of Alexander Spotswood*, I, 46; *Ex. Jour.*, III, 95.)

above. I did not say my prayers but ate milk for breakfast. I discoursed with Mr. G-r-l who came last night and acquainted me that all was well at Falling Creek. It was so hot I could not go to church. Mr. Anderson came and brought me my watch which he had injured by breaking one of the wheels. He drank some cider and went away to church and about 12 Mr. G-r-l went away also. I ate some boiled pork for dinner and was angry with Moll for neglecting to boil some artichokes for dinner. I wrote a letter in answer to Mr. [Gee's] in which he had asked my advice. I read some English. In the evening I took a walk about the plantation, and when I returned drank some syllabub. I said my prayers and had good health, good thoughts, and good humor, thank God Almighty.

11. I rose about 5 o'clock and read two chapters in Hebrew and 200 verses in Homer. I said my prayers and ate cold milk for breakfast. I danced my dance. About 8 o'clock came Mr. Anderson on his way over the river. He stayed about an hour. It was not so hot as it has been because the wind blew hard. I prepared for my journey to Williamsburg. I ate some roast pigeon for dinner. In the afternoon I got everything ready and then took a nap for about an hour and then washed and dressed me and about 5 o'clock was set over the creek and proceeded on my journey. I got to the ferry about 9 o'clock and there drank some milk. I got to Williamsburg about 11 o'clock and after saying my prayers lay on the bed without sheets and slept very well. I had good health, good thoughts, and good humor, thank God Almighty.

12. I rose about 6 o'clock and read 100 verses in Homer and then got ready to shave me. I ate boiled milk for breakfast. Mr. Bland and Mr. Clayton came to see me. About 9 o'clock and past Colonel Duke and I went to wait on the Governor, who received us very kindly. I drank some cider and after staying about an hour we went to court where two men were [tried] for felony and both found guilty. I saw the French prisoners [that] were taken in the privateer by Captain Smith to the number of 88. They made but a poor

figure. About 4 o'clock the court rose and I and Mr.
Holloway settled our difference. I showed Mr. Clayton my
father Parke's will but he could find no error in it. About
5 o'clock I went with four others of the Council to dine with
the Governor. I ate boiled mutton for dinner. About 8
o'clock all the company went away except myself and I
stayed till 12 with the Governor and we drank about two
bottles of French claret but the Doctor was very dull all the
time. Then I went to my lodgings. I neglected to say my
prayers but had good health, good thoughts, and good
humor, thank God Almighty.

13. I rose about 6 o'clock and read nothing because of
going to court early. However I ate my milk first and then
went to the coffeehouse and got my papers together and
went to 'court where one of the prisoners was burnt in the
hand and the other ordered to the whip. Then we went to
council where several things were debated and particularly
the affairs of Carolina which are in great confusion.[1] Kit
Robinson was made naval officer in the room of Colonel
Corbin.[2] The Court of Admiralty of [c-p] to [try] the
privateer and she was made prize. Then we had a meeting
of the directors of the town and agreed to build a market
place to which we all contributed. About 4 o'clock we went
to dine with the Governor and I ate boiled veal for dinner.
I stayed about an hour after dinner and then took my leave
and went to my lodgings to prepare to go home with Colonel
Ludwell. I went and took leave of Mrs. Bland and then
we rode to Green Springs where I found all well. We sat
and talked till about 10 o'clock and I took leave because I
was to go in the morning early. I neglected to say my
prayers and had good health, good thoughts, and good
humor, thank God Almighty.

14. I rose at 4 o'clock and came away without seeing
anybody, notwithstanding it rained. I said my prayers on

---

[1]One Thomas Cary had seized the government and refused to yield to
Hyde, the new governor. For a full account of the confusion which ensued
see the *Official Letters of Alexander Spotswood*, I, 81 ff.
[2]Colonel Gawin Corbin was judged unfit for the office of naval officer of
the Rappahannock District. (*Ex. Jour.*, III, 276.)

the road. When I was got about 12 miles it began to rain and I put in at W-l-k [Wilkes' ?] and drank some milk and when I came away I promised him a pair of wool [cards] if he would fetch them. I stayed there about an hour and then took horse and had good riding half a mile before it rained again very hard. However, I rode through it and got home about 10 o'clock, where I found all well, thank God, but I was wet with the rain. I shaved myself and drank a glass of wine. I ate some pigeon for dinner and Mrs. Dunn dined with us, whom I found here. In the afternoon came Captain Posford came [sic] and told me he had done caulking and tarring my sloop, for which I thanked him as I did for some oatmeal he brought. He stayed about an hour. My wife hid this afternoon, and so did Mrs. Dunn. In the evening I ordered my sloop to be loaded and sent up and we took a walk about the plantation. At night we had a syllabub. I neglected to say my prayers but had good health, good thoughts, and good humor, thank God.

15. I rose about 5 o'clock and read two chapters in Hebrew and 300 verses in Homer. I said my prayers and ate milk for breakfast. I danced my dance. It was very hot today but my wife was well. I wrote some letters to Williamsburg and settled some accounts. We began to weave and blue pieces went into the loom by Mrs. Dunn's direction. I ate some roast mutton for dinner. In the afternoon I settled some other accounts and then ciphered and read some French till the evening. Then I took a walk about the plantation and then swam in the river to wash and refresh myself. At night I drank some syllabub with Mrs. Dunn but my wife was out of humor and would drink none. I said my prayers and had good health, good thoughts, and good humor, thank God Almighty.

16. I rose about 5 o'clock and read two chapters in Hebrew and 300 verses in Homer. I said my prayers and ate milk for breakfast. I danced my dance. About 9 o'clock came [Wilkes ?] for his wool [cards] that I promised him and also Mr. Mumford to tell me all was well at Appomattox. He hindered me from reading but I wrote a letter

to the Governor. Then Mr. Mumford and I played at billiards till dinner. I ate some boiled fish and roast mutton. In the afternoon we played at billiards again and I lost two bits. We ate some cherries and drank some cider. In the evening both Mr. Mumford and Mrs. Dunn returned home and I went to walk about the plantation. I quarrelled with John for letting some bitches run about. At night I drank some syllabub. Then I said my prayers and had good health, good thoughts, and good humor, thank God Almighty.

17. I rose about 5 o'clock and read two chapters in Hebrew and 200 verses in Homer. I said my prayers and ate milk for breakfast. I danced my dance. It was exceedingly hot and my wife was indisposed in the morning. I gave John G-r-l leave to go and see his mother married. I wrote a letter to England about my father Parke's will and desired Mr. Perry to give me [credit] for the £1000 which my father Parke ordered him to pay me. I ate roast mutton for dinner. In the afternoon I gave my wife a flourish and then refreshed myself with a nap. Then I wrote a letter to Mrs. Custis and another to Captain Posford to desire him to deliver my letters at Williamsburg, and his seaman came for them. I read some French till the evening, and then took a walk about the plantation with my wife. Then we returned and ate some milk. Just as we went to bed it began to rain exceedingly and thundered. I said a short prayer and had good health, good thoughts, and good humor, thank God Almighty.

18. I rose about 5 o'clock and read two chapters in Hebrew and 300 verses in Homer. I said my prayers and ate milk for breakfast. I danced my dance. It was cold and threatened more rain. John G-r-l returned about 9 o'clock and told us that Colonel Hardiman's son had the smallpox on board Colonel Harrison's vessel that is come from Barbados and that nobody would go near him. I settled several accounts and then ciphered till dinner. I ate fish for dinner. It rained almost all the morning. In the afternoon I read some French and then ciphered till the

evening. Then I took a walk about the plantation and saw my corn, which was in a good condition and was much the better for that rain. At night I drank some syllabub. I neglected to say my prayers, had good health, good thoughts, and good humor, thank God. It was very cool, the wind at northeast.

19. I rose about 5 o'clock and read two chapters in Hebrew and 400 verses in Homer. I said my prayers and ate boiled milk for breakfast. I danced my dance. It was very cool this morning, the wind at northeast. My people went to mow the marsh this morning. I settled several accounts and wrote some letters for people in the country concerning bills of exchange. I took a walk to see my people mow but could not get at them. I ate some roast mutton for dinner. In the afternoon I read some French till the evening and then took a walk about the plantation with my wife. We went to see the mare and could not find the gray mare. At night I drank some syllabub. My daughter had a cough and my wife ordered some honey and butter for her which did her much good. I said my prayers and had good health, good thoughts, and good humor, thank God Almighty. Will Kennon was married this day to Colonel Frank Eppes his daughter.[1]

20. I rose about 5 o'clock and read two chapters in Hebrew and 200 verses in Homer. I said my prayers and ate milk for breakfast. I danced my dance. The weather was cool which made me resolve to go to Falling Creek but before I went I had a letter [from] Mr. Gee which created a little quarrel between my wife and I, though I was not to blame. About 12 o'clock I took horse and left my wife out of humor. I went to Colonel Hill's where I found Mrs. Harrison. There I dined and ate bacon and fowl. After dinner I went over the river in the Colonel's boat and rode to Falling Creek, where I came before sunset. I found all well, thank God. I looked into everything and then ate milk for supper and talked with Mr. G-r-l about all my business.

---

[1] Anne Eppes.

I read nothing because I was tired. I said my prayers and had good health, good thoughts, and good humor, thank God Almighty.

21. I rose about 6 o'clock and would have risen sooner but that it rained. I read about 100 verses in Homer. I said my prayers and then walked to the mill where I learned that Westminster had had a mischance [behind] his head by a block that fell on it. It held up about 9 o'clock and I rode to the Falls where I found everything well, thank God, and everything in good order. Then I went over the river to visit the quarters on that side and found things pretty well. I corrected old Robin the doctor for threatening to poison Frank. Then I rode to Burkland where I ate some bacon and eggs very heartily. It rained almost all day. However I looked about and returned over the river about 6 o'clock and rode to Falling Creek, where I met Captain Soane[1] who came to offer me his land but we could not agree. Seth Ward brought his patent there to show me that John Giles could not claim the mill because it was out of his bounds. I ate milk for supper. I said my prayers and had good health, good thoughts, and good humor, thank God Almighty.

22. I rose about 6 o'clock and found it continued to rain. I ate some milk for breakfast and said my prayers. I walked to the mill and was out of humor because the hides I sent from Westover were not carried to the tannery. About 8 o'clock [I] got on my horse to return but before I got half way it rained very hard so that I put in at Dr. Bowman's. I stayed there about an hour and then went on and came to Colonel Hill's about 11 o'clock. There it rained again which made me stay to dinner. I ate boiled mutton. It was evening before I went home because it rained extremely. About 6 o'clock I went home where I found my wife indisposed and in danger of miscarriage. I persuaded her to be let blood but she would not consent.

[1]Captain William Soane in 1704 owned 3,841 acres in Henrico County. (*Va. Mag.*, XXVIII, 218.) On April 4, 1712, he sold Byrd 2,200 acres for £77 sterling. (Henrico County Court Records, 1710-14, p. 117.)

I drank some syllabub. I said my prayers and had good health, good thoughts, and good humor, thank God Almighty.

23. I rose about 7 o'clock and read two chapters in Hebrew and about 200 verses in Homer. I said my prayers and ate milk for breakfast. My wife was indisposed and was threatened with miscarriage. I again persuaded to bleed but she could not be persuaded to it. It rained again and I believe it was the rain that disposed my wife to that infirmity at this time. I settled several accounts till dinner. I ate some pig. In the afternoon I read some French till the evening and then the wind was northwest and it held up so that I took a walk about the plantation. I repeated my petition to my wife to be bled and at night she did try but could not suffer it. I drank some syllabub and gave my daughter some with me. I said my prayers and had good health, good thoughts, and good humor, thank God Almighty. I had a small quarrel with my wife because she would not be bled but neither good words nor bad could prevail against her fear which is very uncontrollable.

24. I rose about 7 o'clock and read two chapters in Hebrew but no Greek. I said my prayers and danced my dance. I ate boiled milk for breakfast. My wife was a little better, thank God, and gave me hope she would avoid miscarriage. Mr. Anderson came before church to see if he could do any service to my wife but I thanked him and told him she was better. I went with him to church, where I saw Peter Hamlin, who had no letters from Barbados for me. People were afraid of him because one of his people had the smallpox. Mr. Anderson gave us a good sermon against speaking ill of our neighbors. There was no news. I brought Captain Posford and Captain L-th-m home with me and found Mrs. Dunn there and my wife worse than she was. I ate some pigeon and bacon for dinner. In the afternoon we endeavored to persuade my wife to bleed but she would not. The Captains went away. In the evening I took a walk about the plantation. At night I drank some syllabub. I said my prayers and had good health, good thoughts,

and good humor, thank God Almighty. It was good weather again this day and dried the wheat so well that we resolved to reap tomorrow.

25. I rose about 5 o'clock and read two chapters in Hebrew and 200 verses in Homer. I said my prayers and ate milk for breakfast. I danced my dance. My wife grew worse and after much trial and persuasion was let blood when it was too late. Captain Stith came about some [n-l] he said he lent my father 20 years ago. Mr. Rogers came also about Mrs. Parker's business. My wife grew very ill which made [me] weep for her. I ate roast mutton for dinner. In the afternoon my wife grew worse and voided a prodigious quantity of blood. I settled some accounts till the evening and then took a walk about the plantation. Before I returned my wife sent for me because she was very weak and soon after I came she was delivered of a false conception and then grew better. I sent for Mrs. Hamlin who came presently. I said my prayers and had good health, good thoughts, and good humor, thank God Almighty.

26. I rose about 6 o'clock and read a chapter in Hebrew and 200 verses in Homer. I said my prayers and ate milk for breakfast. Mrs. Dunn went home and so did Mrs. Hamlin. I received a letter from the attorney general[1] to send his accounts, which I did and wrote a letter to Mr. Bland by him. My wife was extremely mended and very cheerful, thank God. I settled some accounts till dinner. I ate some boiled mutton for dinner. In the afternoon I took a nap by my wife and then went and read some French. I lent my wife some pictures to divert her. Then I went and showed my people how to manage some hay they had mowed out of the swamp. In the evening I took a walk about the plantation and drank some warm milk from the cow. I said my prayers and had good health, good thoughts, and good humor, thank God Almighty.

---

[1]Stevens Thomson, attorney general, 1704-1714.

27. I rose before 5 o'clock and read a chapter in Hebrew and 200 verses in Homer. I said my prayers and ate milk for breakfast. I danced my dance. My wife slept ill last night and was indisposed. It threatened rain this morning. I settled several accounts and wrote three bills of lading. I wrote by my wife that she might not tire herself with reading. Then I read some French till dinner. I ate some fish for dinner. In the afternoon I wrote a letter to England to Mr. Perry about my business. In the evening it rained a little, enough to hinder me from walking about the plantation. However, I walked in the garden. I was a little out of order today and had a small looseness. I said my prayers and had good health, good thoughts, and good humor, thank God Almighty. When my wife heard that Peter Hamlin had the smallpox she said that she should have them likewise because his mother had been here two nights ago and she had laid on her sheets.

28. I rose about 5 o'clock and read a chapter in Hebrew and some Greek in Homer. I said my prayers and ate milk for breakfast. I danced my dance. My wife had the headache severely this morning and had a small fever. I wrote a letter to Mr. Randolph and sent Bannister with it. It rained a little this morning. My wife grew worse of her fever and her pain in the head. I comforted her as well as I could. I wrote a letter to England. Captain Posford and Captain L-th-m came just before dinner. I ate broiled mutton for dinner. Soon after dinner the Captains went away, and my wife grew worse and worse. I sent for Mrs. Dunn and would fain have sent for the doctor but my wife would not let me because she said she should be better in the evening and I think her fever did abate a little. Then I took a walk about the plantation. I said my prayers and had good thoughts, good health, and good humor, thank God Almighty. Mrs. Dunn could not come today but would tomorrow morning. I gave my wife some Venice treacle.

29. I rose at 4 o'clock and sent away G-r-l for Dr. Cocke and Tom for Mr. Anderson for my wife was very bad. She could not sleep this night, which made her headache

continue and also her fever. She vomited up her Venice treacle. I read a chapter in Hebrew. I said my prayers and ate some milk for breakfast. About 10 o'clock Mr. Anderson came and advised us to put spirits of [salt] into her drink to stop her vomiting, which it did. My wife grew a little better and got a little sleep. Mr. Rogers came and paid me £166 for Mrs. Parker. I let Mrs. Harrison know my wife was very ill and she came. I ate some dry beef for dinner. In the afternoon my wife grew much better and her fever abated. In the evening the company went away. George Smith came from Manakin Town and told me all was well at the coalpit and Falling Creek. I took a little walk. Just as it grew dark Doctor Cocke came and found my wife pretty well but he brought no news. Mrs. Dunn came a little before him and I ate some dry beef with them for supper. I said a short prayer and had good health, good thoughts, and good humor, thank God Almighty.

30. I rose at 5 o'clock and settled accounts with George Smith and wrote a letter to Falling Creek but could read nothing. I neglected to say my prayers but had milk tea and bread and butter for breakfast with the Doctor. I wrote a letter to England. My wife slept very well and was much better this morning. The Doctor ordered her nothing but a bitter drink made of camomile flowers and ginseng root, which she was to drink morning and evening. My sloop came from Falling Creek and I ordered to unload her. John W-l-s came and told me that the negro I had put to apprentice to him was lame and desired I would order him to be cured. I told him it was his business to take care of that, who had the service of his labor. I ate some roast lamb for dinner. In the afternoon we diverted my wife and were very merry till the evening and then Mrs. Dunn returned home and the Doctor and I went into the river and afterwards drank some syllabub. My wife was better and better, thank God. I said a short prayer and had good health, good thoughts, and good humor, thank God Almighty. Mr. Bland came here without any news from Williamsburg.

July, 1711

1.[1] I rose at 5 o'clock and read two chapters in Hebrew and wrote a letter to Mr. Randolph. I neglected to say my prayers and ate bread and butter and tea for breakfast. I sent my sloop with 14 hogsheads of tobacco to Sandy Point. My wife was much better, thank God. It was very hot. Mr. Anderson called here to inquire how my wife did and stayed till 9 o'clock and then went over the river. I wrote another [letter] to Mr. Randolph and sent Tom with it. I ate some veal for dinner. In the afternoon I gave the Doctor four pieces of gold for his trouble in taking care of my wife, but I gave it him and desired him to give my service to Suky[2] and give her the money. About 3 o'clock he went away. I wrote a letter to England and in the evening took a walk about the plantation. My wife was better and very hungry. She ate some veal for her dinner. I neglected to say my prayers but had good health, good thoughts, and good humor, thank God Almighty.

2. I rose about 5 o'clock and read two chapters in Hebrew and some Greek in Homer. I said my prayers and ate milk for breakfast. I danced my dance. About 9 o'clock there came an express with a letter from the Governor with one from Colonel Hunter, governor of New York, by which I learned there was an expedition on hand which I judged to be against Canada and that all the money in my hands was to be sent there.[3] My wife was indisposed a little and very much out of humor. Mr. Anderson and several other gentlemen of the vestry came down just before dinner. I asked them to dine with me, which they did. I ate veal for dinner, but gave my wife none, which bred a mortal quarrel when the company was gone. I endeavored to reconcile

---

[1]This entry is dated June 31, and at the foot of the page, in longhand, is: "Note this last day shoud have been the 1st of July because June has but 30 days."

[2]Dr. Cocke's maid. Apparently this was Byrd's indirect way of paying his friend, Dr. Cocke, for professional services without offending him.

[3]Revenue due the Crown, in Byrd's hands as receiver-general.

myself to her and to persuade her to eat but she plagued me
a great while before she would. I wrote some accounts and
in the evening took a walk about the plantation, and was out
of humor with everybody. I said my prayers and had good
health, good thoughts, and good humor, thank God Almighty.

3. I rose about 5 o'clock and wrote a letter to the Governor and to Dr. Cocke and then sent away the express. I
read a chapter in Hebrew and some Greek in Homer. My
wife was better, thank God, though her headache continued.
Bannister came back with my tobacco and told me Captain
S-c-r would not take it in. I sent my sloop away to Appomattox for more tobacco. I found myself out of order,
especially in my head. I wrote letters to England till dinner
and I ate some minced veal. I read some French and then
wrote more letters to England till the evening. Then I took
a little walk about the plantation. I continued indisposed
and had but little stomach. I took great care of my wife,
however. I said my prayers and had good thoughts, good
humor, but indifferent health, thank God Almighty.

4.[1] I rose about 5 o'clock but read nothing because I prepared to go to Williamsburg, notwithstanding I was indisposed. I ate some milk for breakfast and said my prayers.
It was a coolish morning so that I thought it would be a cool
day. About 11 o'clock I went over the creek and so rode to
Williamsburg, having commended my family to God Almighty. It proved a hot day and I was very much affected
with my journey. When I came to the ferry I was faint and
drank some milk and water, which was wrong. Then I rode
to Colonel Ludwell's, where I drank abundance of water.
Here I stayed about two hours and then proceeded to Williamsburg where I arrived in the evening. I drank some
cider with Mr. Bland and then went to the Governor's where
I found him just returned from Kiquotan where he had been
concerning matters about the marines that were to go on
the expedition to Carolina. The Governor told me he should

---

[1]In the margin opposite this entry there is an "x."

buy 1000 barrels of pork for Colonel Hunter. Here I drank
some syllabub and then went to my lodgings and went to bed
and was taken with an ague which was succeeded with a
fever which went away in a sweat towards morning. I slept
very little. I said a short prayer to God and had very good
thoughts, good humor, but bad health, but God's will be
done.

5. I rose about 8 o'clock and found myself indisposed.
However I did some business. I said a short prayer and ate
some water gruel for breakfast. My man Tom had a headache and a little fever. I ordered him to be let blood.
About 11 o'clock I went in the President's coach to the
Governor's but before I went the Doctor came to see me.
I drank some tea at the Governor's and was much out of
order. However I went with the rest to Council where I
could not hold up my head. It was agreed in Council that
the revenue of two shillings per hogshead ought not to be
applied to the supply of New York, but only quitrents. It
was also agreed that it was necessary to endeavor to stop
the seditious proceedings in Carolina and send some forces
there and the Governor was pleased to say he would go in
person. About 3 o'clock we went to the Governor's to
dinner and I went among the rest but could eat nothing but
water gruel. I found myself a little better and then took
leave of the Governor and went to my lodgings where I
said my prayers and then went to bed. My man was grown
very ill. God's will be done. I had a bad night of it and
could not sleep well, notwithstanding I had an intermission
of the fits. Poor Peter Hamlin died of the smallpox, for
want of attention.

6. I rose about 8 o'clock and found myself pretty well
but I learned my man continued bad. I said a short prayer
and ate water gruel for breakfast. Several persons came to
see me and I settled several accounts. The captain of the
French privateer came to see me and lamented the necessity
of his going to old France. About 11 o'clock my ague came
with more violence. The Doctor was gone to York and I
resolved to go, sick as I was, to Colonel Ludwell's in order

to go home the next day in Captain Posford's boat. I asked the President to lend me his coach, but he made several excuses and therefore I sent to beg that favor of the Governor, who readily granted it, and about 5 o'clock came in his coach and offered me everything he had. I was very ill; however I went away a little after 5 o'clock and before 7 got to Colonel Ludwell's where they took great care of me, but I went to bed as soon as I could and had a fever all night and could not sleep till morning. God's will be done.

7. I rose about 9 o'clock and was pretty well, thank God, and without much ceremony took my leave and went in the Governor's coach to the water-side where I went into Captain Posford's boat. I gave the Governor's man 10 shillings and in about five hours I came very easily home where I found all well, thank God. I was pretty well the rest of the day but ate nothing but water gruel and drank some apple drink and sugar tea. I ordered Captain Posford's men to be well treated for their care of me. Before I came from Williamsburg I had given the best orders I could about my man Tom and desired Mr. Bland to get an old woman to attend him and had sent Bannister home before me with my horse to prevent my wife going to Williamsburg to take care of me, which would not have been fit for her in her weak condition. I had also made the Governor the compliment that if I had been well I would have waited on him to Carolina. I said a short prayer and went to bed where I slept very indifferently, God's will be done. I took some snakeroot stewed in wine and water to make me sweat. However I sweated but little.

8. I rose about 8 o'clock and was pretty well and ate some water gruel. I said a short prayer and sat up till 1 o'clock and then came my ague violently and Colonel Hill and Mr. Anderson came from church and found me very ill. I went to bed and had a very severe fit. I took more snakeroot and sweated very much with it, but it made my hot fit the worse and last the longer. I was not very dry nor did my head ache at all, or my back. I drank sage tea and some apple drink. At night came Dr. Cocke out of

pure friendship and not as a doctor. He gave me some comfort but said little to me that night because he would not disturb me. Only he did not approve of the sweats that I took. I sweated all night and could not sleep but in the morning the fever went off and left me very weak.

9. This day I was so weak I could not rise but I was without a fever, but the Doctor would not give me the bark because there would not be time before next fit to take quantity enough to prevent the next fit and if it did not prevent it, it would make it worse. I could eat nothing and took little or nothing but sage tea. The Doctor told me he would stay with me till I was safe, notwithstanding he neglected a great deal of other business. Several came to see me but the Doctor would let nobody to me because when people are weak company do them mischief. The Doctor assured me I should have but one fit more which pleased me much in my weak condition. Everybody was concerned for my sickness and my people attended me very well and particularly Mrs. Dunn. The Doctor comforted my wife so that she was very easy, thank God Almighty. I slept very little all night, nor could I command my thoughts enough to pray but I addressed myself to heaven to be restored.

10. I was a little easy this morning but had nothing but sage tea. The weather was [. . .] but I was very hot notwithstanding. I had a good intermission, thank God, but I lived in fear of the next fit, which came about 11 o'clock with terrible violence. My cold fit lasted four hours and the hot fit [. . .]. It was much the most violent I ever had in my life. The Doctor said he had not seen such a one and if I had another he believed it would turn to the quartan fever. It is not possible to describe the uneasy condition I was in but God enabled me to bear it, thanks to His holy name. The fit did not go away till the evening and then the bark was prepared for me and I took it every three hours.

11. This morning about 6 o'clock I began to be easy and continued to take the bark every three hours, but at first it

purged me and gave me four stools. This obliged the Doctor to give me laudanum with the bark and made me drink a drink made of burnt hartshorn.[1] He also gave me barley cinnamon water to stop the purge and it succeeded very well. I swallowed the bark like milk and took two ounces. Mr. Rogers was here yesterday and paid off Mrs. Parker's mortgage and I surrendered it to him. I was very weak-kneed and could eat nothing but bark and drink [whey] drink made of burnt hartshorn. The Doctor was very merry with Mrs. Dunn. In the evening Mr. Clayton came to see me, which was very kind. He brought me no news. My mouth was very clammy and I washed it with water very often to cool it. In the evening I began to look very yellow which the Doctor took for a good sign that the medicine had taken effect. Mr. Clayton lay at Mrs. Harrison's.

12. I was a little better this morning and the bark had thrown the distemper into my skin and I had the yellow jaundice in a great degree for which the Doctor prescribed turmeric and [1-p of s-l-p-n-c] and saffron, and every night and morning I had my [p-s b-k]. This distemper made me very [unclean] and burdensome to myself. Captain Posford sent often to know how I did. Mr. Clayton came this morning, but the Doctor would not let him or anybody else come up to see me. Colonel Hill and Mr. Anderson came to the house and dined here but I saw them not. Blessed be God, I lost my fit this day. The Doctor ordered the bark to be mixed with the turmeric without my knowledge so that I took three ounces of bark in all. I was very weak and had a clammy mouth and no stomach. Nor could I sleep but distracted sleep but I was easy, thank God Almighty.

13. I found myself better this morning though my jaundice was full on me. The Doctor saw me in a good way and so took his leave but he took nothing for all his trouble, which amazed me. However the Doctor did not go till after dinner. I gave him a million of thanks since he would

---

[1]E. Smith, *The Compleat Housewife* (1732), pp. 195, 199.

take nothing else and his man led a horse to Williamsburg for Tom who was perfectly recovered. My jaundice began to clear up and I grew better and ate some rice. I got up just to have my bed made and went to bed again. I was thirsty and drank sage tea. In the evening my wife sang to me but however I could not sleep well. I began to say my prayers in order again and to give God thanks for my recovery. Tony came from Appomattox and told me he had brought in above 400 skins.

14. I found myself a little better and my jaundice vanishing away by degrees. I said my prayers and ate some chicken broth for breakfast. About 10 o'clock I got up and sat in the great chair all day. About 2 o'clock came Tom from Williamsburg and brought me a letter from Mr. Bland. Tom was very well again, thank God. My mouth continued clammy and dry but was otherwise very easy. My [piss] was very yellow and was [b-k constantly] twice every day which I believe did me a great deal of service toward clearing my jaundice. In the evening I said my prayers and my wife and Mrs. Dunn sang to me and I slept better than I had done.

15. I found myself a little better this morning and my jaundice cleared away. I said my prayers and ate rice about 10 o'clock. Mr. Mumford came to see me and told me all was well at Appomattox. About 12 o'clock Colonel Ludwell came to see me but brought no news. I got up about 11 o'clock and went down stairs, thank God, for the first time. My beard was very long but I would not shave it. I gave Bannister leave to go see his mother. I ate rice for dinner and drank some wine and water. I had very little stomach to my victuals. I desired Mr. Mumford to go home and treat with H-sh about letting me have money for bills at 10 per cent. I continued in the hall till the evening and walked about much. In the evening I went to bed but slept indifferently.

16. I rose about 10 o'clock this morning and said my prayers and ate broth for breakfast. Colonel Ludwell went

away about 11 and my wife sent a letter by him to Mr. Bland for me about some business. I continued weak but almost lost my jaundice. Robin Mumford came and wrote some letters for me and I wrote a letter to England myself. I ate some eggs for dinner. In the afternoon I took a little nap which refreshed me much. I set things in order in my closet, but was able to do little business. In the evening I ate eggs again. Sometimes I moistened my mouth with a ripe pear. I cleaned my teeth. Before it was dark I retired to my chamber and went to bed where I said my prayers and had good thoughts, good humor, and indifferent health, thank God Almighty.

17. I slept pretty well last night and was better this morning. I dressed me early and went into the hall. I said my prayers and ate eggs for breakfast. About 10 o'clock Captain L-th-m came and gave me bills of lading. I got him to send his boat for Mrs. Dunn's walnut planks. About 12 o'clock Colonel Hill came and he and I settled accounts. He stayed to dinner and I for my part ate only eggs. Soon after dinner came Captain Llewellyn and desired to alter one of his bills of exchange. Colonel Hill told me Mr. Anderson could not leave his wife, who expected to lie in every moment. The Colonel stayed till the evening. I did a pretty deal of business and tired myself. In the evening I ate more eggs. Then I said my prayers and had good humor, good thoughts, and good hope of health, thank God Almighty.

18. I rose about 8 o'clock and took a bitter drink. I said my prayers and about 9 had tea and bread and butter for breakfast. I was much better and began to get strength and did a pretty deal of business. I wrote a letter for England and set my wife to writing one to the Duke of Argyle.[1] I ventured to eat a pear. I settled several accounts. About 12 o'clock I took a little nap and then went into the library. I ate some broth and lamb for dinner and ate a great deal. In the afternoon I ate some Virginia

---

[1] One of the noblemen whose acquaintance Byrd made in England was the Duke of Argyle. He obtained his portrait and hung it at Westover.

cherries and some watermelon. I took a little walk in the garden. I sent John G-r-l in the morning to Williamsburg with an account of my health to the Doctor and wrote merrily. At night I ate two eggs. Then I said my prayers and had good thoughts, good health, and good hope of health, thank God Almighty. I shaved my beard and head.

19. I rose about 8 o'clock but I did not sleep well last night and seemed to have a little fever in the morning. I said my prayers and had tea and bread and butter for breakfast, which made me a little better. I wrote a letter to England and settled several accounts. G-r-l returned about 11 o'clock and brought me some letters from Williamsburg. My sloop came last night and unloaded this day. I ate some lamb for dinner. In the afternoon Bannister was taken with an ague. Captain Posford came and told me the parson of Manakin Town was ill of a fever. Then came Captain Bolling with letters from the Governor and a warrant for £20. I ate some Virginia cherries. I was very well this afternoon, thank God Almighty. I settled some accounts and took a walk in the garden. I said my prayers and had good thoughts, good humor, and indifferent good health, thank God Almighty. I sent away the sloop to Falling Creek. George Carter came to mend the window.

20. I rose about 7 o'clock and found myself better. I said my prayers and ate bread and butter and drank tea for breakfast. Then I wrote some letters to England and settled several accounts. Bannister was better this day. However I gave him a vomit which worked very well. My wife wrote letters for me to the Duke of Argyle and to Mr. P-g-t. I sent Tom to Drury Stith's for watermelons. I ate two eggs about 11 o'clock; then I wrote more letters till dinner. I ate some boiled lamb for dinner. In the afternoon Tom returned and brought four watermelons, one of which we ate and then wrote more letters till 5 o'clock, when I ate more eggs and in the evening I took a walk to the store and in the garden. I said my prayers and had good health, good thoughts, and good humor, thank God Almighty.

21. I rose about 7 o'clock and was better, thank God. I said my prayers and had bread and butter and tea for breakfast. I wrote my public accounts but was interrupted by Colonel Eppes who came about 10 o'clock and then I ate two eggs. About 11 he went away and I went on with my accounts till 12 and then came Captain Posford who came to take his leave. About 1 o'clock came Mr. Bland's boy with letters from England but they brought no great news. I ate half a chicken for my dinner. In the afternoon I presented Captain Posford with two sheep and two hogs, and then recommended him to God's protection. I wrote more of my accounts till 6 o'clock and then ate some more of my chicken. Then I took a walk in the garden. I said my prayers and had good thoughts, good humor, and indifferent good health, thank God Almighty. I sent Tom to Williamsburg to take the Governor's coach to Green Springs on Monday.

22. I rose about 7 o'clock and slept pretty well last night. I said my prayers and had bread and butter and tea for breakfast. I found myself much better, thank God. I prepared to go to Green Springs in Captain Posford's boat. About 11 o'clock came Captain L-th-m to settle accounts with me, and Mr. Anderson and Colonel Hill came to see me but went away presently to church but I did not go there. However they stayed to dinner and ate some chicken. Captain Posford's boat came to carry me down and the men had dinner. About 2 o'clock I went into the boat but the wind was ahead and the tide against us, so that we went very slowly and could get no further than Major Harrison's before night. There I went ashore but the Major was not at home and his lady lying in. However I ate some eggs and then went to bed. Mr. Henry Harrison's wife was here and did the honors of the house. I said my prayers and had good health, good thoughts, and good humor, thank God Almighty. I slept pretty well but sweated very much.

23. I rose at 5 o'clock and said my prayers. Then I drank some chocolate and then took my leave and went into the boat and got to Colonel Ludwell's landing by 8 o'clock

where Tom was with my horses and I rode to the house and
found them all well. Major Harrison was here and his
brother Hal. Here I ate some bread and butter and drank
some tea. About 10 o'clock the Governor's coach came for
me and Dr. Cocke came in it, and after the horses had
rested about two hours we took leave and went to Williamsburg. I was set down at my lodgings and did some business
till about 2 o'clock and then went to the Governor's where
I found Captain P-s-t-n that came from New York for the
pork bought up here. This gentleman [d-b-ch] one of
Colonel Hyde's [daughters], the Governor of Carolina.
I ate some mutton for dinner and then returned to my lodgings and did more business with the naval officers. I did not
stir out any more this evening but did my business till 9
o'clock and then went to bed but did not sleep very well.
However I said my prayers and had good health, good
thoughts, and good humor, thank God Almighty.

24. I rose about 5 o'clock and said my prayers shortly.
Then I prepared my public accounts. Several people came
to see me which hindered me very much. About 8 o'clock
I ate some water gruel. About 10 came Colonel Ludwell
and examined my accounts and we did not finish till about
2 o'clock. Then we went to Council where my accounts
were passed. There were no more than five members of
the Council beside the Governor, and Mr. Blair was one,
who looked as if he would be [sick] soon. When the
Council was done some of us went to dine at the Governor's
and I had veal for dinner. In the evening I went to my
lodgings and dispatched a great deal of business and settled
several people's accounts till 10 o'clock. Then I said my
prayers shortly and had good health, good thoughts, and
good humor, thank God Almighty, but I did not sleep very
well but sweated very much. Dick Randolph copied some
letters for me.

25. I rose about 6 o'clock and neglected to say my prayers. I began to write my letters to England and wrote
several to Mr. Perry. About 8 I had some water gruel and
then wrote more letters. Several gentlemen came to see me,

and I did business with Mr. Bland and others. About 11
o'clock I went to the coffeehouse and ate some bread and
butter and drank some tea till my room was put in order.
Then I returned and wrote more letters and did more business till about 2 o'clock and then I went to the Governor's
to dinner where I ate some beef. After dinner I returned
soon to my lodgings because I would not hinder the Governor nor myself from writing letters. I wrote several letters
to England and went not out any more that night. About
9 o'clock I went to bed. I said my prayers and had good
thoughts, good health, and good humor, thank God Almighty. I sent my man home for my horses this morning.

26. I rose about 5 o'clock and neglected to say my prayers. I wrote several letters and settled several accounts.
About 8 o'clock I ate some milk and baked pears for breakfast. About 9 my man Tom came from home with my
horses and brought me a letter from my wife with an
account that all was well, thank God. He brought me some
fruit which I sent, some to the Governor and some to Mrs.
Bland. About 11 o'clock I went to the coffeehouse and
drank some tea and ate bread and butter till 12. Then
came Colonel Ludwell and Mr. Custis about business. I
wrote a letter to England and about 2 o'clock went to the
Governor's to dinner. I ate some fowl for dinner. After
dinner I went to my lodgings where I wrote letters till the
evening. I went to see Mrs. Bland and from thence to the
coffeehouse where I drank some tea and about 9 went home
to bed, where I did not sleep very well. I said my prayers
and had good health, good thoughts, and good humor, thank
God Almighty. It was extremely hot. Captain Posford
came and took leave of me.

27. I rose about 5 o'clock and said my prayers. Then I
wrote several letters to England till about 8 o'clock and then
I ate some milk and pears and then wrote more letters and
some accounts. Then I sealed up my letters and at 11 I
went to the coffeehouse and made my second breakfast of
tea and bread and butter. Then I returned to my lodgings
and had several persons come to me so that I could do no

business. About 2 o'clock I went to the Governor's where
was Mrs. Hyde[1] on her way to England and Mr. Lawson,[2]
one of the commissioners for running the boundaries of
Carolina. It was extremely hot so that we sat without our
[capes] notwithstanding the ladies. I ate some boiled beef
for dinner. Here I stayed till about 6 o'clock and then left
my letters with the Governor and took my leave. Then I
went and took leave of Mrs. Bland and then went to Colonel
Ludwell's where was much company and my cousin Harrison
among the rest. I drank some tea and about 10 o'clock
went to bed. Major Harrison lay in the same room and we
talked almost all night for the heat would not let us sleep.
I neglected to say my prayers but had good health, good
thoughts, and good humor, thank God Almighty. This was
the hottest weather I ever felt.

28. I rose about 3 o'clock and prepared to go home and
about 4 got on my horse and by moonshine rode to the ferry
and then it began to be day. When I was over the river I
drank some warm milk and then proceeded on my journey
and got home about 9 o'clock and found everything well,
thank God, except John, who had run a nail into his foot.
Several of my people had been sick but were recovered.
About 10 o'clock came John Woodson and I settled accounts
with him. I drank some tea and ate some bread and butter.
When John Woodson was gone I found myself tired and
laid [sic] down to sleep, and slept about two hours which
refreshed me much. I ate a pigeon for dinner and in the
afternoon took another nap. I said my prayers on the road.
I read nothing but only put my things to rights. In the
evening came an express from the Falls by which I learned
that all was well there, thank God, and I wrote two letters
there. In the evening I drank some warm milk and walked

---

[1] Apparently Governor Hyde's wife accompanied him to Carolina and
now was being sent back to England for safety. In a letter to the Society
for the Propagation of the Gospel, John Urmston, a missionary in North
Carolina, July 17, 1711, says "Madame Hyde the Governor's lady . . . came
over with the same ships," bringing letters and papers to the Lords Proprie-
tors. (*Colonial Records of North Carolina*, ed. W. L. Saunders, I [Raleigh,
1886], 773.)
[2] John Lawson, surveyor general of North Carolina. See note on Graffenriedt, Oct. 8, 1711.

in the garden till it was almost dark. I neglected to say my prayers but had good health, good thoughts, and good humor, thank God Almighty. I slept better this night than I had done since I was sick.

29. I rose about 7 o'clock and read a chapter in Hebrew and some Greek in Homer. I drank some warm milk from the cow and about 9 o'clock had some tea and bread and butter. About 10 came an express from Drury Stith to tell me he was sick of a fever and desired two bottles of cider, which I sent him. I gave Will Eppes leave to go see his mother. Moll at the quarters was sick of a fever for which I gave her a vomit that worked very well. Billy Wilkins was also sick. I ate boiled pigeon and bacon for dinner. In the afternoon we sat and talked till 3 o'clock and then ate some watermelon. Then wrote the entries of my journal and afterwards read some French till the evening and then we took a walk about the plantation. My wife and I had a small quarrel about the trial which made us dumb to each other the rest of the night. I said my prayers and had good health, good thoughts, and indifferent good humor, thank God Almighty.

30. I rose about 6 o'clock and read a chapter in Hebrew and 200 verses in Homer. I said my prayers and had some warm milk from the cow. Dick Hamlin came to ask me whether Dr. Cocke would come to his brother [if] sent for to him, who had the smallpox. I told him he would. About 9 o'clock I had tea and bread and butter. My wife [and I] were reconciled this morning. Old Moll continued sick and I ordered her to be bled, and Billy Wilkins to take a vomit that worked very well. I settled several accounts till dinner and then I ate some roast shoat. In the afternoon I cut the top of my thumb almost off with a chisel in making a buckle for my wife. I settled more accounts till the evening and then I took a long walk about the plantation. Several people halloa'd for the ferry but they would not hear so that I set them over in my boat. In the evening I read some news. I said my prayers and had good health, good thoughts, and good humor, thank God Almighty.

31. I rose about 6 o'clock and read a chapter in Hebrew and 250 verses in Homer. I said my prayers and ate warm milk for breakfast. I danced one dance but a little feebly. Old Moll continued to have the headache and I put on a blister behind her neck. About 9 o'clock I had some bread and butter and tea. Then I settled several accounts. Billy Wilkins had his ague again. John was much better, thank God, and began to work. I ate some roast shoat for dinner. In the afternoon I settled more accounts and read some French till the evening and then I walked in the garden because it threatened rain and as soon as it was dark it began to rain and thundered very much and did so good part of the night. I said my prayers and had good health, good thoughts, and good humor, thank God Almighty.

August, 1711

1. I rose about 6 o'clock and read a chapter in Hebrew and 400 verses in Homer. I drank some warm milk for breakfast. I said my prayers devoutly. Billy Wilkins was better and so was John, thank God. It was court day and I had some business there about the negro woman that was dead. About 11 o'clock came Colonel Hill and Mr. Anderson and Mr. Platt and about 12 I went with them to court and the suit against me was dismissed. I brought the persons mentioned before home to dinner and I ate boiled pork for dinner. In the afternoon I sent a bottle of wine to Mrs. Eppes who could not come from court. I read some French when the company was gone. In the evening it threatened more rain. However I took a walk in the garden. The rain blew over. John Pleasant's mill dam was carried away so that nobody could come from Henrico County to court. I neglected to say my prayers but had good health, good thoughts, and good humor, thank God Almighty.

2. I rose about 5 o'clock and read a chapter in Hebrew and 400 verses in Homer. I neglected to say my prayers because company came, which was Mr. Finney and Captain Webb. They had some fresh butter and cheese and strong beer for breakfast and I had some milk. We played at billiards and then Captain Webb and I settled accounts till dinner. I ate some roast pigeon for dinner. It was cool weather today. Captain Webb had just [received] a letter from Mr. Bradley[1] concerning my tobacco. About 4 o'clock Mr. Finney and Captain Webb went away. I read French this afternoon. In the evening I walked about the plantation. Somebody shot a poor mare and drove her into my lane to make people believe that my people had done it. I suppose it was Mrs. Harrison. I neglected to say my pray-

---

[1] William Byrd I refers constantly in his letters to Captain Bradley. Apparently his brother, Ben Bradley, was an English merchant. (*Va. Mag.,* XXV, 264, 359.)

ers but had good health, good thoughts, good humor, thank God Almighty. The sloop came from Falling Creek with planks and stones. At night I read some Italian.

3. I rose about 5 o'clock and read two chapters in Hebrew and 300 verses in Homer. I said my prayers and ate warm milk for breakfast. The weather was cool and John and my people all well, thank God Almighty. I settled several accounts and mended an error in Mr. Tullitt's account and wrote him a letter about it. The sloop was unloaded. My wife was peevish which made a little quarrel between us. I ate roast lamb for dinner. In the afternoon put several things in order and then I wrote a letter to Falling Creek and sent the sloop away. I also wrote to Mr. Randolph to prepare the release for John Giles who offers to take £20 for his right to Falling Creek. Then I read some Latin and French till the evening and then I took a walk into the orchard where there were few apples. It threatened rain but did not come. I neglected to say my prayers but had good thoughts, good health, and good humor, thank God Almighty. At night I read some Italian.

4. I rose about 5 o'clock and read a chapter in Hebrew and 300 verses in Homer. I said my prayers and ate cold milk for breakfast. I sent Tom to Mr. Randolph. I beat Prue for staying with my milk at the cowpen and telling a lie about it. Mr. Anderson came and desired to be set over the river because the ferry man could not hear him, which was done accordingly. I was indisposed with beating of Prue, and tired. I settled some accounts till dinner. John was recovered of his lameness again. I ate some mutton for dinner. In the afternoon I read some Latin and some French. I could not walk in the evening because there was likely to be a terrible gust of thunder and rain which happened accordingly and it rained exceedingly and thundered, and it seems killed a horse at Captain John Stith's. Captain Drury Stith I heard was recovered of his ague and drank nothing but cold water just drawn from the well. I said my prayers and had good health, good thoughts, and good humor, thank God Almighty.

5. I rose about 6 o'clock and read a chapter in Hebrew and 60 verses in Homer and found myself very dry and out of order. However I drank some warm milk for breakfast but did not say my prayers. I prepared to go to church but as soon as I was dressed I found my ague began to return on me again about 11 o'clock. The ague was not very violent but the fever was and lasted till the evening. Bannister brought me home some English letters from Bradley of an old date with an account from him of 36 shillings a hogshead that went by the "Harrison." This price did not mend my fever. However, about 5 o'clock it began to abate and left me in a sweat. I drank nothing but wine and water and not too much of that because I was not exceedingly dry. I made some short ejaculations but my head was not enough composed for prayers. I went to bed as soon as it was dark but did nothing but sweat and slept very little. God's will be done. I had deserved his judgment.

6. I found myself pretty well in the morning and rose about 8 o'clock and then prepared a vomit of ipecuana and took it and it gave me 3 vomits and much disordered me and soon caused my fever to return with some violence, though I had a short ague. I ate a poached egg which sat heavily on my stomach. My fever took me about 12 o'clock and continued till 5 in the afternoon. In my fever I ate some watermelon and drank some mint water and water with 10 drops of spirits of salt which cooled me exceedingly. The fever went away in a sweat and I was easy all the evening. I ate nothing more but went to bed about 8 o'clock and sweated there after a terrible manner so that I dared not go to sleep for fear of taking cold till I had [sh-v] myself, and then I slept a little, thank God Almighty.

7. I found myself pretty well in the morning and rose about 9 o'clock and ate tea and bread and butter for breakfast. I began to have a small looseness which made me a little weak. However, I came down and walked about till about 12 o'clock and then my ague came which, notwithstanding it was short, disordered me extremely and made me vomit up all I had eaten and drunk that day. This alarmed

me so much that I sent for Dr. Cocke. But when I had done
vomiting I found myself pretty easy again. In the afternoon my fever came with terrible violence and to cool it I
ate some watermelon which Captain John Stith sent me.
This increased my looseness so that I had in the whole day
about 6 stools. However this cooler made my fever short
and it went away about 5 o'clock and left me in a sweat. In
the evening it thundered and rained again but not with great
violence, but it hindered Tom getting to Williamsburg for
he lodged at the ferry. I slept about half the night and rose
for a little stool. I had letters from Manakin Town that
told me their minister Mr. Cairon was like to die. God's
will be done.

8. I found myself very easy this morning and got up
about 8 o'clock. I read a little Greek in Homer, and said
my prayers. Then I ate some tea and bread and butter. I
walked about and found me more strong than I had been
since my sickness. About 12 o'clock came Mrs. Harrison
because the weather was grown cold. Besides business she
had some charity in her visit. She stayed to dinner with
us, and I ate some fish with a stomach. In the afternoon I
continued very easy till about 4 o'clock and then I had a
little shiver which was presently succeeded with a moderate
fever. About 5 o'clock came the Doctor who expected to
find me very ill. However he pronounced me worse than I
thought myself and began to recommend the bark to me
which I refused to take because I thought I should get well
without it. In the evening my sister Custis came because she
heard I was dangerously ill and when she came the Doctor
and the three women made such a hubbub and noise that I
retired upstairs and told the Doctor the bark was a fit
remedy for him to prescribe because it made people deaf.
I slept about half the night, thank God Almighty.

9. I was not so well as yesterday morning but was faint
and weak and lay in bed till 10 o'clock. I ate some rice and
currants for breakfast, which did not well agree with me.
My wife and Mrs. Dunn had a quarrel about several matters, which ended in good humor again presently. About 12

o'clock I found myself very uneasy and went up into my chambers and vomitted a little and then I was better but had a little fever. About 2 o'clock I came down stairs again. The Doctor shook his head and told me I was in a bad condition and believed I could not get well without the bark. However he would not insist on it since I had so much aversion to it but would prescribe me a bitter draught which possibly might cure me but he doubted it. I told him I was better than he thought but that I would take his bitter draught. In the evening I ordered the coach for my sister and the Doctor to go to Mrs. Harrison's but my sister out of her great modesty would not go alone in the coach with the Doctor, and so Mrs. Dunn went with them. My fever was moderate all the evening, thank God Almighty.

10. I was better this morning, thank God; however I lay in bed till 10 o'clock and drank tea there with my sister Custis there [sic]. I had my will signed this morning. About 11 o'clock I took my bitter draught and about 12 I ate some veal broth and at dinner I ate a little veal with a stomach, thank God, and it agreed well with me. I was a little warm in the afternoon, nothing to complain of. About 5 o'clock I ate some watermelon and 2 nectarines and drank some canary after them. In the evening I took my bitter draught again and soon after had a small fever which held about three hours but did not make me uneasy. About 8 o'clock I went to bed and said my prayers and had good thoughts, good health, and good humor, thank God Almighty. I wrote in my journal.

11. I slept very well all night, thank God, and scarcely moved out of one place, and also slept till 10 o'clock in the morning, which I imputed to the drink made of the root of dandelion and whey, of which I drank a bottle full. I read some Greek in Homer and said my prayers. I drank my bitter draught and rose about 11 o'clock and about 12 ate some veal broth. I found myself well but weak and my pulse very slow. Then I ate some watermelon and drank two swallows of sage tea lest it might be too cooling. I drank nothing else till the evening and then I drank my

bitter draught and sat up till 9 o'clock and no news of my
fever. When I went to bed I drank some of the whey drink
but whether that was the cause or that I had a fever I can't
tell, but I did not sleep till 12 o'clock and after very indifferently. However I said my prayers and had good
health, good thoughts, and good humor, thank God Almighty.

12. I slept a little good sleep in the morning and then
drank my bitter draught. I read 200 verses in Homer and
about 10 o'clock rose and found myself disordered for want
of sleep. However I had some tea and bread and butter
which made me sweat and then I was better. I walked
about and was shaved and did several things. I [cleansed]
before dinner and then I ate some boiled chicken with sorrel
sauce. I found myself very easy without fever, thank God.
I ate three roast apples and a little muskmelon and drank
some canary after them. I wrote my journal and walked
about and was very well but weak. At night I drank some
bitter draught and then laid [sic] on the couch and gave
audience to my people. My wife took a [hive of bees] but
it proved an indifferent one. My people are all well, thank
God. I had no fever and went to bed about 9 o'clock and
slept pretty well, thank God. I said my prayers and had
good health, good thoughts, and good humor, thank God
Almighty.

13. I found myself better and when I had drunk my bitter
draught I read 200 verses in Homer. Then I took a nap
and rose about 8 o'clock and found Mr. Mumford here.
I had some tea and bread and butter which put me into a
sweat. Mr. Mumford told me he had been sick but that all
was well at Appomattox, and that my trader went out last
week. He told me the parson of Manakin Town was better
again. We talked of several businesses and particularly a
sickness of which he said he had four hogs perish since he
saw me, which makes 8 in all. We discoursed till dinner
and I ate cold chicken for dinner. In the afternoon I found
myself cheerful and in a broad sweat which I had almost all
day. I read some French and wrote three letters to my

overseers above. In the evening I walked a little in the garden. I said my prayers and had good health, good thoughts, and good humor, thank God Almighty. I slept pretty well this night, thank God.

14. In the morning I found my head a little out of order. However I read 150 verses in Homer. I neglected to say my prayers and had tea and bread and butter for breakfast. This put me into a broad sweat which made me better. I had no fever. About 10 o'clock Mr. Mumford went over the river to court. I read some French and walked about till dinner, and then I ate some crab and four poached eggs. In the afternoon came Bannister's mother to account with me. We found the balance more than £9 which I would not take from her in consideration of her son's good service. She was very thankful and gave me her blessing. It was very hot this afternoon. I ordered Mr. Mumford to let Mrs. Eppes know she need trouble herself to bring her son no more because I would keep nobody that would not follow orders. I ate some watermelon and peaches and drank some canary. I learned that Mr. Rogers was sick and I sent him some Spanish flies.[1] In the evening I ate a poached egg and then took a walk in the garden. I said my prayers and had good health, good thoughts, and good humor, thank God Almighty.

15. I rose about 9 o'clock and before that read 300 verses in Homer and said my prayers. I had tea and bread and butter for breakfast. I found myself pretty well only my head was a little giddy. I read some French. The weather was cool again, with a north wind. My stools were regular once a day. About 12 o'clock came Colonel Eppes who told me Tom Cocke[2] was dead and that Mr. Rogers was very sick. He stayed and dined with us. I ate a snipe for my dinner. In the afternoon I received a letter from the Governor with orders to exercise all the militia under

[1]Cantharides, dried and employed externally as a blister and internally as an irritant and diuretic.
[2]Thomas Cocke IV, son of the third Thomas Cocke, died unmarried. (*Va. Mag.*, IV, 212.)

my command because we were threatened with an invasion, there being 14 French men-of-war designed for these parts. I immediately [sent] to Colonel Eppes to get the militia of this county together and sent orders to Colonel Frank Eppes to do the same in Henrico County. In the evening I wrote a letter to the Governor, to make my excuses for not going to council tomorrow. Then I ate more snipe and took a walk in the garden. I neglected to say my prayers but had good thoughts, good health, and good humor, thank God Almighty.

16. I slept very well and before I rose read 200 verses in Homer and said my prayers and ate some boiled milk for breakfast. About 9 o'clock I rose. Tom returned last night from the Falls and told me all was well there and at Falling Creek. I sent him with my letters to Williamsburg. This was the first day of my dressing myself again and my head was shaved. The weather continued cool. I ate two peaches and drank some canary. I found myself better, thank God, and for dinner ate a partridge and a snipe. In the afternoon I played the fool and ate three peaches but drank some canary after them. I continued well but my head was giddy and out of order. In the evening I rode out about my plantation and ate an apple and the sun was set before I returned and then I drank some warm milk from the cow and was cheerful till about 8 o'clock and then my ague took me again with some violence and then I went to bed and had a fever great part of the night. This new return made me resolve to take the bark the next morning because I thought myself too weak for any other method.

17. In the morning about 6 o'clock I took the bark, taking it in hartshorn water for eight doses running. I lay in bed all day and ate nothing but bark of which I took an ounce. I slept pretty much in the day and sweated. The bark did not purge me as it did last time but it made me deaf and dazed me so much that I lay in the same place and almost in the same position for more than 30 hours together. In the afternoon came Mr. Bland on his way to Williamsburg. He was not well himself. He stayed with me about

two hours and then took his leave. The water I made was not of so red a color as before I took the bark. My wife sat up till 11 o'clock and Mrs. Dunn till 2 to give me my dose of bark and I slept pretty well between whiles, thank God Almighty.

18. I took my last dose of bark about 7 o'clock this morning. I was very deaf and my head was giddy. Mr. Anderson came about 9 o'clock and sat with me an hour and about 10 I rose and had bread and butter and tea for breakfast which I ate with some taste. This made me sweat. My sloop came early this morning with walnut planks and unloaded some of it here and was to carry the rest to Williamsburg. At dinner I ate some apple dumpling. In the afternoon I was a little faint. The weather continued cool, the wind northwest. I abstained from all sorts of fruit and kept myself warm for fear my ague should return in the evening and I went to bed as soon as it was dark. I said my prayers and had good health, good [thoughts] and good humor, and slept all night very well, thank God Almighty.

19. I found myself pretty well this morning and said my prayers and then read 200 verses in Homer. I rose about 9 o'clock and ate some hominy for breakfast. Mr. G-r-l came last night and told me all was well at Falling Creek and at the plantation. I discoursed him about several things till about 12 o'clock and then he went away. My wife and Mrs. Dunn went to church where several people had the goodness to ask for me. About 12 I ate some mutton broth and about 2 I ate two small fish and some roast mutton and ate pretty heartily, thank God. I was better in the afternoon and not so giddy in my head. I read and wrote and walked about. It was warm weather again. I said my prayers and had good health, good thoughts, and good humor, thank God Almighty. I slept pretty well and had a pollution in my dream.

20. I was pretty well this morning and read 300 verses in Homer. I said my prayers and rose about 10 o'clock and had tea and bread and butter for breakfast. About 11 came

[Mr.] Laforce [. . .] me the money I sued him for so we agreed the matter. About 12 came Colonel Hill and Colonel Eppes who dined here and I ate some roast mutton with an indifferent stomach, thank God. Mr. Laforce would not stay to dinner. In the afternoon I read some French and wrote some things. I sent further orders to Colonel Frank Eppes about the militia and gave them to Colonel Littlebury by word of mouth and walked about in the garden pretty much without being tired. I said my prayers and had good health, good thoughts, and good humor, thank God Almighty. I drank some canary and snakeroot when I went to bed but I could not sleep well, I had so many projects come into my head, but I slept the latter end of the night without waking till day, nor had I any polluting dream as I had the night before.

21. I found myself pretty well and read 200 verses in Homer. Then I rose about 8 o'clock and said my prayers and had tea and bread and butter for breakfast. There came a man for 12 rights of land. There came also an express from the Governor concerning the militia, a copy of which I sent to Colonel Eppes with my orders to put it in execution. I wrote to the Governor and to Mr. Band by the express. I ventured to dress myself today and was very easy and well. I ate some mutton for dinner. In the afternoon I prepared some infusions of the bark to take at the end of the week. I read some French and in the evening I wrote to Colonel Frank Eppes to send with a copy of the Governor's letter to me. I took a walk in the garden. I said my prayers and had good health, good thoughts, and good humor, thank God Almighty.

22. I slept well last night and could hardly wake this morning. I said my prayers and read a chapter in Hebrew and 300 verses in Homer. I rose about 9 o'clock and had tea and bread and butter for breakfast. I found myself a little hot but the tea set me right again. I took a walk in the garden. Bannister went this morning to Henrico to carry my letter to Colonel Frank Eppes. I ate some squirrel and onions for dinner. I caused Moll to be beaten for not mak-

ing the shoats [fat]. I cleaned my pistols this afternoon. In the evening it rained a good shower but gave over too soon. Then I took a walk in the garden a little while but the air was a little too damp for me. I said my prayers and had good health, good thoughts, and good humor, thank God Almighty.

23. I slept well this night, especially the first part of it. I said my prayers and then read 300 verses in Homer and a chapter in Hebrew. I rose about 8 o'clock and drank a glass of red wine in which the bark had been steeped, and about 9 had some tea and bread and butter. Then I was shaved. It was cool after the rain. I had a letter from Captain Drury Stith that he had a fever but all the other officers came except John Eppes who was sick likewise. We discoursed of several matters relating to the militia and about the beacons and we agreed on the places where they were to be put. They dined with me and I ate some pigeon. In the afternoon came Colonel Frank Eppes and several gentlemen with him. We settled several matters and named several officers and then they all went away. Soon after they were gone I received a letter from the Governor dated yesterday that two French men-of-war and several privateers were arrived and ordering me to send away to Jamestown 25 gunners out of each county to work on the battery there. I sent away orders after my two colonels this night. My wife was frightened and would hardly go to bed, but was persuaded at last, but I could not sleep for thinking of our condition and what I was to do. I said my prayers devoutly and had good health, good thoughts, and good humor, thank God Almighty. I drank my bark.

24. I rose about 6 o'clock and dispatched several orders. I sent for my guns and ammunition from Appomattox and I sent away the plate and several things of value to Captain Drury Stith's, that place being more secure than this. I sent to Major H-n-t to send an express as soon as any privateer appeared at his house. I got my arms in order and made cartouches. I ate a roast pigeon for dinner. In the afternoon Mrs. Harrison and her daughter and Mr. Cocke came

to hear what news concerning the enemy and were pleased
to hear I had heard no further about them. I told her
when I learned the danger was near I would send her
word and defend her. They went away about 4 o'clock and
I began to read some French and to write in my journal.
Tom returned from Major H-n-t without an answer and
John returned with the cart from Captain Drury Stith's and
said the things got there well but that the Captain was not
at home. In the evening I took a walk to the point and in
the garden. I said my prayers and had good health, good
thoughts, and good humor, thank God Almighty. I drank
my bark and slept well great part of the night.

25. I rose about 6 o'clock and found my sloop come. I
wrote a letter to the Governor, to Dr. Cocke, and Mr.
Bland, and sent some venison to the Governor by Tom. The
people of my sloop told me there was news that our fleet
was taken. My boat came in the night from Appomattox
and brought what ammunition they had there with an account that Mr. Mumford was very sick and therefore I [*or
they*] sent for the Doctor to come to him. About 9 o'clock
came Colonel Hill and Colonel Frank Eppes to give me an
account what he had done. I gave them some bread and
butter and cheese and some strong beer for breakfast.
Colonel Eppes went away again about 11 and soon after his
brother Littlebury came and he told me the beacons would
be all up this day. He and Colonel Hill stayed to dinner
and I ate some chicken with a good stomach. About 3 the
two colonels went away and I read some French and in the
evening took a walk. The Frenchman made me a great
number of cartouches and cleaned my arms. At night I received a letter from Mr. Salle about the affairs of the
Manakin Town. I neglected to say my prayers and had
good health, good thoughts, and good humor, thank God
Almighty.

26. I rose about 7 o'clock and read two chapters in
Hebrew and a chapter in the Greek Testament. I said my
prayers and ate hominy for breakfast. I drank my bark and
found myself very well, thank God. My wife and Mrs.

Dunn rode out this morning with the child. About 12 o'clock Tom returned from Williamsburg with letters from the Doctor and Mr. Bland for the Governor was not at home. They told me that Colonel Milner of Nansemond had sent an express yesterday about noon which said that 15 French men-of-war were come within the Cape and with several other ships and had landed several thousand men on the Eastern Shore. I believe this not all true. I ate a partridge for my dinner. In the afternoon came Billy from the Falls with an account that all was well there, but they were in fear of the Indians and therefore he wanted powder. I sent him a pound and wrote a letter to him and to Tom Osborne. In the evening it rained a good shower after which I took a walk in the garden. I said my prayers and had good health, good thoughts, and good humor, thank God Almighty.

27. I rose about 6 o'clock and I found myself pretty well but I read nothing because I prepared to go to meet my captains in Henrico. I said my prayers and ate roast partridge for breakfast. About 11 o'clock I went to Colonel Hill's where I stayed about an hour and then in his boat I crossed the river and he and Mr. Anderson went with me. When we came to Isham Eppes' I found all my officers there and settled several matters and gave away several troops and particularly one to Frank Eppes. They all seemed to be very vigorous and [polished]. When I came away I recommended to them to inspire the men with vigor and then we passed the river again and I dined at Colonel Hill's and ate some boiled beef. About 4 o'clock Bannister came with a letter from Major H-n-t which told me that the Governor had sent an express to Colonel Ludwell that 7 ships were come up James River and so the militia of James City were ordered to Williamsburg. Upon this I sent orders to Colonel Eppes to march all the militia to the lower part of the county which was done accordingly and an alarm given. I went home, where I found Mrs. Harrison, but heard no more news this night. I read some French. Then I said my prayers and had good health, good thoughts, and good humor, thank God Almighty.

28. I rose about 6 o'clock and read a chapter in Hebrew and 100 verses in Homer. · I said my prayers and had tea and bread and butter for breakfast. Dick Cocke came to hear what news and told me the alarm took through the county and all the people would be together about 2 o'clock. He would not stay to drink. Presently after came Colonel Littlebury Eppes, come for news likewise, and as soon as he was gone came Major Wynne[1] and told me that Prince George County were all in arms because of the alarm of Henrico. I told him the reason of it. He said John Bolling set such a heap of straw on fire in the night that it caused two beacons of Prince George to be set on fire. The Major had his holsters at his girdle and an armor bearer that carried his pistols, which made a good figure. He would not stay to dinner. I ate a roast chicken for dinner. In the afternoon I read some French and Latin. In the evening came Mr. Bland's boy with letters from him and Dr. Cocke that told me the seven ships supposed to be French that entered into James River were English. As soon as I received this account I sent away expresses to the militia of Henrico to let them know it, that they might go home if they pleased. I also sent an account of it to Prince George for the same reason. This was just as I suspected, and everything seemed quiet again, thank God. I said my prayers and had good health, good thoughts, and good humor, thank God Almighty.

29. I rose about 6 o'clock and read nothing but 100 verses in Homer. I neglected to say my prayers but had tea and bread and butter for breakfast. I sent Tom to Colonel Bassett's for my accoutrements and John with the cart for our things at Drury Stith's. I also sent away the sloop to Appomattox for tobacco. I received a letter from Colonel Ludwell with an order to send other men to Jamestown because those I sent before complained of their crops and the danger of their families for which reason he was resolved to discharge them except the Governor ordered him

---

[1]Probably Joshua Wynne, a justice of Prince George County in 1708. (*Va. Mag.,* XIV, 174.)

otherwise. I took this letter ill and sent an answer to it that the Colonel won't like. I ate some crab for dinner, which Will Parish[1] brought over. In the afternoon I read some French and set my closet in order. I unpacked my things that came from Drury Stith's. In the evening I took a walk in the garden. Mr. Chamberlayne brought me a letter from Robin Mumford that told me he was better. After it was dark came Dr. Cocke but he brought no news. I ate some bread and butter with him and we drank a bottle of wine. I neglected to say my prayers but had good health, good thoughts, and good humor, thank God Almighty.

30. I rose about 6 o'clock and read nothing because of the company in the house. I neglected to say my prayers but had tea and bread and butter for breakfast. Then we went into the library and read some French. About 11 o'clock came Drury Stith and soon after him Mr. Anderson, Colonel Hill, and several other gentlemen of the vestry which was to meet this day and I went with them to church. We appointed people to positions of [l-n] of the parish. I brought Colonel Hill and Mr. Anderson home with me to dine with the Doctor. I ate roast duck for dinner. In the afternoon they went away to Mrs. Harrison's and the Doctor and I played at piquet with my wife, and the Doctor won the pool. In the evening we took a walk and then drank a bottle of wine. I neglected to say my prayers but had good health, good thoughts, and good humor, thank God Almighty.

31. I rose about 6 o'clock and read 100 verses in Homer. I neglected to say my prayers and had milk tea and bread and butter for breakfast. I wrote to the Governor and to several others in order to send them by the Doctor, who threatened to go in the morning early but he stayed however till noon. About 12 o'clock the Doctor had some souse[2] fish and soon after went away. Soon after we went to dinner and I ate a pigeon. In the afternoon I received a letter

---

[1]Will Parish owned 100 acres in Charles City County in 1704. (*Va. Mag.,* XXXI, 317.)

[2]*I. e.,* pickled.

from Colonel Ludwell that John [Cross] would not work at Jamestown and desired me to have him punished. Then came Captain H-n-t the master of the ship from Mr. Offley[1] and brought me 77 empty bottles from the vessel that had been taken and lost my cider. In an hour he went away and then I put my library in order till the evening and then I took a walk in the garden. At night I read some French. I said my prayers and had good health, good thoughts, and good humor, thank God Almighty. The negro woman S-r-y was sick and L-s-n had hurt his foot.

---

[1]Henry Offley, an English merchant trading to Virginia and Maryland.

September, 1711

1. I rose about 6 o'clock and read two chapters in Hebrew but no Greek. I neglected to say my prayers but had tea and bread and butter for breakfast. It was very hot. Charles Parish[1] sent me some more fish, for which I ordered him a pair of wool cards. John [Cross'] wife came to try to beg for her husband but she did not succeed. A man brought some peaches for which I likewise ordered him a pair of wool cards. I spent most of the morning in setting right my books in the library. I ate some crab for dinner. In the afternoon I worked very hard again in the library till the evening and then a man came from King William county to compound for land escheated to the Queen and I ordered him some supper. Then I took a walk into the garden because it had rained a good shower and made it wet without. Then I read some French. I said my prayers and had good health, good thoughts, and good humor, thank God Almighty. I began this evening to drink the bark in claret.

2. I rose about 6 o'clock and read a chapter in Hebrew but no Greek because I was fixing matters to go to church. I said my prayers and ate hominy for breakfast. The sloop came last night from Appomattox. It rained very hard last night and was cold this morning. I went on horseback to church, where I found two troops and a company of foot drawn up. I viewed them and found several without arms, four of whom I ordered to Jamestown to relieve as many others. Then we went into church and heard a good sermon from Mr. Anderson fit for the occasion. After church the militia were drawn up again and I viewed them and then returned home and Colonel Eppes went home with me. I ate roast pork for dinner. In the afternoon I put some books in order in the library till the evening and then my wife and I took a walk about the plantation. I said my

---

[1] A Charles City County neighbor. (*Va. Mag.*, XXXI, 317.)

prayers and had good health, good thoughts, and good humor, thank God. Negro S-r-y was well again. I took my bark.

3. I rose about 7 o'clock and read a chapter in Hebrew and 200 verses in Homer. I neglected to say my prayers but ate potatoes and butter for breakfast. The weather was very cold this morning, the wind at northwest. I settled some things in my closet till dinner. I ate wild duck for dinner. In the afternoon came Captain H-n-t and told me the Governor told him his letter of marque was good and he might go when he pleased. I offered him £10 a ton but he said he would ride to York and try his fortune there before he would take that and so he went away. I read some French and Latin till the evening and then I took a walk in the orchard and found very few apples there. I gave orders for the sloop to get ready to sail. I said my prayers and had good health, good thoughts, and good humor, thank God Almighty.

4. I rose about 6 o'clock and read a chapter in Hebrew and 200 verses in Homer. I said my prayers and ate water gruel for breakfast. I danced my dance. I was not well, nor I was not sick, but out of order a little, I believe for want of sleep. I settled several matters in the library. The weather was grown warmer, the wind at southwest. About 12 o'clock came Colonel Frank Eppes and his son Frank and Tom Randolph to discourse about the militia of Henrico. I ordered that every week two troops should range at the head of the river and if they found any Indians on patented land to take away their guns. They stayed to dinner and I ate some salt crab for dinner. In the afternoon the company went away about 4 o'clock and then I read a little Latin and afterwards took a walk about the plantation and finished my walk in the garden. I was a little displeased with my wife for talking impertinently. I said my prayers and had good health, good humor, and good thoughts, thank God Almighty. When I went to bed my ague returned but not with great violence; however I slept very indifferently.

5. I rose about 7 o'clock. My fever was off. I read a chapter in Hebrew and 200 verses in Greek. I said my prayers and had tea and bread and butter for breakfast. It rained all day, the wind northeast. I danced my dance, though with little vigor. Then I read some French. About 12 o'clock Mr. Clayton came from Mrs. Harrison's where he lay last night. He told me the men-of-war and land forces designed against Canada sailed from Boston the first of last month. It rained so that there was no court here. I ate roast beef for dinner. In the afternoon I got some bark prepared and in the evening took two doses which together with the claret in which I took it made me almost drunk, for I was exceedingly giddy. I desired Mr. Clayton to tell the Governor I would send 2000 palisades[1] to Jamestown and Williamsburg. About 9 o'clock came my ague again and I went to bed and had a fever all night. I neglected to say my prayers but had good health, good thoughts, and good humor, thank God Almighty.

6. I was out of order this morning and rose about 9 o'clock. I had taken one dose of bark about 7. I neglected to say my prayers but ate a little bread and butter for breakfast. About 10 Mr. Clayton went away and then I went to bed again because my head ached. I took the bark every three hours and lay and dozed very much and sweated a little. I slept enough to cure my headache. I ate nothing all the rest of the day but bark. My wife gave it me and looked after me with a great deal of tenderness. I was in a perfect state of villainous health and had no [current] thanks. I said a short prayer and had good humor, but very indifferent thoughts and health. I slept pretty well but not much at a time, thank God Almighty.

7. I was pretty well this morning and read 200 verses in Homer. I said a short prayer and then rose about 8 o'clock. I had tea and bread and butter for breakfast. Then I got

---

[1] *LJC*, I, 529, December 19, 1711, records a petition of William Byrd for allowance of "sloop hire for palisadoes." These palisades were intended for the defense of Jamestown and Williamsburg.

ready to go to church, this being fast day.[1] The captain of
the ship called here and told me he had not been at York
as he intended. He seemed resolved not to take less than
£18 a ton. About 11 o'clock I rode to church where I
found two troops and a company drawn up in pretty good
order. Mr. Anderson gave us a good sermon for the occasion. After church I reprimanded Will Irby[2] for not being
at his post and reviewed the men and then came home very
faint so that I could not keep the fast but ate some cold
chicken for dinner. Then I went into the library and read
some English till the family went to supper and I ate some
broiled beef with them and then took a walk till the evening.
There was an express from the Falls that brought some
boots and an account that all was well, thank God. I said
my prayers and had good health, good thoughts, and good
humor, thank God Almighty. I slept pretty well.

8. I wrote two letters to the Falls and sent others to get
the palisades. I read nothing this morning but I said my
prayers and had tea and bread and butter for breakfast. I
found myself pretty well and had a good stomach. We
prepared to ride to Mrs. Randolph's and then ate again
about 12 o'clock and I ate a partridge. It threatened rain;
however we ventured to go about 12 o'clock and got to Mrs.
Randolph's before it rained. By the way Captain [. . .]
overtook us on the road and I asked him to go with us. I
ate two apples and had no wine to drink after them. Mrs.
Randolph received us very kindly and entertained us with
the best she had. Tom Randolph had been sick and was a
little better. At night I ate some cold roast mutton for
supper and drank beer, which I have not done since I came
to Virginia. Captain Bolling came over with Will Randolph

[1]To implore the blessing of God on the Canadian expedition, the Queen
had commanded that a day of public humiliation and fasting be kept. (*Ex.
Jour.*, III, 586-87.)

[2]Later mentioned as "Dr. Irby's son"—probably son of Dr. William Irby,
of Westover Parish, mentioned in Henrico County Records in 1679-93. There
was also a Dr. Joshua Irby in Prince George County. (W. B. Blanton,
Medicine in Virginia in the Eighteenth Century [Richmond, 1931], pp. 382,
384.) William Irby qualified as captain of the Charles City County militia
in 1741. (*Va. Mag.*, XXI, 86.)

and we sat up till 10 o'clock. I said a short prayer and had good health, good humor, and good thoughts, thank God Almighty. It rained hard all the night.

9. I rose about 8 o'clock, having first rogered my wife. I read a little in my commonplace book. I said my prayers and drank chocolate for breakfast. Notwithstanding the bad weather we prepared to go to church but it did not rain, however. Will Randolph's troop waited on me to church and within a quarter of a mile of the church three more troops met me in good order and I took their courtesy very kindly. I viewed all the troops and found them in as good condition as might be expected and we went into church and Mr. Finney gave us a good sermon. After church I reviewed the troops again and spoke several things kindly to them. I saw G-r-l and Tom Turpin who told me all were well at the quarters. I took leave of Colonel Eppes and all the officers and men and after drinking two drams of peach brandy we returned to Mrs. Randolph's but I would not let any of the troops wait on me but returned home. My wife in returning had a gentle fall from her horse. I ate roast mutton for dinner and in the evening took leave of Mrs. Randolph and went to Will Randolph's where I drank more persico.[1] We talked away all evening and then I said a short prayer and had good health, good thoughts, and good humor, thank God Almighty.

10. I rose about 8 o'clock and read some English. I said my prayers and drank chocolate for breakfast. Then we took a walk. The weather was very thick and threatened rain. About 11 o'clock came Ned Randolph and told us that his brother Tom was sick. This news made us all walk to Mrs. Randolph's to see him. When we came he was out of the fainting fit which he had had and was grown easy with a stool which he had. I gave him some sage and snakeroot which I had about me and he found himself better. His distemper was a colic and a fever caused by a violent cold. Then we returned to Will Randolph's to dine,

---

[1] "A kind of cordial prepared by macerating the kernels of peaches, apricots, etc., in spirit."—*New English Dictionary.*

and I ate some mutton. I wrote a letter to Mr. Salle. In the afternoon we took our leave and returned home where we found all well, thank God. I ate some cold roast beef for supper. The women were tired very much and I myself a little. I said my prayers and had good health, good thoughts, and good humor, thank God Almighty. We found Robin Mumford here, who told us all was well at Appomattox.

11. I rose about 7 o'clock and read a chapter in Hebrew but no Greek because Robin Mumford was here. I neglected to say my prayers but ate milk and rhubarb for breakfast. About 11 o'clock came Mr. Bland who told me all was well at Williamsburg but no news at all. He came up to ship tobacco on board the ship at Swinyards. He stayed to dinner with us. I ate [cow h-l] for dinner. In the afternoon Mr. Bland went over the river in my boat, and I went to Mrs. Harrison's. I found her at home and offered her £17 10s. for her coach in the name of Dr. Cocke which she was willing to take if it be made sterling. I ate some peaches and drank some wine. She told me Dr. Blair made her pay 12 per cent between money and sterling. In the evening I returned home and found Captain H-n-t at my house. I ate some cold roast beef with him for supper. He stayed here till about 9 o'clock and then took his leave. I said a short prayer and had good health, good thoughts, and good humor, thank God Almighty. An express to Mrs. Dunn from my sister Custis complained that she had a fever and desired her to go down.

12. I rose about 6 o'clock and read a chapter in Hebrew and some Greek in Lucian. I said my prayers and ate some boiled milk and rhubarb for breakfast. Then I wrote two letters to send by Mrs. Dunn who went this morning to see my sister Custis. A man came for eight rights of land and another man came to be excused from ranging because his wife was sick. The weather was exceedingly hot this day. I ate some boiled beef for dinner. In the afternoon I rode as far as Captain Stith's to see Joe Harwood's troop muster but they were not there, so I went and made Captain Stith

a visit. They were all well but Johnny Stith, who was lame. Captain H-n-t was there. I ate some stewed quince and drank some cider and ate apples till about 5 o'clock and then I returned home and found all well, thank God. My wife met me and we walked together about the plantation. At night I wrote several things. I said my prayers and had good health, good thoughts, and good humor, thank God Almighty.

13. I rose about 6 o'clock and read a chapter in Hebrew and some Greek in Lucian. I said my prayers and ate boiled milk and rhubarb for breakfast. I danced one dance. Then I wrote several things and particularly the [report] of our militia in this and the upper county to send to the Governor. Captain H-n-t sent us some fish. The weather was cold this morning, the wind northeast; however I found myself very well and ate two apples and several figs. I ate fish for dinner with a very good stomach. In the afternoon I set several things to rights and then read some Latin till the evening and then I went to see the people work. I tasted of the perry and found it very good. My wife and I took a walk about the plantation and saw the mare. At night I read some French. I said my prayers and had good health, good thoughts, and good humor, thank God Almighty. I continued very well.

14. I rose about 6 o'clock and took a dose of bark in the powder. Then I read a chapter in Hebrew and some Greek in Lucian. I said my prayers and had tea, bread and butter for breakfast. The weather was cold. About 11 o'clock I took another dose of the bark and then rode out to see my men muster. When I came to Captain Stith's I found Joe Harwood and his troopers which are in good order. I told them of the prizes and set them immediately to running and wrestling. I stayed to see them about an hour and then returned home, where I found Captain Webb and nine of his troops who had brought with them six Indians that were found [hunting] on patented land. I threatened them and sent them away after they had victuals given them. We gave the troops victuals also. I ate some cold roast beef.

Captain Webb and I settled accounts. Mr. Bland came about 4 o'clock on his way to Williamsburg, and went away again in the evening and so did all the rest. My wife and I took a walk. I took four doses of the bark this day. In the evening I said my prayers and had good health, good thoughts, and good humor, thank God Almighty.

15. I rose about 6 o'clock and took the bark again in powder. I read a chapter in Hebrew and some Greek in Lucian. I neglected to say my prayers but had tea and bread and butter for breakfast. My sloop was come from Falling Creek and the people told me that Mr. G-r-l had the ague. Captain H-n-t sent for the nine-hogshead flat. The weather was cold and fair. I took the bark again at 11 o'clock. A man came for two rights of land. I ate some broiled pork for dinner. In the afternoon I read some Latin. G-r-l returned from Mrs. Randolph's, where I sent him in the morning to know how Tom Randolph did, and told me he was perfectly recovered. Mrs. Randolph sent my wife some apples as fine as ever I saw. I ordered John to put 20 hogsheads of tobacco on board the sloop to send to Captain H-n-t. My wife and I took a walk in the evening. I took four doses of bark this day. I neglected to say my prayers but had good health, good thoughts, and good humor, thank God Almighty. Captain [Bond][1] came over about 8 o'clock and brought some letters from England of an old date. He came in the frigate.

16. I rose about 7 o'clock and Captain [Bond] was gone away. I read a chapter in Hebrew and a chapter in the Greek Testament. I said my prayers and ate boiled milk and rhubarb for breakfast. About 10 o'clock there was a cry that Evie's [c-n-f] was lost and I called at the old Frenchman's as being the most likely person to steal it. About 11 o'clock I rode to church and found only Captain Stith's troop and Captain Eppes' company. Mr. Anderson gave us a good sermon. I asked Captain H-n-t and Isham Eppes to go and dine with me. I ate some roast shoat for

---

[1]Perhaps John Bond, master of the merchant ship *Industry* in 1705 (*Va. Mag.*, IX, 257), and pilot in the James River in 1708 (*Ex. Jour.*, III, 192).

dinner. After dinner Mr. G-r-l came to tell me he wanted more 30-penny nails for the dam. He looked thin with the ague which he had had three times. I gave him a vomit and he and the rest of the company went away about 5 o'clock. My wife and I took a walk about the plantation. At night I read some French. I said my prayers and had good health, good thoughts, and good humor, thank God Almighty. Mr. Bland's boy came in the evening with a letter from England of an old date.

17. I rose at 6 o'clock and read a chapter in Hebrew and some Greek in Lucian. My sloop carried 19 hogsheads of tobacco on board Captain H-n-t. I wrote several things. The weather was fair and cold, the wind northeast. I had a letter from Colonel Hill which told me that his ship the "Henrietta" was arrived in the Downs and that Colonel Eppes had an account of £5 a hogshead and that tobacco rose. I ate some blue wing for dinner. In the afternoon I wrote several things till the evening and then I took a walk to see my people at work and my wife met me. At night I read some French and prepared for my journey the next day to Williamsburg. I said my prayers and had good health, good thoughts, and good humor, thank God Almighty. This day Colonel Hardiman was giving a glyster to his race horse and he kicked him on the breast that he died in about 18 hours without leaving a will.

18. I rose about 7 o'clock and read a chapter in Hebrew and some Greek in Lucian. I said my prayers and ate rhubarb and milk for breakfast. Then I got ready for my journey. About 10 o'clock I ate some shoat and then was set over the creek and from thence rode to my brother Duke's but neither he nor my sister was at home. However the negroes set me over the river and I proceeded to Colonel Duke's. I found him among the rubbish for his house was pulled to pieces. He had not been well. In the evening they got me some roast flesh but he had no drink good so that I was forced to drink thick cider. He knew no news. The Colonel was very kind to me and very cross to his old woman according to custom. She was grown very deaf so

that the Colonel conceives some hope of outliving her. We sat and talked till about 9 o'clock and then I retired. I said my prayers and had good health, good humor, and good thoughts, thank God Almighty. Colonel Hardiman died this day of the kick of the horse.

19. I rose about 6 o'clock and read some Greek. Then I said my prayers and ate some milk and rhubarb for breakfast. About 8 o'clock I took leave of the Colonel and rode away to Queen's Creek to visit my sister Custis. I got there about 11 o'clock and found my sister recovered and my brother sick of the ague. I presented my sister with six blue wing which we had dressed for her. About 12 o'clock came the Doctor and Mr. Robinson. There was no news. They told me the Governor would not return till the next day. The Doctor told me Mr. Holloway was sick of the pleurisy and the Attorney General had the gout in his stomach and both were dangerously sick. I ate some beef for dinner. We stayed here till about 4 o'clock and then went to Williamsburg and in the evening played at piquet till about 10 o'clock; in the meantime I saw Mr. Bland, Mr. Clayton, and Mr. Thacker.[1] Then I retired to my lodgings and said my prayers and had good health, good thoughts, and good humor, thank God Almighty.

20. I rose about 6 o'clock and read a chapter in Hebrew and some Greek. I said my prayers and about 9 o'clock went and drank tea with the Doctor and ate some bread and butter. Then I read the news. Here I found a box with dessert knives for me, sent by Mr. B-r-n-t which I sent to my lodgings. About 11 o'clock I went to the coffeehouse but before I went I gave [Harry] four great pomegranates for the Governor which grew at Westover. Mr. Holloway was better this day. About 1 o'clock we went to dinner at the coffeehouse and I ate a fricassee of chicken for dinner. In the afternoon we played at piquet till the evening and then Mr. Robinson and I took a walk to the new house and after viewing that we went to the Governor's and found him at supper. I sat down with him and ate some roast beef.

---

[1]Probably Chicheley Corbin Thacker, clerk of the General Court.

He was extremely tanned. He received me kindly. I delivered him my list and the report of the militia of my counties with which he was well pleased. I stayed with him till about 10 o'clock and then retired to my lodgings where I said my prayers and had good health, good thoughts, and good humor, thank God Almighty.

21. I rose about 6 o'clock and read nothing. I said my prayers and ate milk and pears for breakfast. I settled some affairs with Mr. Bland concerning the pork account and about 9 o'clock went to the Governor's where I drank tea and ate bread and butter. One of the Governor's servants gave me abundance of letters which came from Kiquotan, in one of which was an extraordinary [?] of the Duke of Argyle and the Earl of Orrery.[1] I was a long time in discoursing with the Governor concerning what should be done with obstinate Quakers, and about 11 o'clock took my leave and then rode away to Colonel Duke's. The weather was hot but I got there in 2½ hours. Here I found my brother James Duke who was not very well. About 2 o'clock I ate some stuffed chicken and about 4 we took the Colonel with us and went to my brother's and called at Mr. B-s where we saw the brunette that married Dr. Burbage. We found my sister well and all the family. We drank some thick cider and I ate some milk. Then I retired to my chamber and said my prayers and had good health, good thoughts, and good humor, thank God Almighty.

22. I rose about 6 o'clock and got ready to return home. The weather threatened rain. I said my prayers and ate milk and rhubarb for breakfast. About 7 o'clock I took my leave of the Colonel and all the family and rode home in 2½ hours and found my family well, thank God, only Sue had lost her child and 10 of the Falls cattle were missing. I stayed at home but two hours and then changed horses and rode to Colonel Hill's in order to go over the river to meet my militia. I told the Colonel all the news I knew and then passed the river and found Captain Isham Eppes' troop

---

[1]Charles Boyle, first Earl of Orrery, like the Duke of Argyle, was a friend and correspondent of Byrd's.

of horse and Captain Bolling's troop of dragoons. I reviewed them and then we marched away to Captain Bolling's house where we lighted and drank persico. Here we met Captain Kennon's troop of dragoons and in about half an hour proceeded to Mrs. Kennon's where we dismissed the troops. I was received with great courtesy and ate boiled beef for supper. I ate very heartily, having had no dinner. We sat up about an hour and then I retired to my lodging where I said my prayers and had good health, good thoughts, and good humor, thank God Almighty. Parson Robinson met me at Captain Bolling's.

23. I rose about 7 o'clock and found the weather grown very cold, the wind at northeast. I said my prayers and ate boiled milk for breakfast. All the rest of the company drank drams plentifully. Everybody showed me abundance of respect. About 10 o'clock the whole company went to breakfast and I among them and I ate some stewed fowl. About 11 we went to church with Will Kennon's troop to wait on me and there we found Captain Jefferson's,[1] Captain Bolling's, Captain Eppes', and Captain Worsham's troops and companies which made a good appearance. Everybody respected me like a king. Mr. Robinson gave us a sermon and when church was done I reviewed the troops again and then with all the officers we went to Colonel Eppes' to dinner and I ate boiled beef. All the drink I used was cider. We were very merry all the evening only the Colonel had his ague moderately. I said my prayers and had good health, good thoughts, and good humor, thank God Almighty.

24. I rose about 7 o'clock and said my prayers and then went down to the company. The Colonel was better this morning. About 9 o'clock everybody else went to breakfast on meat but I drank only some chocolate, and about 10 o'clock took our leave and I went attended with about 10 persons, all officers except the Parson Robinson, to Captain Bolling's, who gave us some persico, of which I drank plenti-

---

[1]Captain Thomas Jefferson of Henrico County, ancestor of the famous statesman. His will, and other references to him in county records, show that he was a man of some wealth and importance.

fully and about 2 o'clock we went to dinner and I ate some blue-wing pie. In the afternoon we stayed about an hour and then took our leave but I could not persuade the officers to return but all went with me to the Hundred and saw me safe in the ferryboat. I thanked them all for the honor they had done me. When I got over the river I just called on Colonel Hill and he gave me a piece of a pint bottle of wine. Then I rode home, where I found all well, thank God. I said my prayers and had good health, good thoughts, and good humor, thank God Almighty. I rogered my wife.

25. I rose about 7 o'clock and read a chapter in Hebrew and some Greek in Lucian. I said my prayers and ate boiled milk for breakfast. I danced my dance. Then I settled several accounts and set my business in order. It was clear weather and warm. I wrote to Captain H-n-t and sent John with the letter, but he was not on board. I was displeased with John for giving away the sweetbread of the hog he killed and threatened to whip him. I ate fried pork for dinner. In the afternoon I weighed some money and put several things to rights and settled several accounts, and in the evening took a walk with my wife about the plantation and were very kind to one another. At night I wrote my journal and then read some French. I neglected to say my prayers but had good health, good thoughts, and good humor, thank God Almighty.

26. I rose about 6 o'clock and read a chapter in Hebrew and some Greek in Lucian. I said my prayers and ate milk and rhubarb for breakfast. I danced my dance. I settled several accounts and wrote some of my journal in arrears. It was fine warm weather but there was great want of rain for the grass. I ate roast pork for dinner. In the afternoon I rogered my wife in the billiard room. Captain H-n-t came and told me he had but 70 hogsheads on board and the reason was because people gave notes for tobacco which was not ready. About 4 o'clock I took a walk with him to Mrs. Harrison's to inquire when she would send her tobacco. She gave us apples and wine and told me that Colonel Harrison was very much indisposed and drooped without

being sick and believed he should never see Williamsburg again. In the evening we returned home where all was well, thank God. At night I had several people whipped for being lazy in the morning. I said my prayers and had good health, good thoughts, and good humor, thank God Almighty.

27. I rose about 6 o'clock and read a chapter in Hebrew and some Greek in Lucian. I said my prayers and ate milk and rhubarb for breakfast. I danced my dance. I received a letter from John Bolling that desired my sloop might go up for Captain Webb's tobacco but I excused myself in an answer that I wrote him. I understood that Drury Stith had beaten Dr. Irby's son for being refractory which was well done. I read some Latin in Terence till dinner and then I ate some boiled pork. In the afternoon I went with Bannister to the store to examine my stock of nails. When I returned I read more Latin. About 3 o'clock came my cousin Harrison and her daughter, Betty Bassett and her sister. I gave them wine and cider and was very courteous to them. About an hour after came Mrs. Cargill who told us there was a man-of-war come in. They stayed here till 8 o'clock and then there came so few horses that Betty Bassett and Betty Harrison stayed all night. I ate some bread and butter with them and we were very merry. I said my prayers and had good health, good thoughts, and good humor, thank God Almighty. Mr. Bland's sloop brought my box of knives and forks and spoons.

28. I rose about 6 o'clock and read a chapter in Hebrew and some Greek in Lucian. I said my prayers and ate milk and rhubarb for breakfast. I danced my dance. The young ladies went away after breakfast. The weather was hot and fair. Eugene was whipped for neglecting his business when the company was here yesterday. I read some Latin in Terence till dinner and then I ate some boiled beef. In the afternoon we cleaned the new knives, forks, and spoons. Then I read some Latin again till the evening and then took a walk about the plantation. The weather continued fair and warm. I gave a vomit to a woman that came over to be cured of obstruction. At night I read more Latin in Terence.

I said my prayers and had good health, good thoughts, and good humor, thank God Almighty.

29. I rose about 7 o'clock, having rogered my wife, this morning. I read a chapter in Hebrew and some Greek in Lucian. I said my prayers and ate boiled milk and rhubarb for breakfast. I danced my dance. The weather grew cold with a northwest wind. I sent Tom to Appomattox for the pistols and bullets for the prizes at the general muster. I made an abridgment of the laws concerning the militia till dinner and then I ate some bacon fraise. In the afternoon I wrote again and then looked over my arms that I design for prizes. I read some Latin in Terence and then took a walk [about] the plantation with my wife. A mulatto man came to sell me a steer for 15 [shillings?] because he wanted three rights and I sent him to the master of the ship, who gave him 30. I received a letter from G-r-l in which he complained of a famine at Falling Creek and told me that Tom Osborne was sick at my quarters. At night I read more Latin in Terence. I said my prayers and had good health, good thoughts, and good humor, thank God Almighty.

30. I rose at 7 o'clock and found it very cold. I read a chapter in Hebrew but no Greek. I wrote an answer to G-r-l's letter. The sloop came in the night with 40 hogsheads of tobacco. I said no prayers before I went to church. However I ate milk and rhubarb for breakfast. About 11 o'clock we went to church and heard a good sermon and then received the Sacrament. After church I invited Mr. Anderson and Captain H-n-t to dinner and I ate some blue wing for dinner. In the afternoon I bespoke Mr. Anderson to go with me tomorrow to Henrico. About 5 o'clock the company went away and my wife and I took a walk about the plantation. Johnny that belongs to my sloop had a bad toe that was caught with rolling tobacco. At night I read some Latin in Terence. The weather grew warmer again. I said my prayers and had good health, good thoughts, and good humor, thank God Almighty. This day it is three weeks since it rained here. It was this day three weeks since it rained [sic].

October, 1711

1. I rose about 7 o'clock and read a chapter in Hebrew and some Greek in Lucian. I said my prayers and ate boiled milk for breakfast. I prepared my business to go into the upper county and about 11 o'clock my wife and I ate each of us a blue wing and then committed our family to God's protection and then set out for Colonel Hill's where we got by one o'clock and at 2 we went to dinner and I ate some boiled beef for dinner. I persuaded Mr. Anderson and Nanny B-k-r to go with us over the river and see Captain John Bolling, where we came about 5 o'clock in the evening. He was just come from Henrico court. We had abundance of victuals for supper and I ate boiled beef. Everything was very clean and well dressed beyond any other house in that county. We spent the evening in conversation till about 10 o'clock and then we took leave of the company and retired. I said a short prayer and had good health, good thoughts, and good humor, thank God Almighty.

2. I rose about 7 o'clock and found the weather cold, which was the more troublesome because the chimney smoked. I said my prayers shortly and read nothing because the company was all up. I drank some persico and about 10 o'clock had a family breakfast and I ate some blue-wing pie. After breakfast came Robin Mumford who told us that his wife was very sick, and soon after came Captain Kennon. About 11 we took horse and rode to Captain Jefferson's where the militia of that side of the river was drawn up. I viewed them a little and because they were not all come I went to Captain Jefferson's house where we drank some persico and then returned into the field where I caused the troops to be exercised by each captain and they performed but indifferently for which I reproved them. [Massot] one of the French was drunk and rude to his captain, for which I broke his head in two places. When all was over we went to dine with Captain Jefferson and I ate some roast beef. My horses got out of the house where

they were put and ran away, for which I was angry with
Tom. Most of the company went home with John Bolling
and got drunk, but I said a short prayer and had good
health, good thoughts, and good humor, thank God Almighty.

3. I rose about 7 o'clock and found it had rained a little
but it soon cleared up again. I said a short prayer and
catched [sic] a little cold because the room had no glass
window. We sent several ways for my horses and they were
brought about 10 o'clock. Mr. Anderson was called out of
his bed to go to a woman that wanted to receive the Sacrament. About 11 o'clock I ate some mutton for breakfast,
and several of my captains came to go over the river with
me, where we got about 2 o'clock but in the meantime the
Major had exercised his men on the north side. Then I
ordered the men to be drawn in single [file] along the path
where the men were to run for the prize, and John Hatcher,
one of Captain Randolph's men, won the pistol. Then I
caused the men to be drawn into a square to see the men
play at cudgels and Dick O-l-n won the sword, and of the
wrestling Will Kennon won the gun. Just as the sun went
down our games ended and then I took leave and we went
to Frank Eppes' where I ate boiled beef for supper. Mr.
Anderson and Mr. Finney came over with us and had a long
dispute about several mysterious things in which they were
both lost and Mr. Finney said several inscrutable things.
My cold was increased. I said a short prayer and had good
health, good thoughts, and good humor, thank God Almighty.

4. I rose at 7 o'clock and my wife shaved me with a dull
razor. I persuaded Mr. Anderson to go and visit Tom
Osborne who was very sick, while I went to the militia court,
but we ate our breakfast first and I ate some boiled beef.
About 11 o'clock we went to the militia court, where Captain
Bolling and I had a dispute about fining Mr. M-r-s-l, one of
my overseers, because he affirmed [they ought to buy such
negroes as make a corps]. We fined all the Quakers and
several others and the Captains agreed to send for trophies.

Captain Royall[1] neither came nor returned a list though he had two Quakers in his company. I spoke gently to the Quakers which gave them a good opinion of me and several of them seemed doubtful whether they would be arrested or not for the future. I told them they would certainly be fined five times in a year if they did not do as their fellow subjects did. The sun set before we had finished and then we rode to Frank Eppes' with design to proceed to Captain Webb's, but it was so late I could not persuade my wife to go so we stayed there and I ate beef again for supper. I said my prayers and had good health, good thoughts, and good humor, thank God Almighty.

5. I rose about 7 o'clock and said a short prayer and about 9 we went to breakfast and I ate some bread and cheese. About 10 we took leave of the family and rode to Falling Creek where we got about 12 o'clock and found all well, thank God, and the dam almost finished. Mr. Anderson came to us a little after we got there and told me Tom Osborne was in no danger of his life but was extremely fretful. We went to the tannery and saw everything that was to be seen, which pleased my wife very much. Then we went to the house to dinner and I ate some roast beef. About 3 o'clock we went away to the Hundred where we arrived about 6 o'clock and just called to ask how Mr. Anderson and the rest of the family did and then proceeded home, where we found all well, thank God. We ate some milk and potatoes and then I read some Latin. I said my prayers and had good health, good thoughts, and good humor, thank God Almighty.

6. I rose about 7 o'clock and read some Hebrew but no Greek. I said my prayers and then prepared to go to the general muster of this county. My wife and daughter went in the coach and I rode on horseback and got into the field about 11 o'clock and was there before several of my Captains. However, I found Captain Drury Stith and Captain Eppes there and I caused them to exercise their men till the

---

[1]Captain Joseph Royall, landowner in Henrico County. (*Va. Mag.*, XXVIII, 215; XXXII, 411-12.)

others came. The first had his troop in good order but the last had his very indifferent and did not exercise them himself. When the rest came I reprimanded them for staying so long, nor was any of their men in order. About 2 o'clock our prizes began and Will M-r-l got the prize of running and John S-c-l-s the prize of cudgels and Robin Easely the prize [of] wrestling. All was finished about 4 o'clock and then we went to Captain Stith's to dinner and I ate some boiled beef. Then we took leave and got home about 7 o'clock and found all well, thank God Almighty. I said my prayers and had good health, good thoughts, and good humor, thank God. Mrs. Anderson was taken with a kind of an ague.

7. I rose about 7 o'clock and read a chapter in Hebrew and a chapter in the Greek Testament. I said my prayers and danced my dance. I ate boiled milk for breakfast. The fair weather continued. I received a letter from the Governor by express by which I learned that 60 people had been killed by the Indians at Neuse and about as many at Pamlico in North Carolina and that he would meet me at Major Harrison's. However, I could not go till tomorrow because I had invited company to dine with me and accordingly Mr. Cole, Mr. Roscow,[1] Mr. [Tayloe],[2] and Captain H-n-t came and dined with me. I ate blue wing for dinner. These young men behaved themselves very well and seem to have good understanding. They stayed till about 5 o'clock and then went away in Captain H-n-t's boat. My wife and I took a walk in the evening and at night we had a game at [p-l-y]. I neglected to say my prayers but had good health, good thoughts, and good humor, thank God Almighty. My trader came in yesterday and made a good voyage.

8. I rose about 7 o'clock and read nothing because I prepared myself to ride to Major Harrison's. I said a short prayer and ate boiled milk for breakfast. About 10 o'clock I got over the river and proceeded on my journey but went a little out of my way. However I got there about one o'clock

---

[1] Probably James Roscow, who succeeded Byrd as receiver-general in 1717.
[2] Perhaps one of the Tayloes, of Richmond County.

and found the Governor, Colonel Harrison, and Colonel Ludwell, which last had been sick. They reproached me for staying so long, but I excused myself because the express had not brought me the letter till yesterday. About 2 o'clock we went to dinner and I ate boiled beef for my part. After dinner we sat in council concerning the Indians and some of the Tributaries came before us who promised to be very faithful to us. It was agreed to send Peter Poythress[1] to the Tuscaroras to treat them and to demand the Baron Graffenriedt[2] who was prisoner among the Indians. It was also resolved that the militia of Prince George, Surry, and Isle of Wight should rendezvous at Nottoway[3] town on Wednesday next and the Governor be there with them to show some part of our strength to the Indians. In the evening came several gentlemen and Mr. Bland among them with letters for the Governor from Carolina which told him how backward the people of that country were to [advantage] themselves. About 10 o'clock we went to bed. Colonel Ludwell and I lay together. I neglected to say my prayers but had good health, good thoughts, and good humor, thank God Almighty.

9. I rose about 7 o'clock and got myself ready because I heard the Governor up. We had chocolate for breakfast, of which I drank four cups. About 10 o'clock the Governor went over the river; I begged of him to go to Westover but he told me very kindly that when he went there it was for pleasure but this was not the time to take pleasure in. I told him I would meet him at Colonel Harrison's this day sennight and so took my leave. However I stayed with the Major till dinner and ate boiled beef for my part. The Major would fain insinuate some unkind things against

---

[1] An Indian trader and interpreter.

[2] Baron Christopher de Graffenriedt, a Swiss, who was instrumental in settling Swiss and Palatine Germans in North Carolina. He, with John Lawson, surveyor-general of North Carolina, was responsible for the settlement of New Bern, North Carolina. When the Tuscarora Indians revolted in 1711, De Graffenriedt and Lawson were captured. De Graffenriedt was later released but Lawson was burned at the stake. See the diary for October 19, 1711. Additional information about the two men will be found in the *Dictionary of American Biography.*

[3] Isle of Wight County.

Mr. Mumford which I told him I would inquire into. About 2 o'clock I took my leave with Mr. Bland and got home about 5 o'clock and everybody was well and my wife at Mrs. Harrison's. I went to see what my people had done but saw very little and that not according to my orders, for which I was angry with John. I had a great cold and had some milk and rhubarb for it when I went to bed. I said my prayers and had good health, good thoughts, and good humor, thank God Almighty.

10. I rose about 7 o'clock and read a chapter in Hebrew and some Greek in Lucian. I said my prayers and ate boiled milk for breakfast. I danced my ·dance. When I was dressed I took a walk to see my people at work and directed what I would have done. Then I returned and settled several accounts and wrote in my journal. John [Cross] came to me but would not agree by fair means to go to work at Jamestown but chose rather to go to prison out of pure conscience. I ate boiled beef for dinner. Just after dinner came John Giles to receive the £20 I was to give him for his right to Falling Creek. I wrote three letters and sent by him to desire some of my captains to meet me at Nottoway Town. In the evening I took a walk about the plantation and saw what work my people had done. At night I read some Latin and wrote in my journal. I said my prayers and had good health, good thoughts, and good humor, thank God Almighty.

11. I rose at 7 o'clock and read a chapter in Hebrew and some Greek in Lucian. I said my prayers and ate boiled milk for breakfast. I danced my dance. About 10 o'clock came Captain H-n-t to buy planks and soon after him came Captain Drury Stith and after him Captain John Eppes, Captain Sam Harwood and Captain Hamlin. I persuaded them to stay and dine before we went to the martial court and fined as many people as came to 4500 pounds of tobacco. We made an order that the fines returned by each captain should go towards his trophies. Mr. Bland called on his way to Williamsburg. In the evening I took a walk and beat Jenny for being unmannerly. At night I read some

Latin in Terence. I said my prayers and had good health, good thoughts, and good humor, thank God Almighty. It rained a little in the night.

12. I rose about 7 o'clock and read a chapter in Hebrew and some Greek in Lucian. I said my prayers and ate boiled milk for breakfast. I danced my dance. It rained in the morning but that did not hinder Mr. Mumford from coming to know if I had any service before the General Court. I told him what I had heard at Major Harrison's concerning him but seeming however not to believe it. He protested solemnly he was innocent and I believe he is. About 11 o'clock came Colonel Hill, Mr. Finney, and Mr. Anderson. We diverted ourselves in the library till dinner and then I ate pigeon and bacon. Mr. Finney had appetite of his usual vigor. It threatened rain which hastened away my company, all except Robin Mumford, who had the discretion to stay all night and it was well he did, for it rained extremely. At night we ate some bread and cheese and drank a bottle of cider. I neglected to say my prayers but had good health, good thoughts, and good humor, thank God Almighty.

13. I rose about 7 o'clock and read a chapter in Hebrew and some Greek in Lucian. I said my prayers and ate boiled milk for breakfast. I danced my dance. I had a looseness which gave me above 12 stools but I shit but a little at a time. It did not rain much in the night and was cold this morning. I took a walk to see my people at work and then settled several accounts till dinner. I ate boiled mutton with a good stomach and after dinner cleaned my gilt knives and forks [and] spoons and then I settled more accounts. Mrs. Hamlin came to account with me and would borrow money of me but I had the discretion not to do it. My looseness continued with great violence. In the evening I took a walk about the plantation and at night came one of my people from the Falls and told me Tom Osborne began to recover and walk about, thank God. I read some Latin in Terence and then said my prayers and had good health, good thoughts, and good humor, thank God Almighty. My looseness continued with griping.

14. I rose about 7 o'clock and read a chapter in Hebrew and some Greek in Lucian. I said my prayers and then took a dose of physic for my looseness and worked it with water gruel. The physic griped me extremely and gave me about four stools. This hindered me from going to church but my wife went and everybody was so kind as to ask after me there. I ate a partridge for dinner and I was interrupted by a furious gripe which forced me to rise from table. In the afternoon I began to be easy and because the weather was fine I and my wife took a very long walk, which lasted till the evening and tired us both. In the evening there came one of my people from Falling Creek who told me all was well. They came for stockings for the people there. At night I read some Latin in Terence. Then I said my prayers and had good health, good thoughts, and good humor, thank God Almighty.

15. I rose about 7 o'clock and had two stools with gripes. I read a chapter in Hebrew and some Greek in Lucian. I said my prayers and then wrote a letter to Mr. G-r-l and sent away the messenger with stockings and shirts. Then I took a walk to see my people at work. When I returned I found Tony and Appomattox Tom come with their horses for my baggage. They told me Mrs. Mumford was very sick again. I was easy with my looseness after my two stools in the morning. I ate partridge again for dinner. In the afternoon I read some Latin and then got my things ready for my expedition tomorrow with which I was so busy that I could not take a walk. At night I ate some bread and cheese but read nothing. I neglected to say my prayers but had good health, good thoughts, and good humor, thank God Almighty. It rained in the night.

16. I rose about 6 o'clock and prepared everything for my journey, notwithstanding it threatened rain. I put up my baggage and then ate some boiled milk for breakfast. I recommended my family to the divine protection and went over the river in order to proceed to Colonel Harrison's with my man Bannister with me, and my people that went with the baggage were gone before we got over the river.

It was 2 o'clock before I got to Colonel Harrison's. However I was there two hours before the Governor. The Colonel treated me with strong water. About 3 o'clock came Colonel Hill and Mr. Platt and John Hardiman and after 4 came the Governor and several gentlemen volunteers with him and particularly Dr. Cocke and Mr. Graeme[1] the Governor's cousin. About 5 o'clock we went to supper and I ate some boiled beef. At night some of the volunteers drank hard but I went to bed and said a short prayer and the Doctor lay with me. I had good health, good thoughts, and good humor, thank God Almighty. Will Robinson lay in the room and disturbed us with his groaning.

17. I rose about 7 o'clock and found the Governor up. I drank some strong water. I said a short prayer and about 8 o'clock we sat to a family breakfast and I ate some roast mutton. About 9 we took leave of Colonel Harrison and got on our horses with Captain Hal Harrison's troop to wait on us. Captain John Allen's[2] troop met us on the road and about 3 o'clock we met Colonel Ludwell and soon after got to Nottoway town where we met abundance of the militia. We had just time before night to settle our quarters and to look about us. Several of us lay in the King's cabin with the Governor, where we lay on new mats and our cabin was covered with other mats. I found my baggage well received but one of the horses was sick. No less than eight of my Henrico captains came over to meet the Governor, which compliment he took very kindly. Both they and all the volunteers supped with the Governor under his marquee and I ate venison pasty. The Governor appointed a guard for the fort of about 100 men. Several of the Tributary Indians came here to meet the Governor. The Doctor lay with me but our lodging seemed very hard at first and we were incommoded with the smoke at first. I said a short

---

[1] John Graeme, merchant of Middlesex County, England, now visiting the colony. He returned to Virginia to live in 1725, when he acted as attorney for Spotswood (then in England), and in 1737 was appointed professor of mathematics at William and Mary College. (*Wm. Q. (1)*, XVII, 301; Leonidas Dodson, *Alexander Spotswood* [Philadelphia, 1932], p. 298. *Cf.* Bassett, pp. 359-60.)
[2] Surveyor of Isle of Wight County.

prayer and had good health, good thoughts, and good humor, thank God Almighty. We talked almost all night. We lay in our morning gowns and breeches.

18. About break of day we were waked with the reveille and rose about 6 o'clock and then took a walk about the town to see some Indian girls, with which we played the wag. I ate some gingerbread and drank tea with the Governor for breakfast. Then we got on our horses to take a review of the militia and assigned to each county its post and gave the militia of the Isle of Wight the head because we were in their county. While we were in the field the Governor modelled the horse and put commanders at the head of them. There were about 700 horse besides volunteers and about 900 foot, and there were about 30 volunteers among whom were three parsons. About noon the Governor sent about 30 horses to meet the Tuscarora Indians at the Saponie town. After the Governor had reviewed the horse on both wings he dismissed them about 4 o'clock and sent all except those appointed for the guard that they might provide themselves with lodgings in the neighborhood. About 5 we went to dinner with the Governor and I ate some venison. All the volunteers dined with the Governor. At night we drank a bottle till about 10 o'clock, and then went to bed. I said a short prayer and had good health, good thoughts, and good humor, thank God Almighty.

19. I rose about 6 o'clock and found it cold. We drank chocolate with the Governor and about 9 o'clock got on our horses and waited on the Governor to see him put the foot in order. [He] divided the companies and made them about 50 men each, and made captains over them, though when he came to Surry he found it difficult to get captains because everybody refused the Governor and made him so angry that he swore at several which was a thing he seldom did. The Doctor went away about 10 o'clock privately with pretence of some business but it was to go to Mrs. Russell. We ate gingerbread all day long and saw the Governor exercise the foot. I drew up the volunteers into a company or troop and commanded them under the name of the Gov-

ernor's Guard and we placed ourselves on the right. About 3 o'clock the Tuscarora Indians came with their guard and Mr. Poythress with them. He told the Governor that the Baron was alive and would be released but that Mr. Lawson was killed because he had been so foolish as to threaten the Indian that had taken him. About 6 o'clock we went to dinner and I ate some roast mutton. At night some of my troop went with me into the town to see the girls and kissed them without proceeding any further, and we had like to have been kept out by the captain of the guard. However at last they let us in and we went to bed about 2 o'clock in the morning. I neglected to say my prayers but had good health, good thoughts, and good humor, thank God Almighty.

20. I rose about 6 o'clock and drank tea with the Governor, who made use of this opportunity to make the Indians send some of their great men to the College, and the Nansemonds sent two, the Nottoways two, and the Meherrins two. He also demanded one from every town belonging to the Tuscaroras.[1] About 9 the Governor mounted and we waited on him to see him exercise the horse and when all the militia was drawn up he caused the Indians to walk from one end to the other and they seemed very much afraid lest they should be killed. The Governor did nothing but wheel the foot, and Colonel Ludwell and I assisted him as well as we could. About noon the Governor ordered lists to be taken of the troops and companies that the people might make their claim to be paid, because they had been on the service five days. When this was done he gave liberty to the people to go home, except a troop and company for the guard that night. Then we went and saw the Indian boys shoot and the Indian girls run for a prize. We had likewise

---

[1]Spotswood wrote to the Board of Trade and Plantations on November 17, 1711, giving an account of the expedition to the Nottoway Town; he says in part: "I then proposed to them either to carry a war against those Indians . . . or to join with her Majesty's subjects of Carolina for extirpating those assassins, and that for the better assuring us of their future good behaviour, they should deliver two children of the great men of each town to remain as hostages, and to be educated at our college." (*Official Letters of Alexander Spotswood,* I, 121-22.)

a war dance by the men and a love dance by the women, which sports lasted till it grew dark. Then we went to supper and I ate chicken with a good stomach. We sat with the Governor till he went to bed about 11 o'clock and then we went to Major Harrison's to supper again but the Governor ordered the sentry to keep us out and in revenge about 2 o'clock in the morning we danced a [g-n-t-r] dance just at his bed's head. However we called for the captain of the guard and gave him a word and then we all got in except Colonel Ludwell and we kept him out about quarter of an hour. Jenny, an Indian girl, had got drunk and made us good sport. I neglected to say my prayers and had good health, good thoughts, and good humor, thank God Almighty.

21. I rose about 6 o'clock and we began to pack up our baggage in order to return. We drank chocolate with the Governor and about 10 o'clock we took leave of the Nottoway town and the Indian boys went away with us that were designed for the College. The Governor made three proposals to the Tuscaroras: that they would join with the English to cut off those Indians that had killed the people of Carolina, that they should have 40 shillings for every head they brought in of those guilty Indians and be paid the price of a slave for all they brought in alive, and that they should send one of the chief men's sons out of every town to the College. I waited on the Governor about ten miles and then took leave of him and he went to Mr. Cargill's and I with Colonel Hill, Mr. Platt, and John Hardiman went to Colonel Harrison's where we got about 3 o'clock in the afternoon. About 4 we dined and I ate some boiled beef. My man's horse was lame for which he was let blood. At night I asked a negro girl to kiss me, and when I went to bed I was very cold because I pulled off my clothes after lying in them so long. I neglected to say my prayers but had good health, good thoughts, and good humor, thank God Almighty.

22. I rose about 7 o'clock and understood by Colonel Hill that he [f-s-t] away last night. I said a short prayer and

then drank some chocolate for breakfast. About 9 o'clock we took leave of the Colonel and the rest of the family and rode home with Colonel Hill and Mr. Platt and Mr. Hardiman, who went with me part of the way. I got home about 11 o'clock and found Mrs. Hamlin there who wanted some physic for her son Dick who had the gripes and I gave her a purge. Captain Eppes and Colonel Eppes came just before dinner and sat down with us and I ate venison for dinner. All my family was well, thank God, and so were all my people above, thank God. In the afternoon I settled my affairs to go to Williamsburg tomorrow. In the evening my wife and I took a walk about the plantation. At night I wrote several letters to my overseers above. I said my prayers and had good health, good thoughts, and good humor, thank God Almighty.

23. I rose about 7 o'clock and got ready for my journey, notwithstanding it rained. I said my prayers and ate boiled milk for breakfast. About 9 o'clock I took leave of my wife and daughter and was set over the creek and was angry with Tom for forgetting the strap of my portmantle and I was displeased with Eugene for forgetting his cape. It rained all the way I rode to Williamsburg, where I got about 3 o'clock pretty wet. Then I got ready to go to court that I might not lose my day and accordingly did save it. I made my honors to the Governor and to the gentlemen of the council and took my place. We sat in court till about 5 o'clock and then the Governor took me home to dinner and there I found Mrs. Russell returned from her travels. I ate boiled beef for dinner. The Governor told me that our design upon Canada had miscarried by the fault of the Admiral.[1] About 8 o'clock we went to the coffeehouse where I played and won 50 shillings. About 10 I went to my lodgings and wrote a letter to my wife. I said my prayers and had good health, good thoughts, and good humor, thank God Almighty.

---

[1] Rear-Admiral Sir Hovenden Walker, commander of the fleet which unsuccessfully attacked Canada. For an account of the campaign, see Herbert L. Osgood, *The American Colonies in the Eighteenth Century* (New York, 1924), I, 441-54.

24. I rose about 7 o'clock and read nothing but dispatched Tom home with the horses. I said my prayers and ate boiled milk for breakfast. The Doctor and several gentlemen came to see me. About 9 o'clock I went to court where I sat diligently till noon and then I ate some gingerbread. Nothing very remarkable happened but in all cases they dispensed judgment very equally. We sat till the evening and I went again with the Governor to dine, as he said, to eat some of my own venison. We had a rumor that the Duke of Marlborough had gained another victory in Flanders and that the French had failed in their enterprise upon Brussels. About 8 o'clock I went to the coffeehouse where I fell to playing with some of the young men and won £9. About 10 o'clock I went to my lodgings where I said my prayers and had good health, good thoughts, and good humor, thank God Almighty. There was a Council this morning.

25. I rose about 7 o'clock and read a chapter in Hebrew but no Greek. I settled accounts with some of the naval officers. I had several gentlemen come to see me. I said my prayers and ate boiled milk for breakfast. Colonel Hill called to see me and let me understand all was well above. About 9 o'clock I went to court and heard several cases but none remarkable. About noon I returned to my chambers and wrote in my journal and then went into court again and we sat till it was dark and then I went home again with the Governor because the rest of the Council sneaked away in the dark. I ate some boiled beef for supper. About 8 we went to the coffeehouse and got Mr. Graeme with us. We played at whist and I lost 5 shillings. About 10 o'clock I went to my lodgings where I said a short prayer and had good health, good thoughts, and good humor, thank God Almighty. Billy Beverley came to see me with his father.

26. I rose about 7 o'clock and read nothing but wrote a letter to my wife to send by Colonel Hill to invite her over to see Mrs. Russell. I said a short prayer and ate boiled milk for breakfast. Then I went to the capitol to read some law books and about 9 o'clock went into court, where

I sat till noon and then I went up stairs and wrote in my journal. I ate some gingerbread. Nothing came before us very remarkable; however we sat till about 5 o'clock and then I slipped away lest the Governor should ask me again to dine with him. Several of us went to dine at Marot's where I ate a good fricassee of chicken, and drank Virginia wine that was [tolerable]. When dinner was over we went to the coffeehouse and played at cards and I lost 5 shillings. About 10 o'clock I went to my lodgings where I said a short prayer and had good health, good thoughts, and good humor, thank God Almighty.

27. I rose about 7 o'clock and read two chapters in Hebrew and a little Greek in Homer. I said my prayers and ate boiled milk for breakfast. I wrote another short letter to my wife by Mr. Platt. I had several people come to see me at my chamber. About 10 o'clock I went to court where I sat diligently all day because two of the judges went home. However I got time to settle accounts with Colonel Waters.[1] We sat till it grew dark and dispatched a great deal of business. Then I went home again with the Governor to dinner and ate some salt fish. We drank some French wine till almost 10 o'clock and then we took leave and I went home to my lodgings. Two or three days ago the Governor put Gilbert his coachman into prison for his insolence. I said a short prayer and had good health, good thoughts, and good humor, thank God Almighty. It blew hard in the night and rained much.

28. I rose about 7 o'clock and read a chapter in Hebrew and some Greek in Homer. I said my prayers and ate boiled milk for breakfast. I got Daniel to shave my head. It continued to rain. However I went to church purely because I thought it my duty but I went in the President's coach. There were few people at church and no ladies but Mrs. Russell. Mr. Robinson gave us a good sermon but very sadly delivered. After church the Governor asked me to dine with him but I was engaged to the Commissary. Colonel Carter and I went in the President's coach to the

---

[1]William Waters was naval officer of the Eastern Shore.

Commissary's and I ate roast goose for dinner. Mrs. Blair was in good health and very good humor. It continued to rain; however we took our cloaks and walked home. I went to my lodgings and wrote a great deal in my journal. I read some Latin. I said my prayers and had good thoughts, good health, and good humor, thank God Almighty.

29. I rose about 7 o'clock and read two chapters in Hebrew and some Greek in Homer. I said my prayers and ate boiled milk for breakfast. About 9 o'clock I went to wait on the Governor but he was not at home and I walked after him to the new house and found him there and saw several of the Governor's contrivances, and particularly that for hanging the arms. About 11 o'clock I came with the Governor to court where we sat till about 3 and then I went up stairs and danced my dance and wrote a letter to England. Then I returned to court where we stayed till about 5 and then I went home with the Governor and ate venison for dinner and then drank a bottle till 8 o'clock. Then we went to the coffeehouse, where we played at cards till 10 and I won 25 shillings. Then I returned home and I committed manual uncleanness, for which God forgive me. I neglected to say my prayers but had good health, good humor, but indifferent thoughts.

30. I rose about 7 o'clock and read a chapter in Hebrew and some Greek in Homer. I neglected to say my prayers but ate milk for breakfast. About 10 o'clock I went to court where I sat till about 2 and then went up stairs and danced my dance and wrote a letter to England. Then I returned into court where we sat till about 5. Then I went with the Governor to dinner and found the weather very cold. I ate venison pasty for dinner and then we drank a bottle till 8 o'clock. Afterwards we went to the coffeehouse where I played at piquet and won 5 shillings. In the evening Colonel Smith and Colonel Carter were at Marot's and somebody cast a brick from the street into the room which narrowly missed Colonel Carter. I went home about 10 o'clock and neglected to say my prayers but had good health, good thoughts, and good humor, thank God Almighty.

31. I rose about 7 o'clock and found it very cold. I read a chapter in Hebrew and some Greek in Homer. I neglected to say my prayers but had chocolate for breakfast. About 10 o'clock I went to court where I sat till about 3 and then I went up stairs and danced my dance and wrote a letter to England. About 4 I returned to court and we sat till past 5. Then we went to dine at Marot's and I ate roast veal for dinner. About 8 o'clock we went to the coffeehouse and I had not been there half an hour before Eugene came and told me that my wife was at my lodgings. I instantly went home and found her there. She told me all was well at home, thank God, this morning. I neglected to say my prayers but had good health, good thoughts, and good humor, thank God Almighty. I rogered my wife. The weather was very cold.

November, 1711

1. I rose about 8 o'clock and read nothing because I had a great deal to say to my wife. We sent some ducks and pigeons to the Governor and my wife sent to Mrs. Dunn to come to her. I drank chocolate for breakfast and about 10 o'clock went to court but the Governor was not there. I sat till about 3 o'clock and then went to my lodgings where I wrote in my journal till 4 o'clock, and then went to the Governor's to dinner and found my wife there. I ate venison pasty for dinner. In the evening we played at cards and I won. We put a trick [on] the Doctor who left 10 shillings on the table and we took it when he turned his back and left it for the cards when we had done. About 10 o'clock we went home in the Governor's coach. I neglected to say my prayers and had good health, good thoughts, and good humor, thank God Almighty.

2. I rose about 7 o'clock and read nothing because my wife was there, nor did I say my prayers, but ate boiled milk for breakfast. About 10 o'clock I went to the capitol and sat all day in court without once going away and by night we made an end. Then I waited on the Governor home to dinner where we found Mrs. Churchill and several other ladies and my wife among them. The table was so full that the Doctor and Mrs. Graeme and I had a little table to ourselves and were more merry than the rest of the company. I ate roast beef for supper. In the meantime the Doctor secured two fiddlers and candles were sent to the capitol and then the company followed and we had a ball and danced till about 12 o'clock at night and then everybody went to their lodgings, but I neglected to say my prayers but had good health, good thoughts, and good humor, thank God Almighty. Mrs. Russell was my partner.

3. I rogered my wife this morning and rose about 7 o'clock. I neglected to say my prayers but had boiled milk for breakfast. Mr. Beverley came to see my wife and break-

fasted with us. About 10 o'clock I went to the capitol to write letters because I would not be disturbed, and my wife went to see her sister. The weather was grown warmer. I wrote three letters to England. About 1 o'clock I ate some gingerbread and drank sage and snakeroot, and then wrote more letters. About 5 o'clock I returned to my lodgings and put up my letters and because Mrs. Churchill and Mrs. Beverley were at Colonel Carter's lodgings I went there and found the Colonel with the President and Mr. Clayton almost drunk. They would fain persuade me to drink with them but I refused and persuaded the Colonel not to suffer the ladies to wait on him so long. Then I went to the coffee-house and had the misfortune to affront the President without saying anything to provoke a reasonable man. After that we went to [p-l-y] and I won £18 and got home before 11 o'clock. I neglected to say my prayers but had good health, good thoughts, and good humor, thank God Almighty. I let Mrs. Churchill know that I owed her £40 of which her husband had kept no account.

4. I rose about 7 o'clock and read a chapter in Hebrew and some Greek in Homer. I neglected to say my prayers but ate boiled milk for breakfast. About 10 o'clock came my sister Custis to dress here who told me the Major was better. About 11 the coach was sent by the Governor to carry the women to church and I walked. Mr. Commissary gave us an indifferent sermon. When church was done we went to the Governor's to dinner and I ate some boiled venison, though my stomach was not so good as usual. About 4 o'clock we went to see the new house and there we found Mrs. Blair and Mrs. Harrison. When we had tired ourselves there the coach set the women home and the Governor and I went to the coffeehouse where we stayed about half an hour and then I went home to my lodgings and read some of the public news till about 9 o'clock. I neglected to say my prayers but had good health, good thoughts, and good humor, thank God Almighty.

5. I rose about 7 o'clock and read a chapter in Hebrew and some Greek in Lucian. I said my prayers and ate boiled

milk for breakfast. About 9 o'clock came Mrs. Bland and
invited my wife and Mrs. Dunn to dinner and the Governor
sent and invited me by Mr. Robinson, together with all the
governors of the College that were in town. The College
presented their verses to the Governor by the hands of the
Commissary and the master.[1] About 11 o'clock I went to
the capitol and wrote a letter to England and set G-r-l to
copying letters for me. About 2 o'clock I went to the Governor's to dinner and found there Mr. Commissary and the
master of the College and Johnny Randolph as being the
first scholar, who at dinner sat on the Governor's right hand.
I ate roast mutton for dinner. The Governor was taken sick
before we rose from table but it soon went over. In the
evening Mr. Bland took a walk to the College, and the
Governor, Mrs. Russell, and several ladies came to see the
bonfire made by the boys. At night we went to the Governor's to spend the rest of the evening till 10 o'clock and then
we went home. I neglected to say my prayers but had good
health, good thoughts, and indifferent humor, thank God
Almighty.

6. I rose about 7 o'clock and read two chapters in
Hebrew and some Greek in Homer. I said my prayers and
ate boiled milk for breakfast. My wife and her sister and
Mrs. Dunn waited on Mrs. Russell to Nat Burwell's, but I
could not possibly go with them and therefore committed
them to the care of the Doctor, who gallanted them. About
11 o'clock I went to the capitol, where I danced my dance
and wrote several letters to England. The old Frenchman
came to desire me to get him a passage to England, which
I promised to do when Captain H-n-t comes down. I stayed
and wrote at the capitol till about 5 o'clock because it rained
so hard that I could not get away. However at last I ran
through it to the coffeehouse, where I sat an hour before
anybody came. At last came Mr. Clayton from York but
had no news. Soon after came Mr. Robinson and he played
at piquet with me and we neither won nor lost. About 10

---

[1]The College was obliged by its charter to pay to the Governor on every
November 5 two copies of Latin verses as a quitrent.

I went home to my lodgings where I said my prayers and had good health, good thoughts, and good humor, thank God Almighty.

7. I rose about 7 o'clock and read two chapters in Hebrew and some Greek in Homer. I said my prayers and ate boiled milk for breakfast. I paid £500 to Mr. Tullitt for the College. About 10 I caused my secretary to be brought to my lodgings from the capitol. The wind blew very hard at northwest so that my wife and her company could not come from Gloucester. Some of the burgesses began to come and the House met and adjourned. I dined upon gingerbread because I could find no company to dine with. About 3 o'clock I went to the capitol and wrote letters to England and danced my dance. About 5 o'clock Mr. Clayton came to me and told me my wife and the other gentlewomen were returned from Gloucester and were at my lodgings. I went to them and gave them some victuals and a bottle of wine from Marot's. My sister Custis and Mrs. Dunn went to Queen's Creek and my wife went to bed and I went to the coffeehouse where I won 5 shillings and stayed till 9 o'clock. I neglected to say my prayers and had good health, good thoughts, and good humor, thank God Almighty.

8. I rose about 7 o'clock and read nothing because my wife was preparing to go away home. I neglected to say my prayers and ate boiled milk for breakfast. About 9 we went to the Governor's who showed me his speech. I entreated for Gilbert but could not prevail. I drank some tea till about 11 and then went in the Governor's coach to the capitol where he made his speech to the Council and Burgesses. Then I started a project of paying the ministers in money[1] and laying 3 shillings more on tobacco and everybody was pleased with the reason of it. About 2 o'clock I dined with the Council at Marot's and ate mutton for dinner. Harry W-l-s walked from hence to Jimmy Burwell's and back-again in less than three hours for a wager of two

---

[1] From the early years of colonization, the pay of ministers had generally been reckoned in tobacco.

guineas, but was almost spent. I took a walk to see the College and Governor's house and in the evening returned to the coffeehouse where we played at cards and I won 20 shillings. I returned home about 10 o'clock where I said my prayers and had good health, good humor, and good thoughts, thank God Almighty.

9. I rose about 7 o'clock and read two chapters in Hebrew and some Greek in Homer. I said my prayers and had boiled milk for breakfast. Mr. Bland came to see me and so did Frank [Ballard][1] and told me Mr. D-k was resolved to marry Mrs. Young in spite of all his friends. I went to prayers with the Burgesses and then we met as upper House but did nothing more than adjourn. Then I danced my dance and wrote my proposal but learned that the Governor was against it because it was no provision for more powers than are at present. About 2 o'clock we dined at Marot's and I ate roast veal for dinner. In the afternoon we went to the [?] coffeehouse where we fell into gaming and I won about £8 in all at piquet and dice. About 10 o'clock I returned to my lodgings where I said my prayers and had good health, good thoughts, and good humor, thank God Almighty.

10. I rose about 7 o'clock and read nothing because of writing a letter to Mr. D-k to endeavor to dissuade him from marrying Mrs. Young. I had several people come to see me this afternoon; however I got ready about 9 and went to the Governor's and found him [t-s] with the Commissary. I mentioned to him Mr. D-k's marriage with which he was surprised because he had not heard of it before. I asked the Governor if he had any service at Westover, and took my leave and went to the capitol where I danced my dance and wrote several things and stayed there till 4 o'clock, and then took a walk. About 5 I went to Mr. Bland's and were [sic] there about half an hour. My man Tom brought my horse and a letter from home by which I learned that all was well there, thank God. At night

---

[1]Burgess for Elizabeth City County.

I went to the coffeehouse where came some other gentlemen. I played at cards and won 5 shillings. Then I went to my lodgings where I said my prayers and had good health, good thoughts, and good humor, thank God Almighty. At the coffeehouse I ate some chicken pie and drank a bottle of the President's wine.

11. I rose about 7 o'clock and read nothing because I prepared to go home. However I said my prayers and ate some cranberry tart for breakfast. Mr. Graeme came to go home with me and I gave him some Virginia wine. About 10 o'clock we got on our horses and called at Green Springs where we drank tea and then took our leave and proceeded to Frank Lightfoot's[1] and were conducted there by a dog which we found at the ferry. We designed to take Frank with us home but he was obliged to go to court the next day, but promised to dine with us on Tuesday. I ate boiled beef for dinner. In the afternoon we sent to Major Harrison to come to us and then took a walk and met a pretty girl and kissed her and so returned. About 6 o'clock Major Harrison came to us but we could not persuade him to go with us to Westover. We sat up and were merry till 11 o'clock and then we went to bed. I neglected to say my prayers but had good health, good thoughts, and good humor, thank God Almighty.

12. I rose about 7 o'clock and said my prayers. Then we ate our breakfast of milk and took our leave and proceeded to Westover, where we found all well, thank God Almighty. Mr. Graeme was pleased with the place exceedingly. I showed him the library and then we walked in the garden till dinner and I ate some wild duck. In the afternoon I paid money to several men on accounts of Captain H-n-t and then we took a walk about the plantation and I was displeased with John about the boat which he was building. In the evening we played at piquet and I won a little. About 8 o'clock my wife was taken with the colic violently but it was soon over. Then Mr. Graeme and I drank a bottle

---

[1] Francis Lightfoot of James City County, later made naval officer of the Upper District of the James River.

of pressed wine which he liked very well, as he had done the white madeira. About 10 o'clock I went to bed and rogered my wife. I neglected to say my prayers but had good health, good thoughts, and good humor, thank God Almighty.

13. I rose about 7 o'clock and read nothing because of my company. However I said a short prayer and drank chocolate for breakfast and ate some cake. Then Mr. Graeme and I went out with bows and arrows and shot at partridge and squirrel which gave us abundance of diversion but we lost some of our arrows. We returned about one o'clock but found that Frank Lightfoot had broken his word by not coming to us. About 2 o'clock we went to dinner and I ate some venison pasty and were very merry. In the afternoon we played at billiards and I by accident had almost lost some of my fore teeth by putting the stick in my mouth. Then we went and took a walk with the women and Mr. Graeme diverted himself with Mrs. Dunn. In the evening came Mr. Mumford who told me all was well again at Appomattox. We played at cards and drank some pressed wine and were merry till 10 o'clock. I neglected to say my prayers but rogered my wife, and had good health, good thoughts, and good humor, thank God Almighty.

14. I rose about 7 o'clock and gave all the necessary orders to my people. I recommended myself and family to God and then ate some cold venison pasty for breakfast. I settled my business with Captain H-n-t and delivered my letters to him. Then we took our leave and were set over the creek and then proceeded on our journey and about 3 o'clock we got to Green Springs but neither the Colonel nor his lady were at home and therefore we stayed but half an hour and then went on to Williamsburg where we got about 5. I dressed myself and went to Colonel Bray's where the wedding[1] had been kept and found abundance of company

---

[1] This and later references (Nov. 18, 30) seem to indicate that Angelica, wife of Llewellyn Eppes, was a daughter of David Bray, and that this was the date of the marriage. The wedding mentioned two days later at Mr. Ingles' house was probably the same celebration, as Mungo Ingles married an aunt of the supposed Angelica. On November 27 James Bray's daughter Elizabeth married Arthur Allen.

there. I dined and ate some chicken pie and then we went to dancing and the bride was my partner but because Colonel Bray was sick we went away before 10 o'clock to the coffee-house where I won 5 shillings of the President. I said my prayers and had good thoughts, good health, and good humor, thank God Almighty.

15. I rose about 7 o'clock and read a chapter in Hebrew and some Greek in Homer. I said my prayers and ate boiled milk for breakfast. I wrote a letter to my wife and sent Tom home. About 10 o'clock Colonel Ludwell [came] to my lodgings. He stayed about half an hour and then we went to the capitol where I danced my dance and wrote in my journal. Then I went into council where our address to the Governor was read and Colonel Lewis and myself were ordered to wait on the Governor to know where and when the council should wait on him with it, and I walked him so fast that when he came there he could hardly speak. The Governor gave us some strong water to warm us and then we returned. About 2 o'clock we dined at Marot's and I won 5 shillings. I went home about 9 o'clock and read some Greek. I said my prayers and had good health, good thoughts, and good humor, thank God Almighty.

16. I rose about 7 o'clock and read two chapters in Hebrew and some Greek in Homer. I said my prayers and ate boiled milk for breakfast. About 9 o'clock I went to the Governor's where I stayed about an hour and then went to the capitol where we read a bill concerning rolling houses[1] the first time. About 11 the Governor came and the President read our address to him with an indifferent grace. About 2 o'clock we dined at Marot's and I ate some fish for dinner. My mouth was sore with the blow I had with the billiard stick. About 4 o'clock Jimmy Burwell and I resolved to go to the wedding at Mr. Ingles' and went away in his coach and found all the company ready to go to supper but we ate nothing with them but some custard. After supper we began to dance, first French dances and after

---

[1]The contemporary term for tobacco warehouse. For notes on legislation mentioned during November and December see *JHB*, 1702-1712, pp. 306-49.

country dances till about 11 o'clock and then most of the
company went to Williamsburg but I stayed with Jimmy
Burwell and Jimmy Roscow and James Bray, got drunk and
went home by myself about 12 o'clock. I neglected to say
my prayers but had good health, good thoughts, and good
humor, thank God Almighty.

17. I rose about 7 o'clock and neglected to say my prayers but ate boiled milk for breakfast. Mr. Ingles entertained us very generously and is a very good and courteous
man. We took our leave about 8 o'clock and returned in
Jimmy Burwell's coach to Williamsburg and went away to
the capitol where we read a bill concerning horses the first
time. Then we adjourned and I went to Colonel Duke's
who entertained me with good cider and toast. The weather
threatened rain or snow. About 1 o'clock I went again to
the capitol and danced my dance and wrote in my journal.
Then I read Italian for an hour. After which I took a walk
round the town till about 5 o'clock, and then went to the
coffeehouse and won 5 shillings of the President. About 9
I went to my lodgings where I read nothing but said my
prayers and had good health, good thoughts, and good
humor, thank God Almighty.

18. I rose about 7 o'clock and read two chapters in
Hebrew and some Greek in Homer. I said my prayers and
ate boiled milk for breakfast. About 11 o'clock the President called upon me with his coach to go to church where
Mr. Paxton[1] gave us a sermon that was very good. After
church Colonel Duke and I dined with the Commissary and
I ate roast turkey for dinner. Mrs. Blair was not very well.
In the evening Colonel Duke and I took leave and walked
to Colonel Bray's and found him much better but the design
was to visit Mrs. B-r-d [bride?] before she went up to
Captain Llewellyn [Eppes?]. We diverted ourselves with
the girls till about 9 o'clock and then took our leave and
wished them a good journey the next day. I read some

---

[1]Reverend Zechariah Paxton, invited to Bruton Parish in 1710. (Goodwin,
p. 297.)

English at my lodgings and said my prayers and had good health, good thoughts, and good humor, thank God Almighty.

19. I rose about 7 o'clock and read a chapter in Hebrew and some Greek in Homer. I said my prayers and ate boiled milk for breakfast. It rained a little in the morning. I went to the Governor's but he was gone to the new house and I went there to him and found him putting up the arms. Captain H-n-t came over and could hardly prevail with the Governor to let him go; however I interceded for him and got leave. About 2 o'clock my sister Custis sent horses for me and about 3 I rode to make her a visit and found them pretty well and their whole family. About 6 o'clock we went to supper and I ate some roast beef. Then we talked about dividing the land of old Colonel Parke between them and me.[1] Some words were spoken concerning selling some of Colonel Parke's land to pay his debts but my sister would not hear of it. I said my prayers and had good health, good thoughts, and good humor, thank God Almighty.

20. I rose about 7 o'clock and my brother and I appointed Mr. Bland and Mr. [Keeling] to divide the land of old Colonel Parke and agreed my sister should have the choice. I said my prayers and ate boiled milk for breakfast. About 9 o'clock I took leave and rode to Williamsburg where I found my man Tom with a letter from home, that told me all were well except my daughter, who had fallen down and cut her forehead. I wrote a letter to my wife and sent Tom home. Then I went to the capitol and read some bills. The Governor was there. We sat till two o'clock and I went to dinner at the Governor's and ate roast beef. About 4 we went away and I went and wrote in my journal and afterwards went and recommended the business of the College to some of the burgesses and then went to the coffeehouse where I won of Dr. Cocke 45 shillings at piquet. About 12

---

[1]Colonel Daniel Parke, Sr., grandfather of Mrs. Byrd and Mrs. Custis, had left his land to his son Daniel, and to that son's heirs. It would therefore, after the death of Daniel Parke, Jr., be divided equally between the two daughters. The estates lay mostly in York and James City Counties. (*Va. Mag.*, XIV, 174-76.)

o'clock I went home and said a short prayer and had good thoughts, good humor, and good health, thank God Almighty.

21. I rose about 7 o'clock and read nothing because I went to the committee for making the port bill[1] and stayed there about an hour. Then I returned and said my prayers and had boiled milk for breakfast. Then I went to the capitol and danced my dance and did some business with Mr. Holloway. Then I went down to the Council and read some law and the Governor came among us and stayed about an hour. About 2 o'clock we rose and went to dinner and I ate fish. Then Colonel Smith and I played at billiards and I won half a crown. Then we took a walk and afterwards went to the coffeehouse and played at whisk but lost 15 shillings. Then we played at dice and after losing £10 I recovered my money and won £8, [by holding in 13 hands together]. About 12 o'clock we drank a bottle of wine and then went home. I said my prayers and had good health, good thoughts, and good humor, thank God Almighty.

22. I rose about 7 o'clock and read a chapter in Hebrew and some Greek in Homer. I said my prayers and ate boiled milk for breakfast. Mr. Bland came to see me and told me he would go about the dividing of old Colonel Parke's land as we desired. About 11 I went to the capitol where I found the Governor, who had letters from the Governor of North Carolina which gave a terrible account of the state of Carolina. He had also a letter from the Baron by which he had a relation of his being taken with Mr. Lawson by the Indians and of Mr. Lawson's murder.[2] The House of Burgesses brought their address of thanks to which the Governor answered them that he would thank them when he saw them act with as little self interest as he had done. About 3 o'clock we went to dinner and I ate some roast goose. Then I took a walk to the Governor's new house with Frank W-l-s and then returned to the coffeehouse where I lost 12 pounds 10 shillings and about 10

---

[1]Concerning ports, warehouses, rolling houses, and public landings.
[2]See *The Colonial Records of North Carolina,* I, 990-92.

o'clock returned home very much out of humor to think myself such a fool. I said my prayers and had good health, good thoughts, and good humor, thank God Almighty. It was very hot till about 9 o'clock in the evening and then it grew cold.

23. I rose about 7 o'clock and read a chapter in Hebrew and some Greek in Homer. I said my prayers and ate boiled milk for breakfast. Several gentlemen came to my lodgings. About 10 o'clock I went to the capitol where I danced my dance and then wrote in my journal. It was very cold this morning. About 11 o'clock I went to the coffee-house where the Governor also came and from thence we went to the capitol and read the bill concerning ports the first time. We stayed till 3 o'clock and then went to dinner to Marot's but could get none there and therefore Colonel Lewis and I dined with Colonel Duke and I ate broiled chicken for dinner. After dinner we went to Colonel Carter's room where we had a bowl of punch of French brandy and oranges. We talked very lewdly and were almost drunk and in that condition we went to the coffeehouse and played at dice and I lost £12. We stayed at the coffeehouse till almost 4 o'clock in the morning talking with Major Harrison. Then I went to my lodging, where I committed uncleanness, for which I humbly beg God Almighty's pardon.

24.[1] I rose about 8 o'clock and read a chapter in Hebrew and some Greek in Homer. I said my prayers and ate boiled milk for breakfast. Colonel Carter and several others came to my lodgings to laugh at me for my disorder last night. About 10 I went to the coffeehouse and drank some tea and then we went to the President's and read the law about probate and administration. Then I went to the capitol and danced my dance and wrote in my journal and read Italian. This day I make a solemn resolution never at once to lose more than 50 shillings and to spend less time in gaming, and I beg the God Almighty to give me grace to keep so good a resolution if it be His holy will. I read some

---

[1]Opposite this entry is drawn a pointing hand.

Italian and danced again. Then I took a walk, notwithstanding I had a good cold on me and the weather was also very cold. Then went to the coffeehouse but returned to ›my lodgings about 5 o'clock and wrote two letters to England. I said my prayers and had good health, good thoughts, and good humor, thank God Almighty.

25. I rose about 7 o'clock and found my cold much worse. However I read a chapter in Hebrew and some Greek in Homer. I said my prayers and ate boiled milk for breakfast. I was so disordered with my cold that I could not go to church but read some English. About 11 o'clock Mr. Clayton came to see me and I desired him to lend me his horse to ride to Queen's Creek. About one my brother Custis called on me and I went with him home and found all the family well. Just before we sat to dinner Dr. Cocke came to us. I ate some roast beef for dinner notwithstanding my cold, which continued violently. We were merry till the evening and then we drank a bowl of punch made of French brandy and oranges which I drank for my cold and ate roast apples with it. We sat up till about 10 and then I said a short prayer and had good health, good thoughts, and good humor, thank God Almighty.

26. I rose about 8 o'clock and found myself much better, thank God. It rained and thundered much in the night. I said my prayers and ate boiled milk for breakfast. My sister agreed to divide her grandfather's land without any intervention of [f-r-n] and she also agreed to the sale of some of the land and negroes of her father to pay his debts. About 10 o'clock we took leave and went to Williamsburg but there we did not meet to do business till almost 2 o'clock because we had not enough in town. We read two bills and then went to dinner and I ate chicken pie but was not well after it. In the evening we went to the coffeehouse where I received a letter from Mr. Perry and an account of £5 a hogshead for tobacco. About 9 o'clock I went to my lodgings where I said my prayers and had good health, good thoughts, and good humor, thank God Almighty.

27.[1] I rose about 7 o'clock and read a chapter in Hebrew and some Greek in Homer. I said my prayers and ate boiled milk for breakfast. The weather was very cold and threatened snow. James Bray invited me to the wedding of his daughter[2] this day but the weather was so bad I made my excuses by the Commissary. We sat at the President's house where we had a good fire. I received a letter from home by my sloop that brought some coal on her way to Kiquotan with palisades. We read several bills and the Governor came to us and made his exceptions to some clauses in the bill concerning probate and administration, which we resolved to amend. We sat till about 4 o'clock and then went to dinner and I ate some roast mutton. In the evening we went to the coffeehouse where I played at cards and won 25 shillings. About 9 I returned to my lodgings where I said my prayers and had good health, good thoughts, and good humor, thank God Almighty.

28. I rose about 7 o'clock and found the weather extremely cold. I read a chapter in Hebrew and some Greek in Homer. I said my prayers and ate boiled milk for breakfast. I had a gentleman that came to buy the quitrents of Nansemond County but we could not agree. About 10 o'clock I went to the capitol where I wrote in my journal and danced my dance, and then went to the coffeehouse where I found several of the council but not ready to go to council, and so some of us took a walk to the Governor's house where we found the Governor looking over the workmen. It was exceedingly cold. Then we returned to the President's lodgings where we read some bills and afterwards adjourned to the capitol where the House of Burgesses brought an address to the Governor in which they desired him to make war on the Indians and the council afterwards advised him if no other method would procure satisfaction from the Indians then to make war on them.

---

[1]This has been changed from "28" to "27." A note in longhand at the bottom of the page reads "Mem. that 27th day is omitted and therefore the first of next month shoud be the last of this and the second the first." The following dates, up to the 4th of December, have been altered by Byrd according to this correction.
[2]Elizabeth Bray married Arthur Allen.

About 4 o'clock we went to dinner and I ate some roast beef. In the evening we played at cards till 7 o'clock and then I went home and read some Greek and looked over several papers relating to the estate of old Colonel Parke. I said my prayers and had good health, good thoughts, and good humor, thank God Almighty.

29. I rose about 7 o'clock and read some Hebrew but no Greek because I intended to wait on the Governor. I said my prayers and ate boiled milk for breakfast. About 9 I went to the Governor but he was so busy nobody could speak with him. Then I returned to the coffeehouse where I ate some toast and butter and drank milk tea on it. Here I learned that Captain Smith, commander of the "Enterprise", was come and that Dr. [Barret's] house was burnt last night. It was cold and threatened snow. About 10 o'clock I went to the capitol, where I danced my dance and wrote in my journal and then went to the President's lodgings, with the rest of the Council, and there we read the law about probate of wills and administration, and the Governor came to us and I went in his coach with him to dinner, and I ate some fish. Captain Smith, commander of the "Enterprise", was there also. In the evening I went home where I found Tom with a letter from my wife by which I learned that all was well there, thank God. Then I went to the coffeehouse where I played at cards and won [. . .] shillings. Then I returned to my lodgings and said my prayers and had good health, good thoughts, and good humor, thank God Almighty. Tom brought a wild goose that was very fat and therefore I sent it to the Governor.

30. I rose about 7 o'clock and read nothing because I prepared for my journey home. However I said my prayers and ate boiled milk for breakfast. I sold the quitrents to Mr. Bland and then took my leave of him and got on horseback about 9 o'clock when it was fair weather, but it was overcast before I got to the ferry. Sometimes I walked to get myself warm, and sometimes I rode, and got there about 3 o'clock in the afternoon, and found all my family well, thank God Almighty. My wife and Mrs. Dunn had worked

very hard to put the house in order. In the evening I ate two partridges for my supper and spent the rest of the evening in talking about all the affairs of the neighborhood. My wife told me that Llewellyn Eppes his wife was like not to be very happy because he was cross already to her. I told them all the news of the town and about 8 o'clock we went to bed. I neglected to say my prayers but had good health, good thoughts, and good humor, thank God Almighty. I rogered my wife vigorously.

December, 1711

1. I rose about 9 o'clock and read a chapter in Hebrew and some Greek in Homer. I ate milk for breakfast and then said my prayers. I learned by Robin Jones that all was well above. I let him the plantation that I bought of Sam Good[1] for 30 bushels of wheat. I wrote two letters by him to my overseers. I wrote to Mr. Mumford and sent Tom up with it to Appomattox. L-s-n was taken sick of a vomiting and purging for which I gave him a vomit. The weather was very good but cold and it blew hard. I ate boiled venison for dinner. In the afternoon I had my head shaved but Bannister had set the razor so bad it was practically murder to me. In the evening I took a walk about the plantation and overlooked everything and found several things out of order, for which I scolded at John. At night Peter came from above and brought a wild goose that was very fat. L-s-n seemed to be a little better. My wife and I had a small quarrel about nothing. I neglected to say my prayers but had good health, good thoughts, and good humor, thank God Almighty.

2. I rose about 8 o'clock and read two chapters in Hebrew and a chapter in the New Testament. I said my prayers and had milk for breakfast. The weather was a little warmer and my man L-s-n a little better, thank God. I wrote a letter to my overseers above by little Peter. I gave a vomit to Anaka and Jenny which worked very well. Peter carried up 18 narrow hoes. I ate some wild duck for dinner and in the afternoon took a walk about the plantation and saw everything and considered what was to be done and did not return till the evening and then I found Mr. Mumford come over the river and he told me that Captain Evans and another Indian trader were come from Carolina and

---

[1]In 1704 Samuel Good paid quitrents on 588 acres in Henrico County. (*Va. Mag.,* XXVIII, 212.) In January 1711 Byrd had purchased from him two tracts, 123 acres in Henrico County on the south side of the James, and 423 acres on Stony Creek. (Henrico County Court Records, 1710-14, pp. 108, 111.)

had brought abundance of skins. He told me also that the Tuscarora Indians were come in to tell us what their nation would do. Mr. G-r-l came just at dark and told me all was well above. I ate some stewed duck with them. In the evening I neglected to say my prayers but had good health, good thoughts, and good humor, thank God Almighty. L-s-n was very ill, God preserve him.

3. I rose about 7 o'clock and read nothing in Hebrew and a chapter in the Testament. I said my prayers and ate boiled milk for breakfast. It threatened to snow. Then I went to see L-s-n and found him very ill still and had not rested all night. About 9 o'clock Mr. G-r-l went away and then Mr. Mumford and I took a walk about the plantation and when we returned we found Colonel Hill who came in just before dinner. I ate roast venison for dinner. The Colonel stayed with me till late in the afternoon and then went over the river and so did Mr. Mumford. In the evening it began to snow and snowed almost all night. I wrote a contract with my overseer and then I went to see L-s-n and found him with a pain in his side. I gave him some laudanum and committed him to God Almighty. Then I went in and we were merry all the rest of the evening. I said a short prayer and recommended my sick man to heaven. I had good health, good thoughts, and good humor, thank God Almighty.

4. I rose about 8 o'clock and found a great snow. I said my prayers and ate boiled milk for breakfast. I prepared for my journey to Williamsburg and then went to visit L-s-n and found him very ill and left the best directions I could about him. Then I took my leave and was set over the creek and so proceeded through the snow to Williamsburg. It was very cold so that I was forced to alight off my horse to walk two several times. I got to Williamsburg about 3 and dined with the council and I ate mutton for dinner. Then I went to the Governor's to consult the doctor about L-s-n and he gave me his directions in writing. Then we played at piquet and I won 20 shillings. I went home about 9 o'clock and wrote a letter to my wife and another to Mr.

Ludwell to beg some linseed. I said my prayers and had good health, good thoughts, and good humor, thank God Almighty. It was terribly cold this night that I could not be warm in bed.

5. I rose about 7 o'clock and read a chapter in Hebrew and some Greek in Homer. I said my prayers and ate boiled milk for breakfast. Abundance of company came to my lodgings and some burgesses among them, with whom I discoursed about the unreasonable taxes on several things. I settled some accounts and then I went to the capitol in my boots because of the snow. The wind came to south and it grew a little warmer, thank God. My man Tom returned home. We rejected the bill concerning the gold coin and began to make a bill about negroes. We sat till about 3 o'clock and then went to dinner. I ate some roast chicken. We sat and discoursed till the evening and then went to the coffeehouse where I lost 10 shillings at whisk. It was 11 o'clock when I returned to my lodgings where I said my prayers and had good health, good thoughts, and good humor, thank God Almighty.

6. I rose about 7 o'clock and read two chapters in Hebrew and some Greek in Homer. I said my prayers and ate boiled milk for breakfast. It was warm, thank God, but threatened more snow. I settled several accounts and had several people come to my lodgings and some burgesses among them. About 11 o'clock we went to the capitol and read the horse bill and sent it down with a message that we adhered to our amendment. We made some steps to making another negro bill but made nothing of it. About 3 we adjourned and I went to dine at the Governor's and I ate some venison for dinner. Then I went to the coffeehouse where I lost £4 at piquet. About 11 o'clock I returned to my lodgings, where I said my prayers and had good health, good thoughts, and good humor, thank God Almighty.

7. I rose at 8 o'clock and read a chapter in Hebrew and some Greek in Homer. I said my prayers and ate boiled milk for breakfast. The weather was particularly warm. Several people came to my lodgings and Mr. Custis among

the rest who came about selling some of Colonel Parke's land and negroes to pay his debts. About 11 I went to the capitol, where we sat in council about Mr. Cary's accounts and the Governor insisted that he was incapable of the business and should be turned out and the council were of his opinion.[1] We went to dinner about 3 and I ate some wild duck for dinner. Then Colonel Smith and I took a walk and in the evening went to the coffeehouse, where I played again at piquet and won of the Doctor about £4 and about 11 o'clock went home, where I said my prayers and had good health, good thoughts, and good humor, thank God Almighty. Gilbert, the Governor's man, was sent this day on board the man-of-war.

8. I rose about 8 o'clock and read a chapter in Hebrew but no Greek because Mr. Custis came to me again and several other people. I said my prayers and ate boiled milk for breakfast. Colonel Ludwell invited me to go to Green Springs but I excused myself, notwithstanding several pretty women were there. About 10 o'clock I went to the capitol where the Governor gave audience to the Tuscarora Indians and engaged them to promise to cut off those Indians that committed the murder in Carolina. The weather was warm. About 3 o'clock my man Tom brought me a letter from home that L-s-n was very ill and everybody else well, thank God. Then I went to the Governor's to dinner and I ate some venison. We had some French wine sent by Captain Garlington to the Governor. About 7 o'clock I went home to my lodgings and wrote a letter to my wife with directions concerning L-s-n. I said my prayers and had good health, good thoughts, and good humor, thank God Almighty. I ordered Tom to go away in the morning by break of day.

9. I rose about 7 o'clock and read two chapters in Hebrew and some Greek in Homer. I said my prayers devoutly and ate boiled milk for breakfast. The weather

---

[1] Henry Cary, under pretence of feeding the workmen on the Governor's house, had been appropriating the public funds to feed his own family. On April 28, 1711, he had been cautioned by the Council to be more frugal, but had apparently not profited by the warning. (*Ex. Jour.*, III, 272, 293.)

was warm but cloudy. About 10 o'clock came my brother
Custis and stayed till 11 o'clock and we went to church,
where I saw Billy Cole's wife,[1] who was very pretty. Mr.
Finney gave us a sermon and a very indifferent one. After
I went with my brother and sister Custis to Mrs.
[Whaley's][2] to dinner where we had a turkey and bacon,
very well dressed. In the afternoon we sat and talked till
about 4 o'clock and then I took leave and walked some part
of the way with Mr. Custis, and he told me of some slander
he had heard of me, which came from Mrs. Russell. I had
my usual way of contempt for it. In the evening I went to
visit Colonel Bray where I stayed till about 8 o'clock and
then went to my lodgings where I washed my feet. Then I
said my prayers and had good health, good thoughts, and
good humor, thank God Almighty.

10. I rose at 7 o'clock and read a chapter in Hebrew and
some Greek in Homer. I neglected to say my prayers but
ate custard for breakfast. It was cold, misty weather, the
wind at northeast. I had several gentlemen come to my
lodgings and among them Mr. Custis who desired me to go
to the committee to attest my wife's consent to selling some
of Colonel Parke's estate to pay his debts, which I did
accordingly. Then I went to the capitol where we read the
money bill the first time and heard the treaty they passed
with the Tuscarora Indians. About 3 we went to dinner
and I ate chicken pie and then went to the coffeehouse where
we played at whisk and I won 20 shillings. About 10 I
returned to my lodgings where I said my prayers and had
good health, good thoughts, and good humor, thank God
Almighty.

11. I rose about 7 o'clock and read a little Greek in
Homer and nothing in Hebrew. I neglected to say my
prayers but ate boiled milk for breakfast. Frank Eppes
came to see me but I was in great haste to go to Council,

---

[1] Young William Cole married Mary, daughter of William Roscow.
[2] Probably Mrs. Mary (Page) Whaley, widow of James Whaley, founder
of Mattey's School in Williamsburg; owner of property at Queen's Creek.
(*Wm. Q. (1)*, IV, 3-14.)

where the Tuscarora Indians were to sign the treaty with the Governor, which they performed accordingly. Then we [went] into court where we were sworn as judges of the Court of Oyer and Terminer and then we went to church to hear the Commissary preach the [assize] sermon, which was very indifferent. Then we returned to court where Betty J-r-d-n was convicted of burglary for breaking the Governor's house. About 5 o'clock we went to dinner and I ate some boiled pork for my dinner. Then we went to the coffeehouse, where I won 40 shillings and returned to my lodgings about 11 o'clock, where I said my prayers and had good health, good thoughts, and good humor, thank God Almighty. The weather cleared up and grew cold.

12. I rose about 7 o'clock and read a chapter in Hebrew and some Greek in Homer. I said a short prayer and ate boiled milk for breakfast. I had several people to see me and I settled some accounts with some of them. Then I went to the capitol and we went into court to pronounce sentence of death upon Betty J-r-d-n and she plead her belly. Then we went into Council and excepted against several things in the money bill. We had a hot dispute and Colonel Ludwell and Colonel Carter quarreled before the Governor, who laughed at them to himself. We sat till about 4 o'clock and then went to dinner. The House of Burgesses sent us up several bills and that for selling some of the land and negroes belonging to my sister Custis among them, which we read the first time. I ate some roast chicken for dinner and then went to the coffeehouse where I played at piquet and won 5 shillings of Mr. Walker and about 10 o'clock went home to my lodgings where I said my prayers and had good health, good thoughts, and good humor, thank God Almighty. The weather was very cold again.

13. I rose about 7 o'clock and read a chapter in Hebrew but no Greek. I neglected to say my prayers because there came company that hindered me, but I ate three custards for breakfast. Colonel Bassett came among the rest. I received letters from my overseers above by which I learned that all were well there. About 10 o'clock I went to the

capitol where a jury of matrons were impanelled to inquire if Betty J-r-d-n was quick with child and their verdict was that she was quick. Then we went to Council and read several bills and sent a message concerning amendments to be made to their money bill. We rose about 4 o'clock and then went to dinner and I ate roast duck. My man Tom came from home and told me poor L-s-n died on Sunday morning last but that all else were well, thank God. Then I went to the coffeehouse where I played at piquet and lost 25 shillings. About 10 o'clock I went home and said my prayers and had good health, good thoughts, and good humor, thank God Almighty. Colonel Carter was out of order.

14. I rose about 7 o'clock and read a chapter in Hebrew and some Greek in Homer. I said my prayers and ate boiled milk for breakfast. It threatened rain; however I wrote a letter and sent Eugene home with it to let my wife know why I could not come. Several gentlemen came to my lodgings but about 10 o'clock I went to see Colonel Carter and found him better. Then I walked to the capitol where I danced my dance; then we went to Council and read some bills the third time and particularly Mr. Custis his bill. Then we examined Mr. Cary's accounts and found several articles wrongly charged. It rained very hard almost all day. About 4 o'clock we went to dinner and I ate a fricassee of turkey. Then we went to the coffeehouse and I won £5. About 11 o'clock I went home, where I said my prayers and had good health, good thoughts, and good humor, thank God Almighty.

15. I rose about 7 o'clock and read nothing because I had some business to do and accounts to settle. I neglected to say my prayers but ate boiled milk for breakfast. Several people came to my chambers. About 10 o'clock I went to the capitol where we received an answer from the House of Burgesses to our proposals to amend their money bill, who refused to allow of those amendments. Mr. Robinson told some of the Council that the Governor was for having the bill passed notwithstanding the Burgesses had refused our

amendments. However I was against it though I was very ready to oblige the Governor in anything in which my honor was not concerned. We made some amendments to the bill for raising the land forces and sent it away down and then rose and I walked home with the Governor to dinner and ate some boiled mutton for dinner, and then drank a bottle of French wine till about 8 o'clock and then walked home to my lodgings, where I said my prayers and had good health, good thoughts, and good humor, thank God Almighty. The weather cleared up and was very fair again.

16. I rose about 7 o'clock and read two chapters in Hebrew and some Greek in Homer. I said my prayers and ate boiled milk for breakfast. The weather was very cold. A man came to me for rights and because it was matter of necessity I let him have some rights. I did not go to church but rode to Jimmy Burwell's where I got about one o'clock before the people came from church, but they came about half an hour after. Here I found Colonel Eppes, John Bolling, and Robin [Bolling], which last was ill of the colic. I never had seen Mrs. Burwell, who is a pretty woman, nor did I ever see Suky the Doctor's maid, who was not ugly but much gone to the flesh. About 3 o'clock we went to dinner and I ate some boiled beef. In the afternoon we took a walk, notwithstanding it was very cold, till the evening and then we sat by a good fire and were merry till about 10 o'clock, and then I took my leave and went to bed next door to the nursery. I said my prayers and had good health, good thoughts, and good humor, thank God Almighty. One of Major Burwell's children disturbed me in the night so that I could not sleep.

17. I rose about 7 o'clock and read nothing but a little Dutch. However I said a short prayer and ate boiled milk for breakfast. The weather continued very cold. Robin Bolling was better and he and I went to shoot with bows and arrows. When that was over we returned and I drank some chocolate. About 10 o'clock we took leave and returned to Williamsburg, where we heard that a ship was come into Rappahannock from London which brought word

that our fleet got well to England. The Doctor and my brother Custis came to my chambers and from thence we went to the capitol where we heard that the Indians were forming a conspiracy against the English and that a Notto-way Indian told a negro of it. We had a conference about the bill that lay the taxes but the Burgesses had orders to discourse about the title of the bill and not the substance of it. About 4 o'clock we went to dinner and I ate some broiled pork for my part and then went to the capitol where I drank two dishes of tea and then returned to my lodgings. We learned that Major Robinson's house was burnt. I said my prayers and had good health, good thoughts, and good humor, thank God Almighty.

18. I rose about 7 o'clock and read a chapter in Hebrew and some Greek in Homer. I said my prayers and ate boiled milk for breakfast. Mr. Bland came to my lodgings on his way to the Governor's. It was very cold and had snowed in the night but it melted this morning. I settled the pork account and then went to the capitol where I danced my dance. Then we went into Council and read some of the claims. The Governor let some of us know he would not pass the bill for the impositions. About 12 o'clock I danced my dance again and read some Italian. We settled the rangers and then went to dinner and I went with the Governor home and ate boiled beef for dinner. Then we drank a bottle of claret and then went to the coffeehouse where I lost 30 shillings. About 11 o'clock I returned to my lodgings and had good health, good thoughts, and good humor, thank God Almighty.

19. I rose about 7 o'clock and read a chapter in Hebrew and no Greek because I had company. I said my prayers and ate boiled milk for breakfast. The weather was cold and clear. Captain Holt came to me to favor him in a protested bill by forbearing him, which I did. About 10 I went to the capitol where we sent a message to the Burgesses to confer with them about their imposition bill but they denied us it on account of its being the province of the Burgesses to raise money after which method they pleased.

We resented this usage, but the Governor came and gave
audience to the Saponie Indians and then made the Burgesses a speech which was a severe reflection upon their
proceedings and in which he told them he could not pass
their imposition bill because it was insufficient and [unusual].
Then I went home with the Governor to dinner and ate salt
fish and after dinner we drank a bottle of claret. About 8
I went to the coffeehouse where I won 15 shillings and went
home about 11 o'clock. I said my prayers and had good
health, good thoughts, and good humor, thank God Almighty.

20. I rose about 7 o'clock and read a chapter in Hebrew
and some Greek in Homer. I said my prayers and ate
boiled milk for breakfast. The weather was moderate but
overcast. Several gentlemen came to my lodgings and I
settled several accounts with them and particularly with Dr.
Cocke I settled his [p-l-y] account and he owed me £24.
About 11 I went to the capitol where I danced my dance and
read some Italian. Nothing was done in Council but sign-
ing a warrant and petition though the House of Burgesses
[laid] some faults on us. I danced my dance again because
I was cold. Mr. Custis came to town and would have me
go home with him but I could not because the young men
came to town. About 4 o'clock we went to dinner and I ate
some roast chicken and after dinner we drank a bowl of
punch and were merry with Colonel Carter, who went away
about 7 o'clock in the evening. Then we went to the coffeehouse where we played at dice and I won £4. Then I returned to my lodgings where I said my prayers and had
good health, good thoughts, and good humor, thank God
Almighty.

21. I rose about 7 o'clock and read nothing because I
was to write out the Governor's account, which I did. I
said my prayers and ate custard for breakfast. The weather
was very cold. About 9 o'clock I went to the Governor's to
settle accounts with him but he was not at leisure. When I
returned I went to the coffeehouse where I played a game at
piquet and won 15 shillings. Then I went to Mr. Clayton's

and settled Colonel Churchill's account and desired him to
write a deed of partition between my brother Custis and me
of old Colonel Parke's land.   Then I returned to the capitol
where I danced my dance.   We prepared a protest against
the proposal of the House of Burgesses not to grant us a
conference on the money bill.   About 4 o'clock we went to
dinner and I ate some wild duck for my dinner.   From
thence we went to the coffeehouse where I lost 20 shillings
at piquet and returned to my lodgings about 11 o'clock
where I said my prayers and had good health, good
thoughts, and good humor, thank God Almighty.

22.   I rose about 7 o'clock and read nothing because I
prepared to go to the Governor's to settle his account.   I
neglected to say my prayers but ate boiled milk for breakfast.   [It] snowed last night and this morning.   About 10
o'clock Mr. Bland came and he went with me to the Governor's where we balanced accounts with him and he made me
allow him 6 percent for the difference of money.   I inquired
of him whether I might not pay the contingent charges in
money and charges sterling and he agreed that I might.   I
desired leave to go home, but the Governor told me he
should speak to the House of Burgesses on Monday and
would have the Council there.   About 12 I went to the
coffeehouse where the gentlemen of the Council were and I
told them the Governor's mind and they agreed to be there.
About 2 o'clock I went again to the Governor's in the
President's coach to dinner and ate beefsteak.   In the evening we drank a bottle and about 8 went to the coffeehouse
where I lost 7 shillings at piquet and at 10 went home to my
lodgings, where I said my prayers and had good health,
good thoughts, and good humor, thank God Almighty.   I
endeavored to reconcile the Governor to the Burgesses but
in vain.

23.   I rose about 7 o'clock and read a chapter in Hebrew
and some Greek in Homer.   I said my prayers and ate
boiled milk for breakfast.   I wrote out a chronology of the
Bible which the Governor lent me and did not go to church,
God forgive me.   About 12 o'clock Dr. Cocke came to me

in, order to go to Queen's Creek and we got on horseback about one and rode there and [found] them pretty well. The weather was cold and had hindered them from going to church likewise. We waited till 3 o'clock for dinner and then I ate some turkey and chine and after dinner we sat by a fire and chatted and were merry, without much scandal to our [talk]. The Doctor was very pleasant company, as he commonly is. We had some roast apples and wine, with which we diverted ourselves till about 10 o'clock and then we retired to our lodgings where I said my prayers and had good health, good thoughts, and good humor, thank God Almighty.

24. I rose about 7 o'clock but read nothing because all the company was up. However, I said my prayers and ate boiled milk for breakfast. It was very cold and had frozen very hard. However, about 10 we took leave and rode to Williamsburg. Mr. Bland came to my lodging and told me he had bought Mr. Brodnax's[1] land for me that lay near the Falls and was to give him £165 for it. Then I went to the coffeehouse, where I met all my brothers of the Council that were in town. About 12 o'clock Colonel Ludwell and I went to the Governor's to learn from himself how long he intended to keep us and to persuade him to give leave to the House of Burgesses to adjourn for a month without their asking, which he at last consented to. He asked us to dine but we [. . .] to the rest of the Council and dined with them at the coffeehouse and I ate some beef for dinner. I paid all my debts and about 3 o'clock we went to the capitol to expect the coming of the Governor, who adjourned the assembly till the 24th of January and then we all took leave and went away and I went to Queen's Creek and surprised a good company there. I ate some toast and cider and roast apples and sat and chatted till 10 o'clock and then I recommended the company to the divine protection and said a short prayer and had good thoughts and good health and good humor, thank God Almighty.

---

[1] John Brodnax, of James City County, owned land in Henrico County. (*Va. Mag.*, XLIX, 37-44.) He was keeper of the gaol in Williamsburg.

25. I rose about 7 o'clock and read nothing because I prepared for my journey to Colonel Duke's. However I said my prayers and ate boiled milk for breakfast. The weather threatened snow but it did not frighten me from taking my leave about 11 o'clock, but before that I wrote a letter to Mr. C-s and enclosed to Mr. Graeme who was to go soon in the man-of-war. About 2 o'clock I got to Colonel Duke's and found both him and his old woman in good health, only the last was grown very deaf. We sat and talked till about 4 and then we went to dinner and I ate some wild duck. In the meantime the Colonel sent a negro man to see whether the river was open at my brother Duke's and he brought word it was, and therefore I took leave of the Colonel and his old countess and rode away to the river and with some difficulty got over as soon as it was dark. I found all well there and we drank a bottle of wine. About 9 o'clock I went to bed. I said my prayers and had good health, good thoughts, and good humor, thank God Almighty.

26. I rose about 7 o'clock and read nothing because I prepared for my journey. However I said my prayers and ate boiled milk for breakfast. It was cold and threatened rain or snow. About 9 I took leave and rode towards home and between Captain Stith's and home I met my wife and Mrs. Dunn going to Williamsburg to see what was become of me, but they turned back with me home where I found all well, thank God Almighty, except old Jane who was very ill of a fever. About 3 o'clock we went to dinner and I ate some wild goose. In the afternoon I looked about and found all things in good order. Mr. Anderson dined with me and after dinner gave old Jane the Sacrament. He stayed with me till the evening and then returned home. I inquired of my people how everything was and they told me well. Then I gave them some rum and cider to be merry with and afterwards read some Italian and wrote two letters to my overseers. I said my prayers and had good health, and good thoughts, and good humor, thank God Almighty. I rogered my wife [lustily].

27. I rose about 7 o'clock and read nothing because I put my things in order, but I wrote in my journal. I should have said my prayers but as soon as I had eaten boiled milk for breakfast Colonel Hill and Mrs. Anderson came to see us. My wife had [c-s] some of her [f-x]. The Colonel inquired how matters went below and I acquainted him with everything I knew concerning it. The weather was more moderate than it had been lately. Mr. Anderson would have come likewise but he was obliged to go to marry a couple of his parishioners. About 1 o'clock we went to dinner and I ate some roast beef. The company stayed with me till 4 o'clock and then went away. Then I danced my dance and said my prayers devoutly and then walked in my library because the ground was wet. In the evening I wrote in my journal and caused several of my people to be let blood by way of prevention. Then I read some Latin in Terence till 10 o'clock. I said my prayers and had good health, good thoughts, and good humor, thank God Almighty. I rogered my wife [lustily].

28. I rose about 7 o'clock and read two chapters in Hebrew and some Greek in Lucian. I said my prayers and ate boiled milk for breakfast. The weather was warm but cloudy. I danced my dance. I wrote some accounts and put several matters in order. Poor old Jane was very ill. We had several of the people let blood by way of prevention and Jenny for a sore throat. I ate boiled beef for dinner. In the afternoon settled several accounts till the evening and then I took a walk about the plantation and found matters pretty well, thank God. At night I wrote in my journal and read some Latin in Terence till 10 o'clock. It snowed a little this evening. I said my prayers and had good health, good thoughts, and good humor, thank God Almighty. About 8 o'clock came Mr. G-r-l and George Smith by whom I learned that all was well at Falling Creek and the coal-pit.

29. I rose about 7 o'clock and read two chapters in Hebrew and some Greek in Lucian. I said my prayers and ate boiled milk for breakfast. I had abundance of talk with Mr. G-r-l about the affairs of Falling Creek and he told me

some of his wants and so did George Smith, which I endeavored to supply as well as I could. I gave John G-r-l
leave to go visit his mother. Poor old Jane died this morning. about 9 o'clock and I caused her to be buried as soon as
possible because she stank very much. It was not very cold
today. I danced my dance. Mr. G-r-l and George Smith
went away about 12 o'clock. I ate some broiled goose for
dinner. In the afternoon I set my razor, and then went out
to shoot with bow and arrow till the evening and then I ran
to breathe myself and looked over everything. At night I
read some Latin in Terence till about 10 o'clock. I said my
prayers and had good health, good thoughts, and good
humor, thank God Almighty.

30. I rose about 7 o'clock and read a chapter in Hebrew
and three chapters in the Greek Testament. I said my
prayers very devoutly and ate boiled milk for breakfast.
The weather was very clear and warm so that my wife
walked out with Mrs. Dunn and forgot dinner, for which
I had a little quarrel with her and another afterwards because I was not willing to let her have a book out of the
library. About 12 o'clock came Mr. Bland from Williamsburg but brought no news. He stayed to dinner and I ate
some roast beef. In the afternoon we sat and talked till
about 4 o'clock and then I caused my people to set him over
the river and then I walked with the women about the
plantation till they were very weary. At night we ate some
eggs and drank some Virginia beer and talked very gravely
without reading anything. However I said my prayers and
spoke with all my people. I had good health, good thoughts,
and good humor, thank God Almighty. I danced my dance
in the morning.

31. I rose about 7 o'clock and read a chapter in Hebrew
and six leaves in Lucian. I said my prayers and ate boiled
milk for breakfast. The weather continued warm and clear.
I settled my accounts and wrote several things till dinner. I
danced my dance. I ate some turkey and chine for dinner.
In the afternoon I weighed some money and then read some
Latin in Terence and then Mr. Mumford came and told me

my man Tony had been very sick but he was recovered again, thank God. He told me Robin Bolling had been like to die and that he denied that he was the first to mention the imposition on skins which he certainly did. Then he and I took a walk about the plantation. When I returned I was out of humor to find the negroes all at work in our chambers. At night I ate some broiled turkey with Mr. Mumford and we talked and were merry all the evening. I said my prayers and had good health, good thoughts, and good humor, thank God Almighty. My wife and I had a terrible quarrel about whipping Eugene while Mr. Mumford was there but she had a mind to show her authority before company but I would not suffer it, which she took very ill; however for peace sake I made the first advance towards a reconciliation which I obtained with some difficulty and after abundance of crying. However it spoiled the mirth of the evening, but I was not conscious that I was to blame in that quarrel.

January, 1712

1. I lay abed till 9 o'clock this morning to bring my wife into temper again and rogered her by way of reconciliation. I read nothing because Mr. Mumford was here, nor did I say my prayers, for the same reason. However I ate boiled milk for breakfast, and after my wife tempted me to eat some pancakes with her. Mr. Mumford and I went to shoot with our bows and arrows but shot nothing, and afterwards we played at billiards till dinner, and when we came we found Ben Harrison[1] there, who dined with us. I ate some partridge for dinner. In the afternoon we played at billiards again and I won two bits. I had a letter from Colonel Duke by H-l the bricklayer who came to offer his services to work for me. Mr. Mumford went away in the evening and John Bannister with him to see his mother. I took a walk about the plantation and at night we drank some mead of my wife's making which was very good. I gave the people some cider and a dram to the negroes. I read some Latin in Terence and had good health, good thoughts, and good humor, thank God Almighty. I said my prayers.

2. I rose about 7 o'clock and read two chapters in Hebrew and some Greek in Lucian. I said my prayers and ate boiled milk for breakfast. I danced my dance. It rained pretty much in the night and was cloudy this morning. I settled several accounts and wrote a letter to Colonel Duke. About 12 o'clock came Colonel Eppes but could not stay because he was obliged to go to court. A little before dinner came Ben Harrison in his best clothes, because he happened to come yesterday in his worst. He dined with us and I ate roast beef and before we had done Colonel Hill and Mrs. Harrison came and the Colonel ate some pudding with us, but Mrs. Harrison ate nothing. They went away about 4 o'clock and then my wife and I went to

---

[1]Only son of Benjamin Harrison II of Berkeley.

walk about the plantation and saw some young trees that Tom had planted this day. At night I read some Terence till almost 10 o'clock. I said my prayers and had good health, good thoughts, and good humor, thank God Almighty. My mulatto Jacky came from Falling Creek with a very sore arm and told me all was well there, thank God.

3. I rose about 7 o'clock and read two chapters in Hebrew and some Greek in Lucian. I said my prayers and ate boiled milk for breakfast. I danced my dance and then settled several accounts. The weather was very clear and cold. Mr. Bland's sloop brought two hogsheads of cider and 66 hides from Williamsburg which were put ashore. I read some Latin till dinner and then I ate some roast pork. I gave Anaka a good scolding for letting Billy Brayne have a hole in his stocking. In the afternoon I set my razor and then went to prune the trees in the young orchard and then I took a walk about the plantation and my wife and Mrs. Dunn came to walk with me. At night I read some Latin in Terence and then we drank some cider. I said my prayers and had good health, good thoughts, and good humor, thank God Almighty.

4. I rose about 7 o'clock and read two chapters in Hebrew and some Greek in Homer. I said my prayers and ate boiled milk for breakfast. I danced my dance and then settled several accounts. The weather was clear and warm. My wife was indisposed with the colic but recovered pretty soon again, thank God, by the help of good drams of caraway water. I took a walk in the garden till dinner. I ate no meat this day but only fruit. In the afternoon I weighed some money and then went into the new orchard to trim some trees and stayed there till it was dark almost and then took a little walk about the plantation. In the evening Tom Turpin brought 30 hogs from the Falls and told me all was well, thank God. At night I read some Latin in Terence and said my prayers and had good health, good thoughts, and good humor, thank God Almighty. I ate some broiled turkey for supper.

5. I rose about 7 o'clock and read nothing because Tom Turpin was here. He came with 30 hogs from the Falls. He told me all was well above. I said my prayers and ate boiled milk for breakfast. I danced my dance. About 9 o'clock came Major Harrison and the captain of the "Pelican". I gave them a bottle of sack. Then we played at billiards and I won 7 shillings, and sixpence. About one o'clock we went to dinner and I ate some boiled beef. In the afternoon we were merry and made the Quaker captain drink the Queen's health on his knees. About 2 o'clock came my brother and sister Custis and sat down to dinner. They brought no news. My sister was much tired. In the evening the captain and Major Harrison went away to Mrs. Harrison's where I understood that Mr. Clayton was come. We drank a bottle of wine at night. This day a negro of mine at Falling Creek had a tree fall on his head and had his brains beat out. I neglected to say my prayers and had good health, good thoughts, and good humor, thank God Almighty.

6. I rose about 8 o'clock because my wife made me lie in bed and I rogered her. I read nothing and neglected to say my prayers but had boiled milk for breakfast. About 10 o'clock came Mr. Clayton and brought me two English letters without any news because they were of an old date. I gave him a dram and about 11 o'clock we walked to church where we heard a good sermon from Mr. Anderson. I invited Colonel Hill to dine with me and ate wild goose for dinner. In the afternoon it rained so that Colonel Hill agreed to stay all night. In the evening we drank a supper bottle and were merry with nonsense but Colonel Hill's head ached a little. However it did not mar the supper or conversation. The Colonel is a man of good sense and good principles notwithstanding what has been said of him. I neglected to say my prayers but had good health, good thoughts, and good humor, thank God Almighty.

7. I rose about 7 o'clock and read nothing because we prepared to go to Colonel Hill's. I ate chocolate for breakfast. I said a short prayer. About 10 o'clock our ladies

made a shift to get dressed, when we got on horseback and
my horse was very frolicsome. The weather was cold and
very clear. We called at Captain Llewellyn's and took Lew
Eppes and his wife with us to Colonel Hill's, where we
found all well. We were as merry as we could be, considering there was but little [w—]. About 2 o'clock we went to
dinner and I ate some boiled pork for dinner. In the afternoon we went to see the ship and found them far advanced.
Then we returned and saw my sloop bringing to at the
Hundred, where my people left behind 50 bushels of wheat
from G-r-l. In the evening we were very merry and the
women offered violence to me because I would not dance and
my wife quarrelled with her sister because she would not
dance. About 10 o'clock we went to bed. I recommended
myself and my family to the protection of Almighty God,
and had good health, good thoughts, and good humor, thank
God Almighty.

8. I rose about 7 o'clock and read a little in Horace. I
neglected to say my prayers because the women came in
with a dram of strong water of which I [drank] two drams.
Then I left the women and went to the men and talked
with them. About 9 o'clock came Colonel Frank Eppes to
discourse with me concerning the rangers in the upper county
and he told me nobody would accept of that place because
the pay was too little. I ate some roast beef for breakfast
for breakfast [sic] contrary to my custom. About 10 o'clock
we went away home and found all well, thank God. We
expected Mr. Clayton and Major Harrison from Prince
George court and therefore we ordered dinner late. About
3 o'clock came Dr. Cocke and brought me some English
letters, by which I learned there were plenipotentiaries appointed to agree about a peace, which God prosper. About
5 o'clock came Mr. Clayton, Major Harrison, and his
brother Harry. We went to supper and I ate some boiled
beef. We were very merry and I gave them some of my
best wine. We played at cards and I won 15 shillings. I
neglected to say my prayers because the company kept me

up late but I had good health, good thoughts, and good
humor, thank God Almighty. Parson Finney dined with
us also and stayed all night.

9. I rose about 7 o'clock and found the weather exceedingly cold. I neglected to say my prayers because of the
company. However I drank chocolate for breakfast and
ate some cake. After breakfast we went to [p-l-y] and I
won £10 at cards. About 10 o'clock Major Harrison and
his brother Harry went away but the rest of the company
was persuaded to stay a day longer, only Parson Finney,
who went away likewise. Mr. Clayton and I took a walk
till dinner and then I ate some roast mutton which was very
good. My sloop went away this morning to Falling Creek.
In the afternoon we were merry without drinking but did
not venture out because of the [. . .] cold weather. In the
evening Peter came from the Falls and told me all was well,
thank God. We drank some of my best wine and were
merry but would not let the women part from us. About
10 we ate some bread and cheese and drank a bottle on it,
and about 11 we went to bed. My wife had got some cold
and was disordered in her hip. I neglected to say my
prayers but had good health, good thoughts, and good
humor, thank God Almighty, only I was a little displeased
at a story somebody had told the Governor that I had said
that no Governor ought to be trusted with £20,000.[1] Little
Peter brought a wild goose with him and two ducks.

10. I rose about 7 o'clock and found it terribly cold. My
wife was a little better. I neglected my prayers and ate
boiled milk for breakfast but the company ate some chicken
pie. About 11 o'clock my company took leave and went
away and then I could do everything which too much company had hindered me from. I read this day no Hebrew
nor Greek in Lucian but read my English letters and settled
some accounts. Mr. Chamberlayne came from Appomattox

---

[1]In order to carry on the war against the Tuscaroras, the Burgesses
attempted to raise £20,000 by extraordinary taxes. Byrd's disgruntlement
with the whole scheme appears not only in this remark about trusting the
Governor with such a sum, but also in his indignation against Robin Bolling
(Dec. 31, 1711) who suggested taxing skins. (See *JHB*, 1702-1712, pp. 324-25.)

and told me all was well there, thank God. He would dine
with me whether I asked him or not and I ate roast beef.
In the afternoon I weighed some money and settled some
accounts till the evening and then took a walk about the
plantation. Redskin Peter pretended he fell and hurt himself but it was dissimulation. I had a cow die this day. At
night I read some Latin in Terence. Then I said my prayers
and had good health, good thoughts, and good humor, thank
God Almighty.

11. I rose about 7 o'clock and read two chapters in
Hebrew and some Greek in Lucian. I said my prayers and
ate boiled milk for breakfast. I danced my dance. It was
not so cold as it has been because the wind came to south.
My wife was a little indisposed with a cold. I settled several
accounts and put many things in order till dinner. I ate
some raspberries for dinner. In the afternoon I set my
razor and then went into the new orchard and trimmed the
trees till the evening and then I took a walk about the
plantation. Redskin Peter was very well again after he had
worn the bit 24 hours and went to work very actively. Before I came in I took a run for my health. At night I read
some Latin in Terence. I said my prayers and had thoughts
[sic], good health, and good humor, thank God Almighty.

12. I rose about 8 o'clock and read two chapters in
Hebrew and some Greek in Lucian. I said my prayers
devoutly and ate boiled milk for breakfast. I danced my
dance. Jacky's arm was almost well, thank God. The
weather was warm but the wind was northeast. My wife
was well again, thank God, and went about again as usual.
I read some Latin in Terence till dinner and then I ate some
roast pork. In the afternoon I went into the orchard and
trimmed the young trees till I was called away by one of the
girls who told me that Mr. Peter Butts[1] would speak with
me. His business was to desire me to get a sheriff's place
for his brother and in order to persuade me to it told me
several things of Ned [Goodrich] and how he had once hin-

---

[1] Perhaps the brother of Thomas Butts, appointed sheriff of New Kent
County in April, 1712.

dered my man Tony from paying £30 for lying with an Indian wife. A man came from New Kent concerning a protested bill and he stayed here all night. In the evening I took a walk and at night read some Latin in Terence. I said my prayers and had good health, good thoughts, and good humor, thank God Almighty.

13. I rose about 8 o'clock and read two chapters in Hebrew and some Greek in Lucian. I said my prayers and ate boiled milk for breakfast. I danced my dance. The weather was clear and the wind northeast. My wife was indisposed a little again and went to walk about the plantation. About 12 o'clock Mr. Bland came on his way to Williamsburg. He stayed and dined with us and I ate some boiled beef. In the afternoon we sat and talked about the news that came in my last letters till about 4 o'clock and then Mr. Bland went away to Captain Stith's and I went to walk about the plantation and went into the swamp, which was frozen very hard. In the evening Mr. G-r-l came from Falling Creek and told me all was well there except my negro smith who was lame and they feared had the pox. At night we talked of several things relating to my estate. I said my prayers and had good health, good thoughts, and good humor, thank God Almighty.

14. I rose about 7 o'clock and read two chapters in Hebrew and some Greek in Lucian. I said my prayers and ate boiled milk for breakfast. I danced my dance. I made Mr. G-r-l put on several locks and put up the cornice for my curtains in the library. I settled the accounts he brought with him and found him still in my debt above £40. I settled the Shockoe accounts of Mr. M-r-s-l till dinner and then I ate boiled hare and onions. My wife continued out of order and had sometimes a pain in her side but would not be let blood. In the afternoon I worked in the library with Mr. G-r-l and helped him till the evening and then I took a short walk. At night I wrote out his accounts and had some discourse with him concerning matters at Falling Creek. He complained he had too few people there and however confessed he used them for his business sometimes.

I said a short prayer and had good health, good thoughts, and good humor, thank God Almighty. My wife sweated much in the night.

15. I rose about 7 o'clock but read nothing because I wrote some letters and one especially to Will Randolph concerning what I learned the Governor had [been] informed concerning my saying no Governor ought to be trusted with £20,000, and he owned he had told it because I had said it and he thought it no secret, for which I marked him as a very false friend. I said my prayers and ate boiled milk for breakfast. I had a sore throat this morning. The weather was warm and the wind southwest. Mr. G-r-l made an end of putting up the curtain cornice in the library and then went and showed John to plant fruit trees. Drury Stith, Colonel Hill, Mr. Anderson, and Mr. Platt came to see me and put me in mind of the vestry. However we ate our dinner first and I ate some roast mutton. Then we went to the vestry and among other things agreed to make a well in the churchyard. In the evening I was out of humor because my wife broke open Will Randolph's letter. I read some Terence at night and wrote in my journal. Mr. G-r-l went away in the evening. I said my prayers and had good health, good thoughts, and good humor, thank God Almighty.

16. I rose about 7 o'clock and read a chapter in Hebrew and some Greek in Lucian. I said my prayers and ate boiled milk for breakfast. I danced my dance. My wife was something better and rode out because it was very fine weather and not cold. We killed a beef this morning that came yesterday from Burkland where they were all well, thank God. I settled some accounts till dinner and then I ate some hash of beef. In the afternoon my wife shaved me and then I walked out to see my people plant trees and I was angry with John for mistaking Mr. G-r-l's directions. Then I showed him again and helped him plant several trees. Then I took a walk till night. When I came in my [wife] persuaded me me [sic] to eat skim milk for supper. Then I read some Latin in Terence. I said my prayers and had

good thoughts, good humor, and good health, thank God Almighty. I dreamed a coffin was brought into my house and thrown into the hall.

17. I rose about 7 o'clock and read a chapter in Hebrew and some Greek in Lucian. I said my prayers and ate boiled milk for breakfast. I danced my dance. When I got up I thought to ride to Falling Creek but the weather threatened snow and the wind northeast, which discouraged me from my journey. About 12 o'clock I went to see John and Tom plant the peach orchard where I stayed till dinner was ready. I ate some beefsteak. In the afternoon I looked over some books with pictures for half an hour and then went again to my people to see them plant trees. I stayed there a little time and then went to take a walk about the plantation to examine what the rest had done and was contented with the overseer's management. I also saw all the cattle, which seem to be in good condition. At night I resisted my wife's temptation to eat milk and read some Latin in Terence. I said my prayers and had good health, good thoughts, and good humor, thank God Almighty.

18. I rose about 7 o'clock and read a chapter in Hebrew and some Greek in Lucian. I said my prayers and ate boiled milk for breakfast. I danced my dance. The weather was clear and cold but the wind was northeast. I settled several accounts and then read some Latin in Terence till dinner, and then I ate some boiled beef but I was displeased with my wife for giving the child marrow against my opinion. In the afternoon I read a little more Latin and then went to see my people plant peach trees and afterwards took a great walk about the plantation and found everything in order, for which I praised God. I was entertained with seeing a hawk which had taken a small bird pursued by another hawk, so that he was forced to let go his prey. My walk lasted till the evening and at night I read some Latin in Terence. I said my prayers and had good health, good thoughts, and good humor, thank God Almighty.

19. I rose about 7 o'clock and read a chapter in Hebrew and some Greek in Lucian. I said my prayers and ate boiled

milk for breakfast. I danced my dance. The weather [was] cloudy and rained a little. Two people came here for rights, which I gave them and a dram to comfort them in the bad weather. I read some Latin in Terence till dinner and then I ate some fish. In the afternoon it held up and I took a walk to see my people plant peach trees. I understood by one of the men who came for rights that the Meherrin Indians were removing from their town. The wind was at northeast. One of my sheep was killed in the pasture today. In the evening I took a walk about the plantation. At night we ate skim milk for supper and then I read some Latin in Terence. I said my prayers and had good health, good thoughts, and good humor, thank God Almighty. I dreamed a mourning coach drove into my garden and stopped at the house door.

20. It rained very hard in the beginning of the night and towards morning it snowed exceedingly and continued till about 9 o'clock. I rose about 7 and caused a path to be made to the kitchen, to the library, and to the house office. I read a chapter in Hebrew and some Greek in Lucian. The weather would not permit us to go to church. I said my prayers and ate boiled milk for breakfast. I danced my dance. After 9 o'clock it thawed very much all day. I ate wild goose for dinner. In the afternoon because I could not walk I danced my dance and then walked in the library till night and considered what [obligation] to make to the Governor for saying no Governor ought to be trusted with £20,000. At night I ate some bread and butter and drank some cider but read little or nothing. I said my prayers and had good health, good thoughts, and good humor, thank God Almighty.

21. I rose about 7 o'clock and read a chapter in Hebrew and some Greek in Lucian. I said my prayers and ate boiled milk for breakfast. I danced my dance. The weather was clear and pretty warm. I was out of humor because I missed a book out of the library which I thought my wife had taken for Mrs. Dunn without my knowledge, but she denied it. Mr. Peter Poythress came to our house and

brought me a letter from my brother Custis who told me
the Governor was angry about what I had said concerning
the £20,000. He stayed and dined and I ate roast mutton
for dinner. In the afternoon came Mr. M-r-s-l and told
me all were well at Falling Creek except Jacky who was
grown worse in his arm again. I settled accounts with him.
About 4 o'clock came Mr. Mumford and told me all was
well at Appomattox. In the evening I took a walk. At
night I ate some mutton with Mr. Mumford. I said my
prayers and had good health, good thoughts, and good
humor, thank God Almighty.

22. I rose about 7 o'clock and read nothing because I
prepared to go to Williamsburg. The weather was cloudy
and it rained about 10 o'clock. I said my prayers and ate
boiled milk for breakfast. About 11 o'clock came Colonel
Eppes and Colonel Hill, the first came to inquire what he
should do further about the rangers because people refused.
They stayed [till] 12 o'clock and then went away. I ate
some tripe and then notwithstanding it rained resolved to
ride as far as my brother Duke's and accordingly I recommended my family to heaven and got on my horse about 2
o'clock and got to Mr. Duke's about 5 and there I found the
Colonel and all in good health. In the evening I ate some
roast beef and Mr. Duke gave us a bottle of wine. We sat
up till about 9 o'clock and then I said my prayers and had
good health, good thoughts, and good humor, thank God
Almighty.

23. I rose about 7 o'clock and found it had snowed very
much and continued so to do and the wind blew hard at
northeast. I said my prayers and because I could get no
milk I ate some hashed beef for breakfast. About 10
o'clock the wind began to abate and then we made a shift to
go over the river with our horses and then rode to Colonel
Duke's and there I ate some toast and cider. All this time
it continued to snow but held up about 2 o'clock and then
I took leave of the Colonel, who promised me to follow me
next day, and rode in about three hours to my brother
Custis' and found them all well there. Here I ate nothing

but some boiled milk for supper. We talked about Mrs. Russell and the Governor, not much to the advantage of the first. My sister loves to talk a little scandal of her neighbors. I said my prayers and had good health, good thoughts, and good humor, thank God Almighty.

24. I rose about 7 o'clock and read nothing but said my prayers and ate boiled milk for breakfast. I was a little perplexed what to say to the Governor to extenuate what I had said but I was resolved to say the truth, let the consequence be what it would. About 12 o'clock I and my brother went to town and lighted at my lodgings. Then I went to the coffeehouse where I found Mr. Clayton and he and I went to the Governor. He made us wait half an hour before he was pleased to come out to us and when he came he looked very stiff and cold on me but did not explain himself. At last several of the council came in and paid their compliments to the Governor, who invited us to dinner and six of the council dined there and I ate some boiled pork for dinner. We stayed till it was dark and then went to the coffeehouse where I stayed till 10 o'clock and then went home to my lodgings. I said my prayers and had good health, good thoughts, and good humor, thank God Almighty. There were 25 of the Burgesses met today which was more than could be expected, considering the weather.

25. I rose about 7 o'clock and read two chapters in Hebrew and some Greek in Homer. I said my prayers and put several things in order. I had several people at my chambers with whom I settled some business. We had nothing to do but meet in order to adjourn and the Burgesses did little else unless it was to adhere to their Book of Claims, which put the Governor out of humor with them. The weather was very cold and much snow on the ground, so that I went with boots. About 2 o'clock Colonel Smith and I went to the Governor's to dinner and I ate some cod sounds.[1] I perceived Mrs. Russell to be very cold and stiff

---

[1] The swimming bladder of the cod. Mrs. Elizabeth Raffald, in *The Experienced English Housekeeper* (1778), gives directions for dressing cod sounds.

in her behavior to me. However we were pretty easy. We stayed there till about 7 o'clock and then went to the coffeehouse, where I lost £2 at piquet. About 10 I went to my lodgings where I said my prayers and had good health, good thoughts, and good humor, thank God Almighty.

26. I rose about 7 o'clock and read two chapters in Hebrew and some Greek in Homer. I said my prayers and ate boiled milk for breakfast. I settled several accounts and had several people come to my lodgings. I wrote a letter to my wife. The weather was clear and good; however I wore my boots. The Governor continued stiff to me but I took no notice of it but behaved myself very courteously to him, when he came in my way. About 3 o'clock we dined at Mrs. [Serjanton's]¹ and I ate roast chicken for dinner but we were forced to dine in the kitchen but however it was very good and we made a shift to be very merry and contented. Nothing of moment was done this day either by the Burgesses or us. In the evening we went to the coffee-house where I lost £6 at piquet. John G-r-l fell from one of my horses as he was riding them to water and had like to broke his neck but was bled and so got no hurt. I said my prayers and had good health, good thoughts, and good humor, thank God Almighty.

27. I rose about 7 o'clock and read two chapters in Hebrew and some Greek in Homer. I said my prayers and ate custard for breakfast. The weather was clear and cold. I had my head shaved by my old man Daniel, who told me he was to live with Mr. Page. About 11 o'clock came Colonel Smith. We stayed in town and Colonel Duke and we walked to church where we expected Parson Anderson to preach but he disappointed us so that Mr. Commissary was forced to give us a sermon. After, we went home with the Commissary to dinner and I ate some roast goose and we were very merry with a dream Colonel Duke had concerning Mrs. Harrison. We were well entertained both

¹There was a John Serjanton (Serginton) who owned land in York County in 1704, and a Dr. John Serganton of Williamsburg some time later. (*Va. Mag.*, XXXI, 70; *Wm. Q. (1)*, XVI, 14.)

with victuals and company till about 5 o'clock and then
walked to the coffeehouse where we talked till about 8
o'clock and then I went home and found my man Jack who
had brought the Doctor's coach but was three days in coming. He brought me a letter from my wife by which I found
all were well. I read some English and then said my prayers and had good health, good thoughts, and good humor,
thank God Almighty.

28. I rose about 7 o'clock and read a chapter in Hebrew
and some Greek in Homer. I said my prayers and ate
chocolate for breakfast. I had several gentlemen at my
chambers. I wrote another letter to my wife and sent home
Jack with the coach horses. I settled several accounts and
then went to the capitol, where I danced my dance. The
weather was clear and cold. We dined at 2 o'clock this day
because the Governor was to come at 3 o'clock to make a
speech to the Burgesses. I ate some boiled pork for dinner.
The Governor made a very long speech and much softer
than the last. When that was done we went to the coffeehouse where the governors of the College were to meet
about several matters and particularly about Tanaquil
Faber[1] and they turned him out of his place but gave him,
however, his salary for the whole year. They agreed to
give Mr. Tullitt £400 to build up the College hall. Then
we played at piquet and I lost £7. About 10 I went home
and said my prayers and had good health, good thoughts,
and good humor, thank God Almighty.

29. I rose about 7 o'clock and read two chapters in
Hebrew and some Greek in Homer. I said my prayers and
ate chocolate for breakfast. Several gentlemen came to see
me and particularly Major Harrison, who told me that my
wife came on Friday last to Colonel Harrison's and the
next day to his house with Mrs. Ludwell, where she stayed
till Monday morning. He paid me £3 he owed me. About
12 o'clock I went to the capitol where I danced my dance.
Major Custis came to town and told me all was well at his

---

[1]Or LeFevre. See note under date of April 17, 1711.

house. The Doctor came to me at the capitol and we talked about the Governor being out of humor with what I had said concerning the £20,000. We met just to adjourn and then went to dinner and I ate some wild duck. In the afternoon I took a walk to the Governor's new house and so returned to the coffeehouse where we played at dice and I played with good luck and won 50 shillings clear and the Doctor was among us. About 10 I went home and said a short prayer and had good health, good thoughts, and good humor, thank God Almighty, but in bed I committed uncleanness for which God forgive me. My man Tom brought me a letter from home by which I learned that all were well, thank God, but my little panther which he brought for the Governor died by the way.

30. I rose about 7 o'clock and read 2 chapters in Hebrew and some Greek in Homer. I said my prayers and ate boiled milk for breakfast. I wrote a letter to my wife which I sent home by Tom again with my horse. Several people came to see me and I received 3 pounds, 15 shillings for my first escheat[1] from Major B-s. The weather was warm but cloudy, the wind southeast. The Governor went to church but I did not because I heard of it too late but went to the coffeehouse where I played at piquet and won 50 shillings. Then I went to the capitol where I danced my dance and then read some Italian till 3 o'clock and then went to dinner and ate some roast turkey. After dinner I took a walk to the College and the Governor's great house and then returned to the coffeehouse where I stayed about an hour and then went to my lodgings where I wrote in my journal and then read some English till about 10 o'clock. I said my prayers and had good health, good thoughts, and good humor, thank God Almighty.

31. I rose about 7 o'clock and read two chapters in Hebrew and some Greek in Homer. I said my prayers and ate milk for breakfast. It rained very much this morning

---

[1] See entry for April 22, 1711; Byrd apparently became escheator for the south side of the James River when the place was vacated by the death of William Randolph. (See also *Va. Mag.*, II, 2.)

as well as in the night. About 10 o'clock our doorkeeper
came to me and told me that the Governor was going to the
capitol with the Council. This made me get ready and then
I went to the capitol where I found the Governor complaining that the House of Burgesses had passed several resolutions which made it plain they intended to spend their time
only in dispute and then he commanded Mr. Robinson [i. e.,
Robertson]¹ to order the speaker and the house to attend
him and when they came he dissolved them after a short
speech and then proposed how he should perform the treaty
made with the Indians. Everybody was silent for some time
and then I said notwithstanding there was no money in my
hands belonging to the Queen; however rather than either
Her Majesty's interest or the country's should suffer I would
advance £500 to pay the Indians with in case they performed their treaty. The Governor took [it?] and the
rather because nobody seconded me. Then we rose and I
went home with the Governor in his coach to dine with him.
I ate some boiled goose for dinner. Several of the Burgesses came after dinner to take leave of the Governor and
about 5 o'clock I took my leave and went to the coffeehouse
where I played till about 2 o'clock in the morning and
neither won nor lost. I said a short prayer and had good
health, good thoughts, and good humor, thank God Almighty. I desired the Doctor to give the servants 5 shillings
each for me. I advised the Governor to finish the fort at
Point Comfort and pay it out of the contingency charges,
which he seemed to agree to.

¹William Robertson, clerk of the Assembly.

February, 1712

1. I rose about 7 o'clock but read nothing because several gentlemen came to settle accounts with me and because I prepared to go out of town. I sent a letter home by Frank Eppes to let them know my brother Custis would lend me horses to return home. I ate boiled milk for breakfast and recommended myself to heaven in a short prayer. I took leave of Mrs. Bland and thanked her for all her kindness and ordered G-r-l to give her servants money. Then I went to the coffeehouse to pay my debts and went from thence to the Commissary's where I stayed to dine and I ate goose giblets for dinner. In the evening I went to Major Custis and found him a little out of humor that I had not come there to dinner. However that was soon over. He gave me some very good cider. We talked about all our affairs till about 10 o'clock and then I said my prayers and had good health, good thoughts, and very good humor, thank God Almighty.

2. I rose about 7 o'clock and prepared for my journey. My brother and sister agreed to go with me to Mount Folly. I said my prayers and ate boiled milk for breakfast. About 10 o'clock we were ready and got on horseback and by the way saw Skimino mill and then called on George Keeling and I threatened to arrest him about a bill of exchange. Then we went to Mount Folly and rode about the Neck and found it fit to raise [the stock]. About one o'clock we ate some cold roast beef which we had brought with us and then away we went to Colonel Duke's and by the way my brother Custis and I made a bargain that I should have the land and negroes that were to be sold by act of Assembly, and pay all Colonel Parke's debts.[1] About 4 o'clock we reached

[1] Daniel Parke had left Mrs. Byrd only £1,000 and had bequeathed his Virginia and English property to her older sister, Frances Custis. Parke's debts were charged against this property, and the Assembly had passed an act empowering her to sell a mill [Skimino] and certain lands and negroes to pay the debts. (*JHB*, 1702-1712, p. 356.) Byrd's bargain, to take the lands and pay the debts, proved a hard one, for the debts were a good deal heavier than he had imagined. (*Va. Mag.*, XX, 372; XXXV, 377-79.)

Colonel Duke's just as it began to rain. The Colonel was very kind but had no more than one bottle of wine. I ate some cold chicken for supper and then we sat and talked till 9 o'clock. Then I took my leave and said a short prayer and had good health, good thoughts, and good humor, thank God Almighty. It rained all night pretty hard.

3. I rose about 9 o'clock and the reason I lay so long in bed was to consider about our bargain whether I had best agree to it or no. I said a short prayer and ate boiled milk for breakfast. It rained all day so that we could not start from hence. I was computing the profit of my bargain almost all day. We sat by a good fire and discoursed our affairs till 2 o'clock and then we went to dinner and I ate some roast turkey but we had no wine and only bad cider so that we were dull through the bad weather and had nothing to arm our spirits. However we made a shift to wear out the day in chatting and the Colonel is always good company and is kind as far as he is able. I wrote several heads of agreement between my brother Custis and myself. Colonel Duke and his maid were ready to quarrel several times by which I told I told [sic] him it was plain he was too familiar at other times, but the Colonel denied it stiffly. His man B-n-ch was sick and I caused G-r-l to let him blood. I said my prayers and had good health, good thoughts, and good humor, thank God Almighty.

4. I rose about 7 o'clock and wrote out the articles of agreement between Mr. Custis and his wife and myself. I said my prayers to bring a blessing on our business and ate boiled milk for breakfast. At last we signed and sealed our bargain and God Almighty give it a blessing. The weather was grown clear and warm. I desired the Colonel to take care of my rent tobacco. About 11 o'clock we took our leave of the Colonel and of one another and about two miles from thence I met my brother Duke who turned back with me again and we went over the river to his house, where I found my sister well and her child. My brother's boat was not good but because I came often that way I promised to present him with a boat if he would send for it. I went with

him to his mill and then took my leave of them and rode home, where I got about 4 o'clock and found all well, thank God. I ate some partridge for supper. We talked away the evening and I told my wife of the bargain and she was not pleased with it. I said my prayers in short and had good health, good thoughts, and good humor, thank God Almighty. I found the sloop here.

5. I rose about 8 o'clock, my wife kept me so long in bed where I rogered her. I read nothing because I put my matters in order. I neglected to say my prayers but ate boiled milk for breakfast. My wife caused several of the people to be whipped for their laziness. I settled accounts and put several matters in order till dinner. I ate some boiled beef. In the afternoon I ordered my sloop to go to Colonel Eppes' for some poplar trees for the Governor and then I went to visit Mrs. Harrison that I found in a small way. She entertained me with apples and bad wine and I stayed with her till evening and then I took a walk about my plantation. When I returned I learned Peter Poythress had been here. At night I read some Latin. I said my prayers and had good health, good thoughts, and good humor, thank God Almighty. I rogered my wife again.

6. I rose about 7 o'clock and read two chapters in Hebrew and a little Greek. I said my prayers shortly and ate boiled milk for breakfast. I settled some accounts but was interrupted by John Eppes who came to see me and soon after two masters of ships and I promised 25 hogsheads to one of them that commanded the *Pelican*. Soon after them came Colonel Hill and I walked with him to court where I invited several people to dinner and two masters of ships among the rest. I ate bacon and pigeon for dinner. In the afternoon the company went away and I wrote two letters, one to G-r-l and one to my receiver. Colonel Eppes came and told me that my sloop was at his house and got trees. In the evening I took a walk about the plantation and at night I read some Latin and wrote in my journal. I said my prayers and had good health, good thoughts, and good humor, thank God Almighty.

7. I rose about 7 o'clock and found it raining very hard. I read two chapters in Hebrew and some Greek in Lucian. I said my prayers and ate boiled milk for breakfast. I danced my dance. Jack was indisposed with a cold and looseness for which I bled him and gave him two glasses of broth. Jenny was better, thank God Almighty. About 10 o'clock came the sloop with about 70 poplar trees. It rained hard almost all day. Tom returned about 11 o'clock and brought me several letters by which I learned that the Indians continued still their hostilities in Carolina. I ate some partridge for dinner. In the afternoon I wrote several letters to the Governor and others to send by my sloop. I gave my cousin Harrison leave to put some clapboards on board my sloop to go to Williamsburg. In the evening I danced my dance again because the ground was wet that I could not walk. At night I read some Latin and wrote a letter to Mr. Bland. I said my prayers and had good health, good thoughts, and good humor, thank God Almighty. The wind came to northwest.

8. I rose about 7 o'clock and read two chapters in Hebrew and some Greek in Lucian. I said my prayers and ate boiled milk for breakfast. I danced my dance. I caused my man Jack to be bled again for his pain in the side and then he found himself better. I read some Latin in Terence. About 11 o'clock came Captain Drury Stith partly to make a visit and partly to get some of the quitrents, and soon after him came Colonel Eppes and John Eppes to account with me. However I desired them to dine first and I ate some fish for dinner of which we caught a great quantity this morning. In the afternoon we settled our accounts and about 4 o'clock the company went away and I took a walk about the plantation with the women and we were very merry. The weather was very clear and cold. My sloop went away in the night for Williamsburg with 1,000 feet of planks for the market and some fruit trees for the Governor. At night I read nothing because I wrote four letters. I said my prayers and had good health, good thoughts, and good humor, thank God Almighty. Negro P-t-s-n was taken sick.

9. I rose about 7 o'clock and read a chapter in Hebrew and some Greek in Lucian. I said my prayers and ate boiled milk for breakfast. I danced my dance. My brother Duke sent two negroes for the boat I promised to give him and I sent him the flat of nine hogsheads which I presented him with. I sent Tom to my brother Custis with some fish and a letter concerning our bargain.[1] I also sent Bannister to Falling Creek with my orders to Mr. G-r-l about several things. My sick people were better, thank God. I read some Latin in Terence and settled some accounts till dinner and then I ate some turkey for dinner. In the afternoon I read some more Latin in Terence and played with my girl and then took a walk about the plantation. My wife was a little indisposed with the coming of her moon. At night I read some Latin in Terence and had good health, good thoughts, and good humor, thank God Almighty. I made a visit to the things in the cellar.

10. I rose about 7 o'clock and read two chapters in Hebrew and read some Greek in Lucian. I said my prayers devoutly and danced my dance. It rained a little in the morning a little [sic] but did not last above an hour. I read some Latin and then I went with the women to take a walk about the plantation. My sick people grew better, thank God. About 12 o'clock came Mrs. Stith to visit my wife and Frank P-t-r-m [or B-t-r-m] but neither would dine with us. I ate some roast pigeon for dinner. In the afternoon came Bannister from Falling Creek and told me all were well there and at the plantation. Mrs. Stith stayed with us all the afternoon till the evening and then went away, after which we took a walk and my wife burst herself with laughing. In the evening Tom returned from my brother Duke's and brought me some letters. At night I read nothing but we drank a bottle of wine to the health of all our friends. I said my prayers and had good health, good thoughts, and good humor, thank God Almighty. Negro Sue was taken sick at the quarters and I caused her to be bled.

---

[1] See *Va. Mag.*, XXXV, 380-82, for Byrd's letters to Custis at this time.

11. I rose about 7 o'clock and read nothing because I prepared to go my journey. I said my prayers and ate boiled milk for breakfast. I danced my dance. I recommended my family and particularly my sick people to God's protection and about 10 o'clock rode to Captain Drury Stith's. He told me that Mr. Anderson was very sick of a fever. I would have gone to see him had I not been obliged to meet Mr. Custis. However I desired Captain Stith to tell him if I had anything at my house that he desired it should be at his service. About 2 o'clock I proceeded to Mr. Fleming's where I got about 5 o'clock. Here I met Mr. Custis, who told me his family was well. We were courteously used here, and I saw two pretty daughters of Mr. Fleming. I ate some turkey for supper and ate heartily but it was [late first]. Then we talked till about 10 o'clock and then retired to bed. I said a short prayer and had good health, good thoughts, and good humor, thank God Almighty. We saw three moons.

12. I rose about 7 o'clock and said a short prayer. The weather threatened rain. Mr. Custis and I talked about all our affairs. I sent one of my servants with a negro shoemaker, which I had bought of Mr. Custis, to Falling Creek. About 9 o'clock I ate some chicken for breakfast and about 10 took our leave and rode up to the quarters at Parke [Level]. We saw everything there and then went to Parke Hall where a negro woman was sick of a pain in the side. I caused her to be bled and then ate some bacon and eggs. In the afternoon we went over the river to Parke Meadow and from thence to Parke Manor, which two plantations are in King William County. We found the land extraordinarily good and very level. Then we returned over the river to Parke [Level] where we ate some boiled shoat; then we discoursed of all our affairs. I said a short prayer and had good health, good thoughts, and good humor, thank God Almighty. We made peace between two poor men.

13. I rose about 7 o'clock and said a short prayer and ate milk for breakfast. Mr. Custis removed several of his

negroes and those which I had bought were still on the
plantation. About 10 o'clock we rode to the plantation
called Mount Pleasant and examined everything and I found
all the plantation in good order. Then we returned to
Parke Hall and went over the river and walked about the
low ground at Parke Meadow which had the best timber I
ever saw. It rained a little in the afternoon. I was much
pleased with this land. Captain Anderson came to account
with Mr. Custis and they had a dispute which Mr. D-m-n-y
decided. We returned in the evening to our lodgings where
we ate some roast fowl. Mr. Custis had brought some cider
and I some wine so that we fared well. Mr. Custis told
me several things concerning managing the overseers which
I resolved to remember. I said my prayers and had good
health, good thoughts, and good humor, thank God Almighty.

14. I rose about 7 o'clock and said a short prayer and ate
some boiled shoat for breakfast. I gave directions about
everything and promised Tom Addison I would take him
for my overseer next year for two of my plantations there.
About 10 o'clock I got a man to show me the way across the
country to the falls of James River. I took leave of Mr.
Custis in about two hours. I got to my plantation called
Shockoe about 12 o'clock, where I found all well, thank
God. I went to my two other plantations on that side and
found all things well, only little tobacco made. About 6
o'clock I returned to Shockoe and ate some boiled beef for
supper. Allen [Bailey] had almost finished the storehouse
there. I had not seen this place since the house was built
and hardly knew it again. It was very pretty. I said my
prayers and had good health, good thoughts, and good
humor, thank God Almighty. I lay at Shockoe.

15. I rose about 7 o'clock and said a short prayer and
then gave Tom Osborne orders concerning what I would
have done and then was set over the river to the Falls,
where I found things in a bad way, but little tobacco, and
that not well ordered, for which I reprimanded Tom Turpin. I ate some milk for breakfast and then I rode to

Kensington and found the tobacco as ill managed as at the Falls at which I was angry with the overseer and with old Robin. Then I crossed the northeast way to Falling Creek which was about seven miles and almost all on my land. I found all things very well and Mr. Mumford was there who told me all was well at Appomattox. Poor C-c-r continued lame but everybody else was well. My negro shoemaker was there at work full of promises to do well. I ate some boiled shoat for supper. We walked about and then went in the boat about three miles up the creek to look for a stone quarry and found several and it was late before we returned. I said my prayers and had good health, good thoughts, and good humor, thank God Almighty.

16. I rose about 7 o'clock and said a short prayer and ate boiled milk for breakfast. Then I walked to see C-c-r and the shoemaker. Captain Jefferson was at the sawmill and asked my advice concerning the dispute he is like to have about building a mill which I gave him as well as I could. I gave directions about everything and about 10 o'clock Mr. Mumford and I rode away to the Hundred where we got about one o'clock. I went to Isham Eppes' house where I found the Colonel and Frank Eppes. I stayed with them about half an hour and then went over the river and found Mr. Anderson much better and learned that Dr. Cocke had been with him and that he was gone to my house. I ate some bacon for dinner and about 4 o'clock went home where I found the Doctor and all my family well except Redskin Peter who was very sick. The Doctor brought me several letters from England. I likewise found Tom Randolph and Tom Butts there; the first offered himself to be my general overseer. We drank a bottle till about 10 o'clock. I said my prayers and had good health, good thoughts, and good humor, thank God Almighty.

17. I rose about 7 o'clock but read nothing because here was company, notwithstanding Tom Randolph went away before I was up. I drank chocolate for breakfast. Tom Butts came to buy quitrents and went away about 10 o'clock though I desired him to stay to dinner. I sent to know how

Mr. Anderson did and received word that he was better. My Redskin Peter continued very sick but the Doctor looked after him. I ate fish for dinner. In.the afternoon we took a walk but the wind was at northeast and very cold so that we soon returned. We were very merry as we always are with the Doctor. At night we drank a bottle of wine and ate some bread and cheese. Mrs. Dunn was troubled with a toothache which abated our mirth a little. Colonel Harrison's brigantine arrived from the Madeiras full of wine and brought hopes of a peace. About 10 o'clock we parted. I said a short prayer and had good health, good thoughts, and good humor, thank God Almighty.

18. I rose about 7 o'clock and read nothing. It began to snow about 8 o'clock and snowed almost all day. I said my prayers and ate boiled milk for breakfast. Notwithstanding the weather the Doctor went to see Mr. Anderson and found him better but he returned before dinner. James Bates came to buy Skimino Mill and at last agreed to take it for £248. He brought me a letter from Mr. Custis by which I learned that my sister had been ill. When Bates had secured his bargain he went away home, notwithstanding I would have had him stay to dinner. I ate some fricassee of chicken. It continued to snow all day which confined us in the house. Peter continued very sick. We were forced to play at piquet because we could not walk. I had a little of the piles and 'my wife was indisposed. At night we drank a bottle. I said my prayers and had good health, good thoughts, and good humor, thank God Almighty.

19. I rose about 7 o'clock and read nothing because. I had letters to write by the Doctor and I wrote four. I said my prayers and ate boiled milk for breakfast. Peter was very sick and the Doctor began to doubt of him. However he left directions about him in writing. About 9 o'clock came an express to summon me to the Council which was to be the next day, which made me get ready to go with the Doctor notwithstanding my piles, which were a little better. About 11 o'clock I recommended my family and in particular the sick man to God and we rode away to my brother

Duke's and from thence we went to the Colonel's, who we found very well by his own confession, and then I told him he was to go to Council the next day which made his back ache. Here we ate some milk and then proceeded to Queen's Creek, where we came about 6 o'clock and surprised the family who did not expect us. However they were pleased to see us. About 8 we ate some broiled turkey very heartily after which I grew so sleepy I could not hold open my eyes so that I was forced to go to bed. I said a short prayer and had good health, good thoughts, and good humor, thank God Almighty.

20. I rose about 7 o'clock and said my prayers and ate boiled milk for breakfast. Su Allen[1] came to buy cider and made us some spirits. My sister resolved to go to Williamsburg with us, which made us stay till 10 o'clock and then we all went together. When I had put myself in order I went with several gentlemen of the Council to wait on the Governor but he was not at home. However we saw the Doctor dissect a beaver and take out the castor which is not the stones of the beaver but two glands just above the genitals. Then we returned to the capitol to Council where the Governor laid before us a petition from the people of Carolina to send them some assistance but we after some consultation thought it necessary to answer them with the assurance that we had made a treaty with the Indians in their favor. I told the Council there was a rumor that the people of South Carolina had hired 1,000 Indians to come and cut off the Indians who had committed the massacre, and this proved true for in the evening the Governor had a letter from Governor Hyde with an account that the Assembly of South Carolina had raised £4,000 and sent about 700 Indians and some white people and had destroyed about six towns of the Indians and were about to destroy the rest. I ate some beaver for dinner at the Governor's and about

---

[1] Susannah Allen apparently kept an ordinary near Williamsburg. Her claim for dieting the 81 French prisoners in 1711 had been disallowed by the House of Burgesses and the Council finally paid her out of the "revenue of 2 shillings per hogshead." (*JHB*, 1702-1712, pp. 340, 345; *Ex. Jour.*, III, 329. See also April 19, 1712, in the diary.)

8 o'clock we went to the coffeehouse where I played at cards
till 2 o'clock in the morning and I won 27 shillings. I said a
short prayer and had good health, good thoughts, and good
humor, thank God Almighty.

21. I rose about 7 o'clock and read nothing because I
settled some business with Mr. Clayton and desired him to
draw conveyances for the land, etc., which I had bought of
Mr. Custis. He told me Mrs. Brodnax demanded something to acknowledge her husband's sale of land to me
which I refused with some indignation, but she sent to excuse
it and pretended it to be only in jest. I ate boiled milk for
breakfast. The Governor did me the honor of a visit this
morning without any business and stayed about half an hour.
Daniel Wilkinson came to tell me he was engaged to Mr.
Page or else he would serve me as a general overseer.
About 11 o'clock I went to see the Governor's avenue and
his great house which pleased him. I stayed about an hour
there and then took my leave of him and rode directly home,
where I got about 6 o'clock and found all my family pretty
well, thank God, and Redskin Peter was much better and on
the way to recovery. I ate some battered eggs for supper.
Then I said my prayers and had good health, good thoughts,
and good humor, thank God Almighty.

22. I rose about 8 o'clock and read a chapter in Hebrew
and some Greek in Lucian. I said my prayers devoutly and
ate boiled milk for breakfast. I danced my dance. I settled
several accounts and put many things in order. The weather
was very warm and it rained a little. My wife was grown
much better than when I went to Williamsburg. Redskin
Peter was better also. I ate some fish for dinner. In the
afternoon I settled more accounts and put several things in
order till the evening, and then I took a walk about the
plantation and was displeased to find the cattle was not fed
till very late, for which I reproved the overseer when I
came home and he promised it should be mended. I wrote
two letters to the Falls and wrote also in my journal. My

wife was out of humor about a triviality of nothing. I said my prayers and had good health, good thoughts, and good humor, thank God Almighty.

23. I rose about 7 o'clock and found it had rained. I read a chapter in Hebrew and some Greek in Lucian. I said my prayers and ate boiled milk for breakfast. I danced my dance. I sent Tom L-s-n to Falling Creek with some letters. It continued very warm and rained by showers. Redskin Peter was better but Quarter Jenny was sick, for which I caused her to be bled and to take the oil, which is of great use in all pain in the side and breast and has cured many pleurisies both in negroes and other people. I settled some accounts till dinner and then ate roast meat for dinner. Tom Turpin came from the Falls and told me all was well above and at Falling Creek. I settled accounts with him and owned I was out of humor with Mr. G-r-l who had drawn another note on me for £10, notwithstanding he is already deep in my debt. In the evening I took a walk about the plantation. At night I read in Milton's *Paradise Lost* in Latin.[1] I said my prayers and had good health, good .thoughts, and good humor, thank God Almighty.

24. I rose about 7 o'clock and read two chapters in Hebrew and some Greek in Lucian. I said my prayers and ate boiled milk for breakfast. I danced my dance. My man Peter was better and so was Jenny. The weather was warm and clear. My wife was indisposed. I read some Latin in Milton till dinner. Then I ate some fish for dinner. My people shot two otters this day but could not catch them. In the afternoon came Mrs. Harrison, Betty Bassett, and Betty Harrison to pay us a visit and stayed all the afternoon. In the evening I took a walk about the plantation. At night I read in Milton aloud till I was weary and very sleepy. I wrote a long letter to Mr. G-r-l in which I reprimanded him for his confidence in drawing notes on me when he owed me so much money. I said my prayers and had good health, good thoughts, and good humor, thank God Almighty.

---

[1]Byrd evidently meant Milton's Latin poems, printed with *Paradise Lost.*

25. I rose about 7 o'clock and read two chapters in
Hebrew and some Greek in Lucian. I said my prayers and
ate boiled milk for breakfast. I danced my dance. The
weather was clear and warm. I sent G-r-l and John in the
boat to Mr. Bland's for my things that came from Williamsburg. I read some Latin in Milton. About 11 o'clock came
Colonel Eppes who stayed till dinner and then came also
Colonel Hill. They both dined [with] us and I ate boiled
beef for dinner. In the afternoon came Mr. Platt who
offered to pay the £5 due to the Queen. They went away
about 5 o'clock and then I took a walk about the plantation
and my wife with me who was not well, but better than
yesterday. I wrote a letter to England and read some Latin
in Milton. My sick people was better, thank God. I said
my prayers and had good health, good thoughts, and good
humor, thank God Almighty.

26. I rose about 7 o'clock and read a chapter in Hebrew
and no Greek because I wrote some letters to England and
Williamsburg. I said my prayers and ate boiled milk for
breakfast. I danced my dance. About 10 o'clock came
Tom Butts to purchase quitrents. I sent Tom to Colonel
Hill's with my letters. I settled several accounts. About
12 o'clock came Betty Harrison and Betty Bassett and Mrs.
Anne B-k-r to dine with us and I ate some roast capon for
dinner. In the afternoon Tom Butts went away and Tom
came from Colonel Hill's with a letter by which I learned
that a ship was come from England commanded by Captain
Harvey and about an hour after I had several letters from
England which came by her which put me out of humor.
In the evening the girls went home to Mrs. Harrison's and
I took a walk about the plantation. At night I read some
news from England which gave some hopes of a peace. I
said my prayers and had good health, good thoughts, and
good humor, thank God Almighty.

27. I rose about 7 o'clock and read a chapter in Hebrew
and some Greek in Lucian. I said my prayers and ate
boiled milk for breakfast. I danced my dance. The wind
was northeast and it rained a little all day, a little cold rain.

About 10 o'clock I had letters from my overseers in New Kent by [which] I learned that all was well there, thank God. I wrote some conditions between Tom Randolph and myself in case he undertook to be my general overseer. I ate some roast beef for dinner. In the afternoon I wrote again and settled several accounts and sent away the messenger that came from New Kent. It continued to rain a little. My overseer brought a mustrat [*sic*] which I dissected and got out the musk which is in two glands not far from the anus. In the evening I could not walk and therefore danced my dance, and heard the guns of a ship come to Swinyards. At night I read some Latin in Milton and then said my prayers and had good health, good thoughts, and good humor, thank God Almighty.

28. I rose about 7 o'clock and read a chapter in Hebrew and some Greek in Lucian. I said my prayers and ate boiled milk for breakfast. I danced my dance. It continued to rain, the wind northeast. I read some English and settled some accounts. About 11 o'clock came Tom Randolph to inquire about his place of general overseer and brought me a letter from his brother Will to which I wrote an answer. Tom Randolph and I talked about the business but I desired to stay a week more before I could promise him. Lucy Hamlin came just before dinner and it then began to thunder and rain very violently. I ate some roast beef. In the afternoon Tom Randolph and I discoursed more of the business till about 4 o'clock and then he went away and I read some Latin and because it was too cold to walk I danced my dance. The wind blew very hard and very cold. At night I read some Latin in Milton. I said my prayers and had good health, good thoughts, and good humor, thank God Almighty. The wind blew very violently in the night.

29. I rose about 7 o'clock and read two chapters in Hebrew and some Greek in Lucian. I said my prayers and ate boiled milk for breakfast. I danced my dance. The wind continued to blow very hard. I read some Latin in Milton. About 11 o'clock came Captain Wilcox who came from England the 10th of January last. He brings goods

to purchase his load and then pretends there is no hope of a peace and that tobacco is like to fall again. He would not stay to dinner. My wife was indisposed. I ate some hashed beef for dinner. In the afternoon I set several things in order in my closet and then read some Latin in Milton till the evening and then I took a walk about the plantation. At night I read some Latin again in Milton. I said my prayers and had good health, good thoughts, and good humor, thank God Almighty.

March, 1712

1. I rose about 7 o'clock and read two chapters in Hebrew and some Greek in Lucian. I said my prayers and ate boiled milk for breakfast. I danced my dance. I settled some accounts and wrote a letter to England, and then read some Latin till dinner and then I ate some roast beef. Old Moll at the quarters and Jenny were very sick, for which I caused them to be bled and to take the oil. In the afternoon I set some things in order in my closet and then read some Latin till the evening and then took a walk about the plantation and went to visit the sick people and they complained they were all [. . .]. My wife and Mrs. Dunn came and walked with me till night and then I read some news. About 8 o'clock came Mr. G-r-l and I learned by him that all was well above. I said my prayers and had good health, good thoughts, and good humor, thank God Almighty.

2. I rose about 7 o'clock and read a chapter in Hebrew but no Greek because Mr. G-r-l was here and I wished to talk with him. I ate boiled milk for breakfast and danced my dance. I reprimanded him for drawing so many notes on me. However I told him if he would let me know his debts I would pay them provided he would let a mulatto of mine that is his apprentice come to work at Falling Creek the last two years of his service, which he agreed. I had a terrible quarrel with my wife concerning Jenny that I took away from her when she was beating her with the tongs. She lifted up her hands to strike me but forbore to do it. She gave me abundance of bad words and endeavored to strangle herself, but I believe in jest only. However after acting a mad woman a long time she was passive again. I ate some roast beef for dinner. In the afternoon Mr. G-r-l went away and I took a walk about the plantation. At night we drank some cider by way of reconciliation and I read nothing. I said my prayers and had good health, good thoughts, and good humor, thank God Almighty. I sent Tom

to Williamsburg with some fish to the Governor and my sister Custis. My daughter was indisposed with a small fever.

3. I rose about 7 o'clock and read a chapter in Hebrew and some Greek in Lucian. I said my prayers and ate some boiled milk for breakfast. My daughter was better this morning, thank God. I beat Billy Wilkins for telling a lie. I settled some accounts and read some Latin and then read some news till dinner and then ate some roast beef for dinner. In the afternoon I read more news and then more Latin. I danced my dance and in the evening took a walk about the plantation and my wife with me. In the evening Tom returned from Williamsburg with letters from several persons containing some public [s-s] concerning the Duke of Marlborough being removed from all his places of honor and profit and that it was talked that he was also put into the Tower. I read nothing but said my prayers and had good health, good thoughts, and good humor, thank God Almighty.

4. I rose about 7 o'clock and read some Hebrew but no Greek because I prepared to go to the wedding of Mrs. Anne B-k-r. However I said my prayers and ate boiled milk for breakfast. I danced my dance. It threatened rain but about 10 o'clock it began to snow, but that did not discourage us from our journey and a little after 10 we set out in the coach and got to Colonel Hill's before 12. We did not find much company there but only the relations and some of the next neighbors. About 12 o'clock Mr. Poythress[1] and Mrs. Anne B-k-r were married and about 2 we went to dinner and I ate some boiled tongue for dinner. We continued very grave till the evening and then we danced and were very merry. My daughter went with us and behaved herself very prettily. About 11 o'clock we went to bed. I neglected to say my prayers but had good health, good thoughts, and good humor, thank God Almighty. I was extremely merry.

---

[1] Probably Peter Poythress. In *Wm. Q. (1)*, XV, 45-71, there is a detailed study of the Poythress family. The name of Peter's wife is unknown. But he had an only daughter and heir named Anne born December 13, 1712.

5. I rose about 7 o'clock but read nothing. However I said my prayers and danced my dance before I went out of my chamber. I drank chocolate for breakfast. We were very merry again this morning but poor Colonel Hill had the headache very much. Nothing happened very remarkable. Colonel Eppes came about 11 o'clock from the [. . .] and let me know there was some difficulty in persuading the people to range by turns as they had promised. About one o'clock we went to dinner and I ate some boiled beef for dinner. We took a walk to the ship and about 3 o'clock took leave of the company and went home in the coach but our horses balked at all the hills on the way and my wife was out of humor because we came away. We got home about 5 o'clock and found all pretty well, thank God. Captain H-n had been here and left some spice and some fruit for a present. Frank Lightfoot, Tom Randolph, and Captain H-n came to visit me and stayed and ate some roast beef and Captain B-r-d-f-r came with them. The two first tarried all night. I neglected to say my prayers but had good health, good thoughts, and good humor, thank God Almighty.

6. I rose about 7 o'clock and read nothing because of the company. However I said a short prayer and drank chocolate for breakfast. Then we walked about the garden because it was good weather and then we played at billiards and I won 3 shillings. About 12 o'clock we took a walk and met Mr. Roscow who came from Mrs. Harrison's where he courted Mistress Betty and Colonel Hill also came to dine with us and I ate some pigeon and bacon for dinner. In the afternoon we played again at billiards and then Colonel Hill went away and we took a walk about the plantation till the evening and then Mr. Lightfoot and Mr. Jimmy Roscow took their leave and went to Mrs. Harrison's, one to make love to the mother and the other the daughter. But Tom Randolph stayed and I let him understand that I agreed he should be my general overseer. We discoursed of several things concerning that subject till about 9 o'clock. I neg-

lected to say my prayers but had good health, good thoughts, and good humor, thank God Almighty. John G-r-l was a little out of order.

7. I rose about 7 o'clock and read nothing. However I said my prayers and drank chocolate for breakfast. I danced my dance. About 10 o'clock Tom Randolph went away and notwithstanding the weather threatened rain I walked to Mrs. Harrison's to visit the two gallants and their mistresses, but Frank Lightfoot was gone before I got there, but the rest were there. Poor Jimmy Roscow was melancholy though I did all I could to make him merry. I went into the study and chose some books and about 2 o'clock we went to dinner and I ate some boiled pork. In the afternoon it rained very hard which kept me there till night and then my wife [sent] a horse for me. It thundered and rained very hard. I found all my people well but I quarreled with John about his work and with the overseer for working the ox in the rain. I wrote in my journal and read nothing. I said my prayers and had good health, good thoughts, and good humor, thank God Almighty. John G-r-l was still out of order.

8. I rose about 6 o'clock and read a chapter in Hebrew and some Greek in Lucian. I said my prayers and ate boiled milk for breakfast. I danced my dance. I settled several accounts and then read some French. My sick people were grown better, thank God. The weather was clear and cold, the wind northwest and blowing hard. I found something which Mr. B-l-w thought was an error to be no error. I ate some tripe for dinner. In the afternoon young John L-t came to ask my opinion concerning his wife who had lost the use of her hands and feet for which I advised her to bathe in cold water after taking two purges. I wrote several things and settled several accounts till the evening and then I took a walk about the plantation. A man came from Mr. Duke's where they were all well. At night I read some English. I said my prayers and had good health, good thoughts, and good humor, thank God Almighty.

9. I rose about 6 o'clock and read two chapters in Hebrew and some Greek in Lucian. I said my prayers devoutly and ate boiled milk for breakfast. I danced my dance. The weather was pretty warm and clear, notwithstanding it had been a frost this night. I took a walk about the plantation and my wife with me and then read some English in Milton. The man returned who came from my brother Duke's and promised to come about 14 days hence to work for me, he being a bricklayer. His name is Cornelius H-l, a man of above 80 years old and yet he walked from Mr. Duke's over. I ate some fish for dinner. In the afternoon I read some English in Milton but was ready to fall asleep and therefore I took a walk about the plantation and saw several hogs of other people in my pasture. When I returned I found Mr. Mumford who told me all was well at Appomattox. In the evening the sloop came and brought me news that my negro C-c-r, the smith, was dead. I neglected to say my prayers but had good health, good thoughts, and good humor, thank God Almighty.

10. I rogered my wife this morning and rose about 7 o'clock but read nothing because Mr. Mumford was here and because they set up a case for my clothes. I neglected to say my prayers but had boiled milk for breakfast. I caused the sloop to be unloaded and then sent her away with 25 hogsheads of tobacco on board the [. . .] "Pelican". Mr. Mumford and I took a walk with our bows and then played at billiards and he beat me. I ate some cod sounds for dinner. John G-r-l had a pain in his ear very violently. In the afternoon we played at billiards again and he beat me. Then we took a walk again about the plantation. The weather was warm and clear. At night I read some news but found myself exceedingly sleepy and took a nap in the chair for about an hour and Mr. Mumford took a nap also but the women sang and were merry. I said my prayers and had good health, good thoughts, and good humor, thank God Almighty.

11. I rose about 6 o'clock and read a little Greek but no Hebrew because I prepared for my journey to Major Harri-

son's. I said my prayers and ate boiled milk for breakfast.
About 8 o'clock Mr. Mumford went away. John G-r-l was
not well and I caused him to be bled and then he found
himself better. The weather was clear and cold; however I
went over the river about 11 o'clock and then proceeded on
my journey to Major Harrison's where I got about 3 o'clock
and [found] him at home but he was indisposed in his
breast, for which I persuaded him to enter into a milk diet.
About 5 o'clock I ate some bacon and fowl for dinner. In
the evening Peter Poythress came with 14 of the Tuscarora
Indians whom he was going to conduct to the Governor.
They told us the Carolina men had killed no more than
about 20 old men and women of their people and had taken
about 30 children prisoners when all the young men were
not at home, that the Tuscaroras could [cut] them all off
but that they saw some English among them which hindered
them and their business with the Governor was to give the
reason why they could not perform their articles and to
inquire whether they might defend themselves in case they're
attacked. We were merry till about 9 o'clock and then
retired. I neglected to say my prayers but had good health,
good thoughts, and good humor, thank God Almighty.

12. I rose about 7 o'clock and read a little Latin in
Horace. I said my prayers and ate chocolate for breakfast.
About 10 o'clock came Mr. Cargill the minister, who agreed
to go with [us] on board the "Pelican", but Frank Lightfoot
who had promised broke his word. We took a walk and I
saw the Major's improvements about his [threshing] and
his [c-l-g grass] and I saw him trim his vines. About 12
o'clock we went on board and were saluted with seven guns
and a glass of canary. About 2 o'clock we went to dinner
and I ate some of the beef that was preserved after the new
manner and found it very juicy and not very salt. It is the
best way of saving meat and will preserve it for several
years free from taint and was found out by chance by a poor
carpenter who keeps the secret to himself and gets abundance of money. We did not find Captain Thompson on
board but we found his son who entertained us generously

and gave us 32 guns in all. We stayed till about 10 o'clock and were merry and almost drunk. However we got well to Major Harrison's and behaved ourselves very discreetly. About 11 o'clock we went to bed where I was guilty of uncleanness and neglected to say my prayers but had good health, good humor, but unclean thoughts, for which I am sorry and hope God will please to forgive me.

13. I rose about 7 o'clock and found my head ached a little. I said my prayers and drank some chocolate for breakfast. This day Major began his milk diet and resol ed to continue it till the end of May next. About 9 o'clock I took my leave and the Major went to Colonel Harrison's and so rode some part of the way with me. He again protested to me he would keep strictly to his milk and I wished him good fortune. I found all my family well, thank God, except John G-r-l who continued indisposed still in his ear, and had something broke in it by which accident he found himself better. My sloop had been here and unloaded some planks and was gone to Appomattox for tobacco. My people had sowed my oats since I went from home. Major Harrison told me he believed his father would never go more to Council. I ate pigeon and bacon for dinner. In the afternoon I read some Latin in Petronius. It rained in the afternoon so that I could not walk about the plantation. The old joiner came from Falling Creek and told me all was well there. At night I read some English in Milton. I said my prayers and had good health, good thoughts, and good humor, thank God Almighty.

14. I rose about 6 o'clock and read a chapter in Hebrew and some Greek in Lucian. I said my prayers and ate boiled milk for breakfast. I danced my dance. The weather was cold and wet, the wind northeast. John G-r-l had an imposthume break in his ear and our maid Jenny was sick with a pain in her bones. I wrote two letters to my overseers above by the old joiner who fixed the case for our clothes but the rain would not let him return. I ate some fish for dinner but was out of humor with Moll because she had not made good sauce. In the afternoon I set several

things in order in my closet and then read some Latin in Petronius. I danced my dance because the rain would not let me take a walk in the evening. Bannister told me he heard some guns today and I thought so likewise. At night I read some English in Milton. I said my prayers and had good health, good thoughts, but indifferent humor, thank God Almighty.

15. I rose about 6 o'clock and read a chapter in Hebrew and some Greek in Lucian. I said my prayers and ate boiled milk for breakfast. I danced my dance. The weather was clear but cold and the wind violent at southwest. My wife was indisposed with a sore throat. My man Redskin Peter pretended again to be sick, for which I put him [on the bit] and Billy Wilkins pretended also to be sick but I believed he dissembled. John G-r-l was a little better but Jenny continued with a pain in her bones. I settled several accounts till dinner and then I ate boiled beef. In the afternoon came Colonel Eppes and stayed about half an hour. I read some news and wrote out an account. In the evening I danced my dance because the wind blew so I did not care to walk about. At night I read some English in Milton. I said my prayers and had good health, good thoughts, and good humor, thank God Almighty.

16. I read a chapter in Hebrew and three chapters in the Greek Testament. I said my prayers and ate boiled milk for breakfast. I danced my dance. My wife continued indisposed but G-r-l and Jenny were better. The wind continued violent but not so cold. About 11 o'clock I went to church where Mr. Anderson gave us a good sermon. After, I asked him, Colonel Hill, and the ladies to go with us to dinner and I ate some roast shoat. In the afternoon Peter Poythress came over and told me the Governor received the Tuscaroras very coldly and ordered them to go and help the people of Carolina cut off Hancock town, which they said they would. About 4 o'clock the company went away and I took a walk about the plantation and found all well. At night I read a little English. Both my wife and Mrs.

Dunn were indisposed. I said my prayers and had good health, good thoughts, and good humor, thank God Almighty.

17. I rose about 6 o'clock and read two chapters in Hebrew and some Greek in Lucian. I said my prayers and ate boiled milk for breakfast. I danced my dance. My wife was worse of her cold but everybody else was better. The weather was clear but a little cold. About 10 o'clock I took a walk in the garden and then settled several accounts and read some English in Milton till dinner and I ate some roast shoat but I dined by myself with nobody but the child [or children], for Mrs. Dunn was sick likewise. In the afternoon I went into the garden and trimmed the vines and was angry with Tom for being so lazy there. Then I returned and read some English in Milton till the evening and then I took a walk about the plantation and found things in pretty good order. At night I read a little in Milton and went soon to bed because my wife was indisposed. I said my prayers and had good health, good thoughts, and good humor, thank God Almighty.

18. I rose about 6 o'clock and read a chapter in Latin and some Greek in Lucian. I said my prayers and ate boiled milk for breakfast. I danced my dance. My wife seemed a little better but grew worse again about noon. The weather was very clear and pretty warm and Mrs. Dunn was well again. G-r-l and Jenny were also better, notwithstanding G-r-l's ear continued to discharge matter. I took a walk and then settled several accounts. Afterwards I read some English in Milton till dinner and then I ate some boiled beef. In the afternoon put several things in order and then read more in Milton. About 5 o'clock George came from Burkland and told me several of the people were sick and that Frank had a swelling under his ear. He also told me Shockoe Billy had a wife [aboard] for which I was out of humor. Then I took a walk about the plantation and when I returned I found Robin Hix who came for some rights. I ate some cold beef with him and had the patience to hear

him talk very foolishly till 9 o'clock. My wife was worse. I neglected to say my prayers but had good health, good thoughts, and good humor, thank God Almighty.

19. I rose about 6 o'clock and read a chapter in Hebrew and some Greek in Lucian. I said my prayers and ate boiled milk for breakfast. I dispatched Robin Hix away as soon as I could and another man who came for rights. My wife seemed worse but would neither let me send for the Doctor nor be bled though she tried two or three times. About 12 o'clock came John Randolph to see me. I desired him to go to Williamsburg to present a petition to the Governor as rector of the College that he might be usher and gave him some advice about it. He dined with us and I ate some partridge for dinner. In the afternoon I took him into the library and examined him and found him improved very much. About 4 o'clock he went away and I took a walk about the plantation and when I returned I found my wife much better, thank God. I read a little English but in compliance to my wife went soon to bed. I said my prayers and had good health, good thoughts, and good humor, thank God Almighty. The weather was very clear and warm.

20. I rose about 6 o'clock and read two chapters in Hebrew and some Greek in Lucian. I said my prayers and ate boiled milk for breakfast. I danced my dance. My wife was better, thank God, though her fever rose about 10 o'clock. The weather was clear and warm and I took a walk to see my people work. When I returned I wrote the articles between Tom Randolph and myself till dinner and then I ate some mutton till the evening, and then I took a walk about the plantation. My wife [was] a little better, thank God; however she complains sometimes of a pain in her side but could by no means be persuaded to be bled, so much her fear prevails over her reason. At night I read some English in Milton. I said my prayers and had good health, good thoughts, and good humor, thank God Almighty.

21. I rose about 6 o'clock and read a chapter in Hebrew and some Greek in Lucian. I said my prayers and ate boiled milk for breakfast. I danced my dance. The weather was

clear and warm. I wrote more articles between Tom Randolph and myself. I found that my wife had an intermittent fever and therefore persuaded her to take the bark
and got it ready for her accordingly and gave her the first
dose about dinner. I ate some salt cod sounds for dinner.
In the afternoon I went into the orchard and trimmed some
young trees. I sent Tom L-s-n to Falling Creek to let Mr.
G-r-l know the bricklayer would come on Friday. I read some
English in Milton. My wife took the bark with much reluctance and would eat some fish against my opinion. In the
evening I took a walk about the plantation. At night I read
some English in Milton. I said my prayers and had good
health, good thoughts, and good humor, thank God Almighty.

22. I rose about 6 o'clock and read a chapter in Hebrew
and some Greek in Lucian. I said my prayers and ate boiled
milk for breakfast. I danced my dance. My wife was ill
of her fever, notwithstanding the bark, insomuch that I sent
for Dr. Cocke for fear of the worst. I read some news and
sold some rights before dinner. I ate some fish. The old
bricklayer came just after dinner and told me all was well
at my brother Duke's. It rained a little almost all day so
that I could not walk out. I read more news in the afternoon. My wife's fever abated a little. In the evening I
walked about the garden because the grass was wet everywhere else. Tom L-s-n came from Falling Creek and told
me all was well there and at the plantation, thank God.
At night I read some English in Milton. I said my prayers
and had good health, good thoughts, and good humor, thank
God Almighty.

23. I rose about 6 o'clock and read two chapters in
Hebrew and some Greek in the Greek Testament. I said
my prayers and ate boiled milk for breakfast. I danced my
dance. The sloop came from Appomattox with 60 hogsheads of tobacco. Shockoe Billy came from the Falls and
bore a letter from Tom Turpin which let me know all was
well there. He desired me to provide myself with another
overseer because I found fault with some of his management
and I wrote him word I would do as he desired. I ate some

roast shoat for dinner. My wife had a little fever this morning but it soon went off again. About 2 o'clock Tom Randolph came and was wet with a gust that happened about that time and soon after came Tom from Williamsburg and told me the Doctor was gone to Rappahannock with Mrs. Russell and would not be home before this night. Mr. Randolph and I took a walk about the plantation. At night came G-r-l and told me all was well at Falling Creek. We drank a bottle of cider. I said a short prayer and had good health, good thoughts, and good humor, thank God Almighty. It thundered and rained this evening. My wife [took] another dose of bark.

24. I rose about 8 o'clock and found my wife much disordered with the bark. I read nothing and it rained in the morning that my people could not work but about 10 o'clock it held up. I said a short prayer and ate boiled milk for breakfast. When it had done raining Mr. G-r-l and my people raised the pigeon house to have pillars put under it. My wife [was] very much out of humor and out of order all day. I read some English till dinner and then ate some boiled beef. In the afternoon we walked about to see the people work and then read some more English and endeavored to please my wife but could not till the evening and then [the evil spirit] went off. I ate some bread and butter at night and drank some cider. I said a short prayer and had good health, good thoughts, and good humor, thank God Almighty. The old bricklayer began to work.

25. I rose about 6 o'clock but read nothing because I gave the necessary orders about everything. However I said my prayers and drank chocolate for breakfast. My wife seemed a little better this morning and the weather was likewise very good, so that my people unloaded the sloop and prepared to go away. Mr. G-r-l also went away and the old bricklayer went with him for a set of tools. About 12 o'clock we ate some cold roast beef and then took horses. We called at Captain Drury Stith's but did not light and so proceeded to Charles Fleming's where we got about 5 o'clock. Charles was very courteous to us only he com-

plained he had no good drink but found, however, three bottles of cider. We ate some fowl and bacon for supper and went to bed about 9 o'clock. I said a short prayer and had good health, good thoughts, and good humor, thank God Almighty.

26. I rose about 6 o'clock and read nothing. I said my prayers and ate some boiled milk for breakfast. About 8 o'clock we took our leave and rode up to my plantation where I found all well, thank God, only a little backwards in their business. We rested ourselves a little and then took a walk on the other side the river to show Captain Randolph my land there. We walked about three miles and then returned and ate some bacon and eggs for dinner. I had some wine with me from home. In the afternoon we rode to the rest of the plantations and found everything well. The weather was very good and warm. After we had seen everything and given the necessary orders we rode away to Major Merriweather's but he was not at home. However his wife was very courteous to us and would have got a supper for us but we told her we did not want to eat. We returned about 9 o'clock. I neglected to say my prayers but had good health, good thoughts, and good humor, thank God Almighty.

27. I rose about 7 o'clock and said a short prayer and ate some milk for breakfast. The weather was very good and favored us much. About 8 o'clock we took leave and rode away to the wading place in order to go to Shockoe but the water was so high that we could not pass so we were obliged to go round by the great bridge and was so discouraged with that we were resolved to return home and by the way called at Drury Stith's and found him not [home]. Here we ate some cold beef for dinner. Here we stayed about two hours and rode away home where I found my wife better and Dr. Cocke with her and my sister Custis. My man John had had the beam of the tobacco press fall on his head but it only made his neck stiff, thank God. At night we drank a bottle of wine. I neglected to say my prayers but had good health, good thoughts, and good humor, thank God Almighty.

28. I rose about 6 o'clock and read a chapter in Hebrew and some Greek in Lucian. I said my prayers and ate boiled milk for breakfast. I danced my dance. The weather was hot and it rained a little in the morning but soon cleared up again. I wrote two letters to my overseers at the Falls to let them know that I had appointed Captain Randolph to overlook my plantations. I also wrote a note to forewarn all people from driving their cattle and hogs on my land. My wife was a little better, but Ned was taken sick of a fever and pain in the side. Tom Randolph went away about 10 o'clock. I ate bacon and pigeon for dinner. In the afternoon I had another boy taken sick. We sat with my wife and endeavored to divert her. In the evening we took a walk about the plantation. I said my prayers and had good health, good thoughts, and good humor, thank God Almighty.

29. I rose about 6 o'clock and read a chapter in Hebrew and some Greek in Lucian. I said my prayers and ate boiled milk for breakfast. I danced my dance. My wife was a little better and so were my sick people. The overseer was taken sick also for which I gave him a general purge. I settled some accounts to carry with me to Williamsburg and then took a walk till dinner. I ate some boiled mutton for dinner. In the afternoon we played at billiards and then I took a walk to see my people work. Then I read some English till the evening. My sister Custis made several complaints to Mrs. Dunn concerning the unhappy life she led by Mr. Custis' unkindness but I believe it is owing to her humor, which seems none of the best. However she seems so easy here that she could not have much at heart. At night we drank a bottle of wine and were merry. I said my prayers and had good health, good thoughts, and good humor, thank God Almighty.

30. I rose about 6 o'clock and read a chapter in Hebrew and no Greek because I prepared to go with the Doctor to Major Harrison's. I said my prayers and ate boiled milk for breakfast. My wife and all my sick people were better, thank God, which encouraged me to undertake my journey.

About 11 o'clock came Colonel Hill to go with us. However I ate some roast beef before we went and then I recommended my family to heaven and took my leave and were set over the river in my boat and then proceeded on our journey notwithstanding it threatened rain but did not rain till we came near to Major Harrison's. The Major was gone to Williamsburg but we were courteously entertained by his lady. She told me the Major did not keep very strictly to his milk diet. I ate some boiled beef for dinner. In the evening it rained very much. However we were as merry as we could be without the Major. I neglected to say my prayers but had good health, good thoughts, and good humor, thank God Almighty. I lay with the Doctor. Poor Colonel Hill had the headache terribly.

31. I rose about 7 o'clock and found the weather very clear again. I read nothing but said my prayers. I ate nothing but chocolate for breakfast. We were set over the river with our horses but then we lost our way above six miles and did not reach Green Springs till about 3 o'clock where we met a messenger to the Doctor from Colonel Bassett to go to his wife who was dangerously sick. The Doctor went, though he was much tired, and we proceeded to Williamsburg and found the governors of the College sitting. Colonel Hill was sworn one of the members. Several things were done concerning the tenants and then we chose the Commissary rector. Then we went to the coffeehouse and I ate some cold roast beef and Will Robinson gave me a bottle of wine. Then he and I played at piquet and I lost 50 shillings. About 11 I went home to my lodgings where I said a short prayer and had good health, good thoughts, and good humor, thank God Almighty. We have had abundance of rain this month and I never saw the roads so wet in my life as we found them today. Some of us endeavored to get John Randolph to be usher but it was rejected because there were but 22 boys which was not a number that required an usher.

April, 1712

1. I rose about 6 o'clock and read nothing because several gentlemen came to see me. I did also neglect to say my prayers for the same reason; however I ate some boiled milk for breakfast, and then went to wait on the Governor and settled several accounts with him and talked of several affairs and particularly about my Lord Orkney's business and then we drank some tea. The Governor asked us to come to dinner. Then I waited on the Governor to Council where it was considered how to assist the people of Carolina with 200 men according to the petition of their Governor, Council, and Burgesses, and at last we agreed to do it and pay it out of the quitrents rather than let the Queen's subjects perish for want of help. Then I went with Colonel Hill to dine with the Governor and ate some fish for dinner. Mrs. Russell looked very coldly on me. After dinner we took our leave and rode away to Colonel Duke's but by the way met Dr. Cocke who told us Mrs. Bassett was better. About 7 o'clock we got to Colonel Duke's but he had no drink for us. However we were merry till about 9 o'clock and then I went to bed and committed uncleanness. I neglected to say my prayers but had good health, good humor, but foul thoughts, for which God forgive me.

2. I rose about 7 o'clock and read nothing. However I said a short prayer and ate some potato and milk for breakfast. Then we played at cards and I lost 10 shillings. We could not persuade Colonel Duke to go with us to the club, and therefore we took our leave about 11 o'clock and got to the Brick House[1] before one and found but little company but several more came soon after, among whom were Colonel Bassett and Mr. Holloway, but none of them could tell us any news. About 2 o'clock we went to dinner, about 17 of us, and I ate some roast beef for dinner which was very fat and good. In the evening I went home with

---

[1] An ordinary on the York River, owned by Colonel William Bassett.

Colonel Bassett and found his lady much better and Jimmy Burwell and his wife came there likewise and told us they heard several guns this afternoon. We had a supper but I ate only some milk. Colonel Hill lay with me and snored terribly so that I could not sleep and I wouldn't wake him for fear his head should ache. I neglected to say my prayers but had good health, good thoughts, and good humor, thank God Almighty.

3. I rose about 6 o'clock but neglected to say my prayers. However I had some chocolate for breakfast. The Colonel would have had us stay to the christening of his child but I excused myself because I had left my wife sick and wanted to see her. About 10 o'clock we took our leave and the Colonel went with us to the store, about two miles off, where I bought a maid to look after my spinners. Here we saw the salt works. About 12 Colonel Hill and I went away home and by the way I called at Drury Stith's and let him know that the Governor had promised his brother to be sheriff[1] and my petition came too late for him. Then I went home and found everybody well there, thank God, only some were sick at my quarters above. I found Mr. Salle here. At night I ate some cold roast beef for supper. I neglected to say my prayers but had good health, good thoughts, and good humor, thank God Almighty. I rogered my wife.

4. I rose about 7 o'clock and read a chapter in Hebrew and some Greek in Lucian. I said my prayers and ate boiled milk for breakfast. I wrote two letters to the quarters and one to Williamsburg and sent the last by my sister Custis who would go, notwithstanding it was like to rain. About 11 o'clock Mr. Salle went away likewise. I settled several accounts and wrote in my journal till dinner and then I ate some fish. In the afternoon I rogered my wife again. The weather was very bad and it rained almost all day so that my poor sister was terribly wet except she called at some house. My wife and I took a nap after dinner and after

---

[1] John Stith was appointed sheriff of Charles City County on April 22, 1712. (*Ex. Jour.*, III, 305.)

our roger. I settled several accounts and read some news. It rained till night so that I could not walk. At night came the master of a ship lately come from Lisbon. We gave him some supper and I ate some broiled turkey with him. He told me he would let me have eight dozen of bottles of Lisbon wine. I said my prayers and had good health, good thoughts, and good humor, thank God Almighty.

5. I rose about 6 o'clock and read a chapter in Hebrew and some Greek in Lucian. I said my prayers and ate boiled milk for breakfast. I danced my dance. The captain only drank a dram with me and would not stay to eat any breakfast notwithstanding I asked him. It rained again this morning. About 9 o'clock came Mr. Bland from Williamsburg but brought no news. He gave me an escheat warrant for some land in Prince George County on which I signed an order to the sheriff to summon an inquest. He went away in about an hour. I settled several accounts till dinner and then I ate some fish. In the afternoon I read a little English and then took a walk to [see] my people work. It continued to rain by fits. In the evening I took a walk about the plantation and found some of my boys going to burn some of my hogshead staves, for which I beat them. Colonel Bassett sent the maid that I bought and I wrote him my thanks for it. At night I wrote two letters to my officers to choose men to go to Carolina. I said my prayers and had good health, good thoughts, and good humor, thank God Almighty.

6. I rose about 7 o'clock and read a chapter in Hebrew and some Greek in the Greek Testament. I said my prayers and ate boiled milk for breakfast. I danced my dance. The weather was fair but very cool this morning. My wife was a little indisposed but I persuaded [her] to take a walk which made her better. I read some English. Then my wife and Mrs. Dunn and I took a walk to see the peach orchard and to get us a stomach. Mrs. Harrison came just as we sat to dinner and dined with us. I ate roast beef for my part. In the afternoon my wife went to take the air in the coach and Mrs. Harrison with her. I took a walk and when I re-

turned I read some English. Billy Brayne came to tell me that my wife was at Mrs. Harrison's and desired me to come there, and I walked there and stayed about half an hour and then we returned in the coach. At night I read some French. I said my prayers and had good health, good thoughts, and good humor, thank God Almighty.

8. I rose about 6 o'clock and read a chapter in Hebrew and some Greek in Lucian. I said my prayers and ate boiled milk for breakfast. I danced my dance. The weather was very clear and warm. About 10 o'clock I ate some bacon because I wished to go to Prince George Court and soon after came Colonel Hill to go with me. I expected Captain Wilcox to call on me but he stayed so long that we went in my boat. I impanelled a jury for an escheat on the petition of Mr. Bland. I drank a bottle of canary and sold several rights. About 5 o'clock we returned home and had some fish for supper. Colonel Hill, Captain Wilcox, and Captain Stith came home with me and stayed till almost 8 o'clock. I said my prayers shortly and had good health, good thoughts, and good humor, thank God Almighty.

9. I rose about 6 o'clock and read a chapter in Hebrew and some Greek in Lucian. I said my prayers and ate boiled milk for breakfast. I danced my dance. The weather was clear and warm which tempted me to go to the general muster in Henrico and accordingly I went about 11 o'clock but when I got as far as Colonel Hill's it began to rain so that I resolved to return and send John G-r-l. About 2 o'clock we went to a very indifferent dinner and I ate some bacon and peas but the Colonel would give me no wine, notwithstanding he had it in the house. In the afternoon we went to see the ships that were building and stayed there about an hour. About 6 o'clock G-r-l returned and told me there were 26 volunteers had offered themselves on the south side of James River. Then I took my leave and went home and found all well. I said my prayers and had good health, good thoughts, and good humor, thank God Almighty. My wife had caused Moll to be whipped for not letting the people have what was ordered them.

10. I rose about 6 o'clock and read a chapter in Hebrew and some Greek in Lucian. I said my prayers and ate boiled milk for breakfast. I danced my dance. The weather was very clear and warm but it had rained in the night and thundered. My wife and I took a walk about the garden. I settled several matters and sold some rights to a man. I ate some pigeons and bacon for dinner. In the afternoon I took a walk to see my young trees. Then I wrote a letter to England and afterwards took a walk about the plantation and saw the people at work in the churchyard which Captain D-k was to pale in. I had a letter from Colonel Hill to send him some paint for his ship. At night I ate some bread and butter and drank some cider and my wife and I romped for half an hour till we went to bed. I said my prayers and had good health, good thoughts, and good humor, thank God Almighty. My maid Betty had her ague again. The weather was a little cooler.

11. I rose about 6 o'clock and read two chapters in Hebrew and some Greek in Lucian. I said my prayers and ate boiled milk for breakfast. I danced my dance. The weather was cool, the wind at northwest. Mr. C-k the wire-man came and told me about 30 volunteers offered themselves yesterday to go to Carolina. He made an end of my wire. About 12 o'clock came Colonel Frank Eppes, Major Farrar[1] and Captain Worsham, to return me a list of the volunteers of Henrico which were in all 39. Colonel Littlebury Eppes came also and all these gentlemen dined with me and I ate some boiled beef. In the afternoon all the company went away and I wrote some things to prepare to go to Williamsburg. In the evening I took a walk about the plantation. At night I read some news and drank some cider till about 9 o'clock. I said my prayers and had good health, good thoughts, and good humor, thank God Almighty.

12. I rose about 6 o'clock and read two chapters in Hebrew and some Greek in Lucian. I said my prayers

---

[1] William Farrar, appointed sheriff of Henrico County April 22, 1712. (*Ex. Jour.*, III, 305.)

and ate boiled milk for breakfast. I was a little out of humor this morning and beat Anaka a little unjustly for which I was sorry afterwards. About 11 o'clock I went to Mrs. Harrison's to wait on her to Colonel Hill's to see his ship launched and found Major Burwell and Mrs. Berkeley there. We went all together to Colonel Hill's where we found abundance of company but it was about 3 o'clock before the ship went off and then it went very well. About 4 we went to dinner and I ate some boiled beef. I saw Tom Randolph and Mr. G-r-l, who told me all was well above except Frank who had a swelling in his neck. Tom Randolph went home with me, where I found all well. I said my prayers and had good health, good thoughts, and good humor, thank God Almighty.

13. I rose about 6 o'clock but read nothing because I got ready for my journey to Williamsburg. However I said a short prayer and ate boiled milk for breakfast. About 9 o'clock came Frank Eppes who offered his services to command the men to be sent to Carolina and I promised to recommend him for that post to the Governor. Mr. Clayton had no news except that our men had taken some prizes and carried them to Barbados. About 11 I went to church where Mr. Anderson gave us a good sermon. Major Burwell and Mrs. Berkeley and Mrs. Harrison went home to dine with us and I ate some veal for dinner and soon after dinner we went away to Colonel Duke's and Major Burwell and Mr. Clayton to Williamsburg. Tom Randolph went with me and we got to Colonel Duke's about 8 o'clock. I ate some milk for supper. I said a short prayer and had good health, good thoughts, and good humor, thank God Almighty.

14. I rose about 7 o'clock and wrote a little in my commonplace. I said my prayers and ate milk and potato for breakfast. About 9 o'clock I persuaded Colonel Duke to go and show us my land that lay near him. We went to both my [huts] and saw some of my land and then we took leave of the Colonel and rode away to Mount Folly where we found all well, thank God. Here we ate some fried chicken

and bacon and gave the plantation into Tom Randolph's charge and ordered the overseer to follow his directions in everything. Then we went from there and got to Queen's Creek about 6 o'clock where we found my sister well but my brother was not yet come over the Bay. About 8 o'clock I ate some turkey and received a letter from the Doctor to let me know he would send his coach for me next morning or else come himself and told me the news about what our men-of-war had done in taking the prizes. I neglected to say my prayers but had good health, good thoughts, and good humor, thank God Almighty.

15. I rose about 7 o'clock and read a little in my commonplace. I ate some boiled milk for breakfast and said a short prayer. About 8 o'clock came the Doctor in his coach and kept me here till 10 o'clock and then we took leave of my sister and rode in great haste to Williamsburg. I had not time to wait on the Governor but went into court as soon as I had put myself in order, where we sat till about one o'clock. Then I went home to my lodgings and did some business till 3 o'clock and then we went to dinner and I ate some fried oysters. After dinner I took a walk to see the Governor's house where we found the Governor, who took us home to drink some French claret where I saw the Baron [Graffenriedt], who seems to be a good man. We sat till about 10 and then retired. I said my prayers and had good health, good thoughts, and good humor, thank God Almighty.

16. I rose about 6 o'clock and read a chapter in Hebrew and some Greek in Homer. I said my prayers and ate boiled milk for breakfast. I settled some business and then went to wait on the Governor about some business and drank some chocolate. I stayed about an hour and then retired to my lodgings and did some business and about 11 o'clock went to court where we sat till near 3 o'clock but the Governor went away before. Then Colonel Custis and I went to Mrs. [Whaley's] to meet my sister Custis who did not come because her husband was come home. Then we went to dinner and I ate some roast beef for dinner and afterwards

took a walk till it was dark and then went to the coffeehouse where I was got into a game and won £3 and about 11 o'clock got to my lodgings, where I said a short prayer and had good health, good thoughts, and good humor, thank God Almighty.

17. I rose about 6 o'clock and read a chapter in Hebrew and some Greek in Homer. I said my prayers and ate boiled milk for breakfast. I settled some business till about 10 o'clock and then went to court where I sat till about 2 o'clock and then I returned to my chambers in the capitol where I danced my dance and read a little Latin and then came down again to court and sat till 3 and then went to dinner and ate some pork. After dinner I went to Mrs. [Whaley's] where I saw my sister Custis and my brother who is just returned. Here we drank some tea till the evening and then I took leave and went to the coffeehouse, where I played at cards and won 40 shillings but afterwards I played at dice and lost almost £10. This gave me a resolution to play no more at dice and so I went to my lodgings where I said a short prayer and had good health, good thoughts, and good humor, thank God Almighty.

18. I rose about 6 o'clock and read a chapter in Hebrew and some Greek in Homer. I said my prayers and ate boiled milk for breakfast. The weather was cloudy and threatened rain. Mr. Curle[1] came to my lodgings and told me our Indian hostages were all run away last night. Several other gentlemen came, with whom I settled some business and about 9 o'clock went to the capitol where we sat till about 11 and then went to church, this being Good Friday, and Mr. Commissary gave us a sermon. Then we returned to court again and dispatched some business and then went to dinner and I ate some boiled beef. After dinner I went to Mrs. [Whaley's] where I saw my sister Custis. We stayed till evening and then I took a walk and returned to my lodg-

---

[1]Nicholas Curle, burgess from Elizabeth City County and owner of a sloop employed as a spy ship. (See *JHB*, 1702-1712, p. 345; *Ex. Jour.*, III, 329.)

ings about 8 o'clock where I washed myself very clean.
Then I said my prayers and had good health, good thoughts,
and good humor, thank God Almighty.

19. My brother Custis came this morning before I got up
to tell me that my sister was resolved not to agree to our
bargain concerning the selling of the land and negroes. I
was surprised at it but thought it only a stratagem to prevail
with her husband to live at Williamsburg. I rose about 8
o'clock and found it raining. Several persons came in to do
business and so the Major went away in a very great rage
with his wife. I had a letter from her with many things
very foolish in it. About 11 o'clock I said my prayers and
ate some custard for breakfast. I danced my dance, and
then went to court where we sat till about 3 o'clock and then
went to dinner and I ate some mutton. Then we went to
Council where we had several examinations of Indians taken
by Major Harrison by which we learned that our Indians
knew of the design of the Tuscaroras. We sat till about 8
o'clock and then I went home to my lodgings where I settled
a little business and then said my prayers and had good
health, good thoughts, and good humor, thank God Almighty. Several of our young gentlemen were before Mr.
Bland this morning for a riot committed last night at Su
Allen's and A-t-k-s-n's, but came off with paying 10 shillings
apiece. The gentlemen were Mr. Page, Ralph Wormeley,
John Grymes, Mr. Johnson, and Jimmy Burwell,[1] though
I understand the last was not much in fault.

20. I rose about 6 o'clock and read a chapter in Hebrew
and some Greek in Homer. I said my prayers very devoutly
and ate boiled milk for breakfast. Then wrote some English in my commonplace. It threatened rain all the morning.
About 10 o'clock came the Doctor, to whom I told the
quarrel with my brother and sister Custis. About 11 I went
to visit the President and went with him to church, where

---

[1]Mann Page of Rosewell, Gloucester County; Ralph Wormeley of Rosegill,
Middlesex County; John Grymes of Brandon, Middlesex County; Thomas
Johnson of King and Queen County, and James, son of Lewis Burwell.
Ralph Wormeley died in 1713, but the rest became members of the Assembly
and leading citizens.

Mr. Commissary gave us a good sermon. I took the Holy
Sacrament and then went with Mr. President to dine with
the Governor, where I ate some boiled mutton. In the
afternoon there were four Tuscarora Indians who had been
taken up by the rangers of Prince George and were put into
prison. In the evening I went to the coffeehouse, and then it
began to rain violently and thundered. Here I tarried till
about 9 o'clock, and then returned to my lodgings where I
said my prayers and had good health, good thoughts, and
good humor, thank God Almighty. The Governor told me
privately that he intended to take the militia and march to
the Tuscaroras soon and charged me to let nobody know it.

21. I rose about 6 o'clock and read a chapter in Hebrew
and some Greek in Homer. I said my prayers and ate boiled
milk for breakfast. I danced my dance. It was warm
weather and clear. The Doctor came to see me and we
talked about the unhappiness of my brother and sister
Custis, and in the middle of our discourse my brother Custis
came in and told me my sister would acknowledge conveyances on some articles agreed between them. Several gentlemen came to see me and about 11 o'clock I went to court
where we learned that the fleet was come in yesterday.
About 2 o'clock I went up to my chambers and read some
Italian and then came down to court again and sat till about
4 o'clock and then we went to dinner and then I invited my
brother Custis to dine with us and I ate boiled beef. About
6 my wife came and let me know all was well at home, thank
God. I waited on her to Queen's Creek where I could not
disguise my resentment to my sister. I neglected to say my
prayers but had good health, good thoughts, and good
humor, thank God Almighty. I rogered my wife.

22. I lay with my wife till about 7 o'clock and read nothing, nor did I say my prayers; however I ate boiled milk for
breakfast. About 8 o'clock came Captain B-r-k-l-t who came
with the fleet and let us know all the fleet was come in and
among the rest those that had my goods, thank God. He
told me that Mrs. Cocke also was come in the Harrison and

two of her children.[1] I hastened to Williamsburg and went
to the Governor with this news and was the first to tell him
for certain of the fleet. About 11 o'clock I went to court
where we sat till about 2 and then went to council concerning some cases of land and then concerning the Indians.
About 6 o'clock I went home with the Governor to dinner
and ate some roast beef. Several Nottoway Indians were
brought in to examine. About 8 o'clock I went to the coffeehouse and from thence home, about 10. I said my prayers
and had good health, good thoughts, and good humor, thank
God Almighty.

23. I rose about 6 o'clock and read nothing because I had
company come in continually about business, so that I neglected to say my prayers but I ate some boiled milk for
breakfast. About 9 o'clock came Captain Isham Randolph
and Captain Posford and brought me some letters from
England, by one of which I learned that Dr. Cocke was
Secretary of this colony. About 11 o'clock I went to court
where I sat till 12 and then learned that my wife was come
to town and went to her and had several more letters by
Captain Turner[2] who brought my goods for Williamsburg
to the value of 2,000 first cost. Then I returned again to
court and sat about two hours and then we went into council
about the Indians and sat there till night and then went to
supper and I ate some boiled beef. Then I went to my
lodgings. [?] came to me. About 8 o'clock the Governor's
coach brought Mrs. Cocke and the Doctor to town. My
wife was not very well. 'I again neglected to say my prayers
but had good health, good thoughts, and good humor, thank
God Almighty.

24. I rose about 6 o'clock and read a little Greek in
Homer. I said my prayers and ate some chocolate for
breakfast. Several people came to me about business. My
wife was not well. I left her and her company preparing to
go to visit Mrs. Cocke but much company came in and hin-

[1]Mrs. William Cocke (Elizabeth Catesby) wife of the Doctor. They had
three daughters and one son, born between 1701 and 1705.
[2]Jeremiah Turner. (*Cal. S. P.*, p. 107.)

dered them. About 10 o'clock I went to court where I sat till about 3 and then we went to Council where several things relating to the expedition to Carolina were considered, the officers appointed, and Major Eppes was to command them. It was almost dark before we had done and then we went to dinner and I ate roast beef. The Indian prisoners endeavored to burn the door of the prison and had nearly performed it. About 8 I went home to my lodgings and did abundance of business till my wife came home about 10 and then I neglected to say my prayers but had good health, good thoughts, and good humor, thank God Almighty.

25. I rose about 6 o'clock and my brother and sister Custis came about 7 to perfect the deed between us. There were several little quarrels between my brother and his wife, and my wife could not forbear siding with her sister and they would fain make me believe that I had promised that my brother should make my sister [easy], which was wrong and gave me a bad opinion [of] my sister. However at last everything was agreed between us and we signed and sealed. About 9 o'clock came the Doctor and I gave him joy for his wife's arrival in this country. About 11 I went to court and about 2 came in the women to acknowledge their deed in court. Then I went away with them to my lodgings and returned to court again and sat till 3 and went to take leave of my wife and her sister who went to Queen's Creek. About 4 we went to dinner and I ate some boiled beef. Then Mr. President and I went to wait on Mrs. Cocke who is a pretty sort of woman. Soon after us the two captains of the men-of-war came to the Governor's but had no news. Then I went to my lodgings where I said my prayers and had good health, good thoughts, and good humor, thank God Almighty.

26. I rose about 6 o'clock and read a chapter in Hebrew and some Greek in Homer. I neglected to say my prayers but ate some boiled milk for breakfast. The weather was cold and clear. Several gentlemen came to me about business and among the rest James Bates concerning the mill that I was to sell him. About 10 o'clock I went to court,

where we sat till about 2 and then went to Council concerning the Indians. The hostages were brought back again and were taken up near the Nottoway town. Several men were examined about their trade with the Indians but nothing could be got from them. About 6 I went home with the Governor to dinner and ate some fricassee of veal. The Doctor was returned from Colonel Bassett's and told us his wife was better. About 8 I took my leave and went to the coffeehouse where I sat about an hour and then returned to my lodgings. I said my prayers and had good health, good thoughts, and good humor, thank God Almighty.

27. I rose about 6 o'clock and read a chapter in Hebrew and some Greek in Homer. I said my prayers devoutly and ate boiled milk for breakfast. The weather was warm again. Colonel Duke was still sick and went out of town this morning without taking leave of anybody. It is to be feared he will be buried by his old woman who is more than 80 years old. Colonel Carter went also away yesterday for good and the rest went out of town so that I was the only councillor left in town. About 11 o'clock I walked to church and had a sermon from a new parson.[1] After church the Governor asked me and my wife to go down with them but we were engaged to go to Queen's Creek because Colonel Custis was there. Accordingly we went there and found the Colonel and some other company. About 3 o'clock we went to dinner and I ate some boiled beef. After dinner we took a walk in the orchard and then because my wife was tired she and I went to loll on the bed. There I rogered her. At night we drank some syllabub. I neglected to say my prayers but had good health, good thoughts, and good humor, thank God Almighty.

28. I rose about 7 o'clock and before I could dress me I learned the President was come. I neglected to say my prayers but ate boiled milk for breakfast. The weather was cold this morning. About 9 o'clock Mr. President and I

---

[1]Probably James Worden, who officiated in Jamestown in 1712, and later was minister of Weyanoke and Martin's Brandon Parishes. (Goodwin, p. 314.)

went to Williamsburg in his coach and got there about 10. I did some business at my lodgings and then went to court and sat till 12. Then I went home and my brother and sister Custis passed conveyances to me for part of Colonel Parke's estate and then came and acknowledged them in court. At the same time I made over Skimino Mill to James Bates. We sat in court till about 3 o'clock and then went to dinner and I ate some fowl and bacon but my wife dined at the Governor's. About 6 we went to Council and sat there till 10. Then I went to my lodgings, where I neglected to say my prayers but had good health, good thoughts, and good humor, thank God Almighty.

29. I rose about 6 o'clock but could read nothing because of much business I had to do. I neglected to say my prayers but drank some chocolate for breakfast. My wife prepared to go away to Green Springs, and about 9 o'clock I was sent for to court where we sat till about 3 when we finished all the business and then went to dinner about which time my wife went out of town. I received a letter from Frank Eppes by which I learned that his father would not let him go on the expedition notwithstanding he had engaged the Governor to give him that place. This made me very much out of humor. However I ate some broiled pork for dinner. After dinner I and several of the gentlemen of the Council went to wait on the Governor to let him know this disappointment. The Governor did not seem much moved but asked us to drink a bottle of claret with him. The President and they that stayed in town accepted his invitation. We stayed there till about 10 and then I went to my lodgings where I said a short prayer and had good health, good thoughts, and good humor, thank God Almighty.

30. I rose about 6 o'clock and settled my business and read nothing. I neglected to say my prayers but ate boiled milk for breakfast. The weather was very warm. Several persons came to see me and among them Mr. Tullitt to settle our old account but neither of us had time. I wrote some letters to England and settled several accounts with Mr. Bland and others. I was so taken up that I had not time to

eat all day. The Doctor came to see me and brought his brother-in-law[1] with him whom I invited to come and see me, which the Doctor took well. About 12 o'clock came Colonel Hill who told me all were well at my house on Sunday last. In the evening I went to supper at Mr. Bland's and ate some cold gammon and then went to the coffeehouse where I paid off my score and talked till about 10 o'clock and then returned to my lodgings where I said my prayers and had good health, good thoughts, and good humor, thank God Almighty.

---

[1]Mark Catesby, the naturalist, author of *The Natural History of Carolina, Florida, and the Bahama Islands* (1731). His sister was Dr. Cocke's wife. In 1712 he came to Virginia for a seven years' visit. (See W. B. Blanton, *Medicine in Virginia in the Eighteenth Century*, p. 114.)

May, 1712

1.[1] I rose about 6 o'clock and settled several matters and wrote some letters. I said my prayers and ate boiled milk for breakfast. Colonel Hill came about 7 o'clock and about [. . .] he and I took leave of Mrs. Bland and rode to Green Springs where we found Dr. Cocke and his wife and Mrs. Russell and about 12 came Captain Posford to let us know he had brought his boat to carry us home but we stayed to dinner and I ate some veal. After dinner I and my wife, Mrs. Dunn and the child, and Colonel Hill went to the boat, and [after] six hours we got home about 11 o'clock where I found all well, thank God. I said a short prayer and had good health, good thoughts, and good humor, thank God Almighty.

2. I rose about 7 o'clock but read nothing because I was taken up with opening some of my goods. I said my prayers and ate boiled milk for breakfast. The weather was very warm. My wife was indisposed and had a sort of looseness. I had several boat-loads of goods come ashore from Captain Posford who had one of my flats of nine hogsheads. We opened several goods which proved very indifferent and particularly the saddle which was the worst I ever saw. I ate some pigeon and bacon for dinner. In the afternoon we opened more goods till the evening and then I took a walk with my wife in the garden and found things in good order there. Then I took a walk about the plantation. I said my prayers and had good health, good thoughts, and good humor, thank God Almighty. I rogered my wife in the morning and also wrote a letter to England and settled several accounts.

3. I rose about 6 o'clock and read a chapter in Hebrew and some Greek in Lucian. I said my prayers and ate boiled milk for breakfast. I danced my dance. I wrote a letter

---

[1]This entry appears under April and a longhand note is inserted: "Memorandum this ought to be the first of May."

to England. About 11 o'clock came Tom Randolph and told me all was well above and also Frank's neck had been cut open and a woman had been brought to bed. He told me of all my matters and about 12 o'clock went on board his brother's ship at Swinyards. I had several goods come ashore. I ate some lamb stones for dinner. In the afternoon I took a nap and then wrote a letter to England till the evening and then I walked about the plantation. Tom Osborne came and let me know all was well above at all the quarters. At night my wife was out of humor for nothing. I said a short prayer and had good health, good thoughts, and good humor, thank God Almighty.

4. I rose about 6 o'clock and as I walked before the cellar window I heard something running, at which I went and called the boy and it was a vinegar barrel which had not been well stopped. I read two chapters in Hebrew and two chapters in the Greek Testament. I said my prayers and ate boiled milk for breakfast. Then I danced my dance. About 10 o'clock Tom Randolph came from on board ship and we talked till dinner and then I ate some roast shoat for dinner. In the afternoon I rogered my wife and then took a little nap. About 4 o'clock Mr. Randolph went away with full directions from me how to act. About 5 Mr. Mumford came and told me all was well at Appomattox but he was much concerned we had no goods come in. In the evening we took a walk about the plantation and then I ate some supper with him. I said my prayers and had good health, good thoughts, and good humor, thank God Almighty.

5. [I rose] about 6 o'clock and read a chapter in Hebrew and some Greek in Lucian. I said my prayers and ate cold milk for breakfast. I danced my dance. About 8 o'clock Mr. Mumford went away. The weather threatened rain and was very warm but it cleared up again. I wrote a letter to England. About 11 o'clock came Mr. T-l-r from Williamsburg with a letter from the Governor concerning the debt due to my Lord Orkney. He also had orders to choose some walnut planks. I made him stay to dinner because I

had several things to return to the Governor. I ate some dried beef for dinner. In the afternoon I wrote several letters to send by Mr. T-l-r and he went about 4 o'clock. Then I wrote another letter to England. In the evening I took a walk about the plantation. I ate some milk and strawberries. I said a short prayer and had good health, good thoughts, and good humor, thank God Almighty.

6. I rose about 6 o'clock and read nothing because I wrote several letters to send to Williamsburg. However I said my prayers and ate boiled milk for breakfast. The weather was extremely hot and clear. I set several things in order and made several alterations in the house. About 10 o'clock came Llewellyn Eppes and his wife. I entertained them courteously. About 12 o'clock came Colonel Littlebury Eppes and gave me a letter from the Governor by which I understood that the General of Carolina had made a peace with the Indians and that it would not be necessary to send any men to their assistance.[1] The Colonel would not stay to dinner but the rest of the company did. I ate some roast shoat for dinner. In the afternoon I took a nap and about 5 o'clock the company went away and then came Captain V-n to see bills of lading. Then I took a walk in the garden because it was too late to walk about the plantation. I neglected to say my prayers but had good health, good thoughts, and good humor, thank God Almighty.

7. I rose about 6 o'clock and read a chapter in Hebrew and some Greek in Lucian. I said my prayers and ate boiled milk for breakfast. It threatened rain again but to no purpose for it cleared up and was very hot. I wrote two letters to England. About 11 o'clock came three of the masters and with them Captain John Stith. They stayed till about 12 and then I went with them to court where we made a shift to agree the freight at £8 a ton. Then I brought them home to dine with me and I ate some roast mutton. In the afternoon the company went away and I put several things in order till the evening and then I took a walk about

---

[1]Spotswood made a journey on April 30, 1712, to the border to meet the Governor of North Carolina. (*Wm. Q. (2)*, III, 41.)

the plantation. I wrote a letter to Major Harrison concerning our settling the freight and proposed what ships should go. At night I ate some strawberries and milk. I said my prayers and had good health, good thoughts, and good humor, thank God Almighty.

8. I rose about 6 o'clock and read a chapter in Hebrew and some Greek in Lucian. I said my prayers and drank some whey for breakfast. The weather was very hot again. Captain Posford sent for one of my 12-hogshead flats which I sent him. I settled several things and unpacked my trunks that came from Williamsburg. Then I settled some papers till dinner and then I ate some roast mutton. My people washed the sheep in order to clean them for shearing tomorrow. In the afternoon I set my closet in order and afterwards read some Greek till the evening and then I took a walk about the plantation. At night I ate some strawberries and milk and after eating took a walk in the garden. Tom returned from Williamsburg and brought eight young negroes from Queen's Creek and a letter from Mr. Bland. I said my prayers and had good health, good thoughts, and good humor, thank God Almighty.

9. I rose about 6 o'clock and read two chapters in Hebrew and some Greek in Lucian. I ate some strawberries and milk for breakfast. I said my prayers and danced my dance. It threatened rain again very much but did not rain, however, till the afternoon. About 10 o'clock came Frank and told me all was well above, thank God, only the beef he said lay down in the road and would not drive forward. I wrote two letters to my overseers. My people sheared the sheep this day till noon. I ate some boiled mutton for dinner. In the afternoon it began to rain and grew very cold so that all my people went to plant the tobacco and planted 4,000 plants. I settled some accounts and then read some French till the evening and then I walked in the library because it rained. At night I read some news. I said my prayers and had good health, good thoughts, and good humor, thank God Almighty. Captain Turner was here in the morning.

10. I rose about 6 o'clock and found it extremely cold. I read two chapters in Hebrew and some Greek in Lucian. I said my prayers and ate boiled milk for breakfast. I danced my dance. It rained a cold rain, the wind northeast. However my people went to plant tobacco again and planted about 26,000 this day. I settled several accounts and then read news till dinner and then I ate some stewed lamb. In the afternoon put several things in order and settled more accounts and read some Dutch till the evening and then I took a walk about the plantation and went to M-n-s orchard and there got some cherries and brought them home to my wife. I gave all the people a dram after planting in the rain. At night we ate some bread and butter and drank some Lisbon wine. I said my prayers shortly and had good health, good thoughts, and good humor, thank God Almighty.

11. I rose about 6 o'clock and read two chapters in Hebrew and two chapters in the Greek Testament. I ate some boiled milk for breakfast and said my prayers shortly because Tom Randolph came and hindered me. He told me all was well at my plantations only [Cæsar] the negro was run away for killing a hog. My clothes were brought ashore but when I opened the box I found half the clothes taken out of the box. I sent immediately on board the ship commanded by Turner to let him know I had been robbed and Mr. Randolph was so kind as to go aboard and all the men were searched and their cabins but nothing was found. About 11 we went to church where I saw a man who told us he had read in a gazette that the King of France was dead. Mr. Anderson gave us a good sermon and after church he and several others came to dine with me and I ate some pigeon and bacon for dinner. It rained in the afternoon. However the company went away except Tom Randolph. It rained so that I could not walk and was so cold that we sat by the fire all the evening. I neglected to say my prayers but had good health, good thoughts, and good humor, thank God Almighty.

12. I rose about 7 o'clock and read a chapter in Hebrew
and some Greek in Lucian. I said my prayers and ate boiled
milk for breakfast. I danced my dance. The rain continued; however Tom Randolph went away to his post. Red-,
skin Peter was again sick in pretence but I tied him up by
the leg to cure him and it did cure him. My people planted
tobacco again. I settled several matters till dinner, and
then I ate some dried beef. Just before dinner came Mr.
Custis and told me all was well at Queen's Creek. He came
in order to go with Tom Randolph to share the tobacco at
the quarters in King William. In the afternoon we took a
walk about the plantation and got some cherries. In the
evening my brother Custis complained his head ached and
he would not drink anything. I said my prayers shortly and
had good health, good thoughts, and good humor, thank
God Almighty.

13. I rose about 6 o'clock but read nothing because I
prepared to go with my brother to Falling Creek. I said
my prayers and ate boiled milk for breakfast. The weather
threatened rain but did not discourage us from going but
before we went came several masters of ships and Colonel
Hill and Mr. Bland who told me all was well at Williamsburg. These were going to Prince George court. About
11 o'clock my brother Custis and I set out and rode to
Colonel Hill's where we found Mr. Anderson, who gave us
some cherries. We stayed till our horses got over the river
and then rode to Falling Creek, where we found two negroes
sick and some other things out of order for which I scolded
at Mr. G-r-l. My brother was pleased with the sawmill.
In the evening we ate some bacon and then I discoursed
about several things with G-r-l. I neglected to say my
prayers but had good health, good thoughts, and good
humor, thank God Almighty.

14. I rose about 6 o'clock and said a short prayer and
then went to the mill where we met Tom Randolph who
told us all was well at the plantations. Then I ate some
boiled milk for breakfast. Captain Soanes called and discoursed about the money I owed him for his land. About

9 o'clock I gave the necessary orders and then took my leave of my brother Custis and delivered him into Tom Randolph's hands and returned home and the weather began to clear up again. There was a great noise in the wood made by certain flies by some called drouth flies. About 12 o'clock I got home and found all well, thank God, but my wife was out of humor; that made me so likewise. Mrs. Harrison and Mrs. Hamlin came and dined with us and I ate some broiled shoat. In the evening I took a walk about the plantation and was a little out of humor because my wife was not so kind as I thought she should be. I said my prayers and had good thoughts, good humor, and good health, thank God Almighty.

15. I rose about 6 o'clock and read two chapters in Hebrew and some Greek in Lucian. I said my prayers and ate boiled milk for breakfast. I danced my dance. Mr. T-r-t-n came and I agreed with him to build my sloop next year. I settled some accounts with a man who came from above. The weather was warm and clear again. I settled several accounts till 12 o'clock and then came Captain Posford and Captain Randolph to dine with me and I ate some pigeon and bacon and asparagus. The captains went away soon after dinner and then I settled some accounts and read some Dutch till the evening and then I went to see my people turn the boat and helped them till the evening and then it began to thunder and rained extremely. I gave my people a dram because they had wet themselves and stayed much in the water. I said a short prayer and had good health, good thoughts, and good humor, thank God Almighty. I rogered my wife.

16. I rose about 6 o'clock and read two chapters in Hebrew and some Greek in Lucian. I said my prayers and ate boiled milk for breakfast. I danced my dance. The weather was cloudy and my people went to plant tobacco this morning. About 10 o'clock came Captain [Willis][1] who commands Mr. Offley's ship in York River and with him

[1]Perhaps Francis Willis, mentioned in the *Journal of the Commissioners for Trade and Plantations*, 1714-18, p. 164.

one Mr. Adams.[1] I gave them some cherries and wine and persuaded the first to stay to dinner and I ate some roast shoat. In the afternoon came Mr. Bland and soon after him Mr. Mumford and we settled what goods Mr. Bland should send to Appomattox. It thundered in the afternoon without any rain here. About 5 o'clock I sent my boat with Mr. Bland to Swinyards and Mr. Mumford and I took a walk about the plantation. At night I ate some bread and butter with Mr. Mumford. I neglected to say my prayers but had good health, good thoughts, and good humor, thank God Almighty.

17. I rose about 6 o'clock and read a chapter in Hebrew and some Greek in Lucian. I said my prayers and ate boiled milk for breakfast. I danced my dance. I sent John Bannister on board ship with Mr. Mumford. The weather was clear but not very warm. I settled several accounts and then prepared to put up some pictures. About 12 o'clock Mr. Mumford returned and said none of the masters were aboard. I had little stomach to my dinner and only ate some [c-t] soup. In the afternoon we cleaned and put up some pictures. Then I ate some cherries and afterwards took a walk about the plantation. Mr. Mumford went away over the river. At night I ate some bread and butter. I said my prayers and had good thoughts, good humor, and good health, thank God Almighty.

18. I rose about 6 o'clock and read two chapters in Hebrew and some Greek in Lucian. I said my prayers and ate boiled milk for breakfast. I danced my dance. The weather was clear and cold. I received a letter from one of the masters in York River that he would take my tobacco at £8 a ton but I wrote him word I was engaged already. Then I read some English till dinner and ate some fish only. In the afternoon I took a little nap and my wife went out in the coach. I read some Dutch and English till my wife returned and then I took a walk with her and ate some

---

[1]Possibly James Adams, interpreter to the Pamunkey and Chickahominy Indians. (*LJC*, I. 538.)

cherries. At night I neglected to say my prayers and had good health, good thoughts, and good humor, thank God Almighty.

19. I rose about 6 o'clock and read two chapters in Hebrew and some Greek in Lucian. I said my prayers and ate boiled milk for breakfast. I danced my dance. The weather was clear and cold. I ordered my colt to be branded. There were abundant flies like locusts in the wood which make a shrill noise but do no visible mischief, and the birds eat them so that we saved our cherries and other fruit from them. I settled some accounts. About 12 o'clock came Hal Gee from above and told me Mr. G-r-l had overset himself and was lame but could tell me no particulars. I settled accounts with him. I ate some tongue for dinner. In the afternoon I put several things in order and then went to the store and unpacked several things till the evening and then took a walk about the plantation. I neglected to say my prayers but had good health, good thoughts, and good humor, thank God Almighty.

20. I rose about 6 o'clock and read a chapter in Hebrew and some Greek in Lucian. I said my prayers and ate boiled milk for breakfast. I danced my dance. The weather was hot but cloudy. I settled some accounts till about 10 o'clock and then came Isham Randolph to borrow the 12-hogshead flat which he had and also to get notes for my tobacco in York River. I gave him some cherries and he went away about 12 o'clock and soon after came Tom Randolph from sharing my crops in York River and I found, one with another, I had made 1680 a share with which I was content. I ate some green peas for dinner. In the afternoon I discoursed Tom Randolph concerning several matters and he went away about 4 o'clock, notwithstanding it threatened rain and it did rain soon after he was gone, so that I could not walk but only in the library. I said my prayers and had good health, good thoughts, and good humor, thank God Almighty.

21. I rose about 6 o'clock and read two chapters in Hebrew and some Greek in Lucian. I said my prayers and ate boiled milk for breakfast. I danced my dance. It rained this morning and all the people went to plant tobacco. I settled accounts and wrote out some of my general accounts to send to England. I ate some bacon fraise for dinner. In the afternoon I wrote the other accounts till about 5 o'clock and then I ate some cherries and then wrote a letter to Robin Beverley concerning a protested bill of exchange. In the evening I took a walk about the plantation. At night I received a letter from Dr. Cocke, who desired me to persuade Captain Posford to send his boat to Green Springs for him and his lady. I ate some bread and cheese for supper. I said my prayers and had good health, good thoughts, and good humor, thank God Almighty.

22. I rose about 6 o'clock and read two chapters in Hebrew and some Greek in Lucian. I said my prayers and ate boiled milk for breakfast. I danced my dance. It rained a little this morning. My wife caused Prue to be whipped violently notwithstanding I desired not, which provoked me to have Anaka whipped likewise who had deserved it much more, on which my wife flew into such a passion that she hoped she would be revenged of me. I was moved very much at this but only thanked her for the present lest I should say things foolish in my passion. I wrote more accounts to go to England. My wife was sorry for what she had said and came to ask my pardon and I forgave her in my heart but seemed to resent, that she might be the more sorry for her folly. She ate no dinner nor appeared the whole day. I ate some bacon for dinner. In the afternoon I wrote two more accounts till the evening and then took a walk in the garden. I said my prayers and was reconciled to my wife and gave her a flourish in token of it. I had good health, good thoughts, but was a little out of humor, for which God forgive me.

23. I rose about 6 o'clock and read two chapters in Hebrew and some Greek in Lucian. I said my prayers and ate boiled milk for breakfast. I danced my dance. It was

cloudy and hot this morning. I wrote more public accounts to send to England. My wife and I were very good friends again. Captain Posford sent his boat to Green Springs for Dr. Cocke and his family. I ate bacon fraise for dinner. In the afternoon I put several things in order and then wrote another account but committed so many mistakes that I was forced to write it over again. We had some showers now and then in the day. In the evening I walked about the plantation. I said my prayers and had good health, good thoughts, and good humor, thank God Almighty.

24. I rose about 6 o'clock and read two chapters in Hebrew and some Greek in Lucian. I said my prayers and ate boiled milk for breakfast. I danced my dance. Then I wrote an account over again. The weather was clear and the wind, northeast, was fair for our friends and brought them up [o-v-r]. By 12 o'clock there came the Doctor and his wife and Mr. Catesby and the Doctor's daughter. I received them very courteously and gave them a glass of canary and some cakes to stay their stomachs. There was no news but only that L-r-n T-y had found a silvermine.[1] About 3 o'clock we went to dinner and I ate some beans and bacon for dinner. In the afternoon the daughter, Mr. Catesby, and I went into the swamp to see the nest of a humming bird and the Doctor followed along. However we found a nest with one young and one egg in it. In the evening we took a walk about the plantation and at night we drank a bottle. I neglected to say my prayers but had good health, good thoughts, and good humor, thank God Almighty.

25. I rose about 8 o'clock and read two chapters in Hebrew and no Greek. I said my prayers and ate boiled milk for breakfast. I danced my dance. The weather was very clear and cold. About 11 o'clock we went to church

---

[1] On May 15, 1712, Spotswood wrote to the Board of Trade and Plantations concerning the encouragement of mining and referred to "a general opinion lately revived that there are gold and silver mines" toward the Carolina mountains. (*Official Letters of Alexander Spotswood*, I, 160-162.)

where Mr. Anderson gave us a good sermon. The two Mrs. Thomsons[1] were come up to see Mrs. Eppes and I invited them to come and see us. I took three of the masters of ships home with us to dinner and I ate some dried beef. In the afternoon the masters went away very early and we went to take a walk in the evening. At night we drank a bottle and the women went upstairs by themselves. I said my prayers and was out of humor that my wife did not come to bed soon. I had good health, good humor, and good health [sic], thank God Almighty.

26. I rose about 6 o'clock and read a chapter in Hebrew and some Greek in Lucian. I said my prayers and ate boiled milk for breakfast. I danced my dance. It was cloudy and cold. I wrote several letters to send by the Doctor to Williamsburg who threatened to go tomorrow. I did nothing but write out another account to send to England before dinner. I ate some boiled pork. In the afternoon I wrote more letters till the evening and then took a walk about the plantation with the ladies and afterwards Mr. Catesby and I walked in the garden. [In] the evening we drank a bottle and were merry till about 10 o'clock and then we parted. I said my prayers and had good health, good thoughts, and good humor, thank God Almighty.

27. I rose about 6 o'clock and read a chapter in Hebrew and some Greek in Lucian. I said my prayers and drank some tea and ate bread and butter. I danced my dance. The weather was very hot this morning. About 10 o'clock came my sloop from Falling Creek and brought several things. I caused tobacco to be put on board to send to ships at Swinyards. I settled some accounts till dinner. I ate some beans and bacon. In the afternoon we went into the library to see some prints. We spent the afternoon in conversation and in the evening we took a walk and ate some cherries. At night we had a syllabub and drank a bottle and were merry. I said my prayers and had good health, good thoughts, and good humor, thank God Almighty.

---

[1]Probably Mary and Elizabeth, daughters of Stevens Thomson. (*Wm. Q.* (*1*), X, 141.)

28. I rose about 6 o'clock and read a chapter in Hebrew and some Greek in Lucian. I said my prayers and drank some tea for breakfast. I settled accounts with old P-r-t. The weather was cold in the morning but very hot in the afternoon. I read some Latin in Petronius till dinner. I ate some green goose. In the afternoon I set my razor. and then read some more Latin in Petronius till the evening and then we took a walk about the plantation, notwithstanding it threatened rain and was very hot. At night I drank a bottle with my friends and [we] were very merry. The ladies ate some bread and butter for supper. I neglected to say my prayers but had good health, good thoughts, and good humor, thank God Almighty. Mr. Platt was here in the morning to settle accounts.

29. I rose about 6 o'clock and read two chapters in Hebrew and some Greek in Lucian. I said my prayers and drank milk tea for breakfast. I danced my dance. The weather was hot. My sloop returned from putting my tobacco on board and I set my people to patching the upper works of the sloop. Then I wrote several things and settled some accounts and went into the library and read some Latin. The Doctor went away to Williamsburg on my horse. I ate some tongue for dinner. In the afternoon we talked for about an hour and then I went and read more Latin till the evening. It rained very hard this afternoon but in the evening grew fair [again]. I took a walk about the plantation. At night I reprimanded my overseer for rising so late, as I did also John G-r-l. I ate some bread and butter for supper. I said my prayers and had good health, good thoughts, and good humor, thank God Almighty.

30. I rose about 6 o'clock and read a chapter in Hebrew and some Greek in Lucian. I said my prayers and had tea and bread and butter for breakfast. I danced my dance. It was very cold this morning. Betty Harrison came and told us her mother was better of the cold she had lately had. I wrote an account but did not finish it before Colonel Hill and Mr. Anderson and his wife came and soon after them

Captain Posford. They all dined with us and I ate some calf for dinner. In the afternoon we were very merry till about 6 o'clock and then the company went away. Tom came from Williamsburg and brought me a letter from Mr. Bland. In the evening Mr. Catesby and I took a walk about the plantation and did not return till dark. At night I ate some bread and butter. We talked till about 10 o'clock. I neglected to say my prayers but had good health, good thoughts, and good humor, thank God Almighty.

31. I rose about 6 o'clock and read a chapter in Hebrew and some Greek in Lucian. I said my prayers and ate raspberries and milk for breakfast. I danced my dance. The weather was very hot again. I was angry with Billy Wilkins for not writing yesterday and gave him a salute on the ear. My sloop went away last night to Falling Creek. I wrote one public account and then read some Latin in Petronius till dinner and then I ate some salt fish. In the afternoon came Mr. Salle from Manakin town and Phil W-b-r to renew his bill of exchange. I wrote another account and then my wife and the ladies went out in the coach and in the evening the men and I walked out to meet them. They all ate some supper at night except me who did not find myself very well. I said my prayers and had good health, good thoughts, and good humor, thank God Almighty. The weather was very cool this [. . .], the wind southeast. I was out of humor with my wife for her foolish passions, of which she is often guilty, for which God forgive her and make her repent and amend.

June, 1712

1. I rose about 6 o'clock and read two chapters in Hebrew and some Greek in Lucian. I said my prayers and ate nothing for breakfast because I was indisposed and feared an ague which I had [favorably], thank God, but my wife took no notice of my complaint. Mrs. Cocke had a letter from her husband with an account of two prizes condemned.[1] The weather was cloudy. I grew so ill that about 10 o'clock I was forced to go to bed and soon after had a most violent fever and sore throat. My fever continued with great violence till about 6 o'clock and then it began to abate and then I took the bark, very willingly, to avoid having another fit. Mrs. Cocke had the goodness to come and sit above an hour with me. Mrs. Dunn gave me the bark in the night. I slept indifferently but had no command of my thoughts nor humor, God's will be done.

2. I rose not in the morning but took the bark in bed and sweated much and ate nothing but two eggs all day. I began my two ounces of bark and did not rise till the afternoon for about two hours and then went to bed again. I said a short prayer and found neither my strength nor looks much altered. Mrs. Cocke made me a short visit this day while I lay abed. I endeavored to eat some minced veal but could not eat but very little or nothing. The weather was very hot though I was not very sensible of it, I was so dizzy with the bark. However it removed the fever, thank God, and I was pretty well. I recommended myself to God in a short prayer but had good health, good thoughts, and good humor, thank God Almighty. Tom Randolph came over this morning.

3. I did not rise till about 10 o'clock but continued to take my bark. I found myself very easy, thank God, and had

---

[1]Spotswood in a letter of May 15, 1712 reports that the guard ships have taken 12 ships bound for Martinique, and that the *Bedford* has taken a French merchant ship loaded with sugar, indigo, and cocoa. (*Official Letters of Alexander Spotswood*, I, 163.)

bread and butter and tea for breakfast. I said a short prayer and wrote some things. Mr. Randolph told [me] all was well under his care and gave me several accounts of my matters above. Major Harrison and his wife and my neighbor Harrison came to dine with us. I did not dine with them but ate some meat which made me hot and [o-d-r]. The company went away about 4 o'clock after being very merry and I took a little walk in the garden and the library. I sat up pretty late and when I went to bed could not sleep a great while but when I got to sleep I woke not till morning. I said a short prayer and had good thoughts, good humor, and pretty good health, thank God Almighty. The stonecutter came from Williamsburg to put up my marble chimney piece.

4. I rose about 8 o'clock and found myself pretty well, thank God. I had tea and bread and butter for breakfast after having said a short prayer. About 10 o'clock came Captain Posford to tell me his sloop was ready to take in my things to carry them to York River and I ordered them immediately to be put on board accordingly, and she sailed with a tide and wind down the river. About 12 o'clock came Mrs. Betty Thomson and Mrs. Llewellyn Eppes with Mr. Booth[1] and Llewellyn Eppes and several after them, among whom was Robin Bolling who had not been in the house for several years. Colonel Frank Eppes came to account with me and I gave him a wipe about hindering his son from going to Carolina. We had 11 people at dinner and Mr. Clayton among them but I ate nothing but bread and butter. In the afternoon most of the company went away and Mr. Mumford came and told me all was well at Appomattox. At night I went early to bed but the ladies talked so loud I could not sleep a great while, which made me uneasy. I said my prayers and had indifferent health, no thoughts, and bad humor. God's will be done. The stone[cutter] got some irons made for the marble.

[1]Possibly the Mr. Booth of York County who is said to have married Mary Thomson, daughter of Stevens Thomson.

5. I rose about 9 o'clock and found myself not well for want of sleep. I said my prayers and had tea and bread and butter for breakfast. The stonecutter began to work in the library chimney. I wrote in my journal all that happened since I was sick. The weather was extremely hot. Mr. Mumford went away about 11 o'clock, when it rained a little and would not stay to dinner though I invited him to do it. I ate some boiled mutton for dinner but did not dine with the rest of the company because they would not have the window shut where it rained in. This made me a little out of humor. After dinner I found myself better and walked about the garden all the evening, and Mr. Catesby directed how I should mend my garden and put it into a better fashion than it is at present. I ate two poached eggs for supper and did not go to bed till the rest of the company. I said a short prayer and had good thoughts but indifferent good health and humor, thank God Almighty. I slept very well.

6. I rose about 8 o'clock and found myself much better because of having slept well. I had bread and butter and tea for breakfast. I said my prayers shortly. The weather was pretty cold with the rain that fell yesterday. I read a little English. It rained several times and cleared up again. I was very lazy and did only settle some accounts before dinner. In the afternoon walked about very much and read nothing. About 4 o'clock came Tom [Howlett] and I settled accounts with him. Then I took a walk about the plantation and returned some time before it was dark out of pure discretion, and found Prue with a candle by daylight, for which I gave her a salute with my foot. At night I ate two poached eggs for my supper. I neglected to say my prayers but had good health, good thoughts, and good humor, thank God Almighty.

7. I rose about 8 o'clock and began to take the bark again. I found myself pretty well though I did not sleep well last night. I said my prayers and had tea and bread and butter for breakfast. I settled several accounts. It rained several times before dinner. However Captain Pos-

ford came to know whether [. . .] have the boat on Monday. He stayed to dinner and I ate some tongue for dinner. Soon after dinner came John [Butts][1] to account with me for the quitrents of New Kent. He would not eat. In the afternoon I settled several more accounts and read a little English till the evening and then Mr. Catesby and I took a walk about the plantation and I ventured to eat six cherries. I ate two poached eggs for supper. I took the bark four times this day. I said a short prayer and had good health, good thoughts, and good humor, thank God Almighty. I rogered my wife with vigor.

8. I rose about 8 o'clock and took the bark. I said my prayers and had tea and bread and butter for breakfast. I found myself pretty well this morning. The weather was cool. I took four doses of bark today to make an end. We prepared to go to church where we had a good sermon by Mr. Anderson. It was very hot at church. We stayed to receive the Sacrament which I did devoutly. Nobody came to dine with us. I ate some roast pigeon for dinner. In the afternoon came the Doctor very much fatigued but brought no news. In the evening we took a walk about the plantation and ventured to eat more [cherries]. I ate some bread and cheese for supper. Before I went to bed I drank my last dose of bark. I neglected to say my prayers and had good health, good thoughts, and good humor, thank God Almighty.

9. I rose about 8 o'clock and found myself pretty well. I said my prayers and ate bread and butter for breakfast. I prepared to go to Williamsburg with the Doctor and my sister Custis. The weather was very hot and the boat came not so soon as we expected so that we ate again about 12 o'clock and I ate some roast chicken. The boat came not till almost 3 o'clock and then we took leave and went first on board the "Harrison" where we drank some strong beer and then proceeded in our voyage with a fair wind but it was

---

[1]Possibly a brother of Thomas Butts, who was sheriff of New Kent. John Butts is mentioned as an attorney in 1705 and was a justice of the peace in King William County in 1714. (*Va. Mag.*, II, 7; XXV, 175.)

late before we got to Green Springs. Tom was not at the
landing with the horses but we soon met him. We found all
well at Green Springs and drank some canary. The weather
was exceedingly hot so that I dreaded going to bed. However I ventured about 11 o'clock. I neglected to say my
prayers but had good health, good thoughts, and good
humor, thank God Almighty.

10. I rose about 4 o'clock with design to go away to
Williamsburg but our horses were not ready till 6 and then
the Doctor and I rode to Williamsburg. When I got there
I lay down and took a nap for two hours and then went to
the coffeehouse and drank six dishes of tea and then intended
to go wait on the Governor but he prevented us by coming
to the coffeehouse; however we made him the compliment
that we were just coming to wait on him. About 12 o'clock
we went to the capitol to Council where we agreed that for
the future there should always [exist] a commission of oyer
and terminer whether there were any criminals or not, but
were content to go without pay for this time because no
commission had [existed]. The Governor exposed an
anxiety about his double dealing with the Doctor about his
commission of secretary. About 5 o'clock we went to dine
with the Governor and when we got there happened a
terrible gust. I ate some boiled beef for dinner. At night
the Doctor was sworn secretary.[1] About 11 o'clock the
President set me home in his coach where I neglected to say
my prayers but had good humor, good thoughts, but indifferent health, thank God Almighty. The gust this evening split the mizzen mast of the "Harrison" and had like to
burned the ship.

11. I rose about 6 o'clock and said a short prayer. I
settled some accounts with gentlemen who came to my
chambers and then ate milk for breakfast. About 9 o'clock
I went to the coffeehouse and drank some tea and stayed

---

[1]For an account of this meeting of the Council and Dr. William Cocke's
entry into the office of secretary of state for the colony, see *Ex. Jour.*, III,
313-17. Byrd was apparently security for Cocke, as in 1718 he declined to
continue so (*ibid.*, 481) ; Cocke served until 1720.

there till 12 o'clock and then went to the capitol where Colonel Ludwell and I were to determine the difference between the two Burwells and their sisters and we had the good fortune to do it to their entire satisfaction. About 4 o'clock the Doctor and I went in his coach to the Commissary's where we dined and I ate some fowl and bacon. About 6 we went in the Doctor's coach to Green Springs where we found several people. Here we went to bed for two hours and then rose and went to the landing in the Doctor's coach and there went into the boat in order to return home and we slept in the boat. I said my prayers and had good health, good thoughts, and good humor, thank God Almighty.

12. About 5 o'clock in the morning we went ashore at Major H-n-t where we slept about three hours on beds where there were abundance of chinches. About 11 o'clock we had an indifferent breakfast of bacon and peas and water to drink. About 12 o'clock we got into the boat again and about 3 got on board the "Harrison" where I heard the damage the gust and [. . .] had done her. We ate some [anchovies] and drank some wine and strong beer. About 6 o'clock we proceeded to Westover where we found all well, thank God. We drank some syllabub and talked till about 9 o'clock and then retired. I said a short prayer and had good health, good thoughts, and good humor, thank God Almighty. I rogered my wife with vigor. My sloop went this morning to Williamsburg.

13. I rose about 7 o'clock and read a chapter in Hebrew and some Greek in Lucian. I said my prayers and had bread and butter for breakfast. I wrote in my journal and settled several matters. The weather was very hot. I settled several accounts and put several things in order in the library which I caused to be cleaned. It was 4 o'clock before we went to dinner and I ate some fish. In the afternoon I put things again in order in the library and then walked in the garden. I had a small quarrel with my wife concerning the [nastiness] of the nursery but I would not be provoked. In the evening Mr. Catesby and I took a

walk about the plantation and I drank some warm milk at the cowpen and there discovered that one of the wenches had stolen some apples. I said my prayers and had good health, good thoughts, and good humor, thank God Almighty.

14. I rose about 7 o'clock and read two chapters in Hebrew and some Greek in Lucian. I said my prayers and drank some whey for breakfast. It rained this morning and was pretty cold; however we kept our purpose to go aboard ship; about 12 o'clock the boat came for us and about one we went with a fair wind to Swinyards. All the ships there had their ornaments out and we were received with 11 guns by the "Harrison". About 2 o'clock came Captain Randolph and Captain Turner and then we went to dinner and I ate some ship's beef. We had abundance of guns all day long so that in all we had about 120 from all the ships. Tom Randolph came in the afternoon and told me all was well everywhere. The rain kept us till 10 o'clock and then we returned home and were so merry that Mr. Catesby sang. I neglected to say my prayers but had good health, good thoughts, and good humor, thank God Almighty. Mr. Mumford was at our house and told me all was well at Appomattox.

15. I rose about 7 o'clock and read two chapters in Hebrew and some Greek in Lucian. I said my prayers and had milk and hominy for breakfast. I began again to dance my dance. About 10 Tom Randolph came to let me know Captain Randolph's sloop had left out nine hogsheads of my tobacco in York River because the sloop was leaky. He went away again presently. It was very cold this morning. I ate some veal for dinner. In the afternoon we went in the coach to visit Mrs. Harrison where we had some syllabub and stayed till 8 o'clock. Then we returned home and ate some bread and cheese and drank a bottle. I neglected to say my prayers but had good health, good thoughts, and good humor, thank God Almighty. Mr. [. . .] went away this evening.

16. I rose about 7 o'clock and read a chapter in Hebrew and some Greek in Lucian. I said my prayers and had tea and bread and butter for breakfast. Our company prepared to go away this day. I danced my dance. The weather continued cold, the wind at northeast. We prepared to go aboard Captain Randolph and about 11 o'clock the boat came for us and we got aboard about 12. I had a looseness in the morning. I ate some pea soup for dinner, and some ship's beef which made me out of order, so that I was very dull company till the evening, and then we danced some dances. The wind proved contrary as well as the tide, so that our company returned home with us again about 8 o'clock. We had guns only going and coming. I neglected to say my prayers but had good health, good thoughts, and good humor, thank God Almighty. Mr. Salle was here when we came home.

17. I rose about 6 o'clock and read a chapter in Hebrew and some Greek in Lucian. I said my prayers and had milk tea and bread and butter for breakfast. I [sent] a letter to the Governor by Mr. Salle. About 10 o'clock the Doctor and his lady went away and Colonel Foster[1] came to make up his sheriff's accounts and stayed about an hour. Then I settled some accounts till dinner and I ate some roast veal. In the afternoon noon [sic] I put several things in order in the library and then wrote a letter to England and got Mrs. Dunn to copy it. In the evening I took a walk all about the plantation and found the tobacco in the weed extremely. I said my prayers and had good health, good thoughts, and good humor, thank God Almighty.

18. I rose about 6 o'clock and read a chapter in Hebrew and some Greek in Lucian. I said my prayers and ate boiled milk for breakfast. I danced my dance. The weather began to grow warm again and my people began to reap the wheat. I wrote a letter to England. About 12 o'clock Tom Randolph came from below and told me all was well but that things were very backwards there. I ate some minced

---

[1]Colonel Joseph Foster, sheriff of New Kent County in 1710 and 1711.

veal for dinner. In the afternoon I took a nap and then wrote more letters to England. About 4 o'clock Tom Randolph went away to the Falls. He told me my maid Betty M-l-ng had a negro husband and was good for nothing. In the evening I took a walk and drank some warm milk from the cow. I said my prayers and had good health, good thoughts, and good humor, thank God Almighty.

19. I rose about 6 o'clock and read two chapters in Hebrew and some Greek in Lucian. I said my prayers and had warm milk from the cow. I danced my dance. The weather was very hot and sultry. I wrote a letter to England and then wrote a public account. Then I read some Latin in Sallust till dinner and then I ate some bacon and sallet. In the afternoon I made some punch and put it into bottles and then I wrote another account and afterwards read more Latin in Sallust. In the evening I took a walk about the plantation. A Frenchman that had been courteously entertained here took away my boat across the river, but he brought it again and I gave him a severe reprimand. I said my prayers and had good health, good thoughts, and good humor, thank God Almighty. I drank some milk from the cow.

20. I rose about 5 o'clock and read two chapters in Hebrew and some Greek in Lucian. I said my prayers and drank some warm milk for breakfast. I danced my dance. It was exceedingly hot; however Captain [Salle] came over from Williamsburg and let me know the Governor had, according to my desire, made Mr. T-b cornet of dragoons and had reprimanded them that had mutinied. I wrote a public account before dinner. I ate some dried beef. In the afternoon came Captain Wilcox to give bills of lading and settle accounts and did take several of my letters to England. About 3 o'clock they all went away again and I wrote an account till the evening and then I took a walk about the plantation and found my people had made an end of reaping. I drank some warm milk from the [cow]. I said my prayers and had good health, good thoughts, and good humor, thank God Almighty. I rogered my wife.

21. I rose about 5 o'clock and read two chapters in
Hebrew and some Greek in Lucian. I said my prayers and
drank some warm milk. I danced my dance. The weather
was very hot again. I wrote an account to be sent to England, and then read some Latin in Sallust. My wife was out
of order but three hours' sleep recovered her. Mrs. Dunn
had her face swelled very much. I ate some cold beef and
sallet for dinner. In the afternoon I settled several accounts
and then read more Latin in Sallust. Mrs. Harvey came to
see my wife, who is exceedingly altered from a very pretty
woman. There was a little gust in the evening but it rained
but little and did not hinder me from walking about the
plantation. I drank some warm milk from the cow. I said
my prayers and had good health, good thoughts, and good
humor, thank God Almighty. My sloop came in the night
from Williamsburg.

22. I rose about 5 o'clock and read two chapters in
Hebrew and some Greek in Lucian. I said my prayers and
ate milk and hominy for breakfast. My sloop came up in
the night from Williamsburg and brought abundance of
goods for Mr. Mumford from Mr. Bland. It was a little
cold and cloudy and threatened rain. About 11 o'clock we
went to church and had a good sermon from Mr. Anderson
but it rained so after dinner that the congregation could not
go home. I took the two captains home that belonged to
the ship to dine with me and I ate some roast pig. I heard
this day that Captain Llewellyn died on Thursday last which
surprised me because I knew not that he had been sick.
About 4 o'clock the captains went away and it rained all the
afternoon so that I could not walk. I said my prayers and
had good health, good thoughts, and good humor, thank
God Almighty.

23. I rose about 6 o'clock and found Mr. G-r-l here and
the Dutch joiner. I settled accounts with the last and I got
the first to put up the glass in the library. Mr. Hardiman
came here about the horse that killed his father. I settled
accounts with Allen [Bailey] and Will Bass. I sent the
sloop away to Appomattox. I drank some warm milk for

breakfast. I neglected to say my prayers. The weather
cleared up and I set my people to cutting the oats down.
I ate some fish for dinner. In the afternoon G-r-l went away
and the other man with him. I settled several accounts and
then ate some cherries. In the evening I took a walk about
the plantation and trimmed some trees in the walk. · At
night I drank some milk from the cow. I said a short
prayer and had good health, good thoughts, and good
humor, thank God Almighty. It was cold weather. My
[wife] was sick with being with child.

24. I rose about 6 o'clock and read two chapters in
Hebrew and some Greek in Lucian. I said my prayers and
drank some milk from the cow. I had a letter from Colonel
Eppes to invite me to Captain Llewellyn's funeral. There
was a gust and thunder but it did not reach us, thank God,
for my people continued to cut oats. I settled several accounts and wrote six letters before dinner and then I ate
roast pigeon with an indifferent stomach. Mrs. Dunn continued out of order with a swelled face. In the afternoon
I settled several things in order in the library, and then read
some Latin in Sallust. I had a letter from Mr. Anderson to
borrow 12 sickles but I could not send them because my
people used them. In the evening I took a walk about the
plantation and then drank some milk from the cow. I said
my prayers and had good health, good thoughts, and good
humor, thank God Almighty.

25. I rose about 6 o'clock and read two chapters in
Hebrew and some Greek in Lucian. I said my prayers and
drank warm milk for breakfast. I danced my dance. The
weather was cloudy. Mrs. Dunn continued indisposed. I
settled things in order in the library. My wife was often
indisposed with breeding and very cross. I settled several
accounts and wrote a letter to the Governor and to Tom
Randolph. I ate some broiled bacon and pigeon for dinner.
In the afternoon I set several things in order in the library
and worked very hard till the evening. It rained this afternoon very much but my people made an end of cutting the
oats first, but the rain spoiled my walk. About 6 o'clock

came Captain Posford and brought with him Captain Lee, commander of one of the men-of-war. They had been drinking. They would eat nothing but bread and butter. About 9 o'clock Captain Posford went away and left Captain Lee here. I neglected to say my prayers but had good health, good thoughts, and good humor, thank God Almighty.

26. I rose about 6 o'clock and read two chapters in Hebrew and some Greek in Lucian. I said my prayers and drank some milk from the cow. About 7 o'clock Captain Lee went away and had nothing but a dram. Captain Posford sent me word his sloop was got well from York River with my 54 hogsheads of tobacco. It was very cool, that my wife and I resolved to go to the funeral of Captain Llewellyn. Mrs. Dunn was better but could not go with us. About 11 o'clock we went in the coach and got there soon after 12. There were abundance of people. Mr. Anderson gave us a sermon. We had wine and biscuits according to custom. We stayed there till 6 o'clock and then returned and our horses performed very well. Tom L-s-n was indisposed for which I caused him to be bled. I took a walk about the plantation. I neglected to say my prayers but had good health, good thoughts, and good humor, thank God Almighty.

27. I rose about 6 o'clock and read two chapters in Hebrew and some Greek in Lucian. I said my prayers and drank milk from the cow. I danced my dance. It continued very cold. Tom L-s-n was a little better. I caused Tom G-r-d-n-r to be bled also for the headache. My wife was still out of order with breeding. Jenny at the quarter was out of order likewise and threatened to be brought to bed but was not. I settled some accounts till dinner and then I ate some roast shoat. In the afternoon I put several things in order in the library and then continued to settle some accounts till the evening and then I took a walk about the plantation. I ate a little roast shoat for supper. I said my prayers and had good health, good thoughts, and good

humor, thank God Almighty. Tom L-s-n was a little better. The weather continued cold and fair. I sent for a midwife for Jenny but she was not at home.

28. I rose about 5 o'clock and read two chapters in Hebrew and some Greek in Lucian. I said my prayers and drank warm milk from the cow. I danced my dance. My sick people were better except my wife who seemed to have a little fever with a pain in her legs. The weather continued cool and fair. I gave Bannister leave to go see his mother. I settled some accounts and wrote a letter till dinner and then I ate some broiled pork. In the afternoon I settled more accounts till about 4 o'clock and then came Captain Posford and stayed about an hour and then returned aboard again. In the evening my wife was extremely bad. I took a walk about the plantation and trimmed some of the peach trees. I neglected to say my prayers but had good health, good thoughts, and good humor, thank God Almighty. I slept but indifferently this night but my wife slept better.

29. I rose about 6 o'clock and read two chapters in Hebrew and some Greek in Lucian. I said my prayers and had milk and hominy for breakfast. I danced my dance. My wife was better, thank God. The sloop came about 10 o'clock and brought 13 hogsheads of skins from Appomattox where all was well, thank God Almighty. The weather was warm again. I ate some boiled pork for dinner. In the afternoon I took a nap. I received a letter from the sheriff of King and Queen[1] with a bill of exchange, to which I wrote an answer. Then I read some English till the evening, when I took a walk about the plantation. I said my prayers and had good health, good thoughts, and good humor, thank God Almighty.

30. I rose about 6 o'clock and read two chapters in Hebrew and some Greek in Lucian. I said my prayers and had warm milk from the cow. My wife continued indisposed. The weather was clear and warm. I caused Johnny to be whipped for threatening to strike Jimmy and caused

---

[1]Thomas Pettitt, appointed sheriff on April 22, 1712.

Moll also to be whipped and made them renounce one the other. Prue and Jenny were also whipped. The sloop carried the skins and nine hogsheads of tobacco on board the ship. I wrote a long account of Mr. Tullitt's till dinner. In the afternoon I put things in order in the library and then wrote more accounts till the evening and then I took a walk about the plantation. I neglected to say my prayers but had good health, good thoughts, and good humor, thank God Almighty.

July, 1712

1. I rose about 5 o'clock and read two chapters in Hebrew and some Greek in the Apocrypha. I said my prayers and had warm milk for breakfast. My sloop returned in the night and I caused her to be loaded to go to the Falls. My wife had a pain in her side but could not be bled for pure fear. The weather was cold and clear, the wind northeast. I settled several accounts and put several things in order before dinner and caused several things to be put into the sloop to send to Falling Creek. Colonel Littlebury Eppes came and dined with me and I ate some ship's beef for dinner. In the afternoon I put several things in order and wrote a letter to Mr. Tullitt to send with his accounts and in the evening took a walk about the plantation. Mr. Anderson called here in the evening and told us several ships were come in with news that Mr. W-s is broke and Captain V-n-t taken into France. I said my prayers and had good health, good thoughts, and good humor, thank God Almighty.

2. I rose about 5 o'clock and read two chapters in Hebrew but no Greek for Captain R-s came and brought me about 12 letters from England. I said my prayers and drank milk from the cow. I found by my letters that W-s is broke and Captain V-n-t taken and that it is probable we shall have peace. About 11 o'clock abundance of company came and among them Mr. Rogers concerning Mrs. Parker's business and we made a shift to settle it at last. Then I went to court and brought about six gentlemen with me home to dinner. I ate beans and bacon. In the afternoon the company returned to court but I stayed to write some letters to send to Williamsburg. Then I took a walk about the plantation. My wife was a little better, thank God. The weather continued cold. I neglected to say my prayers but had good health, good thoughts, and good humor, thank God Almighty.

3. I rose about 5 o'clock and read two chapters in Hebrew and three chapters in [the] Greek Apocrypha. I said my prayers and drank milk from the cow. I danced my dance. My [wife] was better. The wind continued northeast and it rained; however I sent some powder to Appomattox in Captain Posford's boat. I read some news and read my letters again in order to answer them the better. I ate some roast mutton for dinner. In the afternoon I put things in order in the library and then wrote a letter to the Governor about a mistake I had committed in bills I sent to my Lord Orkney. The rain would not let me take a walk in the evening. I said my prayers and had good health, good thoughts, and good humor, thank God Almighty.

4. I rose about 5 o'clock and read a chapter in Hebrew and another in Greek. I said my prayers and had milk from the cow for breakfast. My wife was a little better, thank God. The weather was cloudy, the wind southwest. I wrote several letters to send to Williamsburg. It rained several showers in the day but very hard at night. I settled some accounts and wrote some letters till dinner and then I ate some bacon broiled. In the afternoon I settled several matters in the library and then settled more accounts and Bannister wrote out several of my accounts to send to England. It rained in the evening that I could not take a walk about the plantation. I said my prayers and had good health, good thoughts, and good humor, thank God Almighty.

5. I rose about 5 o'clock and read two chapters in Hebrew and four in Greek. I said my prayers and drank milk from the cow. I danced my dance. It was very cloudy again. My wife had the headache very much. I settled several things till dinner and then helped John Bannister to write. In the evening came Tom Osborne and told me all was well above and soon after came Tom Randolph and gave me an account of all matters to my satisfaction. I took a walk with him about the plantation. I said my prayers and had good health, good thoughts, and good humor, thank God Almighty. Captain Posford came from Williamsburg

and brought me a letter from the Doctor wherein he told me he expected peace by a letter from Frank W-l-s to his son later than the rest of the letters.

6. I rose about 6 o'clock and read two chapters in Hebrew and no Greek. I said my prayers and then ate some milk and hominy for breakfast. Then I gave some directions to Tom Randolph about my affairs above. The weather was cloudy and very hot; however I walked to church, where I saw Mr. Bland who gave me a letter from the Governor concerning Colonel Hill's giving bond for the collector's place. It rained while we were at church. Mr. Anderson gave us a good sermon and he, Colonel Hill, and Mrs. Anderson went home with us to dinner and so did Mr. Bland and Tom Randolph. I ate some goose for dinner. In the afternoon they went away and my wife went out in the coach and all the company went away and I took a walk about the plantation. I said my prayers and had good health, good thoughts, and good humor, thank God Almighty.

7. I rose about 5 o'clock and read two chapters in Hebrew and three in Greek. I said my prayers devoutly and had milk from the cow. I danced my dance. The weather was cloudy and hot. My wife was better, thank God. I wrote a long letter to England and settled accounts till dinner and then I ate some good beef for dinner. In the afternoon I put several things in order and then settled some accounts. About 4 o'clock came a gust with rain and thunder. It was violent but did not last. I took a walk in the evening, and Tom returned from Williamsburg and brought me several letters and one from the Governor but no news at all. I said my prayers and had good health, good thoughts, and good humor, thank God Almighty.

8. I rose about 5 o'clock and read two chapters in Hebrew and three in Greek. I said my prayers and had warm milk for breakfast. I danced my dance. It rained small rain in the morning. My wife was pretty well, thank God. I wrote two long letters to England and Bannister

wrote some public accounts till dinner and then I ate some broiled pork. In the afternoon I wrote more letters to England and settled some accounts till about 5 o'clock and then came Captain Turner but he stayed but a little time. In the evening I took a walk about the plantation. The weather cleared up this evening. I said my prayers and had good health, good thoughts, and good humor, thank God Almighty. Captain Posford called here in the morning as he went to Prince George court.

9. I rose about 5 o'clock and read two chapters in Hebrew and two in Greek. I said my prayers and drank some milk from the cow. I danced my dance. Mr. Gee came over to beg time till he could pay his protested bill, which I gave him. The weather was cold and clear. My wife was pretty well again, thank God. I wrote letters to England. We burnt a kiln of lime. Bannister continued to write the public accounts. I ate some boiled pork for dinner. I settled several matters in the library and then wrote more letters to England and settled some accounts till the evening and then I took a walk about the plantation. My wife was much indisposed this afternoon. I said my prayers and had good health, good thoughts, and good humor, thank God Almighty.

10. I rose about 6 o'clock and read two chapters in Hebrew and some Greek in the Apocrypha. I said my prayers and drank milk from the cow. I danced my dance. Mr. Goodwin came to get time to renew his protested bill and I gave him till October next. The weather was cloudy and hot. My wife was still indisposed but would not be bled till after an hour's trying. I wrote an English letter till dinner. My wife was faint after losing her blood. I ate some broiled bacon for dinner. In the afternoon I read some news. George Smith came down and I scolded at him for wasting his time above and sent him up again. Captain Turner and Captain Randolph called here and soon after them Mrs. Harrison and her daughter. In the evening I took a walk about the plantation. This day Mr. Page was

married to Judy Wormeley.[1] I said my prayers and had good health, good thoughts, and good humor, thank God Almighty.

11. I rose about 5 o'clock and read a chapter in Hebrew and three in Greek. I said my prayers and drank milk from the cow. Our house Jenny was taken very sick, for which I caused her to be bled and gave her a vomit. The weather was cloudy and hot. My wife continued weak. I wrote a letter to England and several other matters till about 12 o'clock and then came Colonel Hill to settle accounts with me and gave me bills for the balance. He stayed to dinner with us, and I ate some boiled beef. My wife longed for small beer and I sent to Mrs. Harrison's for some but she had none, so that she drank a bottle of strong almost herself. Tony came from Appomattox and brought a young horse with him and let me know all was well. Colonel Hill went away about 5 o'clock, and soon after it rained, that I could not walk. I neglected to say my prayers but had good health, good thoughts, and good humor, thank God Almighty.

12. I rose about 5 o'clock and read a chapter in Hebrew and three in Greek. I said my prayers and ate no breakfast because I ate too much yesterday. I danced my dance. Our maid Jenny was better, thank God, but my wife was indisposed. The weather was cloudy but it did not rain. I wrote several letters to England and Bannister wrote several accounts till dinner and then I ate some fritters. In the afternoon I put several things in order in the library and then wrote another letter to England. About 5 o'clock the sloop came from Falling Creek with the frame of the tobacco house and part of the granary. In the evening I took a walk about the plantation. I said my prayers and had good health, good thoughts, and good humor, thank God Almighty.

13. I rose about 6 o'clock and read a chapter in Hebrew. I said my prayers and had milk and hominy for breakfast.

---

[1]Mann Page of Rosewell; his first wife was Judith, daughter of Ralph Wormeley of Rosegill.

I received a letter from Dr. Cocke in which he desired me to pay Posford £25 but in my answer I excused myself. The weather was cloudy and very hot. My wife was a little better, thank God. I read some news till dinner and then I ate some roast shoat. In the afternoon I took a nap and then my wife and I had a small dispute which put her into a foolish passion and she continued out of humor all day and would not speak to me. Then I read some news again till the evening and then I took a walk about the plantation. When I returned I spoke kindly to my wife but she would not answer me; however I considered her weakness and bore it. I said my prayers and had good health, good thoughts, and good humor, thank God Almighty.

14. I rose about 6 o'clock and read a chapter in Hebrew and some Greek in the Apocrypha. I said my prayers and drank some milk from the cow. I danced my dance. My wife was still indisposed. The weather was clear and hot. My people took the granary out of the sloop, as much of it as they had brought this trip from above. I wrote some letters to England and settled some accounts till dinner and then I ate some roast pork. After dinner I settled some things in the library and then I wrote more letters to England. The sloop was unloaded and sent away but some of the frame of the granary was rotten. In the evening I took a walk about the plantation. I said my prayers and had good health, good thoughts, and good humor, thank God Almighty.

15. I rose about 6 o'clock and read a chapter in Hebrew and a chapter in Greek. I said my prayers and had milk from the cow. I danced my dance. The weather was clear and very hot. My wife was a little better, thank God. I wrote several letters and settled some accounts to be sent to England. This was the hottest day we have had this year. I ate some roast shoat for dinner. In the afternoon I settled some things in the library. My wife had the headache violently. I wrote more letters to England till the evening and then took a walk about the plantation. I have had three calves die in three days. Mrs. P-l-n-t [Pleasants?] had

halloed a great while for the ferry but could not be heard.
Therefore I desired [her] to go home with me and a boy
set her over the river which she did. She told me that
Colonel Hill had the gout. I neglected to say my prayers
but had good health, good thoughts, and good humor, thank
God Almighty.

16. I rose about 6 o'clock and read a chapter in Hebrew
but no Greek. I said my prayers and had milk from the
cow for breakfast. About 9 o'clock Captain Posford came
but did [not] bring me the box of books. I wrote several
letters to England. About 10 Captain Posford went away
again and I wrote again till about 12 when Colonel Eppes
sent me several letters from Williamsburg. I ate some
boiled pork for dinner. In the after dinner [sic] I took a
little nap and then read some news. G-r-m-r P-n came from
the Falls and told me all was well there. She came to get a
lease of some of my land. Then I wrote more letters to
England till the evening and then took a walk about the
plantation. This was a hotter day still than yesterday. I
wrote a letter to Falling Creek. I neglected to say my
prayers but had good health, good thoughts, and good
humor, thank God. I rogered my wife.

17. I rose about 6 o'clock and wrote a chapter in Hebrew
and a chapter in Greek. I said my prayers and drank some
milk from the cow. The weather continued to be exceedingly hot. My wife was pretty well, thank God. I wrote a
letter to England and a public account till dinner and then
I ate some pigeon. I had invited John Eppes and Mr.
Dennis to come and dine with me but they came not till after
dinner. My wife wished to seal an instrument before two
justices and she did it before them. They stayed all the
afternoon and went away in the evening and then I and my
wife took a little walk in the orchard. I said my prayers and
had good health, good thoughts, and good humor, thank
God Almighty. It rained much in the night with abundance
of thunder and lightning.

18. I rose about 6 o'clock and read a chapter in Hebrew
and no Greek in the Apocrypha. I had milk from the cow

for breakfast. The weather was cloudy and cool. My wife
was indisposed. About 8 o'clock came Captain Posford,
with whom I settled accounts, and soon after came Tom
Randolph and Mr. Finney. They went with Captain Posford to see Isham Randolph. I wrote a letter to England
till dinner and then ate some broiled bacon. In the afternoon I settled some things in the library and then wrote
more letters till the evening and then took a walk about the
plantation. My wife and I had a small quarrel by her
passion. I said my prayers and had good health, good
thoughts, and good humor, thank God Almighty. About 9
o'clock Tom Randolph and Mr. Finney returned from
aboard.

19. I rose about 6 o'clock and read a chapter in Hebrew
and some Greek in the Apocrypha. I had some warm milk
from the cow. I danced my dance. Captain Turner came
to settle accounts and take his leave. The weather was cool.
My wife continued indisposed very much. About 8 o'clock
my company went away and I wrote a letter to England till
dinner and I ate some fritters. In the afternoon I set
several things in order and then prepared for my journey
again tomorrow. In the evening I took a walk about the
plantation and gave the necessary orders about my business.
I said my prayers and had good health, good thoughts, and
good humor, thank God Almighty.

20. I rose about 4 o'clock and got myself ready and then
took my leave of my wife that was abed, and of Mrs. Dunn
who was up, and went over the creek in my boat and then
proceeded to Williamsburg. The weather was very cool and
favored my journey much. By the way I said my prayers.
I got to Williamsburg before church and after I had made
myself ready I went to church with Mr. Bland. I found
Mr. M-s-t-n, a mad person, in our pew, who behaved himself oddly. After church the Governor asked me to go home
with him to dinner. I ate some tongue and udder. Mrs.
Russell was very much out of humor with me. Colonel

Quarry[1] and Captain Smith, commander of our man-of-war, dined with us and we stayed till late and then went home in the Governor's coach. I neglected to say my prayers but had good health, good thoughts, and good humor, thank God Almighty.

21. I rose about 5 o'clock and wrote several things and prepared my public accounts in order for passing this day. I ate some boiled milk for breakfast but neglected to say my prayers. About 9 o'clock came Colonel Ludwell to examine my accounts and then we went to Council where my accounts were passed. Mr. Jeffrys,[2] the surveyor of James County, was accused of having used the Governor's name to several unjust things, [and] was obliged to ask his pardon on his knees before his accusers. The Governor proposed the dispute there was between him and the President whether he should have the salary from the day of his arrival in the country or from his being sworn, but the President would not submit to our judgment. About 4 o'clock we went home to dine with the Governor, and I ate beans and bacon. About 9 o'clock we took leave and went to my lodgings where I wrote several things and about 12 went to bed but I neglected to say my prayers, for which God forgive me, but I had good health, good thoughts, and good humor, thank God Almighty.

22. I rose about 5 o'clock and wrote several letters and accounted with the Commissary and several others and paid them their money. I ate boiled milk for breakfast but neglected again to say my prayers because I was very busy. I wrote several letters and took leave of the masters of ships who went away this morning. I accounted with several of the naval officers and then went to the Governor's and paid him £1000 and then took my leave of him and returned to my lodgings where I continued to write all the rest of the day till the evening and then went to visit Mrs. Bland and

---

[1] In a letter of July 26, 1712, Spotswood mentions Colonel Robert Quarry, who is returning to England after a "short stay" in Virginia. (*Official Letters of Alexander Spotswood,* I, 178.) Though surveyor general of customs for America, Quarry spent little time in the colony.

[2] Simon Jeffrys. (See *Ex. Jour.,* III, 314, 319.)

ate some minced veal and then took a walk and met Mr.
Blackamore, who was drunk. Then I returned to my lodgings where the Doctor came to see me to tell me I was mis-
taken about his note. I wrote another letter to England.
About 10 o'clock I went to bed. I said a short prayer and
had good health, good thoughts, and good humor, thank
God Almighty.

23. I rose about 5 o'clock with intent to go to Queen's
Creek, but the rain prevented me. I wrote another letter
and then went to visit the Doctor and drank tea with him
and his wife. Here I stayed till about 9 o'clock and then
took leave of them and Mr. Bland and rode to Queen's
Creek where I found everybody well. Here I wrote several
notes wherein I promised to give £5 for each of my negroes
run away. About 12 o'clock came the Doctor and his lady.
We were very merry together and about 2 o'clock we went
to dinner and I ate some salt fish, which would have been
good if we had had butter to them. About 5 o'clock I took
leave and rode to Colonel Duke's whom I found sick of a
fever. Here I drank some good ale. In the evening I wrote
a letter to the Governor to let him know the Colonel was
really sick. About 10 o'clock I recommended the Colonel
and myself to heaven and had good health, good thoughts,
and good humor, thank God Almighty.

24. I rose about 5 o'clock and took leave of the Colonel
and rode over to Mr. Duke's where I found all pretty well.
Here I ate some milk and stayed about an hour and then
proceeded on my journey and on the road said my prayers.
About 11 o'clock I got home where I found everybody
pretty well, thank God, and the sloop come from Falling
Creek with the rest of the granary. It rained as soon as I
got home. I learned several people had sent things to my
wife and Will Parish brought some fish, which we ate for
dinner. In the afternoon I put several things in order till
about 4 o'clock and then it rained extremely hard and a
great while together. My wife was better, thank God, than
when I went away. There fell a hail this afternoon that
damaged abundance of tobacco. I could not walk in the

evening because it was very wet. I said my prayers to thank God for my safe return and had good health, good thoughts, and good humor, thank God Almighty.

25. I rose about 5 o'clock and had a letter from Colonel Ludwell to send a statement of the 2 shillings per hogshead, which I did. I read a chapter in Hebrew and also in Greek. I said my prayers and drank some milk from the cow. I danced my dance. My wife was pretty well. The weather was cloudy and hot. I settled several accounts and caused Billy Wilkins to be whipped for not writing well. I ate fish for dinner. In the afternoon I read some news and then went into the library and read some Latin till the evening and then I took a walk to see the carpenter at work. I had a letter from Colonel Hill which I answered. I said a short prayer and had good health, good thoughts, and good humor, thank God Almighty.

26. I rose about 5 o'clock and read two chapters in Hebrew and two chapters in Greek. I said my prayers and drank some milk from the cow. I danced my dance. My wife was pretty well, thank God, but quarter Moll[1] was sick. The weather was cloudy and warm. I settled several accounts and wrote several things till dinner, just before which came Mr. Mumford and told me all was well in Appomattox and while we were at dinner came Tom Randolph who had been getting evidence against the men who entertained my negroes. I ate a roast pigeon for dinner. In the afternoon I discoursed several things with them and then read some Latin and in the evening took a walk with them about the plantation. They stayed and I ate some bread and butter for supper with them. I said my prayers and had good health, good thoughts, and good humor, thank God Almighty.

27. I rose about 5 o'clock and read a chapter in Hebrew and some Greek. I said my prayers and ate milk and hominy for breakfast. I danced my dance. The weather

---

[1]Apparently a slave who lived in the quarters, to distinguish her from the cook Moll.

was cloudy and hot. My wife was pretty well, thank God. About 9 o'clock Mr. Mumford and Tom Randolph went away. I read some English and then a sermon in Tillotson till dinner and then I ate some roast mutton for dinner. In the afternoon I took a nap and then read some news. My wife and Mrs. Dunn went out in the coach and I read some Latin till the evening and then I took a walk about the plantation and in the orchard where there was abundance of fruit. I said my prayers and had good health, good thoughts, and good humor, thank God Almighty. Negro Sue was brought to bed of a boy.

28. I rose about 5 o'clock and read two chapters in Hebrew and three in Greek. I said my prayers and drank some warm milk for breakfast. I danced my dance. The weather was cloudy and hot. My wife was pretty well, thank God. I wrote several things and then read some law till dinner, when I ate some boiled mutton. In the afternoon I walked to see the carpenter at work about the granary and then went to the store which was much out of order. Then I read some more law till the evening and then I took a walk about the plantation. My wife grew worse again this afternoon and was very sick at her stomach. I said my prayers and had good health, good thoughts, and good humor, thank God Almighty.

29. I rose about 5 o'clock and read a chapter in Hebrew and two chapters in Greek. I said my prayers and drank warm milk from the cow. I danced my dance. The weather was cloudy again and hot. My wife was much indisposed again. I read some law and wrote the most remarkable part of it in a book till dinner and then I ate some roast mutton. In the afternoon I put several things in order and then read some news and afterwards read more law till the evening and then I took a walk about the plantation and saw the carpenter work. My wife was a little better this evening. I neglected to say my prayers but had good health, good thoughts, and good humor, thank God Almighty.

30. I rose about 5 o'clock and read a chapter in Hebrew and a chapter in Greek. I said my prayers and drank warm milk. I danced my dance. The weather was clear and hot. My wife was better, thank God. My Indian boy Ned ran away this morning and those I sent after him could not find him. I read some Latin but Colonel Hill and Mr. Anderson came about 10 o'clock and prevented me. The Colonel was still a little lame with the gout. Moll was strapped this morning and so was Jenny. I ate some neat's tongue for dinner. In the afternoon we talked till 4 o'clock and then the company went away and I wrote a letter to Falling Creek and sent Tom away in the evening. I took a walk about the plantation. I neglected to say my prayers but had good health, good thoughts, and good humor, thank God Almighty.

31. I rose about 5 o'clock and read a chapter in Hebrew and two chapters in Greek. I said my prayers and ate milk and hominy for breakfast. Tom returned with two people from Falling Creek with two of my people [sic] to help raise the granary. The weather was clear and cool, the wind northwest. My wife was a little better, thank God. I read some law abridgments which I read till dinner. I ate some broiled bacon. In the afternoon I put things in order in my library and then read more law till the evening and then I took a walk about the plantation. My wife was much indisposed with a small fever. I said my prayers and had good health, good thoughts, and good humor, thank God Almighty. We have had abundance of rain this month and on the 24th there fell some hail that spoiled the corn and tobacco of several neighbors.

August, 1712

1. I rose about 5 o'clock and read a chapter in Hebrew and two chapters in Greek. I said my prayers and had warm milk from the cow for breakfast. Then I danced my dance. My wife was much disordered with a small fever. The weather was clear and hot. I read some law and abridged it in a book. My wife resolved to take the bark. I ate some broiled pork for dinner. Parson Goodwin came just before dinner but would not stay. In the afternoon I took a nap in the library and then read more law till the evening. My wife was better this afternoon. In the evening it threatened rain but we had none. I took a walk to see the granary. I said my prayers and had good health, good thoughts, and good humor, thank God Almighty. The fleet sailed this day out of the Cape.

2. I rose about 5 o'clock and read a chapter in Hebrew and two chapters in Greek. I said my prayers and had milk from the cow. I danced my dance. It was exceedingly hot. My wife was better and took the bark again but she vomited up again and it made her head ache. I read some law and abridged it in my book. It threatened rain but there came none. I ate some fish for dinner sent us by my neighbor Parish. In the afternoon I settled some things in the library and then read more law till the evening and then I took a walk about the plantation and ate some apples. I said my prayers and had good health, good thoughts, and good humor, thank God Almighty. The Governor[1] was much indisposed this whole day and at night was taken with a fever.

3. I rose about 5 o'clock and read two chapters in Hebrew and three chapters in Greek. I said my prayers and ate milk and hominy for breakfast. The weather was cool and clearer than it had lately been. My wife was pretty well in the morning but had a small fever in the middle of

---

[1] In this passage, Byrd may be speaking ironically of his wife.

the day. About 11 o'clock I went to church and heard a good sermon of Mr. Anderson. After church Captain John Stith and Harry D-k's wife and Mr. John Hardiman came to dine with me, and I ate some roast shoat for dinner. In the afternoon I went in the coach to Mrs. Harrison's who they said was very sick, but when I came there I found her pretty well. There we found John Stith's wife. I stayed till the evening and then walked home and found my wife out of order. My sloop came this evening. I neglected to say my prayers but had good health, good thoughts, and good humor, thank God Almighty.

4. I rose about 5 o'clock having rested very ill the whole night, and read two chapters in Hebrew and two in Greek. I said my prayers and had some milk from the cow. I danced my dance. It rained very much for about an hour. My wife was much indisposed with the headache and so continued all day. I read some law till noon and then I ate some boiled pork for dinner. In the afternoon I took a walk in the garden, it being very cool and then I read more law till the evening and then I took a walk to see the house, now the roof was put up this day, notwithstanding the rain which fell often today. I said my prayers and had good health, good thoughts, and good humor, thank God Almighty.

5. I rose about 5 o'clock and read a chapter in Hebrew and a chapter in Greek. I said my prayers and had warm milk for breakfast. It rained a little this morning and continued cloudy. My wife was a little better but not well. I wrote a letter to Mr. Randolph and Mr. G-r-l to send by Billy and [Bob]. Mr. Bland's shallop brought me up some things and some books among the rest, which I looked over, which hindered me from reading the law. Colonel Frank Eppes came just before dinner. I ate some roast pork. After dinner the Colonel and I took a walk to see the granary. He went away about 4 o'clock. I sent Mrs. Hamlin some bark. In the evening my sloop went away and I took a walk. I said my prayers and had good health, good thoughts, and good humor, thank God Almighty.

6. I rose about 5 o'clock and read a chapter in Hebrew and two chapters in Greek. I said my prayers [c-l] and had warm milk from the cow. I danced my dance. The weather was cloudy and hot but did not rain. My wife was indisposed. I read a little law but was interrupted by company. About 9 o'clock came Mr. Rogers with two persons from Chickahominy and soon after came Colonel Hill and Mr. Anderson and dined with me. I ate some boiled goose for dinner. In the afternoon came Mrs. Harrison and stayed about half an hour. She made so much haste because Frank Lightfoot and Major Harrison came over the river to visit her. About 6 o'clock my company went away, and I took a walk about the plantation. The weather cleared up in the afternoon and was very hot. I said my prayers and had good health, good thoughts, and good humor, thank God Almighty.

7. I rose about 5 o'clock and read a chapter in Hebrew and two chapters in Greek. I said my prayers and ate milk and hominy for breakfast. The weather was clear and hot. My wife was pretty well, thank God, but about 10 o'clock was taken with a violent headache. I read a little law but Mr. Bland came about 11 o'clock and brought me several letters. He dined with me and I ate some lamb for dinner. In the afternoon Mr. Bland went over the river and I read French till the evening and then took a walk about the plantation to see how matters went. Mr. Bland told us the Governor, Dr. Cocke, and his wife, and my sister Custis had been sick but were all better again. In the evening my wife and I had a dispute about her taking the bark which put her out of humor. I neglected to say my prayers but had good health, good thoughts, and good humor, thank God Almighty.

8. I rose about 5 o'clock and read two chapters in Hebrew and two chapters in Greek. I said my prayers and had some milk from the cow for breakfast. I wrote a letter to the Governor and sent Bannister to Williamsburg to inquire how the Governor did. I also wrote to the Doctor to consult him concerning my wife, who was pretty well this

morning. The wind was northwest and very cold. I read some law till dinner and then I ate some roast lamb. In the afternoon I took a little nap and then read some law till the evening and then took a walk to see my workmen. My overseer was out of order, for which I gave him a vomit which worked very much. My wife had a good day of it. I said my prayers and had good health, good thoughts, and good humor, thank God Almighty.

9. I rose about 5 o'clock and read two chapters in Hebrew and two chapters in Greek. I said my prayers and had warm milk for breakfast. I danced my dance. My wife was better, thank God. The weather was cold and clear but about 11 o'clock my wife had her fever again. I read some law and abridged it in my book till dinner and then I ate some lamb. In the afternoon I put several things in order in the library and then read some law. My over-seer had an ague for which I gave him a vomit last night which worked very much. In the evening I took a walk about the plantation and went to the tobacco house to see them hang tobacco. I said my prayers and had good health, good thoughts, and good humor, thank God Almighty.

10. I rose about 5 o'clock and read two chapters in Hebrew and three chapters in Greek. I said my prayers and had milk and hominy for breakfast. I danced my dance. My wife was better, thank God, and began to [take] a decoction of the bark with mint water to keep it from coming up. The weather was cloudy and cool, which made us resolve to go visit Drury Stith in the coach·and about 11 we ate some apple pudding and then Mr. G-r-l came and told us all was well at Falling Creek. About 12 we got into the coach and about 3 we got to Drury Stith's where we ate some good mutton and were made welcome and returned home in the evening and the horses performed well. This journey agreed well with my wife. We found all well at home, thank God. I said my prayers and had good health, good thoughts, and good humor, thank God.

11. I rose about 5 o'clock and read a chapter in Hebrew and two chapters in Greek. I said my prayers and had no breakfast because I ate three times yesterday. I danced my dance. The weather was cloudy and cold. My wife was pretty well and continued to take the decoction of the bark with much reluctance. I read some law and abridged it till dinner and then I ate some boiled beef for dinner. In the afternoon I went to the granary to see the people work and then came to the library and put things in order and then settled several accounts till the evening and then I took a walk about the plantation. My overseer took the bark very dourly. I said my prayers and had good health, good thoughts, and good humor, thank God Almighty.

12. I rose about 5 o'clock and read two chapters in Hebrew and two chapters in Greek. I said my prayers and drank warm milk from the cow. I danced my dance. The weather was cloudy and warm. My wife was not very well but took the bark however. I had a letter from Colonel Ludwell concerning our [representation]. I read some law till about 12 o'clock and then came Mr. Dennis to get some Jesuit's bark for Mrs. Irby which I gave him. He stayed to dinner and I ate some fried pork. In the afternoon we took a walk to the house to see the workmen and then he went away. I read law again till the evening and then I took a walk about the plantation. At night I read in the *Tatler*. I said my prayers and had good health, good thoughts, and good humor, thank God Almighty. My overseer took the bark and was well again.

13. I rose about 5 o'clock and read a chapter in Hebrew and a chapter in Greek. I said my prayers and ate milk and hominy for breakfast. My wife was pretty well, thank God. The weather was clear and warm. I read some law and abridged it till dinner and then I ate some roast pork. In the afternoon I set several things in order in the library and then ate some watermelon. Then I read law again till the evening and then I took a walk about the plantation and saw my people hang tobacco. About 6 o'clock came Captain Tom Randolph and let me know all was well above only

there had been a hole in the dam at Falling Creek. I ate a little supper at night. I said my prayers and had good health, good thoughts, and good humor, thank God Almighty.

14. I rose about 5 o'clock and read a chapter in Hebrew and some Greek in Herodian.[1]   I neglected to say my prayers and ate milk and hominy for breakfast. Mr. Randolph and I discoursed about my affairs. About 8 o'clock came Mr. Bland on his way to Williamsburg and I wrote two letters by him. I read no law before dinner. I ate some boiled pork and in the afternoon put several things in order in the library and then read some Latin. I rogered my wife in the library, who was pretty well again. In the evening I took a walk about the plantation and saw a ship come up to buy wheat. At night I read in the *Tatler*. I said my prayers and had good health, good thoughts, and good humor, thank God Almighty.

15. I rose about 5 o'clock and read a chapter in Hebrew and some Greek in Herodian. I said my prayers and drank some milk from the cow. My wife was better, thank God. The weather was cloudy and warm but it did not rain. Captain M-r-l, commander of the prize, came ashore and I lent him a horse to ride to Colonel Hill's to enter. Just as he was gone came Mrs. Harrison and Colonel Eppes and stayed here to dinner. In the afternoon we spent our time in conversation. Captain Eppes went away sooner than Mrs. Harrison, who stayed till the evening. One of Captain M-r-l's seamen showed us some feats of activity in tumbling. I took a walk about the plantation and read at night in the *Tatler*. I said my prayers and had good health, good thoughts, and good humor, thank God Almighty. My wife had a small fever this morning.

16. I rose about 5 o'clock and read a chapter in Hebrew and some Greek in Herodian. I said my prayers and had no breakfast only I ate some muskmelon. I danced my

---

[1] A Greek writer of Roman history whose works were popular in the sixteenth and seventeenth centuries.

dance. My wife was a little better again. It rained in the night and was cloudy and warm this morning and rained several times. About 9 o'clock we made an end of shingling the granary. I read some law till dinner and then ate some bacon fraise. In the afternoon I put several things in order in the library and then read more law. It rained much in the afternoon so that I could not walk about the plantation in the evening. John had an ague but not violently. At night we talked. I said my prayers and had good health, good thoughts, and good humor, thank God Almighty.

17. I rose about 5 o'clock and read nothing because I prepared to go to Colonel Duke's [church]. I said my prayers and ate milk and hominy for breakfast. I ordered my horses over the creek and about 7 o'clock was set across myself. The weather was cooler and cloudy. However in about two hours I got to my brother Duke's where I found them all well, though they had lately been sick. Here I stayed till 11 o'clock and then was set over the river and got to Colonel Duke's about 12 where I found Colonel Hill who had been [a pro-g-r-s] and was full of [folly]. Colonel Duke was well and resolved to go with me next day to Council. About 2 o'clock I ate some boiled beef for dinner. Colonel Duke gave us the best he had and we were very merry. In the evening we took a walk in the orchard and ate some peaches. I neglected to say my prayers but had good health, good thoughts, and good humor, thank God Almighty.

18. I rose about 5 o'clock and resolved to go early but was forced to stay for the two colonels till almost 6 o'clock. I said my prayers and had some milk from the cow. Colonel Duke rode a new horse which he had of Colonel Eppes. We rode together as far as the ordinary and there Colonel Hill parted with us and went to Queen's Creek but Colonel Duke and I proceeded to Williamsburg, where we got about 9 o'clock, and when we were dressed we waited on the Governor with Colonel Carter and Colonel Smith who told me the Commissary was sick. We found the Governor well and Colonel Ludwell with him. We sat at council in the

Governor's house and had the Indians before us, who offered to bring in Hancock[1] to show us their sincere intentions to make peace. We also agreed to have an Assembly the 22nd of October. About 4 o'clock we went to dinner and I ate some boiled beef. Mrs. Russell and I were [g-r] civil. At night we drank two bottles each of good claret and went to our lodgings [at] 11 o'clock in the Governor's coach because it rained. I neglected to say my prayers and committed uncleanness, but had good health and good humor, thank God Almighty.

19. I rose about 5 o'clock and found myself disordered with the claret I drank last night but not so much as Colonel Carter, who was very sick. I neglected to say my prayers. About 7 o'clock I went to Mr. Bland's where I drank tea till about 9 and then rode to my brother Custis' where I found all well but heard nothing of my negroes. Here I stayed till dinner and ate some roast veal. After dinner came Mr. Catesby and told us the Doctor was sick again and very [amiss] or else I would have visited him. In the evening I rode to Green Springs where I found everybody well. Colonel Hill came there also in the evening and we ate some fruit and drank drams and other drinks. The dram was a remedy for the heartburn which the claret I had drunk the night before had given me. I said my prayers and had good health, good thoughts, and good humor, thank God Almighty. In the night Colonel Hill was taken very sick and I rose to his assistance but when he had vomited he was easy.

20. I rose about 4 o'clock and drank some tea and ate bread and butter and at break of day rode away and passed the ferry about sunrise and paid what I owed to the ferryman. The weather was very hot; however before 9 o'clock I got to Captain John Stith's where I ate some quince and milk for breakfast and then took a nap on the couch for about an hour and about 11 o'clock my wife and Mrs. Dunn came there with the child in the coach. She told me she had

---

[1]One of the Tuscarora Indians and a ringleader in the North Carolina massacre. (*Ex. Jour.*, III, 329.)

lost her fits and that our people were well at home. About
3 o'clock we went to dinner and I ate some fowl and bacon.
In the afternoon we sat and talked till about 5 o'clock and
then took leave and returned and got home before dark.
I found all well, thank God, and because we were all weary
we went early to bed. I neglected to say my prayers but had
good health, good thoughts, and good humor, thank God
Almighty. Mrs. Dunn received a letter from Major Custis
about borrowing money of his wife.

21. I rose about 5 o'clock and read a chapter in Hebrew
and some Greek in Herodian. I said my prayers and ate no
breakfast. I danced my dance. The weather was very hot.
My wife was better, thank God. I beat Billy Wilkins for
lying and writing ill. I settled several accounts till dinner
and then I ate some dried beef. In the afternoon I settled
several things in the library and then ate some fruit with my
wife. Afterwards I read some Latin till the evening and
then my wife and I took a walk about the plantation. My
wife was very well again, thank God. At night I read nothing but we sat and talked till about 9 o'clock. I neglected
to say my prayers and had good health, good thoughts, and
good humor, thank God Almighty.

22. I rose about 5 o'clock and read a chapter in Hebrew
and some Greek in Herodian. I said my prayers and had
some warm milk from the cow. I danced my dance. The
weather was exceedingly hot and my wife was pretty well,
thank God. I settled several accounts till about 10 o'clock
and then Mr. Clayton came from Mrs. Harrison's, who told
me that he had heard the peace was broken off again. He
stayed till dinner and I ate a broiled pigeon. In the afternoon it threatened rain but we had none. About 3 o'clock
Mr. Clayton went away and I wrote some Latin till the
evening and then I took a walk about the plantation. I said
my prayers and had good health, good thoughts, and good
humor, thank God Almighty.

23. I rose about 5 o'clock and read a chapter in Hebrew
and some Greek in Herodian. I said my prayers and ate
milk and hominy for breakfast. The weather was exceed-

ingly hot. My wife was indisposed with a headache. I read
some law and abridged it till dinner and then I ate some
boiled beef for dinner. In the afternoon I put several
things in order in the library and then settled some accounts
and afterwards read some Latin till the evening and then I
took a walk about my plantation, and then walked with my
wife in the garden, where she quarreled with me about Mrs.
Dunn. I spoke my mind with calmness. At night I read in
the *Tatler*. I said my prayers and had good health, good
thoughts, and good humor, thank God Almighty.

24. I rose about 5 o'clock and read two chapters in
Hebrew and ten pages in Herodian. I said my prayers and
ate milk and hominy for breakfast. The weather was clear
and hot; however the wind blew and made [it] a little cooler
than it had been. I read in the *Tatler*. My wife was pretty
well in the morning. I ate some broiled bacon for dinner.
The overseer went to the chapel where he saw Robin Mumford who had been very sick and his whole family. In the
afternoon we went in the coach to visit Mrs. Harrison and
found her sick. We stayed there till the evening and then
returned. My wife had her fever again. At night I read
in the *Tatler*. I said my prayers and had good health, good
thoughts, and good humor, thank God Almighty.

25. I rose about 5 o'clock and read a chapter in Hebrew
and 12 pages in Herodian. I said my prayers and had milk
from the cow. I danced my dance. The wind blew much
and made it cool. My wife had a bad rest last night and a
fever for which she resolved to take the bark in powder.
I read some law till dinner and then I ate some pork and
peas. My wife was disappointed in her dinner for which
she cried and I thought would have miscarried but it went
off again. After dinner Colonel Eppes came and stayed an
hour. Then I settled some accounts and afterwards read
some Latin till the evening and then I took a walk about
the plantation. At night I read in the *Tatler*. I said my
prayers and had good health, good thoughts, and good
humor, thank God Almighty.

26. I rose about 5 o'clock and read a chapter in Hebrew and nothing in Greek because I prepared to go abroad with my wife in the coach. However I said my prayers and had milk and hominy for breakfast. I wrote a letter to Falling Creek. The weather was cold but my wife was not well; however she resolved to go to Colonel Eppes's and to strengthen ourselves we ate some fried mutton pie before we went. About 10 o'clock we got into the coach and got to Colonel Eppes's before 12. He was abroad but she was at home. We sent to Colonel Hill and Mr. Anderson who came to us with Drury Stith and Colonel Eppes came soon after. I persuaded Colonel Hill, Colonel Eppes, and Drury Stith to draw lots which two should stand burgesses and the lots fell upon Colonel Hill and Colonel Eppes. About 5 o'clock we had dinner and I ate some roast mutton. In the evening we went to Colonel Hill's and about one o'clock I had sent G-r-l to Falling Creek. We spent the evening in conversation till about 9 o'clock and then we went to bed. I rogered my wife and neglected to say my prayers but had good health, good thoughts, and good humor, thank God Almighty.

27. I rose about 5 o'clock and read in the *Tatler* till 7. Then I dressed and went to the company and drank some chocolate and Mr. Anderson and Mrs. Dunn went to fish and caught some fish and they were dressed for us about 11 o'clock and I ate some fish. Here we stayed till about 2 o'clock and then we all went to Llewellyn Eppes's, where the mistress of the house spent all her time in getting victuals and we hardly saw her. We ate abundance of fruit and were very merry till dinner which came about 4 o'clock. I ate roast mutton again, and poor Mrs. Eppes ate nothing with us. We stayed till near 6 o'clock and then took leave of the company and returned home where we got about 7 o'clock and found all well, thank God. When we had inquired into all the affairs of the family I said my prayers and had good health, good thoughts, and good humor, thank God Almighty. It rained in the night. I rogered my wife.

28. I rose about 5 o'clock and read a chapter in Hebrew and some Greek in Herodian. I said my prayers and ate nothing for breakfast, to settle my stomach after feasting abroad. I danced my dance. The weather was cloudy and warm. My wife was indisposed for want of sleep, having been disturbed by mosquitoes, which we have more of this year than ever I knew. I read some law till dinner and then I ate some hogs' haslet. In the afternoon I went to the granary to see the people work and then returned and read some Latin till the evening and then I took a walk about the plantation and saw my people making cider. My wife was indisposed very much at night which made me go to bed soon. I said my prayers and had good health, good thoughts, but indifferent humor, thank God Almighty. In the night my wife was disturbed with mosquitoes and could not sleep herself nor would she let me sleep.

29. I rose about 5 o'clock and read a chapter in Hebrew and some Greek in Herodian. I said my prayers and had warm milk for breakfast. I danced my dance. The weather was clear and hot. My wife was indisposed for want of sleep. About 10 o'clock came Tom Randolph from Pamunkey and told me all were well there. We discoursed about all our affairs till dinner when I ate some roast pork. In the afternoon Mr. Randolph went to see how the overseer managed the tobacco and found it pretty well. I received a message from Colonel Ludwell who was at Mrs. Harrison's that they were obliged to return tomorrow and could not come to see us. In the evening I read some Latin and then went to walk about the plantation. I read at night in the *Tatler*. I said my prayers and had good health, good thoughts, and good humor, thank God Almighty.

30. I rose about 5 o'clock and read no Hebrew but some Greek in Herodian. I neglected to say my prayers but had warm milk from the cow. About 8 o'clock I took a walk to Mrs. Harrison's and found her better and there I found Colonel Ludwell and his wife who came yesterday. I stayed there and ate some apples and milk and then Colonel Ludwell walked with me to our house. He stayed there till

about 12 o'clock and then went over the river to Colonel
Harrison's who they say is sick. I ate some roast pork for
dinner. In the afternoon came Mr. M-r-s-l who told me
that Mr. Anderson had lost his son who died Thursday
night. This news was confirmed by the master of Colonel
Hill's sloop who came to fetch some canvas to make sails.
In the evening I took a walk about the plantation. At night
I read in the *Tatler*. I neglected to say my prayers and had
good health, good thoughts, and good humor, thank God
Almighty. Tom Osborne came from above and told me
all was well.

31. I rose about 5 o'clock and read a chapter in Hebrew
but no Greek because I discoursed with Tom Osborne and
we\prescribed something for his wife who is indisposed. I
neglected to say my prayers but drank chocolate for breakfast. Then I prepared to go to church. The weather was
very cold and my wife was very well, thank God. I sent to
know how Mr. Anderson and his wife did and condoled
with them on their loss and learned that he could not come
to church. However at 11 o'clock we went to prayers there,
which being performed, Colonel Eppes and Mrs. D-k came
to dine with us but Mrs. Ludwell would not come. I ate
some fricassee of chicken. Our company stayed till about
5 o'clock and then I took a walk with our women about the
plantation. I neglected to say my prayers but had good
thoughts, good humor, and good health, thank God Almighty. This day I gave shirts to the negroes at the
quarters.

September, 1712

1. I rose about 5 o'clock and read a chapter in Hebrew and some Greek in Herodian. I said my prayers and drank chocolate for breakfast. I danced my dance. The weather was cloudy and cool. I sent Billy Brayne to Williamsburg with Tom in order to go to the College and desired Mr. Bland to take care of him. My wife was very well, thank God. I settled several accounts till dinner and then I ate some pork and peas. In the afternoon I took a walk to the granary to see my people work and then settled more accounts. The overseer was sick again and I gave him the bark. I read some Latin and then took a walk about the plantation. At night I read in the *Tatler*. Then I received a letter from Mr. Anderson that told me Mr. T-r-t-n was very sick and desired some Spanish flies and some bark which I sent him. I said my prayers and had good health, good thoughts, and good humor, thank God Almighty. I caused a beef to be killed this day because the weather was cool.

2. I rose about 5 o'clock and read a chapter in Hebrew and some Greek in Herodian. I said my prayers and had milk from the cow for breakfast. I danced my dance. The weather continued cool still and my wife continued well, thank God. I sent John Hardiman several things for his child who was very sick. Then I read some law till about 12 o'clock and took a walk into the orchard till dinner and ate some roast beef. In the afternoon I gave my wife some lawn to make her shifts. Then I read some Latin till the evening and afterwards took a walk about the plantation. At night I read in the *Tatler* and Tom returned and brought me some letters from Williamsburg. My head ached very much this afternoon. I said my prayers and had good health, good thoughts, and good humor, thank God Almighty. My wife had a small fever this afternoon.

3. I rose about 5 o'clock and read a chapter in Hebrew and some Greek in Herodian. I said my prayers and had milk and hominy for breakfast. The weather was exceedingly cold. My wife was pretty well and gave Prue a great whipping for several misdemeanors. I read some Latin till 12 o'clock and then walked to court and invited Colonel Hill and several gentlemen to dinner. I ate some roast beef. There was no news. In the afternoon I went to court to hear a case between Colonel Hill and Mrs. Harrison where Will Randolph behaved himself rudely and so did Colonel Hill, for which I told them both they ought to be put into the stocks. In the evening I took a walk about the plantation. At night I read in the *Tatler* and Jacky brought me a letter from Falling Creek which told me all was well but a little child. I said my prayers and had good health, good thoughts, and good humor, thank God Almighty.

4. I rose about 5 o'clock and read a chapter in Hebrew and some Greek in Herodian. I said my prayers and had warm milk from the cow for breakfast. The weather continued cool but my wife and the overseer were indisposed again. My wife had the headache and a little fever. I read some English. Colonel Ludwell's man called here and told me that Colonel Harrison and Colonel Ludwell were sick. About 12 o'clock came Frank Lightfoot and his brother[1] and dined with us, and I ate some roast beef. In the afternoon we went and played at billiards and [I?] won most games. Then we took a walk to see the granary; then we returned to the house and they took leave and went to Mrs. Harrison's from whence they came. At night I read the *Tatler*. I said my prayers and had good health, good thoughts, and good humor, thank God Almighty.

5. I rose about 5 o'clock and read a chapter in Hebrew and some Greek in Herodian. I said my prayers and had milk from the cow for breakfast. I danced my dance. The weather continued cold. My wife had a fever again and resolved to take the bark for it but the overseer was better.

---

[1]Philip Lightfoot of James City County.

Moll was sick of a fever for which she had a vomit which worked well. I read some law till dinner and then ate some boiled beef. In the afternoon I took a walk to see the granary and then went to the library and there diverted myself till the evening, when I took a walk about the plantation and saw my people mow. At night I read in the *Tatler*. I neglected to say my prayers but had good health, good thoughts, and good humor, thank God Almighty. Just after dinner came Colonel Hill who had a little fever.

6. I rose about 5 o'clock and read a chapter in Hebrew and some Greek in Herodian. I said my prayers and ate milk and hominy for breakfast. John [Stokes][1] came for a right and advised me to mow my maize. My wife had her fever again. The weather continued cool, the wind northeast. My wife took the bark but it did not make her fever intermit. I read law till dinner and then ate some boiled beef. In the afternoon I was shaved and cleaned my teeth and then read a little Latin till the evening and afterwards took a walk about the plantation and found several things out of order, for which I reproved the overseer at night. I settled the time of the boys so that they might have leisure to improve themselves at night. I read in the *Tatler*. I said my prayers and had good health, good thoughts, and good humor, thank God Almighty.

7. I rose about 5 o'clock and read a chapter in Hebrew and some Greek in Herodian. I said my prayers and had chocolate for breakfast. I danced my dance. The weather continued cool and my wife had her fever again, notwithstanding the bark. I diverted myself in the library till dinner and then I ate some boiled pork. Soon after dinner came Peter from above with a letter from Mr. Randolph with an account that he was sick of a fever and a colic for which I sent him some remedy without letting the boy stay. In the afternoon I read some English till the evening and then took a walk with my wife into the orchard and ate some

---

[1] A John Stokes owned 476 acres in Charles City County in 1704. (*Va. Mag.*, XXXI, 317.)

apples. At night I read in *The Whole Duty of Man*.[1] I
said my prayers and had good health, good thoughts, and
good humor, thank God Almighty. The sloop came in the
night from Falling Creek.

8. I rose about 5 o'clock and read a chapter in Hebrew
and some Greek in Herodian. I said my prayers and drank
chocolate for breakfast. I danced my dance. I ordered the
sloop to be unloaded and then came Mr. Mumford and told
me all was well at Appomattox. We took a walk to see the
granary and discoursed of my affairs till dinner and then ate
some roast beef. In the afternoon we went to billiards and
I lost a bit. My wife had an hysteric fit pretty violently
which lasted about an hour. In the evening we took a walk
about the plantation and at night drank a bottle of brandy
punch which rejoiced us very much. I neglected to say my
prayers but had good health, good thoughts, and good
humor, thank God Almighty.

9. I rose about 5 o'clock and read nothing but Greek in
Herodian. I said my prayers and drank chocolate for
breakfast. My wife was better this morning and the weather
was cooler. I gave the necessary orders and prepared for
my journey to Falling Creek. Mr. Mumford went away to
Prince George court and I went towards Falling Creek
about 11 o'clock. I got to Colonel Hill's about 12 but found
nobody at home but Mr. T-r-t-n who thanked me for the
physic I had sent him and said I had saved his life. I went
over the river and got to Falling Creek about 3 where I
found all well, thank God, and learned that Mr. Randolph
was better. He came soon after himself and looked very
indifferent but had lost his fever. He told me that my
prescription had done him much service. About 6 o'clock
I ate some mutton for supper and about 7 o'clock Mr. Curle
came from his sloop. I gave him a bottle of wine. He
stayed till 10 o'clock and then went to his sloop. I said my
prayers and had good health, good thoughts, and good
humor, thank God Almighty.

---

[1] By Richard Allestree, published in 1660.

10. I rose about 6 o'clock and said a short prayer and then walked to the mill where I dicoursed Mr. G-r-l about everything. About 7 o'clock Mr. Curle came to me again and offered to go with me to Captain Webb's where we got about 8 o'clock and Mr. Randolph brought three men there who had robbed my orchard but when they plead guilty I forgave them on condition they would find security for their good behavior. Here I ate some bread and butter and then took leave and went with Mr. Curle to the Falls where I found everything in good order. About 12 o'clock we went over the river and saw the quarters on that side. We returned to the Falls about 5 o'clock and I ate some roast shoat. About 6 o'clock we returned to Falling Creek where I gave my orders to Mr. G-r-l what I would have sent by the sloop and about other matters. I was very much tired and said a short prayer and had good health, good thoughts, and good humor, thank God Almighty. I was pretty well pleased with what I had seen, things being in good order.

11. I rose about 6 o'clock and said my prayers and then went to the mill with Mr. Randolph and Captain Soane came to me. I discoursed with them about the quarters and then ate some milk for breakfast. About 9 o'clock I took leave and returned home and came to Colonel Hill's about 12 where I found a sick family and learned that Colonel Eppes was sick likewise. I stayed to dinner and ate some boiled beef. After dinner it thundered and rained a little but soon held up and I went home where I got about 6 o'clock and found my wife with a [. . .] headache and two or three people sick but on recovery, thank God. Mr. Bland was just going away but had no news at all. After I had inquired into the condition of the family I said my prayers and had good health, good thoughts, and good humor, thank God Almighty.

12. I rose about 5 o'clock and read a chapter in Hebrew and some Greek in Herodian. I said my prayers and ate boiled milk for breakfast. I danced my dance. My wife was a little better and so were the sick people, thank God. I took a walk to see my people at work. The weather was

cold, the wind northeast. My wife had a good a great [*sic*] quarrel with her maid Prue and with good reason; she is growing a most notable girl for stealing and laziness and lying and everything that is bad. I settled several accounts till dinner and then I ate some roast veal. In the afternoon I settled several things in the library and then read some Latin till the evening. Afterwards I took a walk about the plantation. I gave the bark to Moll and Jenny but Tom had a fever again. At night I read in the *Tatler*. I said a short prayer and had good thoughts, good health, and good humor, thank God Almighty. I rogered my wife with vigor.

13. I rose about 5 o'clock and read two chapters in Hebrew and 14 pages in Herodian. I said my prayers and drank chocolate for breakfast. I danced my dance. My wife was better, thank God, and so were all my people. The weather was cooler [*or* clear], the wind northwest. I read some Latin till dinner and then ate some boiled beef. In the afternoon put several things in order and then read more Latin. About 5 o'clock one of my negroes came from Falling Creek with the coach horses and brought a letter from Mr. G-r-l that told me all was well, thank God. In the evening I took a walk about the plantation and at night read in the *Tatler,* after having examined my boys. I said my prayers and had good health, good thoughts, and good humor, thank God Almighty. I rogered my wife again.

14. I read a chapter in Hebrew but no Greek. I went to see the new horses tried in the coach. I said my prayers and ate boiled milk for breakfast. My sick people were all better and so was my wife, thank God. The weather was warm and windy, the wind at south. About 11 o'clock I went to church and heard a good sermon from Mr. Anderson, who with Colonel Hill and Mrs. Harrison and her daughter came to dine with us. I ate some boiled beef for dinner. I told Mrs. Harrison people said she was going to be married and she could not deny it. The company went away about 5 o'clock between which and dinner there was

abundance of rain. In the evening I took a walk in the garden. I said my prayers and had good health, good thoughts, and good humor, thank God Almighty.

15. I read a [. . .] Hebrew and some Greek in Herodian. I said my prayers and ate boiled milk for breakfast. I danced my dance. The weather was cool and clear, the wind northwest. My wife and all the sick people were better, thank God. I settled several accounts. I renewed four rights for a man who had lost so many in his house when it was burnt. I ate some broiled bacon for dinner. In the afternoon I put several things in order in the library and in the evening took a walk with the women about the plantation. Tony brought a horse from Appomattox and told me everything was well there. There came a man also from Mount Folly to agree about renting that plantation. At night I read some Latin. I said my prayers and had good health, good thoughts, and good humor, thank God Almighty.

16. I rose about 6 o'clock and read a chapter in Hebrew and some Greek in Herodian. I said my prayers and ate boiled milk for breakfast. I danced my dance. This morning I sent Tony to Falling Creek with two horses in the room of the two horses I had thence for the coach. The weather was clear and cool and my wife was a little out of order with scolding at the people. I settled some accounts and walked to see the carpenter at work. I ate some boiled veal and bacon for dinner. In the afternoon I settled some things in the library and then settled my accounts till the evening, and then I took a walk about the plantation. At night I read some Latin. I said my prayers and had good health, good thoughts, and good humor, thank God Almighty. My man John was very bad with the piles.

17. I rose about 6 o'clock and read a chapter in Hebrew and some Greek in Herodian. I said my prayers and ate boiled milk for breakfast. I danced my dance. The weather was very cold, the wind northwest. My wife was well, thank God, and John was better. I settled some accounts of conse-

quence till dinner and then I ate some boiled beef. Soon
after dinner came Mr. Catesby from Williamsburg and
brought me a letter from Dr. Cocke by which I learned that
there was great likelihood of peace and that we had possession of Dunkirk[1] and that several of Colonel Parke's murderers were taken and some sent to England in irons. We
gave him some victuals. Then we took a walk about the
plantation. At night we drank some punch and were merry.
I neglected to say my prayers but had good health, good
thoughts, and good humor, thank God Almighty. I had a
little cold.

18. I rose about 6 and had a sore throat; however I rose
and read a chapter in Hebrew and some Greek in Herodian.
I said my prayers and ate boiled milk for breakfast. The
weather was very cool. I wrote three letters, two to Williamsburg, and one to Appomattox. My wife was disordered with her [m-d]. My man John was incommoded
still with the piles. Mr. Catesby and I took a walk and I
found Eugene asleep instead of being at work, for which
I beat him severely. This is the first day we had a fire in
the hall. I settled several accounts and then ate some hog's
haslet. In the afternoon came Sam Good and bought two
negroes of me for £60 towards paying for the land which
I had of him. Then I settled more accounts till the evening
and then took a walk about the plantation. At night I ate
some milk and roast apples for my sore throat. I neglected
to say my prayers but had good health, good thoughts, and
good humor, thank God Almighty. My wife began this
morning to take the bark again.

19. I rose about 6 o'clock and found my throat better. I
read a chapter in Hebrew and some Greek in Herodian. I
said my prayers and ate boiled milk for breakfast. I danced
my dance. The weather continued cold and my man John
continued disordered in his fundament. Two men came for
rights. Then I settled several accounts till dinner. I was
out of order with my cold; however I ate some roast shoat.

---

[1] The English forces took possession of Dunkirk on July 8, 1712.

In the afternoon my wife was taken with another fit of the vapors which came and went three times. Colonel Eppes came to see us and stayed about an hour. Then I settled more accounts till the evening and then took a walk about the plantation. At night I ate a little broiled pudding. My wife was disordered again after the same manner with a fit. I said my prayers and had good health, good thoughts, and good humor, thank God Almighty.

20. I rose about 6 o'clock and read a chapter in Hebrew and made an end of reading in Herodian. I said my prayers and ate boiled milk for breakfast. The weather was cool and my cold continued. My wife was pretty well this morning but my man John continued in the same condition, notwithstanding I took all the care of him I was capable. I settled my accounts till dinner and then ate some fricassee of possum. In the afternoon I put several things in order in the library and then settled more accounts till the evening and then we took a walk about the plantation. Tom Osborne came at night with his daughter and complained he was very sick, for which I prescribed him a remedy. At night I ate some milk and said a short prayer and had good health, good thoughts, and good humor, thank God Almighty.

21. I rose about 6 o'clock and read a little Hebrew and no Greek. I also neglected to say my prayers and had boiled milk for breakfast. My wife was pretty well and the weather was pretty warm, but John continued in the same condition. About 11 o'clock came Tom Randolph and told me all were well above and everywhere. We discoursed about our business till dinner. I ate some dried beef. In the afternoon we sat a little while and talked and then took a walk about the plantation. My cold continued very troublesome. In the evening my brother Custis' boy brought me letters from the Doctor to desire me to meet the Governor and come to Pamunkey Town with Mr. Catesby because Mrs. Russell had told him I only gave myself an air in pretending to wait on the Governor. At night I wrote two

letters to send by the boy. I neglected to say my prayers but had good health, good thoughts, and good humor, thank God Almighty.

22. I rose about 6 o'clock and read a little Hebrew and nothing in Greek because I prepared to go to Mr. Light-foot's on the Pamunkey River in order to meet the Governor next day at the Pamunkey Indian town. I said my prayers and ate some boiled milk for breakfast. About 11 o'clock I left my orders with Bannister concerning the sloop and everything else and took leave of my wife and with Mr. Catesby rode to Drury Stith's where we drank some persico and then proceeded to Mr. Sherwood Lightfoot's[1] where we arrived about 5 o'clock. He received us very courteously and gave us some boiled beef for supper of which I ate heartily. He lives in a good plantation and seems to be very industrious. About 9 o'clock we retired to bed. I said a short prayer and had good health, good thoughts, and good humor, thank God Almighty. Riding cured my cold, thank God.

23. I rose about 7 o'clock and shaved myself. I said a short prayer and about 9 ate some roast beef for breakfast. The weather was cloudy and threatened rain; however about 10 o'clock we rode to Mr. Goodrich Lightfoot's[2] who lives about a mile from thence. It rained as soon as we got on our horses. There we stayed till the Governor and all the company came in by the man-of-war boat. About 12 o'clock they came by and then notwithstanding the rain was violent we went over the river where the Governor received me very kindly and so did all the rest of the company, except Mrs. Russell. It rained violently all day so that the company could see nothing and the Governor's cook could scarcely get the dinner. However he did get one about 2 o'clock and I ate some boiled mutton. We were merry but were forced to stay in one of the Indian cabins all day and

---

[1] Son of John Lightfoot, who died in 1707; a large landowner of New Kent County, and cousin of Francis Lightfoot of James City County mentioned earlier in the diary.
[2] Another son of John Lightfoot.

about 5 o'clock the company were forced to return in the rain to Captain Littlepage's[1] but Mr. Catesby and I returned to Mr. Lightfoot's. Abundance of people came to the Indian town to see the Governor but were very wet and indeed the rain disappointed us all. There is an Indian called P-t W-l who has now his 20 wives. There was also an Indian who was ill of a bite of a rattlesnake but was on the recovery having taken some snakeroot. About 9 o'clock we ate some blue wing and then retired to bed. I neglected to say my prayers but had good health, good thoughts, and good humor, thank God Almighty.

24. I rose about 7 o'clock and we prepared to go to the election of burgesses in New Kent. I said my prayers and ate some beef for breakfast. About 10 o'clock we took leave and Mr. Lightfoot went with us to the courthouse where abundance of people were assembled and about 12 o'clock they chose Major Merriweather and Captain Stanhope[2] their burgesses without opposition. Captain Littlepage told me the Governor resolved to reach home this night. However I resolved to go to Colonel Bassett's because I had promised to meet the Governor there. Accordingly we rode there and arrived about 5 o'clock. The Colonel had been sick but was better but his son was sick. We had some fish for supper. The Colonel and his wife received us kindly. About 9 o'clock we went to bed. I said a short prayer and had good health, good thoughts, and good humor, thank God Almighty.

25. I rose about 7 o'clock and found the weather cloudy which made us resolve to stay here this day. I said a short prayer and drank milk tea and ate plum cake for breakfast. Then Mr. Catesby and I took a walk about the plantation and found it inclosed by marsh and therefore must be very unwholesome. Mr. Catesby killed two snakes in the pasture. About 3 o'clock we went to dinner and I ate some boiled

---

[1]Richard Littlepage, a large landowner in New Kent County. In 1715, as justice of the county, he caused a great stir by incurring the contempt of the House of Burgesses and refusing to acknowledge their authority. (*JHB*, 1712-1726, pp. xxx-xxxii.)

[2]Nicholas Merriweather and John Stanhope (or Stanup).

mutton. In the afternoon Mr. Catesby and I took another walk but the Colonel was not well enough to walk with us. He complained he wanted bark and therefore I promised to give him some if he would send. In the evening the Colonel gave us some [r-d-s-t-r-c] cider very good and about 9 o'clock we retired to bed where I neglected to say my prayers but had good health, good thoughts, and good humor, thank God Almighty.

26. I rose about 7 o'clock and found the weather cloudy; however we resolved to return home. I said a short prayer and we had milk tea and plum cake for breakfast. The Colonel's [godson] was very sick which put them into a fright. About 10 o'clock we took leave and rode home but stopped at the Brick [House] where we learned that Colonel Eppes and Captain Harwood[1] were chosen burgesses and that Dick O-n had 33 votes. Here we ate some plumcake that Mrs. Bassett had given Tom to bring for us. Then we proceeded to Drury Stith's where we drank some persico. Then we took leave and rode home where we got about 5 o'clock and found everybody pretty well, thank God, only somebody had stolen one of my great flats out of the creek. We ate some cold roast beef for supper. I was dead weary and therefore we went soon to bed where I rogered my wife but I neglected to say my prayers but had good health, good thoughts, and good humor, thank God Almighty. In the night the wind came to northwest and was very cold.

27.[2] I rose about 8 o'clock and read a chapter in Hebrew and some Greek in Lucian. I said my prayers and ate boiled milk for breakfast. The weather was cold, and the wind blew hard at northwest. John went to look [for] the boat but could not find it. My wife was pretty well and John was a little better. I settled some accounts and wrote in my journal till dinner, and then ate some blue wing for dinner. In

---

[1]Littlebury Eppes and Samuel Harwood, burgesses for Charles City County. Dick O-n may have been one of the Owens family, who owned small farms in the county. (*Va. Mag.*, XXXI, 316.)

[2]In the margin opposite this entry is an *x*.

the afternoon I found myself a little out of order but did not much regard it. I put several things in order in the library and then I took a walk with Mr. Catesby who was likewise disordered. The women also walked with [. . .]. When I returned I was much worse. However at night I drank more strong drink than usual. When I went .to bed I had an ague which was followed by the fever, which continued most of the night, and I slept very indifferently. I neglected to say my prayers but had good health, good thoughts, and good humor, thank God Almighty.

28. I was pretty well again this morning but did not rise till about 8 o'clock and then I went into the river to prevent another fit of the ague and found myself much better after it. I ate boiled milk for breakfast. Mr. Catesby went in the river with me and had a violent looseness which carried away his fever. I read nothing but said a short prayer. About 11 o'clock we went to church and Mr. Anderson gave us a good sermon. After church Mr. Anderson, Captain Stith and his wife, and Mr. Eppes and his wife went to dinner with us. Captain Stith was taken with an ague just after church and so was Drury Stith's wife. I ate roast beef for dinner. In the evening the company went away and I took a walk and continued very well. I said my prayers and had good health, good thoughts, and good humor, thank God Almighty.

29. I rose about 7 o'clock and went again into the river against my ague. I read a chapter in Hebrew and some Greek in Lucian. I said my prayers and ate boiled milk for breakfast. I danced my dance. I continued very well, thank God. The weather was cold, the wind northeast. My wife was pretty well. About 11 o'clock I was a .little fevered and my head ached a little; however I would not give way to it. I had not much stomach to dinner; however I ate some broiled beef. In the afternoon I put several things in order in the library and at night Mr. Catesby came and told me he had seen a bear. I took Tom L-s-n and went with a gun

and Mr. Catesby shot him. It was only a cub and he sat on a tree to eat grapes. I was better with this diversion and we were merry in the evening. I said my prayers and had good health, good thoughts, and good humor, thank God Almighty.

INDEX*

A

Abingdon Parish, **1709**, Nov. 6.
Aboh, **1710**, Nov. 13.
Abraham (servant), **1709**, Mar. 5.
Accomac, **1709**, May 2; *see* Eastern Shore.
Adams, Mr., **1712**, May 16.
Addison, Thomas, **1712**, Feb. 14.
Allen, Mr., **1710**, July 12.
Allen, Arthur, **1711**, Nov. 14, 27.
Allen, Major Arthur, **1709**, July 29, 30, Dec. 14; **1710**, May 19 (death).
Allen, Captain John, **1711**, Oct. 17.
Allen, Susanna, **1712**, Feb. 20; her ordinary, riot at, Apr. 19.
Allestree, Richard, *Whole Duty of Man,* **1712**, Sept. 7.
Anacreon, **1709**, N. 10—22; **1710**, Mar. 15—Apr. 13, May 2—June 1.
Anacreontics, **1710**, May 28.
Anaka (maid), **1709**, Feb. 22, Apr. 17, June 2, July 29, Aug. 27, Sept. 19, 22; **1710**, Feb. 20, 21, 22, 23, 24, 26, Sept. 3, Oct. 8; **1711**, Apr. 30, May 1, Dec. 2; **1712**, Jan. 3, Apr. 12, May 22.
Anderson, Captain, **1712**, Feb. 13.
Anderson, Reverend Charles, **1709**, Feb. 6, 10 (son christened), 16, Mar. 28, 30, Apr. 1, 3, 12, May 11, 12, 15, 18, 29, June 8, 13, 14, July 2, 3, Aug. 1, 3, 5, 7, 21, Sept. 4, 8, 9, 17, 18, 26, 28, 30, Oct. 9, 12, Dec. 3, 11, 13, 17, 23, 25; **1710**, Jan. 9, 11, 22, 29, Feb. 1, 3, 4, 5, 19, 22, Mar. 5, 10, 11, 15, 24, 26, 29, 31, Apr. 2, 5, 6, 8, 9, 23, 26, May 6, 14, 17, 19, 21, 24, 25, June 1, 3, 6, 17, 27, 29, July 3, 10, 23, Aug. 4, 5, 6, 8, 15, 20, 27, 30, Sept. 3, 21, 23, 24, Oct. 15, Dec. 19; **1711**, Jan. 7, 19, Feb. 4, 10, 18, Mar. 4, 18, 22, 25, Apr. 1, 22, May 11, 12, 13, 20, 26, 28, 29, 30, June 10, 11, 24, 29, July 1, 2, 8, 12, 17, 22, Aug. 1, 4, 18, 27, 30, Sept. 2, 7, 16, 30, Oct. 1, 3, 4, 5, 12, Dec.

26, 27; **1712**, Jan. 6, 15,' 27, Feb. 11, 16, 17, 18, Mar. 16,· Apr. 13, May 11, 13, 25, 30, June 8, 22, 24, 26, July 1, 6, 30, Aug. 3, 6, 26, 27, 30 (death of son), 31, Sept. 1, 14, 28.
Anderson, Mrs. Charles, **1709**, Apr. 12, May 11, June 8, 13, Aug. 7, Sept. 26, Oct. 12, 14; **1710**, Jan. 22, Feb. 14, 19, Mar. 10, 15, Apr. 14, May 19, June 3, 6, 27, July 10, Aug. 5, 15; **1711**, Jan. 3, Feb. 2, July 17, Oct 6, Dec. 27; **1712**, May 30, July 6, Aug. 31.
Anderson, John, **1710**, Jan. 20.
Angelica (ship), **1710**, Mar. 25.
Animals: bear, **1712**, Sept. 29; beaver **1712**, Feb. 20; muskrat, **1712**, Feb. 20.
Anne, Queen of England, **1709**, June 16, 20, 21; **1710**, Jan. 19, Apr. 25, June 23; **1711**, Feb. 6, 7, Sept. 1; **1712**, Jan. 5, 31, Apr. 1.
Antigua, **1709**, Apr. 1.
Apocrypha, **1712**, July 1-20.
Applewhite, Henry, **1710**, Feb. 4.
Appomattox plantation, **1709**, Feb. 7, 8, 12, 25, 28, Mar. 26, 27, May 8, 15, 21, Aug. 31, Sept. 16, Dec. 6; **1710**, Jan. 14, May 4, 10, 17, June 2, 10, 17, 21, 30, July 16, 24, Aug. 6, 12, 15, Sept. 27, 30, Dec. 21, 28; **1711**, Jan. 22, Feb. 19, 25, Mar. 17, May 21, 23, 26, June 8, 16, July 13, Aug. 13, 23, 25, 29, Sept. 1, 10, 29, Nov. 13, Dec. 1; **1712**, Jan. 10, 21, Feb. 15, Mar. 9, 13, 23, May 4, 16, June 4, 14, 23, 29, July 3, 11, 26, Sept. 8, 15, 18.
Argyle, Duke of, **1711**, May 3 (made General), July 18, 20, Sept. 21.
Arlington, **1709**, Nov. 7, 9, 11, 12, 15, 16.
Armistead, Henry, **1710**, May 9.
Armistead, Mrs. Henry (Martha Burwell), **1710**, Apr. 14, May 9; **1711**, May 13.

---

*It would be manifestly impossible to index such a work as this detailed journal with any completeness. We have tried to include all names of persons and places, all important biographical and historical events, and the more important subject references.

The reference is to the date of entry rather than to the printed page. The diarist used the new style calendar throughout.

Footnotes are included in the entry to which they are appended.

Assembly: prorogued, **1710**, Dec. 9;
see Council of State, House of Bur-
gesses.
Attorney General, *see* Thomson,
Stevens.
Auction, **1710**, Feb. 24, June 21, 24,
July 9.
*A-g-y (maid), **1711**, Jan. 2, 4-9.
A-t-k-s-n's (ordinary), riot at, **1712**,
Apr. 19.

B

Back River, **1709**, Nov. 25.
Bacon's Castle, **1709**, July 29.
Bailey, Allen, **1712**, Feb. 14, June 23.
Bailey, *see also* Bayley.
Ballard, Francis, **1711**, Nov. 9.
Balls, **1711**, Feb. 6, Nov. 2.
Bannister (Banister), John, **1709**, July
11, Aug. 11, 24, Sept. 22, Nov. 26;
1710, Jan. 13, Feb. 2, 4, 10, Mar.
8, 22, May 24, June 18, July 8,
Aug. 21, 25; **1711**, Jan. 25, Feb. 19,
20, Mar. 7, 29, May 1, June 4, 28,
July 3, 7, 15, 19, 20, Aug. 5, 14,
22, 27, Sept. 27, Oct. 16, Dec. 1;
1712, Jan. 1, Feb. 9, 10, Mar. 14,
May 17, June 28, July 4, 5, 8, 9,
12, Aug. 8, Sept. 22; sister of, **1709**,
Dec. 1; mother of, **1709**, Aug. 11;
1711, July 15, Aug. 14; **1712**, Jan.
1, June 28; father-in-law of, **1710**,
Feb. 2, 4.
Barbados, **1709**, Feb. 23, Apr. 19,
Aug. 2, 5, 6, 8, Sept. 2; **1710**, Jan.
5, Feb. 1, Mar. 16, 17, 18, June 14,
July 28, Aug. 16, Nov. 20, Dec. 8;
1711, Feb. 12, 13, Apr. 12, 16, May
19, June 18, 24; **1712**, Apr. 13.
Barn Elms, **1709**, May 3.
Barret, Dr., **1709**, Oct. 29, Nov. 2, 3;
1710, Apr. 18; **1711**, Nov. 29 (house
burnt).
Barret, Mrs. Mary, **1709**, Oct. 29.
Bass, William, **1709**, Oct. 2; **1711**,
Jan. 8, 23, 24, June 8; **1712**, June
23.
Bassett, Miss, **1709**, Aug. 28; **1711**,
Apr. 2, Sept. 27.
Bassett, Elizabeth, **1709**, Aug. 28;
1710, May 8; **1711**, Apr. 1, 2, Sept.
27, 28; **1712**, Feb. 24, 26.

---

*Names of unidentified persons and places
are indexed in the skeleton form in which
they appear in the Diary. See Introduction,
vii, xxvii, *n.* 4. The final "y" represents
any vowel.

Bassett, Colonel William, **1709**, Mar.
1, Apr. 10, 12, May 4, 5, July 21,
Sept. 12, Oct. 18, 19, 22, 28; **1710**,
Apr. 20, May 2, Nov. 18; **1711**,
Mar. 10, 24, 25 (agrees to go into
Council), Apr. 10, May 27, Aug.
29, Dec. 13; **1712**, Mar. 31, Apr. 2,
3 (christening of his child), 5, 26,
Sept. 24 (son of), 25 (plantation
criticized by Byrd), 26.
Bassett, Mrs. William (Joanna Bur-
well), **1709**, May 4; **1710**, Apr. 14,
May 2, 8; **1711**, Mar. 10, Apr. 13;
1712, Mar. 31, Apr. 1, 2, 26, Sept.
24, 26.
Bates, James, **1712**, Feb. 18, Apr. 26,
28.
Bates, John, **1711**, Mar. 29.
Bathing, river, **1710**, July 18, 19, 21,
Aug. 19, 22; **1711**, June 15, 30;
1712, Sept. 28, 29.
Bayley, Abraham, **1710**, Apr. 2.
Bedford (ship), **1710**, Sept. 16; **1712**,
June 1.
Berkeley, Captain Edmund, **1709**,
May 3, 4, Nov. 6, 7; **1710**, Apr. 14,
Nov. 12; **1711**, Mar. 9.
Berkeley, Mrs. Edmund (Lucy Bur-
well), **1709**, May 3, Nov. 6, 7, 8;
1710, Apr. 14, 16, June 19, 20;
1712, Apr. 12, 13.
Berkeley (plantation), **1709**, Feb. 11,
23.
Bermuda, **1711**, Apr. 16.
Bermuda Hundred, **1709**, May 11,
Aug. 20, Oct. 2; **1710**, Mar. 4;
1711, May 30, Sept. 24, Oct. 5;
1712, Jan. 7, Feb. 16.
Bernard, William, **1709**, Apr. 30.
Betty (maid), **1712**, Apr. 10.
Betty (negro), **1710**, July 15, 19.
Betty (ship), **1710**, Sept. 27.
Beverley, Mr., **1711**, Nov. 3.
Beverley, Mrs., **1711**, Nov. 3.
Beverley, Elizabeth, **1709**, June 24
(marriage to William Randolph).
Beverley, Major Peter, **1709**, June 24;
1710, Oct. 25 (Speaker of House of
Burgesses), Nov. 28; **1711**, Apr. 21.
Beverley, Robert, **1710**, Oct. 18, Dec.
9; **1711**, Apr. 22, Oct. 25; **1712**,
May 21.
Beverley, William, **1711**, Apr. 22,
Oct. 25.
Bible: infallibility disputed, **1709**,
May 1; Byrd copies chronology,
1711, Dec. 23; *see also* Apocrypha,

Greek Testament, Psalms, Solomon's Song.
Billy (servant), **1710**, Oct. 13; **1711**, Aug. 26; **1712**, Mar. 18, 23, Aug. 5.
Bird, William, **1710**, Nov. 2.
Blackamore, Reverend Arthur, **1709**, June 7, 24, Oct. 28, 29; **1711**, Apr. 25; **1712**, July 22.
Blackman, John, **1709**, Mar. 29, Aug. 13, 14, 19, Oct. 1; **1710**, July 20.
Blair, Mrs., **1710**, Sept. 13, Dec. 1; **1711**, May 25, Nov. 4.
Blair, Dr. Archibald, **1709**, Feb. 6, June 20, 22, Aug. 5, Oct. 9, 15; **1710**, Feb. 8, Mar. 25, 26, 27, Apr. 5, Nov. 30; **1711**, Sept. 11.
Blair, Reverend James: Introduction, x; **1709**, Mar. 1, 2, Apr. 18, 22, 24, 29, June 16, 20, Aug. 4, Sept. 12, 13, Oct. 21, 23, 30, Nov. 3, 4, Dec. 8; **1710**, Apr. 24, 29, May 9, 10, July 13, Sept. 13, Oct. 22, 29, Nov. 1, 19, 21, 22, Dec. 3, 4 (made minister of Bruton Parish), 5, 6; **1711**, Feb. 8, 14, Apr. 17, 23, 28, May 24, 25, July 24, Oct. 28, Nov. 4, 5, 10, 18, 27, Dec. 11; **1712**, Jan. 27, Feb. 1, Mar. 31 (made rector of the College), Apr. 18, 20, June 11, July 22, Aug. 18.
Blair, Mrs. James (Sarah Harrison), **1709**, Mar. 2, Apr. 29; **1710**, Apr. 5, 14; **1711**, Oct. 28, Nov. 18.
Blair, John, **1709**, June 20.
Blakiston, Colonel Nathaniel, **1709**, June 15; **1710**, Mar. 31.
*Bland, Mr., **1709**, Feb. 11, 12, 28, Mar. 1, 2, 4, 5, Apr. 4, 12, 13, 18, 25, 26, 27, 28, 29, May 5, 9, 21, 24, June 4, 16, 20, 21, 25, 27, 29, July 8, 10, 11, 13, 14, 21, 28, Aug. 4, 21, 28, Sept. 9, 12, 14, Oct. 15, 17, 18, 21, 22, 24, 29, Nov. 4, Dec. 8, 9, 12, 24; **1710**, Jan. 4, 19, 20, Feb. 5, 6, 11, Mar. 14, 31, Apr. 5, 21, 22, 24, 25 (governor of the College), 26, June 1, 10, 26, 29, 30, July 5, 6, 11, 12, 13, Aug. 6, 12, 16, 29, Sept. 4, 13, 14, 15, 16, Oct. 3, 22, 23, 27, 30, 31, Nov. 2, 25, 27, 29, Dec. 4, 11, 13, 18, 22, 23; **1711**, Jan. 19, 20, Feb. 9, 13, 18, 26, Mar. 5, 8, 9, 16, Apr. 6, 13, 29, May 21, 25, June 6, 12, 25, 30, July 4, 7,

14, 16, 21, 25, Aug. 17, 21, 25, 26, 28, Sept. 11, 14, 16, 19, 21, Oct. 8, 9, 11, Nov. 5, 9, 10, 20, 22, 30, Dec. 18, 22, 24, 30; **1712**, Jan. 3, 13, Feb. 7, 25, Apr. 8, 19, 30, May 8, 13, 16, 30, June 22, July 6, 20, 23, Aug. 5, 7, 14, 19, Sept. 1, 11.
Bland, Mrs., **1709**, Sept. 14; **1710**, Sept. 16, Dec. 14; **1711**, June 13, 26, 27, Nov. 5; **1712**, Feb. 1, May 1, July 22.
Bland, Mrs. Richard (Elizabeth Randolph), **1711**, Apr. 22.
Blissland Parish, **1709**, May 1.
Bloodletting, treatment by, **1709**, May 25, 26; **1710**, Jan. 8, Feb. 13, Apr. 6, May 24, Aug. 3; **1711**, Feb. 21-22, May 14, June 23; **1712**, Mar. 9, 21, July 10.
Boatwright, **1709**, July 18; **1710**, Mar. 15, Aug. 1, 3, 9, Sept. 27; **1711**, Jan. 21, 29, Mar. 2, 12; *see also* John B-r-d, Mr. T-r-t-n.
Bob (servant), **1712**, Aug. 5.
Bolling, Captain Edward, **1710**, Mar. 14 (death).
Bolling, Captain John, **1709**, Apr. 21, June 19, July 4, Sept. 15; **1710**, Feb. 18, 27, Mar. 27, July 12, Sept. 1 (burgess), Oct. 3; **1711**, Apr. 21, 23, July 19, Aug. 28, Sept. 8, 22, 23, 24, 27, Oct. 1, 2, 4, Dec. 16.
Bolling, Colonel Robert, **1709**, Feb. 26, 27, July 17 (death), 25.
Bolling, Mrs. Robert (Anne Stith), **1710**, Feb. 15; **1711**, Feb. 24.
Bolling, Robert, **1709**, Feb. 11, 15, 27, Apr. 13, May 8, 17, 24, June 6, 8, 9, 21, July 4, 17; **1710**, Aug. 8 (burgess); **1711**, Dec. 16, 17, 31; **1712**, June 4.
Bolling, Mrs. Robert (Anne Meriweather), **1709**, May 18.
Bond, Captain, **1711**, Sept. 15, 16.
Bonesetting, **1709**, Aug. 5, Dec. 17.
Book of Claims, **1710**, Dec. 5; **1711**, Dec. 18; **1712**, Jan. 25.
Books: *Byrd's*, **1709**, June 17, Aug. 11 ff.; **1711**, Mar. 15, 22, Dec. 30; **1712**, Aug. 5; *Dr. Oastler's*, **1709**, Sept. 11; **1710**, Feb. 8 ff.; *Mr. Harrison's*, **1710**, July 14; **1711**, May 14; **1712**, Mar. 7.
Booth, Mr., **1712**, June 4.
Boston, **1711**, Sept. 5.
Bowman, Dr. John, **1709** Mar. 28, Oct. 2; **1710**, Mar. 4, 5, Aug. 5; **1711**, June 22.

---

*No attempt is made here to distinguish between Richard and Theodorick Bland.

Bradby, Captain Joseph, 1710, July
25, 27.
Bradley, Captain, 1711, Aug. 2, 5.
Bradley, Benjamin, 1711, Aug. 2
Branch family, 1711, Apr. 24.
Bray, Colonel David, 1709, Apr. 19,
26, Oct. 23, 24; 1711, Apr. 23, Nov.
14, 18, Dec. 9.
Bray, Elizabeth, 1711, Nov. 14, 27
(marriage).
Bray, James, 1710, Mar. 25; 1711,
Nov. 16, 27 (wedding of his
daughter).
Brayne, Mrs. John (Susan Byrd),
1709, June 16; 1710, June 28, Dec.
11 (death).
Brayne, Susan, 1710, June 28 (arri-
val in Virginia), Aug. 24, 25, Oct.
8; 1711, Jan. 11, Feb. 1.
Brayne, William, 1710, June 28 (arri-
val in Virginia), July 14, Aug. 30,
Sept. 30, Dec. 24; 1712, Jan. 3,
Apr. 7, Sept. 1 (sent to College).
Brick House (ordinary), 1712, Apr. 2,
Sept. 26.
Bricklayer, 1712, Jan. 1, Mar. 9 ff.;
see also H-l, Cornelius.
Brickmaker, 1709, Apr. 5.
Bridger, Mr., 1710, Sept. 8.
Bridger, William, 1709, May 16.
Bridgewater's mill, 1710, Sept. 25.
Bristol Parish, 1710, Jan. 4.
Broadwater, Captain Charles, 1710,
June 28, 29, July 12, 29, 30, 31,
Sept. 11, 26, Oct. 3.
Brodie, Reverend William, 1711, May
28, 29, 30.
Brodnax, Mr., land of, 1711, Dec. 24.
Brodnax, Mrs., 1712, Feb. 21.
Browne, Captain, 1709, June 28, 29,
Oct. 12.
Browne, Captain (of Surry), 1710,
May 30.
Brussels, 1711, Oct. 24.
Bruton Parish, 1709, June 5, Dec. 8;
1710, Dec. 4 (Blair made minister),
Oct. 22; 1711, Nov. 18.
Buckland, 1709, Aug. 1; see Burkland.
Burbage, Dr. Robert, 1710, Sept. 12;
1711, Sept. 21 (marriage).
Burbydge, Captain Richard, 1710,
June 28, July 2, 3, 4, 9, 12, 17, 22,
24, 25, 28, 31, Aug. 8, 10, 18, 19,
24, 26, 27, Sept. 1, 17, 20, 26.
Burkland (plantation), 1709, Aug. 1,
19; 1710, Mar. 3, Aug. 14, Sept. 6;
1711, May 28, June 21; 1712, Jan.
16, Mar. 17.

Burnet, Gilbert, Bp. of Salisbury,
1710, Sept. 3. .
Burton, Robert, 1711, Jan. 20.
Burwell, Mr., 1711, May 17, 18.
Burwell, Mrs., 1709, Nov. 7, 27; 1710,
Mar. 31, Apr. 10, Nov. 12; 1711,
May 17.
Burwell, James, 1709, July 11, Dec. 3,
5, 15; 1710, Mar. 5, 27, 28, June
18, Sept. 3, 26; 1711, Nov. 8, 16, 17,
Dec. 16; 1712, Apr. 2, 19.
Burwell, Mrs. James, 1711, Dec. 16;
1712, Apr. 2.
Burwell, Major Lewis, 1709, Mar. 1,
Apr. 27, 30, May 1, 4, 5, Sept. 21,
23, Nov. 4, 26, 27; 1710, Apr. 30,
May 27, 30, June 20, July 30, Aug.
8, 10, Nov. 29, 30 (Byrd visits),
Dec. 6, 10, 11, 17, 23 (funeral);
1711, Mar. 10 (family), Dec. 16.
Burwell, Major Nathaniel, 1709, Feb.
21 (appointed naval officer), Mar.
1, Apr. 10, May 2, 3, Nov. 5, 6, 7,
9, 27; 1710, Mar. 31, Apr. 2, 3,
May 9, 10, Oct. 1, Nov. 24, 30,
Dec. 6; 1711, Mar. 10, Nov. 6;
1712, Apr. 12, 13.
Burwell, Mrs. Nathaniel (Elizabeth
Carter), 1709, May 2, 3; 1710, Apr.
1, Nov. 30, Dec. 6.
Burwell family, 1712, June 11.
Butler, Samuel, Hudibras, 1710, Sept.
14, Oct. 8.
Butts, John, 1712, June 7.
Butts, Peter, 1712, Jan. 12.
Butts, Thomas, 1711, May 19; 1712,
Feb. 16, 17, 26.
Byrd, Evelyn: Introduction, x; 1709,
Apr. 14, 15, 16, 17, July 16 (birth-
day), Nov. 26; 1710, Jan. 12, 13,
22, 23, Feb. 12, May 21-27, July 31,
Aug. 1-9, 18, Sept. 1, 3, 4, 9, 16, 19,
Nov. 3-5, 7, 22, Dec. 15, 17, 23-31;
1711, Jan. 1, 2, 5, 9, 14, Feb. 9, 20-
24, May 9, 10, June 19, 23, Aug.
26, Sept. 16, Oct. 6, 23, Nov. 20;
1712, Feb. 9, Mar. 2, 3, 4, May 1,
Aug. 20.
Byrd, Mrs. Mary, 1710, Mar. 16
(death).
Byrd, Parke, 1709, Sept. 6 (birth), 11,
28 (christened); 1710, Jan. 3, May
12-June 3 (illness and death), 4, 6
(funeral), 7.
Byrd, Thomas, 1709, May 9, 11, 12;
1710, Feb. 9, 10, 11, Mar. 13
(death), 17, May 20 (estate), June
21 (outcry of estate), 24.

Byrd, William I: Introduction, ix; 1710, Jan. 24 (grave), 28, Feb. 25, Apr. 17 (accounts); 1711, June 25.

Byrd, Mrs. William I (Maria Horsemanden), 1710, Jan. 22 (tomb), Feb. 25.

Byrd, William II: *biographical:* Introduction, ix-xiii; attends christening, 1709, *Feb.* 10; prepares representation on Indian trade, 16; dispatches sloop to Madeira, 19; visits plantations, 23-27; in Williamsburg, 28-*Mar.* 2; visits Green Springs, 2; visits plantations, 28-30; in Williamsburg, *Apr.* 18-30 (Green Springs, 23-25, King's Creek, 30); visits Carter's Creek, *May* 2; and Green Springs, 5; visits plantations, 11-12; petition against, *June* 3 (July 4); wins damages, 3; appointment as Councillor, 16 (21); salary increased, 16 (Oct. 27; 1710, Apr. 17); in Williamsburg, 20-21; visits Green Springs, *Aug.* 4; and Williamsburg, 4; visits plantations, 18-20; son born, *Sept.* 6 (christened, 28); in Williamsburg, 12-14; sworn councillor, 12; attempt to get governorship of Maryland, 16, 19 (1710, Apr. 17); visits plantations, 30-*Oct.* 2; visits Green Springs, 5, 7; in Williamsburg, 6-8, 15; sworn judge of General Court, 15; visits Green Springs, 31; in Williamsburg, *Nov.* 3; visits Eastern Shore, 7-26; at Major Burwell's, 26; at Williamsburg, and Green Springs, 27, 28; at Williamsburg, and Queen's Creek, *Dec.* 8; visits plantations, 23-24; case in Henrico Court, 1710, *Jan.* 31, *Feb.* 1; visits plantations, *Mar.* 2-4, 29-30; attempt to buy governorship of Virginia, 31; in Williamsburg, *Apr.* 17-30; dispute with Blair, 24; accounts passed, 25, warrants passed, 27; appointed commander-in-chief of county militia, 27; visits Queen's Creek, 29; illness of son, *May* 12 ff. (and death, June 3); illness of daughter, 21 ff.; visits plantations, 15-16; welcomes Spotswood at Green Springs, *June* 22; in Williamsburg, 23; name omitted from Council, 23; arrival of sister's children, 28; at Green Springs, *July* 4; in Williamsburg, 5-7; security for

Nathaniel Harrison, 5; at Green Springs, 6; at Prince George County elections, *Aug.* 8; and Charles City County elections, 15; visits plantations, *Sept.* 5-7; in Williamsburg, 12-16; entertains Spotswood at Westover, 20-24; presented to militia as commander-in-chief, 21; in Williamsburg, *Oct.* 9-11, 16—*Nov.* 4; prepares representation on tobacco trade, *Oct.* 30, 31; writes judgment on Charles Parish case, *Nov.* 2; in Williamsburg, 8-11, 13-Dec. 14; prepares money bill, Nov. 16; throws lampoon into House, 24, and is accused by Mason, 26; visits Burwell, 30; draws up address to Governor, *Dec.* 4, 5, which is approved in Council, 5; assigned best pew in church, 18; visits plantations, 19-22; writes key of *Atlantis,* 26 ff.; plague among the slaves, 26—1711, *Jan.* 30; attempt to get offices of Receiver and Auditor joined, 20; buys negroes for Governor, *Feb.* 2, 3; at Queen's Creek, 5-6; in Williamsburg, 6-8; at Governor's Ball, 6; buys trees for Governor, 8; daughter ill, 20 ff.; finds lost child, 28; in Williamsburg, *Mar.* 7-9; at Queen's Creek, 9; tries to have salary increased, 20; entertains Spotswood, 24 ff.; visits plantations, 27-28; in Williamsburg, *Apr.* 15-29; case in General Court, 20, 21; at Queen's Creek, 21; asks for escheator's place, 22, 23; asks leave to go to England, 23; error in accounts, 27; at Green Springs, 29; attracted to Sarah Taylor, 29; makes a will, *May* 23 ff.; goes on expedition to Manakin Town, and to plantations, 28-30; at county court, *June* 6; in Williamsburg, 11-14; at Green Springs, 13; visits plantations, 20-22; in Williamsburg, *July* 4-7; has attack of malarial fever, 4-16 (and Aug. 6-13 ff.); in Williamsburg, *July* 23-27; at Green Springs, 22, 27; court case dismissed, *Aug.* 1; signs will, 10; ordered to call out militia, 15, 21; sends orders to colonels, 15, 20, 21; sends valuables out of danger, 24; hears of French invading Eastern Shore, 26; reviews militia, 27; invasion a false alarm, 28; orders militia to range, *Sept.* 4; sends palisades to Jamestown, 5; reports on militia to Governor, 13; at Queen's Creek, 19; in Williamsburg, 19-21; musters militia, 22-24, *Oct.* 2-4, 6; goes to council on Indians, 8-9, 16; goes with militia to Nottoway Town, 17-21; in Williamsburg, 23-Nov. 11; plays trick on Doctor, *Nov.* 1; affronts the President, 3; project for paying ministers in money, 8-9; visits Frank Lightfoot, 11-12; entertains Mr. Graeme at Westover, 12-14; in Williamsburg, 14-30; wedding at Colonel Bray's, 14; at Queen's Creek, 19; project of selling Parke land, 19 ff.; attends committee on port bill, 24; resolves not to gamble, 24; visits Queen's Creek, 25; sells quitrents, 30; lets a plantation, *Dec.* 1; in Williamsburg, 4-16; discusses unreasonable taxes, 5; discusses Parke's land, 7; slandered by Mrs. Russell, 9; attests Mrs. Byrd's consent to sale of land, 10; sworn a judge of Court of Oyer and Terminer, 11; cannot oblige Governor at risk of honor, 15; visits James Burwell, 16-17; in Williamsburg, 17-24; gets deed of partition of Parke land, 21; refused permission to leave Williamsburg, 22; copies a chronology of the Bible, 23; visits Queen's Creek, 23, 24-25; persuades Governor to adjourn Assembly, 24; prunes trees at Westover, *1712*, Jan. 3 ff.; trouble about remark concerning Governor, 9, 15, 21, 24, 29; in Williamsburg, 22-*Feb.* 1; escheator, *Jan.* 30; advances £500 to colony, 31; advises Governor to finish fort, 31; at Queen's Creek, *Feb.* 1; bargains for Parke land, 2; inspects land in New Kent, 11-14; visits plantations, 14-16; sells Skimino mill, 18 (Apr. 28); at Queen's Creek, 19; in Williamsburg, 20-21; dissects a muskrat, 27; gives medical advice, *Mar.* 8; visits Major Harrison, 11-13, 30-31, and persuades him to a milk diet, 11; in New Kent, 26; at Green Springs, 31; in Williamsburg, 31-*Apr.* 2; visits Colonel Bassett, 2-3; writes about Carolina expedition, 5; goes to general muster, 9; at Queen's Creek, 14, 21, 27; in Williamsburg, 15-*May* 1;

resolves not to gamble, *Apr.* 17; Mrs. Custis refuses to sell land, 19, 21; English goods arrive, 23; makes agreement with Custis, 25 ff.; at Green Springs, *May* 1; disappointed in English goods, 2; goods stolen, 11; visits plantations, 13-14; shares crops in York River, 20; entertains Dr. Cocke, 24-29; and Mrs. Cocke and Mr. Catesby, 24-*June* 17; has an ague, *June* 1 ff.; at Green Springs, 9; in Williamsburg, 10-12; visits Swinyards, 14; in Williamsburg, *July* 20-23; accounts passed in Council, 21; pays councillors, 22; at Queen's Creek, 23; makes law abridgments, *Aug.* 1, ff.; in Williamsburg, 17-20; visits neighbors, 26-27; visits plantations, *Sept.* 9-11; orchard robbed, 10; maligned by Mrs. Russell, 21; goes to Pamunkey Town, 22-24; visits Colonel Bassett, 25; has an ague, 27; *diary:* Introduction, vi; *land:* Introduction, xi-xii; *1709,* Mar. 29, *Apr.* 13, 18, *Oct.* 1, 13; *1711,* May 30, June 21; *Aug.* 3, Nov. 19, Dec. 7, 10, 21, 24; *1712,* Feb. 2 ff., 21, *Apr.* 14 ff., *July* 16, *Sept.* 15, 18; *letters:* Introduction, vi; *writings:* Introduction, vi, xvii-xviii; *1709,* Mar. 26; *1710, Nov.* 21, 24-27, Dec. 15, 18, 21, 23; *1711,* May 14.

Byrd, Mrs. William II (Lucy Parke): Introduction, x, xx; bad housekeeping, *1709, Apr.* 7; in Williamsburg, 29; ill, *May* 1, 7; beats Nurse, 13; extravagance, *June* 14, 15; goods sold by Byrd, 27; Byrd dreams of her death, *July* 15; Byrd cheats at cards, *Aug.* 27; delivered of a son, *Sept.* 6; at Green Springs, *Oct.* 31; in Williamsburg, *Nov.* 1; annoyed by Byrd's attentions to Mrs. Chiswell, 2; divides her mother's good with Mrs. Custis, 3; on the Eastern shore, annoyed by Byrd's manners, 11; returns from Eastern Shore, 26; involved in neighborhood quarrel, *Dec.* 1, 2; reproaches guest for swearing, 5; neglects family, 13; ill, refuses to be bled, *1710, Feb.* 13; miscarries, 14; mourns at death of child, *June* 3, ff.; has portentous dream, 18; doctors Byrd, 27, 28; quarrels over purchases, *July* 9; burns servant with iron, 15; ill, expects to die, 24; quarrels about servants, *Aug.* 12; presented with Indian goods, *Sept.* 29; pregnant, *Oct.* 4; at Williamsburg, *Nov.* 29; at Queen's Creek, *Dec.* 1; at Green Springs, 3, 4; quarrels over Psalm singing, 16; has portentous dream, 31; cruelty, **1711**, *Jan.* 11; insulted, 12; threatens suicide, 31; quarrels over pulling brows, *Feb.* 5; opens Governor's ball, 6; visits the Governor, 7; wishes herself a freak, 16; upset by the parson, *Mar.* 3; offers to care for Miss Digges, 10; entertains Mrs. Russell, 30; tells of Mrs. Dunn's misfortunes, 31; receives news of Colonel Parke's death, *Apr.* 12; miscarries, *June* 25; fears smallpox, 27; writes letters for Byrd, *July* 16 ff.; frightened at threat of invasion, *Aug.* 23; visits Falling Creek, *Oct.* 5; at Williamsburg, 31; visits Governor, *Nov.* 1, 2; visits Burwell's, 6; consents to sale of land, *Dec.* 10; visits Colonel Harrison, **1712**, *Jan.* 29; displeased with Byrd's bargain for land, *Feb.* 4; has servants whipped, 5; acts a mad woman, *Mar.* 2; has intermittent fever, 21 ff.; at Queen's Creek, *Apr.* 21, 22; at Williamsburg, 23, 24; acknowledges deed in court, 25; at Queen's Creek, 27; at Green Springs, 29; pregnant, *June* 25; goes to funeral, 26; is bled, *July* 10; drinks beer, 11; seals instrument, 17; has fever, *Aug.* 1, ff.; visiting, 10, 26; whips maid, *Sept.* 3; ill, 4 ff.; has vapors, 19.

Byrd Park plantation, **1709**, Aug. 19; **1710**, Mar. 3, Sept. 6.

B-k-r (*or* B-r-k), Mrs. Ann, **1709**, Feb. 6, Apr. 12; **1710**, Jan. 22, June 3, 5; **1711**, Oct. 1; **1712**, Feb. 26, Mar. 4 (marriage to Mr. Poythress).

B-l-w, Mr., **1712**, Mar. 8.

B-n, Mr., **1711**, Feb. 19.

B-r-d, John (boatmaker), **1709**, July 20, 22.

B-r-d-f-r, Captain, **1712**, Mar. 5.

B-r-d-r, Mrs., **1709**, Dec. 12.

B-r-k, Captain, **1710**, Mar. 19 (death); **1711**, June 6 (case against).

B-r-k, *see also* B-k-r.

B-r-k-l-t, Captain, **1712**, Apr. 22.

B-r-n-t, Mr., **1711**, Sept. 20.

B-r-x, Robin, **1710**, May 3.

B-s, Mr., **1709**, Dec. 9; **1711**, Feb. 9, Mar. 11, Sept. 21.

B-s, Major, **1712**, Jan. 30.

B-th, George, **1709**, June 10.

B-t-s or P-t-s, Mrs. (midwife), **1709**, July 27, 28, Aug. 31; Sept. 9.

C

Cæsar (negro), **1712**, May 11.

Cairon, Reverend John, **1711**, May 25 (arrival in Virginia), June 6, 7, July 17, Aug. 7, 13; three sons of, **1711**, June 6, 7.

Calabar [Calabria], **1710**, Nov. 13.

Canada, **1709**, June 8; expedition against, **1711**, July 2, Sept. 5, 6, Oct. 23.

Carolina, *see* North Carolina.

Carolina boundaries, commissioners for running, **1711**, July 27.

Cargill, Reverend John, **1709**, Aug. 9, Oct. 23; **1710**, Aug. 18; **1711**, Oct. 21; **1712**, Mar. 12.

Cargill, Mrs. John, **1711**, Sept 27.

Carpenter, **1709**, July 21.

Carter, Elizabeth, **1711**, Feb. 6.

Carter, George, **1710**, Feb. 3; **1711**, May 2, July 19.

Carter, Colonel Robert, **1709**, Mar. 1, Apr. 23, 24, Oct. 25; **1710**, Nov. 1, 16, 19, 20, 23, 27; **1711**, Feb. 6, Oct. 30, Nov. 3, 23, 24, Dec. 12, 13, 14, 20; **1712**, Apr. 27, Aug. 18, 19.

Carter, Mrs. Robert, **1711**, Feb. 6.

Carter's Creek plantation, **1709**, May 2.

Cary, Mr., **1709**, May 11.

Cary, Henry, **1710**, Aug. 21, Nov. 9, 24; **1711**, Jan. 1, 3, Dec. 7, 14.

Cary, Colonel Miles, **1709**, Feb. 16 (death), 21.

Cary, Thomas, **1711**, June 13.

Cassius, **1709**, Oct. 11-14, Nov. 30 — **1710**, Mar. 14 *daily.*

Catesby, Mark, **1712**, Apr. 30, May 24, 26, 30, June 5, 7, 13, 14, Aug. 19, Sept. 17, 18, 21-29.

Chamberlayne, Major, **1710**, July 18.

Chamberlayne, Mr., **1710**, July 8; **1711**, Aug. 29; **1712**, Jan. 10.

Chamberlayne, Edward, **1710**, July 28.

Chapman, Mr. (and Mrs.), **1711**, May 19.

Charles City County: *bill for dividing*, **1710**, Nov. 21; *burgesses*, **1709**, June 3; **1710**, Aug. 15; **1712**, Sept. 26; *militia*, **1709**, Feb. 1; **1711**, Aug

15, 20, 21; *sheriff*, 1709, Feb. 17, Aug. 29; 1712, Apr. 3.

Charles Parish vestry, dispute with parson, 1709, Oct. 22; to be prosecuted, Dec. 8; settled without trial, 1710, June 17; Byrd writes judgment on, Nov. 2.

Cherries: wine from, 1709, June 4; method of preserving, Nov. 7; stewed, 1710, Feb. 2; for stomach ache, May 31; trees, 1711, Feb. 8.

Chester, Edward, 1711, May 25.

Chester, Mrs. Katharine, 1711, May 25.

Chester, Lucy, 1711, May 25.

Chicahominy, 1709, June 13; 1710, Jan. 10; 1712, Aug. 6.

Chicahominy Bridge, 1711, Mar. 24.

Chicahominy Swamp, 1711, Mar. 28.

Children, discipline and training, 1710, May 21, July 14, Oct. 8; 1711, Feb. 1, Dec. 16; 1712, July 25, Aug. 21; *see* Brayne, Susan and William; Byrd, Evelyn.

Chiswell, Charles, 1709, Oct. 29.

Chiswell, Mrs. Charles, 1709, Oct. 29, 30, 31, Nov. 2; 1710, Apr. 18.

Chiswell, Mary, 1709, Oct. 29.

Church: congregation, 1709, May 15, Nov. 13; 1710, Mar. 5; of Abingdon, 1709, Nov. 6; bell, 1709, Dec. 8; on fast day, 1710, Jan. 11; Byrd's pew in, 1710, Dec. 18.

Churchill, Colonel William, 1709, Oct. 27, Nov. 1; 1710, Nov. 12, 14, 16, 28 (death); 1711, Dec. 21 (accounts).

Churchill, Mrs. William, 1711, Nov. 2, 3.

Christian, C-t, 1710, Aug. 22.

Claiborne, Mr., 1709, Apr. 20.

Clayton, John, 1709, May 6, June 20, Sept. 7-10, Oct. 6, 7, Nov. 4, 27; 1710, Jan. 11, Apr. 13, 25 (governor of the College), June 21, July 6, 11, 12, 13, 14, 20, 21, 24, Nov. 4, Dec. 10, 11; 1711, Jan. 3, 10, 11, 12, Feb. 7, Mar. 8, 10, Apr. 4, 5, 7, 22, May 5, 6, 7, 8, 9, June 12, July 11, 12, Sept. 5, 6, 19, Nov. 3, 6, 7, 25, Dec. 21; 1712, Jan. 5, 6, 8, 9, 24, Feb. 21, Apr. 13, June 4, Aug. 22.

Clergy, 1709, June 15; 1710, Nov. 1; 1711, Nov. 8-9; *see also* Charles Parish vestry; Manakin Town disdisorders.

Clergymen: *see* Anderson, Charles; Blackamore; Blair, James; Brodie; Cairon; Cargill; Dunn; Finney; Goodwin, Benjamin; Gray; Le Fevre; Paxton; Phillipe; Robertson, George; Slater; Smith, Guy; Taylor, Daniel; Wallace; Ware; Whateley; Worden.

Clothing, 1712, Aug. 31, Sept. 2.

Coal mine, 1709, July 18, Aug. 13; 1710, Dec. 23; 1711, May 29.

Coaler, 1709, June 15; *see* Smith, George.

Cocke, Mr., 1709, Feb. 18, Dec. 13; 1711, Aug. 24.

Cocke, Mrs., 1709, Aug. 23, Sept. 26.

Cocke, Richard, 1709, Feb. 11, 13, 22, 23, 24, May 9, June 20, July 24, Dec. 11; 1710, Mar. 6, 11, June 14; 1711, Feb. 14, Aug. 28.

Cocke, Thomas, 1709, Feb. 18; 1711, Aug. 15 (death).

Cocke, Dr. William, 1710, June 22 (arrival in Virginia), July 11-13, Aug. 4-6, Sept. 13, 14, Oct. 11, 12, 26, Nov. 8, 11, 12, 15, 30, Dec. 10, 12; 1711, Mar. 8, 24, 26-29, Apr. 2, 20, 25, 29, May 11, 12-15, June 12, 29, 30, July 1, 3, 5, 6, 8-13, 18, 23, 30, Aug. 7-10, 25, 26, 28-31, Sept. 11, 19, 20, Oct. 16-19, 24, Nov. 1, 2, 6, 20, 25, Dec. 4, 7, 16, 17, 20, 23; 1712, Jan. 8, 27, 29, 31, Feb. 16-20, Mar. 22, 23, 27, 29-31, Apr. 1, 14, 15, 20, 21, 23 (made Secretary of State), 25, 26, 30, May 1, 21, 23, 24, 26, 29, June 1, 8, 9, 10 (sworn Secretary), 11, 17, July 5, 13, 22, 23, Aug. 7, 8, 19, Sept. 17, 21.

Cocke, Mrs. William (Elizabeth Catesby), 1712, Apr. 22 (arrival in Virginia), 23-25, May 1, 21, 23, 24, June 1, 2, 17, July 23, Aug. 7; two children of, 1712, Apr. 22, May 23; daughter of, 1712, May 24.

Coke, Sir Edward: Introduction, vii; 1711, Apr. 2.

Cole, William, 1710, Oct. 1; 1711, Oct. 7.

Cole, Mrs. William (Mary Roscow), 1711, Dec. 9.

Cole, Mrs. William (Martha Lear), 1710, Oct. 1.

Collier, Jeremy, *Short view of the immorality and profaneness of the English stage,* 1709, Nov. 23, 24.

Collins, Captain Edward, 1709, June 13, 24, 29, Aug. 10, 20, Sept. 7, 10.

Commissary, the, see Reverend James Blair.

Conner, Mr., 1709, Apr. 19.

Cook, Captain, 1709, Sept. 26-29; 1710, Feb. 16, 21-28, Apr. 25, 28, 29.

Cookery, 1709, Nov. 7; 1710, Oct. 21; 1711, May 29; 1712, Mar. 12.

Cooper, the, 1709, July 2; 1710, Feb. 17.

Coratuck Inlet, 1709, Dec. 8.

Corbin, Colonel Gawin, 1710, Nov. 1; 1711, Mar. 5, June 13 (dismissed as Naval Officer).

Corn: want of, 1709, Oct. 10, Dec. 4; 1710, Jan. 31; protection of, 1709, Dec. 8.

Corn pone, 1710, Mar. 3; 1711, Mar. 2.

Council of State: Introduction, ix, xv; Byrd prepares a representation for, 1709, Feb. 16; Byrd informs of epidemic, 28; Byrd presents a memorial, Mar. 1; opens Indian trade, Apr. 26; examines Byrd's accounts, June 21; Byrd sworn a member, Sept. 12; discusses Indians, Oct. 21; orders vessel to protect the Cape, 1710, Apr. 19; passes Byrd's accounts, 24; disputes about money for College, 24; passes Byrd's warrants, 27; Governor Spotswood's maiden speech, June 23; Governor's instructions read, July 5; keeps ships from sailing, Sept. 15; reads journal of boundary commission, Oct. 10; hears Governor's speech, 24; approves Speaker of House, and passes Byrd's accounts, 26; discusses Post Office, 30; debates money bill, Nov. 14, 15, 18, 23; discusses bill concerning tobacco hogsheads, 17, 18; and tax bill, 25, 27; passes land bill, Dec. 2; reads Book of Claims, 5; settles Commissions of Peace, 7; meets at the Governor's, 1711, Feb. 6; gives patent to Colonel Hill for "gold mines," Apr. 24; hears disputes about land, 25; examines Byrd's accounts, 27, 28; discusses affairs of Carolina, June 13, July 5; discusses aid to New York in Canadian expedition, 5; passes Byrd's accounts, 24; discusses Indian question, Oct. 8; Governor addresses, Nov. 8; addresses Governor, 16; reads bill on warehouses, 16, and

on horses, 17; advises war on Indians, 28; rejects gold coin bill, Dec. 5; prepares bill on negroes, 5, 6; reads bill on horses, 6; turns out Cary as overseer of building, 7; Governor gives audience to Tuscaroras, 8; treaty with Indians, 10, 11; discusses money bill, 10 ff.; reads bill for selling Parke land, 12 ff.; disputes with House over money bill, 15 ff.; reads claims, 18; gives audience to Indians, 19; assembly adjourned, 24; receives petition from Carolina, 1712, Feb. 20; agrees to assist Carolina, Apr. 1; examines Indians, 19; confers on land cases, 22, and on Indians, 22, 23, 26; appoints commanders of forces to Carolina, 24; discusses Court of Oyer and Terminer, June 10; passes Byrd's accounts, July 21; sentences Mr. Jeffrys, 21; disputes salary of the Governor, 21; has Indians before it, Aug. 18.

Court, county: 1709, May 11, July 4 (Byrd in), Sept. 3, Dec. 3; 1710, Feb. 3, May 3, July 3, 12, Aug. 3, Sept. 4 (Mrs. Harrison in), Oct. 3; 1711, Mar. 13, May 1 (records of), June 6 (Byrd in), Aug. 1 (Byrd in); 1712, Sept. 3 (case between Mrs. Harrison and Colonel Hill).

Court, Henrico County, 1710, Jan. 31; 1711, May 7, 8, June 4.

Court, Prince George County, 1709, Feb. 11; 1710, May 10, June 14; 1711, Feb. 13.

Court martial, 1710, Oct. 5; 1711, Oct. 4 (fines Quakers), 12.

Court of Admiralty, 1711, June 13; 1712, June 1.

Court of Oyer and Terminer: Introduction, ix; tries a man for murder, 1710, Dec. 12, 13; judges sworn, 1711, Dec. 11; tries woman for burglary, 11; pronounces sentence of death, and she pleads pregnancy, 12; jury of matrons gives verdict, 13; discussed in Council, 1712, June 10.

Courthouse, 1710, July 1, Aug. 15.

Courts, see also General Court.

Craddock, Robert, 1709, Sept. 17.

Crapeau, Captain, 1709, Apr. 15.

Creed, religious: Introduction, vii, xxviii; 1709, May 30; 1710, Feb. 13.

Crime, 1710, Apr. 20, Oct. 19; 1711, June 12, 13; *Burglary*, 1710, Feb. 3, Mar. 3, July 5; 1711, Dec. 11-13; 1712, May 11, Sept. 10; *Homicide*, 1710, Apr. 27, Dec. 12, 13; *Rape*, 1709, Oct. 19; *Treason*, 1710, Apr. 18, 19, 21.

Cross, John, 1711, Apr. 30, May 2, Aug. 31, Oct. 10.

Cross, Mrs. John, 1711, Sept. 1.

Crow, Mitford, Governor of Barbados, 1709, Aug. 2.

Curle, Nicholas, 1712, Apr. 18, Sept. 9, 10.

Custis, Daniel Parke, 1710, Oct. 28 (christened).

Custis, Frances, 1709, Sept. 13 (birth); Nov. 20.

Custis, Colonel John, 1709, Nov. 12, 13, 14, 16, 21; 1712, Apr. 16, 27.

Custis, Major John, 1709, Apr. 8, 9, 11, 14, 24, 25, 27, 30, May 2, Nov. 9, 16, 22-25, Dec. 9, 10; 1710, Jan. 20, 21, Apr. 18, 29, May 1, June 5, 6, 7, Sept. 12, 15, Oct. 11, 23, 28 (son christened), Dec. 3; 1711, Feb. 5, 9, Mar. 10, Apr. 2, 4, 5, 17, 29, July 26, Sept. 19, Nov. 4, 25, Dec. 7, 9, 10, 14, 17, 20, 21; 1712, Jan. 5, 21, 23, 24, 29; Feb. 1-4, 9-14, 18, 21, Mar. 29, Apr. 14, 16, 17, 19, 20, 21, 25, 28, May 12, 13, 14, Aug. 19, 20, Sept. 21.

Custis, Mrs. John (Frances Parke): Introduction, xi; 1709, Feb. 28, Mar. 2, Apr. 14, 15, 27, 30, May 1, Sept. 13 (daughter born), Oct. 29, 30, Nov. 2, 3, 7, 18, 19, 23, Dec. 8; 1710, Jan. 6, Mar. 4, 7, Apr. 18, 23, 24, 25, June 5, Sept. 12, Oct. 11, 28 (son christened), Dec. 1, 3; 1711, Feb. 5, 6, Mar. 9, 10, 26, Apr. 2, 9, 29, May 25, June 17, Aug. 8, 9, 10, Sept. 11, 12, 19, Nov. 3, 4, 6, 7, 19, 20, 26, Dec. 9, 12; 1712, Jan. 5, 7, 23, Feb. 2, 4, 18, 20, Mar. 2, 27, 29 (complains of husband), Apr. 4, 14, 16, 17-21, 25, 28, June 9, Aug. 7, 20.

Cutlett, Captain Richard, 1709, June 15; *see* C-l-t.

C-k, Mr., of Plymouth, 1709, Aug. 17.

C-k, Dick, the wireman, 1710, Sept. 11, Dec. 10; 1711, Mar. 19; 1712, Apr. 11.

C-l, Captain, 1709, Apr. 27, 29, May 9, 10.

C-l-t, Captain, 1709, June 15, July 4, 23.

C-l-v, Captain, 1709, July 10.

C-l-y, negro, 1711, Jan. 1, 2 (death).

C-n-g-y, servant, 1710, Mar. 5-9 (death).

C-r-l-y, of England, 1709, June 16.

C-r-n-r, old, 1711, May 17.

C-s, Major, 1709, Feb. 23, May 29, June 4, 5, 19, July 17, 31, Aug. 7, Dec. 10; 1710, Jan. 1, 2, 8, 21, 22, Feb. 1, 6, 9, 12, 21, Mar. 5, 10 12, 15, 18, 19, Apr. 4, 12, 15, May 3, 6, 7, 17, 19, 25, 27, 30, June 6, 10, 14, 19, 24, 25, July 1, 8, 9, 11, 18, 19, 21, 24, 25, 26, 27, 28, Aug. 2, 4, 6, 14, 16, 18, 28, 30, Sept. 2, 4, 10, 20, Oct. 1, 4, 8, 15 (leaves for England); 1711, Feb. 12 (in Barbados), Apr. 12, Dec. 25.

C-t's (ordinary), 1710, Apr. 26, June 23, Oct. 17, 23, Dec. 5, 7.

Ch-s-t-r, Captain, 1710, Mar. 14 (death).

D

Dancing, 1709, Feb. 10, Apr. 19, 23, 26, May 4, 6, Oct. 23, 24, 31, Nov. 12; 1710, Mar. 23; 1711, Feb. 6, Apr. 23, Nov. 2.

Dancing, Indian, 1711, Oct. 20.

Day, Dr., 1709, Dec. 28.

Debts, 1709, June 16, 17, 19, Aug. 18, Sept. 1 (paid in tobacco); 12 (paid in negroes); 14, 24, Oct. 3 (tools seized as security); 1710, Jan. 25 (forgiven).

Dennis, Mr., 1709, Aug. 29, Sept. 29, Oct. 9; 1710, May 3; 1712, July 17, Aug. 12.

Digges, Mr., 1711, Mar. 10.

Digges, Colonel Dudley, 1709, Mar. 1, Nov. 3; 1710, June 5, Oct. 9, 11, 17, 24, Nov. 1, 8, 11, 12, 13, 28; 1711, Jan. 20 (death), Feb. 6, Mar. 10 (family).

Digges, Elizabeth, 1711, Mar. 10.

Diet, rules of, 1709, Feb. 11, 19, 20, Apr. 8, June 9; 1711, Jan. 25; 1712, Mar. 11 ff.

Dion Cassius, *see* Cassius.

Distemper, epidemic of, 1709, Feb. 28, Apr. 8, 9 (fast day for), May 18; 1710, Jan 3 ff., 15, Feb. 28, Apr. 31.

Doctors, *see* Barrett; Blair, Archibald; Bowman; Burbage; Cocke, William; Irby; Oastler.

Downs, the (England), **1711**, Jan. 25, Sept. 17.

Doyley (D'Oyley), Mr., **1709**, June 5, July 17; **1710**, Mar. 5, 6, 28, Apr. 13, June 6, July 2, Aug. 15.

Doyley (D'Oyley), Charles, **1709**, June 5, Sept. 22; **1710**, June 18, 24; **1711**, Feb. 22.

Doyley (D'Oyley), Cope, **1709**, June 5; **1710**, Aug. 20 (death).

Dreams and portents: Introduction, xix; **1709**, Apr. 8, 14, July 15; **1710**, Jan. 5, Mar. 31, Apr. 10, June 18, 21, July 21, Aug. 29, Dec. 31; **1712**, Jan. 16, 19.

Drinking and drunkenness, **1709**, Feb. 18, Mar. 2, 4, 28, June 7, 25, July 5, Aug. 27, Oct. 12, 27, 28, Nov. 1, Dec. 14; **1710**, May 3, Aug. 15, 22, Sept. 21, 22, Nov. 10, 26, Dec. 11; **1711**, Feb. 7, Apr. 4, 23, Nov. 3, 23; **1712**, Mar. 12.

Drought, **1709**, July 22-24, Aug. 19, 29.

Dudley, Colonel Joseph, **1710**, Sept. 26.

Duke, Colonel Henry, **1709**, Mar. 1, Apr. 18, 28, Sept. 11, 12, Oct. 18, 19, 22, Dec. 7, 9, 10; **1710**, Feb. 13, Apr. 23, 30, Sept. 12, Oct. 22, 23, 29, Nov. 2, 18, 19, 20, 21; **1711**, Feb. 5, 8, Mar. 7, 10, 11, Apr. 15, 16, June 12, Sept. 18, 19, 21, 22, Nov. 17, 18, 23, Dec. 24; **1712**, Jan. 1, 2, 22, 23, 27, Feb. 2, 3, 19, Apr. 1, 2, 13, 14, 27, July 23, 24, Aug. 17, 18.

Duke, Mrs. Henry, **1711**, Sept. 18, Dec. 25; **1712**, Apr. 27.

Duke, James, **1709**, Feb. 6, 27, Aug. 30, Sept. 11, Dec. 9; **1710**, Feb. 13, Apr. 30, June 6, Sept. 12, Nov. 20; **1711**, Jan. 4, Feb. 4, 9, Mar. 7, 11, Apr. 15, 16, Sept. 18, 21, Dec. 25; **1712**, Jan. 22, Feb. 4, 9, 10, 19, Mar. 8, 9, 22, July 24, Aug. 17.

Duke, Mrs. James, **1709**, Feb. 6 (miscarried); **1710**, Apr. 30 (and her child), June 6, 9, Sept. 12; **1711**, Feb. 4, Mar. 7, May 1, 2, 4, Sept. 18, 21; **1712**, Feb. 4 (and child).

Dunkirk, **1712**, Sept. 17.

Dunn, Reverend, **1709**, Feb. 28, Sept. 13 (married), Nov. 9, 10, 11, 13, 18, 20, 22; **1710**, Jan. 6, Apr. 18, May 13, Oct. 12, 13, Nov. 29, Dec. 14, 15; **1711**, Jan. 4, Feb. 1, 2, 3,

21, 27, 28, Mar. 1, 3, 31, Apr. 2, 3, 4, 6, May 22, 23, June 1, 24.

Dunn, Mrs. (Mrs. J-f-r-y, *q.v.*), **1709**, Sept. 7, 13, Nov. 9, 18, 19, 20, 22; **1710**, Apr. 18, Nov. 29, 30, Dec. 2, 3, 14, 15, 16, 17; **1711**, Jan. 4, 6, 31, Feb. 1, 4, 21, 22, 24, 27, Mar. 4, 26, 31, Apr. 2, 9, 10, May 22, 23, June 1, 3, 14, 15, 16, 26, 28, 29, 30, July 9, 11, 14, 17, Aug. 9, 17, 19, 26, Sept. 11, 12, Nov. 1, 5, 6, 7, 13, 30, Dec. 26, 30; **1712**, Jan. 3, 21, Feb. 17, Mar. 1, 16, 17, 18, 29, Apr. 6, May 1, June 1, 17, 21, 24, 25, 26, July 20, 27, Aug. 20, 23, 27.

D-k, Mr., **1711**, Nov. 9 (to marry Mrs. Young), 10.

D-k, Mrs., **1711**, Apr. 6; **1712**, Aug. 31.

D-k, Captain, **1712**, Apr. 10.

D-k, Harry, wife of, **1712**, Aug. 3.

D-k, Thomas, **1710**, Aug. 18.

D-m-n-y, Mr., **1712**, Feb. 13.

D-r-k, Mr., **1711**, Apr. 22.

E

Easely, Robert, **1709**, May 12, Oct. 2; **1711**, Oct. 6.

Eastern Shore, the, **1709**, Apr. 9, Nov. 7-22 (Byrd visits); **1710**, Aug. 1; **1711**, Mar. 10, Aug. 26.

Education, **1709**, Apr. 25; **1710**, Apr. 7, July 14; **1711**, Mar. 23; **1712**, Mar. 19, Sept. 6; *see also* William and Mary College.

Edwards, Mr., **1709**, May 5, 6.

Elections, *of burgesses,* **1710**, Aug. 8, 15; **1712**, Sept. 24, 26; *declared void,* **1710**, Nov. 2, 3; *of minister,* **1710**, Dec. 4; *see also* names of counties.

Elizabeth City Parish, **1709**, Nov. 25.

Eltham, **1709**, Apr. 10.

England, **1709**, Apr. 25, June 16, July 26, Aug. 31, Sept. 2, 3; **1710**, Jan. 2, 19, 28, Mar. 31, June 7, Aug. 29, Nov. 18; **1711**, Mar. 5, 8.

Enterprise (ship), **1710**, Apr. 19; **1711**, Nov. 29.

Epidemic, **1709**, Dec. 8; **1710**, Dec. 26—**1711**, Jan.; *see also* Distemper; Gripes.

Eppes, Mr., **1709**, June 13; **1712**, Sept. 28.

Eppes, Mrs., **1709**, Apr. 17, June 26, Aug. 20, Sept. 4, 26; **1710**, Mar. 19, May 14; **1711**, Feb. 18, Apr. 11,

May 1, June 6, July 29, Aug. 1, 14; 1712, May 25, Aug. 26, Sept. 27.

Eppes, Captain, 1711, Oct. 6, 22.

Eppes, Colonel, 1709, Mar. 28, Apr. 17, June 3, 8, 13, 26, Aug. 20, Sept. 4, 26, Dec. 3, 11; 1710, Feb. 1, Mar. 15, 19, Apr. 3, May 3, 14, June 2, July 1, 10, Aug. 2, Sept. 2, 18, Oct. 15, Dec. 15; 1711, Jan. 10, Feb. 13, 15, 17, 28, May 1, 2, 4, June 7 (witnesses Byrd's will), July 21, Aug. 2, Sept. 9, 17, 23, 24, Oct. 22, Dec. 16; 1712, Jan. 2, Feb. 5, 6, 8, 16, 25, Mar. 5, 15, June 24, July 16, Aug. 15, 18, 25, 26, 31, Sept. 11, 19.

Eppes, Colonel Francis, 1709, Mar. 28; 1711, Mar. 27, June 19 (daughter married), Aug. 15, 20, 21, 22, 23, 25, Sept. 4; 1712, Jan. 8, 22, Apr. 11, 29, June 4, Aug. 5.

Eppes, Major Francis, 1709, July 4, 22, Aug. 26, Oct. 1, 13; 1710, May 13, Sept. 1, Oct. 6, 7, 15, 17 (commissioned to explore mountains), Dec. 5, 6, 7, 8; 1711, Mar. 2, Apr. 13, 14, May 2, 16, Aug. 27, Sept. 4, Oct. 3, 4, Dec. 11; 1712, Feb. 1, 12, Apr. 13, 24 (to command Carolina forces), 29, June 4.

Eppes, Captain Isham, 1711, Mar. 20, May 2, Aug. 27, Sept. 16, 22, 23; 1712, Feb. 12.

Eppes, Isham, 1709, May 18, Nov. 28 (death), Dec. 23.

Eppes, Mrs. Isham, 1709, May 18.

Eppes, Captain John, 1709, Feb. 17, July 2; 1710, Feb. 9, Mar. 19, May 14, June 12; 1711, Mar. 14, Aug. 23, Oct. 1; 1712, Feb. 6, 8, July 17.

Eppes, Colonel Littlebury, 1709, Mar. 28; 1710, Aug. 15 (burgess); 1711, Aug. 15, 20, 21, 25, 27, 28; 1712, Apr. 11, May 6, July 1, Sept. 26 (burgess).

Eppes, Llewellyn, 1711, Nov. 14, 18, 30; 1712, Jan. 7, May 6, June 4, Aug. 27.

Eppes, Mrs. Llewellyn (Angelica Bray?), 1711, Nov. 14, 18, 30; 1712, Jan. 7, May 6, June 4, Aug. 27.

Eppes, Mary, 1709, Feb. 27.

Eppes, William, 1709, Feb. 27, Sept. 22; 1710, May 3, July 28, Nov. 6, 20 (death).

Eppes, William, 1711, Apr. 11, July 29.

Essex County, burgess, 1709, Apr. 24.

Eugene (servant), 1709, Feb. 8, Apr. 17, June 9, 10, Nov. 30, Dec. 1, 3, 10, 16; 1710, May 4, Aug. 31; 1711, Feb. 2, Apr. 14, Sept. 28, Oct. 23, 31, Dec. 14, 31; 1712, Sept. 18.

Europe, 1709, Apr. 1; 1712, Jan. 8.

Evans, Mr., 1709, May 3, Oct. 4.

Evans, Captain John, 1709, May 3; 1710, June 2; 1711, Dec. 2.

F

Faber, Tanaquil, see Le Fevre.

Faile, John, 1711, Jan. 8.

Falling Creek, 1709, Feb. 6; see also Plantations, Byrd's.

Falls, the, 1709, Feb. 20; see also Plantations, Byrd's.

Farrar, Major, 1712, Apr. 11.

Fashion, 1710, Sept. 11; 1711, Feb. 5.

Fast days, 1709, May 18, Dec. 8; 1710, Jan. 11; 1711, Jan. 30, Sept. 6.

Finance, 1709, Mar. 25, June 16, 21; 1710, Apr. 24, 25; 1712, Jan. 31, July 21, 22; mortgage, 1711, Apr. 10; promissory notes, 1709, Apr. 19, 1710, Jan. 20; see also Money.

Finney, Reverend William, 1710, May 15, June 19, 20, Dec. 19; 1711, Mar. 17, May 28, 29, 30, Aug. 2, Sept. 9, Oct. 3, 12, Dec. 9; 1712, Jan. 8, 9, 18.

Fires, 1709, Apr. 24; 1710, Nov. 13; 1711, Nov. 29, Dec. 17; 1712, Sept. 15.

Fleming, Charles, 1711, Mar. 29, June 5; 1712, Feb. 11, Mar. 25.

Fleming, Judith, 1711, Mar. 29; 1712, Feb. 11.

Fleming, Susannah, 1711, Mar. 29; 1712, Feb. 11.

Fortification, 1711, Aug. 23, Sept. 5; 1712, Jan. 31.

Foster, Colonel Joseph, 1712, June 17.

France, 1709, Apr. 25; 1711, Aug. 15 ff. (rumored French invasion); 1712, July 1; see also Privateers.

Frank (servant), 1709, Feb. 20; 1711, Jan. 1, June 21; 1712, Mar. 18, Apr. 12, May 3, 9.

Freight, 1709, June 15, 17, 23, July 13, 18, 20, 23; 1710, Mar. 21, June 14, July 3, 7, 12, 22, 29; 1711, Mar. 30, Apr. 4; 1712, May 7.

French settlement, see Manakin Town.

French, teaching of, 1710, Jan. 31 ff.

Freshwater, George, 1709, Nov. 10.

Funerals, 1709, July 25, Dec. 17; 1710, Apr. 14, June 6; 1711, May 11; 1712, June 26.

F-c, Captain, 1709, Feb. 6.

G

Gambling, 1711, Nov. 24; 1712, Apr. 17.

Garland (ship), 1709, Sept. 26, Dec. 8, 12, 17; 1710, Feb. 21.

Garlington, Captain, 1710, Oct. 25, Nov. 17, 18; 1711, Dec. 8.

Garth, Sir Samuel, The Dispensary, 1711, Apr. 3.

Gee, Mr., 1709, June 12, 17, Aug. 21; 1710, Jan. 28, Mar. 11, 15, May 1, June 26, Aug. 10, Sept. 8, 16, 25; 1711, Feb. 2, Mar. 7, 12, 31, Apr. 1, 14, May 17, June 10, 20; 1712, May 19, July 9.

General Court: Byrd petitions for land, 1709, Apr. 18; Byrd sworn a judge, Oct. 15; tries man for rape, 19; tries negroes for treason, 1710, Apr. 18, 19, 21; tries felons, 20; tries for manslaughter, 27; orders read, 29; tries criminals, Oct. 19; man reproved for disrespect to clergy, Nov. 1; discusses accounts, 21, 22; prosecutes Mr. S-l-n, 1711, Apr. 19; Byrd vs. Wilkinson, 21; tries case of Branch, 24; Byrd pays fines for absence, 26; tries 2 men for felony, June 12, sentenced, 13; Mrs. Byrd and Mrs. Custis acknowledge deed, 1712, Apr. 25; see also Court of Oyer and Terminer.

George (servant), 1709, June 18, July 1, 5, 11; 1710, Jan. 28, Mar. 15; 1712, Mar. 18.

Gilbert (coachman), 1711, Apr. 7, Oct. 27 (in prison), Nov. 8, Dec. 7 (deported).

Giles, John, 1711, May 6, June 21, Aug. 3, Oct. 10.

Ginseng, 1710, Dec. 23.

Gloucester Town, 1709, Nov. 8; 1710, Sept. 29; 1711, Nov. 7.

Glyster, 1710, May 24, June 5.

Godolphin, Lord Treasurer, 1709, Sept. 13.

Gold mines, 1711, Apr. 24; 1712, May 24.

Good, Samuel, 1711, Dec. 1; 1712, Sept. 18.

Goodrich, Anne, 1710, Apr. 30.

Goodrich, Benjamin, 1710, Apr. 30 (death).

Goodrich, Edward, 1709, May 8, 17, 19, 24; 1710, Aug. 8; 1712, Jan. 12.

Goodrich, Elizabeth, 1710, Apr. 30.

Goodrich, Henry, 1710, Feb. 10.

Goodwin, Mr., 1712, July 10.

Goodwin, Captain, 1710, June 14.

Goodwin, Reverend Benjamin, 1709, June 15, Oct. 30; 1710, May 5; 1711, Mar. 11; 1712, Aug. 1.

Goodwin, Mrs. Benjamin, 1710, May 5.

Gossip, 1710, Jan. 10; 1711, May 5, 11, June 24, Dec. 9; 1712, Jan. 23, Sept. 14, 21.

Governor, the, see Spotswood, Colonel Alexander.

Governor's Guard, 1711, Oct. 19.

Governor's House (Williamsburg), 1710, Aug. 21, Oct. 31, Nov. 17; 1711, Feb. 8, Mar. 8, 9, Oct. 29, Nov. 19, Dec. 7 (Cary turned out), 11 (burglarized).

Graeme, John, 1711, Oct. 16, 25, Nov. 11, 12, 13, Dec. 25.

Graeme, Mrs. John, 1711, Nov. 2.

Graffenriedt, Baron de, 1711, Oct. 8 (taken prisoner by Indians), 19, Nov. 22; 1712, Apr. 15.

Gray, Reverend Samuel, 1709, Oct. 16.

Greek, 1709, Feb. 6 ff.; 1711, Mar. 23; and see Anacreon, Apocrypha, Cassius, Herodian, Homer, Josephus, Lucian, Pindar, Plutarch, Thucydides.

Greek Testament, 1709, Mar. 27, Apr. 3, 10, May 8, Sept. 25, Dec. 11, and passim.

Green Springs plantation, 1709, Mar. 2, Apr. 23, 24, May 5, Aug. 4, Sept. 21, Oct. 5, 7, 31, Nov. 27; 1710, Apr. 23, June 4, 22 (Spotswood visits), 23, July 4, 6, Oct. 11, Dec. 2, 3, 4; 1711, Apr. 29, June 13, July 21, 22, Nov. 11, 14, Dec. 8; 1712, Mar. 31, Apr. 29, May 1, 21, 23, June 9, 11, Aug. 19.

Grills, Richard, 1709, Mar. 4; see also G-r-l.

Gripes, epidemic of, 1709, Feb. 28 ff.

Grotius, Hugo de, Truth of the Christian Religion, 1710, Aug. 20 ff.

Grymes, John, 1712, Apr. 19.

Guy, Mr., 1711, Jan. 5-9, 13, 17.

Guy, Mrs. (Mary Byrd), 1711, Jan. 5.

G-l-s Ordinary, 1710, Jan. 7.

G-l-s W-l, 1709, Feb. 23, Aug. 9.

G-n (J-n), 1709, May 22.

G-p-l-n, Ralph, 1710, Dec. 18.

G-r-d-n-r, Tom, 1712, June 27.
G-r-l (overseer), 1709, Mar. 4, 28, 29, May 8, 9, 11, 12, 14, 29, July 24, Sept. 30, Oct. 12, Nov. 29, Dec. 6, 7; 1710, Jan. 1, 15, 20, 23, 24, Feb. 1, 24, 25, Mar. 4, 30, Apr. 9, May 15, 20, 28, 29, July 9, 11, 16, Aug. 17, Sept. 2, 5, 6, 7, 30, Oct. 1, Nov. 5, Dec. 19, 20; 1711, Jan. 14, 21, 22, 23, Feb. 24, 25, Apr. 14, 15, May 15, 16, 17, 28, June 10, 20, Aug. 19, Sept. 9, 15, 16, 29, 30, Oct. 15, Dec. 2, 3, 28, 29; 1712, Jan. 7, 13, 14, 15, 16, Feb. 6, 9, 23, 24, Mar. 1, 2, 21, 23, 24, 25, Apr. 12, May 13, 19, June 23, Aug. 5, 10, Sept. 10, 13.
G-r-l (brother of overseer), 1709, May 11; 1710, May 15, 28.
G-r-l, John, 1709, July 2, Aug. 7, 27, 30, Sept. 23; 1710, Jan. 20, 22, Feb. 13, May 24, 26, July 8, 19, Aug. 22, 23, 25, Sept. 18, Nov. 29; 1711, Jan. 25, Feb. 1, 19, May 1, 4, June 17 (mother married), 18, 29, July 18, 19, Sept. 15, Nov. 5, Dec. 29; 1712, Jan. 26, Feb. 1, 3, 25, Mar. 6, 7, 10, 11, 13, 14, 15, 16, 18, Apr. 9, May 29, Aug. 26.
G-r-t-l, Mr., 1711, Feb. 10.
G-s, Lady, 1710, Apr. 17.

H

Hamilton, Andrew, 1709, Nov. 14.
Hamilton, John, 1710, Oct. 25, 29, 31, Nov. 1.
Hamlin, Mr., 1709, Dec. 11; 1711, July 30.
Hamlin, Mrs., 1709, Aug. 2, Sept. 6, Dec. 12; 1710, Jan. 23, Feb. 15, Mar. 12, Apr. 4, 5, 9, May 18, 27, Sept. 18, Nov. 4, 5; 1711, Jan. 16, Feb. 10, June 25, 26, 27, Oct. 13, 22; 1712, May 14, Aug. 5.
Hamlin, Captain, 1709, July 3; 1710, Feb. 25; 1711, Oct. 11.
Hamlin, Lucy, 1712, Feb. 28.
Hamlin, Peter, 1709, Mar. 26, July 19, Sept. 29, Dec. 16; 1710, Jan. 15 (goes to England), Sept. 27 (returns); 1711, Feb. 13, Mar. 13, June 24, 27 (has smallpox), July 5 (death).
Hamlin, Richard, 1709, June 11; 1711, Mar. 17, July 30, Oct. 22.
Hamlin, Mrs. Richard (Anne Harrison), 1709, June 11.

Hancock (Indian chief), 1712, Aug. 18.
Hancock, Mrs., 1711, Feb. 25, June 9.
Hancock Town, 1712, Mar. 16.
Hardiman, Mr., 1709, Mar. 26; 1712, June 23.
Hardiman, Francis, 1709, Aug. 16.
Hardiman, Mrs. Francis (Jane Cross), 1711, Apr. 30.
Hardiman, Colonel John, 1709, May 18; 1710, Aug. 8 (burgess); 1711, Apr. 11, June 18, Sept. 17 (death), 18; 1712, June 23.
Hardiman, John, 1709, Aug. 16 (marriage); 1711, Oct. 16, 21, 22; 1712, Aug. 3, Sept. 2 (child).
Harris, Mr., 1709, Nov. 10.
Harrison, Mr., 1709, May 17, 18.
Harrison, Captain, 1709, July 28 (death).
Harrison, Colonel Benjamin, 1709, Apr. 10, 23, May 30, June 16, July 20, Aug. 9, Oct. 23, 28; 1710, Apr. 5, May 22, June 7, 9, 30, July 2, 7, Sept. 28, 29, Oct. 22, Nov. 19; 1711, Jan. 17, Mar. 26, Apr. 7, 23, June 18, Sept. 26, Oct. 8, 9, 16, 17, 21, 22; 1712, Jan. 29, Feb. 17, Mar. 13, Aug. 30, Sept. 4.
Harrison, Benjamin, 1709, Feb. 11, Apr. 4, 10, 11, 12, 16, 24, 28, May 19, 20, 22, 24, 25, 26, 30, June 3, 5, 13, 17, 23, 27, July 3, 11, 26, Aug. 1, 2, 3, 5, 6, 9, 28; Sept. 3, 10, 24, 28, Oct. 9, 12, Dec. 3, 5, 13, 15, 26, 27; 1710, Jan. 9, 11, 19, 22, 29, Feb. 1, 8, 14, 22, 24, 25, Mar. 10, 11, 15, 22, 23, 24, 25, 26, 27, 28, 29, 30, Apr. 1-9, 10 (death), 12, 14 (funeral), Nov. 5 (grave), 22 (accounts).
Harrison, Mrs. Benjamin (Elizabeth Burwell), 1709, Feb. 11, May 24, June 27, July 11, 13, Aug. 6, 9, 14, 15, 28, Sept. 5, 6, 18, 24, 28, Dec. 1, 5, 26; 1710, Jan. 21, 28, 29, Feb. 6, 14, 22, 25, Mar. 6, 10, 11, 15, Apr. 10, 11, 12, 14, 16, May 2, 5, 6, 7, 9, 10, 17, 21, 24, 31, June 3, 6, 7, 9, 20, 21, 25, 30, July 3, 13, 14, 17, 26, 28, 31, Aug. 2, 3, 5, 8, 10, 16, 20, 22, 25, 27, 30, Sept. 1, 3, 4, 21, 26, 28, 29, Oct. 4, 14, 29, Nov. 5, 7, Dec. 17; 1711, Jan. 3, 10, 11, 12, 17, Feb. 2, 3, 13, 16, 18, Mar. 15, 18, Apr. 1, 2, 5, 13, May 6, 8, 13, 14, 17, 25, June 3, 4, 6, 20, 29, July 11, 27, Aug. 2, 8, 9, 24, 27, 30, Sept. 5, 11, 26, 27, Oct. 9, 12, Nov.

4, 23; **1712**, Jan. 2, 5, 27, Feb. 5, 7, 24, 26, Mar. 6, 7, Apr. 6, 12, 13, May 14, 30, June 3, 15, July 10, 11, Aug. 3, 6, 15, 22, 24, 29, 30, Sept. 3, 14.

Harrison, Benjamin III, **1710**, June 6, July 2; **1712**, Jan. 1, 2.

*Harrison, Elizabeth, **1709**, June 27, Aug. 28, Sept. 18, 28, Dec. 5; **1710**, Apr. 14, May 8, June 6, July 10, 31, Aug. 16, Oct. 29; **1711**, Jan. 17, Apr. 1, 2, 12, 13, May 13, 17, 27, Aug. 24, Sept. 27, 28; **1712**, Feb. 24, 26, Mar. 6, May 30, July 10, Sept. 14.

Harrison, Captain Henry, **1709**, Feb. 11, Aug. 9; **1710**, Mar. 26, 27, 28, Apr. 16, May 9, Sept. 29, Nov. 10; **1711**, Jan. 10, Feb. 16, 19, 21 (rumored dead), 23, July 23, Oct. 17; **1712**, Jan. 8, 9.

Harrison, Mrs. Henry (Elizabeth Smith), **1709**, Feb. 11; **1710**, May 9, Sept. 29; **1711**, July 22.

Harrison, Major Nathaniel, **1709**, May 5, 6, Aug. 9; **1710**, Mar. 26, 27, 28, Apr. 3, 16, June 7, 9, 24, July 4, 5 (naval officer), 6, 7, 12, Nov. 16; **1711**, Jan. 10, Apr. 10, July 22, 23, 27, Oct. 7, 8, 9, 20, Nov. 11; **1712**, Jan. 5, 8, 9, 29, Mar. 11, 12, 13, 30, Apr. 19, May 7, June 3, Aug. 6.

Harrison, Mrs. Nathaniel, **1709**, May 5; **1710**, July 4; **1711**, July 22; **1712**, Mar. 30, June 3.

Harrison family, **1711**, May 15.

Harrison (ship), **1710**, Apr. 14, 15; **1711**, Mar. 13, 15, Aug. 5; **1712**, Apr. 22, June 9, 12, 13.

Harry, the Indian, **1710**, Feb. 3, Aug. 21, 23, 24, 25, 26, Nov. 22 (death).

Harvey, Captain, **1710**, July 2, 29, Aug. 12, 14; **1712**, Feb. 26.

Harvey, Mrs., **1709**, Apr. 18, June 22, July 16; **1712**, June 21.

Harvey, William, **1709**, Apr. 17, 18, June 22, July 16, Aug. 4, 5.

Harwood, Mr., **1709**, June 3.

Harwood, Joseph, **1709**, June 3; **1710**, May 3; **1711**. Sept. 12, 14.

Harwood, Captain Samuel, **1709**, June 3; **1710**, Aug. 15 (burgess); **1711**, Oct. 11; **1712**, Sept. 26 (burgess).

Hatcher, John, **1711**, Oct. 3.

Hawkins, Mr., **1709**, Apr. 24, 25.

---

*May be confused with her mother, Mrs. Benjamin Harrison, in some entries.

Haynes, Mr., **1709**, Feb. 17, Mar. 31 (appointed tobacco receiver).

Haynes, Nicholas, **1711**, Jan. 19 (death).

Haynes, Thomas, **1709**, Apr. 17.

Health and sickness, **1709**, Feb. 13, 28, Apr. 10, 14, Nov. 13; **1710**, Feb. 10, May 31, July 30.

Hebrew, **1709**, Feb. 6 *and daily.*

Henrico County, **1711**, May 8, Aug. 1, 15, 22, 27, 28, Sept. 4, 30, Oct. 1, 17; *burgesses,* **1710**, Sept. 1; *court,* **1710**, Jan. 31; *militia,* **1710**, Sept. 22; **1711**, Aug. 15, 20, 21, 27; **1712**, Apr. 9 (general muster), 11 (volunteers for Carolina); *sheriff,* **1712**, Apr. 11.

Henrico Parish, **1709**, Mar. 25; **1710**, May 15.

Henry (servant), **1709**, Apr. 16; **1710**, Aug. 13.

Herodian, **1712**, Aug. 14-Sept. 20 *passim.*

Hides, **1709**, Mar. 26, May 6, 21, Aug. 31; **1710**, June 2; **1711**, Jan. 19.

Higbee, old, **1710**, May 8.

Higginson, Lucy, **1709**, Apr. 30.

Hill, Colonel Edward, **1709**, Aug. 20 (house), Dec. 23 (house); **1710**, Jan. 2 (arrival in Virginia), 4, 8, 9, 22, 27, Feb. 1, 3, 4, 14, 19, 20, 22, 24, 27, Mar. 2, 4, 10, 11, 14, 15, 16, 17, 22, 26, 29, 30, Apr. 3, 4, 14, May 6, 16, 17, 18, 19, 22, June 1, 6, 11, 17, 20, 27, 29, July 3, 4, 5, 13, 15 (launches ship), 18, 27, Aug. 1, 8, 15, 18, 19, 23 (wife's death), 27, 31, Sept. 7, 21, 23, 24, 25, 27, Oct. 12, 19, Nov. 2, Dec. 15, 19; **1711**, Jan. 3, 18, 19, 25, Feb. 2, 10, 11, 13, 17, 28, Mar. 7, 8, 9, 10, 11, 13, 21, 22, 27, Apr. 3, 5, 24, May 2, 4, 11, 12, 25, 30, June 6, 20, 22, July 8, 12, 17, 22, Aug. 1, 20, 25, 27, 30, Sept. 17, 22, 24, Oct. 1, 12, 16, 21, 22, 25, 26, Dec. 3, 27; **1712**, Jan. 2, 6 (Byrd's estimate of), 7, 15, 22, Feb. 6, 25, 26, Mar. 4, 5, 6, 16, 30, 31 (Governor of the College), Apr. 1, 2, 3, 8, 9, 10, 12, 30, May 1, 13, 30, July 6, 11, 15, 25, 30, Aug. 6, 15, 17, 18, 19, 26, 30; Sept. 3, 5, 9, 11, 14.

Hill, Mrs. Edward, **1710**, Aug. 23 (death), 27, 31; **1711**, Jan. 25.

Hix (Hicks), Robert **1709**, July 19; **1710**, June 2; **1712**, Mar. 18, 19.

Holloway, John, **1709**, Oct. 12, 17, 30, Nov. 3, 4; **1710**, Oct. 25, Nov. 2 (trial), 3, Dec. 7, 9; **1711**, Feb. 8, Mar. 9, Apr. 18, 24, June 12, Sept. 19, 20, Nov. 21; **1712**, Apr. 2, 23.

Holt, Captain, **1711**, Dec. 19.

Homer, reading of, **1709**, Apr. 8-May 18, June 6, Aug. 31, Sept. 24, 26, Nov. 22-24; **1710**, Mar. 23, Apr. 18-29, Sept. 4-17, Oct. 19-Nov. 2, 9-Dec. 13; **1711**, Mar. 9, Apr. 17, 18, 24, May 11-July 3, 29-Sept. 7, Oct. 27-Dec. 23; **1712**, Jan. 4, 25-31, Apr. 16-27.

Homer, *Odyssey*, **1709**, Feb. 7-Apr. 7.

Horace, reading of, **1709**, Nov. 17-22; **1712**, Jan. 8, Mar. 12.

Horses, **1709**, July 5, 11, 12, 14, 17, Sept. 14, 21, 25, Nov. 12, 16, 26; **1710**, May 27, Sept. 18, 24; **1711**, Feb. 11, Mar. 28-29; *bill concerning*, **1711**, Nov. 17, Dec. 6; *breeding of*, **1710**, Feb. 26, 28, May 1, 8; *cause of death*, **1711**, Sept. 17; **1712**, June 23; *racing*, **1709**, Aug. 27; **1710**, Oct. 17.

Hospitality: Introduction, xxii; **1709**, Aug. 23; **1710**, Feb. 11, Apr. 12, July 5; *see also* Social life.

House of Burgesses: Introduction, ix; chaplain of, **1709**, *June* 15; clerk of, **1710**, *July* 6; chooses speaker, *Oct.* 25; approved by Governor, 26; Mr. Holloway tried, *Nov.* 3; passes money bill, 9; discusses Governor's House, 17; throws out two bills, 21; Byrd writes verses on, 21; conference on money bill, 23; Byrd lampoons, 24, 26; Governor speaks to, **1711**, *Nov.* 8; Byrd recommends College to, 20; brings address of thanks to Governor, 21; advises war on Indians, 28; Byrd protests taxes, *Dec.* 5; disputes with Council over taxes, 12-24; adjourned, 24; adheres to Book of Claims, **1712**, *Jan.* 25; Governor speaks to, 28; dissolved, 31.

Howlett, Thomas, **1710**, May 30; **1712**, June 6.

Huguenots, *see* Manakin Town.

Hungars, **1709**, Nov. 12, 18.

Hungars Creek, **1709**, Nov. 14.

Hungars Parish, **1709**, Sept. 13.

Hunt, George, **1709**, Apr. 17.

Hunter, Colonel Robert, **1709**, Apr. 25, June 20; **1710**, Jan. 2, Aug. 25, Oct. 31; **1711**, July 2, 4.

Hunting: Introduction, xxiii; **1709**, Sept. 20; **1710**, Jan. 10; **1711**, Mar. 22, Sept. 4, 14.

Hyde, Colonel Edward, **1710**, Sept. 13, **1711**, July 23, Nov. 22; **1712**, Feb. 20.

Hyde, Mrs. Edward, **1710**, Sept. 13; **1711**, July 27.

H-ch, John, **1709**, Aug. 27.

H-l, Cornelius (bricklayer), **1712**, Jan. 1, Mar. 8, 21, 22, 24, 25.

H-l-y, Mrs., **1709**, Apr. 22.

H-m, Mr., **1709**, Feb. 9.

H-m-l-n, Mrs., **1709**, Apr. 17.

H-n, Captain, **1712**, Mar. 5.

H-n-s, Thomas, **1710**, Mar. 1.

H-n-t, Major, **1711**, Aug. 24, 27; **1712**, June 12.

H-n-t, Captain, **1711**, Aug. 31, Sept. 3, 7, 11, 12, 13, 15, 16, 17, 25, 26, 30, Oct. 7, 11, Nov. 6, 12, 14, 19.

H-s, Cousin, **1710**, Sept. 16.

H-sh, **1711**, July 15.

H-s-t, John, **1711**, Apr. 9.

I

Impositions, *see* Taxes.

Indian trade: Introduction, xii; Byrd's representation on, **1709**, *Feb.* 16; 26; to be open, *Apr.* 23, 26; adjusted in England, *June* 16; *July* 19; **1710**, *Jan.* 19; in skins, *June* 2; goods presented to Mrs. Byrd, *Sept.* 29; **1711**, *Dec.* 2; men examined concerning, **1712**, *Apr.* 26.

Indian traders, **1710**, Jan. 19; *see* Evans, John; Hix, Robert.

Indians, **1709**, *Feb.* 23, *Apr.* 8, *Oct.* 21; several tribes complain to Governor, **1711**, *Mar.* 26; hunting on patented land, *Sept.* 4, 14; massacre in North Carolina, *Oct.* 7, *Nov.* 21; militia rendezvous at Nottoway Town, *Oct.* 17-20; to send boys to College, 20, 21; Assembly advises war on, *Nov.* 28; Governor gives audience to, *Dec.* 8, 19; treaty with, read in Council, 10, and signed, 11; conspiracy reported, 17; women, **1712**, *Jan.* 12; treaty with, 31; continue hostilities, *Feb.* 7; towns destroyed in South Carolina, 20; Tuscaroras send delegation to Governor, *Mar.* 11; Governor replies to, 16; hostages run away, *Apr.* 18; examined in Council, 19; put in prison, 20; Governor plans to march against, 20; Council discusses, 22, 23, 26; prisoners try to escape, 24; hostages brought back, 26; peace made between Carolina and Indians, *May* 6; brought before Council, *Aug.* 18; conference at Pamunkey Town, *Sept.* 21-24; Indian with 20 wives, 23; *see also names of tribes:* Meherrin, Nansemond, Nottoway, Pamunkey, Saponie, Tributary, Tuscarora.

Ipecac, 1710, Jan. 20, 22, June 25.

Ingles, Miss, 1709, May 5.

Ingles, Anne, 1710, Nov. 12 (death).

Ingles, Mungo, 1709, May 5; 1710, Apr. 28, Nov. 13; 1711, Nov. 14, 16 (wedding at house of), 17.

Ingles, Mrs. Mungo (Anne Bray), 1709, May 5.

Irby, Dr., 1711, Sept. 7.

Irby, Mrs., 1712, Aug. 12.

Irby, William, 1711, Sept. 7, 27.

Iron, 1710, Aug. 18, 25; 1711, Feb. 10.

Iron works, 1710, Sept. 24.

Isle of Wight County, 1709, May 16 (burgess); 1710, Feb. 4 (sheriff); 1711, Oct. 8 (militia); 17 (surveyor); 18 (militia).

Italian, reading of, 1709, Feb. 8, Mar. 26, 31, Apr. 2, 5, 7, Aug. 12, Nov. 30, Dec. 2; 1710, Jan. 5, May 13 ff.; *and passim.*

J

Jack (servant), 1709, May 14-June 5, Aug. 8, 10, 15; 1710, Jan. 14, Dec. 26; 1711, Apr. 30; 1712, Jan. 27, 28, Feb. 7, 8.

Jackson, Mr., 1709, June 18, Dec. 24, 25; 1710, Jan. 9, Nov. 4; 1711, Jan. 1.

Jacky (mulatto), 1712, Jan. 2, 12, 21, Sept. 3.

Jacquelin, Edward, 1710, Nov. 14.

Jamaica, 1709, June 12; 1711, Apr. 16.

James City County, 1709, Apr. 19 (sheriff); June 18 (surveyor); 1711, Aug. 27 (militia); 1712, July 21 (surveyor).

James River, 1709, Feb. 28; 1711, Aug. 27, 28; 1712, Feb. 14, Apr. 9.

Jamestown, 1709, Apr. 24, May 6; 1711, Aug. 23 (battery at), 29, 31, Sept. 1, 5, Oct. 10.

Jane, old (servant), 1710, Aug. 19; 1711, Dec. 26, 28, 29 (death).

Jane (maid), 1709, Apr. 10 (son born); *see also* Jenny.

Jarrett, Mrs., 1710, June 29; 1711, Apr. 19, 26.

Jefferson, Captain Thomas, 1711, Sept. 23, Oct. 2; 1712, Feb. 16.

Jeffrys, Simon, 1712, July 21.

Jenings, Colonel Edmund, 1709, Feb. 9, 11, 21, 27, 28, Mar. 1, 2, 31, Apr. 13, 18, 20, 23, 28, 30, May 8, 11, 17, 22, June 1, 6, 20, 21, July 5, Aug. 4, Sept. 12, 13, 14, Oct. 6, 7, 8, 15, 16, 20, 22, 23, 27, 30, Nov. 1, 3, Dec. 8; 1710, Jan. 17, 20, Apr. 17, 18, 21, 22, 23, 24, 25, 28, 29, June 23, Oct. 28, Nov. 8, 15, 27, Dec. 4, 10; 1711, Feb. 6, 7, Mar. 2 (intends to go to England), July 5, 6, Oct. 28, Nov. 3, 10, 14, 16-18, 24, 27-29, Dec. 22; 1712, Apr. 20, 25, 27, 29, June 10, July 21.

Jenny (maid), 1709, Feb. 8, Mar. 30, Sept. 3, 16, Nov. 30, Dec. 1; 1710, Jan. 6, Mar. 27, 28, June 17, Sept. 25, Dec. 23; 1711, Jan. 5-7, 28 (child of), Oct. 11, Dec. 2, 28; 1712, Feb. 7, Mar. 2, 14, 15, 16, 18, June 30, July 11, 12, 30, Sept. 12.

Jenny, little, 1710, July 15, Aug. 22, 31; 1711, Feb. 27.

Jenny, Quarter, 1712, Feb. 23, 24, Mar. 1, June 27.

Jimmy (servant), 1710, Jan. 5, 6, June 4, Sept. 2, 30, Dec. 20; 1712, June 30.

John (servant), 1709, Apr. 5, 6, 16, May 19, June 23, 25, Aug. 21; 1710, Apr. 16, July 29, Sept. 7, 8, 20, Dec. 19; 1711, Jan. 29, Feb. 25, Mar. 2-6, Apr. 30, May 1, 5, June 5, 16, July 28, 31, Aug. 1, 4, 24, 29, Sept. 15, 25, Oct. 9, Nov. 12, Dec. 1.; 1712, Jan. 15, 16, 17, Feb. 25, Mar. 7, 27, Aug. 16, Sept. 16, 17-21, 27.

Johnny (sailor), 1710, Dec. 22; 1711, Sept. 30.

Johnson, Thomas, 1712, Apr. 19.

Jones, Mr., 1709, Nov. 27.

Jones, Captain, 1711, June 9.

Jones, Frederick, 1710, Dec. 10.

Jones, Peter, 1710, Nov. 20.

Jones, Robert, 1709, July 23; 1710, June 7; 1711, Dec. 1 (leases plantation).

Jones, Thomas, 1711, Jan. 3, Apr. 4, 5.

Jones, *see also* G-n (J-n).

Jordans (plantation), 1709, Feb. 11; 1711, May 25.

Josephus, 1709, May 10—Oct. 10.

Justin, 1709, Apr. 19.
J—, Mr. (seaman), 1710, June 28.
J— (or G—), 1709, Dec. 13; 1710, May 26.
J-f-r-y, Mrs., 1709, Feb. 28, Mar. 2, 25, May 10, June 1, July 6, Sept. 13 (marriage): *see* Mrs. Dunn *for later references.*
J-k, Mr., 1710, Oct. 12.
J-r-d-n, Betty, 1711, Dec. 11 (convicted of burglary), 12, 13.

K

Keeling, Captain George, 17( ), June 9, 10; 1710, Jan. 3; 1711, Nov. 20; 1712, Feb. 2.
Kemp, Colonel, 1710, Jan. 19.
Kennon, Mr., 1711, Feb. 13.
Kennon, Mrs., 1711, Sept. 22.
Kennon, Richard, 1710, Oct. 15.
Kennon, Captain William, 1710, Oct. 15; 1711, Apr. 13, 14; June 19 (marriage), Sept. 22, 23, Oct. 2, 3.
Kennon, Mrs. William (Anne Eppes), 1711, June 19.
Kensington (plantation), 1709, Aug. 19; 1710, Mar. 3, Sept. 6; 1712, Feb. 15.
King, Miss Mary, 1711, Feb. 9, Mar. 11, Sept. 21 (marriage).
King and Queen County, sheriff of, 1712, June 29.
King William County, 1711, Sept. 1; 1712, Feb. 12, May 12.
King William Parish, 1711, May 25.
King's Creek, 1709, Apr. 30, May 4.
Kingsland, 1711, Apr. 24.
Kippax, 1709, July 17.
Kiquotan, 1709, Oct. 7, Dec. 8; 1710, Apr. 1, 25, June 21, Oct. 26, Nov. 2, 17; 1711, Mar. 9, June 6, July 4, Sept. 21, Nov. 27.

L

Laforce, René, 1710, Sept. 7, Dec. 20; 1711, May 28, June 2, Aug. 20.
Land, 1709, Apr. 18; 1710, Feb. 7 (Treasury Rights), Nov. 28 (bill), Dec. 2; 1711, Feb. 10 ff., Apr. 24, 25; 1712, Apr. 22, 25; *see also,* Byrd, William II, land of.
Lane, Mr., 1711, Mar. 9 (death), 11.
Latimer, Bishop, sermon of, 1710, Dec. 17.
Latin reading, *see* Horace, Milton, Petronius, Sallust, Terence.
Law: study of, encouraged, 1710, June 14; habeas corpus act, July

25, Oct. 25; letters of administration, Sept. 4; alias capias writ, Oct. 25; of Virginia, 1711, Feb. 13, 24; against drunkenness, Apr. 4; concerning militia, Sept. 29; Byrd abridges, 1712, Aug. 1 ff.
Lawsuits, 1709, June 3, July 4; 1710, Jan. 31, Feb. 1; 1711, Apr. 4, 20, 21, May 6, Aug. 1.
Lawyers, 1710, Dec. 7, 9; 1711, May 8: *see* Messrs. Clayton, C-s, Holloway, Randolph (William, Jr.), and Rogers.
Lawson, John, 1711, July 27, Oct. 8, 19, Nov. 22.
Lee, Captain, 1710, Sept. 16; 1712, June 25, 26
Lee, Colonel, ,709, Oct. 24.
Leeward Islands, 1709, Apr. 1; 1710, June 10 (Colonel Parke recalled from); 1711, Apr. 12, May 25.
Le Fevre (*or* Faber), Reverend Tanaquil, 1711, Apr. 17, 25 (made professor in College); 1712, Jan. 28 (turned out).
Lewis, Colonel John, 1709, Mar. 1, Oct. 18; 1710, Oct. 31, Nov. 10, 25; 1711, Nov. 15, 23.
Library, at Westover, 1709, Aug. 11 ff.; 1710, Jan. 23, Mar. 15, 25, June 8, July 12 (Dr. Cocke visits), 18 ff., Aug. 11, Sept. 4 (Parson Robinson visits).
Lightfoot, Frank, 1711, Nov. 11, 13; 1712, Mar. 5, 6, 7, 12, Aug. 6, Sept. 4, 22.
Lightfoot, Goodrich, 1712, Sept. 22, 23, 24.
Lightfoot, John, 1712, Sept. 22.
Lightfoot, Philip, 1712, Sept. 4.
Lightfoot, Sherwood, 1712, Sept. 22.
Ligon, Mr., 1709, Feb. 23.
Ligon, Mrs. Elizabeth, 1709, July 4.
Lister, Martin, *Journey to Paris,* 1709, Apr. 5, 6, 7.
Littlepage, Captain Richard, 1709, Apr. 4; 1712, Sept. 23, 24.
Littleton, Mr., 1709, Nov. 9.
Llewellyn, Captain, 1709, Feb. 10, 20, Apr. 14, June 3, Oct. 12, 15, Dec. 11; 1710, Feb. 3, 5, Aug. 25, Sept. 2; 1711, Jan. 23, July 17; 1712, Jan. 7, June 22 (death), 24, 26 (funeral).
London, 1711, Dec. 17; Byrd in, *see* Introduction, viii.
London, Bishop of, 1710, Oct. 14, 15; 1711, May 25.

Louis XIV, King of France, **1709**, Apr. 19, 20; **1711**, Mar. 11; **1712**, May 11.

Lovelace, John, Baron, **1709**, Feb. 9 (arrival at New York), June 4 (death).

Low, see L—.

Lucian, **1709**, May 1-5, Sept. 13, Oct. 16—Nov. 2; **1710**, Aug. 11—Sept. 30, Oct. 16-18, Nov. 6, 7, Dec. 16— **1711**, Mar. 5, 14—Apr. 13, 20, 22, May 1-10, Sept. 13—Oct. 1, Nov. 5, Dec. 28—**1712**, Jan. 3, 11-21, Feb. 7-10, 22—Mar. 9, 14—Apr. 12, May 3—June 30, Sept. 27-29; in Greek and French, **1710**, Oct. 1-15.

Ludwell, Miss Hannah, **1710**, July 4, 6.

Ludwell, Colonel Philip, **1709**, Mar. 1, Apr. 23, 24, May 6, Aug. 4, 9, 10, Sept. 14, 21, Oct. 5, 7, Nov. 3; **1710**, Mar. 28, Apr. 24, 30, May 9, 28, July 4, 5, Sept. 16, Oct. 11, Dec. 4; **1711**, Jan. 10, Apr. 17, 27, 29, June 13, July 4, 6, 15, 16, 23, 24, 26, 27, Aug. 27, 29, 31, Oct. 8, 17, 20, Nov. 14, 15, Dec. 4, 8, 12, 24; **1712**, Jan. 29, June 11, July 21, 25, Aug. 12, 18, 29, 30, Sept. 4.

Ludwell, Mrs. Philip (Hannah Harrison), **1709**, Aug. 4, 9, Sept. 21, 23, Oct. 9; **1710**, Apr. 14, Oct. 11, 28; **1711**, Apr. 17, Nov. 14; **1712**, Aug. 30, 31.

Ludwell's bay, **1710**, July 4.

Luke, George, **1709**, Apr. 20.

L—, John, **1709**, Sept. 20.

L—, Mrs., **1709**, May 29, July 2, 3, Dec. 11; **1710**, Feb. 6, Apr. 10.

L-d, Tom, **1711**, Jan. 12.

L-s-n (servant), **1709**, July 5; **1710**, June 17, Aug. 27; **1711**, Mar. 2, 3, Aug. 31, Dec. 1, 2, 3, 4, 8, 13 (death).

L-s-n, wife of, **1710**, June 17.

L-s-n, Tom (servant), **1712**, Feb. 23, Mar. 21, 22, June 26, 27, Sept. 29.

L-th-m (or L-th-n), Captain, **1711**, Apr. 10, 13, 14, May 2, June 2, 9, 24, 28, July 17, 22.

L-t, young John and his wife, **1712**, Mar. 8.

M

Madeira, **1709**, Feb. 16, 18, June 29, Oct. 28; **1710**, May 13; **1711**, Jan. 19; **1712**, Feb. 17.

Madness, **1709**, Apr. 17, May 12; **1710**, Dec. 24; **1712**, July 20.

Malarial fever, **1711**, July 4-16, Aug. 6-13 ff.; **1712**, June 1 ff., Sept. 27.

Mallory, Mrs., **1709**, Dec. 1.

Mallory, Captain, **1710**, Feb. 17.

Mallory, Francis, **1709**, May 28.

Manakin Town, **1709**, June 30; **1710**, Sept. 22; **1711**, Mar. 5, May 25, 28, 29, June 1, 29, July 19, Aug. 7, 25; **1712**, May 31; *disorders:* **1709**, May 7, 10, Sept. 15, Oct. 22; **1710**, Sept. 23 (reconciled by Governor); *land grants,* **1710**, Nov. 16; *parson of,* **1709**, May 7, Sept. 15; **1710**, Sept. 23.

Manley, Mrs., *New Atlantis,* **1710**, Dec. 26, 27, 29, 30.

Manners, **1709**, Nov. 11; **1710**, Feb. 25; **1711**, Feb. 6, Mar. 3, 28, 31, Nov. 3; **1712**, Sept. 3.

Markin, Captain Thomas, **1709**, June 15; see M-r-n.

Marlborough, Duke of, **1710**, Mar. 31, Aug. 29; **1711**, Oct. 24; **1712**, Mar. 3 (removal from office).

Marot, Jean, **1710**, Nov. 1, 20, 26; **1711**, Apr. 25, Oct. 26, 30, 31, Nov. 7, 8, 9, 15, 16, 23.

Marshes, **1709**, Feb. 17, Apr. 30, Sept. 20; **1712**, Sept. 25.

Marshall, Major, **1709**, July 4.

Marshall, see M-r-s-l.

Martinique, **1710**, Mar. 14.

Martin's Brandon Parish, **1711**, May 20; **1712**, Apr. 27.

Mary (maid), **1710**, Mar. 6, 7; **1711**, Jan. 12.

Maryland, **1709**, Sept. 16, 19; **1710**, Apr. 17.

Mason, George, **1710**, Nov. 26.

Massot, Mr., **1710**, Aug. 10; **1711**, Oct. 2.

Mattey's School, **1711**, Dec. 9.

Medicine: Introduction, xix; **1712**, Feb. 20, 27; see also Bathing, Bloodletting, Bonesetting, Diet, Distemper, Epidemic, Glyster, Gripes, Health, Madness, Malarial fever, Midwife, Salivation, Smallpox.

Medicines: **1710**, Feb. 8, 15; **1711**, July 4-16, Aug. 6-13 ff.; see also Ginseng, Ipecac, Milk, Snakeroot, Spanish flies.

Meherrin Indians, **1709**, Feb. 23; **1711**, Oct. 20; **1712**, Jan. 19.

Men-of-war, see Ships.

Merriweather, Major Nicholas, **1710**, Feb. 7; **1711**, Mar. 28; **1712**, Mar. 26, Sept. 24 (burgess).

Merriweather, Mrs. Nicholas, 1711, Mar. 28, 1712, Mar. 26.

Middlesex County, 1709, June 16; 1710, Jan. 19.

Midwife, 1709, July 27 ff.; 1710, Oct. 28; 1712, June 27.

Militia: Introduction, xvi; general muster, 1709, Oct. 5; Byrd made commander-in-chief of Henrico and Charles City Counties, 1710, Apr. 27; ordered to attend the Governor, Sept. 17 ff.; general muster, 21-23; called out on threat of French invasion, 1711, Aug. 15 ff.; reviewed, Sept. 2, 7, 9; ordered to range at head of the James, 4; contest for prizes in field sports, 14 (Oct. 3, 6); mustered, Sept. 22-24, Oct. 2-4, 6; rendezvous at Nottoway Town, 8, 16-20; bill for raising land forces read, Dec. 15; rangers discussed in Council, 18; men refuse to act as rangers, 1712, Jan. 8, 22, Mar. 5; general muster, Apr. 9; volunteers for Carolina, 9, 11; Frank Eppes offers to command volunteers, 13; appointed, 24; withdraws, 29; rangers take 4 Indians, 20; Governor to march against Indians, 20; officers appointed for Carolina forces, 24; see also Court martial.

Milk, 1709, Aug. 12, Nov. 13, 17; 1710, May 21, June 15, July 12 ff. (milk tea), Sept. 21 ff.; 1712, Mar. 11 ff. (milk diet).

Miller, Will, stonecutter, 1709, June 25.

Mills: Bridgewater's, 1710, Sept. 25; Jefferson's, 1712, Feb. 16; Pleasants', 1710, Sept. 22; Queen's Creek, 1709, Dec. 10; Skimino, 1712, Feb. 18, Apr. 28; see also Sawmill.

Milner, Colonel (of Nansemond), 1711, Aug. 26.

Milton, John, Latin poems, 1712, Feb. 23 ff.; English, 1712, Mar. 13.

Mines, see Coal mine, Gold mine, Silver mine.

Moll (cook), 1709, Feb. 16, May 23, July 31; 1710, Feb. 22, Mar. 8, July 27, 28; 1711, Jan. 29, 30, Feb. 2, Mar. 16, 20, May 20, June 10, July 29, 30, 31, Aug. 22; 1712, Mar. 1, 14, Apr. 9, June 30, July 30, Sept. 5, 12.

Money, 1709, Feb. 16, 27, Mar. 3, 5 (wool used for), Apr. 19, 27, 28, Aug. 27, Oct. 31; 1710, Jan. 27,

Mar. 31 (weighing of), Apr. 25, 28, June 13, July 14; 1711, Apr. 11, 12 (weighing of), May 8 (Spanish), Sept. 11 (exchange), 25 (weighing of), Dec. 1 (rents reckoned in wheat), 22 (exchange); see also Finance, Taxes.

Money bill, 1710, Nov. 9, 14-18, 23; 1711, Dec. 5-15 ff.

Morals, 1709, Feb. 22, May 19; 1710, June 17; 1711, Apr. 17, May 5.

Morgan, Captain, 1709, May 6.

Mosquitoes, 1710, June 22; 1712, Aug. 28.

Mount Folly plantation, 1712, Feb. 2, Apr. 14, Sept. 15.

Mount Pleasant plantation, 1712, Feb. 13.

Mountains, exploration of, 1710, Oct. 17, Dec. 5, 6.

Mumford, Mrs., 1711, Oct. 15.

Mumford, Robert, 1709, Feb. 27, Mar. 1, 4, Apr. 13, 14, May 8, 10, 11, 17, 19, 24, June 6, 8, 19, 21, July 11, 12, 17, Aug. 10, 21, 22, Sept. 16, 17, Dec. 6; 1710, Jan. 1, 2, 3, 23, Feb. 25, Mar. 17, 18, Apr. 12, 13, May 10, 11, June 2, 21, 24, 27, 28, 29, 30, July 1, Sept. 27, 28, Nov. 20, Dec. 21, 28, 29; 1711, Jan. 22, 23, Feb. 13, 19, Mar. 17, Apr. 13, 14, May 8, 9, 21, 22, June 16, July 15, 16, Aug. 13, 14, 25, 29, Sept. 10, 11, Oct. 2, 9, 12, Nov. 13, Dec. 1, 2, 3, 31; 1712, Jan. 1, 21, Feb. 15, 16, Mar. 9, 10, 11, May 4, 5, 16, 17, June 4, 5, 14, 22, July 26, 27, Aug. 24, Sept. 8, 9.

M-l, Mr., of Madeira, 1709, Feb. 16.

M-l-ng, Betty (maid) 1712, June 18.

M-n-g-y, little, 1710, Dec. 21 (death).

M-n-s (orchard), 1711, May 10; 1712, May 10.

M-r-k-m, Sam, 1710, May 10.

M-r-l, Captain, 1712, Aug. 15.

M-r-l, Will, 1711, Oct. 6.

M-r-n, Captain, 1709, June 15, 25.

M-r-s-l, Mr. (overseer), 1709, Apr. 13; 1710, Jan. 23, 24, July 9, Aug. 17; 1711, Feb. 10, 11, Apr. 9, May 19, Oct. 4; 1712, Jan. 14, 21, Aug. 30.

M-s-t, Captain, 1709, Feb. 18, 19, July 10.

M-s-t-n, Mr., 1712, July 20.

N

Nansemond County, **1711**, Aug. 26, Nov. 28.

Nansemond Indians, **1709**, Feb. 23; **1711**, Oct. 20.

Naval stores, **1710**, Oct. 23.

Ned, Indian, **1710**, Sept. 2, 8, 9, 11; **1712**, July 30.

Negroes, **1709**, Oct. 12; **1710**, Nov. 13 (white negro); **1711**, Jan. 14, Dec. 5, 6 (bill concerning); *see also* Servants, Slaves.

Neuse, N. C., massacre at, **1711**, Oct. 7.

New Bern, N. C., **1711**, Oct. 8.

New England, **1709**, Feb. 28, Mar. 25, 28, June 8; **1710**, Sept. 26.

New Kent County, **1711**, Feb. 12, May 19, June 5; **1712**, Jan. 12, Feb. 27; *burgesses of*, **1712**, Sept. 24; *quit-rents*, **1709**, June 9; **1712**, June 7; *sheriff of*, **1709**, Apr. 4, June 9; **1711**, May 19; **1712**, June 17.

New York, **1709**, Feb. 9 (arrival of Governor), Apr. 25, June 4; **1710**, Jan. 2, Apr. 19, Oct. 21, Dec. 18; **1711**, June 6, July 2 (expedition against Canada), 5, 23.

Nicholson, Sir Francis, **1710**, Sept. 29.

Norris, Dr. John, sermons of, **1709**, Dec. 11; **1710**, Dec. 25; **1711**, Feb. 11.

North Carolina, **1709**, Feb. 26, June 16; **1710**, Jan. 19, Feb. 21, May 15, 20, 28, Sept. 13, Oct. 10 (boundary commission); **1711**, May 25, June 13, July 4 (expedition to), 5, 7, 27, Oct. 7 (Indian uprising), 8, 21, Nov. 21 (discussed in Council), 22, Dec. 2, 8; **1712**, Feb. 7, 20 (petition from), Mar. 11, 16, Apr. 1, 5, 11 (volunteers for), 13, 24, May 6 (peace made with Indians), June 4.

Northampton County, **1709**, Nov. 11.

Nottoway Indians, **1711**, Mar. 26, Oct. 17 (King of), 20, Dec. 17; **1712**, Apr. 22.

Nottoway Town, **1711**, Oct. 8, 9, 17, 21; **1712**, Apr. 26.

Nurse, **1709**, Feb. 22, May 13, 18, 20; **1710**, Jan. 9, Mar. 19, 20, 21, Apr. 8, June 2, 18, Aug. 23, Oct. 12, Dec. 26; **1711**, Jan. 17, 31, Apr. 5, 30, May 4, 5.

N-r-t-n, Mr., **1709**, Aug. 17.

O

Oastler, Dr. William, **1709**, Feb. 13, 21, 22, Mar. 4, 25, Apr. 1, 5, 14, 16, May 11, 17, 28, June 6, 10, July 12, 14, 15, Aug. 1, 2, 10, 13, 22, Sept. 6, 8, Oct. 2, 3, 4, 5, 8-13, Dec. 7, 11-14 (death), 15, 17 (funeral); **1710**, Jan. 9, Feb. 8, 9, 11, 13, 15, 16, 17, 18, 28, Mar. 1, 9, 10, 17, 21, 25, Apr. 4, May 20; **1711**, Jan. 6.

Office, attempts to secure: Introduction, ix-x; **1709**, Sept. 16, 19; **1710**, Mar. 31, Apr. 17, July 6, Nov. 20; **1711**, Jan. 20, Feb. 8, 9, 10, Mar. 5, 10, Apr. 22, 23; **1712**, Aug. 26 (lots drawn for).

Offley, Henry, **1711**, Aug. 31; **1712**, May 16.

Ordinaries, **1712**, Aug. 18; *Allen's*, **1712**, Feb. 20, Apr. 19; *A-t-k-s-n's*, **1712**, Apr. 19; *Brick House*, **1712**, Apr. 2, Sept. 26; *C-t's*, **1710**, Apr. 26, June 23, Oct. 17, 23, Dec. 5, 7; *French ordinary*, **1710**, Dec. 9; *G-l-s*, **1710**, Jan. 7; *Marot's*, **1710**, Nov. 1, 20, 26; **1711**, Apr. 25, Oct. 26, 30, 31, Nov. 7, 8, 9, 15, 16, 23.

Orkney, Lady, **1710**, Mar. 31.

Orkney, Lord: Introduction, x; **1710**, Mar. 31; **1712**, Apr. 1, May 5, July 3.

Orrery, Earl of, **1711**, Sept. 21.

Osborne, Thomas (overseer), **1710**, Dec. 21; **1711**, Jan. 14, 18, Aug. 26, Sept. 29, Oct. 4, 5, 13; **1712**, Feb. 15, May 3, July 5, Aug. 30, 31 (wife), Sept. 20 (daughter).

Osborne family, **1710**, Dec. 21.

Overseers, **1710**, July 9; **1711**, Jan. 13, 15, 22; **1712**, Feb. 27 ff., Mar. 2, 23; *see also names of overseers*: Addison, Blackman, G-r-l, M-r-s-l, Osborne, Turpin, Wilkinson.

Owens family, **1712**, Sept. 26.

O-d-s-n, Ben (servant), **1709**, July 15-17, 20—Aug. 2, 6, 9-12, 15, Sept. 10, Nov. 28 (death).

O-l-n, Dick, **1711**, Oct. 3.

O-n, Dick, **1712**, Sept. 26.

O-s-b-r-n, Mrs., **1711**, Mar. 11.

P

Page, Mr. Mann, **1709**, Feb. 6; **1711**, Mar. 9; **1712**, Jan. 27, Feb. 21, Apr. 19, July 10 (marriage to Judith Wormeley).

Pamlico, N. C., massacre at, **1711**, Oct. 7.

Pamunkey, **1711**, Mar. 28.

Pamunkey Indians, **1709**, Aug. 13.

Pamunkey River, 1711, Mar. 29; 1712, Sept. 22.
Pamunkey Town, 1712, Aug. 29, Sept. 21.
Parish, Mr., 1712, Aug. 2.
Parish, Charles, 1711, Sept. 1.
Parish, William, 1711, Aug. 29; 1712, July 24.
Parke, Colonel Daniel I, land of, 1711, Nov. 19, 20, 22, 26, 28, Dec. 21.
Parke, Colonel Daniel II: Introduction, x, xi; 1709, Apr. 1 (rumor of death), 8, 19, Sept. 7, 14, Oct. 15; 1710, Mar. 1, Apr. 27, June 10 (recalled), Aug. 15; 1711, Mar. 9, Apr. 12 (death), 16, 23, May 11, 25 (will), June 12, 17; *lands of,* 1711, Nov. 19, 26, Dec. 7, 10; 1712, Feb. 2, Apr. 28; *murderers of,* 1712, Sept. 17.
Parke, Mrs. Daniel II (Jane Ludwell), 1709, Nov. 3.
Parke, Frances, *see* Mrs. John Custis.
Parke, Lucy, *see* Mrs. William Byrd II.
Parke Hall, 1712, Feb. 12, 13.
Parke Level, 1712, Feb. 12.
Parke Manor, 1712, Feb. 12.
Parke Meadow, 1712, Feb. 12, 13.
Parker, Thomas, 1709, Feb. 15, 21, Apr. 4, May 26, June 3, Aug. 7, Sept. 4, 21, 25; 1710, Feb. 3, 17, 18, Apr. 3, May 13, July 14, Aug. 15, Nov. 14 (death), 16.
Parker, Mrs. Thomas, 1711, Apr. 10, May 8, June 25, 29, July 11; 1712, July 2.
Paxton, Reverend Zechariah, 1711, Nov. 18.
Pelican (ship), 1712, Jan. 5, Feb. 6, Mar. 10, 12.
Pennsylvania, 1711, May 5, 11.
Perry, Micajah, 1709, May 21, June 17, Aug. 18, Oct. 28, Sept. 12, 14, 24; 1710, Apr. 17, June 30, Aug. 12; 1711, Jan. 12, Mar. 9, May 4, 28, June 17, 27, July 25, Nov. 26.
Perry and Lane (ship), 1709, May 21, 27.
Peter (servant), 1709, Sept. 6; 1711, Jan. 28, Mar. 9; 1712, Sept. 7.
Peter, little, 1710, Sept. 19; 1711, Mar. 4, Apr. 8, Dec. 1, 2; 1712, Jan. 8.
Peter, Indian, 1709, July 5, 6; 1710, Aug. 11, Nov. 3.
Peter, Redskin, 1711, Jan. 22, 23;

1712, Jan. 10, 11, Feb. 16, 17, 18, 19, 21, 22, 23, 24, May 12.
Petronius Arbiter, 1712, Mar. 13 ff., May 28 ff.
Petsworth Parish, 1709, May 3.
Pettitt, Thomas, 1712, June 29.
Phillipe de Richbourgh, Reverend Claude, 1709, May 7, Oct. 22; 1711, May 29, 30.
Pictures, Byrd's, 1710, Aug. 24, Dec. 15; 1711, Mar. 5, 13, 14, Apr. 3.
Pigeon, Justice, 1710, July 12.
Pigot (Pickett) family, 1709, Nov. 8.
Pigot's Hole, 1709, Nov. 8, 24, 25.
Pindar, 1710, June 2, 5, 13.
Plantation management: Introduction, xiii; 1709, Feb. 7, 8, 17, Mar. 4, July 23, 24, Aug. 1, 13, 18 ff.; 1711, Dec. 1; 1712, Jan. 3 ff., May 20; *see also* Overseers.
Plantations, Byrd's, 1709, Feb. 23-27, Mar. 28-30, May 11-12, Aug. 18-20, Sept. 30—Oct. 2, Dec. 23-24; 1710, Mar. 2-4, 29-30, May 15-16, Sept. 5-7, Dec. 19-22; 1711, Mar. 27-28, May 28-30, June 20-22; 1712, Feb. 14-16, Mar. 26, May 13-14, Sept. 9-11.
Platt, Randolph (*or* Randle), 1710, Mar. 9 (marriage), 16, 18, 22, July 15, Aug. 18, 19; 1711, Mar. 1, Aug. 1, Oct. 16, 21, 22, 27; 1712, Jan. 15, Feb. 25, May 28.
Platt, Mrs. Randolph (Mrs. Taylor), 1710, Mar. 9 (marriage), 18, Aug. 18.
Pleasants, John, 1709, May 20, Nov. 14, Dec. 22; 1710, Mar. 6; 1711, Jan. 3, July 1.
Pleasants' Mill, 1710, Sept. 22; 1711, July 1.
Plutarch, *Moralia,* 1709, May 9.
Plymouth, 1709, Aug. 17; 1710, July 10.
Point Comfort, 1712, Jan. 31.
Politics, talk of, 1709, Sept. 8, 9.
Poor, 1709, Apr. 24; 1710, Jan. 25, May 18.
Pork, 1711, July 4, 23, Sept. 21, Dec. 18.
Posford, Captain, 1710, Mar. 14, 21, Apr. 13, May 1, 2, 26, 30, June 10, 12; 1711, Mar. 13, 16, 18, 20-22, 30, Apr. 4, 10, 14, May 2, 3, 5, 8, 15, 24, 25, 31, June 9, 14, 17, 24, 28, July 6, 7, 12, 19, 20, 22, 26; 1712, Apr. 23, May 1, 2, 8, 15, 21,

23, 30, June 4, 7, 25, 26, 28, July 3, 5, 8, 13, 18.

Post Office, 1710, Oct. 30.

Postmaster, *see* John Hamilton.

Poythress, Peter, 1709, Feb. 1; 1711, Oct. 8, 19; 1712, Jan. 21, Feb. 5, Mar. 4 (marriage), 11, 16.

Prayer, 1709, Feb. 6, June 6, Sept. 2, 6, 12; 1710, Jan. 3, Mar. 28, Dec. 29.

Prince George County, *burgesses*, 1709, Mar. 26, May 8; 1710, Aug. 8; *clerk*, 1709, Feb. 9, 11, Mar. 1, Apr. 13, May 8, 11, 17-19, 24, June 1, 6, 8; *court*, 1709, Apr. 13; 1710, May 10, June 14, July 12; 1711, Feb. 13; 1712, Jan. 8, Apr. 8, May 13, July 8, Sept. 9; *justices*, 1709, Feb. 27; 1711, Aug. 28; *land*, 1712, Apr. 5; *militia*, 1711, Aug. 28, Oct. 8; 1712, Apr. 20; *sheriff*, 1709, Feb. 27, May 28; 1710, Nov. 20.

Privateers, 1709, Feb. 28, Apr. 15, 25, May 30, Nov. 8; 1710, Apr. 19, July 2; 1711, Mar. 11, 13, June 8 (captured), 12, 13 (tried by Court of Admiralty); 1712, Apr. 13 (captured), 14, June 1 (condemned).

Profanity, 1709, Aug. 27, Oct. 19, Dec. 5; 1710, Feb. 26; 1711, Jan. 12.

Prue (servant), 1710, Oct. 8; 1711, Apr. 30, May 1, Aug. 4; 1712, May 22, June 6, 30, Sept. 3, 12.

Psalms, 1710, Jan. 30, Feb. 5—Mar. 26; 1711, Apr. 9-15.

Psalm singing, 1710, Dec. 15, 16, 24; 1711, Jan. 25.

Pursell, Philip, 1709, June 3, Sept. 22.

P—, Mr., 1709, Dec. 17-26; 1710, Jan. 2-3.

P-g-t, Mr., 1711, July 20.

P-l-n-t, Mrs., 1712, July 15.

P-n, G-r-m-r, 1712, July 16.

P-r-r, Mr., 1709, Oct. 8.

P-r-s-n, old, 1711, May 30 (death).

P-r-t, old 1712, May 28.

P-s-t-n, Captain, 1711, July 23.

P-t-r-m, Frank, 1712, Feb. 10.

P-t-r-s-n's mill dam, 1709, Feb. 26.

P-t-s-n, negro, 1711, Feb. 25, May 7; 1712, Feb. 9.

Q

Quakers, 1711, Sept. 21, Oct. 4; 1712, Jan. 5.

Quarry, Colonel, 1709, Oct. 31; 1712, July 20.

Queen's Creek plantation, 1709, Nov. 3, Dec. 8; 1710, Mar. 4, Apr. 29, June 4, Sept. 12, Nov. 29, Dec. 1; 1711, Feb. 5, 6, Mar. 9, Apr. 22, Sept. 19, Nov. 7, 25, Dec. 23-25, 1712, Feb. 1, 19, Apr. 14, 21, 25, 27, May 8, 12, July 23, Aug. 18.

Quitrents: Introduction, ix; 1709, Apr. 4, May 16, June 9; 1710, Feb. 3, 4, May 30; 1711, Feb. 3, Nov. 30.

R

Racing, 1709, Apr. 24; 1710, Aug. 19; *see also* Horses.

Rand, Mr., 1709, Sept. 10.

Rand, Mrs. (Ursula Horsemanden), 1709, Sept. 10.

Randolph, Mr., 1709, June 8, 11, Aug. 21, Oct. 12; 1710, Apr. 12, May 10, 18, July 6; 1711, May 1, June 28, July 1, Aug. 3, 4.

Randolph, Captain, 1711, Oct. 3.

Randolph, Edward, 1709, Apr. 11, May 16, June 4, 7; 1710, Aug. 2; 1711, Sept. 10.

Randolph, Henry, 1709, June 27, Aug. 9; 1710, Aug. 2; 1711, Mar. 2, 3.

Randolph, Captain Isham, 1709, Feb. 14, 15, 16, May 20, June 20; Aug. 15, 18, 19, 21, Sept. 27, Dec. 3, 5-7, 23, 26, 29; 1710, Jan. 1, 31, Feb. 1, 3, 10-16, 28, Mar. 1, 7, 10, 11, 14, 16, 17, 18, 20, 22, 24, 26, 27, May 15, 16, June 19, July 18, Sept. 18, 27, Oct. 8, 15, 20; 1712, Apr. 23, May 3, 15, 20, June 14, 15, 16, July 10, 18.

Randolph, John, 1709, Apr. 25, June 24; 1711, Mar. 23, Apr. 10, 14, Nov. 5 (first scholar); 1712, Mar. 19, 31.

Randolph, Richard, 1709, June 18, Oct. 4, Dec. 24, 25; 1710, Jan. 9, 19, 20, July 31; 1711, Jan. 8, 20, July 24.

Randolph, Captain Thomas, 1709, Apr. 13, Aug. 3; 1710, Feb. 27, May 22; 1711, Mar. 17, 29, May 29, Sept. 4, 8, 10, 15; 1712, Feb. 16, 17, 27, 28, Mar. 5, 6 (general overseer for Byrd), 7, 20, 21, 23, 26, 28, Apr. 12, 14, May 3, 4, 11, 12, 14, 20, June 2, 3, 14, 15, 18, 25, July 5, 6, 16, 18, 26, 27, Aug. 5, 13, 14, 29, Sept. 7, 9, 10, 11, 21.

Randolph, Colonel William, 1709,

Feb. 13, 14, 23, Apr. 11, 20, May 8, June 7, Aug. 3, 18, Sept. 14, 24, Oct. 10, 28, Dec. 7, 9, 20, 21; 1710, Jan. 31, Feb. 1, 22, Apr. 14, 15, 24, May 15, 22, 27, June 19, 25, July 27, 31, Aug. 18, Sept. 1 (burgess), 18, 22, Oct. 3, Nov. 27, 28; 1711, Mar. 17, Apr. 4, 6, 10, 20, 21 (death), 22.

Randolph, Mrs. William (Mary Isham), 1709, Aug. 18, Dec. 22; 1710, Apr. 14, May 28; 1711, Sept. 8, 9, 10, 15.

Randolph, William, Jr., 1709, Feb. 23, Apr. 4, 13, 26, 27, May 11, 27, June 3, 24 (marriage), July 4, 13, 22, Aug. 3, 18, 23, Sept. 15, Dec. 20; 1710, Jan. 31, Feb. 1, Mar. 6, 17, May 10, 11, 15, 16, June 25, Nov. 2, 10; 1711, Feb. 13, 24, Apr. 10, May 1, June 6, Sept. 8, 9, 10; 1712, Jan. 15, Feb. 28, Sept. 3.

Randolph, Mrs. William, Jr. (Elizabeth Beverley), 1709, June 24 (marriage), July 13, Aug. 3, 18, 23.

Rappahannock, 1709, Apr. 9; 1711, Dec. 17; 1712, Mar. 23.

Reading and study: Introduction, xvi; see also Allestree, Burnet, Butler, Collier, Day, Garth, Greek, Grotius, Latimer, Latin, Lister, Norris, Sacheverell, Tatler, Tillotson.

Religion: Introduction, xxi; 1709, May 1; 1710, Mar. 31; 1711, Jan. 27, 28; see also Church, Clergy, Creed, Manakin Town, Prayer, Sermons, etc.

Rhett, Colonel William, 1709, Feb. 28.

Richbourgh, Claude Phillipe de, 1709, May 7, Oct. 22; 1711, May 29, 30.

Richmond, City of: Introduction, xii; 1709, Feb. 6, 20, Mar. 29, Aug. 19.

Roberts, Captain John, 1710, Oct. 21, 24, 25, 26.

Robertson, Reverend George, 1710, Jan. 4, Sept. 4; 1711, Sept. 22,, 24, Oct. 28.

Robin (servant), 1710, Mar. 3; 1711, June 21; 1712, Feb. 15.

Robinson (or Robertson), Mr., 1709, Feb. 28, Apr. 28, May 6, June 22, Sept. 26, 29, Nov. 3, 27; 1710, Jan. 11, Apr. 13, 29, Sept. 20; 1711, Sept. 19, 20, 23, Nov. 5, 6, Dec. 15.

Robinson (or Robertson), William, 1709, Oct. 27; 1710, Apr. 20, Nov.

26; 1711, Oct. 16; 1712, Jan. 31, Mar. 31.

Robinson, Colonel, 1711, Apr. 21.

Robinson, Major, 1711, Dec. 17.

Robinson, Christopher, 1711, June 13 (naval officer).

Robinson, Captain Tancred, 1710, Oct. 24.

Rogers, Robert, 1710, Apr. 12; 1711, Mar. 19, May 8, June 25, 29, July 11, Aug. 14, 15; 1712, July 2, Aug. 6.

Roscow, Mr., 1711, Oct. 7.

Roscow, James: Introduction, ix; 1711, Nov. 16; 1712, Mar. 6, 7.

Roscow, Mary, 1711, Dec. 9.

Rosegill, 1709, June 16.

Royall, Captain Joseph, 1711, Oct. 4.

Rum, 1709, Feb. 25, 28, Mar. 3, 25, 28, Apr. 17, June 2, July 21, Aug. 13; 1710, June 18.

Russell, Mrs. Katharine, 1710, June 22, July 18, Aug. 11, Oct. 21, 28, Nov. 8, 10, 30, Dec. 1-4, 9, 10, 13; 1711, Feb. 6, 7, Mar. 9, 24, 29, 30, 31, Apr. 1-9, 16, 18, 28, May 5, 11, Oct. 19, 23, 26, 28, Nov. 2, 5, 6, Dec. 9; 1712, Jan. 23, 25, Mar. 23, Apr. 1, May 1, July 20, Aug. 18, Sept. 21, 23.

R-b-n (Roberts?), Captain, 1709, Sept. 26, 27, 28, 29.

R-b-r-s-n (Robertson?), 1709, Oct. 22.

R-d, Cousin, 1710, May 8.

R-s, Captain, 1712, July 2.

S

Sacheverell, Dr. Henry, 1710, Sept. 1, 3, Oct. 2, 5.

Sailing, 1709, Nov. 7 ff., 25.

St. Peter's Parish, 1709, June 15, Oct. 16; 1711, May 28.

Salivation, 1709, May 25, 26, Nov. 10.

Salle, Abraham, 1709, May 7, 10, June 30, Sept. 15, Oct. 3, 4, 22; 1710, Jan. 10, 12, Aug. 9, Sept. 22, 23, Nov. 14, 16; 1711, Mar. 5, May 29, 30, Aug. 25, Sept. 10; 1712, Apr. 3, 4, May 31, June 16, 17, 20; son of, 1709, June 30.

Salle, Mrs. Abraham, 1709, Oct. 3.

Sallust, 1712, June 19, 21, 24.

Salt, 1711, May 16, 23; 1712, Apr. 3.

Sandy Point, 1710, July 27; 1711, July 1.

Saponie Indians, 1711, Dec. 19.

Saponie Town, 1711, Oct. 18.

Sawmill, 1709, Mar. 29, Nov. 29,

Dec. 23; 1710, Mar. 3, 4, 30, May 16; 1711, Mar. 27; *see also* Mills.
School, 1709, Apr. 11; 1711, Apr. 6.
Schoolhouse, 1709, Aug. 4.
Scott, Walter, 1710, Aug. 14.
Seamen, 1709, Feb. 17, June 23, 29, Dec. 8; 1710, July 18, Oct. 19.
Serjanton, Mrs., 1712, Jan. 26.
Sermons, 1709, Apr. 3, Oct. 17; 1710, Apr. 14, May 7, Nov. 19, Dec. 3.
Servants, 1709, Feb. 8, Apr. 6, July 12, Nov. 18, Dec. 25; 1710, Aug. 5, Dec. 8; 1711, Jan. 26, Feb. 7, Oct. 27, Nov. 8, Dec. 7; *apprentices,* 1711, June 30; 1712, Mar. 2; *bond servants,* 1711, Feb. 24, Apr. 11, Aug. 14; *Indian servants,* 1709, July 5; 1710, Feb. 3, July 21 ff.
Servants, care for, 1709, Feb. 21, July 19, 21, Sept. 4, Nov. 25; 1710, Jan. 20, 22; July 9, 23, Aug. 20; 1712, June 27.
Servants, conduct of, 1709, Feb. 22, May 13, June 2, July 11, Sept. 22; 1710, Jan. 13, 15, Apr. 16, May 26, 28, June 17, Aug. 12, 23; 1711, Feb. 25, Apr. 30; 1712, June 30, Sept. 12.
Servants, health of, 1709, Feb. 24, Apr. 19, May 11, 12, 26, June 27, July 5, Aug. 13, Oct. 8, Nov. 22-23; 1710, Jan. 3, Feb. 20, Mar. 5 ff., May 28, June 6, July 18, 21, 27, Aug. 13, Dec. 24 ff.; 1711, Jan. 1 ff.
Servants, punishment of, 1709, Feb. 8, 16, Apr. 17, May 23, June 10, July 30, Aug. 8, 27, Sept. 3, 16, 19, Nov. 30, Dec. 1, 16; 1710, Jan. 6, Mar. 3, July 15, Aug. 31, Oct. 8, 9; 1711, Feb. 2, 27, Dec. 31; 1712, Mar. 2, May 22.
Servants, runaway, 1709, Mar. 30, June 9, 10, Aug. 8; 1710, June 24, 25, 28, July 1, 2, 8, 15, 19, Aug. 10, Sept. 8, 9, 11, 12, Nov. 6, 13; 1712, July 23 (reward offered).
Seymour, Governor John, 1709, Sept. 9 (death).
Shirley, 1709, Aug. 20.
Ship building, 1709, July 20, 22, Nov. 14; 1710, Feb. 27; 1712, May 15; *see also* Boatwright.
Ships: 1709, Feb. 14, 16, Mar. 1, Apr. 19, May 5, June 8, 29; 1710, Jan. 2, Apr. 19, May 26, June 21, Aug. 18, Sept. 15, Oct. 30, 31; 1711, Mar. 5; 1712, June 14.

Ships, English fleet, 1709, Apr. 1, 4, May 4, June 13, 14, July 18, Aug. 31; 1710, Jan. 2, June 7, 30, Nov. 2, 18; 1711, Jan. 25, Mar. 8 ff., Dec. 17; 1712, Apr. 21, Aug. 1.
Ships, Colonel Hill's, 1710, Feb. 27, Mar. 12, 14, 16, 17, July 15, 18, Oct. 19, Nov. 2; 1711, Feb. 17; 1712, Jan. 7, Apr. 12.
Shipwreck, 1709, May 6, 21, July 10; 1710, Mar. 25; 1711, Apr. 21.
Shipyard, 1710, Oct. 7; *see* Swinyards.
Shockoe (Shacco) plantation, 1709, Mar. 29, Aug. 19; 1710, Jan. 23, Mar. 3, Sept. 6; 1712, Jan. 14, Feb. 14, Mar. 27.
Shoemaker, 1710, Aug. 9.
Shorthand: Introduction, vii-viii.
Si (negro), 1711, Feb. 20, Mar. 12-20.
Silver mine, 1712, May 24.
Simons, John, 1710, Nov. 24; 1711, Feb. 19.
Skimino Mill, 1712, Feb. 2, 18, Apr. 28.
Slater, Reverend James, 1709, Oct. 22; 1710, June 17.
Slaves: Introduction, xii; 1710, Apr. 18-21 (conspiracy of), May 26, June 1, 2, 5; 1711, Jan. 21, Feb. 2, 8; 1712, Sept. 28; *see also* Servants.
Smallpox, 1710, Mar. 14; 1711, June 18, 27, July 5.
Smith, George (the coaler), 1709, June 15, 28, July 18, Aug. 13, 19; 1710, Feb. 24, Aug. 9, Dec. 23; 1711, Jan. 4, May 29, June 29, Dec. 28, 29; 1712, July 10.
Smith, Reverend Guy, 1709, Nov. 6.
Smith, Colonel John, 1709, Apr. 22, Oct. 25; 1710, Nov. 2, 9, 16, Dec. 8; 1711, Apr. 19, 25, 26, Oct. 30, Nov. 21, Dec. 7; 1712, Jan. 25, 27, Aug. 18; son of, 1711, Feb. 6.
Smith, Miss Mary: Introduction, xi.
Smith, Captain Nicholas, 1710, Apr. 19, Nov. 17, 18, 20; 1711, Apr. 7, June 6, 12, Nov. 29; 1712, July 20.
Smith Island, 1709, Nov. 10.
Snakeroot, 1709, Apr. 9; 1712, Sept. 23.
Soane (Soanes), Captain William, 1711, June 21; 1712, May 14, Sept. 11.
Soane's Warehouse, 1709, Dec. 7.
Social life, 1710, Sept. 20-24; 1711, Nov. 12-14; 1712, May 24—June 17, Aug. 26-27; *see also* Hospitality.
Solomon's Song, 1710, Aug. 27.

Somers, John, Lord, **1709**, Apr. 25.

South Carolina, **1712**, Feb. 20.

Southwark Parish, **1709**, Aug. 9.

Southwell, Edward, **1709**, June 20.

Southwell, Lady Elizabeth, **1709**, June 20.

Southwell, Sir Robert, **1709**, June 20.

Spain, **1711**, Mar. 5, May 3.

Spanish flies, **1711**, Aug. 14; **1712**, Sept. 1.

Sports, **1710**, Feb. 20, 25; **1711**, Sept. 14, Oct. 3, 6; **1712**, Aug. 15.

Spotswood, Colonel Alexander: Introduction, ix; **1709**, *Apr.* 19; **1710**, *Mar.* 31; arrival in Virginia, *June* 21, 22; at Williamsburg, speaks to Council, 23; instructions read in Council, *July* 5; family ill, *Aug.* 11; tells history of the war, *Sept.* 14; visits Westover, 20-25, musters militia, 21, 22; visits Manakin Town, 23; favors iron works, 24; commissions Frank Eppes to explore mountains, *Oct.* 17; chosen governor of William and Mary College, 18; approves Byrd's proposal, 23; reads speech to Council, 24; and to House of Burgesses, 26; godfather to Daniel Parke Custis, 28; attitude in Council, *Nov.* 14; gives directions for building Governor's house, 17; flattered in church, 19; finds fault with tax bill, 25, 27; Byrd tries to soften, 28; entertains, 29, 30; visits Mrs. Byrd, *Dec.* 2; address to, 5; prorogues Assembly, 9; birthday celebration, 12; writes to Byrd, **1711**, *Jan.* 1, 22; negroes bought for, *Feb.* 2, 3; gives a ball, 6; entertains Byrds, 7; discusses offices, 8; trees bought for, 8; writes to Byrd, *Mar.* 21; leaves Williamsburg, 23; visits Westover, 24-27; visits Col. Hill, Falling Creek, and the Falls, 27; journey into New Kent, 28, 29; chosen rector of college, *Apr.* 25; displeased with governors of college, 25; writes to Byrd, *May* 22; *July* 2; buys pork for New York, 4; to go to Carolina, 5; writes Byrd, 19; calls out militia, *Aug.* 15, 21, 23, 27; returns to Williamsburg, *Sept.* 20; discusses Quakers, 21; informs Byrd of Indian massacre, *Oct.* 7; council at Major Harrison's, 8; returns to Williamsburg, 9; at Colonel Harrison's, *Oct.* 16;

treats with Indians at Nottoway Town, 17-21; puts coachman in prison, 27; contrivances at the Governor's house, 29; verses presented by college, *Nov.* 5; speech to Assembly, 8; opposes Byrd, 9; Council addresses, 15, 16; puts up arms in new house, 19; dispute with Burgesses, 22; takes exception to bill, 27; advised to declare war on Indians, 28; complains of Cary, *Dec.* 7; gives audience to Indians, 8; signs treaty, 11; wants money bill passed, 15; will not pass tax bill, 18; gives audience to Indians, 19; quarrel with Burgesses, 19-24; adjourns Assembly, 24; hears Byrd's remarks about the £20,000, **1712**, *Jan.* 9, 15, 20, and is angry, 21, 24; gossip about, 23; out of humor with Burgesses, 25; continues stiff toward Byrd, 26, 29; speaks to Burgesses, 28; dissolves House, 31; poplar trees sent to, *Feb.* 5; and fruit trees, 8; lays before Council a petition from Carolina, 20; receives Tuscaroras, *Mar.* 16; discusses Carolina affairs, *Apr.* 1; intends to march against Tuscaroras, 20; writes Byrd, *May* 5, 6; "double dealing," *June* 10; reprimands mutineers, 20; Mr. Jeffrys asks pardon for offenses, *July* 21; paid £1,000 by Byrd, 22; ill, *Aug.* 7, 8; holds council on Indians, 18; at Pamunkey Town, *Sept.* 21-24; *and minor references.*

Stafford County, **1711**, May 22, 23, June 1.

Stanhope (Stanup), Captain John, **1712**, Sept. 24 (burgess).

Star (horse), **1709**, May 13, 20, 22, 23 (death).

Stith, Mr., **1710**, Aug. 3.

Stith, Mrs., **1709**, Feb. 6, Oct. 15, Dec. 1, 2; **1710**, Apr. 4, June 19; **1712**, Feb. 10.

Stith, Captain, **1709**, Feb. 6, Apr. 4, May 15, June 24, Aug. 3, Sept. 6, Oct. 9, 10, 12, Dec. 1, 7, 11, 12, 13, 14, 17; **1710**, Jan. 3, June 13, Sept. 21, 25; **1711**, June 25, Sept. 14, 16, Dec. 26; **1712**, Jan. 13, Apr. 8.

Stith, Captain Drury, **1709**, Feb. 6, 20, Apr. 25, June 13, Sept. 18; **1710**, Jan. 8, Feb. 28, May 14, June 16, Aug. 7, 15, 20, 21, 28, 31, Sept. 4, Oct. 5; **1711**, Jan. 3, Feb. 21, 24,

Mar. 12, 24, May 2, July 20, 29, Aug. 4, 23, 24, 29, 30, Sept. 27, Oct. 6, 11; 1712, Jan. 15, Feb. 8, 11, Mar. 25, 27, Apr. 3, Aug. 10, 26, Sept. 22, 26.

Stith, Mrs. Drury (Susannah Bathurst), 1709, Feb. 20, May 29; 1710, May 14, June 16, Aug. 15, 21; 1711, Mar. 12; 1712, Sept. 28.

Stith, Drury, 1710, Mar. 24; 1711, Mar. 12.

Stith, Captain John, 1709, Feb. 6; 1711, Mar. 18, 23, 26, 30, Apr. 7, Aug. 4, 7, Sept. 12; 1712, May 3, 7, Aug. 3, 20, Sept. 28.

Stith, Mrs. John (Mary Randolph), 1710, Feb. 24, 25, Aug. 6; 1712, Aug. 3, Sept. 28.

Stith, John, 1709, Apr. 25; 1710, Apr. 7; 1711, Sept. 12.

Stokes, John, 1712, Sept. 6.

Stonecutter, 1709, June 25 (death); 1712, June 3, 4, 5.

Stone quarry, 1712, Feb. 15.

Stores: 1709, July 11, Aug. 22; 1710, Apr. 5, July 5, 7, 25, 31, Aug. 25; 1712, Apr. 3, July 28.

Sue (servant), 1711, Sept. 22; 1712, Feb. 10, July 27 (son born).

Suky, 1711, Mar. 5.

Suky (Dr. Cocke's maid), 1711, July 1, Dec. 16.

Sunday, 1709, July 3; 1710, July 9, 23, Aug. 20, Nov. 12.

Surry County, 1710, Oct. 11; 1711, Jan. 17, 19, Oct. 8, 19; *burgess,* 1709, May 5; *sheriff,* 1709, Sept. 2; 1710, May 30.

Surveys, 1709, Oct. 1, 13.

Sweet Hall, 1709, Apr. 20.

Swinyards, 1709, June 14, July 13; 1710, Mar. 12, Aug. 16; 1711, Sept. 11; 1712, Feb. 27, May 3, 16, 27, June 14.

S-c-l-s, John, 1711, Oct. 6.

S-c-r, Captain, 1711, June 6, July 3.

S-c-r-y, Mr., 1710, Sept. 15.

S-d-s-n, Tom, 1709, June 25.

S-k-f-r (sailor), 1710, Mar. 20, 21, 22, July 24, Dec. 20, 22; 1711, Jan. 23.

S-l-n, Mr., 1711, Apr. 19.

S-m-s-n, Mother, 1710, Jan. 25.

S-n-s Bridge, 1709, Dec. 7.

S-n-y (negro), 1711, Jan. 19-21 (death).

S-r-y (negro), 1709, Dec. 19 (death).

S-r-y (servant), 1711, Jan. 6 (death).

S-r-y (negro), 1711, May 28 (death).

S-r-y (negro), 1711, Aug. 31, Sept. 2.

S-t-c, Captain, 1709, Feb. 14, 15, 18, 19, June 19.

T

Tailor, the, 1709, May 12; 1710, Sept. 11, Nov. 6.

Tannery, 1709, May 12, Aug. 19; 1710, Sept. 5; 1711, June 22.

Tar, 1709, Mar. 26; 1710, Aug. 25.

Tatler, The, 1710, July 7, 8; 1711, Mar. 16 ff.; 1712, Aug. 12 ff.

Taxes, 1710, Nov. 25, 27; 1711, Dec. 5, 10, 12-24, 31.

Tayloe, Mr., 1711, Oct. 7.

Taylor, Mr., 1709, Sept. 2, 3.

Taylor, Mrs., 1710, Feb. 3, 27, Mar. 9 (marriage); 1711, Jan. 3.

Taylor, Reverend Daniel, 1709, May 1; 1710, Oct. 29, Nov. 12, Dec. 10.

Taylor, Henrietta Maria, 1709, Aug. 16 (marriage).

Taylor, John, 1709, Aug. 16.

Taylor, Mrs. John, 1709, Aug. 16 (marriage of daughter).

Taylor, Maria (Mrs. William Byrd II): Introduction, xi.

Taylor, Miss Sarah, 1709, Aug. 16; 1710, May 21, Aug. 21; 1711, Feb. 18, Apr. 6, 12, 13, 29.

Temperance, 1709, Mar. 1, Apr. 30.

Terence, 1709, Sept. 13, Oct. 17, 19, 20; 1710, Jan. 7 ff., 25.

Thacker, Mr., 1711, Sept. 19.

Thompson, Captain, 1712, Mar. 12.

Thomson, Miss Elizabeth, 1712, May 25, June 4.

Thomson, Miss Mary, 1709, Apr. 19; 1712, May 25, June 4.

Thomson, Captain Roger, 1709, Apr. 4.

Thomson, Stevens, 1709, Apr. 19, Dec. 8; 1711, June 26, Sept. 19.

Thucydides, 1710, June 14—Aug. 10.

Tillotson, Dr., sermons, 1709, Feb. 13, 20, Apr. 3; 1710, May 7, 21, June 18, July 2, 30, Sept. 10, *and passim.*

Tobacco: receiver of, 1709, Aug. 29; used as money, Sept. 1; 1710, Feb. 3; smoking, 1710, July 22.

Tobacco culture, 1709, Feb. 17, Mar. 26, Apr. 5, 13, May 1, 2, 12, 31, June 1, Aug. 19, 29; 1710, Sept. 6, Dec. 20; 1712, May 9 ff.

Tobacco trade, 1709, Apr. 25, May 6, 21, June 15, 16, 17, 23, Aug. 31; 1710, Jan. 28, June 23, Oct. 30, 31, Nov. 16-21; 1711, Nov. 16.

Todd, Elizabeth, **1709,** Apr. 30; **1710,** July 10, 17.
Todd, Thomas, **1709,** Apr. 30.
Tom (servant), **1709,** Feb. 17, Mar. 4, 5, Apr. 17, May 30, June 27, July 8, 18, 20, 21, Aug. 8, Sept. 23, Dec. 12, 14; **1710,** Jan. 3, 4, June 4, 21, July 27, 28, 30, Aug. 16, Sept. 4, Oct. 28, 29, Nov. 23; **1711,** Jan. 15, 20, 22, 27, Mar. 2, 3, Apr. 16, May 10, 11, 21, 22, 31, June 29, July 1, 5-7, 13, 14, 20, 21, 23, 26, Aug. 4, 7, 16, 24, 25, 26, 29, Sept. 29, Oct. 2, 23, 24, Nov. 10, 15, 20, 29, Dec. 1, 5, 8, 13; **1712,** Jan. 2, 17, 29, 30, Feb. 7, 9, 10, 26, Mar. 2, 3, 17, 23, May 8, 11, 30, June 9, July 7, 30, 31, Sept. 1, 2, 12, 26.
Tom (tailor), **1709,** May 12 (wedding), Sept. 11.
Tony (servant), **1709,** Feb. 12; **1710,** Feb. 3; **1711,** July 13, Oct. 15, Dec. 31; **1712,** Jan. 12, July 11, Sept. 15, 16.
Tooker, Major, **1710,** July 4.
Trade, **1709,** Feb. 18, 19, June 14, 15, 27, 28, 29, July 29, Aug. 2, 8, 17, 31; **1710,** Mar. 14, June 26, 29, 30, July 9, 10, 24, Aug. 12, 16; **1712,** Apr. 23, May 2, 11; *see also* Freight, Indian trade, Tobacco trade.
Translating: Introduction, xviii; **1709,** June 2; **1710,** Aug. 23, 24, 27, 29, Sept. 9; **1711,** May 22; **1712,** Aug. 27, 29.
Trees, **1709,** Nov. 10; **1710,** Apr. 16, May 31; **1711,** Jan. 13, 17, Feb. 8, 23; **1712,** Jan. 3.
Tributary Indians, **1711,** Oct. 8, 17.
Tullitt, John, **1709,** Oct. 31, Dec. 8; **1710,** Dec. 22; **1711,** Jan. 13, May 28, 29, Aug. 3, Nov. 7; **1712,** Jan. 28, Apr. 30, June 30, July 1.
Turpin, Thomas, **1709,** Feb. 13, Mar. 29, Oct. 1; **1710,** Feb. 24, 25, Mar. 4, July 9, Dec. 20; **1711,** Jan. 13, 15, 18, 22, Feb. 3, 4, 10, 14, 16, Sept. 9; **1712,** Jan. 4, 5, Feb. 15, 23, Mar. 23; wife of, **1711,** Feb. 14.
Turner, Captain, **1712,** Apr. 23, May 9, 11, June 14, July 8, 10, 19.
Tuscarora Indians, **1709,** Feb. 23, Apr. 23; **1711,** Oct. 8, 18, 19, 20, 21, Dec. 2, 8, 10 (treaty), 11; **1712,** Mar. 11, 16, Apr. 19, 20.
T-b, Mr., **1712,** June 20.
T-l-r, Mr., **1712,** May 5.
T-r-t-n, Mr., **1712,** May 15, Sept. 1, 9.
T-y, L-r-n, **1712,** May 24.

U

Urmston, John, **1711,** July 27.

V

Virginia, Governor of, **1710,** Jan. 2, Mar. 31, June 7, 21; *see* Hunter, Nicholson, Spotswood.
Virginia, laws, **1711,** Feb. 13.
V-n, Captain, **1712,** May 6.
V-n-t, Captain, **1712,** July 1, 2.

W

Wager, Admiral Charles: Introduction, x; **1709,** June 12.
Wagers, **1709,** Nov. 29, Dec. 29; **1710,** Mar. 30; **1711,** Nov. 8.
Walker, Mr., **1711,** Dec. 12.
Walker, George, **1710,** Aug. 25; **1711,** Apr. 19.
Wallace, Reverend James, **1709,** Nov. 25 (and wife), 26; **1710,** Nov. 19.
Walpole, Sir Robert: Introduction, x.
Ward, Richard, **1710,** Dec. 18.
Ward, Seth, **1711,** June 21.
Ware, Caleb, **1709,** May 8.
Ware, Reverend Jacob, **1709,** Mar. 25.
Ware, Mrs., **1709,** Sept. 2, 15, Dec. 5; **1710,** Jan. 4, 15.
Ware, Susan, **1710,** Jan. 4, 9, 15.
Warwick, **1709,** Oct. 1.
Waters, Colonel William, **1709,** Nov. 11, 12, 15; **1711,** Oct. 27.
Waters, Miss, **1709,** Nov. 20.
Webb, Captain Giles, **1709,** Mar. 29, Apr. 18, Aug. 15, 18, Oct. 1, Nov. 29; **1710,** Sept. 7; **1711,** Mar. 2, 3, 27, 28, May 30, Aug. 2, Sept. 14, 27, Oct. 4; **1712,** Sept. 10.
Webb, Mrs. Giles, **1711,** Mar. 27.
West, John, **1709,** Apr. 1.
West Indies, **1709,** Apr. 1; **1711,** Apr. 7.
Westminster (servant), **1709,** Oct. 1; **1711,** Jan. 21 (wife), June 21.
Westover: Introduction, xii; **1709,** Mar. 3, 4; **1710,** July 11 (Dr. Cocke's visit), Sept. 20-24 (Spotswood's visit), Nov. 22, Dec. 14; **1711,** Feb. 25, Mar. 24-27 (Spotswood's visit), Apr. 20, May 15, 17, June 22, Sept. 20, Oct. 9, Nov. 10, 11, 12; **1712,** June 5 (Mr. Catesby gives garden advice), 12.
Westover Parish, **1710,** Feb. 3, May 3, June 6, Sept. 21, Dec. 18; **1711,** Apr. 4, Aug. 30; **1712,** Jan. 15.

Weyanoke, 1709, June 19, 20; 1710, Aug. 19; 1712, Apr. 27.

Whaley, Mrs., 1711, Dec. 9; 1712, Apr. 16, 17, 18.

Whately, Reverend Solomon, 1710, Oct. 22, Nov. 19 (funeral).

Wilcox, Captain John, 1709, June 16, 22, 26, July 4, 5, 9, 10, 13, 18, 19, 20, 21, 23, Sept. 20; 1711, Mar. 13, 21, 26; 1712, Feb. 29, Apr. 8, June 20.

Wilkins, Mr., 1711, Feb. 24.

Wilkins, Will, 1711, Feb. 17, 24, June 4, July 29, 30, 31, Aug. 1; 1712, Mar. 3, 15, May 31, July 25, Aug. 21.

Wilkinson, Daniel, 1709, Feb. 6, 7, 12, 13, 14, 18, 19, 22, Apr. 19, May 9, June 29, 30, July 10-12, 28-30, Aug. 22, Oct. 8, 10, 22, Dec. 17; 1710, Nov. 19; 1711, Feb. 6, Oct. 28; 1712, Jan. 27, Feb. 21.

Wilkinson, Joseph, 1709, Aug. 1, Sept. 7, Oct. 1, Dec. 19; 1710, Jan. 29, May 28, 29, July 8, 9, 15, Aug. 14, Sept. 1, 6, 19, Oct. 6, 7, 15, 26, Dec. 20 (discharged), 21; 1711, Apr. 4 (case against), 20, 21; wife of, 1711, Jan. 9.

William and Mary College: Indians to attend, 1711, Oct. 20, 21; present verses to Governor, Nov. 5; recommended to burgesses, 20; usher, 1712, Mar. 19, 31; tenants, 31; Indian hostages run away, Apr. 18.

William and Mary College, *building of:* 1709, June 16, 20, Aug. 4, Sept. 13, Oct. 31, Dec. 8; 1710, Apr. 24, 25; 1711, Nov. 7; 1712, Jan. 28.

William and Mary College, *governors of:* 1709, Apr. 20, Aug. 3; 1710, Apr. 25, Oct. 17, 18; 1711, Apr. 25; 1712, Mar. 31.

William and Mary College, *masters of:* 1709, June 7, Oct. 28, 29; 1711, Apr. 17, 25, Oct. 16; 1712, Jan. 28.

William and Mary College, *rectors of:* 1709, Apr. 20 (Randolph); 1711, Apr. 25 (Spotswood); 1712, Mar. 31 (Blair).

William and Mary College, *students of:* 1709, June 5; 1712, Sept. 1.

Williamsburg: Byrd's visits, 1709, Feb. 28—Mar. 2, Apr. 18-30, June 20-21, Aug. 4, Sept. 12-14; Oct. 6-8, 15—Nov. 3, 27, Dec. 8; 1710, Apr. 17-30, June 23, July 5-7, Sept. 12-16, Oct. 9-11, 16—Nov. 4, 8-11, 13—Dec. 14; 1711, Feb. 6-8, Mar. 7-9, Apr. 15-29, June 11-14, July 4-7, 23-27, Sept. 19-21, Oct. 23—Nov. 11, 14-30, Dec. 4-16, 17-24; 1712, Jan. 22—Feb. 1, 20-21, Mar. 31—Apr. 2, 15—May 1, June 10-12, July 20-23, Aug. 17-20.

Williamsburg, Directors of, 1711, June 13.

Williamsburg, capitol, 1710, Aug. 21; 1711, Feb. 6, Nov. 2.

Williamsburg, *see also* Governor's house, Ordinaries.

Willis, Captain Francis, 1712, May 16.

Wills, 1709, Oct. 10 (Dr. Oastler's); 1711, May 23 ff. (Byrd's), May 25 (Parke's), June 12 (Parke's), Aug. 10 (Byrd's); Nov. 24 ff. (law on probate and administration).

Wilson, Colonel William, 1709, Dec. 8-9.

Wine: 1709, Apr. 30, June 4 (making), 29 (price), Sept. 6, 12, Oct. 6, Nov. 18, 23; 1710, Apr. 14, June 6, 15, 23, Sept. 14.

Wireman, the, 1709, Apr. 14; *see* C-k, Dick.

Women, 1709, Mar. 31, June 12, Oct. 19 (at court), Nov. 11, 15, 24, 27, Dec. 1, 2; 1711, Jan. 9, Apr. 3, Aug. 8, 9, Dec. 13 (jury of).

Woodson, John, 1709, May 23, Aug. 8, Oct. 3, Nov. 29; 1710, Mar. 30, May 22, Oct. 13; 1711, July 28.

Woodson, young, 1710, Mar. 27; 1711, June 5.

Worcester, Bishop of, 1710, Mar. 31.

Worden, Reverend James, 1712, Apr. 27.

Workmen, 1710, Jan. 26, July 11; *see* Boatwright, Bricklayer, Brickmaker, Carpenter, Cooper, Shoemaker, Stonecutter, Tailor, Wireman.

Wormeley, Mr., 1709, June 16.

Wormeley, Mrs., 1709, Oct. 5.

Wormeley, Judith, 1711, May 17; 1712, July 10 (marriage to Mann Page).

Wormeley, Ralph, 1712, Apr. 19.

Worsham, Captain, 1709, Feb. 23, Apr. 17, Dec. 23; 1711, Sept. 23; 1712, Apr. 11.

Wynne, Major Joshua, 1711, Aug. 28.

W-b-r, Phil, 1712, May 31.

W-l, P-t (Indian), 1712, Sept. 23.

W-l-k, Colonel, 1709, Oct. 12.
W-l-r-c, John, 1710, June 5.
W-l-s, Mr., 1709, Apr. 19, 24, 25.
W-l-s, Frank, 1709, Dec. 3, 5; 1711, Nov. 22; 1712, July 5.
W-l-s, Harry, 1711, Nov. 8.
W-l-s, John, 1711, June 30.
W-l-s-n, Joe, 1710, Jan. 11.
W-l-x (Wilkes?), 1709, Mar. 3, 5; 1711, June 14, 16.
W-r-t-n, Mr., 1710, Nov. 1.
W-s, Mr., 1712, July 1, 2.

Y

York, 1709, Nov. 8, 25; 1711, July 6, Sept. 3, 7, Nov. 6.
York county court, 1709, June 5.
York river, 1709, Feb. 21, Mar. 1, May 4, July 20; 1710, June 29; 1711, Jan. 25; 1712, May 16, 18, 20, June 4, 15, 26.
Yorktown, 1711, Mar. 10.
Young, Mrs., 1711, Nov. 9, 10 (marriage).
Y-n, C-t, 1709, Apr. 18.

RESEARCH LIBRARY
OF
COLONIAL AMERICANA

An Arno Press Collection

Histories

Acrelius, Israel. **A History of New Sweden;** Or, The Settlements
on the River Delaware . . . Translated with an Introduction
and Notes by William M. Reynolds. Historical Society of
Pennsylvania, MEMOIRS, XI, Philadelphia, 1874.

Belknap, Jeremy. **The History of New Hampshire.** 3 vols., Vol. 1—
Philadelphia, 1784 (Reprinted Boston, 1792), Vol. 2—Boston,
1791, Vol. 3—Boston, 1792.

Browne, Patrick. **The Civil and Natural History of Jamaica.** In
Three Parts . . . London, 1756. Includes 1789 edition
Linnaean index.

[Burke, Edmund]. **An Account of the European Settlements in
America.** In Six Parts . . . London, 1777. Two volumes in one.

Chalmers, George. **An Introduction to the History of the Revolt
of the American Colonies:** Being a Comprehensive View of
Its Origin, Derived From the State Papers Contained in
the Public Offices of Great Britain. London, 1845. Two
volumes in one.

Douglass, William. **A Summary, Historical and Political, of the
First Planting, Progressive Improvements, and Present State
of the British Settlements in North-America.** Boston, 1749–
1752. Two volumes in one.

Edwards, Bryan. **The History, Civil and Commercial, of the
British Colonies in the West Indies.** Dublin, 1793–1794. Two
volumes in one.

Hughes, Griffith. **The Natural History of Barbados.** In Ten Books.
London, 1750.

[Franklin, Benjamin]. **An Historical Review of the Constitution and Government of Pennsylvania, From Its Origin . . .** London, 1759.

Hubbard, William. **A General History of New England, From the Discovery to MDCLXXX.** (*In* Massachusetts Historical Society, COLLECTIONS, Series 2, vol. 5, 6, 1815. Reprinted 1848.)

Hutchinson, Thomas. **The History of the Colony of Massachusetts Bay** . . . 3 vols., Boston, 1764–1828.

Keith, Sir William. **The History of the British Plantations in America** . . . London, 1738.

Long, Edward. **The History of Jamaica:** Or, General Survey of the Antient and Modern State of that Island . . . 3 vols., London, 1774.

Mather, Cotton. **Magnalia Christi Americana;** Or, The Ecclesiastical History of New-England From . . . the Year 1620, Unto the Year . . . 1698. In Seven Books. London, 1702.

Mather, Increase. **A Relation of the Troubles Which Have Hapned in New-England, By Reason of the Indians There From the Year 1614 to the Year 1675** . . . Boston, 1677.

Smith, Samuel. **The History of the Colony of Nova-Caesaria, Or New-Jersey** . . . **to the Year 1721** . . . Burlington, N.J., 1765.

Thomas, Sir Dalby. **An Historical Account of the Rise and Growth of the West-India Collonies,** and of the Great Advantages They are to England, in Respect to Trade. London, 1690.

Trumbull, Benjamin. **A Complete History of Connecticut,** Civil and Ecclesiastical, From the Emigration of Its First Planters, From England, in the Year 1630, to the Year 1764; and to the Close of the Indian Wars . . . New Haven, 1818. Two volumes in one.

Personal Narratives and Promotional Literature

Byrd, William. **The Secret Diary of William Byrd of Westover, 1709–1712,** edited by Louis B. Wright and Marion Tinling. Richmond, Va., 1941.

Byrd, William. **The London Diary (1717–1721) and Other Writings,** edited by Louis B. Wright and Marion Tinling. New York, 1958.

**A Genuine Narrative of the Intended Conspiracy of the Negroes
at Antigua.** Extracted From an Authentic Copy of a Report,
Made to the Chief Governor of the Carabee Islands, by the
Commissioners, or Judges Appointed to Try the Conspirators.
Dublin, 1737.

Gookin, Daniel. **An Historical Account of the Doings and
Sufferings of the Christian Indians in New England in the
Years 1675, 1676, 1677** . . . (*In* American Antiquarian
Society, Worcester, Mass. ARCHAEOLOGIA
AMERICANA. TRANSACTIONS AND COLLECTIONS.
Cambridge, 1836. vol. 2.)

Gookin, Daniel. **Historical Collections of the Indians in New
England.** Of Their Several Nations, Numbers, Customs,
Manners, Religion and Government, Before the English
Planted There . . . Boston, 1792.

Morton, Thomas. **New English Canaan or New Canaan.**
Containing an Abstract of New England, Composed in
Three Books . . . Amsterdam, 1̇637.

Sewall, Samuel. **Diary of Samuel Sewall, 1674–1729.** (*In*
Massachusetts Historical Society. COLLECTIONS, 5th
Series, V–VII, 1878–1882.) Three volumes.

Virginia: Four Personal Narratives. (Hamor, Ralph. *A True
Discourse on the Present Estate of Virginia . . . Till the
18 of June 1614* . . . London, 1615/Hariot, Thomas. *A Briefe
and True Report of the New Found Land of Virginia . . .*
London, 1588/Percy, George. *A Trewe Relacyon of the
Proceedings and Ocurrentes of Momente Which Have
Happened in Virginia From . . . 1609, Until . . . 1612.*
(In *Tyler's Quarterly Historical and Genealogical Magazine*,
Vol. III, 1922.)/Rolf, John. *Virginia in 1616.* (In *Virginia
Historical Register and Literary Advertiser*, Vol. I,
No. III, July, 1848.) New York, 1972.

Winthrop, John. **The History of New England From 1630–1649.**
Edited by James Savage. Boston, 1825–1826. Two volumes
in one.

New England Puritan Tracts of the Seventeenth Century

Cobbett, Thomas. **The Civil Magistrate's Power in Matters of
Religion Modestly Debated** . . . London, 1653.

Cotton, John. **The Bloudy Tenent, Washed, and Made White in
the Bloud of the Lambe** . . . London, 1647.

Cotton, John. **A Brief Exposition with Practical Observations Upon the Whole Book of Canticles.** London, 1655.

Cotton, John. **Christ the Fountaine of Life:** Or, Sundry Choyce Sermons on Part of the Fift Chapter of the First Epistle of St. John. London, 1651.

Cotton, John. **Two Sermons.** (*Gods Mercie Mixed with His Justice* . . . London, 1641/*The True Constitution of a Particular Visible Church, Proved by Scripture* . . . London, 1642.) New York, 1972.

Eliot, John. **The Christian Commonwealth:** Or, The Civil Policy of the Rising Kingdom of Jesus Christ. London, 1659.

Hooker, Thomas. **The Application of Redemption,** By the Effectual Work of the Word, and Spirit of Christ, for the Bringing Home of Lost Sinners to God. London, 1657.

H[ooker], T[homas]. **The Christian's Two Chiefe Lessons,** Viz. Selfe Deniall, and Selfe Tryall . . . London, 1640.

Hooker, Thomas. **A Survey of the Summe of Church-Discipline** Wherein the Way of the Churches of New England is Warranted Out of the Word, and All Exceptions of Weight, Which Are Made Against It, Answered . . . London, 1648.

Increase Mather Vs. Solomon Stoddard: Two Puritan Tracts. (Mather, Increase. *The Order of the Gospel, Professed and Practised by the Churches of Christ in New-England* . . . Boston, 1700/Stoddard, Solomon. *The Doctrine of Instituted Churches Explained, and Proved From the Word of God.* London, 1700.) New York, 1972.

Mather, Cotton. **Ratio Disciplinae Fratrum Nov-Anglorum.** A Faithful Account of the Discipline Professed and Practised, in the Churches of New England. Boston, 1726.

Mather, Richard. **Church Covenant:** Two Tracts. (*Church-Government and Church-Covenant Discussed, in an Answer to the Elders of the Severall Churches in New-England* . . . London, 1643/*An Apologie of the Churches in New-England for Church-Covenant, Or, A Discourse Touching the Covenant Between God and Men, and Especially Concerning Church-Covenant* . . . London, 1643.) New York, 1972.

The Imperial System

[Blenman, Jonathan]. **Remarks on Several Acts of Parliament Relating More Especially to the Colonies Abroad** . . . London, 1742.

British Imperialism: Three Documents. (Berkeley, George.
  *A Proposal for the Better Supplying of Churches in our
  Foreign Plantations, and for Converting the Savage
  Americans to Christianity by a College to be Erected in the
  Summer Islands, Otherwise Called the Isles of Bermuda . . .*
  London, 1724/[Fothergill, John]. *Considerations Relative to
  the North American Colonies.* London, 1765/*A Letter to a
  Member of Parliament Concerning the Naval-Store Bill . . .*
  London, 1720.) New York, 1972.

Coke, Roger. **A Discourse of Trade** . . . London, 1670.

[D'Avenant, Charles]. **An Essay Upon the Government of the
  English Plantations on the Continent of America** (1701).
  An Anonymous Virginian's Proposals for Liberty Under the
  British Crown, With Two Memoranda by William Byrd.
  Edited by Louis B. Wright. San Marino, Calif., 1945.

Dummer, Jeremiah. **A Defence of the New-England Charters** . . .
  London, 1721.

Gee, Joshua. **The Trade and Navigation of Great Britain
  Considered:** Shewing that Surest Way for a Nation to
  Increase in Riches, is to Prevent the Importation of Such
  Foreign Commodities as May Be Rais'd at Home. London,
  1729.

[Little, Otis]. **The State of Trade in the Northern Colonies
  Considered;** With an Account of Their Produce, and a
  Particular Description of Nova Scotia . . . London, 1748.

Tucker, Jos[iah]. **The True Interest of Britain, Set Forth in
  Regard to the Colonies:** And the Only Means of Living in
  Peace and Harmony With Them, Including Five Different
  Plans for Effecting this Desirable Event . . . Philadelphia,
  1776.